Globalization and the Nation State

Scholars have for decades studied the economic determinants and effects of programs sponsored by the Bretton Woods institutions: the International Monetary Fund and the World Bank. Yet, much less systematic attention has been paid to the political factors that influence these international financial institutions. Recent studies of why countries enter into IFI programs and with what effects have led researchers to re-evaluate conventional wisdom.

This book presents the cutting edge of this research agenda, bringing together an international team of leading researchers, all of whom draw on the advanced techniques of the new political economy to evaluate these issues.

Globalization and the Nation State provides openings for new research approaches on the IMF and the World Bank and each contribution can be used as a window on a larger literature in political economy.

This pioneering book should prove to be an essential purchase for all international and development economists and should also be an invaluable tool for policy makers. It is ideal for students seeking an advanced introduction and for scholars looking for fresh thinking on the new political economy of international financial institutions and on how they impinge on the self-determination efforts of borrower countries.

Gustav Ranis is in the Economics Department at Yale University. **James Raymond Vreeland** and **Stephen Kosack** are in the Department of Political Science at Yale University.

Routledge studies in the modern world economy

Globalization and the Nation State

The impact of the IMF and the World Bank

**Edited by Gustav Ranis,
James Raymond Vreeland and
Stephen Kosack**

LONDON AND NEW YORK

First published 2006
by Routledge
2 Park Square, Milton Park, Abingdon, Oxon OX14 4RN

Simultaneously published in the USA and Canada
by Routledge
270 Madison Ave, New York, NY 10016

Routledge is an imprint of the Taylor & Francis Group

Transferred to Digital Printing 2006

Typeset in Baskerville by Wearset Ltd, Boldon, Tyne and Wear

British Library Cataloguing in Publication Data
A catalogue record for this book is available from the British Library

Library of Congress Cataloging in Publication Data
A catalog record for this book has been requested

ISBN10: 0-415-70086-8 (hbk)
ISBN10: 0-415-42629-4 (pbk)

ISBN13: 978-0-415-70086-3 (hbk)
ISBN13: 978-0-415-42629-9 (pbk)

Contents

Figures

Tables

Contributors

M. Rodwan Abouharb is a PhD candidate in political science at Binghamton University. His research examines how domestic and international economic processes affect the likelihood of civil war and repression. He has a forthcoming co-authored book under contract with Cambridge University Press examining the impact of structural adjustment agreements on human rights.

Rouben Atoian is a PhD candidate in economics at the University of North Carolina at Chapel Hill. He is interested in evaluating macroeconomic policy, and has worked on econometric evaluations of the macroeconomic impact of IMF programs. He is also engaged in research on identifying policy preferences and evaluating the monetary policy implications when central banks operate in an open-economy environment.

Graham Bird is Professor of Economics and Director of the Surrey Centre for International Economic Studies at the University of Surrey. He is Visiting Professor at the Fletcher School, Tufts University, and has been a Visiting Scholar in the IMF's Research Department and a high level expert adviser to the Independent Evaluation Office of the IMF. He has written or edited 22 books and monographs and has published over 140 academic papers. One of his most recent books, published by Routledge, is entitled *The IMF and the Future: Issues and Options Facing the Fund*.

Nancy Birdsall is President of the Center for Global Development. Before launching the Center she held senior positions at the Carnegie Endowment for International Peace, the Inter-American Development Bank, and the World Bank. She is the author of several books and more than 75 articles for academic journals.

James Boughton is Historian of the IMF. He holds a PhD in economics from Duke University, and before joining the IMF staff, he was Professor of Economics at Indiana University. His book *Silent Revolution* (2001) is a history of the IMF from 1979 to 1989.

David L. Cingranelli is a Professor of political science at Binghamton University of the State University of New York. He conducts large-scale, comparative research examining the human rights practices of governments around the world. He is the former president of the Human Rights Section of the American Political Science Association.

Stephen Coate is Kiplinger Professor of Public Policy in the Department of Economics at Cornell University. A British citizen, he holds a bachelor's degree from the University of Wales and a PhD from Northwestern University. He has previously taught at Harvard, Penn, and Yale. His main areas of interest are political economy and public economics.

Patrick Conway is Professor of Economics at the University of North Carolina at Chapel Hill. His research is centered upon the role of developing and transition countries in the international economy, with equal attention to trade and financial aspects. His recent publications include the book *Crisis, Stabilization and Growth: Economic Adjustment in Transition Economies* and journal articles in the *American Economic Review,* the *Journal of Development Economics,* and the *Journal of Comparative Economics.*

Allan Drazen is Professor of Economics and Co-Director of the Center for International Economics at the University of Maryland and Jack and Lisa Yael Professor of Comparative Economics at Tel-Aviv University.

Erica R. Gould is an Assistant Professor of Politics at the University of Virginia and received her PhD in political science from Stanford University in 2001. Her research focuses on international organizations, particularly the limits of state control over international organizations. She has a forthcoming book entitled *Money Talks: The International Monetary Fund, Conditionality and Supplementary Financiers* with Stanford University Press.

Ravi Kanbur is T.H. Lee Professor of World Affairs, International Professor of Applied Economics and Management, and Professor of Economics at Cornell University. He has previously taught at the Universities of Oxford, Cambridge, Essex, Warwick, Princeton, and Columbia. He has also served on the senior staff of the World Bank, including as Chief Economist for Africa and as Principal Advisor to the Chief Economist of the World Bank.

Devesh Kapur is the Frederick Danziger Associate Professor of Government at Harvard University. He is the co-author of *The World Bank: Its First Half Century* (Brookings Institution 1997).

Stephen Kosack is a PhD candidate in political economy at Yale University. He has written on foreign aid, foreign direct investment, and democracy for *International Organization* and *World Development,* and on economic growth and human development in Cuba for the Cuba

Transition Project at the University of Miami. His dissertation looks at the political economy of education in developing countries.

Stephen Morris is the Ford Foundation Professor of Economics at Yale University. He obtained a PhD in Economics from Yale University in 1991 and taught at the University of Pennsylvania from 1991 to 1998. His research focuses on game theory and applications of game theory to economics. He worked as an Economist at the Ministry of Planning and Economic Development, Uganda from 1987-89 and has worked as a consultant to the World Bank.

Paul Mosley is Professor and Head of the Department of Economics at the University of Sheffield. He is author of *Aid and Power* (2nd edn, Routledge 1995) and of other works on development, economic history, and international political economy.

Gustav Ranis is the Frank Altschul Professor of International Economics at Yale University. He was Assistant Administrator for Program and Policy for the Agency for International Development/Department of State (1965–67), Director of the Economic Growth Center at Yale (1967–75), and Director of the Pakistan Institute of Development Economics (1958–61). He received an Honorary Degree from Brandeis University in 1982 and has been the subject of two Festschrift conferences. His publications include more than 20 books and 200 articles in professional journals. He was selected as a Carnegie Scholar in 2004.

Dane Rowlands, PhD Economics, University of Toronto, is currently Associate Professor and Associate Director at the Norman Paterson School of International Affairs, Carleton University. His primary research interests are international development finance, the IMF, conflict and peacekeeping, and international migration.

Marcelo Selowsky, a Chilean citizen, is an Assistant Director of the IMF in the newly created Independent Evaluation Office (IEO). He holds a PhD from the University of Chicago and taught at Harvard University from 1967–68 and from 1971–73. He then joined the World Bank where he was Chief Economist, first for Latin America, and later for the transition countries of Europe and Central Asia. He has written extensively on human capital and later on issues surrounding debt and macroeconomic adjustment. He led the IEO evaluation of *Fiscal Adjustment in IMF-Supported Programs,* published by the IEO in 2003.

Alastair Smith is an Associate Professor of Politics at New York University. He is the author of *Election Timing* (Cambridge University Press 2004) and the *Logic of Political Survival* (with Bruce Bueno de Mesquita, Randolph Siverson, and James Morrow, MIT Press 2003). Much of his research focuses on using game theoretic models to examine how domestic political conditions affect relations between nations.

Frances Stewart, MA, DPHIL, OXON is Director of the Centre for Research on Inequality, Human Security and Ethnicity (CRISE) in the University of Oxford. Books include *Adjustment with a Human Face* (with G.A. Cornia and R. Jolly, OUP 1987), *War and Underdevelopment: the Economic and Social Consequences of Conflict* (with Valpy Fitzgerald and others, OUP 2000), and *Group Behaviour and Development* (with Judith Heyer and Rosemary Thorp). She is a Board member and Vice-Chairman of the International Food Policy Research Institute and an Overseer of the Thomas Watson Institute, Brown University.

Strom C. Thacker is an Associate Professor of International Relations at Boston University. His recent books include *Big Business, the State, and Free Trade: Constructing Coalitions in Mexico* (Cambridge 2000) and *Good Government: A Centripetal Theory of Democratic Governance.*

Tsidi Tsikata is senior economist in the Independent Evaluation Office. During his tenure there, he has participated in evaluations on: prolonged use of IMF resources, on fiscal adjustment in IMF-supported programs; and on the IMF's role in preparing Poverty Reduction Strategy Papers. Prior to this, he served as the IMF resident representative in Tanzania, as principal research officer at the Bank of Botswana, and in the Ministry of Finance and Economic Planning of his home nation, Ghana.

James Raymond Vreeland, PhD, New York University 1999, is Associate Professor of Political Science at Yale University. His research has appeared in *International Political Science Review, Journal of Development Economics, Political Analysis,* and *World Development.* He has authored two books on the International Monetary Fund: *The IMF and Economic Development* (Cambridge University Press 2003) and *The IMF: Politics of Conditional Lending* (Routledge).

Michael Wang was educated in economics at Yale, Cambridge, and Oxford. He has worked as a researcher at the Economic Growth Center at Yale, Centre for International Development at Oxford, and Centre for Human Development in Pakistan. He was a contributor to *War and Underdevelopment* (OUP 1999) and *Group Behaviour and Development* (OUP 2000).

Thomas D. Willett is Horton Professor of Economics at Claremont Graduate University and Claremont McKenna College. He has served as Deputy Assistant Secretary of the US Treasury for International Research. He has written widely in the areas of political economy and international money and finance.

Acknowledgments

This book is one of the results of a broad three-year project entitled Globalization and Self-Determination, supported by a grant from Carnegie Corporation of New York, with supplementary assistance from our host, the Yale Center for International and Area Studies, as well as the Coca Cola World Fund at Yale and the Edward J. and Dorothy Clarke Kempf Fund. The project was first conceived in 2000 by Arun Agrawal, Geoffrey Garrett, and Gustav Ranis and came to involve many of our colleagues working on related international issues at Yale University. We are indebted to these colleagues, too numerous to name individually, for their input and involvement in the project. We are especially grateful to Carnegie Corporation and to Stephen Del Rosso, senior program officer, for his interest and support.

This book incorporates the results of a coherent research program presented at a conference on "The Impact of Globalization on the Nation-State from Above: the International Monetary Fund and the World Bank," held at Yale University April 25–27, 2003. Many of the top scholars working on the Bretton Woods institutions contributed. The quality of the contributions exceeded our high hopes, and it was clear that they deserved wider dissemination. We are grateful to all those who presented papers, served as discussants and chairs of the various panels, as well as others who offered helpful suggestions and raised important questions from the floor. These included Reza Baqir, David Cameron, David Dollar, William Easterly, Martin Edwards, Jeffry Frieden, Galina Hale, Joseph Joyce, Tim Lane, Allan Meltzer, Ashoka Mody, Louis Pauly, Rodney Ramcharan, Rose Razaghian, Kenneth Rogoff, Ratna Sahay, Diego Saravia, Kenneth Scheve, T.N. Srinivasan, Randy Stone, Ngaire Woods, and Ernesto Zedillo. For administrative support, we would like to thank Richard Kane, Peg Limbacher, Marilyn Wilkes, Lisa Brennan, and Beverly Kimbro.

The book was assembled and edited during the 2003–04 academic year. We are grateful to our editors at Routledge, Terry Clague and Robert Langham, for their support in this endeavor. In addition, James Vreeland would like to acknowledge support through a one-year residence at the

UCLA International Institute as part of the institute's Global Fellows Program, and Stephen Kosack would like to thank the National Science Foundation for the support of a Graduate Research Fellowship. Any opinions, findings, conclusions, or recommendations expressed in this publication are those of the authors and do not necessarily reflect the views of the supporting institutions.

Introduction

For decades, scholars have studied the economic determinants and effects of programs sponsored by the Bretton Woods institutions: the International Monetary Fund (IMF) and the World Bank. Much less systematic attention has been paid, however, to the political factors that influence these International Financial Institutions (IFIs). Recent methodological innovations in the study of why countries enter into IFI programs and with what effects, as well as newly available data, have led researchers to reevaluate conventional wisdom. This book presents the cutting edge of this research agenda, bringing together scholars working on various dimensions of the frontier.

The contributors address a host of related questions that are highly politicized and often inspire heated public debate. Too often answers to them forfeit analytical clarity to ideological preference or unfounded opinion. This is not surprising, as the issues are vital to both scholars and policy makers, and rightly inspire passionate discussion. Yet this discussion rarely leads us to answers that are well thought through, let alone inspire consensus. This book builds on a growing scholarly literature that tries to approach these issues with thought and rigor.

One of the most important issues is: Who controls the Bretton Woods institutions? According to Roland Vaubel's (1986, 1996) seminal research on this topic, the answer is straightforward: no one. Principal–agent problems are so severe that the bureaucrats of these international organizations simply pursue the objectives of maximizing budget and leisure. The principle funders of the IFIs (the United States, Japan, Germany, France, and the United Kingdom) simply do not have much leverage over how programs are implemented because the institutions' accountability to them is tenuous at best. Certainly the principal–agent problems that plague the IFIs are severe. Yet more recent research suggests that these institutions may indeed be responsive. Thomas Oatley and Jason Yackee (2000), for example, find evidence that United States foreign policy and financial interests play a role in IMF lending. Miles Kahler (1990: 94) notes that the United States has successfully blocked the renewal of IMF Managing Directors when "accomplishments did not meet American expectations." Randall Stone, looking specifically at post-communist countries

(Stone 2002) and African countries (Stone 2004) finds that countries important to the United States' interests are likely to receive favorable treatment from the IMF.

Beyond the influence of international politics, the ways in which domestic political factors influence participation in programs sponsored by the IFIs inspire just as much controversy. Many assume that assistance packages infringe on national sovereignty by inducing domestic decision makers to accept pieces of the Washington Consensus. Yet more and more frequently, especially of late, analysts are arguing that additional resources actually take the pressure off, and thus *reduce* the leverage the IFIs have over decision making in recipient nation states.

A second key question is: Why do countries turn to the IFIs for help? Early research on this subject focused almost entirely on economic factors, and largely ignored the role of political institutions. Consensus developed around the importance of a few economic variables, such as level of economic development: poor countries are more likely to need IFI support. Yet economics never told more than part of the story, and its impact was difficult to pin down. Looking at IMF agreements, Julio Santaella (1996) and Morris Goldstein and Peter Montiel (1986) found that a balance-of-payments deficit predicts participation, but in other work in collaboration with Malcolm Knight (1997), Santaella found it to be unimportant. Other studies also failed to report significant findings on the balance of payments (Bird 1996; Conway 1994; Edwards and Santaella 1993). Inflation, another widely cited determinant, was similarly found to be important in some studies (Edwards and Santaella 1993; Goldstein and Montiel 1986), and insignificant in others (Santaella 1996; Knight and Santaella 1997; Conway 1994).

Robert Putnam (1988) was one of the first to argue that there are political reasons that governments turn to the IFIs. His reasoning is straightforward: governments may enter into international arrangements as a way to push through unpopular policies. If proponents of economic reform face strong domestic opposition to policy change, they may seek out the IMF and the World Bank as allies. Consistent with this, James Vreeland (2003, 2004) found that political systems constrained by many checks and balances are more likely to enter into IMF programs. Countries facing checks and balances are less able to push through sweeping reforms. As Schelling (1960: 28) has argued, "the ability of a democratic government to get itself tied by public opinion may be different from the ability of a totalitarian government to incur such a commitment." But Vreeland also found that the IMF does not necessarily prefer to grant such countries support. Dictatorships are less constrained by public opinion and competitive elections, and thus they make easier negotiation partners. Adam Przeworski (2000) in collaboration with Vreeland found that dictatorships are actually more likely to receive loans from the IMF.

This is the context in which our book appears. The book's breadth reflects the wide range of issues that the IFIs raise. Its contributions also make use of a wide spectrum of methodologies to answer various questions. Yet the chapters are unified in their dedication to the careful presentation of well-articulated arguments using the most highly developed tools in the social sciences. The contributors represent a growing group of scholars working on the Bretton Woods institutions, and in presenting this book we hope to inspire a new generation of students to raise similar questions and use sophisticated approaches in the search for even better answers.

In short, this book should be viewed as an effort to provide openings for new research approaches on the IMF and the World Bank. Each contribution can be used as a window on a larger literature in political economy. It is ideal for students seeking an advanced introduction as well as for scholars looking for some fresh thinking on the new political economy of the Bretton Woods institutions and how they influence the self-determination of borrower countries.

Part I – "Whither conditionality" – presents four chapters that explore the nature of conditionality, with all its pitfalls and promises. The contributors take a sober and dispassionate approach to conditionality, arriving at surprising conclusions about the potential of conditionality to make both parties to IFI agreements – the IFI and the recipient country – better off. They also provide suggestions about improving conditionality, one of the most politically controversial aspects of the economic programs of the Bretton Woods institutions.

When a country enters into an agreement with the IMF or the World Bank, it receives a loan. In return for the loan, however, the country is expected to follow certain prescribed economic policies. These policy conditions usually involve drastic reductions in public expenditures, as well as increasing interest rates and sometimes devaluing the national currency. Hence the arrangements are often called "austerity programs." Critics on the left often see these programs as tools for the imperialist Western IFIs to impose inhumane, exploitative capitalism on rightfully resistant societies, and as being contractionary and particularly hard on labor and the poor. But they have also been criticized by the far right for often subsidizing the maintenance of bad policy, and for not being enforced thoroughly. Thus in popular debates about the World Bank and the IMF, conditionality is often one of the most contentious issues. The common response is that conditionality induces policy makers who would otherwise lack the knowledge, the will, or the ability to carry out desperately needed reforms in crisis-prone economies to act responsibly.

The chapters in this section look far more deeply at the issue and arrive at a more nuanced view of the role, benefits, and costs of conditionality, one built from an appreciation of domestic political constraints and the heterogeneity of domestic interests, and of the process by which governments and IFIs arrive at agreements.

In the first chapter, James Boughton ("Who's in charge? Ownership and conditionality in IMF-supported programs") argues that, despite the appearance of a contradiction between conditionality and "ownership" of an IMF program by the borrowing country, in actuality ownership does not remove the need for conditionality, nor does conditionality necessarily imply a lack of ownership. In fact, Boughton argues that, unless a country has real ownership of a program, conditionality is unlikely to make much difference. In examining ownership, Boughton identifies four features that make assuring ownership difficult. First, a country has an incentive to claim it is willing to implement changes that lenders want, because it wants the loan, i.e. expressions of ownership may not be genuine. Second, loan programs result from negotiation, and therefore they often do not please everyone and are not always the government's favorite option. Ownership of such programs is dynamic and unstable. Third, while the entire country does not have to "own" a program, ownership must extend beyond the ministries who negotiate with the Fund. Fourth, implementability can be an obstacle to ownership, if there is a gap between what the Fund thinks is needed and what the country has the capacity to implement.

Boughton's analysis leads him to a number of recommendations for the way IMF program negotiations should be conducted. In the initial discussion and negotiation, government officials should be allowed to write the first draft of the agreement, which should then be revised in partnership with the IMF. Second, the IMF must add political-economy expertise to its economist-heavy staff, so that it can have a proper appreciation of the domestic political environment. Third, negotiations should make extensive use of participatory domestic processes. Fourth, the IMF must be selective and must refuse to lend where real ownership is lacking. In the program's design phase, the IMF must take care to ensure that evaluation is parsimonious; that conditionality is focused only on those areas that fall within the IMF's mandate and its comparative advantage; that conditionality contains some flexibility; and that the process of evaluation is clear and transparent.

The next chapter by Stephen Coate and Stephen Morris ("Policy conditionality"), takes a broad theoretical approach to the question of why conditionality is necessary if a program is in a country's interest. Rather than assuming that government officials are in some way ignorant – that they favor bad economic policies because they do not know better and that conditionality pushes them onto a better path – Coate and Morris consider the possibility that governments pursue bad policies rationally because they have some political, as opposed to economic, payoff.

This chapter shows that conditionality can be harmful in certain situations. Suppose a government wants to redistribute resources inefficiently to pay off some domestic interest group. If conditionality removes this possibility the government might find some other, even less efficient, method to pay off the interest group. Consequently, the economy as a whole might be worse off than it would have been without conditionality. Their analysis shows that for conditionality to be beneficial, it must either eliminate all possibilities for paying off the interest group – a difficult task – or ensure that the methods that remain do not lead to perverse outcomes.

The authors also examine whether reforms induced by conditionality are likely to persist after the conditionality period is over. The conventional wisdom seems to be that reforms will persist because domestic interest groups that benefit from the reforms will defend them. Coate and Morris suggest that conditionality will have lasting impact only if it provides incentives to individuals to invest in new ways of operating in the reformed environment on a continuing basis.

In the third chapter ("Conditionality and ownership in IMF lending: a political economy approach"), Allan Drazen – like Coate and Morris – suggests that bad economic policies may be the result of rational calculations, rather than ignorance. He also argues that it is unrealistic to think of the "nation" as a unitary actor represented by its monolithic government. Instead, it is more useful to think of the nation state as made up of heterogeneous interests. Conflict between these interests makes true "ownership" of an IMF program difficult but may create a very important role for conditionality.

Drazen examines a hypothetical case in which a country's government is reformist and is the agenda-setter, but a powerful interest group, with veto authority over policy, opposes reform. In this case conditionality plays a key role *even if the government and the IMF agree on reforms*. Suppose, for example, that the interest group would like the country to receive an IMF loan, but would prefer it without having to undertake reforms. The interest group is likely initially to ally itself with the government and agree to reforms, but renege as soon as the loan is received. If, however, receipt of succeeding tranches of a loan is conditional on the continuation of reform policies, it forces the interest group to become reformist after the initial negotiations. Drazen goes on to show that similar outcomes are possible when the interest group has agenda-setting power and the pro-reform government has veto power.

In short, the chapters by Boughton, Coate and Morris, and Drazen acknowledge the importance of domestic politics in IMF negotiations. The last chapter in this section by Patrick Conway ("Empirical implications of endogenous IMF conditionality") examines empirically whether conditionality itself is the result of bargaining through negotiations or whether conditions are simply imposed upon countries. Building on his previous theoretical work, Conway derives and tests an empirical model in which conditionality is not imposed by the Fund but reflects negotiation by both sides. He argues that if conditions are imposed rather than negotiated noncompliance should lead to either more stringent conditions or the cancellation of lending to a country. Conversely, if conditionality is the result of bargaining, noncompliance should lead to *less* stringent conditions.

Historically, IMF conditions have not been made public, so these hypotheses are difficult to test. Conway, however, is able to use the percentage of a loan actually dispersed as a proxy for the extent of compliance with conditions: the more a country complies with IMF conditions, the larger percentage of its loan it should be able to secure. In support of the bargaining model – which he calls "endogenous conditionality" – Conway finds that failed IMF programs are usually followed by programs with less stringent conditionality.

Conway's empirical results confirm what Boughton, Coate and Morris, and Drazen suggest throughout this section: conditionality is the result of negotiation, which must take into account heterogeneous domestic political interests. Thus our original question – Why is conditionality necessary if the required policies are in a country's best interest? – produces another question: *Whose* interest? The domestic politics of any country are built up from widely varied interests. These must be considered by the IFIs along with the economies when they design reform programs.

In Part II, the book turns to the politics of IFI programs. In his 1987 study *The International Monetary Fund and Latin America: Economic Stabilization and Class Conflict,* Manuel Pastor found that "the single most consistent effect the IMF seems to have is the redistribution of income away from workers" (89). With such strong distributional consequences, it is not surprising that politics plays a major role in the decisions of IFI officials and the governments that turn to them for assistance. Indeed, scholarship on the IFIs acknowledges that, although economic imperatives ostensibly guide the design and implementation of IFI programs, both parties to these arrangements – the governments and the IFIs – operate in highly politicized environments.

At the international level, this section addresses questions such as: Who controls the IMF?, What determines World Bank lending patterns?, and Which IFI – the Bank or the Fund – takes the lead when both are involved in a country? At the domestic level, the section addresses the decisions of governments that choose – or fail – to enter into programs with the IFIs. What governments turn to the IFIs? What are the consequences for the ability of governments to remain in power? And do IFI programs ultimately empower or disempower recipient countries? This section presents seven contributions to these various questions about the politics of IFI programs.

Strom Thacker's chapter ("The high politics of IMF lending") addresses whether the US is able to use the IMF to achieve its ends. He argues that it does. Because the US has more power – both formal and informal – over the IMF than any other single country, he argues that the US can influence the lending decisions of the Fund to reward its allies and punish non-allies. Specifically, Thacker proposes that governments who are more closely aligned with the US in the international arena are more likely to get IMF loans and that governments who *re*align themselves more closely with the US are more likely to get IMF loans.

To measure the degree to which a country is allied with the US, Thacker considers voting records at the United Nations. Specifically, he looks at voting records on key issues as identified by the US State Department. Controlling for a host of economic factors, he finds that movement toward the US position increases the likelihood of a loan, but that the distance to the US position mattered only after 1990. This suggests that the politicization of the IMF has actually *increased* since the end of the Cold War.

Like Strom Thacker, Erica R. Gould ("Money talks: supplementary financiers and IMF conditionality") is interested in the question of whose interests the IMF pursues. Her specific focus is on the purpose of the conditionality that IMF loans carry. Why, in the face of overwhelming criticism from activists, economists, and the general public, and from across the political spectrum, does the IMF attach such strict conditions to its lending? Gould's response is that the success of IMF programs depends on the IMF's ability to secure supplementary financing for countries in crisis, and that, over time, this supplementary financing has been increasingly provided by private lending agents. It is these agents who demand that the IMF deploy harsh conditionality, and – to secure their funding – the IMF has no choice but to comply.

Gould supports the argument that IMF conditionality will be influenced by the wishes of private lenders by showing that when private lenders are organized, IMF conditionality is systematically more "bank-friendly." Her large-N study finds further support in two in-depth case studies of Mexico's 1982 Extended Fund Facility Agreement and Turkey's 1978 Stand-by Arrangement. In both cases, well-organized private financiers were clearly able to influence IMF conditionality.

In the next chapter, Paul Mosley ("The World Bank and the reconstruction of the 'social safety net' in Russia and Eastern Europe") considers the politics between the most powerful IFIs – the World Bank and the IMF: When the Bank and the Fund both lend, whose interests prevail? After the fall of communism, Eastern Europe became the focus of unprecedented attention by the IFIs. While the World Bank had a tremendous comparative advantage in helping to alleviate the massive poverty that resulted, Mosley argues that it largely failed to deliver. One reason was that the Bank, anxious to avoid the contentiousness that had previously characterized its interactions with the IMF, allowed the Fund to take the lead in determining macroeconomic policy. In addition, certain reforms, most notably to the tax system, should have but did not provide increased funding for social spending. Third, the politics of reform in Eastern Europe were misunderstood. The Bank's ambivalence about conditionality and its lack of attention to private entrepreneurs meant that it did not sufficiently encourage governments to increase "pro-poor" expenditures. Mosley marshals some evidence that the Bank's aid did effect a modest decrease in poverty, but its impact was far less than if the Bank had not been reluctant to act at odds with the IMF and had given poverty-reducing measures greater priority in its reform efforts.

Rodwan Abouharb and David Cingranelli take a broader approach to the determinants and impacts of World Bank loans ("When the World Bank says yes: determinants of structural adjustment lending"). Using a large-scale systematic analysis of the factors behind World Bank lending, they ask whether the Bank has political goals such as promoting democracy and human rights. They argue that, while ostensibly the Bank's lending is apolitical – motivated solely by countries' economic needs – its actual decision-making process is again partly political. For example, nations with higher respect for workers' rights are more likely to receive loans, as are countries with larger populations, which the authors take as a proxy for importance in the international system. Somewhat surprisingly, given that democracies are the Bank's primary financiers, developing democracies are not more likely to receive Bank loans than developing autocracies. The authors speculate that this lack of bias may, however, represent a type of affirmative action in favor of democracies, since democratic governments are less able to make credible commitments to repay. In addition, they find support for Ranis' concern (see Chapter 16) that the Bank tends to lend over and over again to the same countries. As a whole, the results not only enhance our understanding of how the World Bank lends but will also allow future empirical work on Bank effectiveness to take account of the non-randomness of lending.

In Chapter 9, we turn to the determinants of IMF lending. Graham Bird and Dane Rowlands ("The demand for IMF assistance: what factors influence the decision to turn to the Fund?") note that previous large-N research has been successful at identifying some economic and political factors that are common to all countries with IMF programs, but searching for the remaining factors in single models is fruitless; some proportion of any country's decision to go to the IMF will be necessarily idiosyncratic. Bird and Rowlands argue that the way forward is through disaggregating at the mid-level: somewhere below the level of large-N but above the level of single case studies. If there is not a single pattern to explain all IMF lending, the next step may be to see if several patterns, working together, can approach an explanation.

They start their search on the demand side: Why do governments turn to the IMF? They find that among countries with higher incomes, larger reserves, and less debt, fiscal and balance-of-payments problems will often lead the government to seek IMF assistance. By contrast, these factors are less important in explaining IMF lending to poorer countries with more debt. Bird and Rowlands hope that more empirical work of this type will yield explanations that have thus far eluded researchers.

Alastair Smith and James Vreeland also argue that governments may have different motivations for turning to the IMF. In "The survival of political leaders and IMF programs," they examine the interaction of participation in IMF programs, with domestic political institutions and the pursuit of domestic political goals. They note that governments facing an economic crisis may have different motivations when turning to the IMF than governments facing a political crisis, and that domestic political institutions not only shape these incentives but also influence the impact of IMF programs.

Specifically, Smith and Vreeland ask whether IMF programs help political leaders survive in office. They find that, under democracy, IMF programs can help, especially if the current government inherited the program from a previous administration. The IMF program assists leaders in pushing through policy changes and allows leaders to use the IMF as a scapegoat for economic pain. For dictators, the impact is the opposite. They are less likely to survive in office, especially if they inherit programs from previous governments. They argue that dictatorships benefit from IMF loans but that IMF conditionality limits their ability to spread the necessary patronage to maintain power.

In the final chapter of Part II, Frances Stewart and Michael Wang ("Do PRSPs empower poor countries and disempower the World Bank, or is it the other way around?") ask whether one of the most visible of the World Bank's recent initiatives, Poverty Reduction Strategy Papers (PRSPs), has had its intended effect of empowering poor countries. Their answer is no. If PRSPs indeed empowered country decision makers, they should reflect unique country needs and approaches. Instead, Stewart and Wang show that PRSPs differ little across countries and are heavily concentrated around the private-sector solutions that the Bank tends to favor. While PRSPs have brought an increased swath of domestic society into the decision-making process, the new participants are not necessarily representative of the society. Rather, they are mostly NGOs (foreign and domestic). Thus PRSPs have not accomplished what they were supposed to. At the moment, they may even have increased the Bank's authority, for they have given the perception, if not the reality, of increased country ownership. Yet the authors predict that eventually the reality will force this perception to change. The long term holds little prospect for PRSPs to change the balance of power between the Bank and recipient countries in any fundamental way.

Part III takes up the issue of how the IFIs might be reformed. Recent increased scrutiny of the IFIs has predictably been accompanied by a raft of proposals for their reform. This section examines a number of specific suggestions, focusing first on the IMF, then on the World Bank. The suggestions vary in scope – from narrow but important comments about the accuracy of data employed by the IFIs to make the decisions that they do – to broad recommendations about what general goals the IFIs should pursue. While this section necessarily presents opinion, the opinions are based on sound research and experience.

The first contribution in this section calls for a modest yet extremely important reform: the IFIs need to collect more accurate data. In "Macroeconomic adjustment in IMF-supported programs: projections and reality" Rouben Atoian, Patrick Conway, Marcelo Selowsky, and Tsidi Tsikata turn to the way the IMF assesses an economy in crisis, and how it gauges the economy's progress toward reform. They begin by showing that the economic predictions by the model used by IMF staff differ significantly from a model constructed in hindsight with historical data. This is no surprise, of course – projections inevitably differ from reality – but the authors consider a number of possible reasons for the difference. First, the true model may be different from the model used in the projections. Second, the policies and reforms that are actually implemented may differ from those the IMF thinks will be implemented. Third, the data on initial conditions available to the IMF may not be accurate. Lastly, some of the process under examination may simply be random, and therefore impervious to statistical analysis.

The authors specifically examine IMF projections with respect to the fiscal and current account balances and find that all four aforementioned factors contributed to the flawed projections. The biggest culprit, however, was a lack of accurate data on which to base the model. It is therefore in this area that the greatest potential for improvement rests. In their current incarnation, IMF projections do not much outperform a random walk.

Such a lack of success has led others to demand more dramatic reform of the IMF. In Chapter 13 ("The IMF and capital account crises: the case for a separate lender of last resort and conditionality functions"), Thomas Willett looks at what became of an argument that was prominent in the aftermath of the East Asian Financial Crisis of the late 1990s: that the IFIs should give up conditionality and act purely as international lenders of last resort (ILOLR). This was the primary recommendation of the controversial Meltzer Commission report (International Financial Institution Advisory Commission 2000). But while the Commission concluded that the IMF should be completely retooled as an ILOLR, abandoning its traditional programs, Willett argues that the two roles could be complementary, and that the IMF should take on both. Ideally, he says, the two would operate in sequence: in a crisis, a loan from the IMF-as-ILOLR would act as a sort of bridge loan provider, a way to overcome temporary coordination problems among disparate lenders; following resolution of the crisis, the IMF, now acting in its traditional role, would assist with more fundamental domestic economic support and reform to reduce the likelihood of future crises. The first phase would increase the effectiveness of the second, by allowing the nation state and the IMF enough breathing room to develop an appropriate package of support and reform. Not only would this enhance the country's "ownership" of its eventual program, it should also allow the IMF the time to gauge the commitment of the recipient government. Both should enhance the value of IMF conditionality, the ineffectiveness of which is now one of the Fund's most serious failings. Willett considers a number of the relevant issues his proposal generates, including criteria for determining a country's eligibility for last-resort lending, the appropriate size and length of the loans and questions of moral hazard.

The IMF has also recently come under pressure to return to its "roots" – that is, as strictly a short-term lending facility for countries in balance-of-payments crises. Graham Bird and Paul Mosley ("Should the IMF discontinue its long-term lending role in developing countries?") offer an alternative view. While they acknowledge that empirical evidence shows that IMF programs have largely failed to promote economic growth, when they look just at the Poverty Reduction and Growth Facility (PRGF) – a new program intended for longer-term lending to increase growth – they find positive evidence. They examine pairs of similar countries, one of which received a loan under the PRGF and one that did not, and find that the countries that received loans had higher growth. The typical IMF program involves cuts in expenditure during the reform period. Lending under the PRGF can, if the country seizes the opportunity, soften the impact of these cuts, helping to maintain social capital and minimizing political instability. Even accepting this evidence, some might respond that the IMF should simply hand over this task to the World Bank. Bird and Mosley disagree, noting the poor record of the Bank in structural adjustment lending. Instead they recommend closer coordination with the Bank's work; a combined effort is necessary to make stabilization as effective as possible.

As for the World Bank, recent criticisms have coincided with widespread interest in International Public Goods (IPGs). Ravi Kanbur ("IFIs and IPGs: operational implications for the World Bank") examines the role the World Bank plays in providing public goods. As voters in donor countries have become discouraged with foreign aid – which they perceive to be inefficient and ineffective – the IFIs have increasingly seen themselves as having a role to play in providing IPGs and, indeed, have tended to present whatever they are doing as providing such goods. Kanbur's analysis, however, shows that the concept of IPGs is much subtler than is commonly appreciated and that even those IFI activities that could be considered IPGs – for example, the provision of research on development, or coordination mechanisms for disparate donor efforts – do not always meet the standard in practice. Kanbur finds that the World Bank's research output will likely never be seen as an IPG since the Bank is too widely viewed as beholden to richer countries and the research as aimed at justifying its own policies. However, the Bank, with some modifications, which Kanbur details in the chapter, *could* be successful as a coordination device for global development efforts.

Gustav Ranis also begins with a look at the Bank's research output. In

"Ownership, Dutch disease, and the World Bank," Ranis notes a decided disconnect between this research and the Bank's operations. Instead of paying attention to its own analysis, and enforcing the conditionality it imposes, the Bank is under as much – and perhaps more – pressure to lend as developing countries are to borrow and tends therefore to provide resources even when its policy recommendations are not implemented. This creates a variation on the classic "Dutch disease": the Bank usually does not lend enough to inflate a borrower's exchange rate, making its exports more expensive but, by creating the impression that money ultimately flows even in the absence of policy change, the Bank tacitly accepts the status quo and takes the pressure off borrowers to reform. Indeed the additional resources can help make it possible *not* to reform. To alleviate this problem, Ranis recommends the Bank should act more like a real bank. For example, it must be more selective and must do more to encourage countries themselves to prepare, take the initiative, propose, and thereby truly "own", their reform programs.

The book's final part takes a broader look at the international infrastructure, especially issues of governance. Ostensibly, the primary goal of multilateral aid is the alleviation of global poverty, but the world's poorer nations have little chance to exercise control over the system that awards that aid, or to offer input on its policies. The authors in this section each argue that the meager influence of poor countries is damaging to the system's effectiveness.

In "Why it matters who runs the IMF and the World Bank," Nancy Birdsall shows the importance of global governance for reducing world poverty, and makes a case for the increased representation of developing countries in global governance. She points out a great irony in development: poor countries are left behind by both market failures and market successes. Global market failures can affect poor countries asymmetrically, either because they must bear some of the costs of rich-country behavior (e.g., global pollution), or because they must bear the total cost for something which benefits others beyond their borders (e.g., fighting disease). But the market's success also tends to work against poor countries, because it channels capital to countries that already have more productive assets. Global governance is vital for addressing these concerns. Yet poor countries are decidedly under-represented in the institutions of global governance, particularly the Multilateral Development Banks (MDBs). Birdsall lays out a series of arguments on why this under-representation may reduce the banks' effectiveness; among them: under-representation limits the banks' funding, fosters a feeling that the policies the banks recommend are intrusive, and limits the recipient country's ownership, and therefore the likely success, of bank programs. She backs up her arguments with evidence from a case study of the Inter-American Development Bank whose governance is more representative of developing countries and therefore, she argues, one of the more effective.

At their 2001 summit, the G-7 examined the structure of the Multilateral Development Banks, and agreed on a number of recommendations for reform. In the book's final chapter ("Do as I say not as I do: a critique of G-7 proposals on 'reforming' the MDBs"), Devesh Kapur argues against these recommendations. He begins with the popular suggestion that additional aid be in the form of grants rather than concessional loans. This proposal has much to be said for it, but, if implemented, the reform could damage the financial autonomy of the World Bank. This reform would mean a further transferring of funds to the International Development Association (IDA), which is considerably more dependent on consistent donor (particularly US) goodwill. Such reforms are a reflection of a persistent shift in the control of the Multilateral Development Banks from the recipient countries and the Banks' own governing structures to the donors and shareholders who provide the Banks' capital. Yet debates on accountability and "governance" usually focus on the developing countries and the Banks and so tend to deflect attention from donor or shareholder governance. This is largely to blame for the Banks' ineffectiveness. The G-7 recommendations also encouraged harmonizing policies and removing overlapping jurisdictions within the MDB system in order to reduce the system's high cost of lending. This is a welcome suggestion, but, again, it ignores the issue of governance and control by the donor countries. The high cost of MDB lending is due to over-regulation by donors, not the lack of harmonization or operational overlap. Such overlap may provide poor countries with a modicum of choice in a system that offers them only one unfeasible method of protest: exit.

Lastly, Kapur examines the G-7 recommendation to increase attention to Global Public Goods, as noted by Ravi Kanbur in his chapter (15). Such public goods are surely worth pursuing, but it is not obvious why "fighting infectious diseases, promoting environmental improvement, facilitating trade, and promoting financial stability" should benefit developing countries more than, for example, a continuation of highly successful research into agricultural innovation. But developing countries cannot press for alternating priorities, because they generally lack the capacity to think creatively about their own development options and bring those ideas to the table. Most development research, both inside the IFIs and elsewhere, is conducted in the West and is largely Western-centric. In this sense, not even the research that the World Bank and the IMF provide is really a Global Public Good. Kapur ends his analysis with some policy recommendations countering the G-7 proposals.

While reading through the following chapters, the reader might keep in mind a basic question of great importance: Do IFIs, with their policy conditions along with the provision of resources, shape the ability of governments to determine their own policies of reform? We offer this book as a way to shed some light on this critical question. The answers presented in the pages that follow are provocative. We hope they will serve not only to bring researchers up to date with new research and techniques, but also to inspire new further projects and new ideas. In 2002 William Easterly's best seller, *The Elusive Quest for Growth*, illustrated that efforts to promote development have thus far been largely unsuccessful. With the less-than-successful structural adjustment era behind us and new poverty reduction programs now on offer, this is an opportune time to reassess the relationship between the nation state and the IFIs in their mutual search for economic growth and prosperity, and to consider constructive changes to the role and governance of the IFIs.

References

Bird, Graham. 1996. The International Monetary Fund and Developing Countries: A Review of the Evidence and Policy Options. *International Organization* 50: 477–511.

Conway, Patrick. 1994. IMF Lending Programs: Participation and Impact. *Journal of Development Economics* 45: 365–91.

Easterly, William. 2002. The Elusive Question for Growth: Economists' Adventures and Misadventures in the Tropics. Cambridge, MA: The MIT Press.

Edwards, Sebastian and Julio A. Santaella. 1993. Devaluation Controversies in the Developing Countries: Lessons from the Bretton Woods Era. In *A Retrospective on the Bretton Woods System*, edited by Michael D. Bordo and Barry Eichengreen, pp. 405–55. Chicago: University of Chicago Press.

Goldstein, Morris and Peter J. Montiel. 1986. Evaluating Fund Stabilization Programs with Multicountry Data: Some Methodological Pitfalls. *IMF Staff Papers* 33: 304–44.

International Financial Institution Advisory Commission (Meltzer Commission). 2000. *Report of the International Financial Institution Advisory Commission.* Washington: Government Printing Office.

Kahler, Miles. 1990. The United States and the International Monetary Fund: Declining Influence or Declining Interest? In *The United States and Multilateral Institutions: Patterns of Changing Instrumentality and Influence*, edited by Karen A. Mingst and Margaret P. Karns. Boston: Unwin Hyman.

Knight, Malcolm and Julio A. Santaella. 1997. Economic Determinants of Fund Financial Arrangements. *Journal of Development Economics* 54: 405–36.

Manuel Pastor. 1987. *The International Monetary Fund and Latin America: Economic Stabilization and Class Conflict.* Boulder: Westview Press.

Oatley, Thomas and Jason Yackee. 2000. Political Determinants of IMF Balance of Payments Lending. Unpublished manuscript, University of North Carolina at Chapel Hill.

Przeworski, Adam and James Raymond Vreeland. 2000. The Effect of IMF Programs on Economic Growth. *Journal of Development Economics* 62: 385–421.

Putnam, Robert D. 1988. Diplomacy and Domestic Politics: The Logic of Two-Level Games. *International Organization* 42: 427–60.

Santaella, Julio A. 1996. Stylized Facts Before IMF-Supported Adjustment. *IMF Staff Papers* 43: 502–44.

Stone, Randall W. 2002. *Lending Credibility: The International Monetary Fund and the Post-Communist Transition.* Princeton: Princeton University Press.

Stone, Randall W. 2004. The Political Economy of IMF Lending in Africa. *American Political Science Review*. Forthcoming.

Vaubel, Roland. 1986. A Public Choice Approach to International Organization. *Public Choice* 51: 39–57.

Vaubel, Roland. 1996. Bureaucracy at the IMF and the World Bank: A Comparison of the Evidence. *The World Economy* 19: 195–210.

Vreeland, James Raymond. 2003. *The IMF and Economic Development*. New York: Cambridge University Press.

Vreeland, James Raymond. 2004. Institutional Determinants of IMF Agreements. Paper presented at the Yale University Conference on Globalization and Self-Determination: The Nation-State Under Siege, May 14–15, 2004.

Part I

Whither conditionality?

1 Who's in charge? Ownership and conditionality in IMF-supported programs[*]

James M. Boughton

The IMF extends credit to countries with an external imbalance, conditional on the country's commitment to implement economic policies that will restore equilibrium. That conditionality serves two purposes. First, it ensures that the IMF's financial resources are used for the intended purpose, to the benefit of the country. Second, it ensures that the IMF will operate as a revolving fund for the benefit of all member countries. This simple description, however, gives rise to a conundrum. If the intended purpose is to benefit the borrower, then why is conditionality necessary? Why is it not sufficient to rely on the government to look after its own interests?

Several possible answers are available. The IMF might have superior knowledge or information, it might be relatively free of the distorting influence of short-term political constraints that limit rational policy making, or – more sinister – it might have a hidden agenda of serving the interests of creditor countries rather than borrowers. The country's authorities might *prefer* conditional assistance, as a commitment device, as a means of overcoming domestic opposition, or as a means of enhancing the credibility of their program. The willingness of creditor countries to finance the institution might be enhanced by the perceived discipline conveyed by policy conditionality. But whether any or all of these answers is an adequate explanation is not obvious.

Whatever the story, a second fundamental question must also be considered. Since the country, not the IMF, must implement the agreed economic policies, it is essential that the country's commitment be authentic and sufficiently deep and broad. Is there an inherent conflict, or contradiction, between conditional finance and national commitment? Are national authorities or other agents in the country less likely to "own" an adjustment or reform program simply because it is conditionally financed? Only one of the justifications for conditionality suggested above – the hidden agenda – would clearly imply a conflict, but most of the others could be so construed.

1 What is ownership?

When the IMF embarked on a reexamination of its policies on conditionality in the millennium year 2000, a key objective was to promote national
ownership of policy adjustments and structural reforms. It was clear from
experience and from formal studies (see Schadler *et al.* 1995) that the
main reason for failure of Fund-supported programs to achieve their
objectives was that governments too often did not implement policies to
which they had committed. Whatever could be done to deepen and
strengthen commitment was likely to improve implementation and raise
the success rate (Khan and Sharma 2003). Depth and breadth of genuine
commitment were encapsulated in the phrase "national ownership," but it
was not easy to define that phrase with sufficient precision to make it operational. After much internal debate, the staff settled on the following definition (IMF 2001b: 6):

> Ownership is a willing assumption of responsibility for an agreed
> program of policies, by officials in a borrowing country who have the
> responsibility to formulate and carry out those policies, based on an
> understanding that the program is achievable and is in the country's
> own interest.

This definition incorporates several key elements:

- "Willing assumption of responsibility" is a judgment call. A government seeking financial support has an incentive to express commitment to strengthen its policies, even without genuine ownership. For
  an external agency such as the IMF to make such judgments requires
  a thorough understanding of the political economy in the country.
- Ownership does not require that an IMF-supported program be a
  government's first choice, nor that it be the program that officials
  would have preferred in the absence of IMF involvement. In general,
  programs result from negotiations, the outcome of which – in a successful case – can be supported by all sides. In other words, ownership
  is dynamic and often fragile.
- Ownership does not require that everyone in the country support the
  program, but ownership usually must be broader than just the officials
  who negotiate with the Fund. Broad support throughout the country
  will raise the likelihood that a program will be successfully implemented, and cases will arise when the absence of majority support will
  undermine official ownership and scuttle implementation. In other
  cases, the government may abandon a program that has broad
  popular support if it does not think the program is in its own (possibly
  narrow) interest. In some cases, the country's top political leadership
  might allow or even encourage its finance officials to agree to a Fund-

supported program and then undercut its implementation once it is approved. As a general proposition, what is essential is that the responsible and controlling officials be committed and that opposition can be overcome.

- Achievability can be a major obstacle to ownership when there are gaps between what the Fund judges to be necessary and what country officials think is feasible. If the gap arises because of weak administrative capacity (e.g., all concerned agree that tax reform is needed to shore up the country's fiscal position, but the government lacks the ability to collect revenues from a wide tax base), accommodation might be reachable through technical assistance, external support, or stretching out the length of the program. If the gap arises from political considerations (e.g., parliamentary or provincial opposition), it may be far more difficult to breach. Prolonged discussions between the Fund and country authorities might be needed to find alternative approaches that will still achieve the goals of the program.

2 Is ownership compatible with conditionality?

Much of the criticism of IMF policy conditionality takes the form of saying that the Fund insists on telling the country to take policy actions that the country views as opposed to its own interests. If the country owned the policy changes, then it would implement them without the Fund's requirements, and conditionality would be unnecessary. Hence conditionality and ownership are said to be incompatible. If the Fund insists on national ownership as well, then that amounts to insisting that the country must not only do what the Fund wants, it must also at least pretend to want to do so. The basis for this criticism may be illustrated by a simple macroeconomic model of the type developed by Jacques Polak in the 1950s as a building block for Fund conditionality (see Polak 1998 and Boughton 2001).

The comparative statics of this model are shown in Figure 1.1, which shows a short-run (one-period) equilibrium between output (Y) and foreign exchange reserves (R). (For the mathematics, see the Appendix.) For this exercise, assume that the country has a fixed exchange rate and that its balance of payments is constrained by the availability of exogenously determined capital inflows. Output is determined by the horizontal Y line, which will shift positively with capital inflows (K) or expansionary domestic macro policies, represented here by government consumption spending (G). The balance of payments is determined by the vertical F line, which will shift to the right with K and to the left with G. The initial equilibrium is at Y0, R0 (point 0).

The classic situation forcing the country to seek the assistance of the IMF is an initial position of excess domestic demand, represented by point A in Figure 1.1.[1] The Fund approves a stand-by arrangement with credit

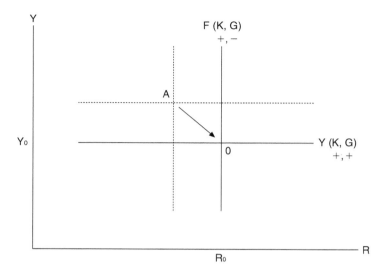

Figure 1.1 Overcoming macro denial.

available in quarterly installments, conditional on the authorities' agreement to adopt restrictive macro policies. In this stylized world, the authorities face a stark choice. They can either pursue their preferred policies until they run out of reserves or are forced to devalue the currency, or they can adjust policies in the direction of point 0 and receive an influx of cash and commitments sufficient to carry the economy the rest of the way. Ownership in this world is simply the recognition that the latter course is in their own interest. Because the initial position and the position required for Fund support are obviously different, the tension between ownership and conditionality is clear.

This basic tension, or what we might call "macro denial," implicitly underpins much of the political science literature on the role of policy conditionality in IMF lending.[2] It is also what Per Jacobsson would have had in mind when he first articulated the importance of ownership for Fund-supported programs in 1959. As Managing Director of the Fund, he was involved in negotiations with General Franco's Spain for a stand-by arrangement. In response to a question from a reporter for Spanish television, he stressed that the Fund could not just impose conditions and expect policy making to improve. "I must emphasize that such programs can only succeed if there is the will to succeed in the countries themselves. The Fund has always found people in these countries who know very well what needs to be done. The Fund does not impose conditions on countries; *they themselves freely have come to the conclusion* that the measures they arrange to take – even when they are sometimes harsh – are in the best interests of their own countries."[3] In that case as in many others, it is unlikely that Franco would have "freely" come to that conclusion without the carrot of the Fund's financial support or the benefit of Jacobsson's persuasive advice.

As a second example, consider the effects of a sudden withdrawal of capital, of the sort that triggered several financial crises in the late 1990s (see Calvo and Reinhart 2000). To maintain simplicity of presentation, assume that the trigger for the crisis is purely exogenous; the economy is initially in equilibrium and then is thrown off balance by a capricious external shock. In Figure 1.2, this moves the economy from 0 to B, with a loss in both income and foreign exchange reserves. In this case, the status quo ante is no longer an option, at least in the short run. The authorities' initially preferred response may be to try to restore internal balance through expansionary macro policies, but this will take them to point C (with a further loss of reserves), not back to 0. The Fund, however, is likely to insist upon a move in the direction of C' in order to restore *external* balance.

This second case – let us call it "Keynesian optimism"[4] – is more nuanced than the first, in that there is more room for debate about the correct policy response. It is no longer a question of whether the government is prepared to bite the bullet, but rather of whether agreement can be reached on a viable path for approaching an undisputed goal. In general, both policy adjustment and new or replacement financing may be warranted, but the mix is not uniquely or clearly determined. The goal of the program is not to restore equilibrium for a given (reduced) level of capital flows, which would force a choice between C and C'. The goal is to

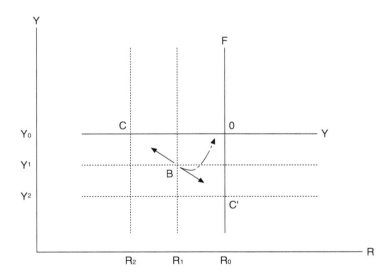

Figure 1.2 Overcoming Keynesian optimism.

instill confidence on the part of both domestic and international investors in order to reverse the initial outflow and ultimately to return the economy to point 0. If the initial position was strong enough, the country might be able to absorb a big loss of reserves or a large depreciation of the exchange rate and instill confidence by demonstrating the economy's ability to keep growing despite the crisis (point C). But if the initial position was that strong, what triggered the crisis? Almost without exception, the appropriate response will be in the direction of C', because confidence cannot be restored without first shoring up the country's external finances. In such cases, negotiations over conditionality will focus on the balance between financing and adjustment, with the mutually agreed goal of trying to move as effectively as possible toward equilibrium along the path indicated by the dotted arrow in Figure 1.2.

More possibilities arise when allowance is made for a flexible exchange rate. Figure 1.3 shows a simple version of a Fleming–Mundell model with autonomous capital flows. Here the exchange rate (E – the domestic price of foreign exchange) replaces reserves (now assumed to be constant) on the horizontal axis. As in the second example, the country is shocked off its initial equilibrium by an outflow of capital. Output falls, and the exchange rate depreciates (point D). The authorities' preferred path might be to raise spending to offset the effect on output and employment, a course that will also bring a further depreciation (to point H). If this

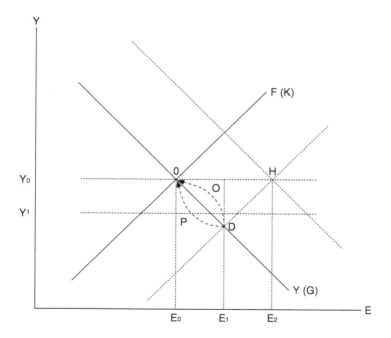

Figure 1.3 Structural optimism/pessimism.

strategy works, then that is the end of the story. The depreciation, however, may destabilize the economy for a number of reasons. It may bring a wave of bankruptcies among firms with substantial currency mismatches on their balance sheets. It may aggravate the initial capital outflow by creating fears of a continuing deterioration. It may weaken consumer or investment outlays by depressing real incomes.

For these and other (including political) reasons, the authorities may wish to put a brake on depreciation and stabilize the exchange rate. To do so without further weakening output in the short run will require additional financing, for which they may turn to the IMF for assistance. Their goal will then be to get direct financial support and a seal of approval that will draw in additional capital from other creditors. In these circumstances, legitimate differences of view will arise regarding feasible paths from point D back toward point 0. An aggressive path would involve using a large injection of official financing to raise expenditure and induce spontaneous inflows of capital that will gradually bring the economy back to equilibrium through point O in Figure 1.3. A more conservative path would involve a strong stabilization program with moderate official financing, aimed at restoring equilibrium through point P. If the authorities are convinced that they can take an expansionary path through point O – "structural optimism" – while IMF officials are convinced that confidence can be restored only by taking a more cautious path through P, then negotiations will be required that might or might not result in a program that the Fund will support and that the authorities will really own.

These simple models abstract from the complications that dominate both theoretical analysis and real-world discussions about economic policy. In most cases where a country applies to the IMF for financial assistance, the economy suffers from a combination of macroeconomic and structural imbalances that are more complex than the situations represented here. In many cases, basic disagreements over economic structure – the development role of the state, control over price and wage decisions, distributional issues – pose greater threats to ownership than the dynamic disputes described here. In all cases, detailed analysis of economic structure, domestic constraints, and dynamic adjustment is needed to determine the best course of action. That course of action must be evaluated in terms of economics (What is the best way to achieve program goals, assuming that the program can and will be carried out?), political economy (What is the best that can realistically be achieved?), and politics (How can the conflicting interests of various parties best be reconciled or balanced?). But even these abstract examples demonstrate that ownership is a much more complicated concept than it appears to be at first blush and that the challenges are linked to the nature of the problem. If ownership is initially lacking, is it primarily because of macro denial, Keynesian optimism, or structural optimism? To what extent is optimism warranted? Or, to turn the point around, is part of the reason for weak ownership that the proposed conditional arrangement is based on overly pessimistic assumptions by the IMF?

Specifically, four points emerge from this analysis that are worth stressing:

- First, establishing ownership is a two-way process. It is not just a matter of the authorities or other agents in the borrowing country coming to accept what is necessary. It also requires the Fund and other involved external agents to be flexible and responsive to the institutional, administrative, and political factors that limit or alter the scope for action in response to adverse shocks.
- Second, as the goals of Fund-supported programs have been broadened beyond the resolution of temporary external financing problems, the need for both ownership and flexibility and the difficulty of achieving them have increased. Particularly when the country or a large portion of its population is impoverished, the goals of the program must include restoration or achievement of strong economic growth, creation of employment opportunities, and a reduction of poverty. Aiming to achieve such goals increases the scope for alternative approaches to economic policy making and may leave substantial room for debate about what policy adjustments or reforms are necessary. Implementing such structural and institutional reforms often requires a broader and deeper national commitment than simply adjusting macroeconomic and financial policies.
- Third, a substantial impediment to ownership is the likelihood of a painful dynamic path toward a favorable but distant and uncertain equilibrium. If output is expected to fall, and unemployment rise, for a lengthy interim period during which the ground is prepared for a healthy rebound, the combination of an adverse reality and an uncertain future will inevitably weaken any government's resolve to own and implement proposed reforms. In these circumstances, it is natural for the government to be overly optimistic about its ability to carry on without major adjustment and for the IMF to be overly optimistic about the magnitude and speed of the growth-enhancing benefits of reform.
- Fourth, a key to coping with these complications is to establish processes of interaction between the international agency and the country that are based on partnership and flexibility. It is no longer enough, if it ever was, to aver that the country must "freely come to the conclusion" that it must undertake harsh measures that are in its own interest. Fostering ownership also requires finding ways to accommodate legitimate concerns within the circle of feasible policy options.

3 How can ownership be strengthened in the presence of conditionality?

If – as the previous section suggests – processes and the specification of conditions matter, then what processes and what conditions will promote ownership and strengthen implementation and success of policy reforms? The IMF's millennium review of conditionality emphasized a number of aspects of interaction between the institution and borrowing countries relating either to the way programs and conditions are negotiated or to the specification of conditions. Many of these were adopted in the guidelines that were approved in September 2002 (see section A of the Appendix) and are now being implemented, but nearly all of them raise difficult issues of balance. How effective these changes will be is an open question that will have to be reviewed regularly.

3.1 Initial discussion and negotiation

3.1.1 Control of the pen

The new guidelines affirm the principle that the country authorities are responsible for the design of their own policies, subject to the understanding that those policies must be acceptable to the Fund if the country is to qualify for financial support. The link between the policy program and Fund support is a Letter of Intent (LOI) addressed to the Managing Director of the IMF from the country's responsible officials, normally the finance minister and central bank governor. The LOI spells out the economic policies that they intend to carry out during the program period (usually one to three years), and it is the basis for the specification of the Fund's conditionality. What the new guidelines mean is twofold. First, before the LOI is drafted, the Fund staff should ascertain the authorities' own preferences and intentions on how to strengthen their policies. The opening gambit should come from the country, not from the Fund. Second, *if the authorities wish*, they should be given the opportunity to write at least the first draft of the LOI themselves. In most situations, this guideline will make little difference, either because it reflects existing practices or because the country's authorities prefer not to take the initiative. In other cases, it has the potential to make a big contribution toward enhancing ownership.

3.1.2 Political economy analysis

Judging the breadth and depth of ownership is a delicate proposition that requires knowledge and understanding of the country's political economy as well as sensitivity to the limits of the Fund's own role. Are the economic officials fully committed? Do they have the support of the country's top political leadership? Is there broad support throughout the country? Are there groups in parliament or elsewhere with the power and the incentive to block implementation? Analyzing such questions does not mean interfering with the country's politics, but it does require an understanding of them. Whether the Fund's staff of highly qualified economists is also well qualified to do this type of political economy analysis is an open question, but the need for a broader perspective than has typically been applied in the past is well understood. Internal training on political economy is being expanded, and the role of the Fund's resident representatives in borrowing countries is being examined.

3.1.3 Participatory processes

When the Fund established the Structural Adjustment Facility (SAF) in 1986, as a vehicle for making loans on concessional terms to low-income countries, it agreed with the World Bank to require borrowers to prepare a Policy Framework Paper (PFP) that would set out the country's overall policy objectives and strategy as a basis for financial support from the two institutions. Although the PFP was supposed to be the country's own document, prepared by the authorities with help from the staffs of the Bank and the Fund, in practice it was usually prepared largely in Washington with help from the authorities. That process continued to be applied through the 1990s under the Enhanced SAF (ESAF). In 1999, however, it was scrapped and replaced by a process that required the preparation of a Poverty Reduction Strategy Paper (PRSP) *in the country itself* and with broad participation by parliamentarians, nongovernmental organizations, and others. The objective was not only to generate more effective policy strategies aimed at reducing poverty and strengthening economic growth. It was also to use the PRSP *process* as a means of enhancing country ownership of policy reforms. Much effort has gone into making it succeed, and much more remains to be done.[5]

Generalizing the use of participatory domestic processes beyond the preparation of PRSPs is an even bigger challenge. Countries requesting to borrow from the Fund's general accounts rather than the concessional facility (now christened the Poverty Reduction and Growth Facility, or PRGF) are required to prepare only an LOI and a more detailed technical memorandum specifying how policy implementation is to be measured and assessed. Especially in crisis cases where program discussions have to be completed very quickly, broad participation may be impractical. For the moment, therefore, the Fund is experimenting with a general injunction to the staff to *encourage* countries to engage in public discussions before deciding on policy reforms or agreeing to conditionality. Whether this recommendation resonates widely or has much impact on ownership remains to be seen.

3.1.4 Selectivity

If ownership is a necessary condition for successful policy implementation, then it follows that the Fund should refuse to lend when ownership is lacking. Applying such a rule, however, is far from straightforward. Ownership is not directly observable, it is not static, and it is assessed in degrees rather than absolutes. Where does one draw a line on an invisible and ever changing path? The Managing Director of the IMF has the responsibility to assess whether a country is sufficiently committed to and capable of carrying out the proposed program and to recommend approval only when he concludes that it will be implemented. This obviously must be a subjective judgment, but it is one that can be evaluated objectively after the fact. Did the country carry out its intended program or not? If not, was there a valid reason, and did the implementation failure cause harm to the economy? If the program was implemented, did it meet its objectives? If post mortems are conducted thoroughly and systematically, the effectiveness of the initial judgments is bound to improve over time.

3.2 Program design

The second set of issues, after the processes discussed above, concerns the specification of conditions on Fund lending and the relationship between conditionality and the overall design of countries' policy reform programs. How can the Fund implement conditionality so as to enhance national ownership?

3.2.1 Parsimony in conditionality

As far as ownership is concerned, limiting conditionality to a few key policy actions is almost axiomatically helpful. Within limits, the fewer conditions the better. The evidence on the implications of this point, however, is a little ambiguous. Empirical studies suggest that programs with large numbers of conditions are implemented at about the same rate as simpler ones.[6] In other words, even if governments prefer simple programs, they are not necessarily less willing or able to meet more complex requirements. The real question is whether a large number of conditions is necessary for a program to succeed in achieving its objectives. If the goal were just to balance a country's external payments position, the answer would surely be no, but when the goal is to solve the payments problem without unduly harming economic growth or the natural environment or neighboring economies while raising the country's potential growth rate and reducing the incidence of poverty, the optimum number of conditions might be considerably larger.

In an ideal world, each country would pursue those broader objectives in its own enlightened interest, but in the real world conditionality can serve as a valuable commitment device that complements and enhances ownership of structural reforms (see Boughton and Mourmouras 2002). The challenge is to determine what policy reforms are of critical import- ance for the success of the program – meaning that without them the program is expected to fail – and to be disciplined in limiting conditional- ity to that set of actions. That challenge must be met case by case. Even if every effort is made to restrict conditionality to what is critical, it is likely that the number of conditions in practice will range from a few to a great many. What matters is the burden of proof: if it is not critically important, then it should not be a condition on Fund lending.

3.2.2 Focus

In addition to limiting conditions to the critical set, it would be helpful if IMF conditionality could be limited to cover only those policies that are within its mandate and comparative advantage. In general, that would cover macroeconomic and exchange rate policies, closely related institu- tional arrangements, and financial system issues. But what should be done if some other policy – say, finding a way to stop a financial hemorrhage from a failing state-run enterprise – is critical for achieving program goals? The compromise embodied in the guidelines is for the Fund to ask the World Bank to design and monitor that part of the program but to con- tinue to include it as a condition on Fund lending and to retain control over whether to disburse in the face of a slippage. Given the Bank's com- parative advantage on such structural policies, this approach should lead over time to better program design and stronger national ownership. To be fully effective, it will also require drawing on country-led development strategies as much as possible. In any event, the overriding principle for coverage of conditionality must be criticality, while comparative advantage governs the focus of each institution's contribution to the process.

3.2.3 Flexibility

As an integral part of the millennium review of conditionality, the Fund held or participated in several seminars around the world to solicit views from country officials, NGOs, and scholars on how to promote ownership and make conditionality more effective.[7] One of the strongest and most consistent criticisms expressed in those consultations was that countries had too little flexibility in deciding how or when to implement reforms. From the Fund's vantage point, the problem is that financing constraints limit a country's flexi- bility and require rapid solutions to financial imbalances. Structural reforms often cannot wait, because delay is expensive and unaffordable. That objec- tion, however, does not apply universally, and the Fund recognized the value of being responsive when it could do so without endangering the success of the program. Three aspects of that response are noteworthy.

First, the use of "prior actions" – requiring the authorities to take certain actions before the Fund approves the program – is being limited to situations where it is critically important that the measure be implemented in this way. If the nature of the policy (e.g., a currency depreciation) requires prior action or if the authorities' ability or incentive to enact it would be weakened by waiting until after approval, then requiring a prior action makes sense. It does not make sense, however, to ask a country to complete reforms in advance as a demonstration of commitment, because such signals are unreliable and the requirement puts an undue burden on the country.

Second, to the extent possible, it makes sense to specify conditions on outcomes rather than on policy instruments, as long as the outcomes are measurable within reasonable time limits and are reasonably within the authorities' indirect control. Again, the key is balance. Setting a condition on the inflation rate seldom makes sense, because the government cannot control it with any precision. Setting a condition on an instrument such as bank reserves may not make sense either, because the instrument may be only weakly related to inflation. Setting several conditions on various policy instruments or on frequent steps toward inflation control may be overly burdensome to administer and monitor. The goal is to allow as much implementation flexibility as possible without sacrificing the assurance that prices will be stabilized.

Third, there may be some scope for linking the timing of disbursements to the completion of reforms, or of steps toward reform, rather than specifying in advance when actions must be completed in order to qualify for financing. These "floating tranches" have been used by the Fund in a few situations, notably for debt relief operations under the Brady Plan and the HIPC initiative.[8] The goal now is to find more general applications as a way of increasing countries' control over the timing of reforms.

3.2.4 Clarity and transparency

One of the original objectives of the Fund's stand-by arrangements when they were inaugurated in 1952 was to provide clear assurances to countries that they would receive financing at specified times as long as they met conditions that were spelled out in advance. As arrangements grew longer and more complex, it became necessary in some cases to include mid-term reviews when conditionality would be respecified in light of economic developments. Quantitative performance criteria were supplemented by benchmarks and indicative targets that would be taken into account in those reviews but that would not necessarily be required for financing to continue. While these innovations were necessary under the circumstances, they undermined the clarity of assurances that the Fund was able to give. In some cases, programs contained substantially more conditions than could reasonably be met, in the expectation that enough targets would be hit to warrant keeping the program going. The cumulative effect was often dispiriting, and it tended to undermine ownership. The new guidelines aim to alleviate this problem, not only by streamlining conditionality but also by requiring that the basis for reviews be specified as clearly as possible at the outset of the arrangement and be based as much as possible on the benchmarks and indicative targets that have been agreed in advance.

4 Conclusions

The thesis of this chapter can be briefly summarized: ownership is operationally important, it need not be undermined by conditionality, and the consistency of the two can be enhanced through sensitivity to processes and products. Doing so is not so easy. As Gustave Flaubert is supposed to have said, "le bon Dieu est dans le detail." The preceding review of changes that are being put into practice at the IMF has tried to convey some of the difficulties that might impede or limit their implementation. Even after taking account of those limitations, however, the cumulative effect on ownership and on program effectiveness should be positive and could eventually be dramatic.

This chapter's focus on processes is not intended to imply that these changes will suffice to solve all ownership and implementation problems or to make all programs succeed. The larger debate must address more fundamental questions of program design: questions of how to extend or modify the so-called Washington Consensus and embed it into the Monterrey Consensus on development finance.[9] Stan Fischer recently summed up that issue neatly by noting that while the Washington Consensus is a "useful shorthand description of a major part of a desirable basic policy orientation" (Fischer 2003: 8), real-world policy recommendations must be more nuanced and comprehensive. How can we assess when macro policies are appropriate to a country's circumstances? What policy changes are needed to restore investor confidence? How much should capital flows be liberalized, and how quickly? Will privatization improve economic efficiency in specific cases? Would a large increase in aid flows improve economic performance or run into administrative bottlenecks and inflationary pressures? As we get better answers to such questions, the effectiveness of conditionality and the depth of national ownership of reforms are bound to improve.

Appendix

Mathematics of the diagrammatic models

Figures 1.1 and 1.2 (Polak model)

One-period model:

Demand for money (L)	$\Delta L = k\Delta Y$
Demand for imports (M)	$M = mY$
Payments identity	$\Delta R = X - M + K$
Supply of money	$\Delta L = q\Delta H$
Sources of monetary base (H)	$\Delta H = \Delta R + \Delta D$

where Y is GNP, X is exports, R is international reserves, K is the net capital inflow, and D is domestic credit of the banking system.

Semi-reduced form (shown in the figures):

$$Y = b_1[kY_{-1} + q(X + K) + \Delta D]$$

$$R = -b_2\Delta D - b_3 Y_{-1} + b_4(X + K) + R_{-1}$$

where b_1 are positive combinations of the structural coefficients m, k, and q. Since D is a positive function of government expenditure (G), it is straightforward to substitute G for D in the solution. Since R is absent from the first equation and the current value of Y is absent from the second, the two lines are horizontal and vertical, respectively.

Figure 1.3 (variant of Fleming–Mundell model)

Keynesian aggregate demand equation

$$Y = C(Y, E) + I(r, K) + G - K$$

Balance of payments

$$F(Y, E) = -K$$

where C, I, G, and F are, respectively, consumption, investment, government expenditure, and net exports; E is the exchange rate; and r is the domestic interest rate.

The line labeled $Y(G)$ in Figure 1.3 is derived by differentiating the demand equation and assuming (1) that the interest rate is fixed by an unchanging monetary policy ($dr = 0$) and (2) that the coefficient $I_K = 1$.

The first assumption allows one to focus on the effects of fiscal policy, while the second simplifies the exposition. If $I_K < 1$, then $Y = Y(G, K)$ with $Y_K < 0$. The slope of this line is $dY/dE = C_E/(1 - C_Y) < 0$. The line labeled $F(K)$ is derived by differentiating the payments equation. Its slope is $-(F_E/F_Y) > 0$.

Notes

* This chapter owes much to my collaboration on conditionality and ownership issues with colleagues at the IMF. I am especially grateful to Rex Ghosh, Graham Hacche, Alex Mourmouras, and conference participants for comments on earlier drafts. Nonetheless, the views expressed in this chapter, and any remaining errors, are mine alone and are not attributable to others or to any institution.

1 This assumption does not necessarily imply that the country has reached point A by pursuing an excessively expansionary macroeconomic policy. It might be that an adverse shock such as a drop in the terms of trade has shifted the internal and/or external balance curves inward and made the initial policy stance unsustainable.

2 The catch phrase is "austerity" being imposed by the IMF and resisted by the government or by veto players in the country. The more sophisticated studies (e.g., Vreeland 2003) use austerity as a metaphor for the whole range of policy reforms covered by Fund-supported programs, but they typically assume that the analysis extends to structural reform without fundamental modifications.

3 Quoted in James (1996: 109), from a transcript of the interview in IMF Central Files (C/Spain/810). Emphasis added here.

4 This line of policy advice, which amounts to applying Keynesian principles to developing-country financial crises, is exemplified by Stiglitz (2002) and has been expressed with considerably more nuance by Corden (1998).

5 As of March 2003, 51 out of 78 eligible countries had prepared either a preliminary paper ("interim" or I-PRSP) or a full PRSP, and most of those had been approved by the Executive Boards of the Bank and the Fund as a basis for lending. Only 24 of those, however, were full PRSPs.

6 The implementation rate for conditions on Fund lending has been estimated (see IMF 2001c: Figure 17) to be positively correlated with the number of conditions, but aside from prior actions the correlation is statistically insignificant. On average, countries implement around 60 percent of Fund conditions regardless of how detailed or extensive the program is.

7 This outreach program also included use of the Fund's website (www.imf.org) to request views from the general public. Comments were posted on the website, and an overview was circulated to Executive Directors as an input to the review (see IMF 2001a).

8 Under the 1989 Brady Plan, the Fund agreed to augment access to its financing to support countries' debt reduction operations such as buybacks of debt owed to external commercial creditors. Under the 1996 initiative for Heavily Indebted Poor Countries, the timing of decision and completion points as triggers for Fund financing is flexible and not determined in advance. Floating tranches are more widely used by the World Bank.

9 John Williamson (1990) coined the term Washington Consensus to characterize the set of policy reforms typically included in an IMF-supported program. The Monterrey Consensus (United Nations 2002) is an international agreement on the mutual accountability of developed and developing countries for their respective responsibilities in fostering economic development.

References

Boughton, James M. 2001. Different Strokes? Common and Uncommon Responses to Financial Crises. IMF Working Paper WP/01/12. http://www.imf.org/external/pubs/ft/wp/2001/wp0112.pdf (January).

Boughton, James M. and Alex Mourmouras. 2002. Whose Programme Is It? Policy Ownership with Conditional Lending. Forthcoming in *The IMF and the International Financial Architecture*, edited by Christopher Gilbert and David Vines. Cambridge University Press. An earlier version is available as Is Policy Ownership an Operational Concept?. IMF Working Paper WP/02/72. http://www.imf.org/external/pubs/cat/longres.cfm?sk=15746.0 (April).

Calvo, Guillermo A. and Carmen M. Reinhart. 2000. When Capital Flows Suddenly Stop: Consequences and Policy Options. In *Reforming the International Monetary and Financial System*, edited by Peter B. Kenen and Alexander K. Swoboda, pp. 175–201. Washington: International Monetary Fund.

Corden, W. Max. 1998. The Asian Crisis: Is there a Way Out? Are the IMF Prescriptions Right?. Manuscript available at www.iseas.edu.sg/pub.html (September).

Fischer, Stanley. 2003. Globalization and its Challenges. Richard T. Ely Lecture. http://www.iie.com/fischer/pdf/fischer011903.pdf (January 3).

IMF. 2001a. Conditionality in Fund-Supported Programs: External Consultations. http://www.imf.org/external/np/pdr/cond/2001/eng/collab/071701.pdf (July 17).

IMF. 2001b. Strengthening Country Ownership of Fund-Supported Programs. http://www.imf.org/external/np/pdr/cond/2001/eng/strength/120501.htm (December 5).

IMF. 2001c. Structural Conditionality in Fund-Supported Programs. http://www.imf.org/external/np/pdr/cond/2001/eng/struct/cond.pdf (February 16).

James, Harold. 1996. *International Monetary Cooperation Since Bretton Woods*. Washington: International Monetary Fund; New York: Oxford University Press.

Khan, Mohsin S. and Sunil Sharma. 2003. IMF Conditionality and Country Ownership of Adjustment Programs. *World Bank Research Observer* 18: 227–48.

Polak, Jacques J. 1998. The IMF Monetary Model at Forty. *Economic Modelling* 15: 395–410.

Schadler, Susan and others. 1995. IMF Conditionality: Experience Under Stand-by and Extended Arrangements, Part I: Key Issues and Findings. Occasional Paper No. 128. Washington: International Monetary Fund.

Stiglitz, Joseph E. 2002. *Globalization and its Discontents*. New York: W.W. Norton.

United Nations. 2002. Report of the International Conference on Financing for Development, Monterrey. Mexico, 18–22 March 2002, A/Conf.198/11. http://ods-dds-ny.un.org/doc/UNDOC/GEN/N02/392/67/PDF/N0239267.pdf?OpenElement.

Vreeland, James Raymond. 2003. *The IMF and Economic Development*. Cambridge, England: Cambridge University Press.

Williamson, John. 1990. *Latin American Adjustment: How Much Has Happened?*. Washington: Institute for International Economics.

2 Policy conditionality*

Stephen Coate and Stephen Morris

It makes considerable sense for the World Bank and other multilateral agencies to push very hard for liberal policies in developing countries, given the demonstrated tendencies of these clients to engage in economically irrational interventions.

(Krugman 1992: 32)

1 Introduction

The World Bank carries out extensive *policy conditionality*: developing country policy makers agree to a program of economic policy reform in exchange for grants and concessionary finance. There are two ways in which policy conditionality might have a beneficial impact. First, policy conditionality may have a *short-term* impact: during the lifetime of policy conditionality, the promise of resources induces policy makers to make beneficial policy changes. Second, policy conditionality may have a *long-term* impact: the short-term implementation of beneficial reforms may alter the political environment in a way that favors the continuation of those policies. In this chapter, we discuss the circumstances under which policy conditionality can have beneficial impacts in the short and long term.

We argue that to analyze the short-term effects of policy conditionality, it is necessary to understand *why* policy makers are choosing the economic policies that the World Bank is trying to reform. Often "economically irrational interventions" (see the above quote) are politically rational and favor interest groups that policy makers wish to favor. Banning the economically irrational interventions may induce policy makers to make transfers to those special interests in more costly ways which cannot be controlled by policy conditionality. In this way, policy conditionality can make all citizens in the recipient country worse off, having an unambiguously negative impact. We discuss the conditions under which this negative unintended consequence of conditionality is likely to arise.

With respect to its long-term effects, we argue that conditionality will only have an impact if there is a tendency for reforms to persist. Thus, it is necessary to understand why short-term implementation of reform policies will alter the political environment in favor of those policies. Without understanding policy persistence, there cannot be much hope of predicting when policy conditionality will have a long-term impact. We discuss some different explanations for policy persistence, and examine their implications for the long-term impact of policy conditionality.

Many authors within and outside the World Bank have conducted theoretical and empirical analyses of policy conditionality (see Haggard and Webb 1995; Mosley *et al.* 1991; Svensson 2000; World Bank 1988). Our methodological contribution in this chapter is to base all our analysis on explicit theories of public choice. We believe that it cannot make sense to employ policy conditionality without a theory of why policy makers in developing countries choose the policies they choose.[1] The remainder of the chapter is organized as follows. Section 2 discusses the short-term impact of conditionality, showing how its welfare consequences depend on the underlying political and policy environment. Section 3 focuses on the long-term impact of conditionality, discussing alternative explanations for policy persistence and their implications for conditionality. Section 4 concludes with a summary of some of the general lessons which emerge from the analysis.

2 The short-term impact of policy conditionality

We will frame our discussion in terms of the following simple example. A developing country policy maker is supporting a domestic cement industry by protecting local producers from international competition. This policy is serving no useful economic objective (encouraging learning by doing, for example), its only role being to make transfers from the population at large (who ultimately consume cement) to the domestic cement industry. In addition, there are significant *deadweight costs* associated with the transfer: that is, the gains from the policy for the cement industry will be less than the cost to the rest of the economy. The World Bank has no desire for transfers to be made to the cement industry, and would like to induce the policy maker to eliminate the protection. The World Bank is considering offering grants, loans, etc. to the country, which would be to the policy maker's benefit. Should it make the granting of this financial package conditional on the removal of this protection? Or would such conditionality make matters worse?

In this section we show that the answer depends on why the policy maker does not want to eliminate the protection. (If he favored reform, he would presumably implement it unilaterally and there would be no role for conditionality.) In much of the discussion of policy conditionality, the implicit assumption is that the policy maker chooses bad policies merely because he does not know any better. For example, perhaps he believes (wrongly) that there is learning by doing in the cement industry so that protection will encourage dynamic economies of scale and create positive externalities in the economy as a whole. In this case, he just needs to be shown that the economy would be better off without the policy and policy conditionality is a convenient way to convey this message. Policy conditionality is therefore obviously beneficial. Suppose, however, that the policy maker is perfectly aware of the effects of the policy and is against eliminating it because he wishes to redistribute to the cement industry. There are many reasons why politicians, in both democratic and authoritarian regimes, wish to make transfers to special interests such as the cement industry. They may expect *political* favors in return, such as votes or financial support for their political movement. They may expect (or negotiate) *personal* favors in return, such as bribes or future employment. The cement industry may be located in a region which the policy maker wishes to favor, either for the above reasons or because he is a benevolent ruler who believes that increasing wealth in that region is necessary to maintain peace. For our purposes, the reason why the politician favors transfers to the cement industry does not matter. What is important is that we must consider how he will respond if this method of redistribution is removed via conditionality. Here we consider this question under two different hypotheses. The first, the *efficient transfers* hypothesis, is that the policy maker favors protection because it is the most efficient way of redistributing to the cement industry. The second, the *hidden transfers* hypothesis, is that the policy maker favors protection because it allows him to hide the fact that he is making transfers to the cement industry.

2.1 Efficient transfers

We are assuming that the policy maker is against eliminating protection because he wishes to redistribute to the cement industry. However, this is not a *sufficient* explanation of why the policy maker favors protection. Presumably the policy maker could have transferred resources to the cement industry in many different ways, for example, by offering production subsidies, government purchases of cement at inflated prices, etc. If the cement industry was favored because of its geographical location, the policy maker could have offered the region new schools, new hospitals, new roads, or more government jobs. From all these possible options, the policy maker chose protection as the transfer mechanism. It is reasonable to assume that this was the *cheapest* method available of making transfers. The Chicago School of Political Economy has long argued that in a democratic environment, transfers will be made in efficient ways: after all, if transfers were being made inefficiently, all voters would have common interest in voting out the policy maker (see Stigler 1982; Becker 1985; Wittman 1989). One might expect that similar pressures would be at work in a non-democratic environment: rational policy makers can only gain by making transfers in the cheapest possible way.

This way of thinking is important because it forces one to consider *the equilibrium effects of policy conditionality on the choice of transfer mechanism.* In particular, if the World Bank provides an incentive to the policy maker to remove the protection program, then is it not possible that the policy maker will simply choose an alternative, less efficient transfer mechanism? If so, is it not possible that such conditionality might make all parties worse off?

To shed light on this consider the following simple model. There are two groups in society: the cement industry and regular citizens; their income is represented by y_c and y_r respectively. The policy maker has smooth, strictly convex preferences over y_c and y_r represented by $u(y_c, y_r)$. This utility function is a reduced form for some more-complex political process. Write $x_i^*(p, y)$ for the value of y_i maximizing $u(y_c, y_r)$ subject to $y_r + py_c \leq y$. Both y_c and y_r are normal goods in the policy maker's utility function, so that $dx_i^*/dy > 0$ for each $i \in \{c, r\}$. The World Bank cares only about y_r (the analysis which follows would generalize as long as the policy maker cares more about transfers to the special interest than the World Bank). Suppose for simplicity that the citizens initially have income y_r^0 while the cement industry has zero income.

To establish a benchmark, let us begin by supposing that the policy maker has only one way of making transfers to the cement industry: protection. This policy has net benefits B for the cement industry and net costs C for the citizens. Assume that $B < C$ so that there is a deadweight cost of protection. The policy maker would choose to implement (or maintain) protection if

$$u(B, y_r^0 - C) > u(0, y_r^0)$$

Assume this condition were true, what could the external agency do to prevent implementation of the policy? A World Bank policy reform package would consist of a payment G that would be made only if protection were removed. The minimum payment necessary, G^*, is implicitly defined by:

$$u(B, y_r^0 - C) = u(0, y_r^0 + G^*)$$

Even though the policy maker cares more about the cement industry than regular citizens, there is some minimum payment that will induce the policy maker not to carry out protection. If the World Bank promises G^* if the policy is not implemented, notice that not only does the citizen not incur the costs of protection, C, but also the citizen will receive the World Bank assistance, G^* (we are assuming that the World Bank assistance benefits the citizen, not the politician directly). The payment of G^* has the effect of increasing the citizen's income by $C + G^*$ (from $y_r^0 - C$ to $y_r^0 + G^*$). In this sense, policy conditionality works and has a multiplier effect.

Now suppose that the policy maker also has the ability to make cash transfers from regular citizens to the cement industry. Specifically, the policy maker can give T to the special interest by taking away $(1+\delta)T$ from the citizen. From a technological point of view, how do cash transfers compare with protection? Notice that the cash transfer mechanism can be used to give B to the special interest at a cost of $(1+\delta)B$; so we say that the policy is an *efficient transfer mechanism* if $C < (1+\delta)B$, i.e. $\frac{B}{C} > \frac{1}{1+\delta}$.

Let us first analyze what would happen if there was no policy conditionality and protection was not available. In this case, the policy maker would choose transfer level $T^* = x_s^*(1+\delta, y_r^0)$. Suppose now that the protection was made available, with $B < T^*$. If protection is not an efficient transfer mechanism, the policy maker will not implement it and will choose transfer level T^*. If protection is efficient, the policy maker will implement it and choose transfer level $T^{**} = x_c^*(1+\delta, y_r^0 + (1+\delta)B - C) - B$. The income of the cement industry is then $x_c^*(1+\delta, y_r^0 + (1+\delta)B - C)$ while the income of regular citizens is $x_r^*(1+\delta, y_r^0 + (1+\delta)B - C)$. If protection is used, it must be efficient and both groups' incomes are higher than if the policy were not implemented. The effect of allowing the cheaper transfer mechanism is to strictly increase the size of the set of income pairs (y_c, y_r) feasible for the policy maker. Now our assumption that citizen and special interest income are both "normal goods" in the policy maker's preferences implies that both are better off.

Let us now analyze policy conditionality. If we allowed financial payments to be made contingent on *both* whether protection were removed *and* the level of cash transfers, the qualitative conclusions would be much as before. But a major practical problem for World Bank policy conditionality is that there are a limited number of actions which can be effectively monitored and thus used as conditions in reform programs. In practice, there will always exist an array of policies (not necessarily with any *budgetary* implications) which have the effect of increasing the utility of one group at the expense of another. Thus we want to consider the case where financial payments are made contingent on whether protection is removed *but not on the level of cash transfers.*

Let us again assume that the World Bank offers a payment G if protection is not implemented. If the policy maker chooses to accept the reform package, the policy maker will not implement protection but will then choose an optimal level of transfers, $T^*(G) = x_c^*(1+\delta, y_r^0 + G)$. If the policy maker refuses the reform package, the policy maker will implement the policy and again choose an optimal level of transfers, $T^{**}(G) = x_c^*(1+\delta, y_r^0 + (1+\delta)B - C) - B$. Thus the minimum cash payment G^* necessary to induce the policy maker not to implement the policy is implicitly defined by:

$$u(T^*(G^*), y_r^0 + G^* - (1+\delta)T^*(G^*)) = u(B + T^{**}, y_r^0 - C - T^{**})$$

The citizen's income in this case is $x_r^*(1 + \delta, y_r^0 + G^*)$. But suppose that the World Bank had instead provided G^* to the developing country with no strings attached. In this case, the policy maker would implement the policy and choose cash transfer $x_c^*(1 + \delta, y_r^0 + G^* + (1 + \delta)B - C) - B$. The citizen's income in this would be $x_r^*(1 + \delta, y_r^0 + G^* + (1 + \delta)B - C)$. The normality of preferences ensures that the citizen would be better off under this scenario than if the policy maker was induced not to implement the project. In this case, therefore, conditionality makes all agents worse off and is unambiguously a bad idea. The two cases considered so far were somewhat extreme. If protection is the only transfer mechanism, or more generally if the World Bank program can monitor all possible transfer mechanisms, then policy conditionality may work well in preventing transfers. If, on the other hand, protection is not the only transfer mechanism and banning the policy does not alter the marginal deadweight cost of transfers, then the only effect of banning the policy is to increase the equilibrium cost of transfers. An intermediate case is one where the World Bank cannot monitor all transfer mechanisms (so an outright ban is impossible) but it can outlaw some methods in such a way that the marginal deadweight cost of transfers increases. The question is then whether increasing the marginal deadweight cost of transfers benefits the citizens or not in equilibrium.

This issue closely parallels one studied by the Virginia School of Political Economy (Brennan and Buchanan 1980: 4–5). Should constitutions allow governments to intervene extensively in the economy? Assuming the government interventions are intended merely as transfer mechanisms, the answer depends on a trade-off. Banning certain interventions merely increases the cost of making transfers, assuming it is not possible to ban all interventions. This implies a relative price effect: fewer transfers will be made because of the higher price. But it also implies a loss of real income, which will tend to reduce the welfare of both winners and losers from the transfer. Thus the overall effect will depend on elasticities (Lott 1997).

These results can be replicated in our setting. We will require two definitions. The cross-price elasticity of the citizen's consumption with respect to the price of the cement industry's consumption is defined as:

$$\eta_{rc} = \frac{\mathrm{d}x_r^*(p, y)}{\mathrm{d}p} / x_r^*(p, y)$$

Cement industry income and citizen income are substitutes (complements) if $\eta_{rc} > 0$ ($\eta_{rc} < 0$). Now the citizens' income is $x_r^*(1 + \delta, y_r^0)$ and thus is increasing in the marginal deadweight cost of transfers if and only if $\eta_{rc} > 0$, i.e. cement industry income and citizen income are substitutes.

Some intuition for this result comes from considering extreme cases. If incomes are perfect complements and the policy maker seeks to maximize the minimum of the incomes of the citizen and the cement industry, then $x_r^*(1 + \delta, y_r^0) = \frac{y_r^0}{2(1+\delta)}$, which is decreasing in δ. If incomes are perfect substitutes, and the policy maker seeks to maximize $(1 + \lambda)y_c + y_r$, then

$$x_r^*(1 + \delta, y_r^0) = \begin{cases} 0, \text{ if } \delta < \lambda \\ y_r^0, \text{ if } \delta > \lambda \end{cases}$$

which is (weakly) increasing in δ. Note that the assumption that only the citizen has income before the transfers matters here. If the special interest had income also, then increasing δ would (by normality) tend to increase y_r via an income effect.

2.2 Hidden transfers

Suppose there exists a technologically feasible and less costly way of making the transfers to the cement industry, say, by offering direct subsidies. But if the policy maker paid direct subsidies to the cement industry, it would be clear to the public he was making transfers to the special interest. They might also suspect that protection was a way of making transfers to the cement industry, but they would not be sure.[2] The policy maker might argue that protection was a Pareto-improving policy because of the dynamic externalities. In both democracies and authoritarian regimes, policy makers have incentives to make transfers to special interests but also have incentives to hide the fact that they are doing so.

Tullock (1983, 1989) proposed this explanation of inefficient transfers. In Coate and Morris (1995), we formalized this story and identified four conditions under which a policy may be an effective hidden transfer mechanism. First, the policy must benefit groups the policy maker wants to benefit (i.e., the policy maker wants to make transfers to the cement industry). Second, there must be ex ante uncertainty about whether the policy also serves a public interest (i.e., the public thinks protection *might* generate dynamic externalities). Third, the public is less informed about the impact of the policy than the policy maker (i.e., the policy maker *knows* that protection helps no one but the cement industry). Fourth, the public never discovers the truth for sure (i.e., the public thinks it possible that the protection served the public interest even after it is implemented). The key to the hidden transfers explanation is that the policy maker is concerned about his reputation (he does not want the public to believe that he is trying to make transfers to the cement industry). The policy maker is then concerned not only about the deadweight costs of alternative transfer mechanisms, but also about the reputational cost to him of carrying out transfers in a transparent way.

It is hard to draw any general conclusions about the desirability of policy conditionality if bad policies are hidden transfer mechanisms. Of course, the World Bank might aim to prevent all transfers (including hidden ones), but we argued above, this was unlikely to be feasible. If one particular hidden transfer mechanism is banned, there is no way to predict ex ante whether the next best, from the point of the view of the policy maker, would entail more deadweight costs or less (it might have lower deadweight costs but be more transparent and thus have a high reputational cost for the policy maker).[3]

3 The long-term impact of policy conditionality

3.1 Internalizing policy reform and policy persistence

Policy conditionality may sometimes be used to persuade policy makers to carry out beneficial reforms which – in the absence of policy conditionality – they would not have carried out. But presumably policy makers will abandon these reforms once the financial incentive disappears. Put simply, if policy conditionality is required in the first place, it is presumably because policy makers do not like the reforms, so our first guess should be that reform will be abandoned once the conditionality disappears.

Yet Bank policy is clearly based on the premise that the reforms induced by policy conditionality will be permanent. Indeed, Bank analysis puts much emphasis on the need to "internalize" policy reform so that the government "owns" the reform program (see, e.g., World Bank 1988: chapter 4). This seems odd, since, we re-iterate, if policy makers were not opposed to the reforms, conditionality would not be required in the first place. One motive for this view would be that policy makers are incompetent and that short-term conditionality allows them to see the error of their ways.

Suppose, however, that policy makers are not incompetent. Are there reasons to believe that short-term conditionality will have long-term effects? This view is certainly implicit in much Bank analysis, although the actual mechanism is not described.[4] Our main purpose in this section is to try and identify reasons why policies might have a tendency to *persist* in the sense that their prior introduction makes it more likely that they will remain in place in the future.[5] In the remainder of this section, we will outline a number of alternative explanations of policy persistence. Each explanation will also have somewhat different implications for the long-term impact of policy conditionality.

3.2 The conventional wisdom

The conventional wisdom is that interest groups representing net beneficiaries will form to defend reforms, so that even when conditionality disappears, there is political pressure to maintain them. The introduction of a reform sets up a system of interest group politics which then dominates political decision taking. Support for this position is garnered from the obvious historical importance of interest groups in the maintenance of many resilient policies.

Unfortunately, this "explanation" is incomplete. In any political system, interest groups will form in response to economic and political incentives. If cement consumers have the capacity and incentives to organize an interest group to successfully lobby to *maintain* the reform, then they would presumably have the capacity and incentives to *introduce* the reform were it not already in place. This being the case, protection would not be operative in the future irrespective of whether it was eliminated in the present. The current introduction of the reform cannot then be held responsible for its future presence. The standard explanation simply fails to answer the key question: what is the *mechanism* by which the introduction of the reform alters incentives in the political process in favor of preserving the reform?

3.3 A private investments explanation

In Coate and Morris (1999), we develop a private investment theory of policy persistence. The idea is that when an economic policy is introduced, agents will often respond by undertaking actions in order to benefit from it. These actions increase their willingness to pay for the policy in the future. This extra willingness to pay will be translated into political pressure to retain the policy and this means that the policy is more likely to be operative in the future.[6]

Consider again the cement industry example. Suppose a protection policy is in place. Industrialists will have responded by making costly investments in domestic cement plants. This investment is sunk. The value to these industrialists of protection is now enhanced by the value of their sunk investments. Their "willingness to pay" for protection has gone up. If the political process is sensitive to the interests of these industrialists, past protection implies a higher likelihood that protection will be in place in the future. In particular, if protection was believed to be the economically optimal policy in the 1950s, it may remain in place in the 1970s even when the policy has been shown to be a pure transfer and even though it would not be in place if it had not been implemented in the 1950s.

Now suppose that protection is removed for the duration of the 1980s. Industrialists will respond by running down their cement plants and investing in outward-oriented industries. Again, this investment is sunk. The industrialists might still wish to see protection for the cement industry. But their willingness to pay for protection has been diminished as a result of sunk investments during the 1980s. In addition, in response to cheaper cement prices, industrial users of cement will have developed greater reliance on cement and will therefore be willing to pay more to prevent protection of the cement industry. Thus if protection was removed by World Bank policy conditionality during the 1980s (against the wishes of the policy makers) it might remain in place in the 1990s (after policy conditionality is removed) because of the induced decrease in the net willingness to pay for the policy.

In Coate and Morris (1999), we presented a simple dynamic model of this phenomenon. We will sketch the idea of the model, in order to make clear what features are required for this explanation of policy persistence. Consider a single firm which can operate in one of two sectors; the cement industry and industry X. The firm can switch sectors at any time, but switching is costly. At the beginning of period one, the firm is operating in the cement industry. There is a public policy (protection) which favors the cement industry. We assume that the impact of the protection is larger than the switching cost, so that the firm's short-term interest is to move out of the cement industry if the policy is not in place and into it if it is, despite the fact that the switching cost must be paid.

For purposes of analyzing the impact of policy conditionality, we can focus on a simple question. Consider a two period model where protection may or may not be enacted in either period. We take the first period policy to be exogenous, but model the choice of second period policy by a policy maker. We suppose that the second period policy maker trades off the welfare of the "citizen" with bribes received from the firm. The payments made by the firm can be interpreted more broadly, however: all that matters for our analysis is that the choice of policy is sensitive to the willingness to pay off the firm.

Now if the policy maker cares mostly about bribes from the firm, he will always enact protection in the second period. If the policy maker cares mostly about the welfare of the citizen, he will never enact protection in the second period. For our *policy persistence* result, we assume that the policy maker's preferences are in some intermediate range, i.e. the policy maker is *moderate*. In this case, we are able to show that protection will be chosen in the second period only if it was (exogenously) in place in the first period.

The logic of the argument is straightforward and comes in two steps. For the first step, we show that protection will be implemented in the second period only if the firm stays in the cement industry in the first period. *If* the firm stays in the cement industry, its willingness to pay for protection in period two is higher than if it had left, and – given our assumption of policy maker moderation – the firm's increased willingness to bribe is enough to maintain protection in the second period. For the second step, we show that the firm's decision as to whether to stay in the cement industry is determined by the first period policy, i.e. the firm stays in the cement industry only if protection is in place. Note that the firm takes into account both its first period profits and the effect of its decision on the second period outcome.

This simple analysis is sufficient to explain a long-term impact of policy conditionality. If the first period policy maker can be induced to abandon protection (by policy conditionality), then the reform will be maintained in the second period *even though there is no policy conditionality in the second period*, and even though protection would have been maintained in the absence of policy conditionality.

The above analysis provides some insights into the likely long-term impact of policy conditionality. It suggests that, if current policy makers can be induced to introduce policy reform, the investments of private agents in response to the policy reform will reduce the net willingness to pay for the policy in the future. In this sense, policy conditionality is internalized.[7] Thus, if part of the purpose of policy conditionality is to make the political climate more favorable to reform policies, the key is to focus on policies which induce the private sector to make investments which can only by protected by their maintenance.[8]

3.4 Asymmetric information about the status quo and reform policies

In a model in which decisions are made by majority rule, Fernandez and Rodrik (1991) show that uncertainty about the distribution of gains and losses from a policy reform can lead to the reform not being undertaken, even if it would be supported once introduced. In such circumstances, the reform would be in place in the future if and only if it were introduced in the present. In their argument, uncertainty alters voters' preferences over policies in ways which, under majority rule, favor the status quo policy. As they note, the point generalizes to decision rules other than majority rule. For example, Olson (1965), Becker (1983), and others argue that a more concentrated distribution of benefits may produce more political pressure than a diffuse distribution. Under this view, eliminating uncertainty will produce more political pressure if the ex ante distribution of benefits is more diffuse than the ex post distribution.

To apply this argument to our example, it would have to be the case that there was uncertainty about the benefits and costs of removing protection from the cement industry. This does not seem unreasonable. Moreover, this uncertainty would have to be such as to make ex ante political support for the reform smaller than ex post support. Again, this does not seem unreasonable. If these conditions are satisfied, policy conditionality can have a beneficial long-term impact. By removing uncertainty about who the winners and losers are under the reform policies, the asymmetry favoring the status quo is removed.

3.5 Entitlements

Others have cited non-economic reasons for policy persistence. Even in the absence of any sunk cost, interest groups may perceive the removal of a policy to be a "loss" of an entitlement and fight harder against its removal than they would have been prepared to fight for its original implementation. This assumes asymmetric attitudes to gains and losses relative to the interest group's perception of the status quo. The psychology literature has documented asymmetric attitudes to "gains" and "losses" that cannot be explained by standard economic theory (Kahneman *et al.* 1991). Tullock (1975) and Baldwin (1989) discuss this phenomenon in the context of taxi licensing and trade policy respectively. While plausible in some instances, it is hard to identify in general what determines the perceived status quo. Thus it is hard to identify the implications for policy conditionality.

To apply this argument to our example, one would have to assume that the cement industry would feel more strongly about its protection being removed than about having it reinstated once it has been removed. Thus, removing the protection would be viewed as a "loss," while reinstating it would be viewed as a "gain." If this were so, policy conditionality by removing the protection could reduce the political pressure for it in the future.

4 Conclusion

This chapter has discussed the circumstances under which policy conditionality can have beneficial impacts in the short and the long term. We will not take a position on whether World Bank policy conditionality has been successful or not. Practitioners may well have used such programs well despite the lack of any explicit rationale of how they were supposed to work (politically). But there is reason to think that old ways of thinking about the Bank's role are potentially misleading. Consider the following typical situation.

> As part of a reform package with policy conditionality, (1) the public investment plan of country X is subject to review (i.e., veto) by the World Bank; (2) the total budget deficit is subject to review (i.e., veto) by the I.M.F.; but (3) the regional distribution of the recurrent budget is not subject to review by anybody. The government proposes building a cement plant in the West of the country. Bank economists argue that the economic rate of return is too low. The cement plant is vetoed.

The analysis of section 2.1 suggests that this may be flawed policy. The very fact that the Government was prepared to incur the deadweight costs associated with transferring resources to the West by building the cement plant suggests that the West is very important in the Government's calculations. Quite possibly, the Government will react by, say, hiring more Westerners in Government positions, a policy which may leave both the East and the West (and thus presumably the World Bank) worse off. The basic flaw of this hypothetical Bank policy was to believe that it makes sense to distinguish "economic" decisions (the investment program) from "political" decisions (the distribution of the recurrent budget).

We will conclude by reviewing some lessons from our analysis.

- A considerable portion of government activity in most countries is devoted to the transfer of resources between different groups. If the "bad" policies that the Bank wishes to ban are in fact transfer mechanisms, then it is necessary to take into account the second order effects of banning them. Bank conditionality never covers all policies, so there will be feed-on effects. Our analysis suggested that if policy makers are using the cheapest ways of making transfers, it is far from obvious what these effects will be (section 2.1).
- Incomplete information about policy can play a number of different roles. If policy makers know which policies are transfers but their political constituencies do not, then policy makers may make transfers in excessively costly ways (section 2.2). But it is far from obvious what policy conditionality can do about it. On the other hand, if policy makers are misinformed, policy conditionality might play a role in forcing them to learn.
- If policy conditionality is to have permanent effects, it must be because there exist political or economic mechanisms which ensure that the implementation of a policy in the past increases the likelihood of it being in place in the future, i.e. policies must persist. If policy conditionality is to have long-term effects, it should be designed with a clear view of the relevant mechanisms creating policy persistence. For example, reform policies which create incentives for private investment will have a tendency to persist not merely because the private investment is beneficial but also because the private investment alters the "willingness to pay" of interest groups for policies in ways which favor the reform policies.

Notes

* The research for this chapter was funded by the World Bank under PRO 680-18, "Analytical Perspectives on Aid Effectiveness in Africa." The views expressed are those of the authors alone. This chapter was written in July 1996. While some references have been brought up to date, we have not attempted to describe recent research that has applied formal methods to understanding policy conditionality. See Drazen (2004) for a recent contribution and references to further work.

1 In the introduction to Haggard and Webb (1995), Summers describes various political problems in economic policy making but argues that "research on political economy does not need to describe in more detail how the mechanisms of these challenges operate. Rather, the task is to find politically acceptable ways of designing institutions to minimize these problems." We believe, on the contrary, that in designing such institutions in general and policy conditionality in particular, it is necessary to be explicit about the political motivation for economic policies.

2 Since the costs of protection are spread widely across the population, it may be that no one has sufficient incentive to become informed.

3 The hidden transfer story also suggests actions other than policy conditionality that might be in the World Bank's interest. If the World Bank could credibly inform the public that protection was just a hidden transfer mechanism, the policy maker would abandon the policy, even without policy conditionality. But again, it is unpredictable what the net effect would be. Another World Bank policy might be to directly transfer resources to the cement industry, thus removing the stigma to the policy maker of having made a transparent transfer. If we believe that policy makers do not carry out economic reforms because the reforms would hurt special interests to which the policy makers are beholden and the political costs of making transparent transfers is too high, then a World Bank policy which had the effect of compensating unpopular losers from economic reform might be cost effective.

4 As Mosley and Toye (1988: 409) point out:

> [The World Bank] has consciously and deliberately laid siege to the high ground of economic policy-making in recipient countries. However, it has done so without any strategy – except the promise of further money – for strengthening the forces supporting its own programme of reform in relation to the forces which oppose it.

5 If an interest group has sufficient power to induce a policy in this period, it is likely that they will have that power next period too. However, this does not reflect policy persistence in our sense unless the introduction of the policy has an effect on the second period choice of policy.

6 This mechanism is also discussed in Rodrik (1991). He argues that the probability that a policy reform is kept in place in the future will depend positively on the responsiveness of private investment to the reform when it is initially introduced. "The greater the investment response, the more likely entrenched interests will be created in favor of the continuation of the reform" (237).

7 To give one concrete example, the Turkish industrial sector once vociferously opposed outward-looking reform policies (Atiyas 1994). However, once those policies were put in place by a military dictatorship, apparently insulated from special interest politics, the same industrialists invested in export markets. Once Turkey returned to democracy, those investments were presumably part of the reason those industrialists no longer opposed the reform policies.

8 Boycko *et al.* (1995) argue that Russia's privatization program was successful precisely because it created the political forces to ensure its success.

References

Atiyas, I. 1994. Governance and Successful Adjustment in Turkey. World Bank.

Baldwin, R. 1989. The Political Economy of Trade Policy. *Journal of Economic Perspectives* 3: 119–35.

Becker, G. 1983. A Theory of Competition among Pressure Groups for Political Influence. *Quarterly Journal of Economics* 98: 371–400.

Becker, G. 1985. Public Policies, Pressure Groups, and Dead Weight Costs. *Journal of Political Economy* 28: 329–47.

Boycko, M., A. Shleifer, and R. Vishny. 1995. *Privatizing Russia*. Cambridge, MA: The MIT Press.

Brennan, G. and J. Buchanan. 1980. *The Power to Tax: Analytical Foundations of a Fiscal Constitution*. New York: Cambridge University Press.

Coate, S. and S. Morris. 1995. On the Form of Transfers to Special Interests. *Journal of Political Economy* 103: 1210–35.

Coate, S and S. Morris. 1999. Policy Persistence. *American Economic Review* 89: 1327–36.

Drazen, A. 2004. Conditionality and Ownership in IMF Lending: A Political Economy Approach. This volume.

Fernandez, R. and D. Rodrik. 1991. Resistance to Reform: Status Quo Bias in the Presence of Individual-Specific Uncertainty. *American Economic Review* 81: 1146–55.

Haggard, S. and S. Webb. 1995. *Voting for Reform: Democracy, Political Liberalization, and Economic Adjustment.* New York: Oxford University Press.

Kahneman, D., J. Knetsch, and R. Thaler. 1991. The Endowment Effect, Loss Aversion and Status Quo Bias. *Journal of Economic Perspectives* 5: 193–206.

Krugman, P. 1992. Toward a Counter-Counterrevolution in Development Theory. Proceedings of the 1992 World Bank Annual Conference on Development Economics, 15–38.

Lott, J. 1997. Does Political Reform Increase Wealth?: Or Why the Difference Between the Chicago and Virginia Schools is Really an Elasticity Question. *Public Choice* 91: 219–27.

Mosley, P., J. Harrigan, and J. Toye. 1991. *Aid and Power: The World Bank and Policy-based Lending.* London: Routledge.

Mosley, P. and J. Toye. 1988. The Design of Structural Adjustment Programmes. *Development Policy Review* 6: 395–414.

Olson, M. 1965. *The Logic of Collective Action.* Cambridge, MA: Harvard University Press.

Rodrik, D. 1991. Policy Uncertainty and Private Investment in Developing Countries. *Journal of Development Economics* 36: 229–42.

Stigler, G. 1982. Economists and Public Policy. *Regulation* 6: 13–17.

Svensson, J. 2000. When is Foreign Aid Policy Credible? Aid Dependence and Conditionality. *Journal of Development Economics* 61: 61–84.

Tullock, G. 1975. The Transitional Gains Trap. *Bell Journal of Economics* 6: 671–8.

Tullock, G. 1983. *Economics of Income Redistribution.* Boston: Kluwer-Nijhoff.

Tullock, G. 1989. *The Economics of Special Privilege and Rent Seeking.* Boston: Kluwer-Nijhoff.

Wittman, D. 1989. Why Democracies Produce Efficient Results. *Journal of Political Economy* 97: 1395–424.

World Bank. 1988. Adjustment Lending: An Evaluation of Ten Years of Experience. Policy and Research Series, Country Economics Department.

3 Conditionality and ownership in IMF lending

A political economy approach[*]

Allan Drazen

The IMF is currently engaged in a wide-ranging and comprehensive reexamination of the nature of its assistance programs. Many of the issues being discussed fall under the general heading of "conditionality" in lending, defined as the "explicit link between the approval or continuation of the IMF's financing and the implementation of certain specific aspects of the government's policy program" (IMF 2001).[1] Conditionality is viewed as a central feature of IMF assistance programs, essential to their success.

The debate on conditionality has raised both pragmatic and conceptual questions. The key pragmatic questions are: How effective has conditionality been in helping IMF or World Bank assistance programs achieve their aims?, and How can it be made more effective? On a very basic conceptual level, there is the question of the "proper" relation between the IMF and sovereign member countries that wish to borrow, with the nature of IMF conditionality indicating (or perhaps even defining) what that relation is in practice. There is the related question of the extent to which the IMF can or should take political factors into consideration in designing assistance programs, a question that touches on the IMF's institutional self-image as technocratic and apolitical. The conceptual debate is very much tied to the more pragmatic issues, since questions of the proper role of IMF conditionality are motivated in no small part by the desire to improve its effectiveness. More concretely, program success depends on successful implementation, which in turn reflects the political constraints, raising the question of the extent to which program design should take these constraints into account.

Intricately tied up with the question of reform of conditionality is that of program "ownership" by a country that participates in an IMF or World Bank program. Ownership of a program, like most terms that sound unambiguously positive, means different things to different people, but may be roughly defined as the extent to which a country is interested in pursuing reforms independently of any incentives provided by multilateral lenders. Here too, conceptual and political dimensions are related to one another, with country ownership seen as fundamental to programs with which the IMF "should" be involved. There is also the pragmatic question of effectiveness. Ownership is widely seen not simply as greatly increasing the chances of program success but as crucial to success since, without ownership, programs are very likely to fail.

In short, reform of conditionality, even from a very pragmatic perspective, requires an understanding of the "politics" of conditionality in the various senses of that term set out two paragraphs above: the role of conditionality in the proper relation between the IMF and borrowing member countries; the effect of domestic political constraints on the design of conditionality; and the extent to which the IMF can and should take these political constraints into account in program design. Unfortunately, none of these questions have received as much discussion in the overall debate on conditionality as they deserve. Hence, it is worthwhile to address these questions in a more formal political economic framework.

The discussion of conditionality and ownership that has taken place is often unclear. It is argued that *both* conditionality *and* ownership are central to assistance programs, even though the latter would seem to negate the need for the former. There has been a significant amount of intellectual effort in IMF documents to argue that the two go "hand-in-hand," much of it striking an outside observer as displaying some extraordinary mental and verbal gymnastics. Moreover, the tension between conditionality and ownership is only one of the points on which the debate on the reform of conditionality is often not clear.

The purpose of this chapter is to shed light on some of these issues. It is not meant to be a comprehensive discussion of conditionality and how it may be reformed, but to focus on the relation between conditionality and ownership. Though it may sound as if the objectives of the chapter are too narrowly defined, the question of how conditionality and ownership can be made consistent gets at the heart of the debate of what conditionality is trying to do, and why it may not be succeeding. Moreover, in addressing this specific question, the chapter will discuss a much wider set of issues. I argue that a political economy perspective may be useful in better understanding the issues, in helping to clear up some points on which the debate has often been unclear and in providing a framework for discussion (and ultimately for analysis). The framework presented is meant to be general, so that it will illustrate some crucial points rather than serve as a vehicle for analysis of specific economic policies. As such, the model is more pedagogic than one aimed directly at policy analysis.

I have argued in Drazen (2000) that heterogeneity of interests is key to political economy; I will argue here that it also must form the basis of any sensible discussion of conditionality and ownership. A political economy perspective also makes clear the importance of distinguishing between economic and political constraints in understanding the limitations of conditionality and in helping to understand how these constraints may interact. It also suggests one way in which conditionality and ownership can be reconciled (or at least disentangled) by focusing on conflict of interests not between the IMF and the borrowing member country but *within* a recipient country. Such an argument has often been made verbally but never really formalized.

1 Conditionality and its discontents

Conditionality has been widely criticized on a number of grounds, but I concentrate on the specific question: *To what extent are conditionality and ownership consistent with one another?* I thus focus on the intellectual discontent with what may be taken as the "official" view on the interaction of conditionality and ownership, where by "official" I mean what can be gleaned from IMF documents on this question. This may be an official view that no IMF official holds any longer, but I think it helps to highlight what seems to be the essential stumbling block that has hindered much of the discussion.

1.1 The "official" view

Conditionality is seen as central to IMF lending, meant to assure a borrowing country that if it takes certain well-specified actions, continued financing will be forthcoming. It is thus seen as allowing the country to "invest" in longer-term policy adjustment by assuring them that if they do so, IMF financing will not be cut off.[2]

To put this in perspective, one may argue that lenders regularly impose conditions on borrowers and monitor the use of loans to make sure that the funds are not used in a way that endangers the probability that the loan will be repaid (commonly known as "moral hazard"). Banks attempt to mitigate or eliminate moral hazard via collateral, contract design, control rights, and reporting requirements. Such safeguards may benefit borrowers by making lending more available, so that it can be in the borrower's interest to agree to these safeguards. Thus, "conditionality" in private lending is consistent with "ownership," that is, with the realization by borrowers that availability of lending requires they act in such a way that loans will be repaid. In contrast to private lending, countries borrowing from the IMF do not possess international collateral or have access to other safeguards available to private borrowers. Explicit IMF conditionality is thus meant to substitute for the lack of safeguards in private lending and, by analogy, to benefit borrowers by making loans more available.[3]

What is taken for granted in private lending is that the interests of lender and borrower will not coincide perfectly, their relation being a prime example of a "principal–agent" problem, with contract design meant to better align these interests. The realization that a conflict of interests underlies the conditions set out in a loan contract causes no problems in *private* lending. Arguing that IMF lending is analogous to private lending, however, raises a difficult question on the relation of the institution to its sovereign members: to what extent is the IMF inducing a country to take actions that the country does not necessarily see in its own best interests? In the extreme, conditionality is viewed as the IMF "imposing conditions" on a country in a way that infringes on its national sovereignty. Hence, use of conditionality is not simply a question of prudent economic behavior, but a potentially politically charged question of the proper relation of the IMF to its members.[4] Many in the IMF find it objectionable even to use the term "principal–agent" in analyzing lending programs, as it "builds in" the assumption of a difference in objectives and is thus inconsistent with the notion of ownership.[5] I return to this point shortly.

The official view is that IMF lending to member countries is characterized not by a conflict of interests but by a commonality of interests. IMF financing and recipient country policies are seen by the IMF as two connected components of a successful program. For example, a country with a balance of payments problem needs to undertake some policy changes but, at the same time, needs short-term financing to weather the payments imbalances while these changes are being undertaken. Lending is thus seen as complementary to policy reform. This may be summed up as:

> The IMF's financing and agreed policy adjustments are intended as two sides of an integrated response to a country's balance-of-payments problem in the context of its overall economic situation. This can best be seen in the stereotypical situation in which a country faces acute external imbalances as a result of excessive monetary financing of a fiscal deficit. In such a situation, the IMF finances short-term external imbalances while the country pursues macroeconomic policies aimed at external adjustment over an agreed time frame, possibly accompanied by structural reforms to enhance the supply response.... In such a situation, the need for adjustment would be clear, with or without the IMF; the IMF essentially provides financing that permits this adjustment to be made in a more gradual and orderly way.
>
> ... Thus, the intended purpose of conditionality is as a mechanism to help bring together a combination of financing and policies as a solution to economic difficulties; it is needed to provide assurances to both authorities and the IMF that both parts of the package are provided together. This concept of conditionality is fully consistent with a cooperative approach to designing and implementing programs.
>
> (IMF 2001: paragraphs 12 and 15)

Under this view of conditionality, country ownership of a program is seen not simply as consistent with conditionality but, in fact, crucial to the success of conditionality (see IMF 2001: paragraph 36). It is argued that in the absence of a high degree of ownership, conditionality won't work, and there is some empirical evidence supporting this view.[6] The basic idea is that if a country is not seriously interested in reform, it will find ways around conditionality, so that conditionality will fail. The multiplicity of potential causes for program failure combined with imperfect observability of a government's actions means that the cause of any particular failure is not necessarily identifiable.

1.2 The basic intellectual conundrum

What should one make of the "official" view? Though great effort has been invested into arguing that conditionality and ownership are not only consistent, but also necessarily complementary, one cannot escape a strong feeling of discontentment. To put it simply, *Why is conditionality needed if it is in a country's best interests to undertake the program in question?* This, to my opinion, is a question with which IMF documents struggle, and which they often talk around. I will argue that it is basically impossible to justify conditionality in the absence of a conflict of interest of some sort. Any attempt to argue that none really exists is not only unconvincing but, ultimately, self-defeating in that it stands in the way of reforming conditionality. This conflict of interests may be due to differences between the borrowing country and IMF, differences between the country and other lenders, or (as I will stress) conflict of interests within the country.[7]

The argument that conditionality only makes sense if there is a conflict of interests does not fully answer the question of how exactly it is related to ownership. Conditionality makes little or no sense if there is full ownership, but it also makes no sense if there is no ownership. How much ownership is needed for conditionality to be effective, and how much lack of ownership justifies conditionality? How can one distinguish those cases in which the lack of ownership is so severe, or the cause of problems so fundamental, that conditionality is a waste of time from those in which conditionality could make a difference? I address these questions in the formal model and present examples that provide specific answers.

The central role of heterogeneity in understanding conditionality also suggests that the principal–agent approach is possibly a useful tool in helping to understand conditionality, both in specific design issues and in more general lessons.[8] The optimal design of an IMF program toward a borrower is a principal–agent problem in the technical sense, even if not in the political sense. If there is a problem, it is in how the principal–agent approach should be applied. I will argue that while the standard principal–agent model refers to a single principal and single agent, the conflict of interests within the borrowing country are more relevant.[9] The principal–agent literature has also largely concentrated on nongovernment principals and agents, also greatly limiting its applicability to the issues being considered. There is beginning to be interesting work on principal–agent models applied to public agencies,[10] and this may eventually provide some useful models specifically applied to IMF lending, but so far there are no such formal models of IMF behavior.[11]

1.3 Attempting to reconcile conditionality and ownership

A number of arguments have been made on how conditionality may play a role in the presence of ownership. In this section, I briefly review some of these arguments and contend that heterogeneity of interests must underlie any such assertion. Put another way, the question is not whether there is heterogeneity of interests, but whether it is between the IMF as lender and the country as borrower (the standard "principal–agent" approach), between the country and other foreign lenders, or between sharply conflicting interests within a country. I focus on the last view as the strongest argument, whereby in the presence of domestic conflict of interests, conditionality may play a role even when the authorities "own" a program.

A standard argument, taken as part of the "official view," is that borrowers may benefit from the imposition of conditions that increase the probability of loan payback if it makes lending more available. As already suggested, this view requires that borrowers' and lenders' interests are not perfectly aligned in the absence of such conditions.

Another argument is that the conflicts are "second-order." For example, it is argued that the overall goals of the program are mutually accepted, but there may be disagreement on the best means of or the "time-frame" for achieving these goals. There may indeed be some cases where the conflict of interests is really how or when to best achieve mutually agreed goals, but this assertion has the flavor of "window-dressing." Unless one contends that agreement on improving the economic situation in the country is an indicator of the absence of a conflict of interest, any observer would have to agree that in the majority of cases, the use of conditionality could not be explained if there is general agreement on a program.

A third argument concerns time inconsistency. Specifically, conditionality is used as a commitment device to overcome a time inconsistency problem. Sachs (1989) and Diwan and Rodrik (1992) argue that policies of recipient governments are time inconsistent, governments accepting ex ante the need for policy change as a condition for receiving loans but having a strong incentive to avoid the change in policy once the loans have been received. Sachs, for example, considers the choice between current consumption and investment. The latter has a high return, so that a country realizes the value of taking a loan to increase investment. The government's discount rate is even higher than the return on investment, however, so that once the loan is received, it will be spent on current consumption. Conditionality thus binds a country to a course of investment and consumption postponement, thus increasing the amount of loans that foreign investors or international financial organizations are willing to make. In the time inconsistency case, commitment is meant to address a conflict of interests between the country and foreign lenders.

Time consistency problems arise even (or especially) when there is full information about a policy maker's preferences. Conditionality may also play an important role when there is asymmetric information about the authorities' commitment or ability to carry out reforms.[12] Investors may be unwilling to make loans to a country if they are unsure how the loans will be used. A government that is committed to the policy changes that the IMF or foreign investors favor may accept conditions to *signal* its commitment and thus separate itself from government types that are less committed.[13] Here, it is the *possibility* of a conflict of interests between the lenders and governments not committed to reform that gives conditionality a role in signaling that a government is interested in reforming.

The approach to reconciling conditionality and ownership that is stressed in this chapter begins with the argument that there are conflicts within a country about policy. A reformist government may be interested in carrying out an IMF program, but it faces internal opposition. Hence, though the authorities may "own" the program, this is not identical with ownership by the country as a whole. More formally put, since policy making is the process of collective choice in the face of conflicting interests, ownership by some important policy makers is not ownership by the "policy making apparatus."[14] Conditionality may then "strengthen the hands" of the reformers who are committed to carrying out reform but face domestic opposition.

Conflict of interest over desired policy may reflect various causes. In the most benign case, there simply may be ideological differences over what is the best way to achieve a commonly agreed goal, a conflict stressed in the "official" IMF view of conditionality. Alternatively, different groups may have different objectives and, hence, desire different policies. This latter view is the one explored in this chapter. In the extreme, powerful interest groups may oppose reforms that reduce their ability to engage in rent seeking. Numerous cases of these latter phenomena could be cited, some of which are discussed in IMF (2001).

2 A political–economic model

I now present a stylized model of the decision of a government of what policy to adopt. The model is highly stylized in order to highlight the political economy dimensions of policy reform in the presence of heterogeneity of interests, both between the IMF and the government of a country and, more importantly, between the government and domestic groups opposed to reform. It is not meant to answer specific policy questions but to highlight the importance of political constraints and their interaction with economic constraints. The model is not explicitly dynamic, even though the process of both lending, especially conditional lending, and reform is inherently dynamic, for the same reason. I begin with the economic model without politics.

2.1 A benchmark economic model

In the benchmark model, there are no political constraints, and the authorities and IMF have identical objectives, namely maximization of economic performance. There are two domestic dimensions to policy, represented by values of two policy instruments, denoted e and τ. The first may represent macroeconomic or exchange rate policy, the second, structural policy. Economic performance (or "output") Y also depends on IMF lending, whose size is denoted S (measured in the same units as Y), so that $Y = Y(e, \tau, S)$.[15] The pre-reform or "status quo"[16] values of the policy variables are e^{SQ} and τ^{SQ}, with the resulting level of output (in the absence of IMF lending) given by $Y^{SQ} = Y(e^{SQ}, \tau^{SQ}, 0)$. A policy reform is a program to increase economic performance via changes in macroeconomic and structural policy.

The following assumptions are made about the effect of policy and lending on Y. First, the output-maximizing level of τ is 0, so that positive τ is simply seen as a structural distortion. Hence, $\partial Y / \partial \tau \equiv Y_\tau < 0$ for $\tau > 0$. Second, in the absence of structural distortions, reducing high e (an "overvalued exchange rate") will increase output when supported by IMF lending. This captures the idea (albeit in a static context) that from an economic perspective, IMF lending is meant to enable a country to address a short-term balance of payments problem (to reduce e) in such a way to increase economic performance (increase Y) rather than reduce it. To model this, it is assumed first that for each value of S, there is a value of e that maximizes $Y(e, 0, S)$. Call this maximizing value $e^+(S)$, which is the authorities' "reaction function" in the absence of political constraints, with $\partial Y(e, 0, S) / \partial e \equiv Y_e < 0$ for $e > e^+(S)$, $Y(e, 0, S)$, and $Y_e > 0$ for $e < e^+(S)$. (More generally, it is assumed that for $\tau > 0$, $\partial Y / \partial e < 0$ for values of e above the output-maximizing level.) The second derivatives of Y with respect to e and τ are assumed to be negative. We naturally assume that $e^{SQ} > e^+(0)$, that is, that e^{SQ} is above the output-maximizing exchange rate in the absence of lending. Assume further that $\partial Y_e / \partial S \equiv Y_{eS} < 0$ for sufficiently high values of e and low values of S, both for $\tau = 0$ and for $\tau > 0$. This assumption means simply that up to a point, more lending increases the effect that reducing e has on increasing Y. This implies that $e^+(S)$ is falling in S up to some level of aid, say $S = S^{max}$. The $e^+(S)$ schedule, summarizing economically constrained policy choices, is shown in Figure 3.1. Finally, it is assumed that $\partial Y / \partial S \equiv Y_S > 0$ (once again, both for zero and positive τ), so that aid can have a positive effect on output even with no change in e.

This model of the effect of lending on economic performance is obviously a gross simplification of a complicated dynamic story, but I think it captures essential elements. Its simplicity allows us to focus on the role of

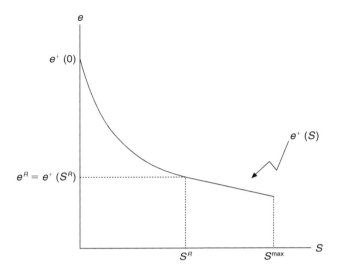

Figure 3.1 Economic equilibrium.

domestic politics. To further simplify the basic model, I assume throughout there is no question of repayment of lending. This is clearly a heroic assumption, which eliminates a major set of arguments for conditionality. However, including issues of sovereign debt repayment and handling them adequately in a political model would be a chapter in itself. Hence, this assumption is made in order to concentrate on the political constraints on the adoption and implementation of programs, and the implications of conditionality and ownership for those questions. It is assumed that a fraction r of any lending must be repaid, so that $1 - r$ is the concessional part of lending. Net output is then $Y(e, \tau, S) - rS$.

Suppose that the country, taken as a unitary actor, chooses policy to maximize net output $Y - rS$. (Implicit in this maximization are any economic constraints on the maximization of Y.) Representing the authorities' objective as $W(e, \tau, S)$, we have:

$$\max_{e, \tau} W(e, \tau, S) = Y(e, \tau, S) - rS \tag{3.1}$$

First-order conditions are:

$$\frac{\partial W}{\partial e} = \frac{\partial Y}{\partial e} = 0$$

$$\frac{\partial W}{\partial \tau} = \frac{\partial Y}{\partial \tau} \leq 0 \tag{3.2}$$

Using our above assumptions, this yields an optimal policy $(e, \tau) = (e^+(S), 0)$.

If the IMF's objective is maximization of net output, it chooses S to maximize $Y - rS$ subject to the first-order conditions in Equation (3.2). This yields a first-order condition for S of:

$$Y_S(e^+(S), 0, S) - r = 0 \tag{3.3}$$

Call the solution to Equation (3.3) S^R and the associated policies (e^R, $\tau^R) = (e^+(S^R), 0))$, where it is assumed that $e^R < e^{SQ}$ and $\tau^R < \tau^{SQ}$. This is the first-best economic reform program, which is both the authorities' and the IMF's preferred solution (given identical objectives). There is no conflict over economic policy. We denote this reform package $P^R \equiv (e^R, 0, S^R)$.

In this simple benchmark, there is no role for conditionality at all. With no heterogeneity of interests, unconditional lending will achieve the goals of the program. In fact, if the government had better information than the IMF about the workings of the economy, unconditional lending would be superior to conditional lending. Lending is simply a "technical" issue meant to improve economic performance without economic dislocations. Conditionality as part of a lending program requires heterogeneity of interests, either between the country and the IMF (or other lenders) or within the country. I consider these in turn.

2.2 Different IMF and country objectives in the economic model

Suppose that the IMF's objective function that $F(e, \tau, S)$ differs from the authorities' objective $W(e, \tau, S)$, where, in the relevant range, $F_e < 0$, $F_S < 0$, $F_{ee} < 0$, and $F_{SS} < 0$. The optimal amount of unconditional lending from the IMF's point of view is the S that maximizes $F(e, \tau, S)$ subject to the constraint that the authorities will choose policy according to Equation (3.2). Diagrammatically, it is given by the point where the IMF's highest attainable indifference curve is just tangent to the curve $e^+(S)$, represented by point U^E in Figure 3.2 (drawn on the assumption that $\tau = 0$). Mathematically, this is given by the conditions:

$$\frac{F_S}{F_e} = \frac{Y_{eS}}{Y_{ee}} \tag{3.4a}$$

$$Y_e(e, 0, S) = 0 \tag{3.4b}$$

the first condition representing tangency of the IMF's indifference curve and the authorities' reaction function; the second, maximization by the authorities implying $e = e^+(S)$.

Conditional lending in this framework would mean the IMF offers not a given amount S, but differing amounts of lending in response to different policies e. Optimal conditional lending from the IMF's point of view would be represented by its choosing the point on the authorities' *indiffer-*

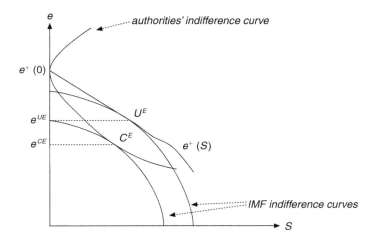

Figure 3.2 Different IMF and authorities' objectives.

ence curve (rather than reaction function) tangent to the highest possible IMF indifference curve. To tie down the equilibrium, one has a *participation* condition, namely that the country (weakly) prefers taking aid to not taking aid at all. Mathematically, these two conditions are:

$$\frac{F_S}{F_e} = \frac{Y_S - r}{Y_e} \tag{3.5a}$$

$$Y(e^+(S), 0, S) = Y(e^+(0), 0, 0) \tag{3.5b}$$

which may be represented in Figure 3.2 by point C^E.[17] Conditional lending makes the IMF better off, but the country worse off, than does unconditional lending.[18] Conditionality induces the country to choose a lower value of e and lets the IMF achieve that objective with less aid. Here, once again, we see that there must be a conflict of interests if conditionality is to play a role.

Why might the IMF's objective differ from that of the country's authorities? One possibility is that the authorities have economic objectives in addition to maximization of output (or whatever macroeconomic goal the IMF is concerned with). Another possibility is that both are concerned about the same general macroeconomic objectives, but the IMF faces financing constraints (opportunity costs of lending to other countries or budgetary constraints), so that its true cost of funds may exceed r. (Or, the IMF is simply concerned with repayment.)

To make explicit the effect of the IMF's financial constraints, it may be informative to write the IMF's objective as $F(e, 0, S) \equiv Y(e, 0, S) + H(e) - f(S)$, where $f(S)$ represents the (total) cost of funds to the IMF and $H(e)$ represents the difference between the IMF's and the authorities' macroeconomic policy objectives. The IMF's financial constraint (and the conflict of interest it implies) is represented by the assumption that $f_S > r$, that the marginal cost of lending to the IMF is above that perceived by the borrowing country. In this case, the slope of the IMF's indifference curve is:

$$\frac{F_S}{F_e} = \frac{Y_S - f_S}{Y_e + H_e} \tag{3.6}$$

where, as assumed at the beginning of the section, both, $F_S < 0$ and $F_e < 0$. The amount of lending in the three cases – of identical objectives, unconditional lending with different objectives, and conditional lending with different objectives – can be represented respectively by the conditions:

$$Y_S - r = 0 \tag{3.7a}$$

$$Y_S - r = (f_S - r) + \frac{Y_{eS}}{Y_{ee}} H_e \tag{3.7b}$$

$$Y_S - r = -\frac{Y_e}{H_e}(f_S - r) \tag{3.7c}$$

In Equation (3.7b), the case of unconditional lending, where we have used the assumption that on the $e^+(S)$ curve, $Y_e = 0$, there are conflicting effects. The financial constraint $f_S > r$ would imply that $Y_S > r$, which reduces IMF lending relative to the case of no conflict of objectives, while its desire to lower the exchange rate relative to what the authorities choose ($F_e = H_e < 0$) would raise lending in order to induce the authorities to choose lower e. In Equation (3.7c), the case of conditional lending, the right-hand side is unambiguously positive when $f_S > r$ (remember that $Y_e > 0$ for $e < e^+(S)$), so that with conditional lending $Y_S > r$ unambiguously, which implies an unambiguously lower level of lending.

2.3 Domestic political constraints

On the basis of actual country experiences with failure to adopt reforms, a political process in which powerful interest groups can block reforms (termed "veto players" in political science[19]) seems especially relevant in studying possible political constraints on IMF lending programs.[20] This ability may flow from a number of sources, including the structure of political institutions and the political power of these groups within this institutional structure, or from their economic power and the ability it gives them to influence political decisions. For simplicity, I work almost entirely with the case of a single domestic interest group that has veto power, since the basic results can be illustrated in this case. Extension to several interest groups is straightforward (see note 22) and does not change the basic results.

Suppose that the government is the agenda setter, in that it determines e and τ subject to the approval of the domestic veto player, who will veto any program lowering its utility $I(e, \tau, S)$ relative to its status quo utility I^{SQ}. Treating the veto player as a unitary actor whose preferences can be summarized by a utility function with standard properties is not a trivial assumption (see, for example, the discussion in chapter 2 of Tsebelis 2002), but is often used in the formal treatment of special interest groups (for example, Grossman and Helpman 2001). The government's choice problem may be written as:

$$\max_{e,\tau} W(e, \tau, S) + \lambda[I(e, \tau, S) - I^{SQ}] \tag{3.8}$$

We begin by assuming that the interest group cares directly only about e and τ, getting no direct utility from IMF lending. Its utility may be represented as $I(e, \tau, S) \equiv V(e, \tau)$, so that $I^{SQ} \equiv V^{SQ} = V(e^{SQ}, \tau^{SQ})$. The formulation in Equation (3.8) makes clear that the constraint on the government is a political constraint, namely any reform must satisfy the constraint of being politically feasible in that it gains the approval of an interest group with veto power.

If the political constraint did not bind, the government would choose its most preferred policy (subject to the economic constraints), namely $(e, \tau) = (e^{+}(S), 0)$, as in Equation (3.1). This would be the case in which the government's preferred policy is also preferred by the interest group to the policy (e^{SQ}, τ^{SQ}). In such a case, a "reform problem" would not arise, and the role of IMF assistance would depend on whether it and the authorities (or the country, which could be treated as a unitary actor) agreed on the objectives or not. If they agreed on objectives, the problem would be "technical" in the sense described above, and there would be no role for conditionality. If the objectives of the IMF were not the same as the authorities, the "standard" principal–agent problem would be present with a single agent.[21]

The more relevant case therefore is when the political constraint in Equation (3.8) is binding. This would be the case, for example, when the interest group's desired policies, which can be denoted (e^{I}, τ^{I}), are closer to (e^{SQ}, τ^{SQ}) than to $(e^{+}(S), 0)$ in a model with spatial preferences (that is, where an actor prefers policies that are spatially closer in Euclidean distance to his first-best policies to policies that are farther away). Put simply, in this case the interest group wants values of e and τ that are above (perhaps substantially) what the government wants. This implies that in the range of policies that maximize Equation (3.8), $\partial V/\partial e > 0$ and $\partial V/\partial \tau > 0$, so that the conflict of interests is clear. (Second derivatives are assumed to be negative.) The government's power is given by its role as the agenda setter, the interest group's power by its ability to veto policies it doesn't want, where the alternative is the status quo.

The maximization problem yields first-order conditions:[22]

$$\frac{W_e(e, \tau, S)}{W_\tau(e, \tau, S)} = \frac{I_e(e, \tau, S)}{I_\tau(e, \tau, S)} \left(= \frac{V_e(e, \tau)}{V_\tau(e, \tau)} \right) \tag{3.9a}$$

$$V_e(e, \tau) = V^{SQ} \tag{3.9b}$$

which can be solved for the equilibrium values of e and τ as functions of S. The politically constrained reaction functions are denoted $e^P(S)$ (which, like $e^+(S)$, is downward sloping in $e-S$ space), and $\tau^P(S)$. When the government's objective is to maximize economic performance net of lending, the left-hand side of Equation (3.9a) is simply Y_e/Y_τ. As in the case of only economically constrained policies in Equation (3.1), these policies are clearly functions of the amount of lending S. In the case of $S=0$, let us denote the solution by (e^o, τ^o).

These conditions have a simple interpretation. Equation (3.9a) is simply the condition that the indifference curve of the government over e and τ is tangent to the indifference curve of the interest group over e and τ. The set of tangencies of these indifference curves yields the "contract curve" of Pareto optimal points from the viewpoint of the two agents. Equation (3.9b) determines which point on the contract curve is the equilibrium. For the interest group's reversion (or "threat") point being the status quo, the government's role as the chooser of policy implies that it "captures all the rents" in that policy in a political–economic equilibrium policy leaves the interest group no better off than in the status quo.[23] Note, however, that along the interest group's indifference curve, e can be reduced from e^{SQ} only by increasing τ.

The determination of equilibrium may be represented as in Figure 3.3, where the upward sloping line represents the contract curve, that is the set of tangencies of the indifference curves defined by Equation (3.9a), SQ represents the "status quo," that is, the pre-reform policy parameters, and G the most preferred point of the government consistent with the constraint in Equation (3.9b) that the interest group is no worse off than the status quo.

One economic interpretation of the solution, which draws the distinction between macroeconomic and nonmacroeconomic policies, would run as follows. Suppose a reform-minded government wants to improve macroeconomic performance Y, which is influenced largely by (exchange rate) policies e. Under the status quo, e is at a high level inconsistent with high Y. The government thus wants to reduce e in order to improve the macroeconomy, but an interest group that has significant political power and can block reform prefers the distorted (that is, high) value of e to a lower value of e. In order to gain the acceptance of reduced e, the government must give the interest group higher τ, which could be thought of as a structural distortion that the interest group may particularly favor. To the extent that the government's objective Y is more sensitive to e than τ (implicit in the argument at the beginning of the paragraph), and the

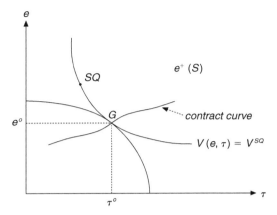

Figure 3.3 Political equilibrium.

interest group's objective is more sensitive to τ than e, the political–economic equilibrium represented by Equation (3.9a) will imply a decrease in e and an increase in τ relative to the status quo.

2.4 Assistance not directly affecting interest group welfare

The nature of IMF lending so as to achieve its policy objectives now induces designing of policy given not only the characteristics of the function $Y(e, \tau, S)$ – representing the economic constraints – but also the nature of the political constraint. It is assumed from here on that the objective of both the authorities and the IMF is maximization of net output $Y(e, \tau, S) - rS$. I begin by deriving the characteristics of the authorities' politically constrained reaction functions and then consider the implications for both unconditional and conditional lending.

When the political constraint is binding, $e^P(S)$ will lie to the northeast of $e^+(S)$, the politically unconstrained reaction function, indicating roughly the extent to which political constraints worsen the policy menu. It may also generally be flatter, most easily seen in the special case in which τ enters the authorities' and the interest group's objectives linearly but with opposite signs (negative for the authorities and positive for the interest group). In this case, the slope of the $e^P(S)$ schedule may be derived from the first-order conditions in Equations (3.9a) and (3.9b) as:

$$\left.\frac{\partial e}{\partial S}\right|_{e^P(S)} = -\frac{Y_{eS}(e^P(S), \tau^P(S), S)}{Y_{ee} + V_{ee}} \tag{3.10}$$

where $e^P(S)$ and $\tau^P(S)$ are defined by those first-order conditions. In contrast, the slope of $e^+(S)$ is $-Y_{eS}(e^+(S), 0, S)/Y_{ee}$. On the assumption that

Y_{eS} is not significantly different in the two cases, $\partial e/\partial S$ will be smaller in absolute value along $e^P(S)$ than along $e^+(S)$. That is, the curve will be flatter.[24]

The effect of increases in S on e and τ may be seen most clearly diagrammatically. Since unconditional aid does not affect the position of the constraint $V(e, \tau) = V^{SQ}$, its effect comes entirely from its effect on the government's indifference curve over e and τ. Whether unconditional aid raises or lowers e (with the opposite effect on τ, since the constraint $V(e, \tau) = V^{SQ}$ is downward sloping in $e - \tau$ space) depends on how it affects the slope of the government's indifference curve. Differentiating the left-hand side of Equation (3.9a) with respect to S for given values of e and τ, one derives:

$$\frac{\partial Y_\tau / Y_e}{\partial S} = - \frac{Y_{eS}\dfrac{Y_\tau}{Y_e} - Y_{\tau S}}{Y_e} \tag{3.11}$$

which shows how the slope of the authorities' indifference curve changes at a given point. Analogous to the assumptions in the pure economic model, I assume that the numerator on the right-hand side of Equation (3.11) is negative, that is, $Y_{eS}(Y_\tau / Y_e) - Y_{\tau S} < 0$, meaning that the effect of increases in S in lowering Y_e is greater than any effect of higher S in lowering Y_τ. In other words, higher lending increases the output gain obtainable from lowering e, not only in absolute terms ($Y_{eS} < 0$) as in the economic model, but also relative to its effect on the output gain from lowering τ. For example, if one interprets e as an exchange rate policy (or more generally a macroeconomic policy) and τ as a structural policy, the assumption is that an IMF assistance program is more economically effective in correcting a balance of payments or exchange rate problem (more exactly, in the effect of such a change on output), than in correcting a structural problem. This seems to be consistent with how one views the effect of assistance programs.

Under this assumption, an increase in S causes the government's indifference curve to become flatter at each point in $e - \tau$ space in Figure 3.4, as in the flatter WW curve in the diagram. The new equilibrium is one with lower e and higher τ, as represented by U^P – the equilibrium with unconditional lending – with a contract curve analogous to that in Figure 3.3 that would go through U^P. (Under the opposite assumption that $Y_{eS}(Y_\tau / Y_e) - Y_{\tau S} > 0$, the government's indifference curve would become steeper with an increase in S, so that higher aid would lead the government to chose higher e and lower τ.) The reaction function for the politically constrained case, which we denote $e^P(S)$, is also downward sloping in $e - S$ space. Note that under the assumption that $\partial Y/\partial S > 0$ at (e^o, τ^o), that is, that IMF lending can improve output even if policy is not affected, unconditional lending unambiguously increases output (and welfare from the point of view of the authorities and the IMF).[25]

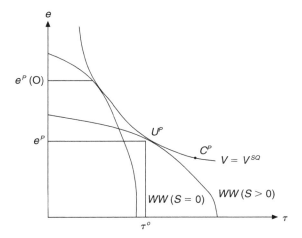

Figure 3.4 Unconditional and conditional lending in political equilibrium.

This result – unconditional lending lowers e in a politically constrained equilibrium (when $Y_{eS}(Y_\tau/Y_e) - Y_{\tau S} < 0$) – may be understood as follows. To begin, suppose that $Y_{\tau S} = 0$, so that our assumption becomes $Y_{eS} < 0$.[26] In other words, higher S raises the responsiveness of Y to e, meaning that the economic benefit of lowering e becomes greater. Since the political cost of lowering e (the need to raise τ to maintain the support of the interest group) is unchanged, the optimal decision is to lower e in response to greater lending, which for an unchanged political constraint means that τ must be raised. The reasoning for the more general case in which $Y_{\tau S} \neq 0$ is identical. Conversely, if $Y_{\tau S} < Y_{eS}(Y_\tau/Y_e)$, the economic benefit of lowering e in terms of higher τ has fallen rather than risen, so the optimal response to more aid would be to lower τ and hence raise e.

Unconditional lending is chosen in essentially the same way as in the purely economic model. The IMF chooses S to maximize $Y(e, \tau, S) - rS$ subject to constraints (Equations (3.9a) and (3.9b)), that is, given the government's politically constrained reaction functions $e^P(S)$ and $\tau^P(S)$. Since lending does not change the position of the $V(e, \tau) = V^{SQ}$ curve, it can only induce a movement along the curve, better macroeconomic or exchange rate policy being "bought" at the price of worse structural policy. The equilibrium value of e would be larger than in the economic model for two reasons. First, the $e^P(S)$ curve lies to the northeast of the $e^+(S)$ curve, implying a higher value of e for any value of S. Second, the $e^P(S)$ curve is flatter than the $e^+(S)$ curve, indicating that the point chosen will be more toward higher e and lower S. Lending meant to maximize a country's welfare will be lower when the authorities face political constraints than when they do not.

The analysis of conditionality in the case of political constraints is also analogous to that in the purely economic model, but with the authorities' reaction function given by $e^P(S)$ rather than $e^+(S)$, and with the authorities' indifference curves similarly defined as taking into account the political constraint. As was seen in the economic model above, conditional lending makes the country worse off when the country and the IMF have different objectives, and can make the country no better off when they have the same objectives.[27] (Point C^P in Figure 3.4 represents this. A diagrammatic analysis would parallel Figure 3.2.)

The source of the weakness of both unconditional and conditional lending reflects two characteristics of the political model. First, and quite crucially, the authorities' role as agenda setter gives it all the "bargaining power," allowing it to pick the point on the interest group's indifference curve it finds optimal. Given this, if IMF lending does not affect the interest group's indifference curve, that is, it does not affect the political constraint directly, it can have relatively little effect. Any equilibrium must be on the $V(e, \tau) = V^{SQ}$ curve, with points on the reaction function $e^P(S)$ giving the optimal response to lending S. Hence the authorities can do no better than when lending is unconditional. For conditionality to have a role when the constraint is the political power of interest groups (whose interests differ from those of the authorities), either lending must directly affect their welfare or it must strengthen the bargaining power of the authorities in a political setup where this power is limited.

2.5 Assistance directly affecting interest group's utility

If lending induces a shift in the $I(e, \tau, S) = I^{SQ}$ curve to the southwest, it will allow choice of an (e, τ) policy closer to what is optimal according to the authorities' (and the IMF's) preferences. Perhaps less obviously, it will also give a role to conditionality. The general point is presented in this section and some examples in section 3.

Consider a reform package $P' = (e', \tau')$ that the interest group prefers to the status quo if lending S' is received, but where lending itself makes the status quo less onerous. Specifically, suppose that the welfare of the interest group displays the following characteristics:

$$I(e^{SQ}, \tau^{SQ}, 0) \leq I(e', \tau', S') \leq I(e^{SQ}, \tau^{SQ}, S') \tag{3.12}$$

That is, the interest group prefers reform with lending to no reform without lending, but prefers lending with no reform to lending with reform. This may be seen diagrammatically in Figure 3.5, in which we consider only one dimension e of domestic policy and draw the interest group's indifference curves over e and S corresponding to the three quantities in Equation (3.12). (Analogous to Figures 3.1 and 3.2, one may think of this as a "slice" of a three-dimensional diagram in which τ is held con-

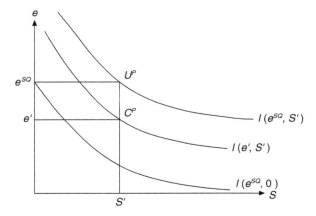

Figure 3.5 Lending affects interest group's utility.

stant.) For any domestic policy, higher lending raises the interest group's welfare. If lending S' is made without any policy conditionality, and the interest group can veto reform programs, it is clear that once the loan has been received the interest group will veto any program P' relative to the status quo if Equation (3.12) holds, implying a point such as U^P. That is, though interest groups would benefit from reform, loans or aid, once given, reduce their willingness to agree to reform. On the other hand, if receipt of the loan S' were made conditional on adopting the program P', that is, if the policy configuration (e^{SQ}, τ^{SQ}, S') (or (e^{SQ}, S') in the diagram) were not an option, the interest group would support the program, implying a point such as C^P.

This case requires that $I(e^{SQ}, \tau^{SQ}, S') > I(e^{SQ}, \tau^{SQ}, 0)$, that is, that lending directly affects the welfare of the interest group, for otherwise the inequalities in Equation (3.12) could not hold. Note further that the conditional lending package does not intervene in the political process per se in the sense of placing political conditions on receipt of loans or in interfering in the domestic political process. It works, however, by taking account of what the political constraints are and designing aid packages with these constraints in mind.

2.6 Limited government agenda-setting power

We have so far assumed that the political mechanism is essentially one in which the authorities choose a policy package that interest groups can either accept or reject. Suppose instead that the policy-making process gave significant bargaining power to the interest group.[28] In this case, even if lending does not affect the interest group's utility directly, it can significantly change the outcome in ways it could not when the government was the agenda setter.

The importance of conditionality when the authorities cannot make "take it, or leave it" offers may be simply illustrated by reversing the roles of the players, and assuming that the interest group is the agenda setter and thus has all the bargaining power. (The representation of bargaining is very simple, and a more complete model would require an explicitly intertemporal framework. However, the basic point made here will still hold true in richer frameworks.) Consider Figure 3.6, showing indifference curves in the absence of lending (where by assumption lending only affects the authorities' indifference curves). If lending were unconditional, the interest group would choose the point $I = U^P$, so that government utility is the same as in the status quo. To support a point such as C^P, just to the northeast of the curve $V(e, \tau) = V^{SQ}$ (so that the interest group is infinitesimally better off than in the status quo), the IMF could offer the following (admittedly extreme) conditional lending package. It provides enough lending if policy remains at SQ so that the authorities prefer SQ to any point on the contract curve northeast of C^P; sufficient lending at C^P so that the government prefers it to SQ; and zero lending otherwise. The government will then reject any program other than C^P and revert to the status quo, but it will accept C^P. In terms of the diagram, conditionality eliminates all points on the contract curve preferred by the interest group to the status quo other than C^P. The interest group knows that the government will reject any offer other than C^P and thus will offer this package.

This example illustrates (albeit starkly) how conditionality can strengthen the "bargaining power" of the government in the case where the policy-making mechanism itself does not give it this ability, as we assumed earlier. Though lending does not affect the interest group directly, it is sufficient that the interest group knows that, because the *government* derives utility from IMF lending, lending changes its payoffs in such a way that it increases their effective bargaining power. This is a "backbone strengthening" effect of conditional lending.

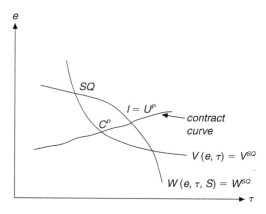

Figure 3.6 Conditionality and bargaining.

This effect could interact with that in the previous section. That is, when IMF lending affects interest group utility and the government does not have all the bargaining power, conditionality could serve both to shift the interest group's indifference curves – and hence the set of points that are preferred to the status quo – as well as to affect which point in the set is chosen. Interesting as this second line of inquiry is, I do not pursue it in this chapter, concentrating instead on the first effect of conditionality outlined earlier in this section.

3 Some examples

I now briefly sketch some specific examples in which the welfare of an interest group may be directly affected by lending, as well as some implications.

3.1 Country ownership

One simple example where assistance directly affects the interest group's welfare is where it depends on both its private interests, as represented by $V(e, \tau)$, and on "social welfare," as represented by $Y(e, \tau, S)$, with weights α and $1 - \alpha$:

$$I(e, \tau, S) = \alpha V(e, \tau) + (1 - \alpha) W(e, \tau, S) \tag{3.13}$$

where $W(e, \tau, S) \equiv Y(e, \tau, S) - rS$. To see the role of conditionality, consider the two inequalities in Equation (3.12) for a specific reform program, for example, the first-best program $P^R \equiv (e^R, 0, S^R)$ as defined by Equation (3.2). In this case, the second inequality in Equation (3.12) becomes:

$$\alpha V(e^{SQ}, \tau^{SQ}) + (1 - \alpha) W(e^{SQ}, \tau^{SQ}, S^R) > \alpha V(e^R, 0) + (1 - \alpha) W(e^R, 0, S^R) \tag{3.14}$$

Equation (3.14) with equality defines a critical value $\alpha^U(P^R)$, such that for $\alpha \leq \alpha^U(P^R)$, the reform will be supported by the interest group (even when lending is unconditional), while for $\alpha > \alpha^U(P^R)$, Equation (3.14) will hold, and the group will veto the reform when lending is unconditional. (Simple algebra shows that the excess of the left-hand over the right-hand side of Equation (3.14) is increasing in α.) It may be said that when $\alpha \leq \alpha^U(P^R)$, ownership is high enough (that is, the domestic interest group puts a high enough weight on social welfare) that conditionality is unnecessary.

To consider the role of conditionality, suppose Equation (3.14) holds (that is, $\alpha > \alpha^{own}(P^R)$), and consider the second inequality for a program P^R. It may be written:

$$\alpha V(e^R, 0) + (1 - \alpha) W(Y(e^R, 0, S^R) \geq \alpha V(e^{SQ}, \tau^{SQ}) + (1 - \alpha) W(e^{SQ}, \tau^{SQ}, 0))$$
(3.15a)

or:

$$V(e^R, 0) + \frac{1 - \alpha}{\alpha} [(Y(e^R, 0, S^R) - rS^R - Y(e^{SQ}, \tau^{SQ}, 0)] \geq V(e^{SQ}, \tau^{SQ})$$ (3.15b)

Note first that though $V(e^R, 0) < V(e^{SQ}, \tau^{SQ})$, the second term on the left-hand side of Equation (3.14b) is positive for an output-increasing reform $(Y(e^R, 0, S^R) - rS^R > Y(e^{SQ}, \tau^{SQ}, 0))$, and it is this factor that allows the reform to be politically acceptable.

Moreover, Equations (3.14) and (3.15) can hold simultaneously. To see this, observe that Equation (3.15a) with equality also defines a critical value $\alpha^C(P^R)$, such that for $\alpha \leq \alpha^C(P^R)$, the reform will be supported by the interest group (and vice versa for $\alpha > \alpha^C(P^R)$) if receipt of the loan S^R is made conditional implementing the reform. Since $W(e^{SQ}, \tau^{SQ}, S^R) > W(e^{SQ}, \tau^{SQ}, 0)$, it is immediate that the value of α that satisfies Equation (3.15) is above the value of α that satisfies Equation (3.14), that is, $\alpha^C(P^R) > \alpha^U(P^R)$. Hence, there is a set of interest group "types," namely, those for which:

$$\alpha^C(P^R) \geq a > \alpha^U(P^R)$$
(3.16)

such that Equations (3.14) and (3.15) hold simultaneously. (For any program P, one can derive similar bounds.) For these types, the reform will be blocked if lending is unconditional but will be supported if lending is conditional on acceptance of reform. To complete the argument, when $\alpha > \alpha^C(P^R)$, so that the economic first-best package is not politically feasible even with conditional lending, Equation (3.15) becomes the binding constraint. The politically constrained second-best reform is that which maximizes $Y(e, \tau, S) - rS$ subject to Equations (3.9a) and (3.15), that is, where $e = e^P(S)$ and $\tau = \tau^P(S)$, and lending is made conditional on adopting these policies.

This discussion illustrates a notion of ownership when there are domestic political constraints, and how it interacts with conditionality. It shows how conditionality can require a certain degree of country (not just government) ownership to be effective, but is unnecessary when there is high enough country ownership. If the IMF and the authorities agree on the objective of maximizing net economic performance Y, so that the authorities own the program, it is the "ownership" of interest groups that is crucial. For any program P, conditionality is unnecessary when $\alpha \leq \alpha^U(P)$ and ineffective when $\alpha > \alpha^C(P)$. When Equation (3.16) holds, conditionality is central to reform, and it indicates how much "ownership" is necessary for conditionality to support reform.

3.2 *Appropriation and selectivity*

Suppose the political process is such that the interest group can appropriate some portion of the aid or lending directly. This approach is motivated by the view that in many cases, assistance programs fail because the lending is simply misappropriated, being used for purposes very different than what was intended.

In Drazen (1999), I considered a formal dynamic model of this phenomenon, in which a government whose objective was to maximize social welfare competes for resources with interest groups who, as in Equation (3.13), care about a weighted sum of social welfare and their own private gains from appropriating resources. A "common property" model was adopted, in which the incentive of interest groups to appropriate a country's resources depends on the level of resources there are to be appropriated. In this setup, "cooperative" behavior of no appropriation cannot be sustained when the amount that can be appropriated in aggregate is too high, with appropriation leading to deterioration in the economy. When the level of resources that can be appropriated becomes low enough, the behavior that interest groups find optimal switches to "cooperative" nonappropriative behavior. A key purpose of the chapter was to present a case for selectivity. If interest groups find appropriation to be a dominant strategy and program design is unable to prevent such behavior, then lending will be wasted, and the IMF can do no better than simply not provide loans, that is, adopt a policy of selectivity. In this setup, there is an even stronger argument for selectivity. Since appropriation of resources is optimal from the point of view of interest groups when the resources to be appropriated are high, but not when they are low, denying loans may serve to put a stop to appropriative behavior sooner than would otherwise be the case.

To represent the arguments simply, suppose that lending can either be appropriated as output-reducing transfers to the interest group (denoted A) or can be used to increase economic performance and reduce e. Hence, if an amount A is appropriated and total lending is S, net lending to affect economic performance is $S - A$, so that net output is:

$$Y = Y(e, \tau + A, S - A) - rS \tag{3.17}$$

The size of A may be constrained by political or institutional features as summarized by a maximum amount of appropriation $\bar{A}$, so that $A \leq \bar{A}$, where $0 \leq \bar{A} \leq S$.

To model interest group decisions over appropriation, suppose the interest group's welfare is given by Equation (3.13):

$$I(e, \tau, S) = \alpha V(e, \tau + A) + (1 - \alpha) Y((e, \tau + A, S - A)) - rS) \tag{3.18}$$

The interest group will choose A to maximize Equation (3.18) subject to the constraint on feasible appropriation, given α, the amount of lending S, and the government's policy rules $e^P(S, A)$ and $\tau^P(S, A)$. When α is close to 1 and $\overline{A} = S$, any unconditional lending will be appropriated and hence is worthless to reformist authorities that share the IMF's objective of increasing economic performance. Since loans have a cost in that some fraction of lending must be repaid, reformist authorities would prefer zero unconditional lending. This would coincide with the IMF's reluctance to make unconditional loans if it is known that all lending will be appropriated, that is, if it is known that α is in the range where the interest group will choose $A = \overline{A}$.

3.3 Unobserved types, pre-conditions on lending, and tranching of loans

In the case of appropriation, it may be reasonable to assume that the IMF cannot observe the extent to which interest groups desire appropriate lending.[29] In a standard application of asymmetric information about types, one might assume that the type of government cannot be observed. Here, I will assume that the IMF knows that the authorities are reformist, but cannot observe how appropriative the interest groups are. (That is, the IMF does not observe the domestic political constraints that the authorities face.) For simplicity, suppose there are two possible types of interest groups, one with low α (high weight on social welfare, or "high ownership"), and the other with high α (low weight on social welfare, or "low ownership"). In a standard principal–agent asymmetric information framework, the principal designs a contract offering different packages, such that the two types reveal his type by the choice of which package they choose. In a model of domestic conflict, even though the authorities' own preferences are known, uncertainty about the "type" of interest group means that the IMF does not know the constrained preferences of the government, that is, its "constrained type." Assume that the IMF can assign probabilities to the types, say probability π that the type is low α and probability $1 - \pi$ that the type is high α. Let's denote by $W^H(e, \tau, S)$ the constrained preferences of a government facing a high α interest group, and by $W^L(e, \tau, S)$ the constrained preferences of a government facing a low α interest group.

Consider two policy packages, (e', τ', S') and (e'', τ'', S''), where these packages are such that the low α type prefers (e', τ', S') to (e'', τ'', S''), and the high α type prefers (e'', τ'', S'') to (e', τ', S'). In a "separating" equilibrium, these packages must obey two sorts of constraints. There are two participation constraints (each type prefers the package "designated" for him to the status quo $(W^L(e', \tau', S') \geq W^L(e^{SQ}, \tau'^{SQ}, 0))$) and analogously for the type with high α for (e'', τ'', S''). There are also incentive compatibility constraints, whereby each type prefers the package intended for it to the package intended for the other group. (Typically in this two-type setup, only two of these four constraints will bind.) The IMF chooses the packages given these constraints to maximize its expected utility.

Conditionality would be a crucial part of this equilibrium, in that different amounts of lending would be offered in "exchange" for different amounts of adjustment. One may easily show that in this case, the package offered the government facing a low α type (that is, where the domestic political system as a whole exhibits high ownership) will have lower *e* and higher *S*. Only conditionality can get types to reveal themselves, allowing optimal use of resources in the face of asymmetric information.

An asymmetric information model in which policy induces self-selection also gives a simple explanation for preconditions in lending, as well as for tranching of loans. Suppose we gave policy choice a time dimension, in that policies were chosen not simultaneously but sequentially. To take a simple example, suppose that we consider τ (a structural policy) chosen before *e* is chosen and before lending *S* is made. Then, if there is asymmetric information about type, an announcement of a loan package conditional on observed policy τ would serve to direct lending to those countries where it will be most effective.

4 Summary and conclusions

This chapter has attempted to show how political economy can inform both the conceptual thinking about conditionality and ownership, and the possibility of modeling specific arguments. I have concentrated on a specific question, namely, what is the role of conditionality if there is ownership, that is, if a government believes it is in a country's best interest to undertake the program reforms. Key to my approach is the realization that a conflict or heterogeneity of interests is central to understanding conditionality. In contrast to approaches that stress a conflict between the borrowing country and the lenders (whether an IFI or a private lender), I stress a conflict of interests *within* a country receiving loans, in order to show the role of conditionality even when the IMF and authorities agree on the goals of an assistance program. Conditionality can be reconciled with ownership by drawing a careful distinction between country and government ownership.

The basic results of the chapter may be summarized as follows. When there are no domestic political constraints on the government, there is no role for conditionality if the IMF and the country agree on the objectives of an assistance program. These objectives can be achieved with unconditional lending, which may be preferable if the government has better information about the economy. When the IMF and a country have different objectives, conditional lending helps the IMF achieve its objectives, but makes the country worse off than unconditional lending.

When a government faces domestic opposition to reform, conditionality can play a role even when the IMF and the government agree on the objectives of an assistance program. These conditions, however, are not sufficient for conditionality to be optimal. When both the government has the power of an agenda setter to make "take it, or leave it" offers to special interests that oppose reform, and IMF assistance does not directly affect the welfare of special interests, conditional lending makes a country no better off than unconditional lending. This holds true even when special interests have the power to veto reform packages, so that a reform must leave them no worse off than the status quo before reform. Assistance leads to policy change to the extent that it changes the government's relative weighting of objectives (for example, if assistance makes it easier to reduce an overvalued exchange rate), but conditionality plays no role per se in helping a government achieve its objectives.

For conditionality to play a role when the IMF and a country's authorities agree on objectives, at least one of two conditions must hold. One possibility is that assistance directly affects the welfare of a domestic interest group that opposes reform, so that lending essentially shifts its indifference curve. Lending thus changes the set of policies that leaves it no worse off than the status quo. Making lending conditional on specific policy changes may be crucial in ensuring that interest groups do not block reform once assistance has been given.

The second possibility is that the government is not the agenda setter. Conditionality may then strengthen the government's bargaining power with interest groups and thus affect policy outcomes. By changing the incentives of the government in a way that interest groups are aware of, IMF lending can affect what special interests offer at the bargaining table even if lending does not affect them directly.

It was also shown how a model in which interest groups are directly affected by lending could be used to formalize and better understand a number of issues connected with conditionality and ownership. For example, if interest groups weight both social welfare and their own private interests, a high enough weight on the former (indicating country and not government ownership) will mean that conditionality is unnecessary, while too low a weight implies that it is ineffective. For intermediate values, conditionality can make some reforms politically acceptable, with a formal model making it possible to derive how much country ownership is required for a specific reform to be politically feasible.

The model can also illustrate the case for denying assistance ("selectivity") if interest groups can appropriate aid for their private uses. When there is asymmetric information about the extent to which interest groups weight social as opposed to private welfare, the model gives a simple explanation for preconditions in lending, as well as for tranching of loans.

To summarize: in short, the chapter demonstrates how a formal political economy approach can both clarify thinking about conditionality and ownership, and provide an apparatus for better understanding when conditionality can help overcome political constraints. As the chapter makes clear, there are a number of interesting unexplored avenues, but that is for future work.

Acknowledgment

This chapter was originally published as: Drazen, Allan. 2002. "Conditionality and Ownership in IMF Lending: A Political Economy Approach," *IMF Staff Papers*, 49, Special Issue. Reprinted with permission.

Notes

* This chapter was originally prepared for the Second Annual IMF Research Conference, Washington, DC, November 29, 30, 2001. I would like to thank my discussants Jeffrey Frieden and Mohsin Khan, conference participants, and especially Jeromin Zettlemeyer for insightful comments. Shir Raz provided excellent research assistance. Some of the research for this chapter was conducted during a visit to the Research Department of the IMF in September 2001, which I wish to thank for its hospitality. Financial support from the Yael Chair in Comparative Economics, Tel Aviv University is gratefully acknowledged.

1 See the IMF website http://www.imf.org under "conditionality" for a number of papers on aspects of this debate.

2 One could argue that conditionality is meant as a form of technical assistance: a country may agree with the overall program objectives set out by the IMF, but be unsure how to implement the program. This is not a really satisfactory answer, however, and is recognized as such. If this were the problem, the solution would be one of technical assistance rather than conditionality, a point widely recognized (see, for example, IMF 2001).

3 For example, Khan and Sharma (2001) argue that the analogy with private bank lending is useful in understanding IMF lending. Tirole (2002) presents a similar argument reconciling conditionality and ownership. Analogous to the commitment arguments made above, he argues that by giving up certain control rights or otherwise constraining himself ex ante, a borrower can commit himself not to take specific actions ex post that a lender would see as detrimental to repayment prospects (see also Federico 2001). In this approach, structural conditionality can be partially justified by the argument that a credible promise of loan repayment requires sustained medium-term improvement in economic performance.

4 This essential tension in terms of what conditionality means about the "political" status of borrowers has long been recognized. It was well stated by Diaz-Alejandro (1984) and forms the basis of recent critiques, such as Killick (1997).

5 "Conditionality is often viewed as an attempt of international financial institutions (or aid donors) to use financing to buy' policy reforms that are not desired by authorities. [This] interpretation of conditionality is often reflected in the use of a principal–agent model, in which the Fund (the principal) establishes a mechanism intended to ensure that reforms will be undertaken by the authorities (the agent), in a setting in which the objectives of the Fund and the authorities do not fully coincide and there are informational asymmetries associated with the fact that the Fund cannot directly observe some aspects of the authorities' actions, objectives and/or circumstances. This presentation

of the Fund as the principal' in this framework is inconsistent with that of country ownership of the program" (IMF 2001: paragraph 16).

6 Many references could be given. See, for example, Haque and Khan (1998). Dollar and Svensson (2000) present convincing evidence that political conditions in the receiving countries are much more important than conditionality in explaining the success or failure of World Bank programs.

7 One should note that the IMF (2001) explicitly acknowledges the importance of heterogeneity within a country, for example, in paragraph 38.

8 For example, the behavior by an agent that can be induced by an optimal contract will depend on the extent to which the interests of the principal and agent are aligned.

9 There is now a growing body of work on multiple-principal, multiple-agent, and multiple-task models, though the application of existing formal models to the specifics of IMF programs is not immediate. It has been suggested that models of "moral hazard in teams" (Holmström 1982) may be relevant. In these models, the outcome is a function of the actions of several agents (and perhaps also a random component), where individual actions are unobservable, so that there is a "free rider" problem. The design of an IMF program would be finding a scheme that induces optimal actions by each agent. On the one hand, team behavior captures the notion that many agents must "sign off" on a program. On the other, the team setup does not seem to describe very well the nature of the economic problem an IMF program is meant to address nor the nature of policy making.

10 Prendergast (1999) and Dixit (2000a) present excellent surveys of principal–agent models as applied to the public sector.

11 Dixit (2000b) provides some suggestions on how conditionality and other aspects of Fund programs may be better understood in terms of formal principal–agent theory.

12 The *type* of conditionality may also demonstrate commitment. For example, structural conditions may more effectively demonstrate the government's commitment to sustainable macroeconomic stability.

13 There are many models of this type. See, for example, Dhonte (1997) or Marchesi and Thomas (1999).

14 As Khan and Sharma (2001: 15): "in pluralistic societies, does ownership refer to the views on program design of and objectives held by key ministers and central bank officials that negotiate the program with the IMF, or to the views of the entire domestic bureaucracy that has to approve the necessary legislation, or to the beliefs of civil society at large?"

15 An IMF program would have no structural component (that is, no reliance on τ) to the extent that the Fund targets Y, and τ has little or no effect on Y. This would represent the case in which the IMF's performance target is narrowly defined so that it is a function only of macroeconomic variables such as e, so that the IMF's narrowly defined objectives imply no role for structural conditionality.

16 The term "status quo" may be slightly misleading, since this could be the state after the economy has suffered a large shock. The idea is that once the economy finds itself in this position, domestic interests may oppose any reform, hence the term "status quo."

17 The authorities' indifference curves are horizontal along $e^+(S)$, since this is a reaction function in which e is chosen optimally for each S.

18 The discussion at the beginning of section 1, whereby conditionality may mean higher welfare for borrowers relates to the case of comparing conditional lending to no lending, the unavailability of lending reflecting problems of

moral hazard, etc. In this discussion, in addition to the absence of such considerations, the lender is assumed to extract all the benefit of conditionality
(Equation (3.5b)), so that the borrower is only weakly better off.

19 Tsebelis (2002) presents a comprehensive discussion of veto player models and
their application.

20 Vreeland (1999, 2001) has used this type of model to study the possible effects
of conditionality in a framework where policy has a single dimension (in his
case, the size of the government budget deficit). Other papers that consider
conditionality from a political economy perspective include Drazen (1999),
Jeanne and Zettelmeyer (2001), Martin (2000), Mayer and Mourmouras (2002),
Svensson (2000), and Willett (2000).

21 There is a slight "catch" in that a conditional lending program itself must be
assumed not to make the domestic political constraint binding.

22 With n interest groups, each concerned about some τ^j, the first-order conditions in a politically constrained equilibrium would be $Y_e(e, \vec{\tau}, S) =$
$$\sum_{j=1}^{n} \frac{Y_j(e, \vec{\tau}, S) \times V_e^j(e, \tau^j, S)}{V_j^j(e, \tau^j, S)}$$ (where $\vec{\tau}$ is the vector of the τ^j and the subscript
j represents the partial derivative with respect to τ^j) in place of (Equation
(3.9a)) and $V^j(e, \tau^j) = V^j(e^{SQ}, \tau^{SQ})$ for every interest group where the veto constraint was binding.

23 Condition (3.9a) is basically equivalent to the first-order condition derived in
Mayer and Mourmouras (2002) in the absence of IMF lending (using a Grossman–Helpman (1994) menu–auction model) when τ, interpreted as a political
contribution, enters linearly and of opposite sign and there are many interest
groups. The difference is in Equation (3.9b), where a menu–auction model
with political contributions has a reservation utility constraint given by the
requirement that the government's utility with positive contributions under
the policy it chooses is the same as what it would get if it ignored the contributions of the interest groups. In terms of Figure 3.3, the equilibrium in the
menu–auction model may be represented by the point on the contract curve
giving the same utility to the government (for a linear formulation for τ) as the
case where $\tau = 0$.

24 In the politically constrained case, e is higher (suggesting aid may be more
effective), but there are both structural distortions and political constraints
(suggesting aid may be less effective). Hence, the difference in the numerator
is ambiguous and may be second order relative to the difference in the numerator.

25 Since (e^o, τ^o) is feasible for $S > 0$, any other point chosen must yield higher
welfare than (e^o, τ^o), which yields higher welfare when S is positive than when it
is zero.

26 The assumption that $Y_{\tau S} = 0$ does not mean that changes in τ do not affect Y,
but rather that a change in S does not change the effect of τ on Y.

27 In the case of different objectives (such as an IMF financial constraint), a
strong distortion due to the political constraint in the sense of $e^P(S)$ being very
much above $e^+(S)$ means that the unconditional and conditional lending solutions will generally be farther apart in the politically constrained case than in
the economically constrained case. In this very limited sense one might argue
that political constraints in themselves give a role for conditionality, but it is a
weak argument given our interest in the case where authorities and the IMF
agree on objectives.

28 Iida (1993, 1996) and Mo (1995) consider bargaining in basic veto player
models.

29 In presenting a case for selectivity in lending, Drazen and Fischer (1997) and Drazen (1999) argue that conditional lending may be ineffective in addressing appropriation because of problems of asymmetric information and nonobservability. For example, suppose not only that the use of loans cannot be observed, but also that neither policy actions nor the connection between policies and outcomes is fully observable. Coate and Morris (1997) suggest that poorly designed conditionality may make things worse if it induces appropriation in especially inefficient ways.

References

Coate, Stephen and Stephen Morris. 1997. Policy Conditionality. Working Paper. Philadelphia: Penn Institute for Economic Research, University of Pennsylvania.

Dhonte, Pierre. 1997. Conditionality as an Instrument of Borrower Credibility. IMF Paper on Policy Analysis and Assessment 97/2. Washington: International Monetary Fund.

Diaz-Alejandro, Carlos F. 1984. IMF Conditionality: What Kind?. *PIDE Tidings* 23 (January–February): 7–9.

Diwan, Ishac and Dani Rodrik. 1992. External Debt, Adjustment, and Burden Sharing: A Unified Framework. Princeton Studies in International Finance 73. Princeton: Princeton University Press.

Dixit, Avinash. 2000a. Incentives and Organizations in the Public Sector: An Interpretative Review. Working Paper. Princeton: Department of Economics, Princeton University.

Dixit, Avinash. 2000b. IMF Programs as Incentive Mechanisms. Unpublished paper. Washington: International Monetary Fund.

Dollar, David and Jakob Svensson. 2000. What Explains the Success or Failure of Bank Supported Adjustment Programs. *The Economic Journal* 110: 894–917.

Drazen, Allan. 1999. What Is Gained By Selectively Withholding Foreign Aid?. Working Paper. College Park: University of Maryland.

Drazen, Allan. 2000. *Political Economy in Macroeconomics.* Princeton: Princeton University Press.

Drazen, Allan and Stanley Fischer. 1997. Conditionality and Selectivity in Lending by International Financial Institutions. Paper presented at a Symposium in Memory of Michael Bruno, Jerusalem, November 23–24, 1997.

Federico, Giulio. 2001. IMF Conditionality. Working Paper. Oxford: Nuffield College, Oxford University.

Grossman, Gene M. and Elhanan Helpman. 1994. Protection for Sale. *American Economic Review* 84: 833–50.

Grossman, Gene M. and Elhanan Helpman. 2001. *Special Interest Politics.* Cambridge, MA: The MIT Press.

Haque, Nadeem Ul and Mohsin S. Khan. 1998. Do IMF-Supported Programs Work?: A Survey of the Cross-Country Empirical Evidence. IMF Working Paper 98/169. Washington: International Monetary Fund.

Holmström, Bengt. 1982. Moral Hazard in Teams. *Bell Journal of Economics* 13: 224–40.

Iida, Keisuke. 1993. When and How Do Domestic Constraints Matter? Two Level Games with Uncertainty. *Journal of Conflict Resolution* 37: 403–26.

Iida, Keisuke. 1996. Involuntary Defection in Two-Level Games. *Public Choice* 89: 283–303.

International Monetary Fund. 2001. Conditionality in Fund-Supported Programs: Policy Issues. Policy Development and Review Department Washington: International Monetary Fund.

Jeanne, Olivier and Jeromin Zettelmeyer. 2001. International Bailouts, Moral Hazard, and Conditionality. Unpublished paper. Washington: International Monetary Fund.

Khan, Mohsin S. and Sunil Sharma. 2001. IMF Conditionality and Country Ownership of Programs. Working Paper 01/142. Washington: International Monetary Fund.

Killick, Tony. 1997. Principals, Agents, and the Failings of Conditionality. *Journal of International Development* 9: 483–95.

Marchesi, Silvia and Jonathon P. Thomas. 1999. IMF Conditionality as a Screening Device. *Economic Journal* 109: C111–25.

Martin, Lisa. 2000. Agency and Delegation in IMF Conditionality. Working Paper. Cambridge, MA: Department of Government, Harvard University.

Mayer, Wolfgang and Alex Mourmouras. 2002. Vested Interests in a Positive Theory of IFI Conditionality. IMF Working Paper 02/73. Washington: International Monetary Fund.

Mo, Jongryn. 1995. Domestic Institutions and International Bargaining: The Role of Agent Veto in Two-Level Games. *American Political Science Review* 89: 914–24.

Prendergast, Candice. 1999. The Provision of Incentives in Firms. *Journal of Economic Literature* 37: 7–63.

Sachs, Jeffrey D. 1989. Conditionality, Debt Relief, and Developing Country Debt Crisis. In *Developing Country Debt and Economic Performance.* Vol. 1. *International Financial System,* edited by Jeffrey Sachs. Chicago: University of Chicago Press.

Svensson, Jakob. 2000. When Is Foreign Aid Policy Credible? Aid Dependence and Conditionality. *Journal of Development Economics* 61: 61–84.

Tirole, Jean. 2002. *Financial Crises, Liquidity, and the International Monetary System.* Princeton: Princeton University Press.

Tsebelis, George. 2002. *Veto Players: How Political Institutions Work.* Princeton: Princeton University Press, forthcoming.

Vreeland, James Raymond. 1999. The IMF: Lender of Last Resort or Scapegoat?. Working Paper. New Haven: Department of Political Science, Yale University.

Vreeland, James Raymond. 2001. Institutional Determinants of IMF Agreements. Working Paper. New Haven: Department of Political Science, Yale University.

Willett, Thomas D. 2000. A Soft-Core Public Choice Analysis of the International Monetary Fund. Working Paper. Claremont, California: Claremont Graduate School.

4 Empirical implications of endogenous IMF conditionality*

Patrick Conway

The Articles of Agreement of the International Monetary Fund created a credit facility to provide temporary balance-of-payments support to member countries.[1] To ensure that this support will be temporary, the Articles of Agreement stipulate that countries participating in this facility must approve conditions limiting the country's macroeconomic policies. These conditions were the "safeguards" devised by IMF staff to "correct balance of payments maladjustments" while not jeopardizing "national or international prosperity." The derivation and use of these conditions has been quite controversial over the years – some critics found the conditions to be too constraining while others found them too loose; some found them too political while others found them not political enough.[2]

The terminology of this debate persists to the present, but should be revised. It does not reflect the reality of IMF credit programs.[3] While the Articles of Agreement are written in the spirit of temporary balance-of-payments support, the practice has become that countries transit from one program directly to another. The effective length of a spell of participation in the IMF credit facilities is for many countries many times longer than the length of a single arrangement.[4] This phenomenon has received widespread attention recently. The International Financial Institutions Advisory Commission (IFIAC) appointed by the US Congress was quite critical of the development.[5] In response, the Independent Evaluation Office (IEO) of the International Monetary Fund recently concluded a thorough investigation of the phenomenon culminating in the report *Evaluation of Prolonged Use of IMF Resources.*[6]

In both of these reports, the conditionality of IMF programs was given a central role in the argument. The authors of IFIAC (2000) concluded that the IMF had ceased to enforce the conditionality it negotiated at the start of each arrangement, thus eliminating its effectiveness. The authors of IEO (2002) concluded that those countries with prolonged access to IMF programs were subject to fewer and less onerous conditions on average, and that conditionality was for these countries poorly "prioritized," so that compliance with some conditions assured continued access to IMF resources while the country's most critical economic problems remained unaddressed.[7]

Both of these critiques of the phenomenon of prolonged use miss a crucial aspect of conditionality: it is a negotiated agreement between the IMF and the participating country, and is thus considered endogenously determined. The conditions, rather than being an independently set list of policy reforms to achieve economic growth and external balance, are the outcome of bargaining between the IMF and the participating country. These conditions are not only policy-reform components of IMF programs, but have become facilitative devices to continued cooperation between the two parties as well. Countries not fulfilling the conditions of an arrangement will often cancel that arrangement – but another arrangement will follow immediately.

Section 1 chronicles this prolonged use of IMF facilities through examination of the histories of Kenya and Pakistan in dealing with the IMF. A number of stylized facts of these relationships will be incorporated into the theoretical model that follows, including the frequent cancelation of an existing IMF arrangement with immediate installation of a new arrangement and the wide variety in percentages drawn down in those arrangements.

While the conditions attached to IMF credit arrangements are closely held by the IMF and the borrowing government, two indicators of non-fulfillment can be found: the premature cancelation of an IMF arrangement and the drawdown of less than 100 percent of the available credit in the arrangement. Section 2 summarizes the implications of a theoretical model of conditionality-setting derived in Conway (2003). Section 3 provides econometric evidence in support of this endogenous-conditionality hypothesis drawn from the IMF Annual Reports. Section 4 explores the implication of this model for cross-country estimation of the determinants of participation in IMF programs. Section 5 examines the implications for cross-country investigations of the impact of IMF programs on economic growth. Section 6 concludes.

1 The prolonged use of IMF credit facilities

In the Articles of Agreement, member use of IMF credit facilities was expected to follow the model of a credit union: periodic use of the facilities, with all members rotating between borrower and lender roles.[8] In practice, however, many borrowing countries have made prolonged use of IMF credit facilities. This prolonged use does not seem to be the exclusive purview of countries meeting the conditions on programs, but rather seems concentrated among those countries for whom it is quite common that arrangements be canceled or funds not drawn down in full.[9] In this section I illustrate this point with evidence from Kenya and Pakistan.

Table 4.1 lays out Kenyan participation in five types of IMF credit facilities: stand-by arrangements (SBA), extended fund facilities (EFF), structural adjustment facilities (SAF), extended structural adjustment facilities

Table 4.1 Kenyan participation in IMF arrangements

Facility	Start date	End date	Cancelled?	Percent drawn down
EFF	7/7/75	7/6/78	No	11
SBA	11/13/78	8/19/79	Yes	100
SBA	8/20/79	10/14/80	Yes	0
SBA	10/15/80	1/7/82	Yes	37
SBA	1/8/82	1/7/83	No	60
SBA	3/21/83	9/20/84	No	100
SBA	2/8/85	2/7/86	No	100
SBA	2/1/88	5/15/89	Yes	74
SAF	2/1/88	5/15/89	Yes	29
ESAF	5/15/89	3/31/93	No	83
ESAF	12/22/93	12/21/94	No	100
ESAF	4/26/96	4/25/99	No	17
PRGF	8/4/00	8/3/03	No	23 (as of 4/30/02)

Source: IMF Annual Reports, various years.

Notes
Also: drawings from Oil Facility and Compensatory Facility in 1974–76, 1979, and early 1980s.

(ESAF), and Poverty Reduction and Growth Facilities (PRGF). These facilities were those for which conditions were necessary for disbursement.

The Kenyan experience provides examples of two phenomena observed in many member countries. First, there are many instances of non-canceled arrangements that nevertheless were characterized by small percentages drawn down. For example, the 1975 EFF agreement between Kenya and the IMF ran its entire term but only 11 percent of the total funds available were disbursed. Second, there were five canceled agreements between Kenya and the IMF during the period since 1975. Each cancelation was followed immediately by the introduction of a new arrangement.

The low percentage drawn down is an indicator of one of two scenarios. The credit available in an IMF arrangement is disbursed in tranches. The tranches are disbursed according to a set timetable on the request of the borrowing country. Later tranches can only be disbursed if the country has met the conditions defined in the Letter of Intent associated with the arrangement. Thus, if the country has not met the conditions, then only the first tranche will be disbursed. Alternatively, the country's external position may improve over time; if the country has no need for the credit it may choose not to request disbursement but hold the arrangement as a credit line against future contingencies. In either case the arrangement continues but the credit is not drawn down.

Cancellation of an arrangement is in theory a more serious step, but in practice it can allow increased access to IMF credit facilities. So long as the current program is in place, its conditions govern the ability of the IMF to disburse credit. If the borrowing country and IMF agree that the conditions of an existing arrangement are no longer appropriate the country can cancel the current arrangement so that a new program, with new conditions, can be introduced. Cancelation is then a signal not of conflict but of cooperation, and is usually followed by immediate agreement on a new program with new conditions.

As Table 4.2 illustrates, Pakistan has a long history as a user of IMF credit facilities. This history can be broken into two parts: the initial generation (1958–78) of non-canceled and nearly completely disbursed arrangements, and a subsequent generation (1980–2000) of arrangements with limited disbursement and frequent cancelation. The initial generation includes a rather rare event – a canceled arrangement in 1959 without a new program immediately negotiated. In the other instances of canceled arrangements (1981, 1994, 1995) there was immediate introduction of a new arrangement in place of the one canceled.

These examples illustrate three features of the history of IMF arrangements that a model should replicate. First, prolonged use should be a possible outcome of the model. Second, the cancelation of an existing arrangement and immediate negotiation of a new program should be an endogenous event in the model. Third, the partial drawdown of arrangements should be an endogenous outcome as well.

Table 4.2 Pakistani participation in IMF facilities

Facility	Start date	End date	Cancelled?	Percent drawn down
SBA	12/8/58	9/22/59	Yes	0
SBA	3/16/65	3/15/66	No	100
SBA	10/17/68	10/16/69	No	100
SBA	5/18/72	5/17/73	No	84
SBA	8/11/73	3/10/74	No	100
SBA	10/16/74	10/15/75	No	100
SBA	3/9/77	3/8/78	No	100
EFF	11/24/80	12/1/81	Yes	0
EFF	12/2/81	11/23/83	No	0
SAF	12/28/88	12/27/91	No	71
SBA	12/28/88	11/30/90	No	71
SBA	9/16/93	2/22/94	Yes	33
ESAF	2/22/94	12/13/95	Yes	28
EFF	2/22/94	12/13/95	Yes	32
SBA	12/13/95	9/30/97	No	52
EFF	10/20/97	10/19/00	No	25
ESAF	10/20/97	10/19/00	No	39
SBA	11/29/00	9/30/01	No	100
PRGF	12/7/01	12/6/04	No	17 (as of 4/30/02)

Source: IMF Annual Reports, various years.

Notes
Also: use of Oil Facility and Commodity Finance Facility in 1970s, early 1980s and early 1990s.

2 Theoretical analysis of conditionality

Participation in an IMF program is an interlocking set of decisions made over time. There are two decision makers: the government of the country applying to participate in the program, and the staff and executive directors of the IMF. When a program is first proposed, there is an initial evaluation by both government and IMF staff as to the desirability of the program. The borrowing country weighs the costs and benefits of requesting a program, while the IMF staff examines the ability of the country to introduce the reforms that are thought to be necessary conditions for re-attaining external equilibrium. If the answer to each is "yes," then the arrangement is approved. The participating government signs a Letter of Intent, indicating its agreement with the conditions of the program. The first tranche of IMF funding is released.

If there is an ongoing arrangement with the country, the IMF staff first examines whether the country has met its conditions. If the country's historical performance has not satisfied the conditions the IMF cannot automatically disburse funds. It will either postpone disbursement or grant a waiver. Otherwise, disbursement will occur upon request of the borrowing country.

2.1 Competing hypotheses

I consider two competing hypotheses on conditionality.

- Hypothesis 1: conditions on IMF programs are derived by the IMF from economic fundamentals of the participating country. If conditions are not met, lending under the program is suspended. For one IMF program to follow another immediately, the conditions attached to the second program must be equal to or more restrictive than the initial program.
- Hypothesis 2: conditions on IMF programs are the outcome of bargaining between IMF staff and participating-country government. If conditions are not met, lending is suspended – but the two actors will look for ways to rewrite the conditions so as to permit disbursement. One method will be to establish an IMF program following another immediately with less restrictive conditionality. Another method will be to cancel the existing program and introduce a new program with reduced conditionality.

In Conway (2003) I derive a theoretical model of this joint decision-making process. The notion that conditionality is endogenous is not new. Drazen (2002), for example, examines the political-economy determinants of conditionality, while Mayer and Mourmouras (2003) provides a model in which the government solves a common-agency problem with principals in the IMF and in the domestic vested interests. The model in Conway (2003) differs from others, however, in that the negotiation between participating government and IMF staff over conditionality is represented as a generalized Nash cooperative equilibrium (see, e.g., Friedman 1990: chapter 6 and Svejnar 1986). This equilibrium is illustrated in Figure 4.1 for participating country j and a single policy variable subject to IMF conditions c_{jt}. The payoffs to the two actors are represented by z_{gjt} for government j and z_{It} for the IMF, both in period t. The "threat point" defined by the bargain is then the origin, while the payoff frontier

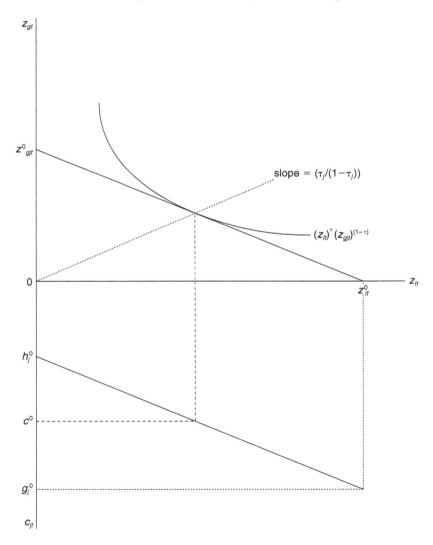

Figure 4.1 The Nash Bargaining Solution: Perfect Foresight.

is defined by varying conditionality on the policy variable between the reservation values of the two actors: g_j^o for the government, and h_j^o for the IMF.

The relative bargaining power of the IMF and country j government is represented by the bargaining weights τ_j and $(1 - \tau_j)$ respectively.[10] The equilibrium conditionality is a weighted average of the reservation values of the two actors. The equilibrium level of conditionality for period $t+1$ is thus based on the period-t value of the variable to which conditions are attached. It is adjusted for the impact of external events, with the weights assigned to those external events determined by the relative bargaining power of the IMF and the participating government. Equilibrium conditionality for an arrangement immediately following another is adjusted upward by the extent to which the country fell short of its conditionality in the preceding program. It also depends upon the difference between the policy variable in period t and its long-term value; the effect of this difference on equilibrium conditionality depends upon the relative bargaining strength of the two actors. If the government is dominant (i.e., τ_j approaching zero) and the country has budget surplus less than its long-term value, then the equilibrium conditionality will be increased proportionally.

When this equilibrium value of conditionality is introduced into the payoffs to IMF and government, there are a number of interesting implications. First, the coefficients on the external variables are now a combination of the coefficients found in the two payoff functions. Second, while in the original form only the IMF payoff depended upon satisfying conditionality, in this "reduced form" both payoffs now depend upon the degree to which conditions were met. Third, one payoff function is a multiple of the other. Estimating either one in this form will provide consistent estimates of these reduced-form coefficients. Fourth, so long as the reservation values are consistent with a program, it will be in both actors' interest to have a continuing cooperative relationship in any period t. Programs would follow one upon another, with conditionality adjusted so as to distribute the benefits from the arrangement between the two actors.

2.2 Uncertainty, cancelation and new arrangements

In the perfect foresight model, there is a clear and one-off decision to create an arrangement. Given perfect foresight, the arrangement once reached is sustained throughout.

It is more realistic to consider a world of uncertain outcomes and incomplete information. Conditionality as represented by c^o is set at the beginning of each program. During the lifetime of a program, the participating country can terminate the program. The IMF will not unilaterally terminate the program, but has the right (and, in fact, the obligation) to deny drawings by the participating country if the country does not satisfy the agreed-upon conditionality. In that case, the participating country does not receive the benefits of the drawdown.

Why might the conditionality not be satisfied? Conway (2003) identifies three potential reasons. First, it may have been violated in the period prior to the program. Such violations contribute directly to violations in the future. Second, the conditions on the policy variable may exceed the long-term value of the policy variable for that country. This will cause a negative component that will grow over time. Third, the accumulated effect of random shocks may cause a violation.

The probability of disbursement for given c^o in period $t + i$ is denoted by $\pi_i(c^o)$. The payoff to the government in the kth period of the arrangement will be lowered relative to the perfect foresight case so long as some $\pi_i(c^o) < 1$.[11] What could cause this probability to decline?

- Negative shocks to policy lower the probability of disbursement in all future periods.
- If the arrangement is predicated upon an incorrectly high target value for policy, then the probability of disbursement will be reduced for all future periods within the program.

Will there be a new arrangement? At the termination of the old arrangement, there is a set of reservation values. Negotiation with unchanged bargaining power will yield a new conditionality program for the new arrangement. This value will fall within the range of reservation values, and will thus be a lower conditionality target. This is thus an illustration of the cancelation clause of Hypothesis 2: when programs are canceled, they will be followed immediately with a new program at reduced conditionality.

3 Evaluating the competing hypotheses of conditionality

The two hypotheses provide two models of the determination of conditionality. Hypothesis 1 will serve as the null hypothesis: conditionality is determined by the fundamentals of the participating country. IMF programs can follow one another, but if conditionality is not met in one program then the subsequent program will have more restrictive conditionality. Hypothesis 2 is the alternative hypothesis, and predicts three potentially observable features. First, there is no reason for programs to be one-off activities; ceteris paribus, programs will be approved in sequence for the same country so long as reservation values conform. Second, conditionality on the programs will be endogenously adjusted at the beginning of the arrangement to reflect the bargaining power and initial conditions of the participating country and the government, including the ability of the participating country to satisfy previous conditionality. If conditions were not satisfied in the previous period, then ceteris paribus the

newly bargained conditionality will be less restrictive. Third, program cancelation is a natural course of events, and will in most cases be followed
immediately by a new program with reduced conditionality.

These implications are difficult to test for two reasons. First, the conditions associated with specific IMF programs have not generally been
made public. Second, there are often many interlinked conditions for
which there is no single sufficient statistic. In this chapter, I deduce the
conditionality associated with IMF programs indirectly by using information on the percentage drawn down of funds made available in IMF programs. The mechanics of IMF lending ensure that a program not meeting
its conditions will be characterized by a smaller percentage drawn down of
the loan amount. I implement this indirect measure using data from IMF
programs between 1993 and 2001.

The IMF policy on disbursements ensures that the percent drawn down
of a program will, ceteris paribus, reflect the strictness of conditionality.
The funds available under an IMF program are drawn down in tranches.
The first tranche can be drawn down upon signing the arrangement, but
for subsequent tranches the IMF staff must either certify that the country
has fulfilled the conditions of the Letter of Intent or must waive the conditions in that instance due to extraordinary events subsequent to signing
that make the conditions unobtainable.

The linkage between percent drawn down and violation of conditionality is not exact. The percent drawn down will depend as well upon the
country government's desire to use its credit line with the IMF. It may
choose not to draw down the resources, either because the country desires
the IMF agreement for reasons (e.g., HIPC consideration) unrelated to
the availability of funds, because it has entered the agreement on precautionary grounds or because events subsequent to signing the agreement
make it unnecessary to use those funds. This possibility must be incorporated in the derivation procedure.

The percent drawn down for any IMF program will be represented as:

$$P_{jt} = \beta_j + \beta_t - \beta_{10}\,\Delta Z_{jt} - \beta_{11}\Delta Z_{jt-1} - \beta_2 Z_{jt-1} + \beta_3(b_{jt} - c_{jt}) + \epsilon_{jt} \qquad (4.1)$$

The Z_{jt} are exogenous variables for country j in time t of importance to the
drawdown decision, and the Δ represents the first difference of those variables. The b_{jt} are the realized levels of policy variables subject to conditions, while c_{jt} are the conditions in time t. The IMF decision to allow
funds to be drawn down is based upon $(b_{jt} - c_{jt})$, the relation of realized
policy variables to the conditions written into the Letter of Intent.[12] Once
the IMF has decided, then the program country government decides
upon the percent drawn down. I hypothesize that this decision will have
both country-specific effects (β_j) and time-specific effects (β_t). The
country may be one to use IMF programs as precautionary lines of credit
or may be interested in the IMF program for other reasons than funding;

the year may matter because world credit market conditions make alternative credit sources more attractive to all IMF program recipients. Positive shocks to macroeconomic variables (ΔZ_{jt}) will reduce the desired percent drawn down, and negative shocks will work conversely. The country's initial macroeconomic situation (Z_{jt-1}) will also affect the desired percent drawn down. I consider two macroeconomic variables Z_{jt}: the ratio of current account surplus to GDP (y_{jt}) and the ratio of government budget surplus to GDP (b_{jt}). Each can be thought of as a policy variable, and thus will have conditions attached. Positive shocks to each should reduce the percent drawn down, while ratios in the previous period that were less negative than average should reduce the percent drawn down as well. If a country outperforms its conditionality (c_{jt}) then it should be able to draw down more of its IMF funds, other things equal. Since I do not observe the government's decision rule with certainty, there will also be an error term (ϵ_{jt}) associated with the predicted rule.

$$P_{jt} - \beta_j - \beta_t + \beta_{10}\Delta Z_{jt} + \beta_{11}\Delta Z_{jt-1} + (\beta_2 - \beta_3)Z_{jt-1} = -\beta_3 c_{jt-1} + \epsilon_{jt} \qquad (4.2)$$

Under either the null or alternative hypothesis, the residual ($-\beta_3 c_{jt-1} + \epsilon_{jt}$) will be an indicator of conditionality. As conditionality is reduced, the percent drawn down not attributed to other factors should be larger.

The programs of special interest to the endogenous-conditionality argument are those that follow immediately upon another IMF program: these will be called "continuation" programs. A specific instance of a continuation program is one that follows immediately on a canceled program: these will be called "post-cancelation" programs. Under the null hypothesis, these programs should be characterized by stricter conditionality than those that they follow. Under the alternative hypothesis, these programs should be characterized by weaker conditionality than those they follow. These hypotheses will be tested using the empirical estimate of the residual ($-\beta_3 c_{jt-1} + \epsilon_{jt}$).

I investigate this hypothesis in two steps. In the first step I estimate (Equation (4.2)) for the 175 IMF programs observed in 75 countries between 1992 and 2001. The data on percent drawn down by the IMF program are taken from various IMF *Annual Reports*, while the data on the current-account and fiscal ratios are taken from the *World Economic Outlook* (WEO) prepared by the IMF. I calculate the estimated value of ($-\beta_3 c_{jt-1} + \epsilon_{jt}$), denoted $\hat{e}_{jt}$, from this first regression. In the second step, I create two dummy variables. The variable d_{xajt} takes the value of one for those IMF programs that are not preceded immediately by another program for that country but are followed immediately by another program, and zero otherwise.[13] The variable d_{xpjt} takes the value of one for those IMF programs that follow immediately another IMF program for the same country, and zero otherwise.[14] In addition, those programs ending in cancelation are represented by the binary variable can_{xajt}, and those following immediately upon a canceled program are presented by the binary variable can_{xpjt}. For nearly all observations, $can_{xpjt} = 1$ is a subset of $d_{xpjt} = 1$, and similarly for can_{xajt} and d_{xajt}.[15] The null hypothesis is that conditionality will be more demanding in follow-on programs, while Hypothesis 2 predicts that continuation programs will have less demanding conditionality. These effects will be heightened in the case of cancelation and immediate adoption of a new program. For post-cancelation countries the net effect on the percent drawn down will be given by the coefficients of d_{xajt} and can_{xajt} or d_{xpjt} and can_{xpjt}.

The first regression, with statistics reported in column (1) of the first part of Table 4.3, replicated (1) exactly with 75 country fixed effects, nine yearly fixed effects, and regressors Δb_{jt}, Δy_{jt}, Δb_{jt-1}, Δy_{jt-1}, Δb_{jt-2}, Δy_{jt-2}, b_{jt-1}, and y_{jt-1}. While the explanatory power of the regression is quite high, with $R^2 = 0.91$, the explanation comes largely through the time and country-specific dummy variables. When the conditionality component $\hat{e}_{jt}$ is exam-

Table 4.3 Estimating the effect of continuing programs on conditionality

Step 1: Deriving an explanatory equation for the percent drawn down

	(1) P_{jt}		(2) P_{jt}		(3) P_{jt}	
	coefficient	s.e.	coefficient	s.e.	coefficient	s.e.
Δy_{jt}	−0.02	0.87	−0.22	0.61	−0.32	0.68
Δb_{jt}	0.61	1.36	0.65	0.89	−0.22	1.03
Δy_{jt-1}	−0.40	0.65	−0.31	0.43	0.31	0.48
Δb_{jt-1}	1.59	1.25	1.25	0.86	1.60*	0.98
Δy_{jt-2}	0.39	0.54	0.70*	0.40	1.00**	0.46
Δb_{jt-2}	0.21	1.00	−0.25	0.67	0.30	0.78
y_{jt-1}	0.92	1.01	0.48	0.34	0.09	0.39
b_{jt-1}	−2.61	1.78	−2.33**	0.82	−3.64**	0.93
T93	82.67**	20.60	64.90**	8.46	40.46**	9.23
T94	75.10**	21.65	68.72**	7.56	56.71**	8.48
T95	76.49**	21.88	64.31**	7.17	48.70**	7.95
T96	63.67**	21.49	53.67**	8.02	38.62**	8.97
T97	71.68**	20.26	59.16**	8.13	38.96**	8.67
T98	69.37**	21.66	62.98**	7.79	52.71**	8.93
T99	44.03**	21.38	40.84**	7.28	31.82**	8.36
T00	66.71**	21.85	45.42**	7.28	35.88**	8.22
T01	33.36**	21.06	12.84	10.70	2.77**	12.37
N	174		174		174	
R^2	0.91		0.84		0.76	
Fixed effects	75 countries, 9 years		9 countries, 9 years		0 countries, 9 years	
F test for excluded variables			F(66, 82) = 0.58		F(9, 157) = 2.83**	

Step 2: Checking the conditionality portion of P_{jt} for sensitivity to nature of program

	(1) $\hat{e}_{jt}$		(2) $\hat{e}_{jt}$		(3) $\hat{e}_{jt}$	
	coefficient	*s.e.*	*coefficient*	*s.e.*	*coefficient*	*s.e.*
Intercept	−0.22	1.80	2.15	2.43	1.83	2.94
d_{xajt}	−4.86	4.68	−12.08*	6.31	−17.94**	7.63
d_{xpjt}	3.51	3.96	−0.69	5.34	0.64	6.46
can_{xajt}	−3.22	6.51	−14.01*	8.78	−3.57	10.62
can_{xpjt}	6.05	6.48	4.23	8.73	7.37	10.56
N	174		174		174	
R^2	0.02		0.04		0.04	
Test: coefficient $d_{xajt} = d_{xpjt}$ F(1, 171) stat	2.19	(0.14)	5.08**	(0.02)	4.07**	(0.04)
Test: coefficients $d_{xajt} + can_{xajt} = d_{xpjt} + can_{xpjt}$	3.28*	(0.07)	2.24	(0.14)	3.45*	(0.06)

Notes
Standard errors in right-hand column. Coefficients significantly different from zero at the 95 percent confidence level marked with**, and at the 90 percent confidence interval with*. P-value in right-hand column for F tests.

ined in the second part of Table 4.3, the signs associated with the coefficients for d_{xajt} and can_{xajt} are negative, as expected under Hypothesis 2, while the coefficients for d_{xpjt} and can_{xpjt} are positive. The difference between the conditionality imposed on the first program and the subsequent programs is significant at the 93 percent level of significance for post-cancelation programs, but at a lesser level for continuation programs in general.

While the country fixed effects contributed significantly to the regression, it was clear in examining the significance of individual coefficients that only a subset of these country effects was important.[16] When insignificant country-specific effects were eliminated, the regression resulted in column (2) of Table 4.3. Those country effects remaining in the regression included those for Costa Rica, Croatia, Egypt, El Salvador, Estonia, Hungary, Latvia, Nigeria, and the Slovak Republic. The coefficients on these country effects were all strongly negative, indicating that for these countries the drawdown percentage is much closer to zero.[17] The hypothesis that the specification in column (1) is significantly different from column (2) is rejected, as shown by the F test in the final row of the first part of the table. When the conditionality residual from this regression is carried to the lower part of the table, it is once again the case that the coefficients on d_{xajt} and can_{xajt} are negative. The coefficient on can_{xpjt} is positive, as expected, while the coefficient on d_{xpjt} differs insignificantly from the implied effect on stand-alone programs. The test that the coefficients on d_{xajt} and d_{xpjt} are equal is rejected by the data.

When all country-specific effects are excluded, as in column (3), the story is quite similar. The initial regression has a similar structure. In the second-step regression the coefficients on d_{xajt} and can_{xajt} are negative, as expected, while the coefficients for d_{xpjt} and can_{xpjt} are positive. Differences in coefficients are significantly different from zero at around the 95 percent level of confidence.

4 Implication for estimation of the determinants of IMF program participation

The evidence cited in the previous section suggests that conditionality is in fact endogenously determined in a manner consistent with the theoretical model. If so, this becomes an important fact to consider when considering the determinants of participation in IMF programs.

There has been substantial empirical work in identifying the determinants of IMF program participation in the last decade: examples include Joyce (1992), Edwards and Santaella (1993), Conway (1994), Bird (1995), Knight and Santaella (1997), Thacker (1999; reprinted as Chapter 5 in this book), Przeworski and Vreeland (2000), Bird and Rowlands (2001), and Dreher and Vaubel (2004). The typical approach used is to specify a probit equation. The binary dependent variable indicates participation or non-participation in an IMF program; the independent variables included have been chosen to reflect both economic and political factors.

The authors have recognized that the decision to participate is jointly determined, but they have typically relied upon a "reduced form" estimation of Equations (4.1) and (4.2) without explicit modeling of conditionality's role in the equations. Knight and Santaella (1997) and Przeworski and Vreeland (2000) went beyond this "reduced form" approach to estimate separately "structural" equations but without consideration of the role of conditionality. Their ability to do so statistically hinged upon their willingness to assign elements of the independent variable matrix Z_{jt} to affect only the government or only the IMF decision. These exclusion restrictions are difficult to justify on a priori grounds. As Dreher and Vaubel (2004) comment about this approach,

> the distinction between demand and supply effects is increasingly blurred. Almost all the additional regressors can be interpreted at the same time as determinants of the government's credit demand and as criteria by which the Fund judges the creditworthiness of its appli-

cants. Thus a meaningful simultaneous or two-state estimation is not feasible. However, for our purpose, ... a reduced-form estimate is sufficient.

(Dreher and Vaubel 2004: 7–8)

While this criticism is valid, the reduced-form estimation approach also has its dangers. In these papers, the authors have appealed to a "reduced form" without stating the endogenous variable that links supply and demand decisions in a reduced form. Without such an endogenous variable, a "reduced form" estimation strategy is potentially biased: the appendix provides an illustration of this bias.[18] In this chapter I identify explicitly the endogenous variable as conditionality: this has surprising implications for the "reduced-form" estimating equation.

4.1 Reconsidering the "reduced-form" specification

The typical approach to "reduced-form" estimation of a participation equation is to include all the exogenous variables thought to be of importance either to the government decision or to the IMF staff decision. If conditionality matters to these decisions, however, this will be misspecified; further, if conditionality is endogenously determined, there are important consequences to the estimating equation.

With the assumption of normality of errors, a univariate probit system of equations can be derived from the endogenous-conditionality solution. The coefficients on the exogenous variables are a weighted sum of the coefficients of the IMF and government payoff functions, with the relative weight defined by the ratio of the marginal cost ω to the government of tightened conditions to the marginal benefit to the IMF. The entire effect is weighted by the bargaining power of the government in setting conditionality. The variables for which conditionality is defined enter twice in contemporaneous form: once as a deviation from long-term value, and once through the impact of conditions carried over from an existing program. If the country participates in an IMF program in the previous period there will be an increase in the payoff of continued participation to the extent that the country's policy variable b_{jt} improves.

4.2 Hypothesis testing

The simplest test implied by the reduced-form derived here takes the null hypothesis that conditionality is not a determinant of either IMF staff or country–government participation decisions. In that case, the two payoffs define a bivariate probit with partial observability similar to that posited by Przeworski and Vreeland (2000). The first panel of Table 4.4 reports the results from such a bivariate probit for annual data on IMF program participation for the period 1991–99.

Table 4.4 Partial observability bivariate probit

1. Null hypothesis

	Country payoff		IMF payoff	
	coefficient	s.e.	coefficient	s.e.
$resimp_{jt-1}$	−0.71**	0.29	−0.27	0.42
$debt_{jt-1}$	1.67**	0.27	0.25**	0.09
y_{jt-1}	−0.08	1.00	1.95**	0.78
cr_{jt-1}	−1.20**	0.24	–	–
b_{jt-1}	−0.48	1.67	6.42**	1.50
$cons_{jt-1}$	4.38**	1.28	−1.91*	1.06
Intercept	−0.57	0.32	1.20**	0.31

N = 744 (period 1991–99); Log-Likelihood: −401.83582; Likelihood Ratio Test: χ^2 = 36.639.

2. Including prior participation

	Country payoff		IMF payoff	
	coefficient	s.e.	coefficient	s.e.
$resimp_{jt-1}$	−1.52**	0.56	−0.58*	0.35
$debt_{jt-1}$	1.33**	0.56	0.25**	0.10
y_{jt-1}	1.31	1.82	1.48**	0.75
b_{jt-1}	−5.78**	2.93	3.75**	1.62
$cons_{jt-1}$	0.53	1.83	−0.18	0.94
cr_{jt-1}	–	–	−0.18	0.23
p_{jt-1}	4.08**	0.72	–	–
np_{jt-1}	–	–	−1.08**	0.18
Intercept	−1.73**	0.53	1.43**	0.31

Notes
N = 744 (period 1991–99); Log-Likelihood: −295.66815; Likelihood Ratio Test: χ^2 = 1.67028. Time-specific dummy variables d91–d98 were included in both equations but their coefficients are excluded from the table. Results are available from the author.

Lagged regressors were used as proxies for contemporaneous variables to avoid the simultaneity bias in the participation decision and these macroeconomic variables. For the exogenous variables I include a number of variables found to be significant in published explanations of participations in IMF programs: the ratio of foreign-exchange reserves to imports ($resimp_{jt-1}$) and the external debt/GDP ratio ($debt_{jt-1}$) enter significantly and with the expected sign.

For policy variables potentially subject to conditionality I include the domestic credit/GDP ratio (cr_{jt-1}) and the government consumption/ GDP ratio ($cons_{jt-1}$); these also enter significantly and with the expected sign. The intercept indicates the country bias, other things equal, against participation. In the IMF payoff the current account/GDP ratio (y_{jt-1}), the government budget surplus/GDP ratio (b_{jt-1}), the government consumption/GDP ratio ($cons_{jt-1}$) and the debt ratio ($debt_{jt-1}$) all enter in a fashion consistent with reported IMF preferences. The intercept indicates a bias toward program approval, other things equal.[19] Year-specific dummy variables were included to control for the influence of shared world economic conditions, but are not reported.

The hypothesis of this chapter suggests that conditionality is endogenous, and simultaneously determined with the participation decision. A complete test of the implied parameter restrictions is left for future work, but here I test a few simple predictions of the endogenous conditionality model.

The first test is of the simplest implication: that payoffs in the current period will be dependent on the participation (or non-participation) in the previous. The endogenous-conditionality model has that implication through the importance of past conditionality in affecting current payoff. When binary variables indicating participation (p_{jt-1}) and non-participation (np_{jt-1}) in the previous period are added to the partial-observability probit, the results (reported in the second panel of Table 4.4) indicate a significant improvement in explanatory power. Comparison of the log-likelihood scores in the two panels demonstrates this improvement. The simple model is rejected in favor of the model including p_{jt-1} and np_{jt-1}.

While the endogenous-conditionality model of this chapter predicts this result, other explanations of participation will do so as well.[20] A more precise test of the endogenous-conditionality model will interact the coefficients on the policy variables subject to conditionality with whether the country participated in a program in the previous period. In Table 4.5 I perform such a test, with the variables subject to conditionality posited to be the current-account ratio (y_{jt-1}), government budget ratio (b_{jt-1}), the growth of domestic credit (cr_{jt-1}), and the government consumption ratio ($cons_{jt-1}$). The first panel of the table is the hypothesis that conditionality does not matter; the second panel reports the specification consistent with the endogenous-conditionality model. Significant coefficients on the interacted variables provide evidence to reject the exogenous-conditionality model in favor of the endogenous-conditionality model.

The upper panel of the table reports a specification derived under the assumption of exogenous conditionality. The variables included are those of the analysis above; other variables (e.g., the terms of trade or the level of per capita income) were introduced but made an insignificant contribution in all cases. If the expected results were those associated with the country's payoff function, the estimates raise a number of questions. An increased reserves/import ratio tends to reduce the probability of participation while the increased external debt ratio increases the probability, as expected. However, the probability of participation is rising significantly in the current account and government budget surplus ratios, and declining significantly in the credit ratio: each of these is counter to expectations of government motivation, but consistent with motivations often attributed to IMF staff.

In the lower panel of Table 4.5, five additional variables are included to

Table 4.5 Probit estimates of the consolidated system

	Ignoring conditionality		Introducing conditionality	
	coefficient	s.e.	coefficient	s.e.
$resimp_{jt-1}$	−0.78**	0.26	−0.86**	0.28
$debt_{jt-1}$	0.55**	0.26	0.33**	0.10
y_{jt-1}	1.46**	0.58	1.52	1.20
cr_{jt-1}	−0.68**	0.17	−0.32	0.43
b_{jt-1}	2.97**	1.10	−0.96	1.53
$cons_{jt-1}$	0.42	0.82	0.45	0.89
$p_{jt-1}*y_{jt-1}$			0.07	1.36
$p_{jt-1}*cr_{jt-1}$			0.04	0.49
$p_{jt-1}*b_{jt-1}$			4.70**	2.26
$p_{jt-1}*cons_{jt-1}$			−0.12	1.60
np_{jt-1}			−1.97**	0.32
Intercept	0.49	0.21	1.24**	0.27
Log-Likelihood	−430.21		−307.99	
Pseudo R^2	0.08		0.34	

Notes
$N = 744$ (period 1991–99). Time-specific dummy variables d91–d98 were included in both equations but their coefficients are excluded from the table. Results are available from the author.

model more precisely the impact of endogeneity. The variable np_{jt-1} is added to capture the initial hurdle effect for the country government; its coefficient should be negative and significant to represent the initial cost to the government of entering an IMF program. The variables $p_{jt-1} \times y_{jt-1}$, $p_{jt-1} \times cr_{jt-1}$, $p_{jt-1} \times b_{jt-1}$, and $p_{jt-1} \times cons_{jt-1}$ interact the binary variable indicating participation in the previous year with the policy variables subject to conditionality. Their coefficients should be positive and significant if conditionality has indeed played a facilitative role in establishing programs.

The results from this specification are more in accord with theory. Once the current account, credit, government budget, and consumption ratios are introduced as target variables for conditionality, the significant paradoxical results of the top panel are eliminated. The estimate of initial entry is negative and significant, as expected. The coefficients on the target variables provide some support to this hypothesis, primarily through the coefficient on $p_{jt-1} \times b_{jt-1}$. As the government budget surplus improves for countries in IMF programs, the probability of continuing the program is increased.

4.3 Unobserved heterogeneity

The preceding regressions were unsatisfactory in that they ignored the impact of the long-term policy value. While this is an unobserved set of variables, its impact can be controlled for in this instance by regressions that correct for unobserved heterogeneity. Ignoring these effects can lead to spurious causation if unobserved heterogeneity in country preferences for or adaptability to IMF programs leads to systematic differences in participation. While it is possible that the heterogeneity is due to consistent policy choice rather than to differences in long-term values, the analysis in this section errs on the side of caution by removing all country-specific variation in the data before testing the endogenous-conditionality hypothesis.

Table 4.6 reports the results of four equations designed to test the endogenous-conditionality hypothesis. There are 735 country/years for which complete data are available, drawn from 88 countries. The variables used include those of the previous section, and a normalized index of the real effective exchange rate lagged one period (rn_{jt-1}).[21] Columns 1 and 3 represent the null hypothesis that conditionality does not facilitate agreement on IMF programs, while columns 2 and 4 incorporate the feedback

Table 4.6 Testing the endogenous-conditionality hypothesis: 1991–2000

	1. No conditionality		2. Conditionality		3. No conditionality – UH		4. Conditionality – UH	
	coefficient	*s.e.*	*coefficient*	*s.e.*	*coefficient*	*s.e.*	*coefficient*	*s.e.*
rn_{jt-1}	−0.00	0.07	0.10	0.14	−0.16	0.13	0.19	0.19
y_{jt-1}	1.15*	0.63	1.26	1.32	3.65**	1.61	2.84	2.12
$resimp_{jt-1}$	−0.87**	0.25	−0.89**	0.29	−0.33	0.64	−1.17*	0.69
b_{jt-1}	2.58**	1.17	−1.15	1.61	11.03**	2.58	6.95**	3.07
$debt_{jt-1}$	0.49**	0.10	0.30**	0.10	1.22**	0.41	1.17**	0.44
$cons_{jt-1}$	1.20	0.96	1.90	1.67	−2.77	2.95	−0.26	3.72
np_{jt-1}			−2.20**	0.34			−1.64**	0.44
$p_{jt-1}^* y_{jt-1}$			0.10	1.49			1.24	1.93
$p_{jt-1}^* b_{jt-1}$			4.84*	2.44			2.87	3.76
$p_{jt-1}^* rn_{jt-1}$			−0.16	0.16			−0.42**	0.22
$p_{jt-1}^* cons_{jt-1}$			−1.98	2.17			−3.55	2.73
N	735		735		735		735	
C	88		88		88		88	
Log-Likelihood	−429.1		−304.4		−249.3		−219.2	
$\chi^2(5)$	249.4**				60.2**			
Degrees of freedom	16		21		102		107	

Notes
All coefficients estimated using probit specification. All estimation results included year-specific dummy variables. The UH analyses also included a country-specific binary variable for each of the 88 countries for which complete data were available. * indicates significance at 90 percent confidence level. ** indicates significance at 95 percent confidence level. The critical value at the 95 percent confidence interval for the $\chi^2(5) = 11.07$.

through target variables. The difference between columns 1 and 2, on the one hand, and 3 and 4 on the other is the inclusion of country-specific dummy variables in the estimation underlying columns 3 and 4. This controls for any country-specific heterogeneity. While some of this heterogeneity may be program-related, some will not be: the estimation results of columns 3 and 4 thus represent a conservative test for the endogenous-conditionality hypothesis.

There is significant evidence for the overall hypothesis, although many of the individual coefficient estimates are insignificantly different from zero. The $\chi^2(5)$ statistics reported at the bottom of columns 1 and 3 report the results of the likelihood ratio test that the additional variables associated with the endogenous-conditionality hypothesis are jointly significant: in both instances, the statistic is significantly different from zero at usual confidence levels. The coefficients on the variable np_{jt-1} represent the estimate of an initial hurdle cost to participation, and these are significantly different from zero in both cases. The individual coefficient estimates all take the expected signs: increases in the current account ratio and the government budget surplus ratio, reduction in the government consumption ratio, and depreciation of the real effective exchange rate all have the effect for a country currently in a program of increasing the likelihood that the program will continue. In each set of estimates only one of these is individually significantly different from zero.

Among the other results from estimation are two robust findings: a larger external debt to GDP ratio is associated with a greater likelihood of an IMF program in the next period, and a larger reserves-to-imports ratio is associated with a reduced likelihood of an IMF program in the following period.

5 Implications for program evaluation

While the results above are interesting in and of themselves, they are also important to the statistical evaluation of the effectiveness of IMF programs. Given that the decision to participate in an IMF program is potentially contemporaneously determined with typical indicators of economic performance, there is a possibility of selection bias in the determination of the program's effect on performance. Two methods of correcting for this bias have been used in the literature. One is based on the "propensity score" for participation, while the other introduces the inverse Mills ratio as a correction for the potential bias. Both will be biased if they do not consider this difference in determinants of participation.

I demonstrate in Table 4.7 the potential for divergent results through use of data on economic growth rates observed for countries participating and not participating in IMF programs over the preceding period. The average economic growth rate for the 816 periods (country/years) in the sample is 5.47 percent. In the 559 periods characterized by participation, the average growth rate was 5.45 percent while for the 257 periods of non-

Table 4.7 Program evaluation: impact of IMF programs on economic growth

1. *Controlling for unobserved heterogeneity in the growth regression*

	Exogenous conditionality first stage			Endogenous conditionality first stage		
	coefficient	s.e.	T-stat	coefficient	s.e.	T-stat
ps_{jt}	−0.077	0.037	2.06	−0.018	0.010	1.77
gy_{jt-1}	0.107	0.041	2.58	0.120	0.036	3.32
y_{jt-1}	−0.174	0.039	4.48	−0.198	0.032	6.17
b_{jt-1}	0.039	0.062	0.63	0.005	0.051	0.09
$rxrn_{jt-1}$	−0.007	0.003	2.05	−0.004	0.003	1.57
$nfig_{jt-1}$	−0.138	0.069	2.01	−0.138	0.059	2.33
ttn_{jt}	−0.300	0.402	0.75	−0.255	0.332	0.77
p_{jt-1}	0.054	0.017	3.13	0.027	0.007	4.04
pp_{jt}	−0.030	0.014	2.15	−0.016	0.009	1.81
N		816			816	
F		14.39			14.12	
R^2		0.68			0.68	

2. *Not controlling for unobserved heterogeneity in the growth regression*

	Exogenous conditionality first stage			Endogenous conditionality first stage		
	coefficient	s.e.	T-stat	coefficient	s.e.	T-stat
ps_{jt}	−0.000	0.009	0.01	−0.003	0.007	0.41
gy_{jt-1}	0.383	0.031	12.34	0.383	0.031	12.37
y_{jt-1}	−0.133	0.023	5.80	−0.132	0.023	5.79
b_{jt-1}	−0.091	0.039	2.30	−0.093	0.039	2.38
$rxrn_{jt-1}$	−0.006	0.002	2.56	−0.006	0.002	2.61
$nfig_{jt-1}$	−0.003	0.031	0.09	−0.002	0.031	0.05
ttn_{jt}	0.073	0.212	0.34	0.075	0.212	0.35
p_{jt-1}	0.020	0.007	2.75	0.021	0.006	3.37
pp_{jt}	−0.001	0.007	0.08	−0.000	0.007	0.06
N		816			816	
F		61.59			61.61	
R^2		0.58			0.58	

Notes
Each regression also includes year-specific regressors. Coefficients are jointly significant, but excluded for brevity.

ps_{jt} is the estimated probability of participation drawn from the first-stage probit analysis. Two different estimates ps_{jt} are used in this table. The first set of columns is derived from a probit model including lagged participation, year-specific fixed effects and country-specific fixed effects but not including the other endogenous-conditionality (EC) regressors. The second set of columns is derived from the same probit model in which all variables had two coefficients: one if the period followed a participation period, and another if the period followed a non-participation period.

The joint significance of the Unobserved Heterogeneity terms cannot be rejected for any of these specifications at the 95 percent level of confidence. For example, the model in the bottom half of the first column is rejected in favor of the model in the top half of the first column, with $F_{87,711} = 2.54$. The critical value for that combination of degrees of freedom is 1.30. The critical two-sided T values for the coefficients in the table: 1.96 for 95 percent level of confidence, and 1.64 for 90 percent level of confidence.

participation, the average growth rate was 5.48 percent. Clearly, the unconditional difference is approximately zero; the question at hand is whether the near equality masks the offsetting effects of more adverse conditions and positive effects of IMF programs (or vice versa).

Table 4.7 is divided into two panels. The top panel reports results in which fixed-effects estimation has been used to control for unobserved heterogeneity in the growth regression, while the bottom panel reports the results with no correction for unobserved heterogeneity in the growth regression. Within each panel are the results of systems regression using two instruments for the country's participation in IMF programs. The first instrument is derived from a first-stage probit of participation on explanatory variables. This specification corresponds to the null hypothesis of this chapter expanded to allow prior participation to matter to current participation. The second instrument expands the specification to include additional effects attributed to endogenous conditionality as suggested by the alternative hypothesis above. Both instruments include controls for unobserved heterogeneity, and thus the instruments correspond to the predicted values derived from the participation equations in columns 3 and 4 in Table 4.7. These predicted values will be denoted by the propensity score (ps_{jt}). The standard errors reported in Table 4.7 represent those from the variance–covariance matrix corrected for the two-stage nature of estimation.

The importance of correcting for unobserved heterogeneity is the most important message of Table 4.7. A comparison of top and bottom panels indicates the wide swings in coefficient estimates that result from inclusion of country fixed-effects terms. While such controls represent a conservative approach to estimation, the large differences in coefficients argue for greater attention to these effects in interpreting such regressions.

The results of Table 4.7 also demonstrate that use of the appropriate propensity score changes the estimates of the impact substantially. The coefficients on the other explanatory variables change insignificantly, but those on IMF-participation variables ps_{jt} and p_{jt-1} are significantly different across the two formulations. Use of the appropriate propensity score leads to significantly larger estimates of the contemporaneous impact of participation on economic growth and a significantly larger cumulative effect of IMF programs.

These estimation results are not meant to be definitive. The choice of explanatory variables used here is based upon a demand-side approach to economic growth, and was selected because of the short time span of the sample. (Supply-side effects then are captured by the "unobserved heterogeneity" fixed effect.) By contrast, Vreeland (2003) reports economic growth equations based upon a supply-side specification. Determining the consistency of the two sets of results can be left for the future; the message of this chapter is the importance of incorporating endogenous conditionality in a program-evaluation exercise.

6 Conclusions

Participation in an IMF program is a joint decision of participating governments and IMF staff. The endogenous determination of conditionality and the ability to cancel an IMF program to introduce another prove to be crucial to this participation equation.

Data on percentages of IMF programs drawn down provide indirect measures of the endogenous-conditionality hypothesis, and these measures indicate behavior consistent with the theoretical construct.

The endogeneity of conditionality has important implications for research on the determinants of IMF participation, and through them on the estimation of the impact of IMF programs on participating-country economic performance. The "endogenous-conditionality" model implies a number of exclusionary restrictions for probit estimation of an IMF participation equation, and these are not rejected by the data. Use of this estimating structure in addition corrects a number of anomalies in the typical reduced-form estimation of the participation equation. Finally, I demonstrate that proper estimation of the economic-growth equation yields estimates of program impact that are significantly different from those estimated on the same data using traditional estimation techniques.

Appendix: use of the reduced-form probit

With bivariate normal errors, and with at least one regressor in z_{gjt} but not in z_{It} and vice versa, bivariate probit can in theory be used to estimate β_{Ij}. β_{gj}, and the correlation coefficient between u_{Ijt} and u_{gjt}.

When the joint decision-making process modeled as a probit is only partially observed, a single "reduced-form" probit can be estimated. The coefficients estimated in this reduced-form probit are in general weighted averages of the two individual probit coefficients.

I created a data set with five exogenous variables $(x_1, x_2, x_3, \epsilon_z, \epsilon_y)$ and 100 observations indexed by t. Each variable was created as a random standard normal variable within STATA. The unobserved decision equations were defined as follows.

$$z^*_{jt} = a_z + x_{1t} + x_{2t} + x_{3t} + \epsilon_{zt}$$

$$y^*_{jt} = a_y + 3x_{1t} - 5x_{2t} + 7x_{3t} + \epsilon_{yt}$$

The binary probit variables were defined P_z and P_y, and were equal to one if z^*_{jt} and y^*_{jt}, respectively, are greater than zero. They were equal to zero otherwise. The intercepts a_z and a_y were set equal to zero for the initial estimation results. The binary variable $P = P_z^* P_y$ was defined as the observed probability.

When P_z and P_y are observed, probit estimation yields solid results for each equation.

The hypothesis that the underlying parameters are those used to create the variables will not be rejected in either of these equations.

Table 4.A1 Binary probit variable estimates

	P_z			P_y		
	coefficient	*s.e.*	*Z-stat*	*coefficient*	*s.e.*	*Z-stat*
Intercept	0.108	0.166	0.65	0.215	0.348	0.62
x_1	0.943	0.208	4.54	3.953	1.233	3.21
x_2	1.249	0.210	5.95	−5.568	1.756	3.17
x_3	1.057	0.238	4.45	7.228	2.074	3.49
Pseudo R^2		0.48			0.88	
N		100			100	

A probit estimation of the joint probability P with respect to the three exogenous variables yields an odd average of the two:

Table 4.A2 Joint probability estimates

	P		
	coefficient	*s.e.*	*Z-stat*
Intercept	−1.122	0.210	5.35
x_1	0.927	0.259	3.58
x_2	0.053	0.170	0.31
x_3	1.352	0.244	5.53
Pseudo R^2		0.416	
N		100	

In the case of the intercept and x_2, we will reject the true parameter from either sample. For x_1 and x_3, the parameters from the z^*_{jt} equation will not be rejected while the parameters from the y^*_{jt} equation will be rejected.

I examine the proposition that this single probit on the joint probability is a weighted average of the two underlying equations through a further simulation exercise. First, I recalculated P for values of the intercept a_z from zero to 10 in increments of 0.10. Second, I recalculated P for values of the intercept a_y from zero to 10 in increments of 0.10. In each instance, after the recalculation, I estimated the single probit on the new joint probability. The following diagram indicates the parameter estimates derived from each of these.[22]

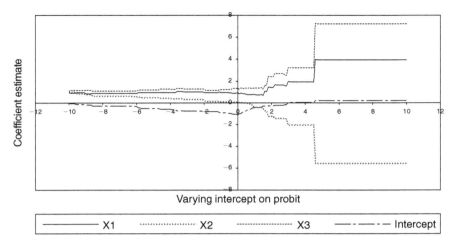

Figure 4.A1 Partially observed joint probit.

As is evident from the coefficient values illustrated in the figure, it is the case that as the intercept of each individual equation rises above five, the estimated coefficients are those of a probit on the other equation. This is sensible, as the increasing intercept makes it increasingly likely that the binary variable calculated from that equation will be one always – and thus the joint probability is determined by the probability from the other equation. It is also evident that for small values of the intercepts the reduced-form coefficients do not bear a recognizable relation to either of the two individual equations. Thus, it will be important in practice to utilize any information available to disentangle these two effects.

Notes

* Thanks to Sergiy Peredriy for assistance in the empirical work, and to Mohsin Khan for discussions that triggered the research of this chapter. Thanks as well for useful comments to participants in the International workshop at the University of North Carolina at Chapel Hill.
1 Article I, section v, states that one goal of the IMF is "(v) To give confidence to members by making the general resources of the Fund temporarily available to them under adequate safeguards, thus providing them with opportunity to correct maladjustments in their balance of payments without resorting to measures destructive of national or international prosperity." A copy of the Articles of Agreement is available from the IMF at http://www.imf.org/external/pubs/ft/aa/aa.pdf.
2 Williamson (1982) is a collection of papers from the years leading up to the debt crisis, and provides evidence of both of these charges. More recently, IFIAC (2000) has charged that the conditions imposed are (a) politically motivated and (b) effective only in perpetuating the dependence of the

borrowing country on the IMF. Other critics of IMF conditions include Sachs (1997) and Feldstein (1998). Rosett (1999) provides a summary of criticisms based on IMF conditions in East Asian countries. Ivanova *et al.* (2003) makes the case that IMF conditions do not have enough political motivation.

3 The IMF has created a number of "facilities" for disbursing credit: these include not only the original stand-by arrangement (SBA), but also the extended fund facility (EFF), the structural adjustment facility (SAF), the extended structural adjustment facility (ESAF), the poverty reduction and growth facility (PRGF), the oil facilities, the compensatory financing facilities, and others. When an individual country approaches the IMF for credit, funds are made available from the appropriate facility.

4 I will use the words "arrangement" and "program" interchangeably to describe the contractual relationship between the IMF and a borrowing country, but that is not quite right. The arrangement is the financial commitment of the country to draw down funds and then repay them, while the program is the set of conditions agreed upon between the IMF and the borrowing country. I will use either term to refer to that single contractual relationship between the two actors.

5 IFIAC (2000).

6 IEO (2002).

7 IEO (2002: 13).

8 Kenen (1986) provides a detailed discussion of this analogy.

9 The notion that conditionality is endogenous to the negotiation process is not a new idea, nor is it limited to these two examples. Dreher (2002) provides a very interesting compilation of the available historical evidence on conditionality and documents trends in design and implementation over time and by groups of countries.

10 The value of τ_j is assumed set exogenously for each country.

11 In this argument I begin from the benchmark, similar to the perfect foresight case, that when the initial negotiation took place both actors believed $\pi_i(c^o) = 1$ for $i = 1, \ldots, n$. If the equilibrium conditionality were based upon some other path of probabilities, then the argument is simply that subsequent events shifted this path downward.

12 If this IMF decision was a once-and-for-all choice in each program, it would be more appropriate to model the percent drawn down as a sequential choice: 0 if the IMF said no, and some positive amount if the IMF said yes. Since for each program there will be at least four determinations based on conditionality, I approximate this IMF "veto power" by the negative linear effect represented in the equation.

13 I define "immediately" here as occurring within a two-month window. In other words, if one program ends on 1 March and another begins on 15 April, then by my definition one follows the other immediately.

14 There are 22 observations for which $d_{xajt} = 1$, and 35 observations for which $d_{xpjt} = 1$. The remaining programs are "stand alone," and have 0 for both these variables. There are more observations for d_{xpjt} because there are a number of countries in which three or more programs follow immediately upon one another. In those cases the first program has $d_{xa} = 1$, while the following programs all have $d_{xp} = 1$.

15 There are 13 observations for which $can_{xajt} = 1$ and 11 observations for which $can_{xpjt} = 1$. For the two programs in the sample for which cancelation did not lead to a new program, $can_{xajt} = 1$ but $d_{xajt} = 0$.

16 Statistical significance is indicated at the 95 percent level of confidence, unless otherwise stated.

17 Why these countries? There is potentially a group of countries in the sample that will not draw down the funds from an IMF program because it has entered the program for precautionary purposes or for benefits other than the availability of funds. One indicator of this type of country will be evidence of zero percent drawdown on IMF programs.

18 If the determination of conditionality were orthogonal to the participation decision, then the estimation of a "reduced form" probit of the participation decision could lead to biased coefficient estimates. The Appendix provides an example of the rather common case where conditions are placed on a policy variable that enters both country and IMF choice functions, but with opposite sign. In that case, the relation between participation and the policy variable is non-linear: estimation using the linear probit technique will lead to bias and imprecision.

19 The identification of the two coefficients in the two probit equations is made econometrically. It is based in part on the curvature of the normal distribution. In this instance it was impossible to identify the two equations separately without imposing a restriction a priori. The lagged credit ratio was included in one set of regressors and not the other to provide this minimal condition for identification.

20 Even if conditionality were not endogenous, one could posit that the participating country pays a fixed cost in terms of popular support for participating in an IMF program. If this cost is less, or non-existent, for subsequent programs the participating country's probit would respond as in Table 4.4. Similarly, the IMF staff may be more comfortable lending to a country with a "track record"; that will also generate the results of Table 4.4.

21 As in the previous section, both terms-of-trade indices and gross domestic product per capita in purchasing-power terms were included. Both were insignificant throughout and were thus excluded.

22 The horizontal axis provides a numeration of the simulations results. For values to the right of zero, each point represents a simulation for a different value of a_y between zero and 10 (and with a_z equal to zero). For each point to the left of zero, the simulation results are indexed by the negative of the value of a_z (with a_y equal to zero).

References

Bird, G. 1995. *IMF Lending to Developing Countries: Issues and Evidence.* London: Routledge.

Bird, G. and D. Rowlands. 2001. IMF Lending: How is it Affected by Economic, Political and Institutional Factors?. *Journal of Policy Reform* 4 (2): 243–70.

Conway, P. 1994. IMF Lending Programs: Participation and Impact. *Journal of Development Economics* 45: 365–91.

Conway, P. 2003. Endogenous IMF Conditionality: Theoretical and Empirical Implications. Processed.

Drazen, A. 2002. Conditionality and Ownership in IMF Lending: A Political Economy Approach. *IMF Staff Papers* 49: 36–67.

Dreher, A. 2002. The Development and Implementation of IMF and World Bank Conditionality. Working paper 165. Hamburg Institute of International Economics.

Dreher, A. and R. Vaubel. 2004. Does the IMF Cause Moral Hazard and Political Business Cycles? Evidence from Panel Data. *Open Economies Review* 15 (1): 5–22.

Edwards, S. and J. Santaella. 1993. Devaluation Controversies in the Developing

Countries: Lessons from the Bretton Woods era. In *A Retrospective on the Bretton Woods System*, edited by M. Bordo and B. Eichengreen, pp. 405–55. Chicago: University of Chicago Press.

Feldstein, M. 1998. Refocusing the IMF. *Foreign Affairs* March/April.

Friedman, J. 1990. *Game Theory with Applications to Economics*, second edition. New York: Oxford University Press.

Independent Evaluation Office (IEO). 2002. Evaluation of Prolonged Use of IMF Resources. Washington, DC: IMF.

International Financial Institution Advisory Commission (IFIAC). 2002. *Report*. Washington, DC: Government Printing Office.

Ivanova, A., W. Mayer, A. Mourmouras, and G. Anayiotos. 2003. What Determines the Implementation of Fund-Supported Programs?. IMF Staff Working Paper.

Joyce, J. 1992. The Economic Characteristics of IMF Program Countries. *Economics Letters* 38: 237–42.

Kenen, P. 1986. *Financing, Adjustment and the International Monetary Fund*. Washington, DC: Brookings.

Knight, M. and J. Santaella. 1997. Economic Determinants of IMF Financial Arrangements?. *Journal of Development Economics* 54: 405–36.

Mayer, W. and A. Mourmouras. 2002. Vested Interests in a Positive Theory of IMF Conditionality. IMF Working Paper 02/73.

Przeworski, A. and J. Vreeland. 2000. The Effect of IMF Programs on Economic Growth. *Journal of Development Economics* 62: 385–421.

Rosett, C. 1999. The World's Poor Pay the Price for the IMF's Failures. Op-ed piece, *Wall Street Journal*, April 22.

Sachs, J. 1997. The Wrong Medicine for Asia. Op-ed piece, *New York Times*, November 3.

Svejnar, J. 1986. Bargaining Power, Fear of Disagreement and Wage Settlements: Evidence from US Industry. *Econometrica* 54/5, September: 1055–78.

Thacker, S. 1999. The High Politics of IMF Lending. *World Politics* 52 (1): 38–75.

Vreeland, J. 2003. *The IMF and Economic Development*. Cambridge, UK: Cambridge University Press.

Williamson, J. (ed.). 1982. *Fund Conditionality*. Washington, DC: Institute for International Economics.

Part II

The international and domestic politics of IFI programs

5 The high politics of IMF lending*

Strom C. Thacker

Considering the degree of scrutiny given to the role of the International Monetary Fund (IMF, or Fund) in the international economy, we know little about the underlying causes of the IMF's behavior.[1] During the 1980s, the IMF became a "lender of last resort" for many developing country governments that had been cut off from private credit markets and faced destabilizing imbalances of payments. After private capital began to return voluntarily to what were called the emerging markets in the early 1990s, the anticipated erosion of the Fund's role in the developing world did not materialize. Faced with recurrent payments' imbalances, pressures for currency devaluation, and the macroeconomic instability associated with crises in Latin America, Asia, and Russia, the developing nations have turned with increasing frequency to IMF credits and stabilization plans. Despite the growing body of research on the IMF's critical role in international finance, we still have few explanations of and only patchy empirical data on why the IMF approves loans to some countries but not others. As the Fund delves further into the management of balance-of-payments and currency crises around the world, both theoretical and practical imperatives dictate that we specify more fully and test more systematically competing explanations of IMF behavior. What factors influence the IMF's decisions to lend? Are these decisions based on technical economic criteria, or do they reflect the political preferences of the Fund's more powerful members? What are those preferences, and how do they affect the IMF's relationship with its developing country clients? In other words, does politics matter? More importantly, *how* does politics matter?

The literature on international institutions and multilateralism suggests that the operation of multilateral economic organizations like the IMF will assume growing importance in a post-hegemonic international order.[2] This body of theory raises several important questions: To what extent do multilateral institutions modify the interests or constrain the behavior of their member states? Can the more powerful states use these organizations as effective instruments of national foreign policy, or are such pressures diluted or transformed in passing through multilateral channels? Finally, what underlying political interests drive the behavior of the large powers within the multilateral institutions, and how do they do so? On the practical side, Gallarotti has shown that poorly managed international organization not only can be ineffective but also can destabilize the international system.[3] The debates surrounding proposed increases in Fund resources and recent loan packages negotiated with South Korea, Indonesia, Russia, and Brazil demonstrate the growing popular recognition of these kinds of problems, but scholarly research has yet to address these questions adequately.

Economists have made inroads in isolating the economic bases of IMF lending, but they are the first to point out that their models remain incomplete. Researchers have found statistically significant results for the impact of a number of economic variables on IMF lending, but the low overall explanatory power of the econometric models reviewed by Bird suggests that "there are probably a range of other non-economic factors which still need to be delineated."[4] One likely source of noneconomic factors is politics, but political scientists have not yet been able to demonstrate the systematic impact of political variables on IMF lending.[5] Several case studies offer suggestive, but not generalizable, evidence of the political bases of IMF lending. Fewer studies have attempted to construct a systematic political explanation of Fund behavior. This chapter attempts to fill some of those gaps in the literature and proposes answers to those questions by developing and testing statistically a political explanation of IMF lending patterns.

The IMF's stated decision-making procedures prohibit the consideration of political factors. Loans are made strictly on the basis of the monetarist "Financial Programming" model and a "Doctrine of Economic Neutrality" that is blind to such factors as international politics and the nature of developing country regimes.[6] The Fund may impose strict lending requirements, but it applies them fairly to all countries. The meetings of the IMF executive board, which approves all Fund programs, are highly secretive.[7] The specific considerations that determine the board's deliberations and decisions are therefore not available in the public domain. For its part, the Fund staff publicly maintains the position of economic neutrality, but evidence presented in numerous case studies leaves open the possibility that political factors play an important role.

There are at least three reasons to suspect that politics matters in the IMF. First, several studies have found extremely low rates of borrower compliance with Fund conditionality, yet the IMF continues to lend to many of these problem debtors even after earlier programs have been canceled for noncompliance.[8] Finch, a former IMF staff member, suggested in the late 1980s that economic factors could not explain these patterns: "Because decisions were no longer based on compatibility with repayment terms, lending was guided increasingly by the political preferences of the leading industrial countries."[9] Second, each country's representative on the Fund's executive board is appointed by his or her home government

(Treasury, in the case of the United States). Thus it should come as no surprise that the positions of those representatives within the Fund reflect the political interests of the national governments they serve.[10] As Smith puts it, "The IMF is itself a political institution. It is managed by politically appointed individuals from member nations, and the political interests of its members influence its decisions."[11] Although the staff is less directly linked to national governments, the executive board must approve all proposed programs. The familiarity of Fund staff members with the preferences of the executive board discourages them from submitting loan packages that the board is likely to veto.[12]

Finally, weighted voting and the decision-making procedures of the Fund also leave room for politics. As of April 1995, the US controlled 17.83 percent of the voting power in the IMF, followed by Germany and Japan with 5.5 percent each, and France and the United Kingdom with 5.0 percent each.[13] An evolving system of special majorities has helped the US maintain its influence beyond that dictated by its gradually decreasing voting share.[14] An 85 percent majority is required for the most important Fund decisions, giving the US alone, and other groups of countries together, veto power. The US can also push through favored programs, which it might not be able to do based on its votes alone. Although the managing director has traditionally been a European, he rarely acts against US preferences.[15] That is not surprising since he is appointed through a process over which the US has veto power.[16] But that power rarely needs to be wielded openly. The managing director typically makes decisions based on a "sense of the meeting," derived from the comments of the various participants and their relative voting power.[17] Other powers can be reluctant to speak against the US for fear that the US will later retaliate by exercising its veto power over their own favored programs.[18] Finally, the US and its like-minded allies together can effect international monetary cooperation by forming subsets, or "k-groups," of countries to push through certain packages that single parties cannot.[19]

Given the possibility that political factors influence IMF decisions, several scholars have argued that the Fund's more powerful members manipulate it to further their own political and economic interests.[20] The US government, for its part, "has repeatedly told foreign governments that it will not intervene in negotiations between the Fund and member governments."[21] Kahler notes, however, that "the U.S. (and other major countries) can still influence programs for friends and clients at the margin."[22] Others suggest that American politicization of Fund lending is more widespread. A series of case studies conducted for a project directed by Killick and Bird reveals that at least one-third of the 17 countries studied secured favorable loan terms on their IMF programs due to the intervention of major shareholding countries on their behalf.[23] Stiles concludes that in only one of seven cases examined did the Fund adopt a politically neutral, technocratic approach to lending.[24]

Such case studies have been useful for providing the kind of rich detailed data that are unavailable by other means, for formulating testable hypotheses, and for providing initial evidence of the role of politics in IMF lending. Despite these advances, we are still unable to say much more than that politics *seems* to matter, at least in some cases. This chapter aims to accomplish two essential tasks. First, it attempts to provide the first systematic quantitative evidence for whether politics affects IMF behavior. Second, it proposes a dynamic explanation of how political factors affect interactions of multilateral organizations with their member states, and tests the statistical formulation of that argument in the case of the IMF. I first propose a simple macroeconomic model and a political explanation of IMF lending. I then operationalize these hypotheses together and report the results of a series of statistical tests conducted on them jointly. I conclude with a discussion of the limitations and broader implications of this research.

1 A simple macroeconomic model

Economists have isolated several important demand- and supply-side macroeconomic determinants of IMF lending. Rather than attempt to replicate such studies, I take them as a starting point for my political analysis. Conway has modeled participation in IMF programs as a function of a country's economic environment and its past economic performance.[25] He finds statistically significant negative results for lagged variables representing the ratio of foreign exchange reserves to imports, the growth rate of real gross national product, the ratio of the current account to GNP, the terms of trade, and the real rate of interest.[26] Variables capturing level of development (proxied by the share of output from the agricultural sector) and long- and short-term debt stocks did not attain conventional levels of statistical significance.

Lindert tests the impact of several variables on the interest rate charged on official creditor lending to 51 countries in 1985.[27] He obtained statistically significant results for only two variables – the log of absolute nominal public and publicly guaranteed debt in 1981 and the log of per capita income – each with a positive coefficient. None of the other variables – the share of debt held by official creditors, the ratio of debt service to GNP, the ratio of reserves to imports, money stock growth, prior default, prior rescheduling, and years since first rescheduling – approached conventional levels of statistical significance.

Summarizing his own and others' research, Bird identifies statistically significant regression results with negative coefficients for balance of payments, per capita income, current account, and reserves.[28] Collectively, these studies find statistically significant positive regression coefficients for inflation, access to private bank credit,[29] domestic credit growth, and government spending. With the exception of Conway, the low predictive power of these models suggests that they are underspecified. Rather than attempt to test the validity of distinct competing macroeconomic models, this chapter draws upon the large body of existing research to identify the putative economic determinants of Fund activities. First, the balance of payments position of a country is the initial baseline upon which its participation in IMF programs is evaluated. An improvement in the balance of payments is the stated primary goal of most IMF lending programs,[30] and without a payments deficit, a country should neither need nor be eligible for Fund lending.[31] When faced with a payments deficit, a country can either run down its reserves or borrow internationally.[32] In the context of the debt crisis, running down reserves was not a viable long-term solution, and the most reliable source of international borrowing was the IMF. Specifically, deterioration in the balance of payments is expected to increase the chances of receiving a loan from the IMF.

Second, a country's debt position should affect its demand for and the supply of an IMF loan for distinct reasons. On the demand side, a heavier debt burden increases developing countries' need for external finance to service that debt. In terms of supply, some have argued that the more heavily indebted countries have more bargaining leverage over the IMF because of their importance to global financial stability.[33] In addition, some view IMF loans as a payoff to foreign creditors.[34] Assuming that those lenders wield influence within the executive board, IMF loans more likely will go to countries where creditors are more heavily exposed. Lindert found that the more heavily indebted countries did receive official creditor loans, but at higher interest rates than the smaller debtors, due to the reluctance of Northern taxpayers to finance more concessionary terms.[35] For the purposes of this study, the fact that the larger debtors were more likely to receive loans is of primary interest.

Third, the level of per capita income of a country also may influence its ability to secure Fund assistance. Killick notes that the IMF's historically narrow focus on balance-of-payments considerations has given way in recent years to a broader view that acknowledges the relationship between the balance of payments and growth.[36] Lindert reports that official favoritism for poor countries resulted in lower interest rates on official loans, and Bird argues that poorer countries are less likely to borrow on private capital markets and therefore to have a higher relative demand for IMF loans.[37] Countries with lower per capita incomes should be more likely to request and receive a loan from the IMF.

Fourth, if the Doctrine of Economic Neutrality is followed, a poor credit history should decrease the chances of receiving a loan. After the massive defaults of the 1930s, the debtor nations were effectively cut off from credit for several years. Many have argued that we should expect similar outcomes now.[38] Specifically, past failures to uphold IMF loan requirements should make it more difficult to receive additional loans.

Finally, both neo-Marxist and modern political economy interpretations would suggest two additional macroeconomic indicators that should affect Fund decisions due to the influence of "low politics": the trade and investment exposure of firms based in the IMF's major principal shareholder, the US. Authors grouped loosely within a neo-Marxist (or dependency) perspective argue that capitalists in the core states, especially the US, dictate IMF policy at the expense of the nations of the periphery.[39] A political economist more concerned with the impact of domestic politics on foreign economic policy might also posit, without necessarily adopting the concomitant exploitation argument, that well-organized export enterprises and multinational corporations (MNCs) pressure the US government to protect their interests on the executive board. Neo-Marxism suggests that higher levels of US exposure lead to a greater likelihood of receiving an IMF loan because the attendant policy conditionality promotes the expansion of global capitalism. A less explored, domestic-politics interpretation yields more ambiguous expectations. The inflow of foreign exchange and the restoration of international creditworthiness would be expected to benefit US exporters and foreign investors, while the demand-reduction components of the typical IMF program would suggest a negative impact for these variables.[40]

2   High politics and the IMF

The international political aspects of IMF lending have received far less rigorous analysis. Two rudimentary strands of thought comprise this genre, but neither has been fully developed nor adequately tested. I label the first, more common strand the "political proximity" hypothesis. Simply put, political friends of the US are more likely to receive loans than are its enemies. In addition to the case studies described above, Bello and Kinley argue that the US disregarded the Fund's economic criteria and pressured the Fund to approve loans to politically friendly South Africa, El Salvador, and Haiti.[41] The IMF has also denied loans to economically worthy political enemies of the US, such as Vietnam.[42] In sum, the more closely a country aligns with the US, the higher the probability it will receive a loan from the IMF.

These arguments have not yet been fully developed conceptually nor thoroughly tested empirically. To illustrate an intuitive analytical foundation for this argument and to facilitate its testing, I construct a continuous voting space, scaled from 0 to 1, where 1 represents total agreement and 0 complete discord with the United States on a single broad dimension of foreign policy affinity (such affinity could be easily measured by votes in a majority-rule international voting arena, such as the United Nations General Assembly). Figure 5.1 is a graphic representation of this space and a schematic portrayal of the political proximity hypothesis. Countries at point A, at the far left-hand side of the voting space, have little chance of receiving a loan, while those at point C, at the far right, are much more

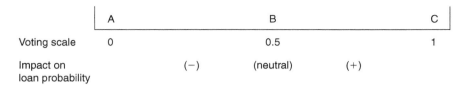

Figure 5.1 The political proximity hypothesis.

likely to receive Fund support. Alignment near the middle, at point B, has little or no effect.

Despite the existence of plentiful case studies, previous research has not effectively evaluated this argument. Furthermore, several studies have documented numerous cases where US "enemies" are rewarded or "friends" punished. In many instances the Fund has made loans to leftist governments, such as Manley's in Jamaica in 1979 and the East European Soviet bloc countries of Hungary, Yugoslavia, and Romania, each of which ranked among the top fifteen IMF loan recipients from 1952 to 1984.[43] This evidence seems to paint a picture of IMF lending as an apolitical technocratic process, economic neutrality at its best. But these loans may not have been justifiable on purely economic grounds, either. Assetto compares the results of a regression equation designed to predict the size of IMF loans based solely on economic criteria with the size of the actual loans received by the three East European countries to conclude that actual lending exceeded predicted lending by a significant margin.[44]

A less static interpretation of these anomalies introduces the "political movement" hypothesis, the less-developed second strand of the political argument. Movement toward or away from the US on international political issues may be at least as important as the absolute political alignment of a particular country. Hinting at this idea, Horowitz asks whether the IMF should use loans to entice countries like Romania and Hungary away from the Soviet bloc.[45] This notion is consistent with Assetto's analysis of the cases of Hungary, Yugoslavia, and Romania, all of whom distanced themselves politically from the Soviet Union (that is, moved closer to the US). In contrast, neither Czechoslovakia nor Poland, more consistently faithful Soviet allies, received any IMF funding in the post-Second World War Cold War period.[46]

Frey applies Hirschman's neutrality model to formulate a model of the bilateral aid-giving process in a bipolar world where aid recipients can play the two superpower donors off one another.[47] On a more general level, McKeown models the aid relationship formally as a sequential bargaining game between the lending principal and borrower.[48] The lender exchanges aid for political realignment by a developing country toward the position of the lender. The borrower moves from its "ideal" point to a new equilibrium point where the marginal utility of additional aid received equals the domestic political loss incurred by another move away from its ideal position. I adapt and extend these central insights to hypothesize that political movement toward the US increases a country's probability of receiving a loan from the IMF.

I portray the lending process as a dynamic game between each borrower and a single lender. I do not model this interaction in formal game-theoretic terms, nor do I model the relationship between the US and IMF. Rather, I assume the US plays the role of principal within the IMF, generate testable hypotheses about the relationship between the Fund and borrowing countries, and evaluate them empirically. If the data confirm these hypotheses, it would strongly suggest, but not directly confirm, a predominant US presence in an increasingly important multilateral organization. Such a conclusion would have important implications for the study of international institutions and regimes, as well as for the multilateral management of the international economy.

Figure 5.2 captures the basic argument of the political movement hypothesis. For simplicity's sake, I present this as a linear relationship, though future research might loosen this assumption. It is based on the same 0–1 voting space. Rather than measure a country's absolute political alignment, however, it charts the change (or realignment) in that position from one time period to another. The maximum distance a country can move vis-à-vis the lender is ±1.0. Countries that make large movements toward the US, such as at point B, have a greater chance of receiving IMF credit than those that make movements away from the US, such as at point A. Figure 5.3 brings the spatial and temporal sides of the story together to illustrate the effect of political realignment from one voting cycle to the next. A country shifting from point A to point B has a better

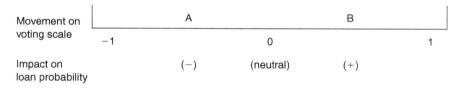

Figure 5.2 The political movement hypothesis.

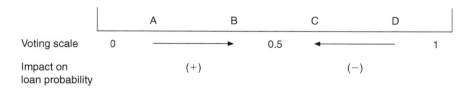

Figure 5.3 The impact of political movement over time.

chance of receiving a loan than one moving from point D to point C, even though point C is still closer to the lender's position than is point B.

5 Operationalization of the hypotheses

Because theory tells us that both economic and political factors affect IMF lending, a model that excludes either category is, by definition, mis-specified. A combined political economy approach addresses one of Bird's main concerns:

> [S]ome countries may be able to muster more support amongst the membership of the Executive Board than others. The problem is that such [political] factors are difficult to model formally and include in econometric estimation, but their exclusion may explain why demand functions which rely exclusively upon economic characteristics will leave much of the story untold.[49]

It may be difficult to model and test political factors econometrically, but it is certainly possible.

The analysis focuses not on the size of the loans, the interest rate, or other conditions but simply on the decision to lend. The structure of the Fund leaves more room for political factors to enter into the process of loan approval than into the formation of the terms of the loans themselves. The politically appointed executive board generally votes yes or no on a complete package that has been assembled by the staff, based largely upon market conditions and its own modeling and forecasting. Furthermore, Fund rules on confidentiality make data collection on most of the terms and conditions of loan packages impossible.[50]

This section presents the hypotheses introduced above in the form of a pooled logit model of IMF lending to 87 developing countries from 1985 to 1994.[51] The dichotomous nature of the dependent variable requires the use of logit estimation, which treats the relationship between a categorical dependent variable (the probability of receiving a loan) and the continuous independent variables as a nonlinear one that approaches both 0 and 1 asymptotically.[52]

The basic logit can be expressed symbolically as:

$$\ln[(P(L=1)_{it})/(1-(P(L=1)_{it})] = b_0 - b_1(\text{BalPay}) + b_2(\text{Debt}) - b_3(\text{PerCapY}) - b_4(\text{Default}) + b_5(\text{USX}) + b_6(\text{USDFI}) + b_7(\text{PolProx}) + b_8(\text{PolMove})$$

L is a dichotomous variable coded 1 if country i received an IMF Stand-by Arrangement (SBA) or Extended Fund Facility (EFF) loan during the calendar year t, 0 if it did not.[53] $P(L=1)_{it}$ is the estimated probability that a country will receive a loan in year t.[54] b_0 is the intercept term. "BalPay" is the balance of payments position; "Debt" is the debt burden; "PerCapY" is per capita income; "Default" is a measure of credit history; "USX" is the amount of US exports to the country; "USDFI" is the amount of US direct foreign investment in the country; "PolProx" is political proximity to the US in the international voting space described above; and "PolMove" is political movement toward the US within the same space. The economic variables are lagged by one year and the political variables by one to two years to establish the direction of causality.

To pose a more challenging test for the political model, I isolate a number of critical macroeconomic factors expected to affect Fund behavior and select several statistical proxies for them. The balance of payments is operationalized into several different variables. BOP_{it-1} is the overall balance of payments of a country in year $t-1$.[55] ΔBOP_{it} is the change in the overall balance of payments from $t-1$ to t. $PCBOP_{it-1}$ and $\Delta PCBOP_{it}$ are per capita balance of payments and change in per capita balance of payments, respectively.[56] $CACCT_{it-1}$ is the current account, and $\Delta CACCT_{it}$ is the change in the current account. $CACCT/GNP_{it-1}$ and $\Delta CACCT/GNP_{it}$ capture the ratio of the current account to GNP and the change in that ratio.[57] Since higher payments deficits are thought to increase the chances of receiving a loan, all coefficients should be negative.

A country's debt burden is measured by the following variables: $DEBT_{it-1}$ is the level of absolute public and publicly guaranteed debt in year $t-1$, and $\Delta DEBT_{it}$ is the change in that level of debt from $t-1$ to t. $PCDEBT_{it-1}$ and $\Delta PCDEBT_{it}$ compute per capita debt figures. A series of ratios captures the debt service burden for each economy. $DEBT/GNP_{it-1}$ is the ratio of long-term total debt stocks (public and private) to GNP, and $\Delta DEBT/GNP_{it}$ tracks the change in that ratio. INT/GNP_{it-1} and $\Delta INT/GNP_{it}$ are the variables for the ratio of interest payments to GNP and its change, and $RES/DEBT_{it-1}$ and $\Delta RES/DEBT_{it}$ measure the ratio of reserves to GNP and the change in that ratio.[58] Because a heavy debt burden increases debtors' demand for loans and because the Fund is hypothesized to give greater supply consideration to the larger debtors,[59] all coefficients should be positive except those for $RES/DEBT_{it-1}$ and $\Delta RES/DEBT_{it}$, which are expected to be negative.

$PCAPY_{it-1}$ represents per capita GNP, computed from data reported in the World Bank's *World Debt Tables* and *Global Development Finance* and in the IMF's *International Financial Statistics*. Lower-income countries should be more likely to receive loans, so a negative coefficient is expected.

$DEFAULT_{it-1}$ is a dummy variable coded 1 if a country has had a prior IMF program canceled any time since 1975 (the first full year of the EFF program) through year $t-1$, 0 otherwise. Since a bad credit history should adversely affect the likelihood of future loans, its coefficient should be negative.[60]

USX_{it-1} is the level of US exports to a country. According to the neo-Marxist hypothesis, it should be positively signed. The domestic-level political economy perspective has ambiguous expectations for the direction of this effect.[61]

USDFI$_{it-1}$ is the value of the stock of US direct investment for all industries in a country. Expectations are similar to those for USX$_{it-1}$.[62]

The voting space depicted in Figures 5.1 to 5.3 is measured by KVOTE$_{it-2}$, an index of political agreement between country *i* and the US in year $t-2$. Calculated as a decimal between 0 and 1, this variable measures the degree of coincidence between the votes of the sample country and the US in the United Nations General Assembly (UNGA) on the approximately 10 to 15 issues in each session that the US Department of State has deemed key votes. Under Congressional mandate, the State Department has compiled the voting records of all UN member nations on these selected issues since the 1983 General Assembly in its annual publication, *Report to Congress on Voting Practices in the United Nations*.[63] The Appendix lists the key votes identified in this report for the years examined here. In accordance with the political proximity hypothesis, a positive coefficient is anticipated.[64]

Using UN voting patterns to measure international political alignment is one solution to the problem of testing political variables lamented by Bird. For its part, the US government has proclaimed that examining UN votes makes it "possible to make judgments about whose values and views are harmonious with our own, whose policies are consistently opposed to ours, and whose practices fall in between."[65] But not all UN votes are equally important. In reference to the key votes, the same report states that the "only votes that can legitimately be read as a measure of support for the United States are those which we identified as important to us, and on which we lobbied other nations."[66] The validity of UNGA voting records has been debated extensively.[67] I adopt the self-identified measure of political alignment of the principal US foreign policy decision-making body: UNGA key votes. There is also evidence that the State Department tracked such data in a similar manner previous to the Congressional mandate, that it considered UN votes a reliable indicator of alignment, and that the US allocated aid on the basis of that alignment. In a 1964 memo to the director of the Food for Peace Program, Dick Reuter, Lansdale noted that "at critical moments in the world's recent history, the US 'bought' votes subtly and indirectly to support its stand in the General Assembly. The 'buying' is in terms of US assistance to the voting country."[68] Furthermore, Lansdale's analysis employed a measure of alignment similar to the current State Department use of key votes, charting only votes on Cold War issues.

It also appears that at least some recipient countries take US vigilance of UN voting seriously. Argentina, for example, previously a leader in the Non-Aligned Movement, modified its voting stance in the UNGA to reflect better its improved relations with the United States in the early 1990s.[69] In a 1997 interview, Carlos Escudé a former adviser to Argentina's minister of foreign relations, revealed that "with respect to some important United Nations resolutions, there was direct contact between Argentina and the United States, and Argentina voted in a manner favorable to the United States."[70] More generally, between 1990 and 1991 Argentina altered its UN votes to move from the fourth, most anti-US stance in the UN to a position similar to that of Turkey.[71]

$MKVOTE_{it-1}$ measures the movement in political alignment between the sample country and the US within the voting space from year $t-2$ to year $t-1$, measured in UNGA key votes.[72] From the political movement hypothesis, I expect a positive coefficient.

4 Findings and interpretations

Table 5.1 presents the results of three different versions of the model. The combination of pooled data and a categorical dependent variable presents unique diagnostic challenges.[73] Column 1 presents the results for the basic logit model, with no correction for autocorrelation. It appears to provide a good overall fit: -2 times the log-likelihood ratio (-2 x LLR) for the model is 124.85, with $p < 0.0001$. We can reject the null hypothesis that none of the independent variables individually or collectively explain a significant amount of variation of the dependent variable.[74] The model correctly predicted 83.25 percent of the outcomes. In terms of individual coefficients, $PCAPY_{it-1}$ and $KVOTE_{it-2}$ are significant at the 0.90 level of confidence; BOP_{it-1} and $PCDEBT_{it-1}$ at 0.95; and $DEBT/GNP_{it-1}$, INT/GNP_{it-1}, $\Delta INT/GNP_{it}$, $RES/DEBT_{it-1}$, and $MKVOTE_{it-1}$ at 0.99; all with the anticipated signs.

To test and correct for autocorrelation, I employed the binary time-series-cross-section estimation technique formulated by Beck, Katz, and Tucker.[75] I constructed a series of nine $(t-1)$ dummy variables coded 1 if it had been $(1, 2, 3, \ldots, t-1)$ years since a country last received an IMF loan, 0 otherwise. If these nine variables collectively are significant in a log-likelihood ratio test, it is an indication of autocorrelation. The correction for autocorrelation is simply the inclusion of the temporal dummy variables in the estimation. Once corrected, the new coefficients for the original variables of interest should better satisfy the assumption of error independence. This test revealed a high likelihood of autocorrelation (log-likelihood ratio = 20.18 with 9 d.f., $p < 0.025$). Columns 2 and 3 in Table 5.1 report the results of the full model and a more refined model correcting for autocorrelation.

Tests were also conducted for multicollinearity and heteroskedasticity. Neither revealed any indications of problems. Despite the presence of a large number of potentially overlapping economic variables, none of the variables in the model exhibited high degrees of collinearity with the other variables (either collectively or individually). To test for heteroskedasticity, I incorporated a variable for GNP to test the impact of

Table 5.1 Logit coefficient estimates of IMF lending, 1985–94

Independent variables	Basic logit (1)	With temporal dummies (2)	Refined with dummies (3)
BOP_{it-1}	-1.907×10^{-4}**	-2.091×10^{-4}**	-1.277×10^{-4}**
	(0.911×10^{-4})	(0.926×10^{-4})	(0.583×10^{-4})
ΔBOP_{it}	-1.200×10^{-6}	1.580×10^{-6}	
	(79.600×10^{-6})	(84.000×10^{-6})	
$PCBOP_{it-1}$	6.642×10^{-4}	8.886×10^{-4}	
	(17.944×10^{-4})	(18.001×10^{-4})	
$\Delta PCBOPt_{it}$	-7.526×10^{-4}	-9.787×10^{-4}	
	(18.621×10^{-4})	(19.023×10^{-4})	
$CACCT_{it-1}$	-1.089×10^{-4}	-1.252×10^{-4}	
	(0.956×10^{-4})	(0.974×10^{-4})	
$\Delta CACCT_{it}$	0.920×10^{-4}	1.192×10^{-4}	1.453×10^{-4}**
	(0.976×10^{-4})	(1.031×10^{-4})	(0.632×10^{-4})
$CACCT/GNP_{it-1}$	-0.020	-0.022	-3.506*
	(0.026)	(0.027)	(2.044)
$\Delta CACCT/GNP_{it}$	0.002	0.003	
	(0.024)	(0.025)	
$DEBT_{it-1}$	-2.400×10^{-6}	-6.600×10^{-6}	
	(11.000×10^{-6})	(11.400×10^{-6})	
$\Delta DEBT_{it}$	-3.320×10^{-5}	-4.760×10^{-5}	
	(6.63×10^{-5})	(6.730×10^{-5})	
$PCDEBT_{it-1}$	9.960×10^{-4}**	8.726×10^{-4}*	8.319×10^{-4}*
	(4.58×10^{-4})	(4.655×10^{-4})	(4.340×10^{-4})
$\Delta PCDEBT_{it}$	5.641×10^{-4}	1.525×10^{-4}	
	(12.84×10^{-4})	(13.253×10^{-4})	
$DEBT/GNP_{it-1}$	-0.011***	-0.010***	-0.010***
	(0.003)	(0.003)	(0.003)
$\Delta DEBT/GNP_{it}$	0.001	0.002	
	(0.003)	(0.004)	
INT/GNP_{it-1}	0.284***	0.274***	0.267***
	(0.065)	(0.069)	(0.065)
$\Delta INT/GNP_{it}$	0.503***	0.519***	0.516***
	(0.100)	(0.102)	(0.099)
$RES/DEBT_{it-1}$	-0.026***	-0.027***	-0.024**
	(0.010)	(0.010)	(0.010)
$\Delta RES/DEBT_{it}$	-4.541×10^{-4}	10.000×10^{-4}	
	(0.021)	(0.022)	
$PCAPY_{it-1}$	-3.638×10^{-4}*	-3.074×10^{-4}	-3.453×10^{-4}*
	(02.112×10^{-4})	(2.122×10^{-4})	(2.052×10^{-4})
$DEFAULT_{it-1}$	0.394*	0.412*	0.467**
	(0.231)	(0.238)	(0.226)
USX_{it-1}	-4.800×10^{-6}	-2.500×10^{-6}	
	(65.300×10^{-6})	(67.300×10^{-6})	
$USDFI_{it-1}$	-9.940×10^{-5}	-8.870×10^{-5}	
	(8.800×10^{-5})	(8.880×10^{-5})	
$KVOTE_{it-2}$	1.247*	1.004	0.898
	(0.716)	(0.728)	(0.677)
$MKVOTE_{it-1}$	2.756***	2.858***	2.711***
	(0.795)	(0.856)	(0.827)
Intercept	-2.294***	-2.243***	-2.247***
	(0.476)	(0.522)	(0.490)
Correctly predicted (%)	83.25	82.98	82.98
Model χ^2	124.85	145.03	140.14
p-value	$p < 0.0001$	$p < 0.0001$	$p < 0.0001$
	24 d.f.	33 d.f.	21 d.f.

Notes

$N = 746$. Standard errors are in parentheses below the estimates. Coefficients for temporal dummies not reported.

* Significant at $p \leq 0.10$ level.

** Significant at $p \leq 0.05$ level.

*** Significant at $p \leq 0.01$ level.

country size and a series of eight dummy variables to capture the effect of geographic region. The results of these tests did not approach conventional levels of statistical significance, so I retained the assumption of homoskedasticity.

The parameter estimates of the corrected full model (column 2) yield several interesting, albeit tentative, findings. The only significant balance of payments variable is the overall balance, BOP_{it-1}. As expected, its coefficient is negatively signed, suggesting that a country with an extra \$100 million payments deficit increases its log-odds of receiving an IMF loan by about 0.02. The insignificant findings for the current account differ from others' results.[76] Controlling for the overall balance, the current account does not seem to matter. Similarly, with the current account controlled for, the negative impact of the balance of payments supports the argument that there is a substitution effect between IMF lending and other foreign capital inflows. Foreign capital inflows (an improvement in the balance of payments) in the year prior to the lending period lower the log-odds of receiving a loan from the IMF.

Several demand-side debt indicators were statistically significant.[77] In particular, the ratio of interest payments to GNP and the change in that ratio seem to have a strong positive impact on the log-odds of receiving a loan. The coefficients for the supply-side aggregate debt indicators $DEBT_{it-1}$ and $\Delta DEBT_{it}$ were not significant. These findings generally confirm the importance of debt in the borrowers' demand functions. They do not, however, support the argument that the IMF gives special treatment to large debtors, either because of their importance to global financial stability or as a payoff to the large creditor banks whose holdings may increase in value if an IMF loan is granted. Special treatment received by any particular debtors may be better explained by political factors than by their position in the international financial system or their relationship with creditor banks. This is a particularly interesting finding in light of the controversies surrounding the US- and IMF-sponsored bailout packages in 1995 in Mexico and in 1997 and 1998 in Asia and Russia.[78]

Per capita income behaves as expected but is no longer significant in the corrected model ($p < 0.1475$). A country's history of default with the IMF is significant at the 0.90 level, but carries a positive sign. This contradicts the notion that economic neutrality drives Fund lending and confirms the pattern of recidivism observed by others.[79] Having had a previous IMF program canceled increases the log-odds of receiving a new loan by 0.41.[80] The coefficients for US exports and US direct foreign investment do not attain statistical significance at conventional levels.[81] The neo-Marxist hypothesis is therefore not confirmed by these data. The potentially mixed interests of US exporters and investors described above makes the domestic politics argument more difficult to assess. Some of the positive and negative impact of exports and investments in different sectors of the economy (for example, traded vs. nontraded, export vs. import competing, consumption vs. intermediate goods) would be expected to work at cross purposes to yield statistically insignificant results overall. Subtler model specification and future research may help clarify these issues.

Both political variables carry the correct sign, but the political proximity hypothesis is not confirmed in the serially corrected model ($p < 0.1682$). The results for the political movement hypothesis are strongly positive and significant at the 0.99 level. A movement toward the US along the 0–1 UNGA key-vote continuum of 0.10 (for example, switching one vote out of ten) raises the log-odds of receiving a loan by 0.29. Politics does matter but not in the manner typically argued. These data suggest that movement toward the US within the political space portrayed in this chapter influences IMF decisions regardless of absolute alignment position. Additionally, the effects of these variables are robust to changes in the specification of the underlying macroeconomic model. I do not report the intermediate results here, but the addition and deletion of various economic variables had little effect on the parameter estimates or the standard errors of the political variables (see Table 5.1, columns 2 and 3).

I added an interactive political variable, $KVOTE_{it-2} \times MKVOTE_{it-1}$, in an attempt to capture some of the potential nonlinear effects of realignment by testing the hypothesis that the impact of a change in political alignment by a country is dependent on that country's starting position. A given movement toward the US by an already tight American ally, whose allegiance is unquestioned by the American government, may not increase the probability of receiving a loan as much as the same degree of movement by a more politically distant country. Expectations for the interactive term were tentative, but a negative coefficient would be consistent with this discussion. I do not report those results here, but the coefficient for this variable was not significant at conventional levels and positively signed.[82] The data suggest that the impact of movement toward the US is consistent across different starting points. This supports the argument depicted in Figure 5.3 that realignment toward the US improves a country's chances of receiving a loan regardless of the starting position.

Table 5.1, column 3, presents the results of a refined statistical model, which largely confirm the above interpretations with the exception of the current account and per capita income variables. I constructed this model by sequentially deleting any previously nonsignificant variables and conducting a series of log-likelihood ratio tests to determine if their inclusion significantly improved the overall fit of the model. With the exception of $KVOTE_{it-2}$, which I retained because of its intrinsic interest, I omitted all variables not meeting these criteria from the refined model.[83] The overall current account balance still does not seem to matter, but its improvement or decline and its weight in the economy do. We detect some impact for the current account by eliminating some potentially overlapping variables.[84] Per capita income is negatively signed and significant at the 0.90 level, a modest improvement from the full model.

Because the logit model is nonlinear, the relative effect of any single variable depends on the value of all the independent variables, which determine where on the curve an estimate lies. To make the parameter estimates more readily interpretable, Table 5.2 uses the refined model results to illustrate the impact of different values of political realignment on the probability of receiving a loan from the IMF in the hypothetical case where the values of all other independent variables in the model are set at their means. Two clear patterns emerge. First, even if we assume that absolute alignment position matters, a political realignment has a much stronger impact on the probability of receiving an IMF lending package than the starting position.[85] Second, the patterns revealed in Table 5.2 are consistent with the scenario portrayed in Figure 5.3. A distant country that starts out at a key-vote index score of 0.0 and moves to 0.25 has a much better chance ($p = 0.121$) of receiving a loan than a country that moves away from perfect alignment with the US (1.0) to a point (0.75) that is still much closer to the US ($p = 0.080$) (Table 5.2, lines 2 and 14). In fact, a country moving from discord to neutrality has a higher loan probability ($p = 0.213$) than a country that starts out and then remains in perfect alignment ($p = 0.147$) (Table 5.2, lines 3 and 15).

Killick raises the possibility that changes in the structure of the international system alter the political dynamics treated here. Specifically, he

Table 5.2 The effect of political realignment on IMF lending[a]

	Original position	*New position*	*Loan probability*
1	0.0	0.0	0.065
2	0.0	0.25	0.121
3	0.0	0.50	0.213
4	0.0	0.75	0.348
5	0.0	1.0	0.513
6	0.5	0.0	0.027
7	0.5	0.25	0.053
8	0.5	0.50	0.099
9	0.5	0.75	0.178
10	0.5	1.0	0.298
11	1.0	0.0	0.011
12	1.0	0.25	0.022
13	1.0	0.50	0.042
14	1.0	0.75	0.080
15	1.0	1.0	0.147

Notes
Moments: $KVOTE_{it-2}$: mean = 0.5156, standard deviation = 0.1857; $MKVOTE_{it-1}$: mean = 0.0082, standard deviation = 0.1555.
a All other variables from Table 5.1, column 3, held at their means.

suggests that the end of the Cold War may dilute the effect of international politics on IMF behavior.[86] If no single power (for example, the USSR) lies at the other end of the 0–1 voting space, does the US still reward political movement? *Does politics matter less after the Cold War?* Table 5.3 presents the full and slightly refined results (using the same refining technique as above) of separate analyses for the 1985–89 and 1990–94 periods. The model provides a good fit for each of the two subsamples, with $-2x$ LLR for all four scenarios yielding $p < 0.0001$. The model had a higher success rate in predicting outcomes in the second period, correctly predicting 88 percent of the outcomes in both the full and restricted versions versus approximately 81 percent in both specifications for the first period.

The underlying macroeconomic models appear to differ slightly for the two periods. Balance-of-payments considerations have a greater impact during the Cold War years (Table 5.3, columns 1 and 3). The overall balance is correctly signed and significant at the 0.95 level. In the refined model, the change in the balance of payments is also significant at the 0.95 level and correctly signed. The coefficients for the current account and the change in the current account approach but do not quite attain statistical significance at the 0.90 level in both Cold War specifications. No balance-of-payments variables even approach statistical significance in the post-Cold War period (Table 5.3, columns 2 and 4). The relevant debt indicators for each subsample differ slightly, but both periods generally confirm the borrower needs hypothesis with the exception of the incorrectly signed debt-to-GNP coefficient. The results for per capita income help clarify the ambiguous results for this variable in the full sample specifications by suggesting that while per capita GNP did not affect IMF decisions during the Cold War, it has become more important in the post-Cold War period. That confirms an apparent trend toward placing greater emphasis on economic growth in formulating IMF programs in recent years.[87] The default variable does not reach statistical significance in either period, possibly due to the smaller sample size. Again, the economic neutrality hypothesis is not confirmed. Finally, US exports and US direct foreign investment are not statistically significant in either subsample, though the USX_{it-1} variable comes reasonably close to attaining 90 percent confidence in the cold war period.

The differences between the impact of the economic variables across the two samples imply two tentative conclusions. First, similar models may produce divergent results if they are tested on different time periods. This may help explain the contradictory results of several seemingly similar econometric studies. Second, splitting larger time series into subsamples may be one good way to compare competing macroeconomic models and to chart their evolution over time.

The impact of politics also varies across the two subsamples but not in the way Killick anticipates. If anything, these results suggest that politics

Table 5.3 Logit coefficient estimates of IMF lending, 1985–89 and 1990–94

Independent variables	Cold War (1)	Post-Cold War (2)	Cold War refined (3)	Post-Cold War refined (4)
BOP_{it-1}	-4.072×10^{-4}***	-1.08×10^{-4}	-4.331×10^{-4}***	-0.931×10^{-4}
	(1.736×10^{-4})	(1.623×10^{-4})	(1.72×10^{-4})	(1.596×10^{-4})
ΔBOP_{it}	-2.273×10^{-4}	-0.166×10^{-4}	-2.784×10^{-4}***	0.304×10^{-4}
	(1.468×10^{-4})	(1.378×10^{-4})	(1.317×10^{-4})	(1.235×10^{-4})
$PCBOP_{it-1}$	0.004	3.88×10^{-4}	0.005*	-2.057×10^{-4}
	(0.003)	(28.569×10^{-4})	(0.003)	(24.936×10^{-4})
$\Delta PCBOPt_{it}$	-0.002	0.002		
	(0.003)	(0.003)		
$CACCT_{it-1}$	-2.776×10^{-4}	-0.535×10^{-4}	-2.880×10^{-4}	-0.572×10^{-4}
	(1.855×10^{-4})	(1.529×10^{-4})	(1.777×10^{-4})	(1.523×10^{-4})
$\Delta CACCT_{it}$	3.040×10^{-4}	0.193×10^{-4}	3.023×10^{-4}	0.031×10^{-4}
	(1.857×10^{-4})	(1.311×10^{-4})	(1.844×10^{-4})	(1.274×10^{-4})
$CACCT/GNP_{it-1}$	-0.046	-0.013	-0.054	-0.011
	(0.039)	(0.044)	(0.036)	(0.044)
$\Delta CACCT/GNP_{it}$	-0.031	0.045	-0.042	0.053
	(0.035)	(0.043)	(0.031)	(0.042)
$DEBT_{it-1}$	-1.93×10^{-5}	2.144×10^{-5}	-2.110×10^{-5}	1.976×10^{-5}
	(2.12×10^{-5})	(1.62×10^{-5})	(2.13×10^{-5})	(1.61×10^{-5})
$\Delta DEBT_{it}$	-1.639×10^{-4}	0.856×10^{-4}	-1.591×10^{-4}*	0.875×10^{-4}
	(1.035×10^{-4})	(1.602×10^{-4})	(0.945×10^{-4})	(1.504×10^{-4})
$PCDEBT_{it-1}$	1.577×10^{-4}	0.002***	1.205×10^{-4}	0.002***
	(7.045×10^{-4})	(0.001)	(6.823×10^{-4})	(0.001)
$\Delta PCDEBT_{it}$	2.425×10^{-4}	0.001		
	(19.369×10^{-4})	(0.002)		
$DEBT/GNP_{it-1}$	-0.007	-0.016***	-0.007	-0.016***
	(0.005)	(0.005)	(0.005)	(0.005)
$\Delta DEBT/GNP_{it}$	-6.81×10^{-5}	0.001		
	(417.55×10^{-5})	(0.012)		
INT/GNP_{it-1}	0.362***	0.183	0.363***	0.197
	(0.094)	(0.142)	(0.092)	(0.135)

	(1)	(2)	(3)	(4)
ΔINT/GNP$_{it}$	0.530***	0.646***	0.530***	0.655***
	(0.153)	(0.184)	(0.151)	(0.173)
RES/DEBT$_{it-1}$	−0.056***	−0.009	−0.052***	−0.009
	(0.019)	(0.012)	(0.017)	(0.012)
ΔRES/DEBT$_{it}$	−0.022	0.020		
	(0.044)	(0.028)		
PCAP$_{it-1}$	-1.753×10^{-4}	-7.171×10^{-4}**	-1.288×10^{-4}	-7.021×10^{-4}**
	(3.345×10^{-4})	(3.188×10^{-4})	(3.096×10^{-4})	(3.16×10^{-4})
DEFAULT$_{it-1}$	0.447	0.345	0.438	0.350
	(0.322)	(0.404)	(0.320)	(0.400)
USX$_{it-1}$	1.757×10^{-4}	-1.041×10^{-4}	1.841×10^{-4}	-1.099×10^{-4}
	(1.141×10^{-4})	(1.508×10^{-4})	(1.131×10^{-4})	(1.528×10^{-4})
USDFI$_{it-1}$	-2.848×10^{-4}	-0.395×10^{-4}	-2.901×10^{-4}	-0.344×10^{-4}
	(1.972×10^{-4})	(1.036×10^{-4})	(1.997×10^{-4})	(1.02×10^{-4})
KVOTE$_{it-2}$	0.599	3.115**	0.566	2.967**
	(0.955)	(1.510)	(0.951)	(1.488)
MKVOTE$_{it-1}$	3.609**	4.333***	3.551**	4.192***
	(1.492)	(1.401)	(1.485)	(1.363)
Intercept	−1.949***	−3.570***	−2.008***	−3.468***
	(0.730)	(0.928)	(0.728)	(0.911)
Correctly predicted (%)	81.17	88.10	80.66	88.10
Model χ^2	96.75	72.04	95.81	70.64
p-value	$p < 0.0001$	$p < 0.0001$	$p < 0.0001$	$p < 0.0001$
	28 d.f.	28 d.f.	24 d.f.	24 d.f.

Notes

$N = 393$ for Cold War, $N = 353$ for post-Cold War. Standard errors are in parentheses below the estimates. All specifications include temporal dummy variables (coefficients not reported).

* Significant at $p \leq 0.10$ level.

** Significant at $p \leq 0.05$ level.

*** Significant at $p \leq 0.01$ level.

may be *more* important now than ever. The manner in which the US treats its allies and potential allies within the Fund seems to have changed in important ways since 1990. The coefficient for alignment position does not approach statistical significance in the 1985–89 period, but movement is positively signed and statistically significant. Based on this sample, the US appears to have been playing a Cold War game of encouraging movement toward it without regard for original alignment position.

Since the end of the Cold War, however, both alignment position and movement are statistically significant and positively signed. This suggests that the US is both playing the realignment game as vigorously as ever and is rewarding the allegiance of those who stay close without necessarily moving any closer. Once a country reaches perfect agreement with the US, it cannot move any closer. These results imply that during the Cold War such a country would have had to move away from the US and then back toward it to secure favorable treatment from the IMF. By rewarding such behavior, the US may have encouraged countries to move toward the median voting position in the UN. Countries might also employ dual tactics of backscratching and blackmail to parlay political realignments and potential realignments into material gains.[88] Such maneuverings may no longer be necessary for close US allies in the post-Cold War period. More generally, these results suggest that the ability of the US to influence IMF behavior to achieve its own political goals has not eroded. These goals may have simply shifted according to changes in the structure of the international system, and the US still seems willing and able to exercise its weight within the executive board of the IMF to pursue them. The case of the IMF suggests that multilateralism, while useful for facilitating cooperation among a small number of like-minded states, may not be an effective buffer of US power in the modern global political economy.

5 Limitations

This section highlights some of the limitations of this study's approach and data analysis with an eye toward future research. First and foremost, does voting in the UN General Assembly really matter, even on issues that the US has deemed important? The UN itself has little power, and measures adopted within the UNGA in particular (as opposed to the Security Council) are largely symbolic.[89] In a similar vein, this study does not distinguish between countries according to their strategic and domestic characteristics. It could be argued that UN voting patterns are just a proxy for more fundamental variables. In particular, as countries democratize and open their economies to market forces, they may also be likely to alter their UN votes to reflect these underlying political and economic changes. The United States and the IMF may be rewarding the political and economic shifts themselves, rather than the reflection of those shifts within the UNGA. This line of thinking is not necessarily inconsistent with the argument of this chapter, but it merits further consideration. In fact, if UN voting does capture these more fundamental characteristics of countries, then it could be a very useful summary measure of them. I ran several new regressions to address these concerns empirically. I included commercial energy production (ENERGY_{it-1}) as a measure of strategic importance to explain why the US might treat some countries differently from others. Measures of money supply (M/GDP_{it-1}), money supply growth (MGROW_{it-1}), budget deficits (DEFICIT_{it-1}), and trade openness (OPEN_{it-1} = exports plus imports, divided by GNP) captured the relative degree of "economic freedom."[90] Finally, several indicators of democracy, including the Polity III democracy (DEM_{it-1}) and authoritarianism (AUTH_{it-1}) scores and the Freedom House rankings on political rights (PR_{it-1}) and civil liberties (CL_{it-1}), helped assess the impact of regime type and democratization (change in regime type from one year to the next). Table 5.4 presents these results. Interestingly, none of these new variables yielded statistically significant results, and their inclusion in the estimation did not significantly alter the effects of the voting variables.[91] In sum, the model presented here appears robust to the inclusion of these factors.

Second, I have kept the underlying macroeconomic model as broad and simple as possible. This makes a direct comparison of theoretically distinct macroeconomic models more difficult, but the inclusion of a large number and wide range of economic variables raises the level of confidence in the statistical significance of the results obtained for the political variables, my more immediate concern. Further refinement or inclusion of additional economic variables could be undertaken if justified by other research.

Third, this chapter treats the IMF essentially as an instrument of the US government to test indirectly the proposition that relatively straight-forward power considerations help explain the behavior of multilateral economic organizations. But the more powerful Fund members are likely to agree on many UNGA votes. Multidimensional scaling analyses conducted by Pallansch and Zinni suggest that the UNGA voting patterns of the G-7 countries tend to congregate together in a Euclidian space.[92] Future work should explore internal executive board politics and expand the focus to include Germany, Japan, France, and the United Kingdom. An approach centered around the formation and operation of subsets, or "k-groups," of countries within the organization could lead to a more complex specification of intraorganizational politics.[93]

Fourth, more careful consideration of the possible impact of US domestic politics would help clarify and respecify those aspects of the problem. Specifically, the influence of domestic interest groups (for example, exporters and foreign investors) and the relations between different government agencies (particularly State and Treasury) merit further attention. Finally, I do not test directly for the impact of a country's past agreements with the IMF, nor do I exclude cases from the data sample that already have a program in effect. The former is partially

Table 5.4 Logit coefficient estimates with control variables, 1985–94

Independent variables	Using Polity III measures (1)	Using Freedom House measures (2)
BOP_{it-1}	-1.201×10^{-4}	-1.041×10^{-4}
	(1.184×10^{-4})	(1.192×10^{-4})
ΔBOP_{it}	6.235×10^{-5}	7.452×10^{-5}
	(11.02×10^{-5})	(11.19×10^{-5})
$PCBOP_{it-1}$	-0.002	-0.002
	(0.003)	(0.003)
$\Delta PCBOP_{it}$	-0.003	-0.003
	(0.003)	(0.003)
$CACCT_{it-1}$	9.496×10^{-5}	9.373×10^{-5}
	(13.09×10^{-5})	(13.14×10^{-5})
$\Delta CACCT_{it}$	2.163×10^{-4}	2.052×10^{-4}
	(1.332×10^{-4})	(11.327×10^{-4})
$CACCT/GNP_{it-1}$	$-0.082*$	$-0.089*$
	(0.049)	(0.049)
$\Delta CACCT/GNP_{it}$	-0.020	-0.021
	(0.043)	(0.043)
$DEBT_{it-1}$	1.933×10^{-5}	2.475×10^{-5}
	(2.01×10^{-5})	(2.00×10^{-5})
$\Delta DEBT_{it}$	-3.45×10^{-5}	-2.97×10^{-5}
	(8.35×10^{-5})	(8.21×10^{-5})
$PCDEBT_{it-1}$	0.001	$0.002*$
	(0.001)	(0.001)
$\Delta PCDEBT_{it}$	0.001	0.001
	(0.002)	(0.002)
$DEBT/GNP_{it-1}$	$-0.014***$	$-0.016***$
	(0.005)	(0.005)
$\Delta DEBT/GNP_{it}$	9.460×10^{-4}	6.491×10^{-4}
	(62.071×10^{-4})	(61.295×10^{-4})
INT/GNP_{it-1}	0.168	0.153
	(0.107)	(0.106)
$\Delta INT/GNP_{it}$	$0.642***$	$0.663***$
	(0.160)	(0.160)
$RES/DEBT_{it-1}$	$-0.030*$	$-0.026*$
	(0.018)	(0.017)
$\Delta RES/DEBT_{it}$	-0.026	-0.022
	(0.035)	(0.035)
$PCAPY_{it-1}$	$-4.716 \times 10^{-4}*$	$-6.376 \times 10^{-4}*$
	(4.072×10^{-4})	(3.833×10^{-4})
$DEFAULT_{it-1}$	$0.653*$	$0.684*$
	(0.361)	(0.364)
USX_{it-1}	1.079×10^{-4}	1.09×10^{-4}
	(0.928×10^{-4})	(0.897×10^{-4})
$USDFI_{it-1}$	-1.328×10^{-4}	-1.452×10^{-4}
	(1.03×10^{-4})	(1.037×10^{-4})
$KVOTE_{it-2}$	1.095	1.350
	(1.209)	(1.203)
$MKVOTE_{it-1}$	$4.138***$	$4.464***$
	(1.270)	(1.265)

Table 5.4 continued

Independent variables	Using Polity III measures (1)	Using Freedom House measures (2)
ENERGY$_{it-1}$	-1.11×10^{-5}	-1.13×10^{-5}
	(0.86×10^{-5})	(0.85×10^{-5})
M/GDP$_{it-1}$	0.017	0.015
	(0.012)	(0.011)
MGROW$_{it-1}$	-1.032×10^{-4}	-0.715×10^{-4}
	(3.026×10^{-4})	(3.033×10^{-4})
DEFICIT$_{it-1}$	0.062	0.062
	(0.050)	(0.050)
OPEN$_{it-1}$	-0.538	-0.490
	(0.694)	(0.688)
DEM$_{it-1}$	-0.033	
	(0.103)	
AUTH$_{it-1}$	-0.055	
	(0.123)	
Pr$_{it-1}$		0.099
		(0.168)
Cl$_{it-1}$		-0.134
		(0.214)
Intercept	$-2.253*$	$-2.533**$
	(1.247)	(1.170)
Correctly predicted (%)	83.72	84.84
Model χ^2	99.94	106.79
p-value	$p < 0.0001$	$p < 0.0001$
	40 d.f.	40 d.f.

Notes
$N = 436$ for column 1, $N = 455$ for column 2. Standard errors are in parentheses below the estimates. Both specifications include temporal dummy variables (coefficients not reported).
* Significant at $p \leq 0.10$ level.
** Significant at $p \leq 0.05$ level.
*** Significant at $p \leq 0.01$ level.

captured by the default variable. The latter is much less of a problem than it appears because loans are often canceled and immediately replaced, suggesting that having a program in effect at a given moment does not exclude a country from the eligible sample.

6 Implications

This chapter has two central goals: 1) to determine the degree to which high politics affects IMF lending patterns; and 2) to develop and test a more precise and more general explanation of *how* high politics influences the behavior of multilateral organizations. Most researchers of the politics of IMF lending argue that the US punishes enemies and rewards friends via its influence within the Fund's executive board. Those who introduce a somewhat greater degree of complexity do not adequately develop nor test the dynamic impact of international political realignment. Previous research on foreign aid more generally has attempted but generally failed to find a statistically significant relationship between aid flows and political conditionality.[94] This chapter provides the first systematic evidence that politics does affect IMF lending, and its conceptual framework and statistical analysis demonstrate the political factors that are most important, the mechanisms through which they influence Fund behavior, and the more general relationship between multilateral organizations and their member states. The results obtained here show that movement toward the United States within a defined international political space (like that measured by UN voting patterns) can significantly increase a country's chances of receiving a loan from the IMF. This suggests that the US has been more concerned with attracting new allies and punishing defectors than rewarding loyal friends. It has been able to do so through multilateral channels like the IMF.

The evidence presented here also suggests that changes in the structure of the international system may have altered US and IMF behavior but not in the predicted manner. In fact, these initial results suggest that the end of the Cold War has been associated with the increasing politicization of the IMF by the US. There is evidence that the US has been willing to reward friends and punish enemies only since 1990. During the Cold War (at least in its last few years), unless they were moving closer to the US politically, allies of the US had no greater chance than its adversaries of receiving assistance from the Fund. Only in the post-Cold War period have these countries been able to cash in on their political allegiance.

The demonstration of the systematic impact of international politics on IMF lending poses interesting methodological, theoretical, and practical implications. Methodologically, the use of key UNGA votes provides a more easily quantifiable and temporally sensitive alternative to traditional indicators of international political alignment, such as security alliances, military base locations, treaties, and content analysis. The use of this indicator may facilitate research in other areas of inquiry.

On a theoretical level, the evidence presented here suggests that multilateral organizations like the IMF, despite their enhanced influence in the developing world, are still most profitably analyzed within the parameters of an international political context shaped primarily by the industrialized nations. More specifically, there is strong evidence that the political interests of the US drive much of the behavior of one of the most important multilateral organizations in the post-hegemonic global economy. I do not explore the reverse causal relationship – the impact of the IMF on US interests and behavior[95] – but these results suggest more generally that the multilateral institutions are still quite sensitive to direct political pressures and influences from their more powerful member states. These influences translate into particular modes of behavior by the multilateral organizations themselves that can be analyzed conceptually, observed empirically, and tested statistically. The study of the role of international institutions and multilateral organizations must take into account not simply the fact that international political factors help determine their behavior on the input side. Such research should also view the operation of such entities as a tool used by the great powers to achieve specific, identifiable, political goals on the output side, such as realignment within the international system. The ability of the US to employ such tools underscores the practical limits of multilateralism and confirms the rather dramatized fears of one of the original architects of the postwar international economic order, John Maynard Keynes:

> There is scarcely any enduringly successful experience of an international body which has fulfilled the hopes of its progenitors. Either an institution has become diverted to the instrument of a limited group or else it has been a puppet – sawdust through which the breath of life does not blow.[96]

On the practical side, the experience of the IMF suggests that Keynes's first fear has been partially realized. To an extent, the US has been able to use the IMF to further its own international political agenda. On perhaps a more positive note, his second fear of irrelevance appears to be a distant one, despite the relative economic decline of the US and the end of the Cold War. While undermining the principle of multilateralism, the continued strength of national influence over Fund behavior may well help maintain the stability of great power support for the multilateral organizations if those powers continue to reap important gains from them that may be more economically or politically costly to obtain bilaterally.[97] Such conclusions could help allay the fears of those within the US Congress who question US support for the IMF based on concerns that it would strengthen multilateralism at the expense of US power.

Finally, as a multilateral organization, the IMF is in a sense a difficult or crucial case for political theories of international finance. It is easy to see how bilateral capital flows could be subjected to the push and pull of international and domestic politics, but on the executive board of the IMF any single country's power is diluted by the presence of other principals within the decision-making body. The structure of the Fund leaves the door open, but a priori we would expect to see less of an impact for politics in the IMF than in bilateral financial flows. If high politics affects IMF lending, then it should have an even stronger impact on national policies. A confirmation of the impact of political realignment on IMF lending therefore provides stronger corroboration of this theory than that which could be obtained in a study of bilateral capital flows and suggests that such ideas may be fruitfully applied to other areas of international finance and international relations more generally.

Acknowledgment

This chapter was originally published as: Thacker, Strom Cronan. 1999. The High Politics of IMF Lending. *World Politics* 52 (1): 38–75. © The Johns Hopkins University Press. Reprinted with permission of The Johns Hopkins University Press.

Notes

* A preliminary version of this chapter was presented at the 1997 annual meeting of the American Political Science Association in Washington, DC. I would like to thank Tim McKeown, Patrick Conway, William Bernhard, Mary Matthews, Dane Rowlands, the participants in the faculty research seminar in the Department of International Relations at Boston University, and the anonymous *World Politics* referees for their insightful comments and suggestions. Yvonne Ochoa and Jaya Badiga provided able research assistance. The usual disclaimers apply.

1 The literature on the IMF is extensive. For useful surveys, see Graham Bird, "The International Monetary Fund and the Developing Countries: A Review of the Evidence and Policy Options," *International Organization* 50, no. 3 (1996); idem, *IMF Lending to Developing Countries: Issues and Evidence* (London: Routledge, 1995); Sebastian Edwards, "The International Monetary Fund and the Developing Countries: A Critical Evaluation," NBER Working Paper, no. 2909 (1989); Tony Killick, *IMF Programs in Developing Countries: Design and Impact* (London: Routledge, 1995); John Williamson, ed., *The Lending Practices of the International Monetary Fund* (Washington, DC: Institute for International Economics, 1982); and idem, *IMF Conditionality* (Washington, DC: Institute for International Economics, 1983).

2 For effective treatments of these and related issues, see Robert O. Keohane, *After Hegemony: Cooperation and Discord in the World Political Economy* (Princeton, NJ: Princeton University Press, 1984); idem, *International Institutions and State Power: Essays in International Relations Theory* (Boulder, CO: Westview, 1989); idem, "Multilateralism: An Agenda for Research," *International Journal* 45, no. 1 (1990); John Gerard Ruggie, ed., *Multilateralism Matters: The Theory and Praxis of an Institutional Form* (New York: Columbia University Press, 1993); Stephen D. Krasner, ed., *International Regimes* (Ithaca, NY: Cornell University Press, 1983); and Kenneth A. Oye, ed., *Cooperation under Anarchy* (Princeton, NJ: Princeton University Press, 1986).

International institutions and multilateralism are not necessarily equivalent. The IMF fits Ruggie's definition in *Multilateralism Matters* of multilateral organization as "defined by such generalized decision-making rules as voting or consensus procedures" (p. 14). On IMF decision-making procedures, see Frank Southard, "The Evolution of the International Monetary Fund," Princeton Essays in International Finance, no. 135 (1979); and Frederick K. Lister, *Decision-Making Strategies for International Organizations*, vol. 20, *World Affairs* (Denver, CO: Graduate School of International Studies, University of Denver, 1984).

3 Giulio M. Gallarotti, "The Limits of International Organization: Systematic Failure in the Management of International Relations," *International Organization* 45, no. 2 (1991).

4 Bird (fn. 1, 1995), 124.

5 Dane Rowlands, "Political and Economic Determinants of IMF Conditional

Credit Arrangements: 1973–1989" (Manuscript, Norman Paterson School of International Affairs, Carleton University, Ottawa, Ontario, 1995).

6 Jacques J. Polak, "Monetary Analysis of Income Formation and Payments Problems," IMF Staff Papers, no. 6 (1957), cited in Edwards (fn. 1); and idem, "The Changing Nature of IMF Conditionality," Princeton Essays in International Finance, no. 184 (1991); and Richard Swedberg, "The Doctrine of Economic Neutrality of the IMF and the World Bank," *Journal of Peace Research* 23, no. 4 (1986).

7 R.S. Eckaus, "How the IMF Lives with Its Conditionality," *Policy Sciences* 19 (October 1986).

8 Southard (fn. 2), 13; Edwards (fn. 1); C. David Finch, "The IMF: The Record and the Prospects," Princeton Essays in International Finance, no. 175 (1989); and John Spraos, "IMF Conditionality: Ineffectual, Inefficient, Mistargeted," Princeton Essays in International Finance, no. 166 (1986).

9 Finch (fn. 8), 2.

10 Lars Schoultz, "Politics, Economics, and U.S. Participation in Multilateral Development Banks," *International Organization* 36, no. 3 (1982); Benjamin J. Cohen, "International Debt and Linkage Strategies: Some Foreign Policy Implications for the United States," in Miles Kahler, ed., *The Politics of International Debt* (Ithaca, NY: Cornell University Press, 1986).

11 Fred L. Smith, "The Politics of IMF Lending," *Cato Journal* 4 (Spring/Summer 1984). The US representative is "ordered by law to clear his or her decisions with the Secretary of the Treasury." Swedberg (fn. 6), 379.

12 Kendall W. Stiles, *Negotiating Debt: The IMF Lending Process* (Boulder, CO: Westview, 1991).

13 *IMF Annual Report* (Washington, DC: IMF, 1995), 216.

14 See Lister (fn. 2).

15 Samuel Lichtensztejn and Mónica Baer, *Fondo Monetario Internacional y Banco Mundial: Estrategias y Políticas del Poder Financiero* (Mexico City: Ediciones de Cultura Popular, 1987), 60–1.

16 Miles Kahler notes that the US has in the past refused to support a renewal of the managing director's tenure when his "accomplishments did not meet American expectations." Kahler, "The United States and the International Monetary Fund," in Margaret P. Karns and Karen A. Mingst, eds, *The United States and Multilateral Institutions* (Boston, MA: Unwin Hyman, 1990), 94.

17 The origins of this procedure date back to the Fund's early years, when the US executive director went to great lengths to muffle the strong voice of US power, which nevertheless was decisive. See Southard (fn. 2), 5–6, 19–20.

18 Eckaus (fn. 7), 237; Stiles (fn. 12), 37.

19 Ruggie (fn. 2), chapter 1; James A. Caporaso and Miles Kahler attribute part of the postwar economic cooperation to this type of "minilateralism." The creation of the Bretton Woods monetary order through US and British coordination and the subsequent adjustments made by the G-7 after its breakdown (for example, the Plaza and Louvre accords) can be profitably understood in these terms. Caporaso, "International Relations Theory and Multilateralism: The Search for Foundations," and Kahler, "Multilateralism with Small and Large Numbers," in Ruggie (fn. 2).

20 Cheryl Payer, *The Debt Trap: The International Monetary Fund and the Third World* (New York: Monthly Review Press, 1974); and Swedberg (fn. 6).

21 Kahler (fn. 16), 110.

22 Ibid.

23 Killick (fn. 1), 118–19.

24 Stiles (fn. 12), 196–7.

25 Patrick Conway, "IMF Lending Programs: Participation and Impact," *Journal of Development Economics* 45, no. 2 (1994).

26 He finds statistically significant positive results for prior participation and the percentage of available funds drawn down. A series of dummy variables for each year had generally significant results.

27 Peter H. Lindert, "Response to Debt Crisis: What Is Different About the 1980s?" in Barry J. Eichengreen and Lindert, eds, *The International Debt Crisis in Historical Perspective* (Cambridge, MA: MIT Press, 1989).

28 Bird (fn. 1, 1995).

29 This result supports the catalytic impact of IMF lending as providing a "seal of approval" that encourages private banks to resume lending to a country that has negotiated an agreement with the Fund. Bird (fn. 1, 1995), 122. A negative result would suggest a substitution effect between IMF and private lending.

30 Spraos (fn. 8); and Finch (fn. 8).

31 Bird (fn. 1, 1995), 109.

32 Ibid., 23.

33 See Jahangir Amuzegar, "The IMF under Fire," *Foreign Policy* 64 (Fall 1986).

34 See Walden Bello and David Kinley, "The IMF: An Analysis of the International Monetary Fund's Role in the Third World Debt Crisis, Its Relation to Big Banks, and the Forces Influencing Its Decisions," *Multinational Monitor* 4 (1983).

35 Lindert (fn. 27), 245.

36 Killick (fn. 1).

37 Lindert (fn. 27), 243; Bird (fn. 1, 1995), 112.

38 Barry Eichengreen has questioned the impact of the "default penalty" on future credit access. Eichengreen, "The U.S. Capital Market and Foreign Lending, 1920–1955," in Jeffrey D. Sachs, ed., *Developing Country Debt and the World Economy* (Chicago, IL: University of Chicago Press, 1989), 247. Cf. Jonathan Eaton and Mark Gersovitz, "Debt with Potential Repudiation: Theoretical and Empirical Analysis," *Review of Economic Studies* 48 (April 1981).

39 See E.A. Brett, "The World's View of the IMF," in Latin America Bureau, ed., *The Poverty Brokers: The IMF and Latin America* (London: Latin America Bureau, 1983); Manuel Pastor, "The Effects of IMF Programs in the Third World: Debate and Evidence from Latin America," *World Development* 15 (Fall 1987); and Swedberg (fn. 6).

40 The net effect of DFI exposure may depend on the sectoral location of the investment. If it serves primarily the domestic market, a negative result might be expected. If it serves mostly export markets, a positive result would be more likely. The impact of export exposure may depend on whether the product exported is a final consumption good (negative) or an input into the export sector (positive).

41 Bello and Kinley (fn. 34), 14.

42 Susumu Awanohara, "Fiscal Interdiction: U.S., Japan Block IMF Effort to Support Vietnam," *Far Eastern Economic Review*, September 28, 1989.

43 Amuzegar (fn. 33); Valerie J. Assetto, *The Soviet Bloc in the IMF and the IBRD* (Boulder, CO: Westview, 1988).

44 Ibid., 50.

45 Irving Louis Horowitz, "The 'Rashomon Effect': Ideological Proclivities and Political Dilemmas of the IMF," in Robert J. Myers, ed., *The Political Morality of the International Monetary Fund* (New Brunswick, NJ: Transaction Books, 1987), 96.

46 In fact, both countries left the IMF in the early 1950s in the midst of politically charged disputes with the Fund. (Assetto (fn. 43), 73–4, 82–7, 184.)

47 Bruno S. Frey, *International Political Economics* (London: Basil Blackwell, 1984), chapter 5; Albert O. Hirschman, "The Stability of Neutralism: A Geometrical Note," *American Economic Review* 54 (March 1964).

48 Timothy J. McKeown, "Resolving the 'Conditionality Paradox' in U.S. Bilateral Foreign Aid" (Manuscript, University of North Carolina, Chapel Hill, n.d.).

49 Bird (fn. 1, 1995), 149–50.

50 Regressions were run on the amount of the loan divided by GNP, and the general results were similar to those reported here, particularly for the political variables.

51 This figure represents all of the developing countries, as defined by the IMF, for which data were available. See IMF, *Annual Report* (Washington, DC: IMF, 1986), 162. Data for the indicator of political alignment used here are not available before 1983. For some countries, data are available only for certain years. See Appendix B for a list of countries used in the data analysis.

52 See John H. Aldrich and Forrest D. Nelson, *Linear Probability, Logit, and Probit Models* (Beverly Hills, CA: Sage, 1984).

53 Two other IMF lending programs, the Structural Adjustment Facility (SAF) and the Enhanced Structural Adjustment Facility (ESAF), are not included in this analysis for a number of reasons. First, only low-income developing countries qualify for SAF and ESAF loans. A large number of countries in the sample would therefore not qualify for these programs, while all are eligible for SBA and EFF packages. Second, the SAF and ESAF are structural adjustment rather than economic stabilization programs. To include them in the analysis would require a different underlying macroeconomic model than that specified for SABs and EFFs. Third, 1987 was the first full year of operation for the SAF and 1988 for the ESAF. Only SBA and EFF programs were operational throughout the entire time period examined here. See Polak (fn. 6, 1991); and Susan Schadler, Adam Bennett, Maria Carkovic, Louis Dicks-Mireaux, Mauro Mecagni, James H.J. Morisink, and Miguel A. Savastano, "IMF Conditionality: Experience under Stand-By and Extended Arrangements. Part I: Key Issues and Findings," IMF Occasional Paper, no. 128 (1995). Compared to the number of SBAs and EEFs, there have been few SAF and ESAF loans made. Regressions run on a variable including all of these programs together yielded results generally consistent with those reported in the following section.

54 Logit transforms this variable, which has a nonlinear relationship to the independent variables, into the log-odds of receiving a loan, which has a linear relationship to the independent variables. The new dependent variable, or logit, is then regressed on the independent variables using maximum likelihood estimation (MLE). Data for this variable were gathered from IMF, *Annual Report* (Washington, DC: IMF, various issues).

55 All economic variables except ratios are expressed in millions of 1990 US dollars, using the 1990 US GDP deflator reported in IMF, *International Financial Statistics Yearbook* (Washington, DC: IMF, various issues).

56 These variables make the figures for large and small countries more comparable. I also tested the ratio of balance of payments to GNP and the change in that ratio with the same substantive results. Data are from IMF, *International Financial Statistics Yearbook* (Washington, DC: IMF, various issues).

57 The World Bank's debt ratios (DEBT/GNP, INT/GNP, and RES/DEBT) appear to have been multiplied by 100. To make comparisons across units consistent, I multiplied the CACCT/GNP ratios calculated from (but not listed in) World Bank data by 100. World Bank, *World Debt Tables* (Washington, DC: World Bank, various issues); and idem, *Global Development Finance* (Washington, DC: World Bank, various issues).

58 These figures are from the World Bank, *World Debt Tables* (Washington, DC: World Bank, various issues); and idem, *Global Development Finance* (Washington, DC: World Bank, various issues); with population data taken from IMF, *International Financial Statistics Yearbook* (Washington, DC: IMF, various issues).

59 Adequate data on the exposure of US banks in particular countries are unavailable. In any event, the largest creditor banks are likely to be based in the US and the IMF's other principal shareholder countries.

60 A variable measuring the total number of cancellations that a country experienced from 1975 through $t-1$ did not yield statistically significant results. Data were gathered from IMF, *Annual Report* (Washington, DC: IMF, various issues).

61 Data are from IMF, *Direction of Trade Statistics Yearbook* (Washington, DC: IMF, various issues).

62 Data have been taken from the US Department of Commerce, *Survey of Current Business*, various issues.

63 Using these annual reports, I coded votes in agreement with the US 1.0, votes in disagreement with the US 0.0, and abstentions or absences by the sample country 0.5. I then added and divided these numbers by the total number of key votes each year to come up with the annual decimal measure for each country. This method differs slightly from the technique of discarding absences and abstentions from the total count of UNGA votes used in Charles W. Kegley Jr and Steven W. Hook, "U.S. Foreign Aid and U.N. Voting: Did Reagan's Linkage Strategy Buy Deference or Defiance?" *International Studies Quarterly* 35 (September 1991). Rather than not count those nonvotes on "key" issues, I interpret them as neutral.

64 The transmission of United States foreign policy preferences from the State Department is not necessarily direct in the case of the multilateral development banks and the IMF, where Treasury plays a critical role. See Schoultz (fn. 10). The (American) deputy managing director has typically been "a 'Treasury man,' reinforcing the close ties between that agency of the U.S. government and the IMF." Kahler (fn. 16), 94. Furthermore, Kahler argues that Treasury maintains tight control over US-Fund relations and that "other agencies that might attempt to politicize the IMF for broader foreign policy goals tended to be excluded from direct access to it." Kahler (fn. 16) 94, 97. On the other hand, Joanne Gowa notes that Treasury has adopted an ordering of priorities that "subordinates the demands of the international monetary order to the imperatives of domestic economic policy and foreign security policy," suggesting some coordination – or at least compatibility – between different agencies within the executive branch. Gowa, *Closing the Gold Window: Domestic Politics and the End of Bretton Woods* (Ithaca, NY: Cornell University Press, 1983). The present analysis of policy output (as opposed to interagency input) is an indirect test of these two competing hypotheses. Future work should address the interagency dynamics more directly.

65 US Department of State, *Report to Congress on Voting Practices in the United Nations* (1985), 2.

66 Ibid., 4.

67 See Soo Yeon Kim and Bruce Russett, "The New Politics of Voting Alignments in the United Nations General Assembly," *International Organization* 50, no. 4 (1996); Steven K. Holloway and Rodney Tomlinson, "The New World Order and the General Assembly: Bloc Realignment at the UN in the Post-Cold War World," *Canadian Journal of Political Science* 28, no. 2 (1995); Leona Pallansch and Frank Zinni Jr, "Demise of Voting Blocs in the General Assembly of the UN? A Multidimensional Scaling Analysis" (Paper presented at the annual

meeting of the Southern Political Science Association, Atlanta, 1996); Brian W. Tomlin, "Measurement Validation: Lessons from the Use and Misuse of UN General Assembly Roll-Call Votes," *International Organization* 39, no. 1 (1985); and Kenneth J. Menkhaus and Charles W. Kegley Jr, "The Compliant Foreign Policy of the Dependent State Revisited: Empirical Linkages and Lessons from the Case of Somalia," *Comparative Political Studies* 21, no. 3 (1988).

68 Ed Lansdale, "Memo Re: Long Range Impact FPF-II," April 24, 1964, National Archives, Record Group 59, Lot file 67D554, Under Secretary for Political Affairs, Records of the Special Assistant 1963–65, Box 2. I thank Tim McKeown for providing me with a transcription of this document.

69 For example, Argentina sent troops to the 1991 Persian Gulf conflict. Carlos Escudé "Entrevista a Escudérealizada por Lorena Kniaz" (1997), cited May 19, 1999, http://www.geocities.com/CapitolHill/Congress/4359/reporta.html.

70 Ibid.

71 Ibid.; Carlos EscudéE-mail from the author, February 16, 1999.

72 Because of the UNGA's voting calendar, the voting variables have a longer lag structure than the economic variables. The fact that UNGA votes are taken in the last four months of the calendar year means that there is a 67 percent chance that a given loan decision will be made before the UNGA meets in a given year. The chances that such a decision will be made before the session is complete and final votes are tallied approaches 100 percent. Conversely, movement at $t-1$ occurs immediately before the next calendar year's loan cycle begins.

73 James A. Stimson, "Regression in Space and Time: A Statistical Essay," *American Journal of Political Science* 29, no. 4 (1985); Nathaniel Beck, Jonathan N. Katz, and Richard Tucker, "Taking Time Seriously: Time-Series-Cross-Section Analysis with a Binary Dependent Variable," *American Journal Political Science* 42, no. 4 (1998).

74 This assumes a Chi Square distribution for the $-2*$ LLR figure. While this assumption may not be entirely valid for individual level data, the strong results are still encouraging.

75 Beck, Katz, and Tucker (fn. 73). This approach is designed for longitudinally dominant data with typically 20 or more time periods. The authors have not yet tested this exploratory method on shorter time periods like the one used here ($t = 10$). Richard Tucker, conversation with the author, August 1998. We may therefore have somewhat less confidence in a negative diagnostic for autocorrelation than in the positive one obtained here.

76 Conway (fn. 25).

77 Per capita debt reached the 0.90 level of confidence, and the following variables attained the 0.99 level: the debt to GNP ratio, the interest to GNP ratio, the change in the interest to GNP ratio, and the ratio of reserves to debt. Curiously, the coefficient for debt to GNP is negative (all others are correctly signed). I have no explanation for this anomalous result, except to surmise that the impact of high relative levels of debt may be sensitive to the burden of repayment as captured by the interest to GNP ratio.

78 On the Mexican crisis, see Riordan Roett, "The Mexican Devaluation and the U.S. Response: Potomac Politics, 1995-Style," in Riordan Roett, ed., *The Mexican Peso Crisis: International Perspectives* (Boulder, CO: Lynne Rienner, 1996).

79 Bird (fn. 1, 1995).

80 This result may be spurious. Bird suggests that requesting a loan from the IMF has a threshold effect; once a country requests one loan, it is more likely to request additional loans. Since any country that has a loan canceled has

already crossed this threshold, it may be more likely to receive loans in the future. Bird (fn. 1, 1995).

81 Regressions were also run using each variable without the other, yielding similar negative results.

82 There was a possible collinearity problem with this variable. Specifically, it correlated strongly with $MKVOTE_{it-1}$. Because the inclusion of the interactive term is likely to have inflated the standard error of the movement variable and because its inclusion did not significantly improve the model's fit, I did not retain it.

83 Because of the potential for omitted variable bias and the negative diagnostic for multicollinearity in the original specification, I have greater confidence in the results of the full model. I therefore present the refined model results for the interested reader but focus most of the substantive interpretations on the full model.

84 The change in the current account from $t-1$ to t is significant at the 0.95 level, and the ratio of the current account to GNP is significant at the 0.90 level. The unexpectedly positive coefficient for the change in the current account from $t-1$ to t could be due to the fact that an IMF loan at time t can itself cause an improvement in the balance of payments at time t.

85 I retained absolute alignment position here to facilitate a clearer comparison of the hypothetical scenarios and to create more difficult conditions for demonstrating the strength of the impact of political realignment. Omitting $KVOTE_{it-2}$ would lower the probability for the static US ally even more, relative to any country moving toward the US.

86 Killick (fn. 1), 128.

87 Killick (fn. 1).

88 See McKeown (fn. 48).

89 Only one developing country (China) is a permanent member of the Security Council, so we cannot use Security Council votes to measure alignment.

90 Data from World Bank, *World Development Indicators 1998* (Washington, DC: World Bank, various issues); idem, *World Debt Tables* (Washington, DC: World Bank, various issues); and idem, *World Bank Global Development Finance* (Washington, DC: World Bank, various issues).

91 The results for some of the economic variables differ from those in Table 5.1. Given the smaller number of cases used in Table 5.4 (a result of data availability), I base my substantive interpretations on the results presented in Tables 5.1 and 5.3. Several intermediate and refined specifications yielded similar results.

92 Pallansch and Zinni (fn. 67).

93 Ruggie (fn. 2).

94 See McKeown (fn. 48).

95 See Kahler (fn. 16), 93

96 Cited in Nick Butler, *The IMF, Time for Reform* (London: Fabian Society, 1982), 24.

97 Cf. Ruggie (fn. 2), chapter 1.

6 Money talks

Supplementary financiers and IMF conditionality[*]

Erica R. Gould

> One reason why the program was so severe ... perhaps lay in the inability of the Fund to find enough resources on its own to finance the entire adjustment, including the payment of arrears and other debt. Thus, the Fund was also faced with trying to design stand-by programs that would attract additional sources of finance that would enhance such programs' chances of success.
>
> (British Alternative Executive Director Pendarell Kent's remarks at Executive Board meeting 79/7 discussing Ghana's 1979 stand-by arrangement)[1]

1 Introduction

The International Monetary Fund (IMF or Fund) was originally created to monitor and maintain the Bretton Woods par value exchange rate system, and loaned resources on a revolving basis for the narrow purpose of helping members offset short-term payments imbalances in order to defend their exchange rates. In 1952, the Fund first attached conditions to its loans, and since then Fund conditionality has changed dramatically. The number of conditions that a borrowing member must meet in order to receive timely installments of a Fund loan has increased. The types of conditions have evolved, from broad macroeconomic targets in the 1950s and 1960s to the "microconditionality" today, which specifies conditions pertaining to policy implementation in great detail. The Fund's loans are now generally larger, longer term, and tackle new problems. Today the Fund offers advice and sets conditions not only on policies from areas of long-standing focus like exchange rates and credit expansion, but also on new areas of concentration, including governance and enterprise reform. These changes in the terms of Fund conditional loan agreements influence the policies and the political and economic trajectories of numerous borrowing states. In the 2000/2001 fiscal year alone, 80 countries participated in Fund conditional loan agreements.[2]

In the wake of the Asian financial crisis, IMF "conditionality" – or the terms of these conditional loan programs – has again become the subject of international scrutiny. Critics initially focused on the conditional loan programs for South Korea and Indonesia. Many argued that these programs required South Korea and Indonesia to meet too many – and perhaps the wrong – conditions in return for disbursements of the Fund loan. Over time, the critics diversified and the scope of their criticism broadened. Now everyone from economists to activists, from politicians to the Fund's staff, and from the left and the right seems to agree that Fund conditionality has expanded beyond the Fund's original mandate and that, for various reasons, this expansion is bad.[3] These critics make strange bedfellows. Their overwhelming consensus about the inappropriateness of Fund conditionality raises the question: why are Fund conditional loan arrangements designed this way? Which factors, or actors, influence Fund conditionality and have contributed to its change over time?

In this chapter, I offer an alternative to the conventional explanations that point to powerful states or bureaucratic interests alone in order to explain international organizational activity, including Fund conditionality. I argue that Fund conditionality is influenced by the private and official financiers who supplement the Fund's loan to borrowers. These *supplementary financiers* are able to influence the terms of Fund conditional loan arrangements because their financing is necessary for the success of Fund-designed programs. Thus they appeal to the interests of the Fund staff and management who actually design these programs. Supplementary financiers may be creditor states, private financial institutions or multilateral organizations, but this chapter limits its scope to the influence of one type of supplementary financier on IMF conditionality: private financial institutions.

The chapter will proceed as follows. First I introduce the general supplementary financier argument in more detail, including the logic of why, how, and when supplementary financiers are able to exercise leverage over the Fund. Special attention will be given to private financial institutions (PFIs) since their influence on Fund conditionality programs is the focus of the two empirical sections. Almost exclusively, the evidence used to test if and illustrate how supplementary financiers are able to influence Fund conditionality arrangements was gathered directly from the Fund's archives in Washington, DC. Two types of Fund archival evidence are employed. The third section uses the Conditionality Dataset, an original dataset of 249 conditional loan arrangements from 1952 to 1995 coded according to their terms. This section provides descriptive statistics and statistical tests, which suggest that PFIs have influenced the terms of Fund conditional loan arrangements in ways the supplementary financier argument predicts. The fourth section discusses the mechanisms of PFI influence in more depth, employing memos and documents from the individual country files and program files from the Fund archives. In this section, two cases of Fund conditional loan arrangements are analyzed. Finally, the chapter concludes with a discussion of the implications of this argument and these findings both for the debates on Fund conditionality and current understandings of international organizations.

2 Theory

I argue that International Monetary Fund conditionality is influenced by supplementary financiers. The Fund often provides only a fraction of the amount of money that a country needs to balance its payments that year and implement the Fund's recommended program. Supplementary financiers provide financing that supplements the Fund's loans to borrowing member states. The Fund relies on this supplementary, external financing to ensure the success of its programs. This gives the supplementary financiers some leverage over the design of Fund programs. The financiers are able to make demands on the Fund, stipulating which conditions must be included in a particular Fund program in order for their financing to be forthcoming.

Supplementary financiers include three types of actors: creditor states, PFIs, and multilateral organizations. Each type has different reasons for providing financing to borrowing states, and therefore different preferences about how Fund programs should be designed. Creditor states, PFIs, and multilateral organizations thus try to influence the terms of Fund conditionality in systematically different ways. Many of the over-time changes in Fund conditionality and cross-sectional variation between Fund programs have been caused by the shifting mix of supplementary financiers. In 1952, when Fund conditionality began, nearly all of the supplementary financing came from creditor states, mainly from the US. Now borrowers receive supplementary financing from a diverse set of creditor states, private financial institutions and multilateral organizations. This shift in supplementary financing – for instance as PFIs came to play more of a role in the provision of supplementary financing through commercial bank lending from the late 1960s through the early 1980s, loan restructurings in the 1980s and the bond markets in the 1990s – has led to new demands on the Fund, and subsequently has contributed to the changes in the design of Fund conditionality agreements.[4]

2.1 Theoretical antecedents

This argument is built on the central insights from two strands of liberal theory: first, that non-state actors may influence international outcomes, and second that international institutions and organizations (IIs and IOs) help facilitate mutually-beneficial exchange between international actors.[5] In other words, I am trying to harness the powerful insights of the neoliberal institutionalist turn, without accepting its state-centric ontology. This section focuses on the neoliberal institutionalist (hereafter neoliberal) insights and the reasons for broadening our analysis of the Fund to include non-state actors.

The trademark neoliberal insight about IIs and IOs, including the IMF, is that they are Pareto-improving. Absent cooperation, state interaction often results in a Pareto-suboptimal outcome. IIs and IOs help states over-come barriers to cooperation and reach mutually-beneficial outcomes by restructuring their incentives.[6] IIs and IOs, like the Fund, thereby serve the collective interests of states. For example, George von Furstenberg has argued that the Fund promotes efficient exchange – namely financing – between debtor and creditor states and thus helps them achieve a more efficient outcome.[7]

For neoliberals, the key actors are states and therefore IIs and IOs help facilitate exchange between states. While this simplifying assumption may be analytically useful and even accurate in the case of some IIs and IOs, it is misleading in the case of the IMF. The Fund's main activities – promot-ing exchange rate stability, helping countries resolve payments imbal-ances, etc. – are no longer exclusively the domain of states.[8] For instance, creditor states are no longer the main source of balance-of-payments financing, and are therefore not the only actor that might benefit from the Fund's capacity to make borrowers' commitments more credible, monitor their policies, and provide signals about borrower creditworthiness.

Consequently previous studies of the Fund have relaxed the state-as-actor assumption, for instance focusing on the Fund's role in promoting efficient exchange – again, financing – between state and non-state actors. Both Benjamin Cohen and Charles Lipson argued that the Fund, in reac-tion to the changes in balance-of-payments financing in the 1970s and 1980s, evolved from an organization focused on providing financing from its own coffers or facilitating the flow from creditor states to one focused on facilitating the flow of balance-of-payments financing from private sources.[9] They separately identified an important relationship between the IMF, borrowing states, and financiers – both official and private.

The argument presented here draws heavily on their insights, and extends their implications. It not only acknowledges the role of the Fund in facilitating supplementary financing to borrowers, but also the supple-mentary financiers' leverage over the Fund and their influence on its activities. The Fund is not simply a neutral arbiter, stamping programs it deems acceptable, monitoring country adherence to these programs and thereby helping both financiers and borrowers overcome their credibility problem. The Fund itself has a vested interest in the success of its pro-grams, and as a result is susceptible to influence from the financiers.

2.2 Why supplementary financiers influence the Fund

Supplementary financiers and the IMF are locked in a mutually-dependent relationship. The Fund depends on supplementary financiers to help ensure the success of its loan programs and its future bargaining leverage with borrowers. In turn, supplementary financiers depend on the Fund to help facilitate their financing transactions and make borrowers' commitments more credible. As a result, supplementary financiers are both able and willing to influence the Fund's activities.

First, consider why supplementary financiers are able to influence the IMF. The Fund is an actor with interests and supplementary financiers help the Fund maximize those interests. The Fund is comprised of an international staff of economists, most trained at a few select US and Western European universities.[10] Despite their diverse national backgrounds, new staff and management join the Fund with remarkably similar shared assumptions and principles influenced by their education. Both the Fund's staff and its management have been trained as economists and want to be successful economists, influencing the direction of the international economy at large and the economies of individual borrowers by applying theoretical principles.[11] The failure of an implemented Fund program damages not only the reputations of the individual staff members who designed it, but also the organization's reputation and the credibility of the principles that have been applied. Therefore individually and collectively, the staff want Fund programs to succeed in measurably improving the economies in which they intervene.[12] Supplementary financiers are able to exercise leverage over the Fund and its activities because their financing affects both the success of Fund programs and the Fund's future bargaining leverage with borrowers.

Supplementary financing is often crucial for the short-term success of individual Fund programs since the Fund provides only a fraction of the amount of money necessary for a borrowing country to balance its payments and implement the Fund-designed program successfully.[13] These financing gaps were well publicized during the 1980s debt crisis, as were the Fund's efforts to line up supplementary financing. Gaps between borrower need and Fund loans have been commonplace throughout the history of Fund conditionality. For instance between 1954 and 1960, in 77 percent of the cases of Fund stabilization programs with Latin American countries, 50 percent or more of the country's external financing came from supplementary financiers, not from the Fund.[14] In 64 percent of the cases from the 1952–95 Conditionality Dataset, the country's current account deficit was more than the amount of the entire Fund loan agreement, indicating a likely financing gap.[15] This comparison is admittedly flawed, not least because it underestimates the frequency of the financing gap. Fund loans are generally not delivered in full when the agreement is signed, but instead in segments over several months or years. For the 36 percent whose Fund loan was larger than their current account deficit that year, the Fund loan was delivered in five segments over 19 months on average. Since the loan was not delivered in full the first year, there is a strong chance that, even for these 36 percent, the country's financing needs exceeded the Fund loan disbursements. Thus in most, if not all, cases the Fund provided only a fraction of the financing needed to balance its payments that year.

Consequently, Fund programs are designed with an assumption of a certain amount of supplementary financing. Countries come to the Fund when they face payments imbalances. The Fund programs are designed to bring them back into balance through a combination of adjustment, often demand-contraction measures that are intended to reduce the existing current account deficit, and financing of the remaining deficits with Fund loans and supplementary financing.[16] Supplementary financing has been factored into these programs since the 1950s when Fund conditionality began. For example, Venezuela's 1960 stand-by arrangement stated that their deficit would be "covered" by loans from PFIs. The stand-by "proposed to finance this deficit by credits now being negotiated with foreign commercial banks."[17] Fund agreements not only stated that supplementary financing was being sought and was necessary for the country to balance, but sometimes required a specific amount of supplementary financing as a condition of the Fund agreement. An early, and at that time rare, example of this was Argentina's 1958 stand-by arrangement, which required Argentina "to request financial assistance from sources other than the Fund" and to borrow from the Fund and those "other credit facilities" in a "proportion of 1 to at least $2\frac{1}{2}$."[18]

In order for a country to balance its payments and implement the Fund's program, supplementary financing was almost always needed and expected. Fund programs explicitly mentioned supplementary financing, factored it in and even required borrowers to secure it as a condition of the Fund program. Without the additional financing, the countries would not have been able to balance their payments that year and would have been forced to abandon a Fund program designed with an assumption of incoming supplementary financing.[19]

Supplementary financing is key to not only the short-term success of Fund programs, but also the Fund's future bargaining leverage with borrowers and thus the perceived future success of Fund programs.[20] Borrowing countries enter into Fund programs not only for Fund financing, but also for the supplementary financing that often accompanies it. Fund staffers have consistently articulated this point. For instance Jorge Del Canto, then head of the Fund's Western Hemisphere division, emphasized how stand-by agreements should help borrowing countries secure supplementary financing. He wrote that:

> In some cases it is the establishment of confidence rather than the use of Fund resources that is the prime objective of a stand-by arrangement ... [and that] the confidence ... is registered directly through a flow of supporting assistance from other sources, the availability and volume of which is tied to observance of conditions in the Fund stand-by arrangement.[21]

In Del Canto's words, borrowers often enter Fund programs for the "flow of supporting assistance from other sources," or supplementary financing. As a result, if a borrowing country signs a Fund agreement and the supplementary financing is not forthcoming, future borrowing member states may be less likely to agree to the Fund's conditions or even turn to the Fund at all. Without the inflow of supplementary financing, Fund programs may be a much less attractive prospect for many Fund borrowers.

Supplementary financing impacts both the success of Fund programs and the Fund's future bargaining leverage with borrowers. As a result, the Fund has an incentive to help secure supplementary financing, particularly since many of the other factors that influence the success of Fund programs – including *inter alia* natural calamities, contraction of international demand for primary product exports and regional political instability – are outside of the Fund's control. The inflow of supplementary financing, on the other hand, is neither random nor automatic.

Earlier scholarship argued that the inflow of supplementary financing was more or less automatic. According to the standard "catalytic effect" argument, a Fund loan program often serves as a "good housekeeping seal of approval," increasing the creditworthiness of debtor countries and provoking an automatic inflow of outside financing.[22] Recent empirical work has challenged that argument, demonstrating that Fund programs have not been followed by an automatic inflow of private capital.[23] The way the inflow of supplementary financing works is different from the spontaneous reaction to the signing of a Fund program suggested by the "catalytic effect" argument and disputed by recent empirical literature on catalysis. Instead, much of the supplementary financing, the so-called "catalytic" finance, is explicitly negotiated and controlled.[24] Supplementary financing almost always accompanies Fund programs.[25] Sometimes it comes mainly from PFIs, other times from creditor states or other multilateral organizations. The Fund plays an integral role in securing these fresh funds and coordinating lenders to restructure existing debt.[26] Supplementary financing packages are often negotiated concurrently with Fund program negotiations. The Fund often acts as a mediator between financier and borrower, and helps the borrower secure necessary financing.

Supplementary financiers are not only able, but also willing to influence the terms of Fund conditionality agreements. They often want to influence the content of the Fund's conditionality arrangements in order to increase the likelihood that the borrowing country will use its financing in ways the financier deems appropriate. Supplementary financiers and borrowers often face a credibility problem. A supplementary financier wants to provide financing as long as it is used in certain ways (e.g., invested rather than consumed), and the borrowing country often pledges to use the financing just as the financier prefers. However, the borrower's pledge may not be credible for two reasons. First, due to informational asymmetries, the supplementary financier may not know a borrower's "type" or their true preferences regarding the use of this financing (e.g., their willingness to invest rather than consume). The Fund program can serve as a signal of borrower creditworthiness and thereby help financiers and borrowers overcome this impediment to mutually-beneficial financing. Scholars have argued that the Fund agreement serves as a signal – either the borrower's costly signal of its commitment to reform, or the Fund's costly signal of its assessment of borrower "type" based on its own expertise and access to private information.[27]

Second, and more importantly for this chapter, is the so-called time-consistency problem.[28] Even if the borrower is earnest in pledging to use the financing as the financier prefers, the supplementary financier knows that the borrower's incentives may change once this financing is disbursed. The Fund can help financiers overcome this problem by influencing the borrower's *ex post* incentives via its conditionality agreements. Despite notoriously uneven compliance, IMF conditionality agreements do include different mechanisms that shift states' incentives and allow them to make more credible commitments.[29] First, IMF financing and supplementary financing, including loans from PFIs, are often tied to the country meeting its binding conditions. The loans are often split into separate segments, and each segment is conditioned on borrower compliance with certain conditions. Thus, borrowers' "hands are tied," in that costs will be suffered *ex post* if they defect from the agreed policy program.[30] Second, IMF conditionality programs allow the Fund to monitor borrowing country policies in detail and publicize transgressions, thereby "reviving the reputation mechanism."[31] The IMF, through its conditionality, facilitates cooperation between creditors and borrowers by vouching for a borrower's reputation and enabling it to more credibly commit to a particular course of action. The financiers often want to influence borrower incentives and the content of this Fund conditionality program in order to better serve their own interests.

In sum, supplementary financiers are both willing and able to exercise leverage over the design of Fund conditionality agreements. The Fund is vulnerable to supplementary financier influence since their financing is necessary for the short-term success and feasibility of Fund programs and for the Fund's future bargaining leverage with borrowers, and is not automatic. Supplementary financiers want to influence Fund conditionality because they want to control how their financing is utilized and Fund conditionality arrangements help them do that.

2.3 What kind of influence?

As previously discussed, there are three types of supplementary financiers: creditor states, PFIs, and multilateral organizations.[32] This article focuses on PFIs. They are of particular interest because they lack the institutionalized mechanisms of influence that states and other multilateral organizations have at their disposal. Scholars often consider PFIs' interests to be subservient to, or subsumed by, state interests, rather than in competition with them.[33] As a result, PFIs are a hard case and provide a good test of the supplementary financier argument.

PFIs provide financing to Fund borrowers in order to make a profit.[34] They extend loans to and make investments in countries when they expect a positive return, and they want Fund programs to help ensure their profitable return. For most of the period under investigation, the main PFI supplementary financiers were commercial banks, and they wanted Fund loan agreements to increase the probability that their loans would be paid back. This interest may manifest itself in different preferences regarding the terms of Fund agreements. The empirical section focuses on one element of the design of Fund programs which isolates the influence of PFIs best: a certain class of binding conditions, labeled "bank-friendly" conditions, which specify that the country must pay back a commercial bank creditor as a condition of its Fund loan.

While the focus of this chapter is on PFIs, the influence of creditor states is also considered, mainly because the realist and supplementary financier arguments have opposing predictions about the nature of that influence on conditionality agreements. The realist model, discussed further in the testing section, predicts that powerful (creditor) states prefer *more* stringent agreements. According to the supplementary financier argument, creditor states provide financing for political ends. They are less concerned with being paid back than PFIs. Aid and bilateral loans are political, not financial, investments. Aid is often given to allies and therefore creditor states are often interested in preserving political stability.[35] In practice, that means that they generally prefer Fund conditional loan arrangements to be relatively *less* stringent than PFIs.[36] While creditor states want borrowers to agree to certain conditions, they prefer Fund arrangements to allow borrowers to maintain some political room for maneuver.

Different types of supplementary financiers – like creditor states and PFIs – may try to influence Fund loan arrangements in systematically different ways, but when should we expect this influence to result in changes in Fund programs, and how much change should we observe? Supplementary financiers and the Fund are engaged in a bargaining relationship. The Fund is not entirely beholden to supplementary financiers. Financiers do not simply communicate an ideal program design and then the Fund's activities fall in line with those preferences. When supplementary financiers influence Fund programs, the influence is often at the margins. They try to add certain requirements that are particularly important to them or remove other conditions that they find particularly onerous.

Creditor states and multilateral organizations have legitimate mechanisms to coordinate their demands and influence the Fund, for instance through the Executive Board or joint Fund-Bank missions, respectively. As a result, their influence on Fund programs should be directly proportional to their relative contribution of supplementary financing. PFIs, by contrast, do not have legitimate, established mechanisms of influence. Officially, they are not supposed to influence the content of Fund programs at all. As a result, PFI influence should not be directly proportional to their relative contribution of supplementary financing. Instead, PFI influence hinges on their ability to generate a credible threat that substantial financing will be lost if Fund activities do not conform to their preferences.

Often, however, PFIs cannot credibly generate this threat for two related reasons. First, when there are multiple PFIs involved in negotiations with a potential Fund borrower, they face a collective action problem. The PFIs may all benefit from a Fund conditionality agreement with "bank-friendly" conditions, but individually they may not want to commit to withhold financing if the bank-friendly condition is omitted and provide financing if the condition is included in the borrower's Fund agreement. These constraints and commitments are themselves costly. They also may not want to engage in costly negotiations with the Fund, and may not agree on how much financing should be provided or withheld if the conditions are included or omitted, respectively.[37] PFIs will be able to overcome this collective action problem when a single financier dominates the group or, more often, when they get organized.[38] Previous scholars have studied when PFI organization is more or less likely, and what forms it is likely to take. For instance, Charles Lipson has studied how and when private creditors organize themselves, for instance through syndicate lending and during debt rescheduling negotiations.[39] For the purposes of this chapter, PFI organization of some sort is necessary so that PFIs can coordinate their demands on the Fund and generate the threat in the first place.

Second and relatedly, in order for this generated threat to be credible, the PFIs' *ex post* incentives must support enforcement of the threat. As North and Weingast have argued, "while parties may have strong incentives to strike a bargain, their incentives after the fact are not always compatible with maintaining the agreement."[40] Under certain circumstances, PFIs may prefer the Fund to include a bank-friendly condition in its agreement, but the inclusion or exclusion of this condition will not change the PFIs' incentives enough to induce them to provide or withhold the necessary supplementary financing, respectively. Given that PFIs are less likely to expend the energy to lobby the Fund in the first instance, we are more concerned about the second instance: when PFIs would be willing to provide supplementary financing even if the Fund agreement did not include a bank-friendly condition. The threat to withhold financing must be *ex post* incentive compatible in order to be credible. Unless PFIs are disinterested enough to walk away from a potential financing opportunity, their threat will not be credible and the Fund has no incentive to change the terms of its agreement. In order to operationalize PFI influence, I use a variable that captures both the idea of PFI organization and the willingness to withhold supplementary financing: whether or not PFIs are engaged in private debt renegotiations around the time of the Fund loan negotiations. Further discussion of why this is an appropriate proxy and of its potential biases is provided in the testing section that follows.

In short, the supplementary-financier argument suggests that PFIs will be able to influence the terms of Fund conditionality arrangements when they can generate a credible threat to withhold necessary supplementary financing if their demands are not met. The PFI threat will only be credible under certain conditions: if they are organized and if the threat is *ex post* incentive compatible. The supplementary financier argument thus generates the following testable hypotheses:

Hypothesis 1: If PFIs are organized and can credibly threaten to withhold/provide financing from/for a particular country, then that country's Fund program should be systematically more likely to include "bank-friendly" conditions, holding other variables constant.

Hypothesis 2: If a borrower receives relatively more supplementary financing from creditor states, then its Fund program should be relatively less stringent, holding other variables constant.

3 Testing

3.1 Conditionality dataset

This section tests whether PFIs have influenced Fund conditionality in systematic ways by using a data set of 249 IMF conditional loan arrangements (stand-by arrangements, EFF, SAF, and ESAF) from twenty countries between 1952 and 1995. An observation is a unique conditional loan arrangement, in other words a unique country-loan-year. True random sampling, while methodologically preferable, was not viable given the organization and resources of the Fund archives. The Fund archives organize documents by country; staff time – to pull, vet, and declassify documents – is minimized by requesting multiple agreements from a single country, rather than single agreements from multiple countries. Consequently I selected representative countries and then, data and access permitting, included all relevant agreements for that country between 1952 (when conditionality began) and 1995 (after which many arrangements remained classified at the time of data gathering). The 249 cases came from the following twenty countries: Argentina, Bangladesh, Bolivia, Brazil, the Central African Republic, the Côte D'Ivoire, El Salvador, Ghana, Haiti, Korea, Mali, Mexico, Morocco, Niger, the Philippines, Romania, South Africa, Turkey, the United Kingdom and Yugoslavia.

Despite this atypical case selection method, the 249 cases are generally representative, both by region and arrangement type. Tables 6A.1 and 6A.2 in the Appendix compare the dataset with the entire population of 759 stand-by EFF, SAF, and ESAF loan agreements between 1952 and 1991. The sample very closely approximates (within three percentage points) the proportion of cases from all regions except Africa, which is under-represented, and Europe, which is over-represented in comparison to the 1952–91 universe. The sample is also generally representative with respect to arrangement type. The European over-representation is warranted since the "universe" comprises only cases between 1952 and 1991, while the sample comprises cases between 1952 and 1995. Since 1991, the Fund has seen an absolute and proportional increase in European agreements, particularly from the former Soviet Union and Eastern Europe.

The Conditionality Dataset codes each loan agreement according to its terms as stated in the original loan agreement, including the letter of intent, attachments, and the resulting press release. A typical Fund loan agreement includes a letter from the borrowing country's finance minister requesting a loan and detailing an extensive policy program concerning many different sectors of the economy and government. The arrangement itself, often a second document, generally outlines more policy proposals and the program's schedule of reviews, and often in the penultimate paragraph specifies which conditions are binding. Binding conditions trigger the suspension of the Fund loan if they are violated. Most arrangements have numerous other conditions that are also listed in the policy program but are not binding; in other words, there are no specified consequences if they are violated.[41] Each case was coded according to 31 separate criteria questions and 52 different binding conditions. The dataset also contains information on a variety of other characteristics of the original program other than binding conditions, including the provisions for phasing, reviews and consultations.

3.2 The dependent variable

PFIs provide supplementary financing to borrowing member states because they hope to make a profit from that loan or investment. For PFIs, Fund conditionality agreements are useful because they may increase the probability of a profitable return. This study focuses on the one change in the terms of Fund conditional loan arrangements that seems to best isolate the influence of PFIs: the inclusion of a certain class of conditions that seem to be clearly serving the interests of PFIs. These conditions, labeled bank-friendly conditions, provide PFIs with more direct assurances that their commercial bank loans will be repaid. Bank-friendly conditions specify that the borrowing country has to pay back a commercial bank creditor as a condition of its Fund loan. As a result, these conditions make it more costly for a borrower to default on a bank loan, thereby increasing the likelihood of repayment.

Table 6.1 lists the five types of bank-friendly conditions from the sampled Fund conditional loan arrangements. One example is from Ghana's 1983 stand-by arrangement. The arrangement included "irrevocable instructions" that the stand-by loan be deposited directly in a Bank of Ghana account at the Bank of England; the Bank of England would follow irrevocable instructions that these deposits would then be directly transferred to the Standard Chartered Bank to re-pay a short-term bridging loan. In other words, Fund financing was being directly funneled to a commercial bank creditor, rather than to Ghana itself.[42] Argentina's 1992 Extended Fund Facility included "set asides to support future debt-reduction operations with Argentina's commercial bank creditor" and if Argentina "incurs [sic] any new external payments arrears after June 30, 1992," then its loan would be suspended.[43] Sixty-one arrangements in the sample (or 25 percent) include a bank-friendly binding condition. Interestingly, all 61 include only one bank-friendly condition as binding. As a result, the dependent variable is binary: whether or not a given conditionality agreement includes a bank-friendly binding condition.

The use of bank-friendly conditions has increased dramatically over the period from 1952 to 1995. Before the 1973 oil crisis, when private commercial bank lending to middle- and low-income countries was still relatively rare, only 3 percent of sampled Fund conditional loan arrangements (or two agreements) required that a bank-friendly condition be met. Between the oil crisis and the debt crisis (from about 1974 until 1982), when commercial bank lending to developing countries surged, 20 percent of sampled Fund loan agreements included at least one bank-friendly condition. After the debt crisis, when private supplementary financing was scarce and discriminating, over 70 percent of Fund loan agreements included a bank-friendly condition. Seventy-nine percent of sampled arrangements between 1983 and 1990 required a bank-friendly condition, while 73 percent of sampled arrangements between 1991 and 1995 required a bank-friendly condition. The increase in bank-friendly conditions is one facet of the broader changes in Fund conditionality, including the increase in the total number of binding conditions and the

Table 6.1 Examples of bank-friendly conditions

---

1   The borrowing country is required to set-aside certain fiscal revenues to match or "complement" international loans with fiscal revenues
2   A percentage of the Fund loan must be set-aside for debt reduction payments or replenishment of reserves
3   The country must make debt service payments, as agreed with commercial banks and/or official creditors
4   The country must limit financial intermediation by national banks and/or move financial intermediation to the private sector
5   The government must meet a target for reducing government's external payments arrears

---

changes in the types of binding conditions. Figure 6.1 provides a portrait of the increase in the use of bank-friendly conditions, as compared to the overall increase in the number of binding conditions over the 1952 to 1995 period for 230 cases for which data was available from the Conditionality Dataset. The measure of bank-friendly conditions is a three-year moving average of the proportion of the sampled arrangements in a given year that required a bank-friendly condition as binding; it varies between 0 and 1. The measure of the number of binding conditions is the average number of binding conditions required by all sampled arrangements started in a given year; it varies between 0 and 13.5.

3.3 The independent variables

According to the supplementary financier argument, PFIs prefer Fund conditional loan arrangements to include bank-friendly conditions. We should expect PFIs to exercise leverage over the Fund when they are an important source of supplementary financing for the borrowing country and are organized enough to articulate their preferences and credibly threaten to withhold financing.

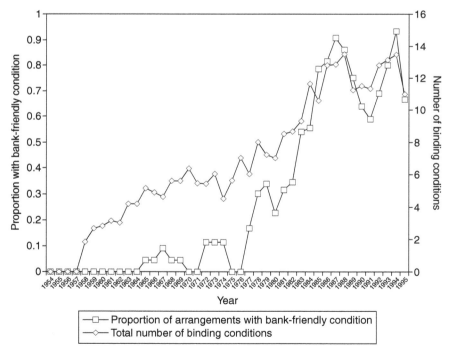

Figure 6.1 Change in number of binding conditions and use of bank-friendly conditions (source: Conditionality Dataset).

The amount of private financing or proportion of external financing that comes from private sources may appear to be the most obvious proxy for private influence; however, it does not capture the logic of the supplementary financier argument.[44] One could imagine PFIs providing (relatively and absolutely) abundant financing to borrowers and yet exercising little or no leverage over the Fund, for instance during most of the "petrodollar recycling" period when PFIs were less organized (despite syndicated lending) and could certainly not credibly threaten to withhold financing since the sovereign loans were considered so lucrative. In other words, the supplementary financier argument does not predict a stable over-time relationship between the amount of private financing and their leverage over the Fund.[45]

In order to test the supplementary financier argument, I instead used a proxy for private influence ("private") which captures the idea that PFIs would be able to exercise leverage when they are organized and can credibly threaten to withhold financing: a binary variable that is coded "1" when the borrowing country restructured their private debt in that or the previous year.[46] Private debt restructuring is a key moment when PFIs may be able to organize themselves, develop a coherent bargaining strategy and articulate their preferences to Fund representatives. Scholarly attention has turned to private debt restructuring as an important form of commercial bank cooperation before.[47] Admittedly, this is only one of the possible ways that PFIs could organize themselves and credibly threaten to withhold borrower financing if their preferred terms are not included in the Fund program. PFIs may be able to influence Fund conditionality in other situations not captured by this proxy that may result in a negative bias (against the hypothesized relationship). The supplementary financier argument predicts that the coefficient on the private influence variable should be positive and significant.

A plausible alternative hypothesis is that Fund activity – including the design of Fund conditionality agreements – is driven externally by powerful states. Realist scholars have argued that powerful states, most often the United States, use international organizations like the Fund as tools to achieve their foreign policy goals. For realists, IIs and IOs are themselves epiphenomenal, reflecting and acting directly according to the interests and preferences of powerful states.[48] For instance, Strom Thacker argues that the United States' political preferences and the international balance of power are the "underlying causes of the IMF's behavior."[49] This seems particularly plausible in the case of the IMF, whose weighted voting system institutionalizes the greater influence of powerful states, particularly the US.

In order to test this argument and control for the influence of powerful states, the "US" variable is included as a proxy for US influence. It is the total amount of US loans and grants to the given borrowing country in the year of the Fund arrangement, divided by (and normalized by) the amount of the IMF loan agreement; it varies between 0 and 33.49.[50] The logic behind this proxy is that the US contributes more resources to those countries in which it is interested, and in turn should have more influence over their Fund conditional loan arrangements.[51] If we expect, as realists do, that changes in Fund conditionality including the introduction of new conditions like bank-friendly conditions have been driven by powerful states, then the coefficient on this variable should be positive. If we believe powerful states drove the observed changes in Fund conditionality, then we should see powerful state influence positively related to these changes.

The supplementary financier also considers the potential influence of powerful creditor states. However, it contends that the US and other powerful states have not been the driving force behind the introduction of new conditions and the increases in Fund conditionality, instead they have actually pushed for reductions in Fund conditionality and worked against many of the observed changes in Fund conditionality. The supplementary financier argument therefore predicts that the coefficient on the US variable should be negative, while the realist argument predicts it should be positive.

Another plausible alternative hypothesis is that Fund conditionality and the changes in Fund conditionality have been driven by the Fund's bureaucracy. Scholars argue that the IMF should be understood as an actor unto itself, not just a conduit for state preferences, with autonomy to pursue its own interest or goals. Those from the rationalist school tend to argue that IOs achieve a degree of autonomy due to principal–agent issues of informational asymmetry and incomplete monitoring.[52] IOs use their autonomy to pursue "power, prestige, and amenities." For instance in a series of articles Roland Vaubel focuses on the Fund bureaucracy's efforts to "maximize their budget, their staff, and their independence." Vaubel views Fund conditionality as a mechanism to pursue those interests.[53] He uses staff size and average salaries as proxies for bureaucratic power and autonomy. To test this argument, I included the "salary increase" variable.[54] This is the proportional increase in the average staff salary since the previous year; it varies between -0.016 and 0.192.[55] The logic is that as Fund bureaucratic power and autonomy increase (indicated in an increase in average salaries that year), it is more likely to insert "discretionary" conditions – like bank-friendly conditions – that serve to further "increase its power."[56] The coefficient on this variable should therefore be positive and significant.

The Fund may also interact with borrowers differently based on borrower attributes. Scholars have considered the influence of borrower attributes on borrower demand for Fund loans.[57] Less work has been done on the supply-side (how borrower attributes may influence Fund activity, including the design of Fund programs) despite the fact that the Fund often claims that programs are tailored to the specific needs and demands of borrowers, or to borrower attributes. It certainly seems plausible that

Fund conditionality agreements would vary systematically based on borrower attributes.

Three variables are included to test the general premise that Fund conditionality is responsive to the changing needs or demands of borrowers. Fund lending was originally intended to help countries offset temporary payments imbalances. Over time the Fund has increasingly lent to countries facing "protracted balance of payments problems" and impediments to growth.[58] The Fund has argued that Fund program design has changed to meet the objective needs of borrowers facing increasingly severe payments imbalances and economic crises.[59] To control for the severity of the borrower's balance-of-payments problem, I include the "reserves" variable, which is the ratio of foreign reserves to imports in the year that the country began its Fund conditional loan agreement. This measure should be negatively related to the dependent variable.[60]

Second, the Fund has also argued that less developed countries require different Fund conditionality – including more or different binding conditions – than more developed countries.[61] As a result, the Fund has created new lending facilities for less-developed countries, like the SAF, ESAF, and now the Poverty Reduction and Growth Facility, that require more detailed conditionality.[62] A constant GNP per capita variable is included in the analysis to control for this effect.[63] The predicted coefficient should also be negative for this variable.

Third, democracies may interact differently with the Fund. Democracies may tend to have systematically higher conditionality programs because they demand increased conditionality in order to tie their own hands.[64] Alternatively, democracies may have systematically lower conditionality programs because they resist tougher conditions out of fear of voter retribution. A regime-type variable, that ranges from −10 (full autocracy) to +10 (full democracy), is included to capture this effect.[65]

The seventh independent variable tests the general Fund's policy on loans: that larger loans (in relation to the country's quota) require more "justification" or stricter conditionality.[66] The "tranche" variable tests whether the Fund actually follows this policy. It is the amount of the Fund loan, divided by the amount of the country's Fund quota. The predicted relationship between this variable and the presence of bank-friendly conditions is positive.

The eighth independent variable tests whether the borrower's size influences the terms of its Fund conditional loan agreement. Some have argued that certain countries are "too big to fail" and have therefore received special, perhaps easier treatment from the Fund.[67] As a result, I have included the borrower's gross national product (GNP) at market prices in billions of constant 1995 US dollars.[68] The coefficient on this variable should be negative if larger countries receive easier terms.

Given that this data set has time-series properties – in other words it includes multiple over-time observations – there may be an over-time effect which is not being absorbed by the model. The terms of the Fund's EFF with Mexico in 1982 may have influenced the Fund's stand-by arrangement with Mexico in 1986 or the Fund's EFF with Brazil in 1983. One of the key assumptions in typical regression models is that all of the observations are independent. If a model is based on that assumption, but the observations are actually dependent on each other, the result is inefficient parameters and biased standard errors. [69] In Gary King's words, the model should capture "the underlying process by which the random observations vary and covary over time. In a sense, the task of time series analysis is to model how history repeats itself or how it influences future events." [70] The explanatory variables previously discussed suggest different reasons for over-time change. The last independent variable – a simple linear time trend – is included to represent alternative theories of over-time change. The year is coded 0 in 1952 and 43 in 1995. If this variable is significant, then clearly there is an aspect of the "underlying process" which is not being captured by the explanatory variables in the model. [71]

3.4 The results

Do private financial institutions systematically influence the terms of Fund conditional loan arrangements? The private independent variable and bank-friendly condition dependent variable are positively correlated; the simple pair-wise correlation is 0.359 with a *p*-value of 0.0000. This positive and significant relationship lends initial support to the argument that PFIs have influenced the terms of Fund conditional loan arrangements. The multivariate results offer stronger confirmation.

Table 6.2 provides estimations of three logit models that test whether or not organized PFIs increase the likelihood of the inclusion of bank-friendly conditions in Fund loan agreements. [72] There are some severe missing data problems with three of the economic independent variables: reserves-to-imports ratio, the constant GNP per capita, and the constant GNP. [73] As a result, Model 1 omits those independent variables plagued by the highest rates of missingness in order to establish if the predicted relationship between the private influence variable and the presence of bank-friendly conditions exists for the bulk of the sample. In Model 1, the private influence variable is positive and significant, as is the year tracking variable. None of the other variables are significant. The impact of private financier influence on the probability of having a bank-friendly condition is strong. Holding other variables in the model at their means, an increase in the private influence variable from 0 (its minimum) to 1 (its maximum) results in an increase in the likelihood that the Fund conditional loan arrangement will require a bank-friendly condition ($y = 1$) from 7 percent to 25 percent. [74]

Model 2 includes the three economic variables mentioned above, and the number of cases drops to 76. The coefficients on constant GNP per

Table 6.2 Change in the inclusion of bank-friendly conditions (Logit)

Variable	Model 1	Model 2	Model 3	% missing
Private influence	1.57 (0.70)**	5.89 (2.35)**	6.00 (2.14)**	0
US influence	−0.04 (0.09)	−0.47 (0.28)*	−0.06 (0.14)	13
Salary increase	−8.56 (6.36)	−11.46 (8.75)	−8.62 (8.08)	8
Reserves		0.16 (0.24)		53
GNP per capita		−0.0001 (0.0004)		21
Regime	0.03 (0.04)	0.07 (0.08)	0.05 (0.06)	2
Tranche	−0.26 (0.26)	−0.35 (0.38)	−0.24 (0.34)	3
Constant GNP		−0.02 (0.01)	−0.02 (0.01)**	19
Year	0.23 (0.04)**	0.18 (0.08)**	0.21 (0.04)**	0
Constant	−6.15 (1.26)**	−3.31 (3.08)	−4.73 (1.33)**	
N	201	76	154	
Log-likelihood	−55.17	−29.49	−41.01	
Mean L-L	−0.275	−0.388	−0.266	
Pseudo R^2	0.4777	0.4400	0.5405	
Null model (modal outcome)	78.1% (157 when $y=0$)	51.3% (39 when $y=1$)	73.4% (113 when $y=0$)	
PCP	89.6%	86.8%	90.3%	

Notes
** $p<0.05$.
* $p\le0.1$.

capita and the reserves-to-imports ratio are not significant. The coefficient on constant GNP is negative, and nearly meets the significance criteria with a *p*-value of 0.102. In other words, larger countries (measured by GNP) are less likely to be required to meet a bank-friendly condition, holding other variables constant. Most of the coefficients on the other independent variables change in magnitude, but not sign or significance, from Model 1. One exception is the US influence variable, which is significant in this specification. As US influence (measured by US relative financing) increases, the likelihood of a country being required to meet a bank-friendly condition decreases. This negative coefficient conflicts with the predictions of the realist argument, and is consistent with the predictions of the supplementary financier argument that powerful states push for weaker conditionality.[75] When the US exercises its influence on a particular Fund program, the probability of a bank-friendly condition being included decreases. This suggests that the impetus for this expansion of Fund conditionality might not have originated from the US, as realists would contend.

Model 3 omits only the reserves-to-imports ratio and GNP per capita, the two variables that have the highest rates of missingness but are not significantly related to the dependent variable, and retains the constant GNP.[76] Model 3 appears to have the best model fit, with the highest mean log-likelihood (Mean L-L) ratio, percent correctly predicted (PCP) and pseudo R^2. The percent correctly predicted is the percent of predicted outcomes that equal the actual outcomes, when predicted probabilities greater than 0.5 are rounded to 1 and less than or equal to 0.5 are rounded to 0.[77] Model 3's percent correctly predicted (90.3 percent) is usefully compared to the null model's percent correctly predicted (73.4 percent).

The results from Model 3 support the conclusion that PFIs have been successful at influencing the terms of Fund conditional loan arrangements. The influence of PFIs is even more striking in Models 2 and 3 than it was in Model 1. Comparative statics elucidate this. For a hypothetical loan agreement with a hypothetical country where all other independent variables in the model are held at their means, if one increases the value of the private influence variable from 0 (its minimum) to 1 (its maximum), the probability that the Fund loan agreement requires a bank-friendly binding condition increases from 30 percent to 99 percent in Model 2 and from only 5 percent to 96 percent in Model 3.

Model 3 also casts doubt on some of the alternative arguments, which focus on powerful states and bureaucratic actors. Neither the US influence nor the bureaucratic influence variables – measured by US relative financing and the increase in average Fund salaries, respectively – are in the direction predicted by these alternative arguments or are significant. The tranche variable is also not in the predicted direction and also not significant. The other significant variable in Model 3 is the constant GNP, which suggests that larger countries do receive less stringent arrangements from the Fund, and the year tracking variable, which suggests that some other over-time change process is not captured by the model.

In short, these results lend support to the supplementary financier argument, and cast doubt on the realist and bureaucratic alternative arguments. There is a strong relationship between the private influence variable and the bank-friendly dependent variable. The next section clarifies how that relationship works.

4 Mechanisms

The previous section suggests that private financial institutions systematically influence the terms of Fund conditional loan arrangements. It identifies a relationship between variables. This result provides some support for the supplementary financier argument, which predicts that PFIs should be able to influence Fund conditionality agreements when they are organized and therefore can articulate their interests and threaten to withhold financing.

PFIs do not have access to the legitimate channels of influence that other supplementary financiers (creditor states and multilateral organizations) often do. Therefore, it is not obvious how they exercise their influence. In order to clarify how PFIs influence Fund loan agreements, I first discuss the mechanism highlighted in the previous section – how PFIs influence Fund arrangements during private debt restructuring – and one case when a country's debt was restructured and its conditionality program included a bank-friendly condition. Then I discuss one case when a country's private debt was not restructured but a bank-friendly binding condition was included in the country's Fund program.

4.1 Influence during private debt restructuring

When PFIs are organized during debt restructuring, they are able to exercise leverage over the Fund. Of the 29 cases which had their private debt restructured in that or the previous year, 69 percent included a bank-friendly condition as compared to 27 percent of the total cases from the Conditionality Dataset.

This finding seems to contradict received wisdom, which points instead to the Fund's influence over the banks during these meetings. During debt restructuring negotiations, the Fund could threaten to "sabotage any agreement between creditors and the debtor" and thereby "provide residual coordination for the banks ... to provide new credits to the impoverished debtor."[78] The accepted interpretation has thus been that the Fund is often the strongman in debt renegotiations, demanding new credits from and exercising leverage over the banks. The underlying reasoning behind this interpretation has been that default – or no restructuring agreement – would be the most costly option for banks, but presumably not for the Fund. The Fund could therefore more credibly threaten to walk away from an agreement than could the banks.

This assumption is curious. How credible would a Fund threat to "sabotage any agreement between creditors and debtor" really be? The Fund has certainly been able to exercise leverage over some banks, providing a focal point solution to the "bankers' dilemma" and helping them achieve their collective self-interest. But the banks are also often able to exercise leverage, and they are poised to do so when they are organized via creditor committees that can articulate common preferences and a threat to withhold financing from several – often hundreds – of banks. Moreover, the Fund's policy, through much of this period, of not lending to countries with external (including private) payments arrears and at times requiring financing assurances from PFIs gave these PFIs renegotiating debt in arrears a "de facto veto over Fund lending," according to one Executive Board decision.[79] If the banks did not agree to renegotiate outstanding debt or provide financing assurances, the Fund program would either not be approved or would be automatically suspended.[80] Since 1989, the Executive Board has revised its policies on external arrears three times in order to loosen PFI control over the approval of Fund programs during these critical junctures.[81]

4.2 Mexico's 1982 extended fund facility agreement

Meetings between the Fund's management or staff and representatives from commercial banks provided an opportunity for the Fund to communicate how much financing the banks needed to provide given the design of the program, and for the banks to communicate the terms of the Fund program needed for them to commit their supplementary financing. Probably the most famous meeting between the Fund's management and bankers was the November 1982 meeting between the Fund's Managing Director Jacques de Larosière and international bankers preceding Mexico's 1982 Extended Fund Facility (EFF) loan agreement.

Mexico faced an enormous external debt burden, reduced export earnings, pressure on its already-devalued currency, and was on the brink of defaulting on its commercial debts. A complicated rescue package was negotiated. The US and the Bank for International Settlements offered initial bridging loans to allow time to negotiate a Fund agreement. The Fund program itself was designed with two primary ingredients to ensure a balance: a condition that the fiscal deficit be reduced (from about 16.5 percent of GDP in 1982 to 8.5 percent of GDP in 1983) and an assumption of $2 billion in official supplementary financing and $5 billion in private supplementary financing (new medium-term credits) in 1983.[82] The Fund loan itself was $3.75 billion (plus a $220 million unconditional first credit tranche loan). This supplementary financing assumption was key, allowing the Fund and Mexico to agree to (what was thought to be) a politically-feasible demand contraction.

Many other scholars have discussed the dramatic negotiations preceding this Fund loan agreement.[83] Most focus on de Larosière's influence over the commercial banks, or as Kraft put it, the Fund's "imposing a forced loan on major private banks."[84] On November 16, 1982, de Larosière met in New York with a group of representatives from 17 major commercial banks and explained the dilemmas of the Mexican crisis, including Mexico's need for about $8.25 billion of which only $1.3 billion could come from the IMF and $2 billion from other official sources.[85] Famously, he demanded that the banks increase their financing to Mexico by $5 billion (that is, new loans) in 1983, "roll over existing short-term credits," develop an agreement to reschedule Mexico's medium- and long-term debt and "'clean-up' $1½ billion in private sector interest arrears that would be outstanding by the end of 1982," or else the Fund would not agree to its loan program with Mexico.[86] Scholars have focused on the Fund's influence on these banks. As Lipson wrote, "Never before had the Fund intervened so directly in the affairs of commercial lenders."[87]

The banks were in a notoriously weak bargaining position since many US and Japanese banks were heavily exposed in Mexico.[88] However, the Fund also had a lot riding on a resolution of the Mexican crisis, which many thought threatened to destabilize the international financial system.

The credibility of de Larosière's November 16 threat is therefore questionable. The Fund not only pressured the banks to provide fresh financing. It also bent over backwards to accommodate the banks' concerns, as it would in future negotiations. The commercial bankers, particularly the ones on the Advisory Committee, did not want Mexico to default, and therefore were willing to provide financing. However, they wanted the Fund to provide them with more direct assurances that private arrears would be paid down. (This, as you might recall, is one of the bank-friendly conditions.) At the November 16 meeting, the bankers expressed the concern that:

> the authorities could do more to solve the problems of private sector arrears to banks. In some cases, companies that could afford to meet their interest payments were being blocked by regulations prohibiting them from using foreign exchange for that purpose.

De Larosière "was reluctant to put the IMF in the middle of the effort to settle private sector arrears, [but] he promised to speak to the Mexican officials about it."[89]

The initial Fund loan agreement with Mexico had already been drafted and signed by the Mexican authorities on November 10, before de Larosière's meeting with the bankers. The letter of intent did discuss Mexico's current external debt, its projected debt servicing requirements and its need for foreign financing, but its discussion of private sector arrears to PFIs was vague and brief, indicating only that Mexico hoped to get banks to postpone private external credit repayments. Clearly the original agreement reached between the Fund and the Mexican authorities had not included provisions for the reduction of private sector arrears to PFIs that the bankers demanded. Fund staffers returned to Mexico from December 13 to 17, 1982, before the commercial bankers secured the required financing. They discussed additional conditions for the Fund program with the Mexican authorities and addressed the bankers' concerns.

On December 21, after the Fund staff returned from Mexico, the staff sent an update to the Executive Board, notifying them of modifications to the Fund agreement and indicating that the bankers' demands had been met. It stated that "the Mexican Government established special procedures for the settlement of arrears on interest payments due by Mexican private borrowers to commercial banks abroad."[90] These procedures allowed private borrowers to deposit their interest payments in local currency in PFI accounts established with the Bank of Mexico, and then the Bank would begin paying PFIs these interest payments in foreign currency starting January 31, 1983.

Two days after this memo was sent, the banks raised the "critical mass" of the $5 billion in new money and the Executive Board approved

Mexico's EFF agreement. It included ten binding conditions. The seventh stated that Mexico would not borrow from the Fund if a "counterpart deposit scheme, without exchange rate guarantee, [had not been] . . . set up to provide for the identification and orderly reduction of arrears" by December 31, 1983.[91]

Mexico's 1982 EFF is just one example, and an unlikely one given the received wisdom about these negotiations, of PFI influence on the terms of Fund conditional loan arrangements. PFIs were able to insert a binding condition in the Fund agreement that was of particular interest to them. In later years, as banks became more reluctant to reschedule and the Fund maintained the policy of requiring financing assurances, their leverage over the Fund became even stronger.

4.3 Alternative mechanisms of influence and Turkey's 1978 stand-by arrangement

Sixty-seven percent of the cases of Fund agreements with bank-friendly binding conditions in the Conditionality Dataset (41 cases) did not have their private debt restructured in that or the previous year. Either another mechanism of PFI influence is at work, or another factor is contributing to the inclusion of this condition. In this section, I discuss one of these 41 cases in order to clarify why the bank-friendly conditions are included, and if PFIs exercise influence in other ways: Turkey's 1978 stand-by arrangement.

Turkey's 1978 stand-by arrangement is a useful case for a few reasons. First, Turkey is a strategically important country, one in which certain powerful creditor states also took a keen interest at this time. As a result, we might expect powerful states' influence to eclipse PFI influence, particularly for this case. However, Turkey and the Fund were dependent on private sources of supplementary financing for Turkey at this time. By 1978, Turkey already owed private creditors over $6 billion.[92] Turkey received a large (but rapidly decreasing) chunk of its supplementary financing – 24.5 percent of Turkey's public or publicly-guaranteed debt commitments in 1978 – from private sources.[93] As a result, there is also good reason to believe that PFIs might also be successful in exercising leverage, if they could organize themselves. Second, this case is one of the earlier cases (in the group of agreements with bank-friendly binding conditions that did not have their private debt restructured in that or the previous year). One might expect PFI pressure on the Fund to be more overt and transparent in earlier cases, when they may have been communicating their preferences about Fund conditionality agreements for the first time. In later cases, Fund staff may be able to anticipate PFI preferences and thus their influence may be less observable. Finally, this case was selected for practical reasons. The Fund files for this case include documents that helped me recreate the negotiation process, while other case files were relatively bare.

In the wake of the oil crisis of 1973–74, Turkey's current account swung sharply from a surplus of $534 million in 1973 to a deficit of $3.4 billion in 1977. Most of this deficit, about 81 percent, had been financed by foreign borrowing; much of it, about 54 percent in 1977, by short-term credits.[94] In 1977, PFIs began curtailing net lending and Turkey plunged into a debt crisis; arrears began to accumulate, growth dropped sharply from 8.9 to 4.9 percent that year, and inflation climbed from 15.6 to 24.1 percent.[95] Turkey approached the IMF for a loan program in 1977, and a Fund mission visited Ankara in September of that year.[96]

The PFIs were organized in their dealings with Turkey and the Fund, even if they did not successfully renegotiate debt in 1978. In fact one banker was quoted at that time as stating "The requirements of this situation sparked an effort of cooperation I haven't seen before in country lending."[97] By December 1977, representatives from several exposed commercial banks were meeting on Wednesdays in New York to address the mounting Turkish debt crisis.[98] In March and April 1978, eight commercial banks organized as a coordinating committee, representing about 220 PFIs in total, to negotiate new credits and reschedulings of existing short-term debt with Turkey.[99] These negotiations did not bear fruit until the summer of 1979 (when a different stand-by arrangement was in place), but the PFIs were still quite organized during the negotiations of Turkey's 1978 stand-by arrangement.

The PFIs were also directly in contact with the Fund during these negotiations. For instance, executives from Chase Manhattan Bank contacted Lord Alan Whittome, the head of the Fund's European division responsible for constructing Turkey's stand-by arrangement, about the pending Fund program. Whittome kept in contact with official and private supplementary financiers during this negotiation period and considered PFI financing particularly crucial.[100] The Chase executives served as representatives for a number of commercial banks and told Whittome that:

> they have talked to banks in a number of countries and throughout the United States. They are reasonably sure that net new lending totaling $1 billion could be available in four equal tranches over a 12-month period provided a stand-by arrangement with the Fund was concluded and *was thought to be adequate*. (My informant said that he had met some fears that given our experience in Egypt we might now be content to take a too lenient attitude.)[101]

The Chase representatives also indicated through several additional phone calls and contacts that the PFIs "would not come to any agreement with the Turks prior to a *satisfactory* arrangement with the Fund."[102] Thus the PFIs organized themselves and indicated that an "adequate" Fund program was necessary in order to ensure that their financing be forthcoming.

From December 11 until December 20, 1977, a Fund mission returned to Turkey to negotiate the 1978 arrangement. On December 16, in the middle of that mission visit, "a meeting of the major US, German and Swiss banks to determine the banks' attitudes vis-à-vis Turkey" was held.[103] The timing of this meeting suggests that it was planned to assess and influence Turkey's 1978 stand-by arrangement; however, details of the meeting are unknown.

The resulting two-year stand-by arrangement was ultimately approved in April 1978.[104] It required eight binding conditions, including a bank-friendly condition that specified that Turkey must devise a schedule to pay down existing arrears by November 1, 1978 and must not allow any new arrears to "arise."[105] In turn, the commercial banks "made disbursement of any part of the new loan conditional upon a program being prepared for dealing with arrears."[106] However, Turkey had trouble meeting this condition. In September 1978, the Fund waived this and other conditions due to non-compliance.[107] By November 1978, Turkey had not devised a schedule to pay down its arrears and the Fund considered suspending the next installment of its loan, but the Fund staff did not want to provoke a further withdrawal of private financing. An internal memo discussed the:

> need to avoid any impression that there has been any break in our discussions with the Turks in order not to give the commercial banks a heaven sent excuse to delay further their agreement both to the rescheduling of $3 billion of bank debt and the provision of a new loan of (hopefully) around half a billion dollars.[108]

The PFIs continued to drag their feet regarding both reschedulings and new loans, while the Fund and Turkey waited anxiously for the promised infusion of private financing. In December 1978, Whittome continued to try to convince the PFIs to dispense the promised supplementary financing to Turkey.[109] He wrote that the Fund had "been fairly constantly involved in talks with the banks and I have deliberately much exceeded the lines laid down by the Board by encouraging individual banks to think sympathetically." However, Turkey did not establish a schedule for paying down arrears on schedule, as was required by the 1978 stand-by arrangement and demanded by the PFIs, and their financing was not forthcoming.[110] This stand-by was eventually canceled in 1979.

Turkey's 1978 stand-by arrangement provides an example of an agreement that was not correctly predicted by the private influence proxy alone, but does fit the broader logic of the supplementary financier argument. PFIs organized themselves to coordinate their provision of financing to Turkey and also to coordinate their demands on the Fund. The Fund agreement included a bank-friendly binding condition that addressed the PFIs' main concern: arrears. However, this condition was never met, and the private financing never came.

The postscript to this stand-by arrangement is equally interesting. A new Turkish stand-by arrangement was approved in July 1979. This agreement, like Mexico's 1982 EFF, is known for being heavily influenced by big creditor countries (particularly the US and Germany) concerned about Turkey's recent flirtings with the Soviet Union.[111] However, Fund negotiators were also keenly interested in addressing the concerns of the PFIs. Staff-generated instructions to the Fund's April 1979 mission to Turkey stated explicitly:

> It is worth noting also that a satisfactory settlement of the issue of overdue suppliers' credits is regarded as a condition for the disbursement of any new loan by foreign commercial banks. A schedule, with the status of a performance criteria [or binding condition], will need to be established for the gradual elimination of nonguaranteed arrears.[112]

While the negotiating and drafting process of the 1979 arrangement was long and contentious, the final agreement did include a bank-friendly condition addressing the PFIs' concerns and did result in a nearly concurrent pledge of supplementary financing from the PFIs, including a $407 million syndicated loan and rescheduling of $2698 million in debt by August 1979.[113] In 1979, 68.7 percent of Turkey's public or publicly-guaranteed debt commitments were from PFIs.[114]

5 Conclusion

Which actors have influenced the terms of Fund conditional loan arrangements and caused them to change so dramatically? This chapter argues that the design of IMF conditionality programs and the changes in Fund conditionality cannot be explained on the basis of powerful states' or bureaucratic interests alone. Supplementary financiers – which include creditor states, private financial institutions, and multilateral organizations – are able to influence the Fund because their financing is necessary for the success of Fund programs and the Fund's future bargaining leverage with borrowers, two things the Fund holds quite dear. In this chapter, I have focused on one type of supplementary financier – private financial institutions – and their influence on one aspect of Fund conditionality – the inclusion of bank-friendly conditions. The data analysis suggests that PFIs have been able to alter the terms of Fund conditionality arrangements systematically. The mechanisms section discusses two cases – Mexico's 1982 EFF and Turkey's 1978 stand-by arrangement – which demonstrate how PFIs have been able to exercise this leverage over the Fund.

This argument and these findings have important implications both for the specific debate about IMF conditionality and, I believe, for our broader understanding of international organizations. The debates about

Fund conditionality have centered mainly on whether it is right for an international organization to dictate policies to a borrowing country or whether it is effective for a lender of last resort to get its hands dirty with thorny questions of development. This chapter suggests that the International Monetary Fund acts as a facilitator of financing. Many of the conditions actually originate as demands from supplementary financiers, and the borrowers agree to these conditions in order to receive Fund and supplementary financing. Moreover, the Fund's mission is not the narrow resolving of short-term balance-of-payments problems by mustering its own resources and sage advice anymore. Instead, it helps maintain economic stability by encouraging flows of supplementary financing. In this new understanding of Fund activities and Fund purpose, is the expansion of Fund conditionality right or wrong or simply practical?

This chapter also encourages a broader understanding of the influences on international organizations. The International Monetary Fund is influenced by states and by non-state supplementary financiers, like PFIs. And yet their influence is not random at all. There is a clear logic behind these diverse actors' influence on the Fund. Supplementary financiers appeal to the Fund's own interests – in designing successful loan programs and in maintaining their bargaining leverage with borrowers – and therefore we can predict when creditor states or private financial institutions should be able to influence the Fund and also when we should observe the stamp of their influence on Fund conditionality agreements. Many elements of international relations work this way. Multiple actors influence outcomes and yet there is a logic to understanding which actors should influence outcomes at any given time. Our challenge as scholars is to identify why actors exercise influence and then which actors should be able to exercise influence and impact outcomes. Our world does not consist of single types of actors, nor of single causal arrows. Our theories should simplify and clarify, but also recognize and attempt to unpack this diversity.

Acknowledgment

This chapter was originally published as: Gould, Erica R. 2003. "Money Talks: Supplementary Financiers and International Monetary Fund Conditionality," *International Organization*, 57: 551–86. Reprinted with permission of the Cambridge University Press.

Appendix

Comparing conditionality dataset with entire population of arrangements, by region and type

Table 6A.1 Region

	Universe		Sample	
	Total number	Total %	Sample number	Sample %
Africa	269	35	67	27
Asia	115	15	46	18
Europe	41	5	33	13
Middle East	12	2	–	–
Western hemisphere	286	38	92	37
Developed	36	5	11	4

(rounded, add to 99)

Table 6A.2 Arrangement type

	Universe		Sample	
	Total number	Total %	Sample number	Sample %
Stand-by	664	87	217	87
EFF	41	5	14	6
SAF	35	5	7	3
ESAF	19	3	8	3
Missing	–	–	3	1

Source: Conditionality Dataset and International Monetary Fund Annual Reports, 1952–92.

Notes
"Universe" includes all Stand-by, EFF, SAF, and ESAF arrangements between 1952–91; $n = 759$. The sample includes 249 arrangements between 1952–95.

Notes

* Many thanks to Judy Goldstein, Steve Krasner, and Tom Willett for reading multiple versions of this chapter and providing incisive, constructive comments each time. I am also grateful to David Andrews, Timothy Bei, Stephen Haber, Peter Henry, Simon Jackman, Jeff Legro, Lisa Martin, John Owen, Louis Pauly, Herman Schwartz, Jim Vreeland, and two external reviewers for helpful comments on earlier drafts. Errors are entirely my own. Many thanks also to the staff of the International Monetary Fund archives who generously assisted me in my research. I also gratefully acknowledge support from the University of Virginia and the following Stanford University sources: the Graduate School of Business, the Graduate Research Opportunity program, the Admiral and Mrs John E. Lee Fund of the Social Science History Institute, and the O'Bie Schultz Fellowship in International Studies from the Institute for International Studies.

Documents from the International Monetary Fund archives are fully cited in the footnotes.

1 EBM/79/7, January 10, 1979: 8.
2 International Monetary Fund 2001: 110–13.
3 Willett 2001.
4 This chapter concerns some of the changes driven by PFIs and the PFIs' influence on the Fund. Elsewhere I have discussed more comprehensively how the changes in supplementary financing have contributed to changes in Fund conditionality. See Gould 2001.
5 For the first, see Keohane and Nye 1972, 1977. For the second, see Keohane 1984. Scholarship on the influence of transnational actors has exploded since the end of the Cold War, see Risse 2002.
6 Keohane 1984: 91 and chapter 6.
7 von Furstenberg 1987: 122.
8 For the Fund's purposes as laid out in the Articles of Agreement, see Horsefield 1969: 188–9.
9 Cohen 1983; Lipson 1981.
10 Clark 1996: 182 cited in Kapur 2001: 33.
11 Interestingly, the Managing Director has not always been credentialed.
12 International Monetary Fund 2000: 259.
13 These financing gaps are both due to objective limits in the amount the Fund can lend to individual countries and a Fund philosophy that they should not provide all of the financing a country needs to balance its payments. The Fund's financing is supposed to "supplement" financing from private and official lenders, sic Masson and Mussa 1995: 23.
14 Memo from Robicheck, February 17, 1960.
15 Current account data is from World Bank 2000. This is the percentage of cases in the Conditionality Dataset for which current account data was available.
16 The Fund also advises countries to implement supply-side measures.
17 EBS/60/32, March 29, 1960.
18 EBS/58/76, Supplement 2, December 18, 1958. This was a binding condition.
19 Capital inflow is both a stated goal of the Fund program and an internal measure of the success of Fund programs, which further compounds its reliance on supplementary financiers. See Schadler *et al.* 1995.
20 Lipson 1986: 232 makes a similar point.
21 Memo from Del Canto, December 2, 1963: 3.
22 McCauley 1986; Goreux 1989. See Marchesi and Thomas 1999 for a recent formalization of this argument where the Fund program signals country type.
23 For instance Edwards 2000; Bird and Rowlands 1997; Faini *et al.* 1991.
24 Einhorn 1979; Polak 1991: 58; Schadler *et al.* 1995: 14.
25 Much of the empirical literature considers only private catalysis, Rowlands 2001 also includes official.
26 Lipson 1986.
27 Marchesi and Thomas 1999 for the first, Masson and Mussa 1995: 25 for the second.
28 Sachs 1989: 259; Diwan and Rodrik 1992; Dhonte 1997; Crawford 1987.
29 Rodrik 1995 argues that the Fund may be more likely to influence borrowers due to the advantage of being "less politicized."
30 Fearon 1997; Kahler 1992: 111; North and Weingast 1989; Root 1989.
31 Milgrom *et al.* 1989: 808.
32 It is useful to distinguish between the three because each has a different interest in providing financing, and hence different preferences over the design of

Fund conditionality programs. As a result, states, private financial institutions, and multilateral organizations try to influence the Fund's activities in systematically different ways.

33 Wellons 1987.
34 For a concurrent perspective from someone who worked at the Fund, Citibank, and First Boston Corporation, see Friedman 1983: 120–1. Although this profit motive may seem obvious, others have argued that PFIs' loans and investments reflect their country's political interests, rather than a profit motive. See Feis 1974; Krasner 1999; Wellons 1987.
35 Scholars are mainly divided between those who view foreign aid as motivated by humanitarian concerns (e.g., Lumsdaine 1993) and those who view foreign aid as motivated by state political interests (e.g., Schraeder *et al.* 1998). The dominant approaches to understanding states' foreign policy in international relations are interest-based and conceive of those interests as political, and I side with that interpretation. For example, Waltz 1986: 85; Keohane 1984: especially chapters 5–6.
36 Or than other multilateral organizations for that matter. When states get involved in influencing the terms of Fund conditionality arrangements, they also usually push for weaker conditionality than the staff. This is a prediction of the argument and also borne out by evidence. See Finch 1989; De Gregorio *et al.* 1999.
37 See Lipson 1985 on the different incentives of small and large banks.
38 Olson 1971.
39 Lipson 1981; Lipson 1985; see also Aggarwal 1987.
40 North and Weingast 1989: 806.
41 The dataset does not code preconditions, which are required before the program goes into effect. Preconditions are often agreed upon by the Fund staff and borrowing countries and often are a key element of conditionality, but are difficult to code since they are not consistently mentioned in the actual agreement.
42 Letter from Mohammed, April 2, 1983; IMF Interfund Message from Zulu, May 3, 1983; IMF Official Cable from Rahman, July 1, 1983; IMF Official Interfund Message from Zulu, July 1, 1983.
43 Press Release No. 92/27, March 31, 1992; EBS/92/46 Supplement 1, April 13, 1992.
44 In addition, data problems make this an unwieldy metric. Financing data is generally not available before 1970. Post-1970 private financing data continues to be spotty.
45 And, in fact there is basically no relationship between the two. The presence of bank-friendly conditions and the proportion of aggregate net flows that come from private sources (portfolio flows plus debt flows) is only correlated at 0.02.
46 Hardy 1982: 4–5; OECD 1981: tables 12–13; World Bank 1997: 72–8; Frank 1970: 27.
47 Lipson 1985; Aggarwal 1987.
48 Krasner 1993; Mearsheimer 1994–95.
49 Thacker 1999 and this volume; Kapur 2001 offers a more nuanced version of this argument.
50 US AID 1998. This variable equals US military aid plus US economic aid plus the amount pledged from the Exchange Stabilization Fund plus the larger of the quantity of Export–Import Bank loans or loans listed under "Other Loans" in the abovementioned publication, divided by the amount of the Fund loan agreement in that year. All numbers are in current US$ millions,

but are normalized by the division. The source for the Exchange Stabilization Fund is Henning 1999. The ESF and the Fund loan amounts were not necessarily drawn upon or fully drawn down.

51 Kapur 2001: 27 offers an opposing interpretation that the "less the size of foreign aid programs of major shareholders, the less the agency of the IMF" and the more the influence of powerful states over the Fund. He views foreign aid and multilateral financing as substitutes. My argument and evidence suggests they are complements.

52 Moe 1984; Niskanen 1971. Martin 2000 argues that states strategically delegate authority to the bureaucracy when it serves their interests. Finnemore 2000 offers an analysis of the Fund from the sociological organizations school.

53 Quotes from Vaubel 1996: 195; see also Vaubel 1991 and Vaubel 1986.

54 Vaubel 1991; Vaubel 1996. Staff and year are almost perfectly correlated (at 0.99), suggesting this is a flawed proxy.

55 Data from 1952 to 1970 are derived from Vaubel 1991: 223. Data from 1971 and 1995 are presented in Boughton 2001: 1051 and were obtained via correspondence with the author.

56 Sic, Vaubel 1996: 195.

57 Vreeland 2001; Conway 1994.

58 This is language describing the Fund's ESAF, revamped in 1999 to be the Poverty Reduction and Growth Facility.

59 Polak 1994; Guitián 1981: 24.

60 World Bank 2000.

61 For instance, Polak 1994: 8 contends that the Fund's changing "clientele" led "the Fund in the 1970s [to begin] to tailor its credit facilities to the specific needs of developing countries." Kapur 2001 argues that the shift in clientele reduced the risk to creditor countries of pushing for increases in conditionality.

62 See for instance, International Monetary Fund 1999a.

63 World Bank 2000. GNP per capita is constant in 1995 US dollars.

64 Vreeland 2001 is concerned with borrower demand for Fund programs. He argues that governments with more veto players (which also tend to be more democratic by his measure) are more likely to enter Fund programs because they need conditionality to help them overcome domestic opposition and enact their preferred policies. If we accept that Fund conditionality is variable, an extension to this argument is that democracies may demand higher conditionality programs than authoritarian governments with fewer veto players.

65 The Polity IV score for the borrowing countries in the first year of their Fund loan arrangement.

66 SM/66/14, January 24, 1966: 1–2.

67 For instance Meltzer 1998.

68 World Bank 2000.

69 Sic, King 1989: 163.

70 Ibid., 163.

71 I also ran these models using a variable representing an alternative theory of over-time change: the lagged-dependent variable. The result holds, although the magnitude of the coefficients change. The model fit is generally better using the linear time trend than the lagged dependent variable.

72 The data set is not a traditional "rectangular" cross-sectional, time series panel dataset, which includes observations for each cross-sectional unit during each unit of time; therefore, the analysis does not use typical panel data techniques, e.g., Beck and Katz 1995.

73 Efforts to impute the missing data (e.g., via *Amelia*) – the preferred way to deal with missing data problems – have been unsuccessful.

74 Long 1997: 49.
75 Stone 2002 reports similar results that powerful states push for weaker Fund treatment of borrowers.
76 I also tried a specification with only the reserves-to-imports ratio omitted, but Model 3's specification was a better fit by all three metrics.
77 Jackman 2001: 15. The null model predicts that 100 percent of the cases are equal to 1 if more than 50 percent of the cases are equal to 1, and predicts 100 percent of the cases are equal to 0 if less than 50 percent of the cases are equal to 1. As a result, it correctly predicts the largest of the actual distribution of *y*.
78 Lipson 1985: 202.
79 EBM/99/64, June 14, 1999. On the external arrears policy, see De Vries 1976b: 214–15. See also De Vries 1976a: 531–2. This decision was first revised in 1980 (see EBS/80/190 reprinted in Boughton 2001: 531–2), then in 1983 (see EBS/83/58 reprinted in Boughton 2001: 532–3).
80 Boughton 2001: 477 and 498–9. See also Polak 1991: 15.
81 In 1989, the policy was first revised to "tolerate" private, not official, arrears. EBM/89/61, May 23, 1989 reprinted in Boughton 2001: 533–5. Two more formal revisions of the Fund's arrears policy were passed in 1998 and 1999, both intended to reduce PFI influence further. The 1998 decision extended the 1989 policy of sanctioned lending into private arrears to non-bank private creditors (e.g., bondholders) and non-sovereign arrears. The 1999 decision relaxed the criteria when the Fund could lend into private arrears in order again. EBM/99/64, June 14, 1999 reprinted in International Monetary Fund 1999b.
82 Sic, Boughton 2001: 304.
83 Most notably, Kraft 1984; see also Boughton 2001.
84 Kraft 1984: 1. Both Lipson 1986: 229 and Boughton 2001: 299 discuss these negotiations as a turning point in the Fund's relationship with commercial banks.
85 The banks represented at this meeting included Bank of America, Bank of Montreal, Bank of Tokyo, Bankers Trust, Chase, Chemical, Citibank, Deutsche Bank, Lloyds, Manufacturers Hanover, Morgan, Société Générale, and Swiss Bank Corporation. Another meeting on November 21 in London also included Paribas. The Fund's EFF loan was eventually $3.75 billion. Kraft 1984: 48.
86 Sic, Boughton 2001: 307.
87 Lipson 1986: 229.
88 Kraft 1984: 9; Aggarwal 1987: 336–44.
89 Boughton 2001: 308; Aggarwal 1997: 342.
90 EBS/82/208, Supplement 3, December 21, 1982: 2.
91 EBS/82/208, Supplement 4, December 30, 1982.
92 Bleakley 1978: 50; Celâsun and Rodrik 1989: 639.
93 World Bank 2000. This is the total amount of private public or publicly-guaranteed debt commitments in that year, divided by the total amount of public or publicly-guaranteed debt commitments in that year (private or official). This ratio omits private non-guaranteed debt, due to lack of availability.
94 Celâsun and Rodrik 1989: 638.
95 Ibid.: 630–1.
96 Memo from Woodward, September 20, 1977; Briefing Paper, September 1977.
97 Bleakley 1978: 48.
98 Ibid.: 50.
99 Celâsun and Rodrik 1989: 754. Swiss Bank Corporation dropped out of the coordinating committee midway through; thus it ended up being a group of seven banks, see Bleakley 1978: 58.
100 Memo from L.A. Whittome, November 16, 1977.

101 Italics added. Memo from L.A. Whittome, November 9, 1977.
102 Memorandum for the files, November 10, 1977; Memorandum for the files, November 16, 1977 (italics added).
103 Memo from U. Baumgartner, December 9, 1977.
104 EBM/78/65, April 24, 1978.
105 EBS/78/154, Supplement 4, April 25, 1978: 7.
106 Memo from L.A. Whittome, November 20, 1977.
107 EBM/78/151, September 20, 1978.
108 Memo from L.A. Whittome, November 3, 1978; Memo for the files from L.A. Whittome, December 6, 1978.
109 Memo from L.A. Whittome, December 1978.
110 Memo from A.C. Woodward, March 30, 1979: 3. In 1978, PPG debt disbursements from commercial banks only totaled US$305.7 million, whereas in 1979 PPG debt disbursements from commercial banks totaled US$3028.3 million. World Bank 1999.
111 Celâsun and Rodrik 1989: 757; Memo for the files, February 16, 1979; Memo for the files, February 22, 1979.
112 Turkey – Staff Visit Under Stand-by Arrangement, April 20, 1979: 8.
113 Celâsun and Rodrik 1989: 755, n. 1.
114 World Bank 2000.

References

Aggarwal, Vinod K. 1987. *International Debt Threat: Bargaining Among Creditors and Debtors in the 1980s*. Berkeley: Institute for International Studies, University of California.

Beck, Nathaniel and Jonathan N. Katz. 1995. Nuisance vs. Substance: Specifying and Estimating Time-Series-Cross-Sectional Models. *Political Analysis* 6: 1–36.

Bird, Graham and Dane Rowlands. 1997. The Catalytic Effect of Lending by the International Financial Institutions. *The World Economy* 20 (7): 967–91.

Bleakley, Fred T. 1978. The Rush to Rescue Turkey. *Institutional Investor* (International Edition) November: 47–64.

Boughton, James. 2001. *Silent Revolution: The International Monetary Fund, 1979–1989*. Washington, DC: International Monetary Fund.

Celâsun, Merih and Dani Rodrik. 1989. Debt, Adjustment, and Growth: Turkey. In *Developing Country Debt and Economic Performance*, Vol. III, edited by Jeffrey D. Sachs, pp. 615–808. Chicago: University of Chicago Press.

Clark, Ian D. 1996. Inside the IMF: Comparisons with Policy-Making Organizations in Canadian Governments. *Canadian Public Administration* 39 (2): 157–91.

Cohen, Benjamin J. 1983. Balance of Payments Financing: Evolution of a Regime. In *International Regimes*, edited by Stephen D. Krasner, pp. 315–36. Ithaca: Cornell University Press.

Conway, Patrick. 1994. IMF Lending Programs: Participation and Impact. *Journal of Development Economics* 45: 365–91.

Crawford, Vincent P. 1987. *International Lending, Long-Term Credit Relationships, and Dynamic Contract Theory*. Essays in International Finance, No. 59, March. Princeton: International Finance Section, Dept. of Economics, Princeton University.

De Gregorio, Jose, Barry Eichengreen, Takatoshi Ito, and Charles Wyplosz. 1999. *An Independent and Accountable IMF*. Geneva Reports on the World Economy No. 1. London: Centre for Economic Policy Research.

De Vries, Margaret Garritsen. 1976a. *The International Monetary Fund 1966–1971: The System Under Stress.* Vol. I: *Narrative.* Washington, DC: International Monetary Fund.

De Vries, Margaret Garritsen. 1976b. *The International Monetary Fund 1966–1971: The System Under Stress.* Vol. II: *Documents.* Washington, DC: International Monetary Fund.

Dhonte, Pierre. 1997. Conditionality as an Instrument of Borrower Credibility. *IMG Paper on Policy Analysis and Assessment* (February). Available from http://www.imf.org/external/pubs/cat/longres.cfm?sk=2109.0. Accessed 12 April 2002.

Diwan, Ishac and Dani Rodrik. 1992. *External Debt, Adjustment, and Burden Sharing: A Unified Framework.* Essays in International Finance, No. 73, November. Princeton: International Finance Section, Dept. of Economics, Princeton University.

Edwards, Martin S. 2000. Reevaluating the "Catalytic" Effect of IMF Programs. *Columbia International Affairs Online.* Available from http://www.ciaonet.org/wps/edm01/edm01.html. Accessed 12 April 2002.

Einhorn, Jessica P. 1979. Cooperation Between Public and Private Lenders to the Third World. *The World Economy* 2 (May): 229–41.

Faini, Riccardo, Jaime de Melo, Abdel Senhadji-Semlali, and Julie Stanton. 1991. Macro Performance Under Adjustment Lending. In *Restructuring Economies in Distress*, edited by Vinod Thomas, Ajay Chibber, Mansoor Dailami, and Jaime de Melo, pp. 222–42. New York: Oxford University Press.

Fearon, James D. 1997. Tying Hands Versus Sinking Costs. *Journal of Conflict Resolution* 41 (1): 68–90.

Feis, Herbert. 1974. *Europe The World's Banker 1870–1914: An Account of European Foreign Investment and the Connection of World Finance with Diplomacy Before the War.* Clifton: Augustus M. Kelley Publishers.

Finch, C. David. 1989. *The IMF: The Record and Prospect.* Essays in International Finance No. 175. Princeton: Princeton University Press.

Finnemore, Martha. 2000. Expertise and Bureaucratic Power at the International Monetary Fund. Unpublished manuscript, George Washington University, Washington, DC.

Frank, Charles R. Jr. 1970. *Debt and Terms of Aid.* Washington, DC: Overseas Development Council.

Friedman, Irving S. 1983. Private Bank Conditionality: Comparison with the IMF and the World Bank. In *IMF Conditionality*, edited by John Williamson, pp. 109–24. Washington, DC: Institute for International Economics.

Goreux, Louis M. 1989. The Fund and the Low-Income Countries. In *The International Monetary Fund in a Multipolar World: Pulling Together*, edited by Catherine Gwin, Richard E. Feinberg and contributors, pp. 141–64. New Brunswick: Transaction Books.

Gould, Erica R. 2001. Financiers as Fund Principals: An Alternative Explanation of Changes in the Activities of the International Monetary Fund. PhD diss., Stanford University.

Guitián, Manuel. 1981. *Fund Conditionality: Evolution of Principles and Practices.* Washington, DC: International Monetary Fund.

Hardy, Chandra S. 1982. *Rescheduling Developing-Country Debts, 1956–1981: Lessons and Recommendations.* Washington, DC: Overseas Development Council.

Henning, C. Randall. 1999. *The Exchange Stabilization Fund: Slush Money or War Chest?* Washington, DC: Institute for International Economics.

Horsefield, J. Keith (ed.). 1969. *The International Monetary Fund, 1945–65*. Vol. III. Washington, DC: International Monetary Fund.

International Monetary Fund. 1999a. IMF Concessional Financing Through ESAF. 5 September. http://www.imf.org/external/np/exr/facts/esaf.htm. Accessed on 19 July 2002.

International Monetary Fund. 1999b. IMF Policy on Lending into Arrears to Private Creditors. 14 June. http://www.imf.org/external/pub/ft/privcred. Accessed on 17 December 2002.

International Monetary Fund. 2000. Streamlining Structural Conditionality. 18 September. Available from http//www.imf.org/external/np/pdr/cond/2001/eng/091800.pdf. Accessed on 12 April 2002.

International Monetary Fund. 2001. *Annual Report of the Executive Board for the Financial Year Ended April 30, 2001*. Washington, DC: International Monetary Fund.

Jackman, Simon. 2001. Binary Outcomes and Proportions. Unpublished manuscript, Stanford University, Stanford.

Kahler, Miles. 1992. External Influence, Conditionality and the Politics of Adjustment. In *The Politics of Economic Adjustment*, edited by Stephan Haggard and Robert R. Kaufman. Princeton: Princeton University Press.

Kapur, Devesh. 2001. Risk and Reward: Agency, Contracts, and the Expansion of IMF Conditionality. Paper presented at the 104th Annual Meeting of the American Political Science Association, August, San Francisco.

Keohane, Robert O. 1984. *After Hegemony: Cooperation and Discord in the World Political Economy*. Princeton: Princeton University Press.

Keohane, Robert O. and Joseph Nye. 1972. Transnational Relations and World Politics: An Introduction. In *Transnational Relations and World Politics*, edited by Robert O. Keohane and Joseph S. Nye, Jr, pp. ix–xxix. Cambridge: Harvard University Press.

Keohane, Robert O. and Joseph Nye. 1977. *Power and Interdependence: World Politics in Transition*. Boston: Little, Brown.

King, Gary. 1989. *Unifying Political Methodology: The Likelihood Theory of Statistical Inference*. New York: Cambridge University Press.

Kraft, Joseph. 1984. *The Mexican Rescue*. New York: Group of Thirty.

Krasner, Stephen D. 1993. Global Communications and National Power: Life on the Pareto Frontier. In *Neorealism and Neoliberalism: The Contemporary Debate*, edited by David A. Baldwin, pp. 234–49. New York: Columbia University Press.

Krasner, Stephen D. 1999. *Sovereignty: Organized Hypocrisy*. Princeton: Princeton University Press.

Lipson, Charles. 1981. The International Organization of Third World Debt. *International Organization* 35 (4): 603–31.

Lipson, Charles. 1985. Bankers' Dilemmas: Private Cooperation in Rescheduling Sovereign Debts. *World Politics* 38 (1): 200–25.

Lipson, Charles. 1986. International Debt and International Institutions. In *The Politics of International Debt*, edited by Miles Kahler, pp. 219–43. Ithaca: Cornell University Press.

Long, J. Scott. 1997. *Regression Models for Categorical and Limited Dependent Variables*. Thousand Oaks: Sage.

Lumsdaine, David Halloran. 1993. *Moral Vision in International Politics: The Foreign Aid Regime, 1949–89*. Princeton: Princeton University Press.

Marchesi, Silvia and Jonathan P. Thomas. 1999. IMF Conditionality as a Screening Device. *The Economic Journal* 109 (454) (March): 111–25.

Marshall, Monty G. and Keith Jaggers. 2000. *Polity IV Project: Political Regime Characteristics and Transitions, 1800–1999. Polity IV Dataset Version 2000 <p4v2000>*.

Martin, Lisa L. 2000. Agency and Delegation in IMF Conditionality. Unpublished manuscript, Harvard University, Cambridge.

Masson, Paul R. and Michael Mussa. 1995. *The Role of the IMF: Financing and Its Internations with Adjustment and Surveillance*. Washington, DC: International Monetary Fund.

McCauley, Robert N. 1986. IMF: Managed Lending. In *World Debt Crisis: International Lending on Trial*, edited by Michael P. Claudon, pp. 123–45. Cambridge: Ballinger Publishing Co.

Mearsheimer, John J. 1994. The False Promise of International Institutions. *International Security* 19 (3): 5–49.

Meltzer, Allan H. 1998. Asian Problems and the IMF. *CATO Journal* 17 (3).

Milgrom, Paul R., Douglass C. North, and Barry R. Weingast. 1990. The Role of Institutions in the Revival of Trade: The Law Merchant, Private Judges, and the Champagne Fairs. *Economics and Politics* 2 (1): 1–26.

Moe, Terry M. 1984. The New Economics of Organization. *American Journal of Political Science* 28 (4): 739–77.

Niskanen, William A. 1971. *Bureaucracy and Representative Government*. Chicago: Rand McNally.

North, Douglass and Barry R. Weingast. 1989. Constitutions and Credible Commitments: The Evolution of the Institutions of Public Choice in 17th Century England. *Journal of Economic History* 49 (4): 803–32.

Olson, Mancur. 1971. *The Logic of Collective Action: Public Goods and The Theory of Groups*. Cambridge: Harvard University Press.

Organization for Economic Cooperation and Development. 1981. *External Debt of Developing Countries*. (October) Paris: OECD.

Polak, Jacques J. 1991. *The Changing Nature of IMF Conditionality*. Essays in International Finance, No. 184, September. Princeton: International Finance Section, Dept. of Economics, Princeton University.

Polak, Jacques J. 1994. *The World Bank and the IMF: A Changing Relationship*. Washington, DC: The Brookings Institution.

Risse, Thomas. 2002. Transnational Actors and World Politics. In *Handbook of International Relations*, edited by Walter Carlsnaes, Thomas Risse, and Beth A. Simmons, pp. 255–74. London: Sage Publications.

Rodrik, Dani. 1995. Why is There Multilateral Lending? Working Paper 5160. Cambridge: National Bureau of Economic Research.

Root, Hilton L. 1989. Tying the King's Hands: Credible Commitments and Royal Fiscal Policy During the Old Regime. *Rationality and Society* 1 (2): 240–58.

Rowlands, Dane. 2001. The Response of Other Lenders to the IMF. *Review of International Economics* 9 (3): 531–46

Sachs, Jeffrey D. 1989. Conditionality, Debt Relief, and the Developing Country Debt Crisis. In *Developing Country Debt and Economic Performance*. Vol. I, edited by Jeffrey D. Sachs, pp. 255–95. Chicago: University of Chicago Press.

Schadler, Susan, Adam Bennett, Maria Carkovic, Louis Dicks-Mireaux, Mauro Mecagni, James H.J. Morsink, and Miguel Savastano. 1995. *IMF Conditionality:*

Experience Under Stand-By and Extended Arrangements. Part I: Key Issues and Findings. Washington, DC: International Monetary Fund.

Schraeder, Peter J., Steven W. Hook, and Bruce Taylor. 1998. Clarifying the Foreign Aid Puzzle: A Comparison of American, Japanese, French and Swedish Aid Flows. *World Politics* 50 (2): 294–323.

Stone, Randall W. 2002. *Lending Credibility: The International Monetary Fund and the Post-Communist Transition.* Princeton: Princeton University Press.

Thacker, Strom C. 1999. The High Politics of IMF Lending. *World Politics* 52 (1): 38–75.

United States Agency for International Development (US AID). 1998. *U.S. Overseas Loans and Grants and Assistance from International Organizations.* Washington, DC: Office of Planning and Budgeting, Bureau for Program Policy and Co-ordination, Agency for International Development.

Vaubel, Roland. 1986. A Public Choice Approach to International Organization. *Public Choice* 51 (1): 39–57.

Vaubel, Roland. 1991. The Political Economy of the International Monetary Fund: A Public Choice Analysis. In *The Political Economy of International Organizations. A Public Choice Approach,* edited by Roland Vaubel and Thomas D. Willett, pp. 204–44. Boulder: Westview Press.

Vaubel, Roland. 1996. Bureaucracy at the IMF and the World Bank. *The World Economy* 19 (2): 195–210.

von Furstenberg, George. 1987. The IMF as Market-Maker for Official Business Between Nations. In *The Political Morality of the IMF,* edited by Robert J. Meyers, pp. 111–26. New Brunswick: Transaction Books.

Vreeland, James Raymond. 2001. Institutional Determinants of IMF Agreements. Paper presented at the 104th Annual Meeting of the American Political Science Association, August, San Francisco.

Waltz, Kenneth N. 1986. Political Structures. In *Neorealism and Its Critics,* edited by Robert O. Keohane, pp. 70–97. New York: Columbia University Press.

Wellons, Philip A. 1987. *Passing the Buck: Banks, Governments and Third World Debt.* Boston: Harvard Business School Press.

Willett, Thomas D. 2001. Understanding the IMF Debate. *The Independent Review* 5 (4): 593–610.

World Bank. 1997. *Global Development Finance.* Vol. I. Washington, DC: World Bank.

World Bank. 1999. *Global Development Finance* CD-ROM. Washington, DC: World Bank.

World Bank. 2000. *World Development Indicators* CD-ROM. Washington, DC: World Bank.

7 The World Bank and the reconstruction of the 'social safety net' in Russia and eastern Europe

Paul Mosley

1 Introduction

Since its inception the World Bank has been gradually expanding its functions, with a particular kink in the curve during the age of structural adjustment in the 1980s. In that decade, Moises Naim, a Colombian Executive Director of the Bank, compiled the following list of alternative conceptions of the Bank which were current at the time:

1 'The Bank as a Bank': the function in the original Articles of Agreement, of lending at a profit for developmental purposes, usually the provision of infrastructure.
2 'The Bank as a Fund': the provision of concessional lending directed at the relief of poverty, which came in with the International Development Association (IDA) in the 1960s and has enjoyed surges of popularity particularly under McNamara in the 1970s and again in the new poverty strategies from the 1990s until the present time.
3 'The Knowledge Bank': the provision and dissemination of knowledge and skills relevant to development, most particularly policy-making and institution-building skills as an adjunct to lending.
4 'The Bank as instrument of global governance': the provision of global public goods, from environmental protection to agricultural research to the Multilateral Investment Guarantee Authority.

Since that time, there has been intense debate, particularly during the period surrounding the Bank and Fund's half-century in 1995, about which of these and other possible functions the Bank should specialise in. The debate, of course, is political rather than simply intellectual: the expansion of the Bank's functions into the provision of 'knowledge' concerning macro-policy, tariff policy and public enterprise reform involved it in a whole series of clashes with the Fund during the era of structural adjustment (Mosley *et al.* 1995: chapter 2), which calmed down for a time but then reignited during the period of the East Asian crisis (Stiglitz 2003: *passim* but especially chapters 1, 5 and 7).

In this chapter we consider the implications for the Bank's role in of the Russian and east European crisis of the 1990s. The dimensions of the crisis are familiar but are brought up to date in Table 7.1: during the period from 1989 to 1994, under the impetus of stabilisation and severe redundancies across the whole of state-owned industry, all measures of poverty increased, and increased very sharply in every east European country except Hungary and the Czech Republic. In Russia, headcount poverty increased by a factor of two and a half between these years and the Gini coefficient of inequality increased from one of the lowest levels in the world to a level exceeding that of the United States (Stone 2002; 64–5). The more long-term indicators worsened also: out of 29 welfare indicators recorded by UNICEF, only two (maternal mortality and the 1–4 death rate) showed an improvement between 1989 and 1994. The crisis 'entailed a steep rise in overall mortality, which particularly affected adult men but also adolescents, the elderly and in some cases even infants'. As a result, life expectancy at birth, the most comprehensive health indicator, deteriorated in seven countries since the onset of the transition. Health and education conditions also showed a high frequency of deteriorations, as shown by a massive surge in new tuberculosis and low birth weight cases, which clearly confirmed an increase in poverty. Finally, there is evidence that primary and secondary education rates moved downward in a majority of countries examined, and that 'with rising youth unemployment, skyrocketing costs of securing a living place and overall uncertainty about the future, marriage, remarriage and birth rates plummeted in all countries' (Cornia 1994b: 602–3).

This predicament clearly went far beyond everything which had been entailed by the phrase 'social costs of adjustment' in other countries, and offered an enormous challenge to the Bank, particularly in terms of two of its 'new' roles listed above. In terms of the fourth role mentioned by Naim – the geo-political role – there was obviously the need to try and create a stable post-Cold War international economic order. And in terms of the second – 'the Bank as a fund' – there was the equally transparent and related need to reverse the trend towards increasing poverty. The Bank made it quite clear that it intended to take up the challenge: 'the major thrust of our portfolio (in the transitional countries) consists of social-sector lending. That is where it has to be to offset the terrible increases in poverty of the last few years' (James Wolfensohn, World Bank President, speech at House of Commons, London, 19 April 1997).

In this chapter, we consider the implementation of this commitment, and the implications which it has had for the Bank's role. The following section considers the evolution of the Bank's lending operations in Russia and eastern Europe, and section 3 incorporates the findings of this section into an experimental 'poverty function' designed to estimate the poverty impact of financial support provided by the Bank and other donors. The final section examines the policy implications.

Table 7.1 Evolution of poverty in Russia and eastern Europe, 1989–2002

	Russia			Poland			Hungary			Romania			The Slovak Republic		
	Headcount (national poverty line)	'Extreme' poverty ($2/day)	Gini coefficient	Headcount (national poverty line)	'Extreme' poverty ($2/day)	Gini coefficient	Headcount (national poverty line)	'Extreme' poverty ($2/day)	Gini coefficient	Headcount (national poverty line)	'Extreme' poverty ($2/day)	Gini coefficient	Headcount (national poverty line)	'Extreme' poverty ($2/day)	Gini coefficient
1980	11.3[a]		27.6[a]												
1989	10.1	14.3	28.4	22.9[c]	5.1[c]		12.3[c]	5.1[c]		29.9[c]	7.7[c]		5.7[c]	0.2[c]	
1990	11.4		26.5	38.3	11.3					17.6	2.4		6.2	0.2	
1991	23.1		28.7	33.9	8.1		13.9	1.5		25.1	6.8		24.9	2.4	19.5
1992	24.7		34.6	35.7	10.4		14.5			44.3	15.2		30.3	2.9	
1993			40.9	23.8	10.5								34.5		
1994	26.0	13.3	38.1												
1995	21.0		37.5							21.5	27.5	28.2		2.4	25.8
1996						32.9			30.8						
1997							17.3								
1998	55.0[b]	25.1	48.7		2.0	31.6		1.7	24.4			28.2			
1999		18.8	45.6												
2000	33.0[b]										5.2	30.3			
2001															

Sources: Wherever possible from World Bank, *World Development Indicators*, 2003b edition, with interpolations from: a, Klugman and Braithwaite (1998); b, World Bank OED (2003); c, Cornia (1994a).

2 The composition and execution of World Bank programmes in Russia and eastern Europe

2.1 The overall picture

In the early 1990s, the World Bank found itself with a unique opportunity to entrench its influence across a huge new kingdom in which it had historically been weakly represented, and was determined not to squander the build-up of that influence through internecine wrangling with the IMF of a kind which had done damage in Latin America and Africa. Accordingly, it graciously allowed the Fund to lead on macro-economic policy, and as a consequence allowed itself to be sucked into the slipstream of the Fund's large stand-bys to Russia, granting two large structural adjustment loans (SALs) of its own in 1993 and 1996. Following the precedent of previous large SALs in Brazil and Mexico, these loans had minimal conditionality attached (World Bank 2003a).

But within all of this, as illustrated by Table 7.1, the status of the social sectors was minor and receded further when, as Stone puts it, 'the Clinton administration completed the transition from treating Russia as a potential superpower to treating Russia as a regional power' (2002: 158). For as long as it could be reasonably represented to the world that keeping the Russian and Ukrainian nuclear missiles in safe hands depended on something radical being done about poverty in eastern Europe – broadly from 1992 to 1996 – there was certainly an impetus for extraordinary action within the social sectors, although, as Table 7.2b shows, even that took time to materialise, reaching its peak in 2000. But thereafter, the game was lost: the transitional region ceased to be perceived as a special case, even though its sufferings continued on a scale to warrant it being treated as one. Except in 2000, percentage allocations to social sectors within the eastern European region have at all times been lower than within the Bank's global budget.

If, therefore, geo-politics were a major factor pushing the Bank away from its proclaimed poverty focus in eastern Europe, other factors were also important. A fundamental one, particularly in Russia, was the failure of revenue policy at the macro-economic level. The same botched tax reforms which failed to achieve a stabilisation of the Russian budget, and hence macro-economy, in 1998 (World Bank 2003a; Stone 2002: 116) also failed to deliver the revenue needed to finance an expansion of social protection spending. A second, certainly, was awareness that instruments other than social protection were available to reduce poverty. But maybe the most crucial was the fact that not only Russia but nearly the whole of eastern Europe lacked the kind of politics which other parts of the world had to put vital impetus behind the Bank's poverty reduction programmes.

The model of Figure 7.1 may help explain the process of prioritisation within eastern European governments which has been described. We assume that governments associate reform with a long-term economic

Table 7.2(a) World Bank commitments to Russia ($ millions)

	1992–95	1996	1997	1998	1999	2000	2001	Cancelled	Total
Rehabilitation loans	1200	0	0	0	0	0	0	0	1200
SALs	0	500	1400	1500	0			1100	3900
Oil, gas and energy	1180	528	40				85	352	981
Social sectors	110	470	137	29	0	0	130	120	755
Private sector development/ financial sector development/ infrastructure	1519	763	216	0	400	0	182	1069	2012
Agriculture/environment	529	80	0	0	0	60	226	118	777
Public sector management	70	21	58	0	30	30	0	2	195
% to social sectors	15.1	47.9	6.6	13.4	0	0	21.4		9.6
Total	729	981	2086	2172	657	606	605		7836

Source: World Bank 2003b: table 2.1, p. 9.

Table 7.2(b) Social sector commitments to Russia, eastern Europe and comparators (percentage of total portfolio)

	1993–97 annual average	1998–99 annual average	2000	2001	2002
Eastern Europe and Central Asia:					
Social sector lending[a] $million	290.0	702.5	573.7	446.3	552.7
Other sector lending[b] $million	3980.0	4553.0	2469.0	2247.0	4971.0
Total	4270.2	5255.1	3042.2	2693.1	5523.6
Social sectors % of total	6.7	13.3	18.8	16.5	10.0
World:					
Social sector lending $million	2262.0	3974.4	2695.0	3120.0	2469.9
Total	21510.5	28794.8	15276.2	17250.6	19519.4
Social sectors % of total	10.5	13.8	17.6	18.1	12.6

Source: World Bank 2002: tables 2.2, p. 30 and table 5.4, p. 102.

Notes
a 'Social protection and risk management' plus 'social development, gender and inclusion'.
b Economic management, public sector governance, rule of law, financial and private sector development, trade and integration, human development, urban development, rural development, environmental and natural resource management.

gain (measured on the vertical axis) and a short-term risk of political loss; both of them increase with the speed and extent of reform. Collectively, the government has to decide where to position itself on the trade-off between the two (the curved line on Figure 7.1): to determine what position on the eventual trade-off will optimise its welfare, taking note of the likely future course of negotiations with any international financial institution or group of such institutions. Above all it wants to avoid being blown across the 'catastrophe line' – a combination of high risk of political defeat and incomplete reform which it sees as being lethal for its chances of holding on to power. Negative shocks such as natural disasters and market collapse (e.g. for Russia a collapse in the oil price, for Bulgaria a collapse in the wine market, etc.) will push the trade-off south-east, and the question is what will blow it in the opposite direction. We would argue that the following may be treated a priori as assets which will raise the 'productivity' of reform and thus raise the 'production function' by which the risk-taking involved in reform is turned into a political dividend:

1 *A reduction in corruption levels* – mentioned ubiquitously by small businesses, most particularly in Russia and eastern Europe, as a key determinant of the cost of doing business, and thence of intentions to invest. Its importance in the present context is that it increases the economic, and hence the political, payoff to liberalisation measures (World Bank 1997).

2 *An increase in social capital* – measured here by the *World Values Survey* measure of trust. Social capital has consistently shown significant impacts on growth, and thence on poverty (Whiteley 2000; Knack and

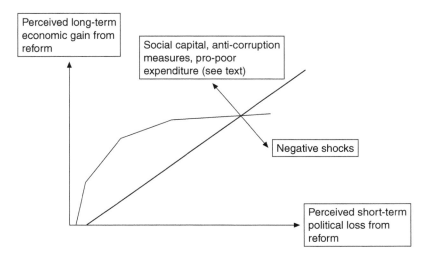

Figure 7.1 Reform decisions as seen by government: a stylised view.

Keefer 1997); more specifically, social sector programmes explicitly seek to build linkages within and between communities, and between communities and levels of government. The gravity of the livelihood shocks inflicted by *perestroika* added particular value to whatever networks individuals were able to retain, and the lower strata of transitional societies have been described by Kennedy *et al.* (1998: 2039) as an environment in which 'those who have access to social capital get ahead; those who do not get sick and die'. This does not imply, of course, that social capital can be constructed like a building, and many programmes which have tried to operationalise this kind of metaphor have fallen flat on their faces; nonetheless, to the extent that survey data give evidence of trust having increased, this again will reduce transaction costs, including those of policy makers. Intra-community equality is strongly associated with social capital.

3   *An increase in 'pro-poor' expenditure* – of which social sector expenditure is a component. Any type of public expenditure which raises the poverty elasticity of growth – either by increasing labour-intensity (World Bank 1990), or by providing services consumed by poor people, or through any other channel, counts as pro-poor expenditure. The empirical characteristics of pro-poor expenditure are discussed in the Appendix. Pro-poor expenditure, in principle, has the ability to deliver the political support of a broad base of low-income people by visibly compensating them, in kind, for the costs of reform. In practice, we have been able to show that the use of this instrument has delivered support for stabilisation programmes across a range of developing and transitional countries (Mosley 2004); we speculate here, and wish to test, that it may also be able to deliver support for programmes of structural reform as well.

These assets may be seen as components of a portfolio which is juggled in accordance with a 'survival decision rule', much as resource-constrained households also have to manage such assets as may contribute to their own survival. But the manner in which this portfolio of assets is juggled in order to move towards 'security' – i.e. leftwards on the diagram – and indeed, the extent to which they are seen as assets at all varies according to states' initial conditions, the personalities of their leadership elite and the strategies which they see as being feasible.[1]

2.2 The social protection programmes

By contrast with poorer developing economies, most transitional economies had a range of social benefits in position in 1990 – old-age pensions, employment-related benefits, and subsidised entitlements to particular services such as housing and utilities. These benefits were embedded in the process of central planning, and few of them were related to levels of individual income or wealth. As the World Bank has become more involved in the process of lending to transitional countries, it has sought to bring about reform in the social protection system through a series of financial and advisory operations, which are listed for our sample countries in Table 7.3.

From the table we may note, first of all, the differentiated way in which social protection schemes evolved after the transition. Although there was a worrying tendency for the real value of benefits, and child benefits in particular, to be seriously eroded by general fiscal weakness, this does not occur everywhere, and in the Slovak Republic and Poland there was a significant increase in their real value. In the eastern European countries, but much less in Russia and central Asia, there was a tendency for subsidies on the consumption of housing and utilities to be converted into cash benefits. In some but not all transitional countries, specific unemployment benefits were introduced.

The main thrust of the World Bank's approach may be described as:

1   to get rid of the distortions in the price system associated with heavily subsidised housing and utilities;
2   to persuade client countries to move away from universalism towards a means-tested system in which benefits are provided according to need;
3   to complement existing systems of benefit provision for those in need with systems which look forward and provide protection for those who are vulnerable to being in need, as per the approach of the *2000 World Development Report* and;
4   in a few cases, to provide supplementary financing for the social security system, in particular by means of *social investment funds* – financial intermediaries which channel resources for the provision of social, health or educational services to private and public organisations and community groups.

As shown by Table 7.3, the Bank did not provide financial assistance everywhere, and in a number of places, such as Poland, functioned purely as a 'Knowledge Bank'. Where financial assistance was provided, as with the Bank's social protection adjustment operations in Russia, it often found itself frustrated by an inability to get the government to accept co-ownership of the objectives it had announced:

The (1992) Employment Services and Social Protection Loan was a technical assistance loan intended to help deal with the anticipated loss of jobs caused by enterprise restructuring. It also was intended to help develop plans for reforming the pension system and other aspects of the social safety net, but the government was not prepared to address these areas at a time when it had more pressing concerns, such as stabilisation and market policy reforms ... Insufficient

Table 7.3 World Bank support for social protection in selected transitional countries

	Economic performance: 1995 per capita GDP (1989 = 100)[b]	Nature of WB intervention[c]	Family allowances as % of GDP 2000 (1989 in brackets)[d]	Evolution: selectivity[e]
Russia	60	1993: Employment Services and Social Protection Loan 1997: Social Protection Adjustment and Implementation Loans	0.7[a] (0.5)	
Poland	98	Poverty assessments only. No financial operations in this sector	3.0[a] (2.0)	35% of households receiving benefits were non-poor in 1998[e]
Hungary				87% of households receiving benefits were non-poor in 1998[e]
Romania	82	1995: Employment services and Social Protection Loan 1996: Community Social Infrastructure Loan 1998: Child Welfare Reform Loan	0.7 (2.9)	
The Slovak Republic	87	1999: Social Benefits Reform Loan	5.0 (2.8)	
Ukraine	42	1997: Social Protection Supplementation Loan 2001: Social Sector Adjustment Loan	(0.1)	
Bulgaria	76			

Notes and sources
a Provisional figure.
b World Bank 2003b.
c World Bank Social Protection Paper by Andrews and Ringold (1999), annex 2.
d Andrews and Ringold 1999: table 4.1, p. 24, updated to 2001 with data from World Bank 2003a.
e Braithwaite *et al.* 1998.

attention was given to social assistance targeting, even as poverty was increasing.

(World Bank 2003a: 23)

Indeed, it was only in Poland and the Czech Republic that the Bank was able to convince the government to implement systems for the effective targeting of welfare benefits, along the lines now widely adopted in industrialised countries (Gough *et al.* 1996). Elsewhere it was frustrated either by lack of government commitment, by lack of government capacity or, as in Hungary, by neither of the above but simply a serene commitment to whatever could be preserved of a universalistic welfare state in defiance of the Bank's homilies in favour of targeting. In areas of social protection specifically emphasised as priorities by the Bank, such as child allowances and child protection, expenditures nonetheless declined in some countries (Table 7.3 above). But within the limits to which it had set itself, some important successes were achieved by the Bank, perhaps especially in the smaller countries – in Romania through a series of social protection operations, in Albania through the Social Investment Fund and in Bulgaria through both.[2] But even in Russia, an experimental spirit has emerged in the design of social protection schemes through the process of decentralisation, for which the Bank modestly disclaims any credit in its OED report cited above, but which may nonetheless be traceable in however indirect a way to its intellectual influence.[3]

There is one limitation of the Bank's social protection strategies in Russia and eastern Europe to which specific attention must be drawn. This is the absence of any integration between social protection and policies to develop financial institutions – indeed, the latter are not even mentioned in the Bank's checklist of social protection options for the region (see Appendix) even though they have become increasingly fundamental for the relief of poverty in developing countries, in the Bank's strategies for those countries and even for community development in industrialised countries such as the UK and the US (United Kingdom 1999; Mosley and Steel 2002). Policy, of course, has increasingly become focused on the individual coping strategies and informal networks developed by the poor – in Russia characterised as an 'hourglass society' in which individuals have a high degree of trust in their immediate social networks of friends, relatives and other face-to-face groups, and a high degree of distrust in the state, even the reformed state. In this climate, far more people rely on informal social capital than on formal institutions of state to deal with their problems, in particular as a source of social protection.[4] It is into these informal networks that microfinance institutions have lent: globally, but maybe with particular success in countries such as Bolivia and Bangladesh, but this also applies to Russia, with damaged state banking sectors and a vibrant informal economy. As they have done so, they have in many cases provided externalities – into the empowerment of women, into the financing of school fees, into the building of social capital, and maybe most relevantly for eastern Europe, into the reduction of corruption. In other environments, including indeed Bangladesh, the Bank has lent for social protection direct into these institutions by means of NGO sector loans; but not in the transitional region.

What differentiates the transitional region from other parts of the world was that small-scale private economic activity was, until the early 1990s, actually illegal, and in Russia carried severe penalties including imprisonment (Klugman and Braithwaite 1998: 42). Even after 1992, as one of our interviewees put it to us, 'initially, entrepreneurs were hiding from everyone – they didn't want to admit what they were'.[5] In such an environment, small entrepreneurs need special support, going beyond finance into training, legal advice and social capital formation (for example through the formation of solidarity groups). Most of this has been forthcoming from NGOs (for example Opportunity International in Russia), but there has also been intervention from international financial organisations such as the EBRD's Russian Small Business Fund. As we have argued above, the form in which social protection is given may determine the externalities it is able to give to the poverty reduction process, in particular by reducing corruption and building social capital. It may be that if these externalities are to be maximised, the Bank needs to complement its 'conventional' social protection support with support for the emergent bottom end of the financial market.

2.3 Outcomes for poverty and other variables

Thus the Bank's ability to reduce poverty, over the course of the transition, was heavily limited by geo-politics and by internal politics, as well as, we have argued, by factors internal to the design of social protection. Nonetheless, within these limits, there was on the fragile evidence of Table 7.1 some poverty reduction in the later 1990s in all the eastern European countries, and even in 2000 in Russia. What was the Bank able, within the limits mentioned, to add to this process and what are the implications for policy? Section 3 considers these questions.

2.3.1 Development assistance and poverty: an explanatory model

As indicated by Table 7.1, it appears as if poverty in the transitional region may at last have begun to fall. To what extent is this due to the influence of aid from the World Bank group and elsewhere? To begin to answer this question, we run a single-equation regression model in Table 7.4 to estimate the impact of aid flows from the World Bank and other donors on poverty levels. We use two kinds of poverty indicator as a dependent variable (the headcount index and the level of under-five mortality) and we reproduce, in the right-hand part of the table, results already obtained from a regression of this type for all developing and transitional countries for which data are available. Three of the independent variables are the ones which we have argued, in our discussion of Figure 7.1, to be likely to shift the balance between risk and return 'north-westwards', by increasing the ability of the recipient government to manage crises: pro-poor expenditure (which diminishes inequality and attracts political support from lower income groups), inequality itself, social capital (assessed by the *World Values Survey* measure of interpersonal trust) which we interpret in terms of the degree of linkage between citizens and government and therefore governability. The fourth, corruption, is simply a measure of the cost of doing business which will impact on levels of enterprise, investment and poverty. All four variables we see as shift parameters which are potentially able to influence the relationship between aid and poverty; in this respect, they play the same role as the 'good policy' variable in the analysis of Burnside and Dollar (2000), without which aid is ineffective, but the components of that measure are mainly macro variables, whereas the one considered here is more micro in nature.

Estimation is by two-stage (or in one case three-stage) least squares, to allow for probable feedbacks from poverty to aid.

The results of Table 7.3 suggest that low levels of corruption, low levels of inequality and high levels of social capital are apparently able, in eastern Europe, as well as globally, to increase the 'poverty-leverage' of aid, and may have contributed to the poverty reduction which at last seems to be occurring. Pro-poor expenditure, in eastern Europe, has a smaller and less significant coefficient than elsewhere (particularly so when the grant element of World Bank lending is used as the indicator of aid!) although still significant at the 5 percent level in relation to the headcount measure of poverty; our interpretation of this, and one of the key messages of this chapter, is that overtly redistributive measures appear to enjoy less political leverage in eastern Europe than elsewhere. Aid itself, holding constant these 'facilitative' variables, is a just-significant influence in relation to headcount poverty only.

A first message which we take from this analysis is that if the 'social sectors' are to have maximum impact on poverty, they need to maximise the level of impact achieved through *indirect* linkages such as the four mentioned above, rather than simply focusing through direct linkages to clients. Examples of such indirect linkages, particularly relevant to the transitional region, are:

1   microfinance and support services to small businesses (as we have seen, somewhat neglected by the Bank in the transitional region), by making possible credit from uncorrupt sources of supply, lower the cost of doing business and raise the rate of investment;
2   aid given to help labour markets operate more flexibly (for example by subsidising child-care services or carers) flattens the labour-supply curve to *all sectors of the economy* (especially of groups with a high

Table 7.4 Estimates of aid's impact on poverty and possible influences on it

Equation number	1	2	3	4	5	6	7
Sample	Russia and Eastern Europe				Global comparisons		
Dependent variable (poverty indicator)	Infant mortality rate			Poverty headcount (at national poverty line)	Infant mortality rate	Infant mortality rate	Poverty headcount (at international poverty line)
Number of observations					117	117	88
Estimation method	OLS[a]	2SLS	2SLS	2SLS[c]	2SLS	2SLS	3SLS[e]
Regression coefficients on independent variables:							
Constant	7.79** (4.61)	8.21* (4.61)		4.65** (5.22)	8.92** (21.04)	8.99** (18.63)	5.53** (6.74)
Aid		-0.14 (1.34)		-0.09* (1.97)	0.04 (0.03)	-0.11* (1.85)	-0.29 (1.47)
Aid from World Bank group only	-0.21* (2.04)						
Gini coefficient of inequality	0.065** (3.34)	0.053** (3.61)		0.078** (4.66)		0.034* (2.31)	0.058** (5.51)
PPE index (as %GDP)[b]	-0.037 (1.13)	-0.049 (1.77)		-0.145* (2.44)	-0.085** (3.45)	-0.25* (1.90)	-0.198** (3.17)
PPE squared						0.045 (0.31)	
Social capital indicator	-0.043* (2.15)	-0.007* (1.98)		-0.013* (2.39)			
Social protection spending	-0.037* (1.99)	-0.026 (1.65)		-0.009 (1.34)			
Health spending/GNP							0.234* (2.21)
Transparency International corruption indicator	-0.34** (4.47)	-0.27** (3.98)		-0.38** (6.32)			-0.22* (2.13)

	(1)	(2)	(3)	(4)	(5)	(6)
Composite policy indicator[c]					−0.00188 (1.54)	
Log (GDP per capita)				−0.635** (10.67)	−0.64** (9.91)	−0.49** (4.15)
R^2	0.43	0.53	0.37	0.68	0.82	0.49

Sources: Poverty headcount index is calculated at national poverty lines from data in World Bank, *World Development Reports*, successive issues from 1990 onward – data arrays available from the author on request. PPE index is from IMF *Government Expenditure Statistics Yearbook*, for full details see Appendix. *Transparency International* corruption indicator from Transparency International website (http://www.gwdg.de/~uwvw/icr.htm).

Notes

Figures in parentheses below coefficients are Student's *t*-statistics. ** denotes significance of a coefficient at the 1 percent level and * denotes significance at the 5 percent level.

a Using White's correction for heteroscedasticity.

b PPE index is a measure of the extent to which public expenditure is intensive in 'priority' sectors likely to have a poverty-reducing effect. It is calculated as (1.69* (log education/GNP) + 0.77** (log housing and amenities') + 0.244 log agriculture/GDP) −0.71** (log military expenditure/GDP); for derivation see Appendix.

c The 'Burnside-Dollar' good policy index – a weighted sum of inflation, budget deficit and openness.

d In regressions 3 to 6, instruments for aid are:

'recipient need': STAB-inflation in 1990s as a percentage of its average value in the 1980s.

DEBTSERV – debt service as a percentage of GNP.

recipient characteristics and ability to absorb aid:

MILPERLF – military expenditure as a percentage of GNP, serving as a quasi-war dummy.

POPTOT – total population.

The instrumenting equation is: log(aid/GNP) = 0.081 − 0.107*(LNSTAB)

(1.85)

+ 0.092(MILPERLF) − 1.34**E-09(POPTOT) + 0.014*(DEBTSERV); r^2 0.087

(1.24)   (3.16)   (1.89)

e In 3SLS (Equation 7) endogenous variables, in addition to poverty, are aid, PPE and health expenditure.

probability of being poor such as single parents) and thereby increases competitiveness;

3   social investment funds generate both human capital (by the provision of local schools and health centres) but also social capital (by developing democratic community decision-taking procedures in the allocation of funds); and finally

4   aid given direct to the NGO sector reduces the various bureaucratic costs associated with dealing through government.

In addition, these results suggest a possible role for conditionality, applied in particular to the catalytic variables mentioned above. As we have seen, conditionality has been somewhat disowned by the Bank in recent years, and has not done well in Russia. But it has done better in smaller countries, witness the case of the Romanian Child Protection Loan (and see Stone 2002 for the parallel case of IMF lending to eastern Europe). Success depends not only on bargaining relationships and country size, but also on pre-existing trust relationships between Bank and recipient country and on the ease with which a target variable can be altered; thus it is easier to increase the level of pro-poor expenditure than to achieve press-button increases in social capital or decreases in corruption. But we have evidence of the success of conditionality applied to pro-poor expenditure in Africa (Mosley *et al.* 2003) and there is evidence of strong increases in the coefficient of pro-poor expenditure in Hungary, Poland and Romania within our sample. It would not be unreasonable to suggest that analysis of the characteristics of pro-poor expenditure within the smaller countries of our sample, and the ability of specific social expenditures to increase it, might yield a poverty dividend through this route.

3 Conclusions and policy messages

In the way we have described,[6] a great idealistic crusade against the ravages of the transition, which the Bank at one time visualised as offering a distinct extension of its global influence, has turned into something of a damp squib. The Bank has missed an opportunity to consolidate its comparative advantage in the poverty reduction field in relation to the Fund, in part because it deemed that eastern Europe was not a suitable stage on which to confront the Fund and, unlike the Fund, had come to feel ambivalent about the use of conditionality. Social protection expenditures never attained the salience within the Bank budget which would have made an extension of its influence possible, even during Russia's period of maximum reverse leverage during the mid-1990s; and from that climacteric they have gradually receded. We give various reasons for this in the text, including the failure to produce innovative institutional ideas to support the small business sector, lagging tax revenue, and maybe most importantly the inability of the Bank to find seriously pro-poor partners within the political structure of transitional countries which had the power to achieve a serious increase in social spending within those countries. In relation to Naim's typology of Bank functions, the idea of 'the Bank as a fund', even out inequalities on a global scale, has given way to the other functions, in particular the geo-political one.

Nonetheless, in several transitional countries a modest increase in social spending, and more broadly in 'pro-poor' spending, did occur, and most importantly a modest decline in poverty did finally happen in a majority of them – but in the case of Russia not until the very end of the 1990s. We have made an attempt to assess the relationship between changes in poverty and a range of variables which the World Bank has tried to influence, including social capital, corruption, inequality and what we call 'pro-poor' expenditures, which is a complex of expenditures of which social spending is a part. All of these turn out to have some bearing on poverty reduction, both globally and within the eastern European/transitional region, although there are econometric problems still to be resolved and the impact coefficient is often weaker in eastern Europe than in the global sample. The implication is that the Bank 'missed a trick': had it exercised more leverage, it could well have helped reduce more poverty, although we emphasise that our model is crude, and that there are some 'industrial country-type' linkages increasingly relevant to transitional economies which we have not attempted to model, including the effects of benefit levels on the incentive to work.

For these reasons, any policy messages drawn from this chapter need to be taken as particularly tentative. The one we would offer at this stage, beyond that which the Bank has already drawn about the need for pro-poor policies to be backed by a proper constituency within the recipient country, is that social protection policies need to be assessed not only in terms of their direct impact, but also in terms of their ability to confer 'multipliers' or 'externalities' into the influences on poverty mentioned above. We have criticised Bank social protection policies for not linking with policies to stimulate the bottom end of the financial sector, precisely for this reason – because microfinance has a proven ability to generate social capital and reduce the costs of corruption. But more broadly, any social protection policy which is able to increase the level of other pro-poor expenditures, or which increases intra-community trust, or which in any other way represents an investment in social capital, is likely on the evidence here presented to reduce poverty through the back as well as the front door. Work to assess the extent and significance of these multipliers in particular empirical contexts represents, in our judgement, an important research priority.

The 'pro-poor expenditure index'

We believe that the intersectoral mix of government (and other) expenditures has an important influence on poverty through at least three channels:

Appendix

World Bank taxonomy of social protection options

<table>
<tr><th colspan="2">Cash benefits</th><th colspan="2">In-kind benefits</th></tr>
<tr><th>Universal eligibility</th><th>Categorical eligibility</th><th>Universal eligibility</th><th>Categorical eligibility</th></tr>
<tr>
<td colspan="4">Not targeted</td>
</tr>
<tr>
<td>None</td>
<td>Child allowances (all)
Child allowances (age cut off)
Single parents
Divorced parents
Families with many children
Disabled children
Military families
Orphans
Unemployment assistance
Student stipends

Foster-parent allowances
Employer benefits
Union benefits
War veterans' benefits</td>
<td>Food subsidies
Energy subsidies
Transportation subsidies
Housing subsidies</td>
<td>School lunches
Student transportation
Transportation for aged
Transportation for disabled
Services for aged
Services for disabled
Student scholarships
Services for alcoholism
Services for drug abuse
Emergency programmes (war, flood, natural disaster)
Employer benefits

Homes for the aged
Orphanages
Programmes for national/ethnic groups</td>
</tr>
<tr>
<td colspan="4">Targeted
i. Means-testing
ii. Indicator-testing
iii. Self-targeting</td>
</tr>
<tr>
<td>Social assistance
Housing allowances</td>
<td>Child allowances (all)
Child allowances (age cut off)
Single parents
Divorced parents
Families with many children
Disabled children
Unemployment assistance
Student stipends
Assistance for elderly
Assistance for disabled

Emergency aid
One-off benefits</td>
<td>Food subsidies
Energy subsidies
Transportation subsidies
Housing subsidies</td>
<td>School lunches
Student transportation
Transportation for aged
Transportation for disabled
Services for aged
Services for disabled
Student scholarships
Services for alcoholism
Services for drug abuse
Emergency programmes (war, flood, natural disaster)
Homes for the aged</td>
</tr>
</table>

Source: Andersen and Ringold 1999: 62.

a   some expenditures are more intensive in the labour of the poor and
      hence generate greater labour-market benefits;
b   some expenditures provide more services for low-income consumers
      (and in some cases generate externalities for them as well);
c   some expenditures are better at generating social networks which are
      economically beneficial ('social capital').

Through all of these channels it reduces inequality, and thereby very possibly acts as a conflict prevention device in the manner described by
Collier and Dollar (2002: 1485–8).

   The idea of designing a 'poverty sensitive' pattern of public expenditures has been often articulated (notably by Ferroni and Kanbur (1991)),
but to our knowledge such a pattern has not been empirically documented. No approach is likely to be perfect because of the range of poverty
impacts which are conceivable, but the following 'quick and dirty' methods
can be visualised. The first two cover only one channel of impact (and we
only have data for a few countries), whereas the last two are more general:

•   *A labour-intensity approach* – covering effect (a) – the definition of 'pro-
    poor expenditure' as those expenditure sectors which are most
    labour-intensive.
•   *A benefit incidence approach* – covering effect (b) – the definition of
    'pro-poor expenditure' as those sectors whose output, on the evidence
    of household budget surveys, is consumed by the poor.
•   *A regression approach* – the definition of 'pro-poor expenditure' as
    those sectors where expenditure exhibits correlation with poverty.
•   *A CGE approach* – which here is tried experimentally in Uganda only but,
    better than the other methods, can hope to trace comprehensively the
    effects of expenditure on poverty through multiple channels of effect.

   Labour-intensity. We know of no statistical exercises which measure the
propensity of different public expenditure sectors to take on low-income
labour. However, the governments of the two most effective exercises in
poverty reduction within low-income countries – Uganda and Ethiopia –
prioritised the same expenditure sectors, explicitly on the grounds that
they are labour-intensive. These are: primary health and education, agricultural research and extension, rural water and sanitation.
   Benefit incidence. Sahn and Younger (2000), drawing on household
budget surveys in eight low-income African countries, have assessed the
extent to which different public expenditures fall on low-income groups.
They conclude that expenditures on primary and secondary education,
and all types of healthcare (but not university education), can be considered progressive and do reduce inequality. Nonetheless, they warn
(344), 'expectations that social sector spending has a substantial
redistributive impact are misplaced' and 'African governments would do
well to consider how to better target their expenditures'.

The CGE approach. For Uganda only, McDonald and Chant (2002) have conducted simulations which examine the impact of different expenditures on poverty through *all* market channels, not just the two examined above. For education, health and 'social sector' expenditures only, they find that the impact of increasing the share of public spending dedicated to those expenditure sectors is poverty-reducing.

The regression approach. Finally, we turn to regression analysis in the hope of both achieving comprehensiveness of coverage and examining tendencies across a wide range of countries. OLS regressions for 34 countries for the years 1980–98 produced the results:

Without military expenditure:

Log (poverty at international poverty line) = 12.4 − 1.05 (log GDP per capita)

(3.46) (2.33)

− 1.86* (log education expenditure/GDP) + 1.84** (log health expenditure/GDP)

(2.43)   (3.17)

− 0.96** (log housing and amenities) − 0.43 (log agriculture/GDP)

(3.21)   (1.10)

− 0.71** (log military expenditure/GDP); $r^2 = 0.660$

(2.17)

Note: **denotes significance of a coefficient at the 1 percent level; * denotes significance at the 5 percent level.

With military expenditure:

Log (poverty at international poverty line) = 13.8 − 1.21 (log GDP per capita)

(4.31) (3.01)

− 1.69* (log education expenditure/GDP) + 1.66** (log health expenditure/GDP)

(2.50)   (3.24)

− 0.77** (log housing and amenities) − 0.24 (log agriculture/GDP)

(2.79)   (0.69)

− 0.71** (log military expenditure/GDP); $r^2 = 0.762$

(2.16)

Note: **denotes significance of a coefficient at the 1 percent level; * denotes significance at the 5 percent level.

Number of observations: 34

Data sources: public expenditure (PPE) data from IMF *Government Statistics Yearbooks* and UNESCO *Statistical Yearbooks;* poverty data from World Bank *World Development Reports.* The full PPE data set is discussed in more detail by Mosley *et al.* (2002).[6]

This set of results obtained by different procedures may be summarised by means of Table 7.5; effects which are ambiguous or insignificant according to a particular methodology are bracketed.

From Table 7.5 it is very clear that educational and 'social' (in the World Bank's classification, 'housing and amenities') expenditure belong in any pro-poor expenditure index. Health and agricultural expenditure are ambiguous. Health very strongly 'refuses to behave' in both regressions in spite of Sahn and Younger's weakly positive results on benefit incidence, and agriculture has the right sign but is insignificant in the regressions. Military expenditure is negative and significant for poverty in the regressions but there is a lack of supporting evidence from other methodologies. In the last cut we decided to omit health given the complete absence of supportive evidence from any comprehensive methodology. The statistical evidence in support of agriculture is weak but we include it in the light of very strong case-study evidence, in particular from Uganda and Ethiopia (Morrissey and Verschoor 2002; Rock 2003), that the prioritisation of agricultural spending made a very important difference to poverty impact from the early 1990s onward.

Hence, in the regressions of Table 7.4 above, we present the 'pro-poor expenditure' (PPE) index in two forms:

Without military expenditure: PPE1 = 0.431x (log of agriculture as %GDP) + 0.964* (log housing, water, sanitation and social security as %GDP) + 1.866 (log education as %GDP)
With military expenditure: PPE2 = 0.431x (log of agriculture as %GDP) + 0.964* (log housing, water, sanitation and social security as %GDP) + 1.866 (log education as %GDP) − 0.71 (military expenditure as %GDP).
Note: *denotes significance at the 5 percent level.

In each index, the weights are the regression coefficients set out on pages 194–5.

Table 7.5 'Poverty elasticity' of components of public expenditure: summary of findings

Methodologies	'Single-channel' methodologies		'Comprehensive' methodologies	
Components of expenditure	Benefit incidence	CGE (Uganda only)	Regression	Labour-intensity (Uganda only)
Educational expenditure	+	+	+	+
Health expenditure	+	+	−	+
Agricultural expenditure			(+)	+
'Social' expenditure		+	+	+
Military expenditure			−	

Sources: For regressions see this Appendix; benefit incidence, see Sahn and Younger (2000); CGE, see McDonald and Chant (2002); labour-intensity, see Uganda (2002).

Notes
+, sector indicated has a significant poverty-reducing effect through the methodology stated; (+) sector indicated has a significant negative effect on poverty through the methodology stated; − sector indicated has a significant poverty-increasing effect through the methodology stated.

Notes

1 For an attempt to estimate such a model and derive principles of 'optimal conditionality', see Mosley (2003: chapter 9).
2 It is almost axiomatic that the influence of a donor wishing to impose conditionality is greater in small countries. See Mosley *et al.* (1995: chapter 3), or for an extended exposition of the argument in relation to the IMF in eastern Europe, Stone (2002).
3 Social assistance in Russia is a discretionary benefit paid at the local level and has become increasingly decentralised to the regional and municipal levels. 'With (World) Bank support the Government has been experimenting with three different targeting methodologies in three pilot oblasts including (i) proxy-means-testing; (ii) a "categorical filter" which pre-screens applicants first on the basis of household characteristics and then applies a means test; and (iii) a complex means-testing formula which estimates potential household earnings' (Andrews and Ringold 1999: 26).
4 Two-thirds of Russians say that they have a friend who could lend them up to a week's wages if their household was short of money, and more than two-thirds know someone who would help them if they were ill (Rose *et al.* 1996).
5 Interview, Novgorod State Fund for Support of Entrepreneurship, Veliki Novgorod, 10 September 2002.
6 More detail can also be obtained by email from the authors: p.mosley @sheffield.ac.uk or a.verschoor@uea.ac.uk.

References

Alexeeva, Elena, Paul Mosley, and Daniela Olejarova. 2003. Microfinance, Social Capital Formation and Political Development in Russia and Eastern Europe: a Pilot Study of Programmes in Russia and Slovakia. Unpublished report, Ford Foundation IMPACT Microfinance Programme.
Andrews, Emily and D. Ringold. 1999. *Safety Nets in Transition Economies: Toward a Reform Strategy.* Washington, DC: World Bank Social Protection Discussion Paper 9914.
Benfoddova, Monika, Allan Bussard, and Marek Markus. 2000. *The Problem of Corruption in Small and Medium Enterprises in Slovakia.* Bratislava: INTEGRA Foundation.
Brainerd, Elizabeth. 1998. Market Reform and Mortality in Transition Economies. *World Development* 26: 2013–27.
Burnside, Craig and David Dollar. 2000. Aid Policies and Growth. *American Economics Review* 90: 847–68.
Collier, P. and D. Dollar. 2002. Aid Allocation and Poverty Reduction. *European Economic Review* 50(1): 133–62.
Cornia, G. 1994a. Income Distribution, Poverty and Welfare in Transitional Economies: A Comparison Between Eastern Europe and China. *Journal of International Development* 6: 569–609.
Cornia, G. 1994b. Structural Adjustment and Living Standards in Transitional Economies. *Journal of International Development* 6 (July): 602–3.
Ferroni, M. and R. Kanbur. 1991. Poverty Conscious Restructuring of Public Expenditures. In *Economic Reform in Sub-Saharan Africa,* edited by A. Chibber and S. Fischer (eds), pp. 90–105. Washington, DC: World Bank.
Gough, I. *et al.* 1996. Social Assistance in OECD Countries. *Journal of European Social Policy* 7: 17–43.
Kennedy, Bruce, I. Kawachi, and E. Brainerd. 1998. The Role of Social Capital in the Russian Mortality Crisis. *World Development* 26: 2029–43.

Klugman, Jeni and J. Braithwaite. 1998. Poverty in Russia During the Transition: An Overview. *World Bank Research Observer* 13: 37–58.

Knack, S. and P. Keefer. 1997. Does Socal Capital have an Economic Payoff? A Cross-country Investigation. *Quarterly Journal of Economics* 112 (4): 1252–88.

Lokshin, M. and R. Yemtsov. 2001. *Household Strategies for Coping with Poverty and Social Exclusion in Post-Crisis Russia*. Washington, DC: World Bank Policy Research Working Paper 2556.

McDonald, S. and L. Chant. 2002. A Computable General Equilibrium Model for Uganda: Technical Documentation. Unpublished paper, University of Sheffield.

Morrissey, O. and A. Verschoor. 2002. Is Ownership a Meaningful Concept in Policy Reform? Policy Learning and the Evolution of Pro-poor Policies in Uganda, mimeo, DFID Research Program on Risk Labor Markets and Pro-poor Growth, Sheffield, Nottingham, Cambridge and Open University.

Mosley, Paul. 2003. *Risk and Underdevelopment*. Forthcoming, Oxford University Press.

Mosley, Paul. 2004. Pro-Poor Politics and the New Political Economy of Stabilisation. *New Political Economy*. Forthcoming May.

Mosley, Paul and Yelena Kalyuzhnova. 2000. Are Poverty and Social Goals Attainable in the Transitional Region?. *Development Policy Review* 18 (March): 107–20.

Mosley, Paul and Lucy Steel. 2002. A Tale of Three Cities: Microfinance, Social Capital and Public Policy in Three UK Cities. Unpublished paper, Universities of Sheffield and Glasgow.

Mosley, Paul, J. Harrigan, and J. Toye. 1995. *Aid and Power: The World Bank and Policy-Based Lending*, second edition. London: Routledge.

Mosley, P., J. Hudson and K. Gomanee. 2002. Aid, Poverty Reduction and the 'New Conditionality'. Pro-poor Growth, Occasional Paper No. 5, University of Sheffield, February.

Mosley, Paul, J. Hudson and A. Verschoor. 2003. Aid, Poverty Reduction and the 'New Conditionality'. *Economic Journal* 114: 217–44.

Naim, Moises. 1994. From Supplicants to Shareholders: Developing Countries and the World Bank. In *International Monetary and Financial Issues for the 1990s*. Vol. IV. New York for UNCTAD, Geneva.

Rock, J. 2003. Donors, Aid, Policy Learning and the Evolution of Pro-poor Policies in Ethiopia, mimeo, DFID Research Program on Risk Labor Markets, and Pro-poor Growth, Sheffield, Nottingham, Cambridge and Open University.

Rose, Richard, W. Mischler, and C. Haerfer. 1996. Getting Real: Social Capital in Post-Communist Societies. Paper presented to Conference on The Erosion of Confidence in Advanced Democracies. Brussels, November 7–9.

Sahn, D. and S. Younger. 2000. Expenditure Incidence in Africa: Microeconomic Evidence. *Fiscal Studies* 21: 329–47.

Stiglitz, J. 2003. *Globalisation and Its Discontents*. London: Penguin.

Stone, Randall W. 2002. *Lending Credibility: The International Monetary Fund and the Post-Communist Transition*. Princeton: Princeton University Press.

United Kingdom. 1999. *National Neighbourhood Strategy*. London: Her Majesty's Stationery Office.

Vreeland, James. 2003. *The IMF and Economic Development*. Cambridge: Cambridge University Press.

Whiteley, P. 2000. Economic Growth and Social Capital. *Political Studies* 48: 443–66.

World Bank. 1990. *World Development Report 1990*. Washington, DC: World Bank.

World Bank. 2002. *Annual Report 2002*. Washington, DC: World Bank.

World Bank. 2003a. *Assisting Russia's Transition; An Unprecedented Challenge*. Washington, DC: World Bank Operations Evaluation Department.

World Bank. 2003b. *World Development Indicators 2003*. Washington, DC: World Bank.

8 When the World Bank says yes

Determinants of structural adjustment lending[*]

M. Rodwan Abouharb and David L. Cingranelli

"Ends"

Oh, some as soon would throw it all
As throw a part away.
And some will say all sorts of things,
But some mean what they say.
          Robert Frost (1874–1963)

1 Introduction

The World Bank along with the International Monetary Fund (IMF) play a crucial role in determining how much capital developing countries will receive from external sources. Thus, it is not surprising that there has been much controversy over the lending practices of these international financial institutions. Most of the controversy has been centered upon the fairness of the structural adjustment conditions imposed by both institutions upon loan recipients and the effects of the loans on economic development. In recent years, scholars have also focused attention on country characteristics used by the Bank to determine which governments will receive loans and which will not. In this chapter, the factors that increased or decreased the probability of a country's government receiving a World Bank structural adjustment loan (SAL) in the 20-year period from 1981–2000 are identified. The governments of 161 countries of the world are included in the analysis. This is the first large-*n*, comparative study of the selection criteria of the World Bank. The results have both theoretical and practical importance.

There are at least four different and partly contradictory theoretical perspectives that could be used to describe or explain the selection criteria of the World Bank: classical economic theory (Van De Laar 1980), the theory of two-level games in international affairs (Putnam 1988; Milner 1997), the opposing "credible commitments" argument (Leeds 1999; Martin 2000), and dependency theory (Pion-Berlin 1984). These theoretical perspectives and the results of previous empirical research suggest the potential importance of the likelihood of economic or political conflict, and human rights performance criteria in the World Bank's decisions to award loans. The results provide some support for expectations generated by classical economic theory, some support for expectations generated by the theory of two-level games, and almost none for those associated with dependency theory and the arguments concerning credible commitments.

The results of our study indicate that states associated with a higher probability of receiving a World Bank loan during this period were in economic need, had larger populations, higher levels of government respect for workers' rights, and had a Japanese colonial experience. States that had previously received a World Bank loan were less likely to receive another in the short term. In comparison, states associated with a lower probability of receiving a World Bank loan during this period experienced increased levels of domestic unrest. While some previous research on the selection criteria of the IMF had found that the IMF preferred to give loans to more authoritarian states, we found no evidence of bias for or against democracies or a preference of military over civilian regimes. Finally, we found no evidence that the World Bank favored countries that repressed their populations at large, were allied, or had a colonial/dependent relationship with the United States or that were more globalized economically.

Understanding the selection criteria of the World Bank is also of crucial practical importance to any estimation of the effects of World Bank loans. Simply comparing recipient to non-recipient as some previous research has done (Harrigan and Mosley 1991) will not advance our knowledge of loan impacts because a non-random process generated which countries became recipients and which countries did not (Achen 1986; Heckman 1988; Przeworski and Vreeland 2000; Vreeland 2002, 2003). This means that in order to isolate the impact of World Bank loans future work needs to "disentangle" (Collier 1991) the selection criteria in World Bank loan receipt from the actual impact of the loan itself in addition to controlling for alternative explanations that may impact the dependent variable of interest. Disentangling this process will allow future research to answer the question: All other things being equal, was it the loans or the pre-existing situation that account for the impact attributed to World Bank structural adjustment loans?

The chapter follows in four sections. The first describes the four theoretical arguments, the second reviews some of the previous findings and generates a number of hypotheses, the third describes our research design, and the fourth discusses our findings and conclusions.

2 Theoretical arguments

We assume that the governments of all developing countries would like to receive money from the World Bank, because the Bank makes loans at rates of interest and with other repayment terms that are far superior to what can be found on the open market (Van De Laar 1980). Loan recipients also seek the "seal of approval" from the Bank. The leaders of the governments of developing countries know that the US government, the governments of other wealthy countries, and private banks will be less willing to provide grants and loans unless the IMF and World Bank are willing to extend international credit as well (Pion-Berlin 1984; Przeworski and Vreeland 2000).

Which governments receive World Bank loans is decided by the Bank's Board of Directors. The World Bank uses a weighted voting system for determining which loans are approved and which are denied. The weights assigned are roughly in proportion to the share of the Bank's development funds contributed by each of the member governments. For the last 25 years, the United States, Japan, and Germany have accounted for more than half of all funds contributed (Banks and Muller 2002), so it is reasonable to assume that the preferences of their country representatives have dominated the preferences of other members of the Bank's Board of Directors. World Bank representatives protest against any allegations that their lending policies are motivated by political considerations, but the internal decision-making process of the World Bank privileges the ideological perspectives of some governments over others, allows for logrolling and vote trading, and in all other respects provides fertile ground for what, in any other context, would be called "politics."

The stated goal of the Bank is to promote economic growth and to reduce poverty in less developed countries (World Bank 1992). Through its public policy statements, the Bank has announced some of its selection criteria. The code of practices by which the Bank operates recommends that the Bank give preference to applicants that have a capitalist ideology, have not nationalized private industry without providing fair compensation to the owners, are not able to borrow on the private market, and are creditworthy (Van De Laar 1980). These criteria created an unabashed bias against making loans to communist countries (though some communist countries including the formerly communist Yugoslavia and Romania did receive them). The publicly stated criteria also are ambiguous enough to provide the Bank's Board of Directors considerable discretion. Terms such as "capitalist ideology" and "creditworthy" must be defined and applied to specific applicants. It is also likely that many governments not able to borrow on the private market also are not creditworthy. The Board must decide how to reconcile these criteria. The Bank provides loans to the poorest countries with the worst credit ratings through the International Development Association and to wealthier countries that have better credit rating through the International Bank for Reconstruction and Development (World Bank 2002a). Wealthier countries pay a higher rate of interest and have a shorter loan repayment period.

All structural adjustment loan recipients are required to comply with certain conditions mainly demonstrating their adherence to capitalist ideology. In essence these conditions represent other publicly announced selection criteria of the Bank. They are political in the sense that they have been the subject of contentious debate among scholars, policy makers, and social activists in the United States and abroad. The purpose of these structural adjustment conditions is to encourage recipient governments to put on what Thomas Friedman (2000: 105) calls "the Golden Straightjacket":

> To fit into the Golden Straightjacket a country must either adopt, or be seen as moving toward, the following golden rules: making the private sector the primary engine of its economic growth, maintaining a low rate of inflation and price stability, shrinking the size of its state bureaucracy, maintaining as close to a balanced budget as possible, if not a surplus, eliminating and lowering tariffs on imported goods, removing restrictions on foreign investment, getting rid of quotas and domestic monopolies, increasing exports, privatizing state-owned industries and utilities, deregulating capital markets, making its currency convertible, opening its industries, stock and bond markets to direct foreign ownership and investment, deregulating its economy to promote as much domestic competition as possible, [and] eliminating government corruption, subsidies, and kickbacks as much as possible.[1]

While exact measures insisted upon between the World Bank and recipient countries differ on a case by case basis, common steps often cited by critics of the World Bank (Bello *et al.* 1994; Palast 2003) include reductions of social spending for such things as education, health services, income subsidies, housing, and reductions in public employment.

2.1 Classical economic theory

Classical economic theory is the basis of the mainstream argument used by the World Bank, IMF, and economically developed countries to justify support for economic stabilization and structural adjustment conditions agreed upon with loan recipient countries. The intention of these conditions is to encourage the economic growth of loan recipients (Przeworski and Vreeland 2000; Harrigan and Mosley 1991) which the Bank's Board of Directors equate with economic development. Structural adjustment programs reduce the size and role of government in the economy and free monies to be used more productively in the private sector. A minimalist state produces and encourages the economic growth that will lead to a better society (Rapley 1996: 58).

Limited government empowers individuals by giving them more personal freedom, making it more likely that individuals will realize their potential. The ability to realize one's potential, according to this line of reasoning, leads to individual responsibility and self-reliance. Both classical and neo-classical economic theory advocate limited government with individuals acting in their own self-interest, maximizing any opportunities and possible gains. Reduction in the size of the state reduces the opportunity for corruption and releases talented people into the private sector (Rapley 1996: 59). Neo-classical thought also promotes strategies of export-led growth through free trade. Essentially trade is a synonym for growth (Rapley 1996: 59). This suggests that conditions of economic underdevelopment or economic slow-down should increase the probability of both IMF and World Bank loan receipt.

Though economists associated with the IMF and World Bank use classical economic theory to justify structural adjustment policy, others use the same theory to criticize structural adjustment loans. Their criticisms take many forms including the arguments that the Fund and Bank use a conception of development that is too focused on economic growth, have misdiagnosed the obstacles to development in the less developed countries, have failed to appreciate the value of government interventions into the private economy, and have insisted that structural adjustment reforms be implemented too quickly.

Some argue that the Fund and Bank have been too focused on Gross Domestic Product (GDP) per capita and growth in GDP per capita as the only indicators of development. They suggest this focus is too narrow since economic growth does not necessarily translate into development if the profits from such growth are not spent on health care, education, and infrastructure, improving the situation for most people rather than just a small ruling elite (Stiglitz 1999; Knack and Keefer 1997). Indeed, Joseph Stiglitz, formerly chief economist at the World Bank, has even argued that the developing countries that are likely to develop the fastest are those that avoid loans from the IMF and World Bank. He notes that China, a country that has received no help from the IMF or the World Bank is probably the most successful of the low-income countries, both in terms of aggregate economic growth and in terms of poverty reduction. Moreover, unlike Russia, China has avoided a rapid increase in economic inequality (Stiglitz 2001, 2002).

Some critics also argue that the real obstacles to economic growth in less developed countries have little to do with the size of government or its role in the economy. Among the real obstacles not addressed by SALs, they contend, are the need for land reform, inelasticities in foreign demand for primary products produced in the developing world, and low internal rates of saving in the private sector (Pion-Berlin 1984). The critics argue that there are no short-term solutions to these problems. Long-term solutions include land reform to raise agricultural output, government investment in infrastructure and capital-creating industries (Moyo 2001; Pion-Berlin 1984). In the formerly communist countries, the absence of a well-developed system of private property is also a major obstacle (Stiglitz 2002).

Critics of the Bank and Fund also contend that the structural adjustment policies of the Bank and Fund impose a shock therapy approach on poorly performing economies, especially in the formerly communist world (Stiglitz 2002). In many cases, they argue, an incremental and adaptive longer-term approach would be more effective (Stiglitz 2002; Murrel 1992). In many formerly communist countries major problems have been created because privatization preceded the development of regulatory and corporate governance institutions and even banks (Schleifer and Vishny 1997; Stiglitz and Squire 1998). While classical economic theory provides one rationale for the types of factors the World Bank would take into account in determining SAL loan receipt, other theories, which focus on the ability of countries to negotiate at the international level may also provide some purchase in understanding the selection criteria of the Bank.

2.2 Two level games: domestic politics and credible commitments

Two contrasting theories appear in the literature concerning the impact of domestic politics on the abilities of states to cooperate. Putnam's (1988) and Milner's (1997) work on the impacts of both domestic and international politics in international affairs suggests that, unless the Bank adopts a kind of "affirmative action policy" toward democracies, they will be at a disadvantage in their attempts to negotiate loans. Critics of the IMF have also noted its preference for working with authoritarian regimes (Przeworski and Vreeland 2000). However, there is a contrasting theoretical argument suggesting that democracies have an advantage when negotiating international agreements, because their governments can make more credible agreements (Leeds 1999; Martin 2000).

Putnam's theory of two level games and a similar argument put forward by Milner (1997) both provide an explanation for the finding in the literature that the IMF prefers lending to authoritarian regimes (Pion-Berlin 1984; Przeworski and Vreeland 2000; Stiglitz 2002). Putnam (1988) suggests that negotiations between an international agency like the Bank or IMF and the leaders of a nation state can be thought of as a two-level negotiation game. Level I negotiation occurs between the leaders of the Bank or Fund and the leaders of the potential loan recipient country. Level II is played between the country leaders and their citizens. A formal model of this game would be exceedingly complex, since the negotiations at both levels are interdependent.[2]

At level I, the leaders of the Bank and Fund behave as autonomous, unitary actors in the model. They are hierarchically organized and they express clear preferences. At the risk of oversimplification, the preferences of the Bank and Fund are that decision makers in recipient countries agree to a set of economic reforms, that these reforms be implemented faithfully, that the economy of the recipient country improve, and that the loans be paid back in a timely fashion (Williamson 1990). The mix of factors that change the size of win-sets can be both "sweet and sour" according to Putnam. That is domestic opposition may improve one's negotiating ability (Schelling 1960) and so improve the terms of any agreement but domestic opposition also makes it harder to reach any agreement. Domestic opposition might arise as a result of the efforts of domestic interest groups and opposition political parties, electoral cycles, and even institutional arrangements requiring legislative approval of international agreements.

Putnam notes that the prospective inability to have an agreement ratified at the domestic level will reverberate at the international level, curtailing the possibility of signing an agreement in the first place. From this perspective Putnam contends that the greater the autonomy of country leaders at level I from influence by their level II constituents, the greater the likelihood of achieving international agreement. At level I, the leaders of authoritarian states can negotiate with greater authority and independence from domestic forces at level II. A bias against democracies in the selection processes of the Bank and Fund is, thus, a predicted outcome of the model. It is the natural result of the rational preferences of both sides of the negotiations at level I. Democratic leaders prefer not to lose the support of their constituents, and Bank and Fund leaders prefer not to give loans with conditions that may not be met by the loan recipient.

The second contrasting perspective concentrates on the ability of democracies to make credible commitments that inform other players in the international system of their intent with respect to an international agreement. Both Leeds (1999) and Martin (2000) argue that the properties of democratic accountability and institutionalized cooperation afford democracies the ability to send clear and credible signals concerning their ability to cooperate. These signals increase the probability of cooperation. Martin (2000) makes a strong argument concerning the ability of democracies to implement agreements signed at the international level. The informational properties of democratic regimes in comparison to non-democratic regimes increase the level of certainty players in the international system have about the probability that any signed agreement is implemented in democratic states rather than non-democratic states. While Martin's (2000) argument is limited to advanced industrialized democracies, research by Dollar and Svensson (2000) suggests that Martin's contentions may be generalizable to less developed democracies as well. They provide convincing evidence that democracies are much more likely to implement the World Bank structural adjustment conditions their governments accept. Martin's (2000) theoretical argument and the Dollar and Svensson findings lead us to expect that democracies generally are more likely to receive World Bank loans, all other things being equal.

While the two perspectives differ in their expectations about the abilities of democracies to negotiate successfully, one expectation that does appear common to both is that any domestic factor or international behavior that makes it less likely that the SAL conditions be implemented faithfully would discourage the leaders of the Bank and Fund from concluding an agreement.

2.3 Dependency theory

The most controversial perspective comes from dependency theorists who argue that governments of less developed (peripheral) countries often are forced to depend upon the IMF and the World Bank for external capital (Moyo 2001).[3] They contend that the relationship between countries on the periphery of the world economic system and the international banks is far more coercive than the leaders of the Bank and the Fund are willing to acknowledge. Furthermore, because of the weighted voting systems these institutions employ, lending policies are strongly influenced by the preferences of US leaders and other major contributors to the Bank such as Japan and Germany (Parenti 1989). Indeed, malevolent intent by leaders of the Bank, the Fund, and the major contributors underlies much of this perspective. Core countries use the structure of the international financial system to maintain a core–periphery relationship, since the periphery provides cheap areas of production and helps maintain the profits of companies in the core.

Structural adjustment conditions, especially conditions that increase unemployment and reduce wages, serve to maximize profits for MNCs operating in recipient countries. However, these policies tend to produce threats to the regime, because they require that decision makers enact unpopular policies. These policies cause hardships, especially among the poorest citizens, who are most dependent upon social programs. These hardships, in turn, often provoke protests, that may turn violent (Auyero 2001), and which tend to elicit government repression (Davenport 1995), increasing the level of human rights abuse. Members of the lower class are not only the most direct victims of the new policies, but are also the most common victims of personal integrity rights abuse (Richards 1999).

From the perspective of dependency theory, therefore, government violations of physical integrity rights in periphery states are encouraged by international institutions like the World Bank and the IMF that do the bidding of the core states (Parenti 1989). Repression is likely to be rewarded with bilateral foreign aid from core states and with loans from the World Bank. Structural adjustment loan programs ensure that the core receives cheap goods and that multinational corporations based in core states receive large profits. It is even possible that this arrangement allows elites in recipient countries to receive extra rents at the expense of their own populations (Berkeley 2001).[4] Dependency theorists see the World Bank as an institution designed to maintain the dependency of less developed countries on core states like the United States. Thus, they would expect the Bank to give more loans to states that were authoritarian (but not communist), that showed little respect for the rights of workers (Myers 1994; Pion-Berlin 1984) and that violated the physical integrity rights of their citizens.

3 Previous research

There are broad theoretical reasons to believe that certain non-random processes underlie the loan selection criteria of the Bank. Thus, if one is interested in assessing the impact of World Bank SALs, then methods that compare countries that did and did not receive loans (e.g., Harrigan and Mosley 1991), or engage in before and after assessments of a particular country, are potentially misleading. All the previous work on World Bank SAL lending ignores these issues of selection and randomization. Thus, we have no way of knowing whether the positive or negative impact attributed to SALs are a result of World Bank policy or because of the pre-existing situation in the country under examination. It is then critical to determine the process that increases or reduces the probability of World Bank loan receipt before any research can make substantive claims concerning the impact of World Bank loans on the particular dependent variable of interest.

The theories described above suggest four categories of selection criteria, that determine the probability of receiving a World Bank structural adjustment loan. Considering the paucity of work that specifically investigates the determinants of World Bank lending practices, many of our arguments arise out of the literature concerning the World Bank's sister organization the IMF. The first concerns economic issues. The second concerns political issues. The third concerns issues of domestic and international conflict, and the fourth concerns issues of human rights. Since both the IMF and the World Bank insist upon the imposition of structural adjustment conditions for loan recipients and since both use a similar weighted voting system for deciding upon loan applications, one would expect that the selection criteria of both institutions would be similar. To this extent we build upon some of the insights gained from studies which examined the IMF, and apply them to the World Bank.

3.1 *Economic determinants of receiving a World Bank SAL*

The Commonwealth Secretariat (1989: 19–22), Harrigan and Mosley (1991), and Mehra (1991) argue that the economic slowdown in the 1970s and early 1980s and its impact in terms of increased debt, deteriorating economic growth, and balance of payments problems in developing countries in general necessitated the need for major adjustment. With reference to specific regions of the World, in Africa generally (Adepoju 1993: 2; Lele 1991; Sahn 1996: 3; Sahn and Haddad 1991) and also in specific countries: Argentina (Pion-Berlin 1984), Cameroon (Ndongko 1993: 119–21; Subramanian 1996: 62), Ghana (Konadu-Agyemang 2001; Sowa 1993: 8–9), India (Sukhamte 1989), Ivory Coast (Stryker and Tuluy 1989); Jamaica (Handa and King 1997; Klak 1996), Malawi (Chipeta 1993: 105–7; Frausum and Sahn 1996: 311), Niger (Dorosh *et al.* 1996: 147), Nigeria (Dennis 1992, Ihonvbere 1992), Peru (Tanski 1994), Sierra Leone (Eliott 1993: 40–2), Senegal (Kane 1993), South Korea (Krueger *et al.* 1989), Turkey (Ğ ǎtay 1994; Krueger and Ruttan 1989a), Tanzania (Vuorela 1991), Zambia (Mwanawina 1993: 69–71), and Zimbabwe (Kanji and Jazdowska 1995: 134–6; Riphenburg 1997: 33–4), all the authors note a litany of economic misery including declining exports, increasing imports, inflation, state control of the economy, government spending outstripping government revenues, decline in the inflow of concessionary capital, deteriorating terms of trade, overvalued currencies, corruption, political instability, poor economic growth, high debt, severe financial imbalances, and unfavorable weather conditions, as situations found in African countries prior to the receipt of structural adjustment loans.

Focusing on such factors, Frey and Schneider (1986) conducted a study of 60 loan recipients in 1981 and 1982, examining the characteristics of countries most likely to receive the largest loans from the World Bank. One important contribution of their study was that it derived theoretical propositions and tested them empirically for the first time. Among the loan recipients, loans were bigger if the loan recipient showed a high degree of economic need (per capita income was low, the rate of inflation was high, external debt was high, and past economic growth was poor). They received bigger loans from the IBRD if they were politically stable and they had a good "capitalist climate."

The authors also presented two types of evidence suggesting that dependency theory carried some weight in explaining loan amounts. First, they found that the former colonies of the United Kingdom, France, and the United States received larger loans. Their analysis also indicated that dependence was important because larger loans were made to countries that had relatively large imports from the United Kingdom, France, and the United States, three major contributors to the Bank. The authors suggested that the larger loans were approved by the donor countries, so that the loan recipients could pay for those imports (Frey and Schneider 1986: 242). Since Dollar and Svensson (2000) and Frey and Schneider (1986) only sought to answer questions about World Bank loan recipients, they tell us nothing about the selection criteria of the Bank.

Building upon previous research, Joyce (1992) models the economic characteristics of IMF program countries in comparison to non-recipients. His work assesses a range of economic factors that impact the probability of program receipt. Measures of foreign exchange reserves and other economic factors play some role in loan receipt, but Joyce (1992: 242) notes that purely economic models exclude institutional and social factors that affect a government's decision on acceptance of Fund assistance. This work builds upon these arguments applying them to the World Bank, where there is reason to believe that, in addition to economic criteria, political and social factors impact the probability of loan receipt.

With the exception of a small body of research conducted to estimate determinants (Joyce 1992) and effects of IMF loans on economic growth (Przeworski and Vreeland 2000), the factors that affect which countries the IMF and World Bank decide to make loans to has been ignored by those who have conducted both large- and small-*n* comparative studies. Systematic biases in the types of countries selected to receive SALs could affect the conclusions concerning the impacts of these loans. Adepoju (1993: 5) rightly asks how one distinguishes between the impact of structural adjustment and that of broader economic difficulties. This crucial question, however, is given little examination, other than to note that the authors' in Adepoju's edited volume approach the problem by examining the situation pre and post SAL (e.g., Sowa 1993) and that while this might be a "conceptual dilemma ... the general trend is apparent-deterioration in the social sectors" (Adepoju 1993: 5).

Others attempt to disentangle these impacts through the use of statistical comparison of paired samples, similar countries that did and did not receive loans (Harrigan and Mosley 1991). Harrigan and Mosley (1991: 69) suggest that their results, which concern the effects of World Bank loans "cannot be explained by non-randomness of SAL selection." However, they do not address the question of why their counterfactual countries, constructed to control for as many macroeconomic differences as possible, did not receive a SAL? More recent work has used simulations to distinguish between the impacts of adjustment and pre-existing factors (Sahn 1996; Subramanian 1996; Dorosh *et al.* 1996; Frausum and Sahn 1996). While admirable in intention and sophisticated in execution, this work still does not adequately deal with selection processes of the Bank.

All of the previous large-n, comparative studies which account for issues of selection have been conducted by scholars operating within the classical-economics or critical-economics schools, and have sought to discover whether acceptance of IMF conditions leads to greater economic growth. Thus, the emphasis has been on economic characteristics of potential loan recipients that make them more or less likely that they will sign an IMF agreement accepting a SAL. According to IMF policies, a balance of payments deficit or a foreign reserves crisis is the prerequisite for signing an IMF agreement (Przeworski and Vreeland 2000). Even so, previous research results have been divided on whether a balance of payments deficit is sufficient to explain whether a government will receive an IMF loan (Goldstein and Montiel 1986) or not (Przeworski and Vreeland 2000; Knight and Santaella 1997; Bird 1996; Edwards and Santaella 1993). Przeworski and Vreeland (2000) also conclude that a large balance of payments deficit is not sufficient to explain agreements.

3.2 Political determinants of receiving World Bank SALs

Economic factors are part of the explanation, but the literature suggests that they do not provide a complete picture. For example, governments in about a third of the cases, which received IMF loans with conditionality stipulations in Przeworski and Vreeland's (2000) work did not have balance of payments difficulties. Is there an explanation of why governments would accept IMF conditions when they are not in economic difficulty? There is much work that argues that the leaders of developing countries have no choice but to go to the IMF for external capital necessary for development. However, many believe that some governments enter into IMF or World Bank agreements because they want conditions to be imposed (Bjork 1995; Dixit 1996; Edwards and Santaella 1993; Przeworski and Vreeland 2000; Putnam 1988; Remmer 1986; Stein 1992; Vaubel 1986; Vreeland 1999). Government leaders may know that some areas of their economy need restructuring to be more efficient and competitive. Yet reform, while possibly necessary and in the long-term interests of most people in a particular country, may pose significant electoral hazards for leaders. These leaders need to blame the IMF or World Bank for imposing them. In short, politics matters and may be a key consideration in the determinants of loan receipt. A more controversial version of this argument suggests that not only do political considerations on the part of domestic governments matter, but also that governments seeking loans may restrict the rights of some of their citizens in order to make themselves more attractive to international financial institutions (Pion-Berlin 1984).

In their broad comparative study Przeworski and Vreeland (2000: 394) delineate the determinants of IMF selection criteria. They examine the effect of regime type on the probability of a government signing an IMF agreement and find that "the IMF is more likely to sign with dictatorships." There is also some case study evidence suggesting that the IMF has shown a preference for military dictatorships by financially rewarding military governments that overthrew democratically elected administrations (Pion-Berlin 1984; Meyers 1998: 186). Discussing the actions of a military government in Argentina led by General Ongania, Pion-Berlin (1984: 116) contends that the Ongania administration engaged in "preemptive coercion" including the banning of unions, freezing of union accounts, and the use of force to break up strikes to convince the IMF that Argentina was worthy of a loan. He contends that Argentina was quickly rewarded by the IMF for these policies. In yet another case, he describes the IMF's unwillingness to give loans to the democratically elected government of Isabel Perón. When that government was toppled in a military coup in 1976, he writes that "the international credit came pouring in" including a substantial IMF loan (Pion-Berlin 1984: 118). In comparison, there is some reason to believe that the World Bank in comparison to the

IMF may not pay much attention to regime type. Nelson (2000) notes that the World Bank is restricted from becoming involved in political matters. Thus from this perspective the World Bank does not discriminate between democratic and non-democratic regimes and so we would not expect to find a bias with respect to either kind of regime.

The size of a country's population is another important political determinant of adjustment lending. The governments of more populous countries are likely to have greater influence over Bank policies. More-populous countries tend to have more influence in the international system, even if they are still developing. China is a good example.

Finally, the end of the Cold War also had a significant impact on changing the calculation of decision makers. There was a strong case for Western-backed development in the former communist countries, which had, in practice, been ineligible for World Bank loans during the Cold War (van de Laar 1980). The West supported development in these newly independent countries to cement both democratic and pro-Western attitudes. Multilateral institutions like the World Bank are key tools to achieving these foreign policy goals of Western states (Tarnoff and Nowels 2001). In addition, after the end of the Cold War, many of the major bilateral foreign aid providers channelled more of their aid through international financial institutions such as the World Bank. Thus, as a result of the end of the Cold War, all countries have a higher probability of receiving loans from international financial institutions.

3.3 International and domestic conflict determinants of receiving World Bank SALs

No previous study has examined the impact of international conflict and domestic unrest on the selection criteria of the World Bank. There is some discussion in the literature that when structural adjustment conditionality is imposed the effect on the recipients of IMF and World Bank loans often leads to increases in domestic unrest (Bello *et al.* 1994; Pion-Berlin 1984; Przeworski and Vreeland 2000). However, there has been little if any attention to how likelihood of conflict domestically or internationally affects the probability of getting a loan from either international financial institution. If the Bank does operate along classical economic lines, it would view both domestic and international conflict as factors reducing the probability of prospective agreements being implemented and existing loans being repaid in a timely manner. Countries in conflict are a poor investment. If there is domestic unrest, a new government may be installed. Previous agreements made by the government, including those made with the World Bank, may not be honored. Argentina is a good example where large-scale riots led to a revolving door of presidents, most recently during 2001–02, generating considerable uncertainty about likelihood of IMF loan repayment. Similarly, if a potential recipient is involved in a war with another state, the governments of the warring parties may be conquered and replaced.

3.4 Human rights determinants of World Bank SALs

Finally, there is some work suggesting that the human rights situation in potential recipient countries, including both respect for workers' rights and personal integrity rights, are important determinants of World Bank loan receipts. For example, Klak's (1996) argument with reference to the Caribbean basin in general and Jamaica specifically is that there are indirect incentives for limiting workers' rights in order to be more competitive internationally. He notes the establishment of Export Processing Zones, where international corporations are encouraged to invest for export purposes, which have 10–15-year exemptions from taxes and duties. These EPZs are looked upon favorably by the World Bank (Klak 1996: 358). In an effort to make these EPZs as competitive as possible, Klak notes (1996: 358) that governments put downward pressure on wages and rental rates for industrial space. Thus, labor loses out in order to make countries as attractive as possible to international investors. In comparison, more recent work (Nelson 2000) argues that the Bank has in fact had a long-standing commitment to maintaining rights, which promote economic growth. From this perspective, maintaining workers' rights may actually increase the probability of receiving structural adjustment loans if the Bank views respect for those rights as beneficial to economic growth.

As noted earlier, Pion-Berlin (1984) makes a more controversial case that the IMF actively seeks out loan recipients willing to be tough, even repressive in the face of domestic protest against the implementation of liberal economic policies. Each time Argentina was successful in attracting IMF loans, repression of labor, especially organized labor, which rebelled against the new policies, increased dramatically. Referring to the Frondizi administration in 1958, Pion-Berlin (1984: 115) writes that "the government thought that its use of force to end a railroad strike in November would enhance its chances of gaining IMF credit. Apparently it was right."

3.5 Hypotheses

Relevant theories and previous research suggest several hypotheses concerning the criteria by which the World Bank selects recipients for loans. Those potential biases are reflected in the hypotheses described in Table 8.1. A number of competing theoretical perspectives provide the same expectations about the conditions under which countries are more likely to receive a SAL. For example, both classical economic theory and dependency theory suggest that countries that engage in increased international trade will be more likely to receive a SAL, though the reasoning, as we have already noted, is very different. There is an over-abundance of

Table 8.1 Hypotheses: multiple theoretical perspectives

Variables	Classical economic theory	Classical economic theory critics	Dependency theory	Democratic credibility	Two-level games
Economic					
Positive percent change GDP per capita	Reduces				
Larger foreign currency reserves	Reduces				
Lower exchange rate value	Reduces				
Higher GDP per capita	Reduces				
Extent of international trade	Increases		Increases		
Human rights					
More respect for personal integrity rights		No relationship	Reduces		
Higher levels of respect for workers' rights	Increases	No relationship	Reduces		
Political					
Alliance with the United States		Increases	Increases		
Higher levels of democracy		No relationship	Reduces	Increases	Reduces
Military regimes		No relationship	Increases	Reduces	Increases
France, UK, US, and Japanese dependent/colonial experience			Increases		
Conflict proneness					
More domestic conflict		Reduces			Reduces
More external conflict		Reduces			Reduces

theory (Ikenberry 1999) with multiple theoretical explanations for similar outcomes concerning the impact of democracy, military regimes, and the extent of domestic and international conflict on the probability of SAL receipt. If relationships with multiple theoretical explanations prove significant, the next stage of theory development would be to provide discriminating tests between these competing perspectives (Schultz 1999). The theoretical perspectives also provide a number of discriminating hypotheses concerning the impact of personal integrity and labor rights, and to a lesser extent the impact of democracy on the probability of SAL receipt. If significant, these hypotheses will provide a stronger basis from which to adjudicate between competing theoretical perspectives.

4 Research design

This study uses a cross-national, annual time-series dataset comprised of all nations of the world having a population of at least 500000 in 1981. The data span the time period from 1981 to 2000. The World Bank has given SALs to a number of more economically developed countries. During the 1981–2000 period, the World Bank awarded a total of 473 SALs to countries in our sample, with a GDP per capita as high as $15878. For this reason, the analysis includes all countries in the world, not just less developed countries. Table 8.2 provides a summary of the operationalization of variables.

5 Results

Table 8.3 shows the probability of receiving a World Bank SAL during the period 1981–2000. As Table 8.3 shows, several of the factors examined increased the probability of SAL loan receipt. In the post-Cold War period countries were more likely to receive loans. Countries were also more likely to receive loans if they were poor, if they had larger populations, if their governments provided greater respect for workers' rights and, if they had previously received a loan from the World Bank. The relationship between previous receipt of a World Bank loan and the likelihood of receipt of a new loan appears curvilinear (at the 0.06 level of probability). Immediately after receiving a loan, governments were less likely to receive another, but as time passed the probability of receiving another loan increased geometrically. Colonial/dependent relationships with Japan also increased the probability of SAL receipt.

As expected, increased levels of GDP per capita and higher levels of foreign currency reserves reduced the probability of SAL loan receipt. Higher levels of domestic unrest also reduced the probability of SAL loan receipt. In comparison, percentage change in GDP per capita, level of exchange rate, extent of international trade, level of respect for personal integrity rights, alliance with the United States, the level of democracy,

Table 8.2 Operationalization of variables

Independent variable	Indicator	Source
Economic		
Growth in GDP per capita	% change in GDP per capita current US$ (purchasing power parity)	World Bank (2002b)
Larger foreign currency reserves	Average government foreign reserves to reflect monthly imports	World Bank (2002b)
Higher exchange rate value	Average annual official exchange rate local currency unit per US$	World Bank (2002b)
Higher GDP per capita	GDP per capita current US$ (purchasing power parity)	World Bank (2002b)
Extent of international trade	Trade percentage of GDP	World Bank (2002b)
Political		
Alliance with the United States	Correlates of war alliance variable	COW Alliance Data-Set
Higher level of democracy	Level of democracy measure	POLITY IV (2000)
Military regimes	Type of regime: civilian or military	Banks (2002)
Larger populations	Logged midyear country population	US Government Census: IDB
(End of) Cold War	Dichotomous	Banks and Muller (2002)
Conflict proneness		
Higher levels of interstate conflict	Ordinal level of interstate conflict	Strand *et al.* (2002)
Higher levels of domestic unrest	Riots: any violent demonstration or clash of more than 100 citizens involving the use of physical force	Banks, Arthur (2002)
Human rights		
More respect for human rights	Index of killing, disappearances, torture, and imprisonment	Cingranelli and Richards (1999)
More respect for workers' rights	0 = not protected by government; 1 = somewhat protected by government; 2 = protected by government	Cingranelli (2002)
France, UK, US, and Japanese dependent/colonial experience	The rule of the most recent possessor identifies the relationships under examination	Hensel (1999)
Temporal dependence		
Number of years since last SAL	Beck *et al.* (1998) BTCS Method	
Number of years since last SAL^2	Beck *et al.* (1998) BTCS Method	
Splines	Beck *et al.* (1998) BTCS Method	
Dependent variable		
World Bank SAL receipt	Dichotomous	Correspondence with World Bank

Table 8.3 Probit regression results of World Bank selection criteria, 1981–2000

Independent variable	Coefficient
Economic variables	
Percentage change in GDP per capita	−0.006
	(0.005)
Average foreign currency reserves	−0.027*
	(0.016)
Exchange rate value	0.000001
	(0.000001)
GDP per capita	−0.0001***
	(0.00001)
Extent of international trade	−0.001
	(0.001)
Human rights	
Level of respect for personal integrity rights	−0.025
	(0.021)
Level of respect for workers' rights	0.177**
	(0.061)
Political variables	
Alliance with United States	0.104
	(0.092)
Level of democracy	−0.009
	(0.013)
Military regime	0.129
	(0.12)
Log of population	0.113***
	(0.033)
Cold War	0.299***
	(0.086)
French dependent/colonial experience	−0.082
	(0.113)
UK dependent/colonial experience	−0.119
	(0.093)
USA dependent/colonial experience	0.08
	(0.451)
Japanese dependent/colonial experience	0.562*
	(0.335)
Conflict proneness variables	
Domestic unrest	−0-.081**
	(0.033)
Interstate conflict	−0.131
	(0.113)
Control variables	
Number of years since previous SAL	−0.307***
	(0.086)
Number of years since previous SAL^2	0.039
	(0.024)
Constant	−2.13***
	(0.582)
Pseudo R^2 15.01	$N = 1893$

Notes
One Tailed Test (splines used to control for temporal dependence).
$P > 0.05$*; $P > 0.01$**; $P > 0.001$***.

and the level of interstate conflict had no statistically significant impact on the probability of loan receipt.

5.1 Predicted probabilities

The predicted probabilities for the statistically significant variables of interest are shown in Table 8.4. The predicted probabilities provide a measure of the magnitude of relationship between the independent and dependent variables of interest. Holding all other variables at their mean or modal value allows us to assess the impact of a change in the value of the independent variable. We chose to describe the impact of changing the independent variables from their minimum to maximum value.

With respect to economic factors changing the average foreign currency reserves from their minimum to maximum value reduces the probability of SAL loan receipt by 0.09. In comparison changing from the lowest to highest GDP per capita reduces the probability of SAL loan receipt by 0.25. The extent of respect for workers' rights also impacts the probability of loan receipt. Moving from a country with no respect for workers' rights to those with full respect for workers' rights increases the probability of loan receipt by 0.06. Political factors are important too. Moving from the smallest to largest country increased the probability of loan receipt by 0.20. The end of the Cold War increased the probability of loan receipt by 0.06. The extent of domestic unrest also plays an important role. Countries that are experiencing the highest levels of rioting are less likely to receive a loan by 0.12.

Table 8.4 Change in predicted probabilities[a]

Independent variables	Change in probability of SAL receipt[b]
Economic	
Average foreign currency reserves	−0.09
GDP per capita	−0.25
Human rights	
Level of respect for workers' rights	0.06
Political variables	
Log of population	0.20
Cold War	0.06
Japanese dependent/colonial experience	0.14
Conflict proneness	
Level of domestic unrest	−0.12

Notes
a Holding all variables at their mean or modal values.
b When variable value from minimum to maximum.

6 Conclusions

In this chapter, the factors that increased or decreased the probability of a country's government receiving a World Bank structural adjustment loan in the 20-year period from 1981–2000 were identified. The governments of 161 countries of the world were included in the analysis. This is the first large-*n*, comparative study of the selection criteria of the World Bank. Four different and partly contradictory theoretical perspectives were advanced that could be used to describe or explain the selection criteria of the World Bank: classical economic theory (Van De Laar 1980), the theory of two-level games in international affairs (Putnam 1988; Milner 1997), the logic of credible commitments (Leeds 1999; Martin 2000), and dependency theory (Pion-Berlin 1984). Hypotheses were derived from each of these perspectives and tested.

The results provided substantial support for the idea that the Bank's operational code based on classical economic theory does, indeed, guide loan selection decisions. That code of practice stipulates that the Bank give loans to countries that are poor, have a capitalist ideology, and are creditworthy. The findings indicated that the poorest countries were more likely to receive SALs from the World Bank than others. This was one of the strongest relationships discovered in the study. The only indicator used to test commitment to capitalism was a measure of involvement in international trade, and it proved to have no relationship to the probability of receiving a loan. It was argued that involvement in domestic or international conflict reduced potential loan recipient's creditworthiness, and significant support was found for the arguments that domestic unrest was found to reduce the probability of getting a SAL from the Bank.

One of the most important political questions examined in this chapter was whether the selection processes of the Bank were biased against democratic regimes. This question is important for both theoretical and practical reasons. Putnam's theory of two-level games led us to expect that democracies would be less likely to be selected. The idea that democratic regimes can make more credible commitments in international negotiations implied that democracies would be more likely to be selected. Mainstream critics of the bank have argued that the World Bank pays little attention to nurturing democracies, implying that democracies would be neither more or less likely to receive loans from the Bank.

The easiest interpretation of the lack of relationship between degree of democracy and the probability of receiving a loan is that it supports the mainstream critical view. However, the findings do not clearly run against Putnam's argument about the disadvantages democracies face in international negotiations or the argument that democracies make more credible commitments in international negotiations. It is possible that the lack of discrimination against democratic governments is a result of an "affirmative action policy" on the part of the Bank that ensures they are not disadvantaged. Without such a policy, authoritarian governments might have had an advantage. The finding that military governments were no more likely to receive SALs than democratic governments lends little support to the critics of the Bank that little attention is paid to regime type, but contrast with those of Przeworski and Vreeland (2000), who find a bias in the IMF toward military regimes.

Similarly, the research conducted by Dollar and Svensson (2000) provides convincing evidence that the commitments made by democratic governments to implement economic reforms are much more credible than commitments made by civilian authoritarian or military governments. Our findings simply suggest that the officials of the Bank either have not recognized that fact in the past or have refused to take it into account in the loan selection process. If the Bank was more biased toward democratic regimes in the loan selection process, there would be fewer cases where reform commitments would not be honored by loan recipients.

One of the strongest findings to emerge from our study was that countries with larger populations were much more likely to receive SALs from the World Bank. While it is possible to treat population size as a technical control variable, we think that the bias toward large countries is political. More populated countries like India and Indonesia carry greater weight in the international system, and it is likely that preferences toward such countries in the selection process are due to this fact.

Another important finding to emerge from this analysis is that the Bank tends to give SALs to the same set of countries over and over again. One possibility is that this finding reflects the fact that the Bank continues to work closely with cooperative governments of developing countries. New loans are rewards for good past performance. However, this finding is also consistent with the Dollar and Svensson (2000: 896) finding that, "once a bad loan is made, there is a tendency to put a lot of resources into salvaging it." Their findings indicate that these tactics are fruitless.

The only theory to receive almost no support from these findings was the dependency theory. The "bad motives" arguments of dependency theorists led us to expect that the World Bank would provide a disproportionate share of its loans to governments allied with the United States, governments extensively involved in international trade, authoritarian governments, and governments that did not protect the personal integrity rights of their citizens. None of these hypotheses were confirmed. Those arguments also led us to hypothesize that the World Bank would provide more loans to governments that did not respect the rights of workers, but the opposite proved to be true. The Bank, in contrast with the claims of protestors in London, Washington, DC, Prague, and Paris, is not encouraging a race to the bottom by rewarding countries that limit the rights of the workers.

Understanding the selection criteria of the World Bank is of crucial practical importance to any estimation of the effects of World Bank loans. Since there are selection criteria, simply comparing recipient to non-recipient as some previous research has done (Harrigan and Mosley 1991) will not advance our knowledge of loan impacts because a non-random process generated which countries became recipients and which countries did not. This means that in order to isolate the impact of World Bank loans future work needs to "disentangle" the selection criteria in World Bank loan receipt from the actual impact of the loan itself in addition to controlling for alternative explanations that may impact the dependent variable of interest. Disentangling this process will allow future research to answer the question: All other things being equal, was it the loans or the pre-existing situation that account for the impact attributed to World Bank structural adjustment loans?

Notes

* We would like to thank David Clark for his help and assistance with this project. Any errors are entirely our own.
1 The perspective found in the World Bank Structural Adjustment Loan Policy Operational Manual (World Bank 1992) is less elaborate. It notes that:

> Success with stabilization usually requires a sustainable mixture of cuts in government spending, reductions in public enterprise losses, tightening of domestic credit, and increases in tax revenues. Central bank losses that result from the provision of credit subsidies to particular sectors, often through the exchange rate or banking system, are frequently an important source of inflationary pressure that need to be eliminated immediately.

2 See Milner (1997) for some examples of formal models of these relationships. Vreeland (2001) also uses a number of formal models to generate expectations about countries with which the IMF prefers to sign agreements. His expectations suggest that the IMF prefers to deal with regimes that have fewer veto players.
3 For an excellent review of this literature, see Richards *et al.* (2001)
4 One especially nefarious variant of the dependency perspective is that elites in peripheral countries benefit from the core periphery system. While they may endure some internal threats due to measures that serve to maximize profits for MNCs they are rewarded with informal acquiescence of the international financial community and MNCs through corruptly creaming off inflows of foreign capital for themselves. For example the Mobutu regime in Zimbabwe allegedly shipped foreign aid out to private personal accounts abroad almost as fast as it arrived (Berkeley 2001).

References

Achen, Christopher H. 1986. *The Statistical Analysis of Quasi Experiments.* Berkley: University of California Press.

Adepoju, Aderanti. 1993. Introduction. In *The Impact of Structural Adjustment on the Population of Africa*, edited by Aderanti Adepoju, pp. 1–6. United Nations Population Fund, New Hampshire: Heinemann.

Auyero, J. 2001. Global Riots. *International Sociology* 16 (1) (March): 33–53.

Banks, Arthur S. 2002. *Cross-National Time-Series Data Archive* [computer file]. Binghamton: Computer Solutions Unlimited.

Banks, Arthur S. and Thomas Muller. 2002. *Political Handbook of the World.* Binghamton: Binghamton University.

Beck, Nathaniel, Jonathan N. Katz, and Richard Tucker. 1998. Taking Time Seriously in Binary Time-Series Cross-Section Analysis. *American Journal of Political Science* 42 (4): 1260–88.

Bello, Walden F., Cunningham Shea, and Bill Rau. 1994. *Dark Victory: The United States, Structural Adjustment, and Global Poverty.* London: Pluto: Institute for Food and Development Policy.

Berkeley, Bill. 2001. *The Graves Are Not Yet Full: Race, Tribe and Power in the Heart of Africa.* New York: Basic Books,

Bird, G. 1996. Borrowing from the IMF: the Policy Implications of Recent Empirical Research. *World Development* 24: 1753–60.

Bjork, J. 1995. The Uses of Conditionality. *East European Quarterly* 29: 89–124.

Çağatay, Nilfer. 1994. Turkish Women and Structural Adjustment. In *The Strategic Silence Gender and Economic Policy*, edited by Isabella Bakker. London: Zed Books.

Chipeta, C. 1993. Malawi. In *The Impact of Structural Adjustment on the Population of Africa*, edited by Aderanti Adepoju, pp. 105–18. United Nations Population Fund, New Hampshire: Heinemann.

Cingranelli, David L. and David L. Richards. 1999. Measuring the Level, Pattern, and Sequence of Government Respect for Physical Integrity Rights. *International Studies Quarterly* 43 (2) (June): 407–18.

Collier, David. 1991. The Comparative Method: Two Decades of Change. In *Comparative Political Dynamics: Global Research Perspectives*, edited by Dankwart Rustow and Kenneth Erickson. New York: HarperCollins.

Commonwealth Secretariat. 1989. *Engendering Adjustment for the 1990s: Report of a Commonwealth Expert Group on Women and Structural Adjustment.* London: Commonwealth Secretariat.

Davenport, Christian. 1995. Multi-Dimensional Threat Perception and State Repression: An Inquiry into Why States Apply Negative Sanctions. *American Journal of Political Science* 39 (3) (August): 683–713.

Dennis, Carolyne. 1992. The Christian Churches and Women's Experience of Structural Adjustment in Nigeria. In *Women and Adjustment Policies in the Third World*, edited by Haleh Afshar and Carolyne Dennis. New York: St. Martins Press.

Dixit. A.K. 1996. *The Making of Economic Policy: A Transaction-Cost Perspective.* Cambridge: MIT Press.

Dollar, David and Jakob Svensson. 2000. What Explains the Success or Failure of Structural Adjustment Programmes?. *The Economic Journal* 110 (October): 894–917.

Dorosh, Paul, B. Essama-Nssah, and Ousmane Samba-Manadou. 1996. Terms of Trade and the Real Exchange Rate in the CFA Zone: Implication for Income and Distribution in Niger. In *Economic Reform and the Poor in Africa*, edited by David E. Sahn. Oxford: Oxford University Press.

Edwards, S. and J.A. Santaella. 1993. Devaluation Controversies in the Developing Countries: Lessons from the Bretton Woods Era. In *A Retrospective on the Bretton Woods System*, edited by M.D. Bordo and B. Eichengreen, pp. 405–55. University of Chicago Press.

Eliott, Josie W. 1993. Sierra Leone. In *The Impact of Structural Adjustment on the Population of Africa*, edited by Aderanti Adepoju, pp. 105–18. United Nations Population Fund, New Hampshire: Heinemann.

Frausum, Yves Van and David E. Sahn. 1996. Perpetuating Poverty for Malawi's Smallholders: External Shocks and Policy Distortions. In *Economic Reform and the Poor in Africa*, edited by David E. Sahn. Oxford: Oxford University Press.

Frey, Bruno S. and Friedrich Schneider. 1986. Competing Models of International Lending Activity. *Journal of Development Economics* 20: 225–45.

Friedman, Thomas L. 2000. *The Lexus and the Olive Tree.* New York: Anchor Books.

Gibney, Mark and Matthew Dalton. 1996. The Political Terror Scale. In *Human Rights and Developing Countries*, edited by David L. Cingranelli, pp. 73–84. Greenwich: JAI Press, Inc.

Goldstein, M. and P.J. Montiel. 1986. Evaluating Fund Stabilization Programs with Multicountry Data: Some Methodological Pitfalls. *IMF Staff Papers* 33: 304–44.

Handa, Sudhanshu and Damien King. 1997. Structural Adjustment Policies, Income Distribution and Poverty: A Review of the Jamaican Experience. *World Development* 25 (6): 915–30.

Harrigan, Jane and Paul Mosley. 1991. Assessing the Impact of World Bank Structural Development Lending 1980–1987. *Journal of Development Studies* 27 (3): 63–94.

Heckman, J.J. 1988. The Microeconomic Evaluation of Social Programs and Economic Institutions. In *Chung-Hua Series of Lectures by Invited Eminent Economists*, No. 14. Taipei: The Institute of Economics Academia Sinica.

Hensel, Paul R. 1999. *ICOW Colonial History Data Set* (Version 0.1). Available from http://garnet.acns.fsu.edu/~phensel/icowdata.html#colonies (Acessed 6.11.03).

Ihonvbere, Jo. 1992. The Military and Political Engineering Under Structural Adjustment: The Nigerian Experience Since 1985. *Journal of Political and Military Sociology* 20 (1): 107–31.

Ikenberry, G. John. 1999. *American Foreign Policy: Theoretical Essays*, 3rd edition. New York: Longman.

Joyce, Joseph P. 1992. The Economic Characteristics of IMF Program Countries. *Economics Letters* 38: 237–42.

Kane, Karamoko. 1993. Senegal. In *The Impact of Structural Adjustment on the Population of Africa*, edited by Aderanti Adepoju, pp. 60–8. United Nations Population Fund, New Hampshire: Heinemann.

Kanji, Nazneen and Niki Jazdowska. 1995. Gender, Structural Adjustment and Employment in Urban Zimbabwe. *TWPR* 17 (2): 133–54.

Klak, Thomas. 1996. Distributional Impacts of the "Free Zone" Component of Structural Adjustment: The Jamaican Experience. *Growth and Change* 27 (Summer): 352–87.

Knack, S. and P. Keefer. 1997. Why Don't Poor Countries Catch Up? A Cross-national Test of an Institutional Explanation. *Economic Inquiry* 35 (July): 590–602.

Knight, M. and J.A. Santaella. 1997. Economic Determinants of Fund Financial Arrangements. *Journal of Development Economics* 54: 405–36.

Konadu-Agyemang, K. 2001. Structural Adjustment Programs and Housing Affordability in Accra, Ghana. *Canadian Geographer* 45 (4) (Winter): 528–44.

Krueger, Anne O. and Vernon W. Ruttan. 1989a. Assistance to Korea. In *Aid and Development*, edited by Anne O. Krueger, Constantine Michalopoulos, and Vernon W. Ruttan, pp. 226–49. Baltimore: The Johns Hopkins University Press.

Krueger, Anne O. and Vernon W. Ruttan. 1989b. Assistance to Turkey. In *Aid and Development*, edited by Anne O. Krueger, Constantine Michalopoulos, and Vernon W. Ruttan, pp. 250–68. Baltimore: The Johns Hopkins University Press.

Krueger, Anne O., Constantine Michalopoulos, and Vernon W. Ruttan (eds). 1989. *Aid and Development*. Baltimore: The Johns Hopkins University Press.

Leeds, Brett Ashley. 1999. Domestic Political Institutions, Credible Commitments and International Co-operation. *American Journal of Political Science* 43 (4): 979–1002.

Lele, Uma. 1991. The Gendered Impacts of Structural Adjustment Programs in Africa. *American Journal of Agricultural Economics* (December): 1452–5.

Martin, Lisa. 2000. *Democratic Commitments: Legislatures and International Cooperation*. Princeton: Princeton University Press.

Mehra, Rekha. 1991. Can Structural Adjustment Work for Women Farmers. *American Journal of Agricultural Economics* (December): 1440–7.

Meyers, William H. 1998. *Human Rights and International Political Economy in Third World Nations: Multinational Corporations, Foreign Aid, and Repression*. Westport: Greenwood.

Milner, Helen. 1997. *Interests, Institutions, and Information: Domestic Politics and International Relations*. Princeton: Princeton University Press.

Moyo, S. 2001. The Land Occupation Movement and Democratisation in Zimbabwe: Contradictions of Neoliberalism. *Millennium Journal of International Studies* 30 (2): 311–30.

Murrel, P. 1992. Conservative Political-Philosophy and the Strategy of Economic Transition. *East European Politics and Societies* 6 (1) (Winter): 3–16.

Mwanawina, I. 1993. Zambia. In *The Impact of Structural Adjustment on the Population of Africa*, edited by Aderanti Adepoju, pp. 105–18. United Nations Population Fund, New Hampshire: Heinemann.

Myers, David J. 1994. Brazil: The Quest for Influence, the Possibility of Hegemony. *International Journal on World Peace* 1 (1): 25.

Ndongko. 1993. Cameroon. *The Impact of Structural Adjustment on the Population of Africa*, edited by Aderanti Adepoju, pp. 119–29. United Nations Population Fund, New Hampshire: Heinemann.

Nelson, P. 2000. Whose Civil Society? Whose Governance? Decision-Making and Practice in the New Agenda at the Inter-American Development Bank and the World Bank. *Global Governance* 6 (4) (October–December): 405–31.

Palast, Greg. 2003. *The Best Democracy Money Can Buy: An Investigative Reporter Exposes the Truth About Globalization Corporate Cons and High Finance Fraudsters*. New York: Penguin.

Parenti, Michael. 1989. *The Sword and the Dollar*. New York: St. Martin Press.

Payer, Cheryl. 1982. *The World Bank: A Critical Analysis*. New York: Monthly Review Press.

Pion-Berlin, David. 1984. The Political Economy of State Repression in Argentina. In *The State as Terrorist: The Dynamics of Governmental Violence and Repression*, edited by Michael Stohl and George A. Lopez, pp. 99–123. Westport: Greenwood Press.

Polity IV. 2000. *Polity IV*. Available from http://weber.ucsd.edu/~kgledits/Polity.html (Accessed 8.6.02).

Przeworski, Adam and James Raymond Vreeland. 2000. The Effects of IMF Programs on Economic Growth. *The Journal of Development Economics* 62: 385–421.

Putnam, Robert D. 1988. Diplomacy and Domestic Politics: The Logic of Two-Level Games. *International Organization* 42 (3) (Summer): 427–60.

Rapley, John. 1996. *Understanding Development: Theory and Practice in the Third World.* Boulder: Lynne Rienner Publishers.

Remmer, K.L. 1986. The Politics of Economic Stabilization, IMF Standby Programs in Latin America, 1954–1984. *Comparative Politics* 19: 1–24.

Richards, David L. 1999. Death Takes a Holiday: National Elections, Political Parties and Government Respect for Human Rights. PhD diss. State University of New York at Binghamton.

Richards, David L., Ronald D. Gelleny, and David H. Sacko. 2001. Money With a Mean Streak? Foreign Economic Penetration and Government Respect for Human Rights in Developing Countries. *International Studies Quarterly* 45 (2) (June): 219–39.

Riphenburg, Claudia. 1997. Women's Status and Cultural Expression: Changing Gender Relations and Structural Adjustment in Zimbabwe. *Africa Today* 44 (1) (January–March): 33–49.

Sahn, David E. 1996. Economic Reform and Poverty: An Overview. In *Economic Reform and the Poor in Africa*, edited by David E. Sahn. Oxford: Oxford University Press.

Sahn, David E. and Lawrence Haddad. 1991. The Gendered Impacts of Structural Adjustment Programs in Africa: Discussion. *American Journal of Agricultural Economics* (December): 1448–51.

Schelling, Thomas C. 1960. *The Strategy of Conflict.* Cambridge: Harvard University Press.

Schleifer, Andrei and Robert Vishny. 1997. A Survey of Corporate Governance. *Journal of Finance* 52 (2) (June): 737–83.

Schultz, K.A. 1999. Do Democratic Institutions Constrain or Inform? Contrasting Two Institutional Perspectives on Democracy and War. *International Organization* 53 (2) (Spring): 233–57.

Sowa, Nii Kwaku. 1993. Ghana. In *The Impact of Structural Adjustment on the Population of Africa*, edited by Aderanti Adepoju, pp. 7–24. United Nations Population Fund, New Hampshire: Heinemann.

Stein, H. 1992. Economic Policy and the IMF in Tanzania: Conditionality, Conflict, and Convergence. In *Tanzania and the IMF: The Dynamics of Liberalization*, edited by H. Campbell and H. Stein, pp. 59–83. Boulder: Westview.

Stiglitz, Joseph E. 1999. The World Bank at the Millennium. *Economic Journal* 109 (November): F577–97.

Stiglitz, Joseph E. 2002. *Globalization and Its Discontents.* New York: W.W. Norton.

Stiglitz, Joseph E. and Lyn Squire. 1998. International Development: Is it Possible?. *Foreign Policy* (Spring): 138–51.

Strand, Håvard, Lars Wilhelmsen, and Nils Petter Gleditsch. 2002. *Armed Conflict Dataset Codebook 1* Version 1.1, 9 September. Available from http://www.prio.no/cwp/ArmedConflict/ (Accessed 3.16.03).

Stryker, J. Dirkch and Hassan A. Tuluy. 1989. Assistance to Ghana and the Ivory Coast. In *Aid and Development*, edited by Anne O. Krueger, Constantine Michalopoulos, and Vernon W. Ruttan, pp. 269–302. Baltimore: The Johns Hopkins University Press.

Subramanian, Shankar. 1996. Vulnerability to Price Shocks under Alternative Policies in Cameroon. In *Economic Reform and the Poor in Africa*, edited by David E. Sahn. Oxford: Oxford University Press.

Sukhamte, Vasant. 1989. Assistance to India. In *Aid and Development*, edited by Anne O. Krueger, Constantine Michalopoulos, and Vernon W. Ruttan, pp. 203–25. Baltimore: The Johns Hopkins University Press.

Tanski, Janet M. 1994. The Impact of Crisis, Stabilization and Structural Adjustment on Women in Lima, Peru. *World Development* 22: 1627–42.

Tarnoff, Curt and Larry Nowels. 2001. Foreign Aid: An Introductory Overview of U.S. Programs and Policy. Congressional Research Service: The Library of Congress (April 6) Order Code 98-916 F.

Van de Laar, Aart. 1980. *The World Bank and the Poor.* Boston: Niijhoff.

Vaubel, R. 1986. A Public Choice Approach to International Organization. *Public* 51.

Vreeland, James Raymond. 1999. The IMF: Lender of Last Resort or Scapegoat?. Unpublished paper presented at the Annual Meeting of the International Studies Association Conference, Washington, DC.

Vreeland, James Raymond. 2001. Institutional determinants of IMF agreements. Available from http://pantheon.yale.edu/~jrv9/Veto.pdf (Accessed 8.6.02).

Vreeland, James Raymond. 2002. The Effect of IMF Programs on Labor. *World Development* 30 (1) (January): 121–39.

Vreeland, James Raymond. 2003. *The IMF and Economic Development.* Cambridge University Press.

Vuorela, Ulla. 1991. The Informal Sector, Social Reproduction and the Impact of Economic Crisis on Women. In *Tanzania and the IMF: Dynamics of Liberalization,* edited by Horace Campbell and Howard Stein. Harare, Zimbabwe: Southern Africa Political Economy Series Trust.

Williamson, J. 1990. The Debt Crisis at the Turn of the Decade. *IDS Bulletin – Institute of Development Studies* 21 (2) (April): 4–6.

World Bank. 1992. The World Bank Operational Manual: Operational Directive Adjustment Lending Policy (OD 8.60). Available from http:wbln0018.worldbank.org/institutional/manuals/opmanual.nsf (Accessed 3.24.03).

World Bank. 2002a. Country Eligibility for Borrowing from the World Bank (IBRD/IDA). http://www.worldbank.org/about/organization/members/eligibility.htm. (Accessed 21.5.02).

World Bank. 2002b. *World Development Indicators,* CD-ROM.

9 The demand for IMF assistance

What factors influence the decision to turn to the Fund?

Graham Bird and Dane Rowlands

1 Introduction

Under what circumstances do countries – or more precisely governments – decide to turn to the IMF for financial assistance? The answer might, at first glance, appear to be relatively straightforward. Surely they turn to the IMF when they are in an economic crisis and have nowhere else to go. They visit the IMF "doctor" when they are economically "ill," for diagnosis, prescription, and medication. By taking the prescribed medicine they recover and, as a result, further visits to the "doctor" become unnecessary. According to this approach, all one has to do in order to come up with an explanation of the decision to turn to the Fund is provide a description of economic illness and the availability of alternative therapies, such as borrowing from elsewhere.

In this vein, it has conventionally been assumed that countries will borrow from the IMF under certain sets of economic circumstances. Traditional indicators of economic ill-health in the form of balance of payments crises, falling international reserves, high inflation and low rates of economic growth will, according to this approach, be associated with borrowing from the IMF; particularly when countries no longer have access to private capital. The problem is that the evidence on IMF lending is frustratingly inconsistent with this initially appealing story. Although econometric research confirms that certain economic variables exhibit a statistically significant relationship with IMF lending, regression equations incorporating these variables have also failed to add much predictive capacity. If countries turn to the Fund when they are economically ill, there seems to be no one common economic illness from which they are all suffering. Moreover, it appears that some countries are able to circumvent the IMF in spite of poor economic performance, while others may turn to the Fund even when their economic situation is not critical. So it would seem that the decision whether or not to go to the IMF for assistance is more complex than might initially appear.

The purpose of this chapter is to consider these complexities. At this stage, we do not attempt to construct a formal model of the demand for

IMF assistance. Instead we more modestly build a descriptive "mental model." In other words we attempt to set up an informal analytical structure within which a country's decision to turn to the Fund (or not) may be considered. Since we have no formal model, we have nothing to formally test against the data. However, we are able to investigate whether the implications of our mental model are consistent with the existing empirical evidence on IMF lending. We also undertake some new empirical analysis to see whether we can establish significant differences in terms of specific economic characteristics as between those countries that turn to the IMF and those that do not. To anticipate slightly, we argue that existing empirical research into IMF lending – including our own previous work – has lacked a secure analytical foundation. As a consequence, results have often been interpreted as disappointing. In this chapter we argue that once a more thoughtful analytical structure is put in place, the results are in fact no more or less than might have been expected. In essence the results are akin to demonstrating that not all patients who visit their doctor have the same illness. In future research we shall attempt to further explore what the most common economic illnesses are that lead countries to seek assistance from the IMF.

The lay-out of the chapter is as follows. Section 2 provides a brief critical summary of existing research into IMF lending. Section 3 describes an analytical framework within the context of which a country's decision whether or not to turn to the IMF may be examined. Section 4 explores the implications of this analysis in terms of identifying a series of testable propositions. It goes on to provide a preliminary evaluation of these propositions against available empirical evidence. Section 5 presents new empirical evidence, which provides further support for the conjectures we are putting forward in section 3. Section 6 offers a few concluding remarks largely focusing on the directions for future research and the implications for policy.

2 Previous research

Although our focus in this chapter is on the demand for IMF assistance, empirical evidence does not allow us to isolate demand side factors. What we observe is either a country having a program with the IMF or not having a program. For there to be a program it is necessary but not sufficient for a country to apply to the Fund for assistance. From this point of view it is also necessary for governments to be able to negotiate programs that are acceptable to both themselves and the Fund's staff and Executive Board. IMF lending therefore reflects a mix of demand and supply factors. Do countries demand them and will the Fund supply them?

Early research into IMF lending attempted to explain the amount of IMF lending in terms of key economic variables making little distinction between demand and supply influences (Bird and Orme 1981; Cornelius

1987). Later research, while continuing to emphasize economic determinants, used econometric approaches which sought to explain whether or not countries had programs rather than seeking to explain the amount of lending (Joyce 1992; Conway 1994; Santaella 1996; Knight and Santaella 1997). As studies multiplied and became more sophisticated, they also tended to encompass a wider range of potential explanatory variables, but these continued to emphasize the economic dimensions of IMF borrowing and lending. Over time areas of consensus emerged. There were some economic variables that appeared to be significant according to most if not all studies. However, there were other economic variables that were found to be significant in some studies but not in others (Bird 1996). The mere existence of a current account balance of payments deficit did not appear, in itself, to make it probable that a country would demand resources from the IMF. Beyond this, the adoption of Fund programs did seem to be linked to low levels of reserve holdings, overvalued exchange rates, a near term record of past programs, and low levels of income and development. Some studies further suggested that the incidence of programs was connected positively to levels of external debt and to terms of trade shocks, although this was not universally found to be the case. Similarly, there was somewhat mixed evidence relating to the significance of fiscal deficits, monetary expansion and inflation as determinants of IMF lending.

A common feature of this genre of research was its arguably low explanatory power overall. While the percentage of correct predictions was often between 80 and 90 percent, it has to be recalled that these numbers corresponded roughly to the percentage of countries without agreements. Hence a blind guess of "no agreement" would have been correct roughly 80 to 85 percent of the time, depending on the actual sample. Therefore, while these studies did identify important relationships and regularities, it was not always clear how powerful the within-sample and out-of-sample predictive capacity of the models were.

In an attempt to improve this, researchers began to include political factors, in part relating to the politics of the demand for IMF assistance but more so relating to the politics of supply. The objective was often to test the claim that IMF lending had become politicized and was being driven by the interests of the Fund's major shareholders, in particular the United States. Some studies found empirical support for a "US effect" (Thacker 1999; Barro and Lee 2001) while others were much more circumspect (Rowlands 1995; Bird and Rowlands 2002). A further recent development in the literature has been to incorporate institutional variables as well as political and economic ones to see whether there is empirical support for public choice and bureaucratic explanations of IMF lending which view the IMF as an institution with its own objective function that it is seeking to maximize (Bird and Rowlands 2002; Vreeland 2003).

Table 9.1 summarizes the results of a large sample study undertaken by the authors that included standard economic variables, combined with a range of political and institutional variables. Although the findings relating to economic determinants are largely consistent with previous research and although some individual political factors appear to be significant, the principal conclusion is that including the selected political

Table 9.1 Estimation results for the two models

Variables	Economic model	Supplemented model
Constant	−0.794*** (−5.31)	−0.962*** (−2.73)
GNP per capita	−0.101** (−2.13)	−0.0391 (−0.74)
GDP growth	−0.00186 (−0.49)	−0.00263 (−0.67)
Reserves/imports	−0.990*** (−4.14)	−0.904*** (−3.46)
Change in reserves	−0.218** (−2.27)	−0.264*** (−2.55)
Current account/GDP	−0.0124* (−1.66)	−0.0171** (−2.16)
Real exchange rate change	0.77*** (2.58)	0.234*** (2.89)
Debt–service ratio	1.41*** (3.72)	1.59*** (3.66)
Change in debt–service ratio	−0.000295 (−0.80)	−0.000288 (−0.72)
Debt/GDP	−0.257* (−1.83)	−0.307** (−1.98)
Arrears/debt	−0.485 (−0.72)	−0.0508 (−0.07)
Past reschedulings	0.338*** (4.64)	0.186*** (2.31)
Real LIBOR	−0.0279 (−1.31)	−0.036 (−1.39)
Change in real LIBOR	0.0759*** (3.02)	0.0929*** (3.16)
US exports	–	−0.813** (−2.10)
French exports (Africa)	–	−0.0113 (−0.84)
Socialist	–	−0.828** (−1.99)
Recent government	–	−0.392 (−1.34)
Civil freedom	–	0.0151 (0.378)
Change in civil freedom	–	0.122** (1.96)
Coup frequency	–	0.326* (1.73)
Past incomplete programs	–	0.0443 (0.76)
Imminent quota review	–	−0.0358 (−0.27)
IMF liquidity	–	−0.229 (−0.49)
Gross real GDP	–	0.117 (1.03)
Imminent rescheduling	2.49*** (3.54)	2.63*** (3.61)
Imminent new government	–	−0.234* (−1.74)
Past IMF agreements	–	0.0411*** (5.00)
Number of observations	1041	1041
% correct predictions	82.22	82.71
Number of correct predictions	856	861
Number of positive observations	189	189
R^2	0.129	0.185

Notes
The *t*-statistics appear in parentheses. Coefficient estimates marked *, **, and *** are statistically significant at the 0.05, 0.025, and 0.01 levels of confidence for a one-tailed test. The dependent variable indicates a signing of an SBA (Stand-by Arrangement), EFF or ESAF (Enhanced Structural Adjustment Facility) arrangement. No country or year dummies were used in the regression.

and institutional variables alongside a reasonably comprehensive list of economic variables does not significantly improve our ability to explain IMF lending. Again this large sample exercise offers little value-added over and above a straight guess of "no program."

What does this imply? It may imply that the equation that is being used continues to be mis-specified. Important determining variables may have been omitted. The challenge is then to find these variables. The reward will be an equation that accurately explains IMF lending. In Bird and Rowlands (2002) we make some move in this direction by examining, in detail, occasions where the model incorporated in Table 9.1 fails quite badly to explain what happens. We examine the outliers; cases where a program was put in place but was not predicted by the model and cases where no program was introduced in spite of the model's prediction that it would be. What were we missing in these cases? From this structured examination of case studies that are inconsistent with the basic model we isolate additional potential explanatory factors that we then add to the model. These include budgetary deficits and terms of trade shocks. However, these additional variables did little to increase the model's overall explanatory power.

This forces us to consider another possibility. Perhaps we are searching for something that does not exist. Perhaps there is no general theory of IMF borrowing and lending. Perhaps certain things are important in some cases but unimportant in others, with the result that their significance effectively cancels out in large sample studies.

Consequently, if we are to better understand IMF borrowing and lending we need to adopt a more disaggregated approach; we need to allow for the possibility that different countries or groups of countries may turn to the Fund in different sets of circumstances. An important first step is to do something that none of the studies mentioned above does. In all of them the analysis is empirically driven. Although explanatory variables are not picked randomly there is little or no attempt to provide an analytical structure which identifies the variables that may be important in explaining IMF lending. Such analysis will ultimately need to consider both the demand and supply side. However, in the next section we make a start by focusing on the factors that may, in principle, influence a government's decision to turn to the IMF for assistance. In subsequent sections we then consider the extent to which available evidence is consistent with the theoretical analysis.

3 An analytical framework

The IMF is a balance of payments agency and in seeking to understand why countries turn to it for assistance it seems sensible to start with their balance of payments. According to its Articles of Agreement, countries are only permitted to draw resources from the IMF where they have a balance of payments "need." However, the concept of need is ill-defined. More useful is the notion of balance of payments "sustainability" (Milesi-Ferretti and Razin 1996). It may reasonably be assumed that countries will be under pressure to turn to the IMF when they have a current account balance of payments deficit that they can no longer sustain.

But what determines balance of payments sustainability? A country's balance of payments becomes unsustainable in circumstances where current policies cannot be continued into the indefinite future; a fundamental policy change becomes required. The loss of sustainability may, on some occasions, be a gradual process but, on others, it may be connected to a sudden discrete event. However, sustainability of a current account balance of payments deficit depends not only on the size of the deficit and the factors that influence it, but also on a country's willingness to borrow and the willingness of creditors to lend. It follows that while basic balance of payments theory helps to identify the factors that may induce a transition from sustainability to unsustainability it may not provide the full story. It will also be necessary to consider capital account factors. A loss of sustainability may involve increasing domestic expenditure or absorption associated with falling domestic private sector saving, increasing private sector investment or an increasing public sector deficit. It may also involve structural features such as the composition of exports and imports, the degree of openness, the size and composition of external liabilities, and the nature of the country's financial structure. For example, an open economy that is heavily reliant on a limited number of exports may be vulnerable to trade shocks, and disadvantageous trade shocks may certainly contribute to a loss of balance of payments sustainability. But current account deficits will, in principle and in isolation, be a poor indicator of unsustainability. Forward-looking agents may anticipate a reversal in the current account and be prepared to provide the resources necessary to finance contemporary current account deficits. Sustainability will therefore depend to a significant degree upon a country's access to external finance and ultimately the factors that determine this, including those that influence creditors' perceptions of return and risk.

This analysis implies that the shift from sustainability to unsustainability may be associated with developments that increase a country's current account deficit, without there being an equivalent increase in its ability to finance it, or with a decline in its ability to finance a given current account deficit because of a loss of creditworthiness. In the former case, the principal determinants may be found in traditional balance of payments theory, although it is important to examine why capital markets are not prepared to fill the increased financing gap. In the latter case, the principal determinants may be found by examining factors influencing capital flows.

The transition in the balance of payments may also be examined in terms of whether or not the causal factors leading to unsustainability are endogenous or exogenous. Exogenous factors may relate to the current account and include a decline in export receipts or a more general decline in the income terms of trade, or they may relate to a general loss of market confidence that affects capital flows. Endogenous factors may include a deteriorating fiscal imbalance.

One way of portraying the structure of the balance of payments and its connection to endogenous domestic factors is to combine simple national income accounting identities. Thus the current account balance is often written as:

$$X - M = (S - I) + (T - G)$$

where X is exports of goods and services, M is imports, S is private saving, I is private investment, T is tax revenue and G is government expenditure. Consequently the balance of payments identity implies that:

$$R = KA + [(S - I) + (T - G)]$$

where R is foreign reserve accumulation and KA is the balance on the capital account. This simple identity facilitates the analysis of five routes toward a loss of sustainability associated with: reserves, the capital account, the current account, the domestic private sector, and the domestic government deficit.

A government deficit, for example, may be financed in various ways. First, it may be offset by a private sector surplus ($S > I$) implying that the government effectively borrows from the private sector. Such a policy will be sustainable for as long as the private sector is willing to directly or indirectly purchase government debt. Hence a government deficit need not imply a current account deficit, and will not always lead a government to turn to the IMF.[1]

If the private and public sectors are jointly in deficit, then a current account deficit will result. This may be financed by foreign capital inflows ($KA > 0$), either in the form of the investments in domestic public debt (government deficit) or the domestic private sector (when $S < I$). Again, the presence of the current account deficit (or a deficit in either its public or private components) does not automatically necessitate a need for IMF assistance.

Finally, if the capital account surplus is insufficient to finance a current account deficit, the third financing mechanism is via the decumulation of international reserves which may be used directly by the government to finance a fiscal deficit, or indirectly to finance a private sector deficit. As long as reserves are sufficient for the purpose, the IMF may again be avoided.

In all three of these cases there is either an accumulation of debt by domestic or foreign investors, or a decumulation of government assets in the form of reduced foreign exchange reserves. The three processes also encounter limits on their sustainability. Reserves are finite and will eventually run out. The demand for a government's debt by foreign and domestic agents will eventually decline, especially when they perceive problems of repayment. Foreign capital markets may also become less enthusiastic about a country's private investment opportunities. The exhaustion of the debt-financing route may be gradual, accompanied by rising interest charges, or sudden, as when it is connected to a capital account crisis. In either case, however, the perceptions of investors become a crucial, and often unpredictable, determinant of sustainability.

A loss of confidence within capital markets will reduce an indebted country's ability to roll over its debt. Meanwhile an appreciation in the currency in which its debt is denominated, or a rise in global interest rates, will exogenously increase the domestic currency cost of servicing debt. This will tend to increase further both the domestic fiscal deficit and the current account deficit, and require yet more debt accumulation or reserve loss. With this dynamic at work debt accumulation may again become unsustainable. Where trade taxes are an important source of revenue fiscal problems may also arise exogenously in association with trade shocks.

A further complication in the analysis of balance of payments sustainability arises from the need to incorporate exchange rate policy. With completely flexible exchange rates, overall balance of payments deficits should, in principle, be eliminated by appropriate equilibrating movements in the values of currencies. As a consequence, countries with flexible exchange rates should avoid unsustainable current account deficits. The mirror image to this is that countries attempting to peg the values of their currencies at too high a level are more likely to encounter situations where their balance of payments becomes unsustainable since they will need external finance to protect the peg.

How does the above analysis of balance of payments sustainability help in conceptualizing the demand for IMF assistance? What is clear is that countries exhibiting similar economic characteristics may have very different needs for IMF assistance. For example, countries with large current account deficits need not turn to the Fund if they can finance them through private capital markets or via aid flows that effectively make the deficit sustainable, but countries without such access may find a similar current account deficit unsustainable, and therefore be encouraged to turn to the Fund. The routes to unsustainability, however, are multiple. For some countries exogenous current account shocks may have been the key factor. For others it may have been fiscal deficits, external debt accumulation and a loss of market confidence, combined perhaps with exogenous shocks affecting the capital account. The probability of reaching the threshold of sustainability will also be influenced by exchange rate policy. Countries with pegged exchange rates are more likely to reach it than those that have opted for flexible exchange rates. Thus, while it is possible to identify a range of factors that may be associated with countries turning to the Fund, it is not possible to identify a unique combination of these factors.

Even when faced with an unsustainable balance of payments it is not certain that governments will turn to the IMF. Different governments may respond in different ways, though respond they must since unsustainability means that policies must change. Turning to the IMF for assistance is one option, but they could also change policy independently of the Fund. In some cases the choice will be strictly limited since debt rescheduling or aid flows may be directly linked to the negotiation or existence of an IMF program. However, in principle, the option of not turning to the IMF remains. If, in practice, some countries exercise this option, it follows that factors influencing the sustainability of the balance of payments will only provide a partial explanation of the demand for IMF assistance. A complete explanation will require us to add in the factors that influence a government's decision once the threshold of sustainability has been reached. Factors influencing sustainability, as outlined above, will be an important part of the story but they will not be the whole story.

Whether or not a government chooses to go to the IMF depends on their assessment of the relative costs and benefits of alternative policy strategies. Remaining outside the auspices of the Fund will not allow countries facing binding financing constraints to avoid economic adjustment. Unless there is spare productive capacity or short-term potential for economic growth, adjustment will involve a cost in terms of reduced consumption. Indeed, without the Fund, the external financing constraint may be yet more binding and the need for short-term adjustment more pressing. The advantage of by-passing the IMF is therefore not the ability to avoid adjustment but rather the ability to retain discretion over the policy means by which adjustment is brought about. Governments will have their own ideas about the likely economic effects of individual policy instruments and will certainly consider the political repercussions of these effects. They will formulate a view about the political and economic costs of pursuing the policies favored by the IMF as compared with the alternatives.

The central benefit from turning to the IMF will be the additional external financing that will become available both directly and via any catalytic effect that it generates. This will allow adjustment to be cushioned, in as much as there will be a somewhat smaller external financing gap. Other things being given, the probability of countries that have reached the threshold of balance of payments sustainability turning to the IMF for assistance will rise with the amount of financial support they anticipate receiving and fall with the anticipated costs of IMF conditionality.

At heart, politics will exert an important influence over a government's policy preferences and therefore the probability of it turning to the IMF in circumstances where the economic situation is unsustainable. Governments want to retain power and will therefore assess the likely effects of different economic policies and strategies on their ability to achieve this goal. They will consider the income redistributive effects of alternative economic policies and the political power of those who are adversely affected. Are those who lose in a position to mount effective opposition? This implies that governments may be less likely to turn to the IMF where the policies that the Fund is likely to support will be strongly opposed by powerful interest groups. It also implies that the nature of the political regime – authoritarian or democratic – may be important, in as much as this affects the ability of the government to deal with or suppress political opposition. Within a democracy the proximity of elections is also likely in principle to exert an influence on the decision whether or not to turn to the Fund since involving the IMF may be interpreted as an indicator that the economic policies pursued by the government in power have failed; something that the political opposition could latch onto with electoral benefit. After an election an incoming administration may be more likely to turn to the Fund since the previous government can be blamed.

It follows then that political factors will need to be superimposed on economic ones in order to understand the decision to turn to the IMF. Countries in similar economic situations may reach different decisions about involving the IMF because of differences in the political environment in which they find themselves.

Politics may be relevant not only at the national level but also in terms of a country's relationship with the Fund. If a government believes that conditionality is endogenous and that it will be able to "cut a favorable deal," it will be more inclined to turn to the IMF for assistance. This may depend on the country's bargaining position; is it of strategic military, political or economic importance to the industrialized countries? Where it believes that it can exert a significant positive influence over conditionality and can expect to receive a large amount of financial support a government may indeed not wait until the economic situation is unsustainable before turning to the Fund; the benefit–cost ratio will be favorable ahead of the balance of payments becoming unsustainable. Similarly, the Fund's involvement may be used to "tip the balance" domestically in favor of policies preferred by the government. Or the Fund may be used as a scapegoat by the government in an attempt to deflect the political costs of policy choices. Alternatively, the IMF may be used to endorse a program of economic reform and as a way of signalling a government's commitment to reform (Bird 2002). While these motivations may come into play in situations of unsustainability they may also be seen as ways of trying to avert unsustainability ex ante. In these cases the government does not perceive IMF conditionality as a cost. The irrelevance of IMF conditionality may also emerge when the government is not genuinely committed to compliance and intends to renege on its commitments. But things may be more nuanced than this. Thus, a government may attach higher costs to some components of conditionality than others. It may intend to negotiate a program that allows it to postpone policies that it regards as less palatable until late in the program, at which point it will simply fail to implement these elements. If it had not been confident of being able to negotiate a delayed schedule for the policies it opposes the government would have been less likely to turn to the Fund in the first place. There is also the possibility that turning to the IMF may transmit a negative signal to private capital markets and therefore make the balance of payments less sustainable than it would otherwise have been.

The connection between conditionality and a government's willingness to turn to the Fund becomes yet more complicated when it is recalled that governments may wish to retain national sovereignty over policy formulation irrespective of the precise nature of the policies. It is therefore possible that a government which is not opposed to the broad policy content of conditionality may nonetheless decide not to turn to the Fund whereas one that is more heavily opposed to it ends up turning to the Fund.

Just as there may be economic thresholds involved in the decision to turn to the IMF, there may be political thresholds as well. A central one is whether the incumbent government believes it can survive the involvement of the Fund. Rising political costs may not exert an effect on the government's decision if it believes it can survive in spite of them. In terms of national sovereignty over policy selection, countries may resist turning to the Fund for as long as they can. Once circumstances have forced them into the Fund subsequent resistance may decline with the result that future near-term programs become more likely.

The above discussion suggests that governments may go through sophisticated policy analysis before seeking assistance from the Fund. This may often be the case. However, and as noted earlier, there are, no doubt, other cases where the choice is less complex. There may be an effective economic imperative such as the need to reschedule external debt. Here, inasmuch as a choice is being made, it is that between rescheduling under the auspices of an IMF-based programme or unilateral default. The decision to turn to the Fund is therefore a reflection of the government's assessment of the net costs of default. This example suggests that the threshold at which the Fund becomes involved may on some occasions be uni-dimensional and on others be multi-dimensional. Certainly we should not expect to see a unique set of circumstances under which countries will turn to the IMF. Countries that appear to be similar in terms of certain economic characteristics may make different decisions. However, at the same time, this does not mean that the decision to turn to the Fund is random. It just means that it is much more complex than has been implicitly assumed in some studies of IMF lending. Nor does it mean that there is no pattern, with each country representing a separate case. It may be that there are reasonably common combinations of characteristics across certain country groupings. Rather than there being one universal "model" that explains the demand for IMF assistance, there may be a larger but still limited number of models that better fit some groups of countries than others.

For example, it may be that poor countries with a high degree of export concentration in primary products encounter a secular weakening in their current account balance of payments as well as trade-related crises from export shortfalls. They may rely on foreign aid to help close their external financing gap but may need to involve the IMF in order to gain access to foreign aid. They may have passed beyond any political threshold that constrains them from turning to the Fund and have become resigned to using the Fund on a long-term basis. To the extent that the policies incorporated in Fund programs have a negative effect on growth the hope is that aid will offset this effect by narrowing the financing gap as compared with what it would be without the Fund. In any case they may believe that they will not be heavily penalized for slippage in complying with conditionality. For emerging economies there may be a different scenario. Here, balance of payments problems may be more closely connected to the capital account and, by implication, debt accumulation and debt rescheduling with private capital markets. The fiscal deficits that resulted in debt accumulation may be more important than current account deficits associated with trade shocks or adverse movements in the terms of trade in explaining the decision to turn to the Fund.

To the extent that there is any general theory of the demand for IMF assistance it is that countries have reached the threshold of balance of payments sustainability such that a change in policy is required. For those that turn to the IMF the ratio of benefits to costs favors this course of action as opposed to alternatives. In principle, an advantageous benefit–cost ratio may arise ahead of unsustainability; although countries will have to be able to demonstrate a balance of payments need for IMF assistance. Beyond this general statement, the factors that cause the balance of payments to become unsustainable are likely to differ quite widely, as may also the factors that influence the perceived costs and benefits from turning to the Fund. A priori reasoning therefore suggests that while it may be possible to construct a list of variables that are important in seeking to explain why countries turn to the IMF for assistance, with this list comprising both economic and political variables, it is unlikely that one model will fit all countries.

How do these ideas coincide with the empirical evidence on IMF lending? Has research identified universal systematic influences or, as the above discussion suggests, are the results more idiosyncratic? In the next section we move on to examine this question drawing on research findings that have already been published. In the subsequent section we examine some preliminary new findings.

4 Formulating testable propositions

The discussion in the previous section leads to some testable propositions. First, while the underlying economics would lead us to expect certain variables to exert a significant impact on IMF lending, we would also expect to find no clear single overall explanation. Hence the predictive power of one overall equation is likely to be relatively poor. Second, we might expect fundamentals such as fiscal deficits and related external debt accumulation to be more important in explaining IMF programs than other variables such as monetary expansion that have a more indirect effect on sustainability. Third, we might expect previous devaluations to have been more common in countries turning to the Fund because of the implied preference for pegged exchange rate regimes, especially if past devaluations were conducted outside the auspices of the IMF and were unsuccessful. We might also, as a consequence, anticipate currency overvaluation to be a common feature among countries turning to the Fund. Fourth, and as a consequence of defending a pegged exchange rate, we might also anticipate that countries turning to the Fund will have experienced a decumulation of reserves to a low level, which eliminates one financing option. Finally, we would expect the importance of variables in aggregate to vary over time as the nature of balance of payments problems change, with capital account crises becoming increasingly important in relation to current account deficits as capital has itself become increasingly mobile internationally.

In terms of political variables it is perhaps more difficult to delineate a priori expectations. An exception relates to the electoral cycle where it seems reasonable to assume that incumbent governments of long duration will be reluctant to turn to the IMF, as will those that have a strong sense of national sovereignty over policy formulation or are particularly hostile to the market friendly policies perceived to be favored by the IMF. The existence of veto players or powerful opposition groups could either encourage a government to turn to the Fund in order to tip the balance or supply a scapegoat, or discourage them because of the anticipated opposition (Vreeland 2003). Similarly, it is unclear in principle whether more authoritarian or democratic regimes would be more or less likely to turn to the IMF.

Much of what the available empirical evidence shows is consistent with these theoretical priors. As noted in section 2, large sample studies of IMF lending have identified statistically significant economic variables along the lines that theory suggests (fiscal deficits, high debt, low income and growth, currency overvaluation, reserve decumulation). Simultaneously, these models have failed to exhibit powerful predictive capacity (Joyce 1992; Conway 1994; Knight and Santaella 1997), implying that borrowing from the IMF is somewhat idiosyncratic.

The same message relating to relatively poor predictive capacity also emerges from attempts to include political variables, where few have been found to exert a systematic influence over the decision to turn to the Fund (Bird and Rowlands 2001; Vreeland 2003). Studies of the circumstances under which countries embark on IMF programs confirm that both domestic macroeconomic policy and performance and exogenous shocks play a part (Killick 1995; Bird 1995). Detailed econometric investigation has found that fiscal deficits are more significant than domestic monetary expansion and that devaluation has been more common in countries that turn to the Fund than in those that don't (Santaella 1996). Many studies show that the existence of previous programs increases the probability of subsequent ones (Joyce 1992; Conway 1994; Killick 1995; Knight and Santaella 1997; Bird 1995). This finding is consistent with the idea of a political threshold, and also with the notion that countries may not always concern themselves too much with conditionality because they believe that non-compliance will not be penalized by impaired access to IMF resources in the long term.

The nature of the political regime, authoritarian or democratic, has been found to be ambiguous (Vreeland 2003) although there is some evidence to suggest that socialist governments may be less inclined to turn to the Fund (Bird and Rowlands 2001). Certainly the stage of the electoral cycle seems to make a difference, with governments unlikely to turn to the Fund shortly before elections and more likely to exercise this option after being elected (Bird and Rowlands 2001; Dreher and Vaubel 2001; Dreher 2002; Vreeland 2003).

In conclusion, while the large sample studies that exist have sometimes been presented as failing to specify an equation that neatly explains IMF lending, we would argue that what we get from such exercises is what we should expect. By including everything in one equation the significance of individual factors cancels out across the sample. Much of the other available empirical evidence is consistent with the discussion in section 3.

5 New evidence

We begin our empirical analysis by asking the simple question of whether there are significant differences in the current account, reserves, and fiscal performance of countries that turn to the IMF and those that do not. As stated in the Introduction it might superficially be expected that signing countries would be performing less well in terms of all these variables. However, our discussion in section 3 raises a priori doubts. In that section we suggested that it is combinations of circumstances that drive countries to the Fund. On this basis we would not necessarily expect there to be significant differences between signing and non-signing countries in terms of individual variables. Indeed the data illustrated in Figures 9.1, 9.2, and 9.3 fail to reveal stark differences in the current account, reserve loss, or government deficit performance between countries which choose

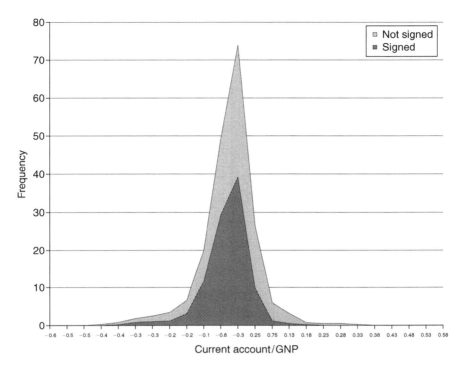

Figure 9.1 Current account distribution.

to turn to the IMF and those that do not, and there is certainly no simple dividing line of sustainability.

However, patterns may still exist. It may be that they are contingent on other characteristics such as the nature of the exchange rate regime, indebtedness and the level of income and reserve adequacy. To test this further we have undertaken additional empirical analysis. The analysis was conducted using a database constructed out of World Bank and IMF sources. Data on 161 countries were collected for the years 1965 to 2000. Many of the resulting 5796 observations could not be used, however, due to missing data. Countries were first identified on the basis of whether they had signed an upper tranche agreement with the IMF in a specific year or not (IMF Annual Reports). Four categories of exchange rate regime were identified: fixed, limited flexibility, managed floating, and pure floating (IMF Annual Report on Exchange Arrangements and Exchange Restrictions). Countries were classified into four different categories of income per capita, and by level of indebtedness (World Development Report, Global Development Finance CD-ROM). Reserve adequacy was measured using the reserves-to-total debt service payments ratio (World Development Indicators, Global Development Finance).

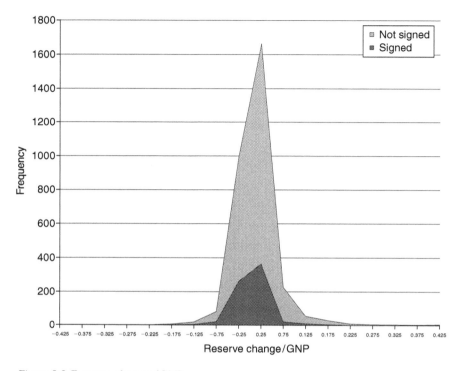

Figure 9.2 Reserve change/GNP.

Data were then collected for the current account balance as a proportion of GDP, the year-on-year change in reserves as a proportion of GNP, and the overall budget deficit as a proportion of GDP. These last three variables represent the key variables for analysis, while the previous variables were used to sort the data into categories.

Several problems with the data should be noted, aside from traditional concerns over accuracy and comparability. The sample was limited to years in which a country had a reasonable opportunity to sign an IMF agreement, so that countries under an IMF agreement or which had their previous agreement expire in the last two months of a calendar year were taken out of the sample. Due to breaks in the method the IMF used to identify exchange rate regimes there is also some possibility that countries have been incorrectly classified. The income classification is based on current status and may be inaccurate for some countries that have either dramatically increased or decreased their per capita income levels, relative to other countries, over the sample period. Similarly the measure of debt burden was extrapolated backwards from current assigned levels using the debt-to-GDP and debt service-to-exports ratio upon which the World Bank

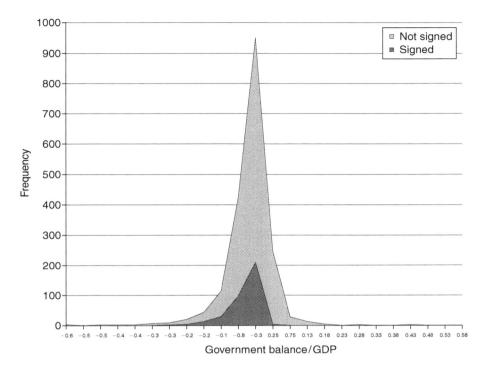

Figure 9.3 Government.

bases its classification; in some instances, however, elements of subjectivity and judgement may have affected the classification.

The reserves-to-total debt service measure was taken as a measure of reserve adequacy instead of the more traditional reserves-to-imports ratio, partly to reflect the more recent emphasis on capital-related flows over current transactions, but mostly to reflect real payments pressures on the government. In addition, the countries were sorted on the basis of the previous year's reserve adequacy measure to avoid the possibility that IMF agreements and associated reserve flows affect the results. The categories of reserve adequacy were also subjective: reserves-to-debt service ratios below six were treated as low, and reserves-to-debt service ratios above nine were treated as high. For similar reasons the current account and reserve change variables were also both lagged by one year, though tests on unlagged data were also performed. These caveats alone draw attention to the complexity of the data problems that surround this type of analysis.

The analysis focused on the three variables that, in some sense, reflect the presence of a financial problem that the government might seek to address by using IMF resources. The current account balance (as a pro-portion of GNP) reflects the more traditional concerns of the IMF. The reserve change variable was used to approximate the overall balance of payments, and thus encompasses capital account movements as well. The budget deficit variable measures the direct fiscal need of the government. In all three cases the analysis consisted of testing for differences in the mean of the "need" variable between countries that signed an IMF agreement and those that did not.

As noted earlier, however, it is not legitimate to expect that all countries with similar balance of payments deficits or government deficits will make the same decision about turning to the IMF. A country with a balance of payments problem but with a floating exchange rate may be content to let balance be restored through exchange rate depreciation. Some countries with fixed exchange rates may have adequate reserves or sufficient capacity to borrow privately to finance exchange market interventions. Similarly, wealthier countries may be able to sustain a government deficit by other borrowing, especially if they are not currently carrying much debt. The data therefore need to be explored according to these other criteria as well.

We have used the following criteria to divide up the sample. We tested the means of the "need" variables between countries that signed IMF agreements and those that did not according to the following categories: all countries, four time periods, income, indebtedness, reserve adequacy, and exchange rate regime. In addition, some of these variables were combined to examine categories of countries such as those with fixed exchange rates, low reserve adequacy, low income and high indebtedness. The relevant summary data and the results of the tests are presented in Tables 9.2 to 9.5. What do the results show?

Several past econometric investigations into IMF program signing have used the current account variable as one of the explanatory variables, with mixed results. The results here indicate that countries that sign IMF agreements tend to have significantly worse current account BoP deficits than countries that do not sign agreements. This difference, however, seems limited to the period immediately following the collapse of the Bretton Woods fixed exchange rate system (1974–81), persisting only weakly into the 1982–90 debt crisis years. Prior to 1973 and after 1990, no significant difference in performance is discernible. As expected, the difference is also most pronounced for countries with more rigid exchange rate regimes. For countries with exchange rates that are fixed or have only limited flexibility, poor current account balance of payments performance is associated with subsequent IMF agreements. The difference between the current account position of program and non-program countries does not appear to be strongly linked to either reserve adequacy or wealth (according to standard levels of statistical significance). For countries with low debt burdens a larger current account deficit is associated with signing a program in the next year. Finally, for poor countries with low reserves, high debt, and rigid exchange rate structures there is no significant difference in current account structures between program and non-program countries. But it should be noted that for this category of economically disadvantaged countries there was a higher proportion of agreements being signed than for other groups.

The reserve change ratio exhibits much starker differences between signing and non-signing countries. Not only is the difference in means statistically different over the full sample, it is present for the two earliest periods in the sample (1966–73 and 1974–81). The differences between program and non-program countries weaken over the debt crisis years and disappear after 1990. As with the current account balance measure, the reserve change variable analysis supports the hypothesis concerning the importance of exchange rate regimes. Countries with more rigid exchange rate structures that sign IMF agreements have significantly lower reserve accumulations than their non-signing counterparts. The few high reserve countries that did sign an IMF agreement experienced significantly poorer reserve performance than non-signing countries with high reserves. Not surprisingly, low reserve countries had much higher rates of signing IMF programs than their high reserve counterparts. Reserve accumulation was also significantly different between signing and non-signing countries in the two middle-income groups of countries. For both low-income and high-income countries reserve performance did not appear to be a significant trigger for seeking an IMF loan. In their case, other factors may have motivated the signing of an agreement. The importance of reserve performance differences between signing and non-signing countries diminishes with indebtedness. While the overall balance of payments may be an important factor driving low-debt countries to seek IMF assistance, high-debt countries that sign agreements do not appear to be distinguishable from non-signers on the basis of reserve changes.

Government budget problems were also associated with a different likelihood of signing agreements with the IMF. Government deficits were relatively higher for signing countries overall, and in the 1974–81 period. Similarly, countries with more rigid exchange rates that signed an agreement had larger fiscal deficits. It appears that government deficits were especially important as a motivation for high-income countries to seek IMF resources, but were not a feature that affected whether low and medium indebted countries turned to the Fund. Highly indebted program countries, however, tended to have significantly better fiscal performance. This rather unexpected result also seems to be true for poor, highly indebted countries.

Some general lessons can be derived from this preliminary data analysis. The link between standard measures of balance of payments structure and the signing of an IMF agreement does seem to be present, but it is far more complex than is generally portrayed. While differences are present

Table 9.2 Means and variances of the current account balance-to-GNP variable

Sample	Signing status	Number of observations	Mean	Variance	t-Statistic
All observations	Signed	607	−0.05771	0.004567	−3.20802
	Not signed	2270	−0.04114	0.014984	
1966–73	Signed	43	−0.03822	0.001083	−0.5177
	Not signed	192	−0.03085	0.008448	
1974–81	Signed	144	−0.0729	0.005864	−5.51504
	Not signed	565	−0.01823	0.012648	
1982–90	Signed	195	−0.06416	0.00335	−1.76161
	Not signed	699	−0.04894	0.013617	
1991–2000	Signed	225	−0.04614	0.005116	0.699369
	Not signed	814	−0.05276	0.018791	
Fixed exchange rates	Signed	345	−0.066	0.004796	−3.09747
	Not signed	1588	−0.04334	0.017412	
Fixed or limited flexibility	Signed	352	−0.06609	0.00484	−3.24103
	Not signed	1648	−0.04254	0.017535	
Managed or pure floating	Signed	254	−0.04621	0.003992	−1.56649
	Not signed	619	−0.03653	0.008056	
Pure floating exchange rates	Signed	105	−0.04599	0.004651	−0.89535
	Not signed	191	−0.03755	0.006757	
High reserves	Signed	60	−0.06316	0.007048	−1.81894
	Not signed	441	−0.03938	0.009291	
Low reserves	Signed	488	−0.05763	0.004322	−1.13999
	Not signed	1140	−0.05236	0.008569	
Low income	Signed	281	−0.06953	0.006237	−0.43531
	Not signed	725	−0.06625	0.013532	
Low-middle income	Signed	231	−0.05155	0.003281	−1.20379
	Not signed	923	−0.04354	0.009397	
High-middle income	Signed	90	−0.03447	0.001686	−1.44662
	Not signed	472	−0.01006	0.025272	

		Count			
High income	Signed	5	-0.09661	0.003097	-1.61373
	Not signed	150	-0.00272	0.016735	
Low debt	Signed	231	-0.04974	0.00345	-2.23594
	Not signed	1458	-0.02992	0.017601	
Medium debt	Signed	202	-0.04739	0.003011	-1.01861
	Not signed	519	-0.04155	0.005471	
High debt	Signed	174	-0.08028	0.007193	1.504527
	Not signed	293	-0.09621	0.015233	
Less flexible, low reserves	Signed	284	-0.06489	0.004221	-1.07878
	Not signed	787	-0.05807	0.009808	
Inflexible, low reserves, poor, high debt	Signed	51	-0.09678	0.004017	0.713799
	Not signed	63	-0.11134	0.017947	

Table 9.3 Means and variances of the reserve change-to-GNP variable

Sample	Signing status	Number of observations	Mean	Variance	t-Statistic
All observations	Signed	676	0.00464	0.008766	−3.88407
	Not signed	2426	0.015079	0.002442	
1966–73	Signed	131	0.00298	0.000158	−3.33599
	Not signed	409	0.014685	0.00156	
1974–81	Signed	144	0.005252	0.001196	−4.56046
	Not signed	565	0.028785	0.003527	
1982–90	Signed	189	−0.00189	0.000595	−1.8967
	Not signed	677	0.005355	0.002593	
1991–2000	Signed	212	0.011174	0.001285	−0.82643
	Not signed	775	0.01379	0.001773	
Fixed exchange rates	Signed	426	0.003534	0.000896	−4.71995
	Not signed	1736	0.014576	0.002111	
Fixed or limited flexibility	Signed	433	0.003717	0.000899	−4.52732
	Not signed	1818	0.014184	0.0021	
Managed or pure floating	Signed	240	0.006312	0.000846	−2.86512
	Not signed	604	0.017737	0.003478	
Pure floating exchange rates	Signed	97	0.006146	0.000878	−1.58472
	Not signed	197	0.01936	0.006303	
High reserves	Signed	56	0.012602	0.002009	−2.00848
	Not signed	457	0.033504	0.005812	
Low reserves	Signed	488	0.004013	0.000809	−1.12343
	Not signed	1161	0.00575	0.000827	
Low income	Signed	308	0.005485	0.001035	−0.7147
	Not signed	742	0.007031	0.001012	
Low-middle income	Signed	263	0.003846	0.000677	−3.77119
	Not signed	949	0.017095	0.003057	
High-middle income	Signed	100	0.003208	0.000846	−2.67747
	Not signed	539	0.018998	0.003318	

High income	Signed	5	0.022973	0.002636	−0.09822
	Not signed	196	0.025017	0.002101	−3.71632
Low debt	Signed	288	0.005749	0.000794	−2.76639
	Not signed	1639	0.018133	0.003057	
Medium debt	Signed	217	0.00294	0.000573	−0.17111
	Not signed	531	0.009649	0.001042	
High debt	Signed	171	0.004928	0.001406	−0.25914
	Not signed	256	0.005533	0.001199	
Less flexible, low reserves	Signed	285	0.00397	0.000829	2.508903
	Not signed	801	0.004476	0.000792	
Inflexible, low reserves, poor, high debt	Signed	51	0.012555	0.000793	
	Not signed	64	−0.0019	0.001059	

Table 9.4 Means and variances of the government deficit variable

Sample	Signing status	Number of observations	Mean	Variance	t-Statistic
All observations	Signed	398	-5.03393	35.7954	-4.20392
	Not signed	1516	-3.45051	47.06154	
1966–73	Signed	33	-4.16046	19.96843	-1.45632
	Not signed	115	-2.85967	20.59478	
1974–81	Signed	126	-6.24523	43.43931	-3.57704
	Not signed	456	-3.38439	68.56098	
1982–90	Signed	132	-4.53032	26.11182	0.058798
	Not signed	505	-4.57147	57.79075	
1991–2000	Signed	124	-2.44874	15.75233	1.061166
	Not signed	435	-2.96931	25.33835	
Fixed exchange rates	Signed	237	-4.8772	39.21843	-2.89662
	Not signed	1029	-3.3994	52.64647	
Fixed or limited flexibility	Signed	242	-4.8846	38.77577	-2.79745
	Not signed	1088	-3.45861	54.24772	
Managed or pure floating	Signed	173	-3.7212	16.57473	0.640882
	Not signed	423	-4.04117	36.32448	
Pure floating exchange rates	Signed	61	-3.63452	19.43135	1.447188
	Not signed	114	-4.79853	29.04001	
High reserves	Signed	40	-2.61431	17.42538	-0.03019
	Not signed	283	-2.58468	36.01929	
Low reserves	Signed	333	-4.64852	30.6868	-0.51669
	Not signed	762	-4.43321	44.4064	
Low income	Signed	167	-5.90175	43.00649	0.595793
	Not signed	401	-6.32581	66.66706	
Low-middle income	Signed	162	-3.35196	15.04155	-1.38379
	Not signed	584	-2.7661	24.85571	
High-middle income	Signed	81	-2.78101	14.52191	-0.20127
	Not signed	373	-2.59964	62.5359	

High income	Signed	5	−14.3936	85.90053	−4.18952
	Not signed	153	−2.29189	39.20125	
Low debt	Signed	173	−4.54143	29.6107	−2.67487
	Not signed	1022	−3.02961	50.23725	
Medium debt	Signed	143	−4.71692	37.04273	−2.42482
	Not signed	348	−3.50797	20.34487	
High debt	Signed	99	−3.69345	19.51023	4.37488
	Not signed	141	−8.19397	90.97981	
Less flexible, low reserves	Signed	191	−5.24454	39.04879	−0.68966
	Not signed	524	−4.82345	56.95585	
Inflexible, low reserves, poor, high debt	Signed	27	−4.43841	8.41144	3.729474
	Not signed	36	−14.1404	175.7271	
Low reserves, poor, high debt	Signed	43	−5.00933	20.78112	3.500367
	Not signed	53	−11.6568	137.9849	

Table 9.5 Differences in variable means for key country groupings

Group	Variable	Program	Mean	Standard deviation	t-Statistic
Fixed exchange rates 352/1383	Reserves	Signed	7.44339	39.65294	−2.66477
		Not signed	15.56026	53.527	
	Income	Signed	1.56534	0.70911	−5.27797
		Not signed	1.79103	0.71808	
	Debt	Signed	0.87216	0.79752	8.952515
		Not signed	0.49241	0.68669	
Floating exchange rates 101/175	Reserves	Signed	7.33693	19.06302	−2.57811
		Not signed	34.88925	106.343	
	Income	Signed	1.65347	0.65476	−0.88799
		Not signed	1.73143	0.72863	
	Debt	Signed	1.18812	0.82113	3.465448
		Not signed	0.82286	0.85604	
Low income 526/1548	Reserves	Signed	6.744	33.49664	−3.02905
		Not signed	14.79413	57.73388	
	Debt	Signed	0.92205	0.80924	8.314841
		Not signed	0.60207	0.74598	
	Fixed	Signed	0.59696	0.49098	−6.65618
		Not signed	0.74781	0.4339	
High income 83/346	Reserves	Signed	3.63245	7.44867	−2.64735
		Not signed	21.53483	61.44624	
	Debt	Signed	0.86747	0.82301	6.172467
		Not signed	0.3815	0.59379	
	Fixed	Signed	0.54217	0.50125	−2.75179
		Not signed	0.69942	0.45917	
High debt 176/265	Reserves	Signed	2.70512	4.25537	−1.81765
		Not signed	10.69724	58.20695	
	Income	Signed	1.51136	0.71705	1.724616
		Not signed	1.4	0.62644	

Group	Category		Value 1	Value 2	Value 3
Low debt 228/1095	Fixed	Signed	0.53409	0.50026	−1.21126
		Not signed	0.59245	0.49231	
	Reserves	Signed	12.06539	49.81353	−2.2429
		Not signed	23.05077	70.36545	
	Income	Signed	1.77193	0.69021	−2.70163
		Not signed	1.91142	0.71316	
	Fixed	Signed	0.60965	0.4889	−5.75041
		Not signed	0.78721	0.40946	
Low reserves 518/1231	Reserves	Signed	1.80974	1.45699	−7.74383
		Not signed	2.43968	1.59198	
	Income	Signed	1.67181	0.71216	−3.28011
		Not signed	1.79529	0.72157	
	Debt	Signed	0.98842	0.79399	7.15983
		Not signed	0.70349	0.74505	
	Fixed	Signed	0.58494	0.49321	−4.48272
		Not signed	0.69537	0.46044	
High reserves 61/488	Reserves	Signed	44.06043	90.89598	−0.65629
		Not signed	53.42692	106.71	
	Income	Signed	1.62295	0.68712	−2.08401
		Not signed	1.82172	0.70418	
	Debt	Signed	0.4918	0.76644	2.647669
		Not signed	0.26844	0.60088	
	Fixed	Signed	0.62295	0.48867	−4.01707
		Not signed	0.83402	0.37245	

between signing and non-signing countries for the whole sample, the effects are not consistent over time, nor are they stark. Instead, these economic fundamentals seem most closely linked to IMF activity in the 1973–81 period. For the most part the data support the arguments regarding the role of intervening variables. Poor balance of payments performance (and government fiscal performance as well) is likely to provide a stronger motivation for turning to the IMF when there is a fixed exchange rate system. For countries with higher incomes, higher reserve adequacy, and lower debt levels, there is some evidence to suggest that poorer basic balance of payments and government fiscal performance are more closely associated with program countries. This observation, while initially counter-intuitive, may be reasonable. For those better-off countries it is fundamentally poorer performance that seems to be associated with their going to the IMF. For poorer, more heavily indebted countries with low reserves, any number of factors may be sufficient to drive them to seek IMF help. These countries exhibit higher rates of Fund signings, but such events are not themselves closely linked to specifically bad fiscal or external balance performance.

Further preliminary insights into the characteristics that may combine to lead some countries to demand assistance from the Fund, or that may discourage others from turning to it when economic performance would appear to make it probable, may be gleaned from the structured case studies reported by the authors elsewhere (Bird and Rowlands 2002). Outliers were identified on the basis of the large sample model described in Table 9.1. In some cases, such as Barbados in 1982 and 1992 and Guatemala in 1992, it seems to have been exogenous trade shocks that shifted countries over the threshold of sustainability and pushed them toward the Fund. In the case of Argentina in 1984 it seems to have been the particularly weak budgetary position that was perhaps the decisive factor. In Ghana in 1983 and 1984, and in Nepal in 1992, political factors may have been important as domestic regime changes in favour of stabilization and more market-based policies facilitated referral to the Fund. Political factors also seem to have been important in the cases of Brazil in 1987 and Nigeria in 1988 where strong feelings of national sovereignty over policy design delayed referral to the Fund, although in both these cases economic factors eventually overcame this political resistance.

We also surmise that the demand for Fund assistance by East Asian economies in 1998 would not have been predicted by models that focus on the current account. In these cases it is widely acknowledged that it was capital account problems that pushed them toward the Fund, although in the case of Malaysia ex ante resistance to conventional IMF conditionality discouraged referral. With capital account crises becoming more common during the 1980s and 1990s it might be expected that overall current account explanations of the demand for IMF assistance would appear statistically more deficient as our aggregate empirical data suggest. Ability to explain crises might be reasonably closely correlated with ability to explain drawings on the IMF, although not perfectly. The question is then the extent to which these examples can be generalized; are they typical of groups of countries? The key research issue as we perceive it is the extent to which there is scope for delineating typical combinations of economic and political factors. Does the absence of a uniform model of the demand for IMF assistance mean that each country is different or are there common themes with a limited number of scenarios within the context of which the demand can be explained. Our results are too preliminary to allow a firm judgement to be reached on this issue and resolving it represents an agenda for future research.

6 Concluding remarks

Can we explain the pattern of IMF lending? There are an increasing number of studies that attempt to do this, but up until now they have exhibited what we would argue is only limited success. A recent development in the literature has been to include political and institutional variables alongside economic ones in the belief that the low explanatory power of previous models may be accounted for by their tendency to exclude political variables. If, as some researchers claim, IMF lending is a political phenomenon, it is hardly surprising that economics-only models statistically fail to explain it. It would certainly be convenient if the issue could be that easily resolved.

Our suggestion in this chapter is that it cannot be. IMF lending is complex and, to some extent, idiosyncratic. The implication is that no overall single equation tested against large sample data will provide "good" results in terms of explanatory power. The inclusion of political variables will do little to change this. The analysis in this chapter suggests that some specific economic variables will be important in some cases but not in others and this will undermine large sample studies. Similarly, political variables may exert an influence in different ways in different cases. If this is correct, there is little mileage left in standard large sample econometric studies of IMF lending. Instead a more disaggregated approach is needed.

Part of the disaggregation is to distinguish analytically between factors that influence the decision that governments make as to whether or not to turn to the IMF for assistance and factors that influence the IMF's response. In this chapter we focus on the demand side. Another part of the disaggregation is to allow for the possibility that different sets of economic circumstances will drive countries to a threshold where turning to the IMF is actively considered as an option. In examining the economics of the demand for IMF assistance there may be a range of stories, with the range being more than one but less than the total number of countries that arrive at the threshold. Thus the failure to find one universal pattern of IMF lending does not mean that there is no pattern. We anticipate that it means that there is a limited series of patterns, with different patterns or combinations of economic and political characteristics fitting different countries or groups of countries.

Having reached a threshold, which is largely associated with economic factors, governments then have to make the decision about turning to the Fund; it will be a politically driven decision. This implies not only that countries turning to the Fund will exhibit different sets of economic circumstances but also that countries with similar economic circumstances may make different decisions with regards to turning to the IMF.

The new empirical section of this chapter concentrates on economic variables but we also draw on other evidence to inform the political dimension. The findings are consistent with this more complex and nuanced account of the demand for IMF assistance. Not only does the account help to explain the disappointing results of large sample studies of IMF lending, but it also allows us to formulate propositions that may be tested against the findings of existing empirical research as well as the results of new empirical investigation. This we do. However, while we offer some empirical support for the claim that there will be no unique systematic explanation of the demand for IMF assistance, at present we only conjecture as to what the more common combinations of characteristics might be that lead to the decision to turn to the Fund. Further research beyond the preliminary empirical findings offered here will be required to see whether statistical analysis allows us to delineate these more clearly. Furthermore, as noted earlier, the demand for IMF assistance is only one part of the story of IMF lending. In order to fully understand it, analysis of the demand for IMF assistance will have to be combined with analysis of the IMF's response.

In some ways the contribution of this chapter may seem to be a negative one inasmuch as we cast doubt on the benefits of large sample studies of IMF lending. However, we prefer to view it as positive; much as in warning a motorist that he or she is travelling along a dead-end street. Our suspicion is that there is an interesting story to be told about patterns of IMF lending but that to tell it requires us to step back a stage or two before progressing. In offering an analytical structure within the context of which the decision to turn to the IMF for assistance may be discussed, and in examining its consistency with available empirical evidence, we hope that we have made a positive contribution that may be constructively built on in the future. In formalizing such a structure we may also be able to identify more appropriate large-sample estimation models that appropriately nest and endogenize the multiplicity of paths by which countries reach – or fail to reach – an agreement with the IMF.

Our general message has important policy implications. If countries turning to the Fund exhibit different combinations of economic and political circumstances this provides further support for the argument that the design of IMF conditionality needs to differentiate between client groups.

We interpret our findings as providing further support for those who reject a "one size fits all" approach to IMF conditionality. However, should further research fail to identify patterns, and instead suggest that there are no statistically significant differences between countries that sign agreements with the Fund and those that don't, there are again important ramifications. Not only would the selection bias problem that bedevils evaluative studies be non-existent, but more fundamental questions would be posed about the very rationale of the IMF itself.

Note

1   An alternative financing mechanism is through monetization of the government deficit by borrowing from the monetary authority and expanding the money supply. While the balance of payments effects will depend on the exchange rate regime, a consequence of monetary expansion will be inflation, which may lead to an appreciating real exchange rate, a current account deficit, and an unsustainable balance of payments.

References

Barro, Robert J. and Jong-Wha Lee. 2001. IMF Programs: Who Is Chosen and What Are the Effects?. Paper presented at Second IMF Research Conference, Washington, DC: IMF.

Bird, Graham. 1995. *IMF Lending to Developing Countries: Issues and Evidence.* London, Routledge.

Bird, Graham. 1996. Borrowing from the IMF: The Policy Implications of Recent Empirical Research. *World Development* 29 (11): 1849–65.

Bird, Graham. 2002. The Credibility and Signalling Effect of IMF Programmes. *Journal of Policy Modelling* 24: 799–811.

Bird, Graham and Timothy Orme. 1981. An Analysis of Drawings on the International Monetary Fund by Developing Countries. *World Development* 9: 563–8.

Bird, Graham and Dane Rowlands. 2001. IMF Lending: How Is It Affected by Economic, Political and Institutional Factors?. *Journal of Policy Reform* 4 (3): 243–70.

Bird, Graham and Dane Rowlands. 2002. The Pattern of IMF Lending: An Analysis of Prediction Failures. *Journal of Policy Reform* 5 (3): 173–86.

Conway, Patrick. 1994. IMF Lending Programs: Participation and Impact. *Journal of Development Economics* 45: 365–91.

Cornelius, Peter. 1987. The Demand for IMF Credits by Sub-Saharan African Countries. *Economic Letters* 23: 99–102.

Dreher, Axel. 2002. The Influence of Elections of Program Interruptions. Mimeographed, forthcoming in *Journal of Development Studies*.

Dreher, Axel and Roland Vaubel. 2001. Does the IMF Cause Moral Hazard and Political Business Cycle? Evidence from Panel Data. Mimeographed, forthcoming in *Journal of Policy Reform*.

Joyce, Joseph. 1992. The Economic Characteristics of IMF Program Countries. *Economics Letters* 38: 37–242.

Killick, Tony. 1995. *IMF Programs in Developing Countries: Design and Impact*. London: Routledge.

Knight, Malcolm and Julio Santaella. 1997. Economic Determinants of IMF Financial Arrangements. *Journal of Development Economics* 54 (2): 405–36.

Milesi-Ferretti, Gian and Assaf Razin. 1996. *Current Account Sustainability*. Princeton Studies in International Finance, 81. New Jersey: Princeton University.

Rowlands, Dane. 1995. Political and Economic Determinants of IMF Conditional Credit Allocations: 1973–1989. Norman Paterson School of International Affairs Development Working Paper. Ottawa: NPSIA.

Santaella, Julio A. 1996. Stylized Facts Before IMF-Supported Macroeconomic Adjustment. *IMF Staff Papers* 43 (3): 502–44.

Thacker, Strom. 1999. The High Politics of IMF Lending. *World Politics* 52 (1): 38–75. Reprinted this volume (Chapter 5).

Vreeland, James Raymond. 2003. *The IMF and Economic Development*. Cambridge: Cambridge University Press.

10 The survival of political leaders and IMF programs

Alastair Smith and James Raymond Vreeland

The primary motive of political leaders is to keep their jobs. The policies that best fulfill these goals depend upon the institutional context in which leaders serve. What constitutes effective public policy under one set of institutions constitutes political suicide under other institutions. With this in mind it is hardly surprising that the reasons that leaders turn to the IMF and their behavior under these programs also depends upon the institutional context. In this study we examine how IMF agreements affect the survival of leaders, and how this survival depends upon both domestic political institutions and the context under which leaders seek IMF programs.

1 Background

Why do governments enter into IMF arrangements? The conventional understanding posits that governments turn to the IMF for a straightforward reason: they need a loan of foreign exchange. Indeed, according to the IMF Articles of Agreement, "A member shall be entitled to purchase the currencies of other members from the Fund . . . [provided] the member represents that it has a need . . . because of its balance of payments or its reserve position or developments in its reserves" (IMF Articles of Agreement Article V, Section 3). Perhaps because it seemed obvious why governments would turn to the IMF, early on this question was ignored in the literature evaluating IMF programs (e.g., Reichmann and Stillson 1978; Connors 1979; Gylfason 1987).

Initial efforts to address the question, however, revealed that the answer was anything but straightforward. While Santaella (1996) and Goldstein and Montiel (1986) found that countries were more likely to turn to the IMF when the balance of payments deficit increased, Knight and Santaella (1997), Conway (1994), and Edwards and Santaella (1993) did not find that the balance of payments mattered. A consensus did emerge around other economic factors, such as level of foreign reserves and level of development (reported in Bird 1996), but economic factors appeared to tell only part of the story.

A political story seemed plausible. Putnam (1988: 457), following Spaventa (1983), argued that IMF arrangements "sometimes enable government leaders to do what they privately wish to do, but are powerless to do domestically ... this pattern characterizes many stabilization programs that are (misleadingly) said to be 'imposed' by the IMF." Others also developed this theme. Vaubel (1986: 45) claimed that the IMF enables politicians "to shirk domestic responsibility for unpopular policies." Remmer (1986: 7, 21) contended that the presence of the IMF "allows authorities to attempt to shift blame for austerity to the Fund." Edwards and Santaella (1993: 425) argued that governments facing domestic opposition to devaluation get the IMF to do their "dirty work." Dixit (1996: 86) noted that developing countries use the IMF as a "delegate" to impose fiscal and monetary restraint.

These arguments suggest two political motivations for entering IMF agreements: "leveraging," where governments use the IMF to increase bargaining leverage with domestic actors opposed to economic reform,[1] and "scapegoating," where governments use the IMF to escape the blame for economic austerity. In contrast to the conventional need-based story where governments turn to the IMF because they *need* a loan, this suggests that there are political *discretionary* motives for governments to turn to the IMF.

While these political arguments have floated around the literature for decades, they have only recently received systematic attention. Various mechanisms have been proposed. Drazen (2005) argues that reform-oriented executives use the IMF loan as a carrot to get opponents of reform to accept IMF conditions. Vreeland (2000, 2003) argues that reform-oriented executives use the IMF threat of punishment as a stick to get opponents of reform to accept IMF conditions. Ramcharan (2003) suggests that governments sign IMF agreements to signal the credibility of their resolve to push economic reform past opponents. All of this work has considered the implications of discretionary motives to turn to the IMF for policy change. In our study, however, we focus on the implications for leadership survival.

Previous studies related to leadership survival have considered how elections play a role. Dreher (2002, 2003a) shows that governments are not likely to enter into IMF agreements within six months before elections, and Przeworski and Vreeland (2000) show that governments are more likely to enter into IMF programs after elections are over. Yet Nelson (1992) and Killick (1995) report that the governments that actually do sign IMF agreements before elections are more likely to be reelected. Dreher (2003b) addresses this puzzle. He argues that entering into an IMF program can send a negative signal of government competence, but only in certain situations. If economic conditions are the result of government competence and random economic shocks, even highly competent governments turn to the IMF when hit by a bad enough shock.

If the economic situation is such that both competent and incompetent governments need a loan from the IMF, incompetent governments can masquerade as the competent type, and both types are reelected despite signing an IMF agreement. When the economic crisis is less severe, competent governments can get sufficient financing from sources other than the IMF, but incompetent governments have only the IMF as a source of funding and must enter into an IMF agreement. So, when the economy is in moderate shape, only incompetent governments sign IMF agreements, and they are not reelected. Dreher's empirical evidence supports his claims. He finds that while there are fewer IMF programs concluded before elections, governments are more likely to be reelected if they do sign an IMF agreement before elections, but less likely to be reelected if they sign the agreement and the economy is in good shape (if growth is high). This is an important counterintuitive result. Note, however, that Dreher addresses the effect of IMF agreements on reelection, not survival in general. The hazards faced by leaders in developing countries are many, and elections tell only part of the story. Furthermore, the hazards facing leaders vary over their tenure according to the institutional context (Bueno de Mesquita *et al.* 2003). It is therefore important to account for duration dependence. Also, Dreher's argument returns to the conventional need-based story of IMF participation: governments turn to the IMF for a loan. There is no scapegoating – governments are reelected despite signing an IMF agreement only if they are perceived as competent. But as our discussion above illustrates, discretionary motives play a role.

In our work below, we emphasize the two competing motives that political leaders have to turn to the IMF: *need* and *discretion*. Clearly some governments turn to the IMF because they sorely need a loan to help their financial difficulties. Yet, as our discussion of leverage and scapegoating points out, leaders often use the IMF for reasons other than financial need. Whether a leader's motivations are need-based or discretionary has implications for performance under IMF programs. In this chapter we examine how IMF programs affect leader survival, and show how this effect depends on the contingencies under which leaders initiate programs, as well as the domestic political institutions they face.

2 Institutions, policy choice, and the survival of leaders

Leaders want to keep their jobs. The ease with which they can do so and how they go about doing so depends on the institutional context in which they serve. We utilize Bueno de Mesquita *et al.*'s (2003) and Bueno de Mesquita *et al.*'s (1999, 2002 – hereafter BdM2S2), concept of selectorate and winning coalition size to characterize domestic political institutions. They analyze how the size of the selectorate and winning coalition shape the policy priorities of leaders and the ability of leaders to retain office.

The selectorate, S, is the set of people with a say about who can be leader. For instance, in democratic societies the selectorate is typically all citizens, while in other societies the selectorate can be a small group. In monarchies the choice of king resides with the aristocracy, and in military juntas senior military officers choose the leader. The most important quality of the selectorate is that it constitutes the pool of potential supporters from which leaders and potential leaders draw supporters to form a winning coalition.

The winning coalition, W, is the set of supporters a leader requires in order to retain power. In democracies, the winning coalition is a large proportion of a large selectorate. In other systems, such as elected monarchies, W might also be a majority of S, but with W obviously being much smaller. Leaders in autocracies often only require a small number of supporters to retain power (small W). Unlike categorical classifications of regimes, such as democracy and autocracy, W and S are conceptually continuous variables that allow not only for comparison between nominal groups, but also for comparison within groups. For instance, the winning coalition for a directly elected president is half the selectorate. In contrast, the winning coalition for leader requiring a majority of single-member electoral districts in a two-party system, such as the Westminster system, is a quarter of the selectorate.

Institutions shape the policies leaders pursue. Many policies improve the welfare of all members of society, be they members of a leader's coalition or not. In contrast, other policies, such as trade protection and patronage, reward the few. BdM2S2 distinguish between these policies as "public" and "private" goods. Of course in reality there are few pure public or pure private goods. However, institutions – specifically coalition size – determine the focus leaders have between these goals.

When a leader is beholden to a small coalition she can reward her supporters through private goods. As the coalition size increases so that rewards need to be given to more people, the focus of policy shifts toward public goods. The types of policies governments pursue thus depend on the institutions under which leaders serve.

Coalition size (W) and its interaction with selectorate size (S) influence how leaders survive in office. When supporters of the incumbent leader contemplate defection to support a challenger, they consider the potential costs of supporting the new leader. Although a supporter might have been critical in bringing a new leader into office, once ensconced the new leader is free to reorganize his coalition. When supporters defect, they risk being excluded from future coalitions. This risk is increasing in the size of the pool of potential supporters (S) and decreasing in the number of supporters a leader needs (W). The cost of exclusion is decreasing in W. Hence when W is small (and particularly when S is large) supporters of the incumbent are particularly reluctant to defect because while the incumbent's inclusion of them in the current coalition demonstrates they will be included in future coalitions, challengers can only offer them inclusion in future coalitions probabilistically (W/S). Small coalitions make it easier to survive in office, and conditional upon a small coalition, large selectorates increase tenure in office.

Leaders of small coalition systems survive by providing private goods. This focus on private goods induces a "loyalty norm." Once supporters are assured of their place in future coalitions they are intensely loyal to the incumbent, since a challenger cannot offer them guaranteed access to future private goods. This suggests an important dynamic in the survival of leaders. In large coalition systems, leaders are always in jeopardy since survival depends upon the provision of good public policy and the competition for ideas is intense. In contrast, survival in small W systems depends on the provision of private goods. Once an autocrat is established, her supporters can be fairly certain of future inclusion in the coalition. This is not so during the initial transition period. Although a leader might have relied on a coalition to come to power, once in power she wants to replace its members with those selectors that for idiosyncratic reasons she believes will be more loyal or for whom she has greater affinity. Members of the current leader's coalition who suspect they will be dumped in the future are particularly keen to defect to a challenger. Hence, recently installed autocrats find survival extremely difficult, but once established their tenure in office becomes secure. As BdM2S2 observe, and we shall replicate here, the risk of deposition for large coalition leaders always remains high, but for small coalition leaders risk starts high and declines rapidly.[2]

BdM2S2's theory provides a basis from which to examine policy choice and leader survival. Leaders from large coalition systems pursue public goods, while the provision of private goods is the key to survival in small coalition systems. Although leaders in both systems like economic success, small coalition leaders do not follow policies likely to promote economic success at the expense of paying off their supporters.

Having established a basis for the policy choices of leaders and their survival prospects under different regimes we have a platform from which to explore the decision to go to the IMF and the consequences of doing so.

3 Competing reasons to enter IMF agreements

Leaders have different motives to turn to the IMF, as we discussed above. We dichotomize these reasons into *need-based* and *discretion*.

Needing a loan is perhaps the easiest category to describe, as it is the stated purpose of IMF arrangements. When a government faces a BOP, reserves or currency crisis it turns to the Fund for a loan. While IMF loans are typically small, they may have a catalytic effect on financing (Bird and Rowlands 2000; Edwards 2000) and may be necessary to enter into debt rescheduling negotiations (Callaghy 1997, 2002). Many private lenders use the IMF's willingness to lend as a signal as to whether they should extend credit. The presence of the IMF has also been shown to increase the value of assets that are privatized (Brune *et al.* 2003).

Apart from needing a loan, a leader may enter into an IMF program for discretionary reasons. The IMF attaches conditions to its loans. While this conditionality limits a government's policy discretion, this is often beneficial for leaders attempting to implement reforms that some domestic actors would like to block. By accepting conditionality, leaders can raise the cost for others of scuttling their reform package. The IMF can also make a convenient scapegoat. Rather than accepting responsibility for domestic policy failures, leaders may dilute accountability by blaming IMF conditionality for problems.

So leaders might turn to the IMF because they need a loan, because they have some discretionary desire for conditionality, or for some combination of need and discretion. The circumstances under which these motives are likely to arise, as well as the impact of the IMF agreement itself, depend on the political institutions under which leaders serve. We now examine conditions that induce leaders to seek IMF agreements under each scenario and the consequences of such agreements.

3.1 Need-based IMF programs

Countries facing high debt service, poor balance of payments, low and/or declining reserves, large budget deficits, and who have experienced a recent currency crisis are likely to need an IMF agreement to help stabilize their international financial position. Such a situation may be indicative of policy failure. Democrats, who are dependent upon large coalitions and who are hence sensitive to policy failures, should be particularly attracted to IMF agreements to help solve their problems. Not only does the IMF program provide a loan but also a convenient scapegoat for the economic pain that economic reforms may bring. Unfortunately for them, IMF agreements under such circumstances cut two ways. While agreements may help improve economic fundamentals and provide a needed loan, they are also indicative of policy failure in the first place. That a democrat needs to enter an agreement under such circumstances is a bad sign, but this is offset by the extent to which an IMF agreement may help. Thus we predict that being under a need-based loan agreement is generally good for the survival of large coalition leaders, but needing such a loan in the first place is bad. Which effect dominates is an empirical question. Fortunately, we can distinguish between the benefit and the signal of prior failure in our subsequent tests, since in many cases leadership changes while countries are under IMF programs. A leader installed while under an IMF program is advantaged by the loan, the possible policy benefits of IMF programs, and the scapegoat for the pain of reform without suffering the stigma of prior policy failure.

The situation for small coalition leaders is more complex. Remember that their survival is not linked directly to public policy successes but rather to the ability to pay off their supporters with private goods. Economic failure harms autocrats' tenure only to the extent that it limits their ability to reward supporters. In general, small coalition leaders face mixed incentives. On the one hand, they value loans as they provide another source of income to expropriate. On the other hand, these loans come with conditions that may constrain a small coalition leader's ability to spread patronage. So, for small coalition leaders, entering into a loan program is a mixed blessing. It increases access to funds but pushes policy toward "public" rather than the politically expedient private orientation. Again we are fortunate in that our econometric tests allow us to distinguish between these effects. While leaders who sign IMF programs have to contend with IMF conditionality, they are also well positioned to ensure their supporters gain from the loan. In contrast, when leadership changes during an IMF program, the new leader, while still saddled with IMF conditionality, finds it harder to redirect funds as she struggles to establish her rule and reorganize her winning coalition. Small coalition leaders who inherit IMF programs from their predecessors find survival harder than corresponding leaders who sign IMF agreements.

3.2 Discretionary loan

IMF agreements come with conditions, and these can often be useful in overcoming veto players (Tsebelis 1995, 2002) who wish to block reforms. So, despite having no pressing financial need for a loan, political leaders can find IMF programs useful for political purposes. Large coalition leaders, in particular, want to improve policy. Doing so helps their survival. When large coalition leaders enter into an IMF agreement but economic conditions such as the BOP and reserves do not warrant it, we should suspect a discretionary motive. Loans made under such discretionary conditions should correlate with political survival. The mechanism is twofold. The first is a selection argument. Large coalition leaders who do not need a loan would be unlikely to enter an agreement if such an agreement would cost them their job. Second, conditionality allows them to implement their desired reforms, which may improve the quality of public policy. Hence, we predict that when large coalition leaders enter into IMF agreements without any pressing need to do so we should expect the agreement to help their survival.

Discretionary IMF loans affect the survival of small coalition leaders quite differently – they are likely to harm the survival of small coalition leaders. While IMF programs help leaders implement policy reform, autocrats pursuing policy reform are not undertaking those policies most beneficial to their survival. Autocrats might still sign discretionary loans for their scapegoating properties; however, small coalition leaders in need of a scapegoat are already in serious trouble and likely to be deposed, especially when IMF conditions limit their ability to spread patronage to their supporters after the initial tranche of the loan has been spent.

3.3 Data

This project is data intensive and requires data from various sources. In particular we require data on political leaders, political institutions, the timing of IMF agreements, and economic conditions. The data on political leaders and institutions are taken from BdM2S2 (2003). Their study describes the date political leaders enter and leave office. It also provides a measure of winning coalition (W) and selectorate (S) size. These variables are measured on a five and a three point scale, respectively, and are both scaled between zero and one. Since the impact of selectorate size is only really important in small W systems, we construct the variable "effective S," $eS = (1 - W)S$. We hypothesize when this variable is large, i.e., in a small W, large S system, that political survival is easier than when winning coalitions are large or when the selectorate is small.

The data on IMF agreements are taken from IMF Annual Reports (various issues). We look at IMF programs only from 1960 onwards. Data on economic conditions are taken primarily from the World Bank Development Indicators (2002) CD-ROM and the IMF's International Financial Statistics (2003) CD-ROM. Table 10.1 lists the major variables used and the data source.

Our primary question is how IMF programs affect the survival of leaders. To address this problem we need to know when governments enter into IMF agreements, when they leave IMF agreements and the dates of leader entry and exit. Figure 10.1 shows the basic setup of the data for Britain during the later half of the 1970s. The figure starts in 1975 at which time Harold Wilson was Prime Minister. He resigned and was replaced by James Callaghan on April 5, 1976. Margaret Thatcher became Prime Minister on May 4, 1979. Britain entered into two separate IMF agreements during this time. The first was entered into by Wilson on December 31, 1975 and it expired during Callaghan's term on December 30, 1976. Callaghan rapidly reentered an agreement on January 3, 1977 and this agreement continued until January 2, 1979.

Figure 10.1 shows how we code whether a leader is under an IMF agreement. The line marked by circles shows whether a leader is UNDER any IMF agreement. This variable is coded one between 12/31/1975 and 12/30/1976 and between 1/3/1977 and 1/2/1979. Since leaders might inherit IMF agreements from their predecessors rather than enter into them themselves we create an alternative dummy variable, Signed, which indicates whether or not a leader is under an IMF agreement that he or she actually signed. For clarity of presentation this dummy variable is plotted at 0.5 in Figure 10.1, but it is actually coded 0/1 in the data. Although James Callaghan is coded as UNDER an IMF agreement in the

Table 10.1 Summary of key variables

Variable	Definition	Source/format
UNDER	Country is under an IMF agreement during period	IMF Annual Reports
Signed	Leader is under an IMF agreement that she signed	IMF Annual Reports
	Obviously signed implies UNDER, but the contrary is not true	
signX	The value of the variable X at the time a leader signed an agreement (or renewed an agreement); zero if signed = 0	
W	Winning coalition size: (BdM2S2 2003) scale: 0–1. $W = 0$ are small exclusionary regimes such as juntas, monarchies and some autocracies. $W = 1$ are large inclusionary systems, such as Democracies	BdM2S2, annual data
eS	Effective selectorate size $= S(1 - W)$ where S is the size of the selectorate (the size of the pool from which W is chosen). Scale: 0–1, see BdM2S2 (2003)	BdM2S2, annual data
Growth	Annual rate of growth: WDI in constant 1995 $	WDI, annual data
DebtService	Debt Service: % of GNP	WDI, annual data
ΔExchange	Largest monthly devaluation in either current or previous two months	IFS, monthly data
ΔReserve	Change in total reserves: smallest change (i.e. largest decline) over current or two previous months	IFS, monthly data
Reserves/ imports	$Ln(1 + reserves/imports)$: reserves/imports the number of months of imports that can be paid for by total reserves	IFS, quarterly data
Year	Calendar year – 1975	Annual data
Cumulative agreements	$Ln(1 + cumulative$ agreements signed by country)	IMF Annual Reports
P	Predicted probability that IMF program is discretionary: $P = \Phi(X_{1i}\hat{\beta}_1) / (\Phi(X_{1i}\hat{\beta}_1) + \Phi(X_{2i}\hat{\beta}_2))$	Predicted from Model 5
NEED[a]	Index of financial need for an IMF loan	IFS and WDBI

Note

a NEED is a composite index of the financial need for an IMF loan. It is constructed as follows: First set NEED = 0 then add points according to the following rules. A) Add one if total reserves decline by more than 10 percent (in current or either of two previous months). B) Add one if reserves decline by more than 30 percent. C) Add one if reserves are less than two months of imports (quarterly IFS data). D) Add one if reserves are less than one month of imports. E) Add one if currency exchange rate increases (devaluation) by more than 2 percent in the current or either of the preceding months. F) Add one if currency exchange rate increases by more than 10 percent in the current or either of the two preceding months. G) Add one if inflation rate increases by more than 20 percent (quarterly IFS data). H) Add one if inflation rate greater than 15 percent. I) Add one if inflation rate is over 50 percent. J) Add one if BOP divided by GDP (quarterly BOP and annual GDP data from IFS and WDI respectively) is less than −0.005 (i.e. 0.5 percent imbalance). K) Add one if BOP divided by GDP (quarterly BOP and annual GDP data from IFS and WDI respectively) is less than −0.04 (i.e. 4 percent imbalance). L) Add one if foreign debt (in terms of GDP) is more than 50 percent. M) Add one if foreign debt (in terms of GDP) is more than 100 percent.

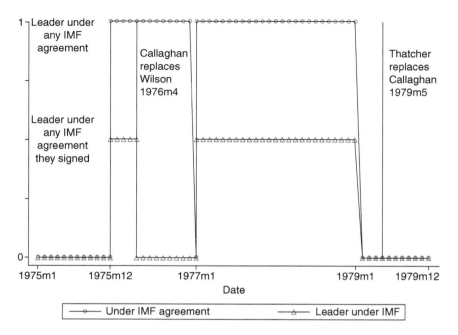

Figure 10.1 British leadership changes and IMF agreements during the 1970s.

first part of his term, he is not coded as having Signed because he inherited the IMF agreement rather than signed it himself. While Signed = 1 implies UNDER = 1, the reverse is not necessarily true.

Our conceptual framework argues that the context in which loans are undertaken influences the subsequent impact of agreements. Thus, we create versions of many of our variables that record the value of the variable at the time a leader enters an agreement. If, for instance, we consider variable X, then the variable signX is coded as the value of variable X at the time the IMF agreement was signed for as long as the country remains under the IMF program and the leader remains in office. For those periods when no IMF agreement is in place, or when the leader inherited the IMF program rather than signed it herself the variable signX takes value zero.[3]

For our hazard analysis, we use Weibull regression, a parametric hazard model. In particular, the Weibull model assumes the hazard rate, the probability of deposition conditional upon not having already been deposed, is $h(t) = p*exp(X\beta)*t^{(p-1)}$, where $X\beta$ represents the standard vectors of covariates and parameter coefficients, t is time in years, and p is an ancillary parameter that describes the overall shape of the hazard function (which can be increasing, decreasing, or constant). The theory and prior analyses (BdM2S2 2003) suggest that while the hazard remains relatively constant for large coalition leaders, the risk of deposition that small coalition leaders face declines rapidly over time. To capture this, we model the ancillary parameter p as a function of coalition size (W).

4 Results

When we control for domestic political institutions and the contingent circumstances that motivated the agreement, IMF programs have clear impacts on survival. To appreciate the impact of IMF programs we need to first accurately describe survival prospects. In Table 10.2 we examine a baseline model of leader survival. It is against this backdrop that we examine the impact of IMF agreements.

4.1 Baseline survival

Model 1 provides a baseline assessment of the effects of institutions on leader survival. Model 1 is a Weibull model in which we control for winning coalition size (W), selectorate size (eS) and economic growth. Additionally, we model the ancillary Weibull parameter, p, as a function of W.

Winning coalition and selectorate sizes strongly influence survival. The ancillary parameter p is increasing in W. The estimates of p in small and large coalitions are 0.706 and 0.946, respectively. Since we find $p < 1$, the overall hazard function is decreasing over time. This implies that all leaders find it easier to survive in office as their tenure increases. However, the risk declines faster for small coalition leaders than for large coalition leaders, who always face significant risk to their tenure. Consistent with theoretical arguments and earlier empirical findings (BdM2S2 2003) this implies that survival for leaders in large coalition systems remains hard, while for small coalition systems, political survival becomes increasingly easy over time. For autocrats, the difficulty is staying in office over the first few years. Once this is achieved, they find continued tenure relatively easy. In contrast, the incumbency advantage of leaders in large W systems does not grow as rapidly. This is most easily seen graphically. Figure 10.2 plots the hazard rate for large (W = 1) and small (W = 0) coalition systems (evaluated at eS = 0 and a growth rate of zero). The figure indicates that while it is initially harder for autocrats to survive in office (the negative coefficient of −0.463 for W in the Xβ component of the hazard rate), as affinities are revealed, and hence supporters become more certain of being retained in future coalitions, the loyalty norm increases and the threat of removal decreases. The negative coefficient of −1.497 for the effective S variable (eS) means that survival is particularly easy in large selectorate, small coalition systems. For the small coalition systems (W = 0) moving from a small (S = 0) to a large selectorate (S = 1) reduces the risk of deposition by 78 percent.

Table 10.2 The impact of institutions and IMF agreements on the survival of leaders: Weibull survival analysis with the ancillary parameter modeled

	Model 1 coefficient (standard error)	Model 2 coefficient (standard error)	Model 3 coefficient (standard error)
W	-0.463* (0.217)	-0.477* (0.214)	-0.308 (0.238)
eS	-1.497** (0.252)	-1.468** (0.245)	-1.444** (0.244)
Growth	-0.046** (0.007)	-0.046** (0.007)	-0.046** (0.007)
Growth*W	0.015 (0.014)	0.014 (0.014)	0.014 (0.014)
UNDER		-0.115 (0.092)	0.382* (0.214)
UNDER*W			-0.845* (0.380)
LEADER_UNDER			-0.275 (0.334)
LEADER_UNDER *W			0.479 (0.520)
Constant	-0.719** (0.140)	-0.688** (0.142)	-0.814** (0.161)
Ln(p)			
W	0.292** (0.111)	0.295** (0.111)	0.262* (0.116)
Constant	-0.348** (0.083)	-0.350** (0.082)	-0.326** (0.087)
Leaders	1066	1066	1066
Observation (monthly)	59245	59245	59245
LogLikelihood	-1555.60	-1554.72	-1552.25

Notes
Standard error in parentheses.
* $p < 0.05$, ** $p < 0.01$ (one tailed tests).

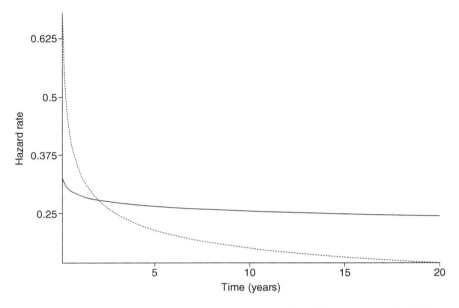

Figure 10.2 Hazard rate over time for large and small coalition systems (solid line: W = 1, dotted line: W = 0; time in years).

High economic growth improves survival in all political systems. The coefficient of −0.046 on the economic growth variable translates to a hazard ratio of 0.995, meaning that a 1 percent improvement in economic growth reduces the risk of deposition by 4.5 percent. Although the coefficient on the interaction of W and growth is positive, the effect of growth on survival is statistically indistinguishable from its effect in small coalition systems. Political institutions and economic growth shape the survival prospects of political leaders. We now turn to the impact of IMF agreements on the survival of leaders.

4.2 IMF agreements and leader survival

Model 2 assesses the aggregate effect of being under an IMF agreement. The variable UNDER is coded one if a leader is under an IMF agreement and zero otherwise. The coefficient on UNDER is −0.115, indicating IMF programs reduce the hazard to leader survival by 11 percent (the corresponding hazard ratio is 0.89). This might be evidence of successful scapegoating – controlling for political institutions and growth, participating in an IMF program reduces the risk of deposition for leaders – however, the effect is statistically insignificant.

We conjectured above that IMF agreements have different impacts under different institutional arrangements. It also matters whether the current leader chose to enter an IMF agreement or whether they inherited such a program from their predecessor. Model 3 examines these differences. The variable Signed is coded one if an IMF program is in effect and the current leader entered the agreement (and coded zero otherwise). Recall that UNDER records only whether a country is under an agreement and does not control for whether or not the incumbent chose to enter the program. As predicted, leader survival depends upon both the institutional context and whether the current leader chose to enter the agreement. Although the coefficients on the Signed variables are statistically insignificant, we examine them in detail here for several reasons. First, joint hypothesis tests suggest that the set of coefficients relating IMF programs are jointly significant. Second, the pattern observed in Model 3 is repeated throughout subsequent analyses (where they are of greater statistical significance).

The coefficient on UNDER is positive, indicating that IMF programs increase the risk of deposition that small coalition leaders face. However, the coefficient on Signed is negative, which indicates that while IMF programs increase the risk of deposition, being the leader that actually signs the agreement largely mitigates the risk. Table 10.3 calculates how the risk of deposition changes relative to not being under an IMF program and how this depends upon coalition size and Signed. Small coalition leaders who sign IMF agreements experience a modest increase in their risk of deposition, 11 percent. In contrast, small coalition leaders who inherit IMF programs but do not initiate them face a much greater increase in risk to tenure of 47 percent.

The effects of IMF programs for large coalition leaders are reversed. The negative coefficient on UNDER*W indicates that IMF programs help large coalition leaders survive. The positive coefficient on Signed*W suggests that being a large coalition leader who signed an IMF agreement reduces the beneficial effect of the IMF program. Calculating the net impact of IMF programs for large coalition leaders requires consideration of all four coefficients. Table 10.3 shows that being under an IMF

Table 10.3 The relative hazard of IMF agreements. The table shows how the hazard ratio of being under an IMF agreement (relative to being under no agreement) depends upon coalition size and whether the leader entered the agreement

Hazard ratio of IMF agreement	Small coalition (W = 0)	Large coalition (W = 1)
Leader entered agreement (Signed = 1)	11% **increase** in the risk of deposition	23% **decrease** in the risk of deposition
Leader did not enter agreement (Signed = 0)	47% **increase** in risk of deposition	33% **decrease** in the risk of deposition

program, on average, helps large coalition leaders, reducing the hazard by 33 percent. However, being the leader who signs the letter of intent diminishes the value of IMF programs: the reduction in the hazard rate is 23 percent.

Domestic institutions alter the impact of IMF agreements on the survival of leaders: IMF programs hurt the survival of small coalition leaders and help the survival of large coalition leaders. IMF programs hurt survival most when small coalition leaders inherit programs, and they help survival the most when large coalition leaders inherit them.

4.3 Assessing the motivations for loans

Leaders enter into IMF programs for a variety of reasons. Our theory suggests the survival consequences of being under an agreement differ according to the motivations for the loan. Hence, in order to proceed we need to be able to assess the extent to which a loan is *discretionary* or *need-based*. In this section, we follow Gordon and Smith's (2004) methodology to estimate the probability that an IMF program is discretionary rather than need-based. The model is described in detail in the Appendix.

Gordon and Smith (2004) propose using qualitative data to assign causal mechanisms for a limited subset of the data, a model they refer to as "trubit." While in general we cannot tell why a country entered an IMF program, in selected cases we can bring additional case study evidence to bear, which resolves the ambiguity. For instance, Vreeland (2002, 2003) discusses why Uruguay repeatedly entered IMF agreements despite extremely healthy foreign reserves. IMF programs helped Uruguay's leaders enact policy reform. This is clearly a case of discretion. Through the use of Monte Carlo testing, Gordon and Smith (2004) show that by assigning even a small percentage of events as discernible causes radically improves the reliability of estimates.

We rely on Vreeland (2002, 2003) to specify other definitive cases. Of 575 entry decisions in our data we assign 3 as discernible cases of discretion (mechanism 1) and 16 as discernible cases of need (mechanism 2). Due to missing data, in the analysis reported below there are 226 decisions to go under IMF programs of which 1 and 5 cases are assigned to discretion and need, respectively.[4] There is a strong tradeoff in assigning cause. Collecting qualitative information to assign cases is costly. As we become less certain about particular cases, we risk biasing our results by erroneously assigning cause. On the other hand, increasing the number of assigned cases improves the reliability of the estimator (see Gordon and Smith 2004). Here, we adopt a minimalist approach, assigning only a limited number of cases we are certain of. More grandiose assignments of definitive cause are shown in Model 5 and lead to similar substantive conclusions.

Table 10.4 shows MLE estimates of the trubit model. The first equation

Table 10.4 Trubit estimate of the determinants of discretionary and need-based loans

	Model 4: six cases defined as discernible causes based on Vreeland (2002, 2003)	Model 5: additional cases defined as discernible causes (33 cases of $Y_1 = 1$; 17 cases of $Y_2 = 1)^a$
Equation 1: Discretion		
W	−0.472 (0.521)	0.025 (0.374)
Tenure	−0.007 (0.020)	−0.003 (0.014)
Tenure*W	−0.009 (0.037)	−0.007 (0.025)
Year	0.017 (0.014)	0.014 (0.011)
Year*W	0.008 (0.023)	0.0005 (0.0179)
Cumulative agreements	0.113 (0.187)	0.184 (0.150)
Cumulative agreements*W	0.635 (0.616)	0.120 (0.437)
Growth	0.021 (0.018)	0.0125 (0.015)
Growth*W	−0.093** (0.033)	−0.045* (0.027)
Constant	−2.633** (0.299)	−2.601** (0.225)
Equation 2: Need		
W	1.989** (0.795)	2.715** (1.003)
Debt service	0.091** (0.028)	0.102** (0.030)
Debt service*W	−0.055 (0.035)	−0.061 (0.039)
ΔExchange	1.273** (0.350)	1.530** (0.363)
ΔExchange*W	−1.642** (0.480)	−1.970** (0.498)
ΔReserve	−1.121 (0.984)	−1.875 (1.181)
ΔReserve*W	2.459 (1.557)	2.829 (1.806)
Reserves/imports	−0.013 (0.244)	0.096 (0.329)
Reserves/imports*W	−0.749* (0.377)	−1.082* (0.494)
Growth	0.005 (0.020)	0.012 (0.026)
Growth*W	−0.017 (0.033)	−0.056 (0.042)
Constant	−3.235** (0.570)	−3.847** (0.719)
Observations	11799	11799
LogLikelihood	−1037.37	−1057.49

Notes
Standard error in parentheses.
* $p < 0.05$, ** $p < 0.01$ (one tailed tests).
a Additional definitive causes code as $Y_1 = 1$ if NEED = 0 and $Y_2 = 1$ if NEED > 5.

corresponds to discretionary motivations, the second equation relates to need-driven decisions to enter IMF programs.

Vreeland (2003) argues that the "audience" or "sovereignty" costs of entering into IMF agreements decreases when other governments – either historically within the country or governments around the world – also have participated in IMF agreements. Discretionary agreements are likely only when these costs are low. Also, Przeworski and Vreeland (2000) argue that dictatorships (small coalition political systems) are less likely to turn to the IMF for discretionary purposes. Thus, the discretion equation includes the variables W, Tenure, year (measured as the calendar year minus 1975), the cumulative agreements (measured as the natural logarithm of the total number of that country's prior agreements plus one) and the interactions of the latter variables with W. The results suggest that individually none of these factors significantly increase the likelihood of a discretionary IMF program. However, as a group they are highly statistically significant, with the likelihood of an IMF agreement being highest early in a leader's tenure (especially for large W), when countries have participated in many prior IMF programs and as year increases. The estimates also suggest economic growth increases the likelihood of agreement in small W and reduces it in large W. However, the effect is only statistically significant in large coalition systems. A stalled economy provides the impetus to initiate discretionary IMF programs.

The various literatures on the causes of IMF programs suggest the inclusion of additional variables such as number of veto players, levels of domestic violence and variables corresponding to the electoral cycle. Unfortunately, inclusion of these variables reduces the number of observations, sometimes drastically. Therefore, the results presented here do not attempt to capture these concepts.

The second equation corresponds to need-based causes for loans. It includes the country's debt service, change in exchange rate, change in reserves, level of reserves, growth and each of these variables interacted with W. Both Models 4 and 5 indicate that high levels of debt service increase the likelihood of a need-based IMF loan. The effect is stronger for small coalition systems. However, the result remains significant even for large coalition systems. In small coalition systems devaluation of the national currency increases the probability of a need-based IMF loan. As the exchange rate rises (i.e., the local currency devalues) debts denominated in foreign currencies such as the US dollar effectively increase. Given this, it is surprising that we see the opposite effect in large coalition systems. Devaluation reduces the likelihood of a need-based IMF program (the aggregate impact of the ΔExchange and ΔExchange*W variables is significant at the 2 percent level). This later result is contrary to expectations.

Reserves affect the likelihood of a need-based IMF program. As a country's reserves decline it becomes more likely to enter an IMF program. This of course was one of the ostensible purposes of the IMF. The effect is weak and statistically insignificant for small W, but in large coalitions the impact of reserve levels is strong and highly significant. While the actual level of reserves strongly influences the likelihood of a need-based IMF program, changes in reserve levels have a far weaker impact. Although the coefficients suggest a decline in reserves makes loans more likely in small W systems and less likely in large W systems, the effects are statistically insignificant.[5] Economic growth has no significant impact on the likelihood of need-based IMF loans once financial considerations are controlled.

The estimates in Table 10.4 suggest discretionary loans are most likely when leaders first come to power, when many previous agreements have been signed in the country's past, as the calendar year increases and when economic growth slows in large W systems. Need-based loans occur when countries service high debts and have low reserves. These estimates provide the basis from which to discriminate between the competing motives for a loan. In particular, if a country takes out a loan in the 1960s, having never previously entered an IMF program, when the leader is well established, economic growth is robust but reserves are low and the country is highly indebted then it is likely that such a loan is need-based. More systematically, we can use the results from Model 4 to estimate the relative probability that a loan is discretionary rather than need-based. The probability of entering a discretionary loan at time t is $\Phi(X_{1t}\hat{\beta}_1)$ where $\Phi()$ is the standard normal distribution, X_{1t} is the vector of covariates associated with mechanism 1 and $\hat{\beta}_1$ are the coefficient estimates for Equation 1. The corresponding probability of entering a need-based loan at time t is $\Phi(X_{2t}\hat{\beta}_2)$. Given these estimates, if a government enters into an IMF program at time t then the probability that this loan is discretionary rather than need-based is $P = \Phi(X_{1t}\hat{\beta}_1) / (\Phi(X_{1t}\hat{\beta}_1) + \Phi(X_{2t}\hat{\beta}_2))$ (see the Appendix for details).

Our theory predicts that the effects of IMF programs on leader survival depend upon the motivation to enter the IMF program in the first place. Using P as an estimate of the probability that a loan is discretionary we now test these predictions.

4.4 Motivations for IMF agreements and the survival of political leaders

IMF programs are anticipated to have different effects on leader survival depending upon why the program was undertaken and the institutional context in which leaders serve. The variable P estimates the probability that a loan is discretionary rather than need-based. Using the same naming convention as earlier, the variable signP represents the motivation for the loan at the time the leader entered the loan. It takes this value for as long as the leader remains in power and the country remains under the IMF program. If the country is not under an IMF program, or the incumbent leader inherited the IMF program rather than signed it herself, then signP = 0. Results are presented in Table 10.5

The impact on IMF programs depends upon whether the leader signed the agreement, the motivation for the loan, and the institutional context of the loan. Thus, in addition to the variables included in Model 3, Model 6 contains the variable signP, which measures the extent to which a loan is discretionary, and its interaction with W. Rather than examine the coefficients themselves, we move directly to an interpretation of the substantive effects. Using the results from Model 6, Table 10.6 compares how an IMF

Table 10.5 How the motivations for IMF programs impacts leader survival (estimate of motives based on Model 4)

	Model 6	Model 7	Model 8
W	0.362	−0.301	−0.317
	(0.368)	(0.658)	(0.441)
eS	−0.995**	−0.988**	−0.998**
	(0.415)	(0.424)	(0.417)
Growth	−0.080**	−0.085**	−0.075**
	(0.027)	(0.028)	(0.029)
Growth*W	0.068**	0.088*	0.069
	(0.040)	(0.043)	(0.046)
UNDER	0.482	0.445	0.460
	(0.368)	(0.367)	(0.377)
UNDER*W	−1.754**	−1.676**	−1.747*
	(0.748)	(0.713)	(0.772)
Leader_UNDER	−1.985**	−1.639*	−2.027**
	(0.763)	(0.785)	(0.734)
Leader_UNDER*W	3.231**	3.062**	3.248**
	(1.086)	(1.136)	(1.043)
signP	2.637**	2.099*	2.739**
	(0.924)	(0.933)	(0.872)
signP*W	−3.388**	−3.451**	−3.453**
	(1.308)	(1.259)	(1.274)
P		0.761	
		(0.628)	
P*W		0.065	
		(0.824)	
NEED			0.062
			(0.097)
NEED*W			−0.019
			(0.145)
Constant	−0.758**	−1.303**	−0.896**
	(0.217)	(0.533)	(0.301)
Ancillary parameter, ln(p)			
W	0.188	0.203	0.191
	(0.269)	(0.262)	(0.268)
Constant	−0.285*	−0.258*	−0.285*
	(0.154)	(0.154)	(0.153)
Observations	18399, 385	18399, 385	18399, 385
LogLikelihood	−455.04	−450.88	−454.25

Notes
Standard error in parentheses.
* $p < 0.05$, ** $p < 0.01$ (one tailed tests).

program alters the risk of deposition relative to no IMF program for both small and large coalition systems. The top row examines the case where countries are under IMF programs but the incumbent leader inherited rather than signed the agreement (UNDER = 1, Signed = 0, signP = 0). The center row is calculated assuming a loan is known to be discretionary and signed by the incumbent leader (UNDER = 1, Signed = 1, signP = 1). The bottom row examines need-based loans signed by the incumbent (UNDER = 1, Signed = 1, signP = 0).

The top row of Table 10.6 shows the effect of being under IMF programs that the current leader did not sign. Small coalition leaders, who find themselves encumbered by IMF programs that they did not initiate, are more likely to be deposed. The increase in risk is 62 percent (hazard ratio = 1.620), although this is not statistically significant. In contrast, IMF loans improve the survival of large coalition leaders who inherit IMF programs. Specifically, inheriting an IMF program reduces the risk of deposition by 72 percent (hazard ratio = 0.280). This is a statistically significant finding. This may be evidence that scapegoating is the most effective for democrats who inherit programs from their predecessors. It may also be that the economic pain associated with IMF economic reforms occurs when the country first participates in the IMF program.

The center row corresponds to the impact of leaders signing discretionary loans. Such discretionary loans badly damage the survival prospects of small coalition leaders, increasing the risk of deposition by more than threefold. In contrast, need-based loans help small coalition leaders survive, reducing the risk of deposition by 78 percent. Recall that small coalition leaders survive in office by paying off their supporters. These leaders survive by distributing the spoils. To the extent that IMF programs constrain autocrats from such activities, they hurt survival prospects.

Table 10.6 The survival impact of IMF programs controlling for motivation. The table shows how the hazard ratio of signing an IMF agreement (relative to being under no agreement) depends upon coalition size and whether the loan is discretionary or need-based

Hazard ratio of signing IMF agreement	Small coalition (W = 0)	Large coalition (W = 1)
Inherited loan: UNDER = 1, Signed = 0, signP = 0	62% **increase** in the risk of deposition	72%* **decrease** in the risk of deposition
Discretionary loan: UNDER = 1, Signed = 1, signP = 1	311%* **increase** in the risk of deposition	54%* **decrease** in the risk of deposition
Need-based loan: UNDER = 1, Signed = 1, signP = 0	78%* **decrease** in the risk of deposition	3% **decrease** in the risk of deposition

Note
* $p < 0.05$.

While small coalition leaders are aided by need-based loans and harmed by discretionary loans the opposite pattern is found for large coalition leaders. If a large coalition leader signs an IMF agreement for need-based reasons then the risk of deposition is similar to that the leader faces from not signing an IMF agreement. However, this risk to tenure is considerably higher than if the leader signed an IMF program for discretionary purposes. Under this latter contingency leaders reduce their risk of being deposed by 54 percent. It is useful to remember that large coalition leaders that inherit IMF program fare best of all, reducing their risk of deposition by 72 percent relative to no IMF program.

One reasonable criticism of these results is that they derive as a function of the underlying economic conditions and have little to do with whether an IMF program is need ($-$) or discretion (2x) based. Models 7 and 8 control for this possibility. Model 7 includes the variable P and its interaction with W. Since P measures the extent to which a loan is discretionary, high P values indicate little need for a loan. Hence Model 7 controls for the underlying need of a loan in each month. Model 8 also controls for economic need through the inclusion of NEED, an index of financial need for a loan. The construction of this index is described in Table 10.1. In neither Model 7 nor Model 8 are these control variables statistically significant; nor do they alter the substantive impact or significance of other variables.

5 Conclusions

The impact of IMF programs depends on domestic political institutions and the context under which IMF agreements are signed. The extant literature suggests governments go under IMF programs for a variety of reasons. Our analyses suggest that the effect of participating in IMF programs depends on what these reasons are. The results are clear: The contingencies under which a leader enters an IMF program and the institutional context in which such a leader serves shape survival.

Democrats that enter into IMF programs generally help their survival prospects. *Inheriting* an IMF program improves survival the most, which may be the result of blaming the previous leader for the IMF program and/or because the economic pain of IMF economic reforms is felt during the earliest years of the program. Entering into *discretionary* IMF programs also helps survival for democrats, perhaps because these discretionary programs are only initiated when IMF economic reforms are expected to improve economic growth and because if the policy changes go awry, the IMF provides a convenient scapegoat. Entering into a *need-based* IMF program has negligible effects for the survival of democratic leaders, probably because the political benefits are mitigated by the fact that the economic situation was poor in the first place.

For autocrats, being under IMF programs hurts survival if the program is *inherited* or initiated for *discretionary* purposes. We have proposed that this is because the constraints imposed by IMF programs go against the means by which dictatorships survive in office: distributing spoils. IMF programs only help autocrats if they are *need-based*, probably because the initial loan allows them to continue distributing spoils before conditionality constrains them.

To the best of our knowledge this study is the first to explore different motivations for IMF programs through the context of leader survival. Many extensions of this study remain to be pursued. For example, we dichotomized the motivations for loans into two categories: need and discretion. While this is clearly better than lumping all causes for loans into a single mechanism, it still conflates competing mechanisms. For instance, we do not distinguish between discretionary loans for scapegoating and discretionary loans for leverage to push through policy reform. Note that it is not necessary for both political causes to operate. On the one hand, a government could enter into a program purely for political leverage, taking full responsibility for the economic austerity, indeed even advocating it. On the other hand, a government could enter into a program without any belief that IMF conditions will effect positive change, but – expecting bad economic performance – seeks the IMF program for a scapegoat down the road. We suspect that loans undertaken for scapegoating are likely to indicate a leader already in trouble and hence such loans are likely to be followed by deposition. In contrast, discretionary loans undertaken for leverage are more likely to improve tenure, at least in large coalition systems where policy performance matters. Leaders would be unlikely to embark on reform otherwise. The data support this conjecture. As small coalition leaders have little interest in policy reform, efficient public policy not being their *modus operandi*, their discretionary loans are more likely to be for scapegoating than is the case for large coalition leaders. As we saw, discretionary loans drastically reduce the tenure of small coalition leaders but aid the survival of large coalition leaders. Fortunately, the methods outlined in this study can be readily adapted to account for multiple mechanisms, although it requires substantial additional case knowledge to identify cases corresponding to all three mechanisms – need, leverage, and scapegoating.

Throughout this chapter we assume the IMF is always ready to lend. This is not the case. IMF programs are joint agreements between the IMF and a government, as Przeworski and Vreeland (2002) show. Fortunately, the method proposed here could be extended to capture this in a manner similar to Przeworski and Vreeland's (2002) model. As we detail in the Appendix, however, to effectively implement such a model one must first identify key cases of the IMF refusing loans that governments wanted and other cases of governments refusing loans that the IMF offered.[6]

These limitations notwithstanding, as the first large-n study of the effect of IMF programs on leadership survival under all regime types, this chapter presents interesting results. IMF programs tend to improve the survival prospects of leaders in democracies, while it hurts survival prospects in autocracies. These effects are augmented when the leader inherits an IMF program from a previous leader rather than entering into it himself.

The study also has further implications for the evaluation of IMF program effectiveness in general, a subject that has been studied since the earliest days of IMF arrangements. Our results indicate that the effect of IMF programs depends not just on economic circumstances, but political conditions as well. The motivations of leaders – whether programs are need-based, discretionary, or simply inherited from previous leaders – play a role, as do the political institutions under which leaders serve. Since all IMF arrangements are not the same, these factors should be addressed in the study of the impacts of IMF programs.

Appendix

We assume there are two mechanisms or "causes" by which an IMF program arises: discretion and need. For each mechanism there is an associated latent variable representation: $Y_{1t}^* = X_{1t}\beta_1 + \epsilon_{1t}$ and $Y_{2t}^* = X_{2t}\beta_2 + \epsilon_{2t}$ where X_{1t} is a vector of independent variables associated with the discretionary mechanism at time t, X_{2t} is a vector of independent variables associated with the need mechanism, β_1 and β_2 are the associated coefficients and ϵ_{1t} and ϵ_{2t} are iid normally distributed stochastic errors with mean zero and variance one. For each mechanism this is a classic probit setup. If the latent variable $Y_{1t}^* > 0$ then the government enters into an IMF program for discretionary reasons (if $Y_{1t}^* > 0$ then $Y_{1t} = 1$, otherwise $Y_{1t} = 0$). Similarly if $Y_{2t}^* > 0$ then the government enters into an IMF program for need reasons (if $Y_{2t}^* > 0$ then $Y_{2t} = 1$, otherwise $Y_{2t} = 0$).

If, as analysts, we observed Y_{1t} and Y_{2t} directly then we could estimate each mechanism separately using standard probit models. Unfortunately, all we typically observe is whether a government entered an IMF program or not: if $Y_{1t} = 1$ or $Y_{2t} = 1$ then $Y_t = 1$; if $Y_{1t} = 0$ and $Y_{2t} = 0$ then $Y_t = 0$, where Y_t is a dummy variable indicating whether or not a country enters into an IMF program. Although we do not observe Y_{1t} and Y_{2t} directly, given certain identification restrictions, we can in principle estimate this model (Poirier 1980; Abowd and Farber 1982; Przeworski and Vreeland 2002; Braumoeller 2003). In particular, $\Pr(Y_t = 1) = 1 - (1 - \Phi(X_{1t}\beta_1))(1 - \Phi(X_{2t}\beta_2))$ and $\Pr(Y_t = 0) = (1 - \Phi(X_{1t}\beta_1))(1 - \Phi(X_{2t}\beta_2))$, where $\Phi()$ is the standard normal distribution function; β_1 and β_2 can be estimated by maximum likelihood estimation. Poirier (1980) refers to this as partial observability probit and Braumoeller (2003) calls it Boolean probit. Although Poirier shows that with certain exclusion restrictions the model is technically identified, Gordon and Smith (2004) show, using Monte Carlo studies, that in finite samples this estimator often performs poorly.

Boolean probit estimates are particularly poor when the sample is skewed (few $Y_t = 1$ and many $Y_t = 0$). Since $Y_t = 1$ corresponds to entry into an IMF arrangement, which happens relatively infrequently, these concerns are particularly pertinent here.

The limitation of the Boolean probit estimator stems from two problems, identification and labeling. It is useful to explain these in terms of Przeworski and Vreeland's (2002) related model. In their model they assume, correctly, that IMF agreements require the assent of both the government and the IMF. Analogous to the problem here, they construct a two equation model, one of which refers to the government's decision and the other of which refers to the IMF's decision. In order to identify their model, they need to have at least one variable that is unique to one of the equations. Unfortunately, finding such a variable is not straightforward. They use a country's overall balance of payments (in absolute terms not relative to GDP), contending that it belongs in the IMF decision equation. While they argue that this absolute size of imbalance is important to the IMF, since its job is maintaining global balance, it is hard to imagine BOP imbalances not also influencing governments.

The lack of a strong identifying restriction raises a second problem: labeling. Although the estimator produces estimates for each of the equations, the allocation of each equation to the government and IMF relies upon the relatively arbitrary exclusion restriction. One might tentatively argue that the IMF's estimates belong to the government and vice versa. Przeworski and Vreeland (2002) estimate two decisions: the decision to enter into IMF programs and the decision to continue such programs. While both decisions are clearly pertinent, we examine only the former. Our methodological goal is to estimate the contingent circumstances of IMF programs. In our study, we assume the IMF is willing to make loans. However, this need not be the case. An appropriate solution, for future development, is to model the IMF's decision as a latent variable Y_{IMFt}^{*} and assume entry into an IMF program requires either ($Y_{1t}^{*} > 0$ and $Y_{IMFt}^{*} > 0$) or ($Y_{2t}^{*} > 0$ and $Y_{IMFt}^{*} > 0$).

Gordon and Smith get around the labeling problem by assigning a small percentage of events as discernible causes, which also radically improves the reliability of estimates. Gordon and Smith estimate their trubit model using a Bayesian Markov Chain Monte Carlo method. Here we use a maximum likelihood estimation, where the likelihood is $L = 1 - (1 - \Phi(X_{1t}\beta_1))(1 - \Phi(X_{2t}\beta_2))$ if $Y_t = 1$ (and no discernible cause is identified), $L = (1 - \Phi(X_{1t}\beta_1))(1 - \Phi(X_{2t}\beta_2))$ if $Y_t = 0$, $L = \Phi(X_{1t}\beta_1)$ if $Y_{1t} = 1$ (i.e., a discernible case of discretion) and $L = \Phi(X_{2t}\beta_1)$ if $Y_{2t} = 1$ (i.e., a discernible case of need). The MCMC procedure generates similar results. Gordon and Smith (2004) also discuss how to extend the model to deal with probabilistic statements as to discernible causes.

Notes

1 Also called the "tip the balance" story (Bird 2001).
2 Bueno de Mesquita *et al.* (BdM2S2 2002; Bueno de Mesquita *et al.* 2003) formally model the shifting of coalitions through the revelation of affinities.
3 Although not presented here, we examined variables of the form underX, which take the value of variable X at the time a nation enters an IMF program and retains this value for as long as the nation is under the IMF even if the leader changes. When no IMF program is in force underX = 0.
4 In particular Uruguay's agreement in March 1979 is coded a definitive case of discretion, while Côte d'Ivoire's loans in February 1981, August 1984, June 1985 and June 1986 are coded as need-based.
5 One potential explanation for this result is that IMF programs help boost reserves. This produces offsetting effects. Declining reserves increase the likelihood of IMF programs but these programs in return boost reserves. This is an issue that could only be resolved with more detailed data that indicates the precise dates of changes in reserves and the disbursement of IMF loans. We do not yet have these data.
6 Given a latent variable representation for a nation's need, leverage, and scapegoat incentive, and a latent variable representation for the IMF's willingness to lend, the signing of an IMF program ($Y_t = 1$ requires either ($Y_{NEED,t}^* > 0$ and $Y_{IMF,t}^* > 0$) or ($Y_{leverage,t}^* > 0$ and $Y_{IMF,t}^* > 0$) or ($Y_{scapegoat,t}^* > 0$ and $Y_{IMF,t}^* > 0$).

References

Abowd, John M. and Henry S. Farber. 1982. Job Queues and the Union Status of Workers. *Industrial and Labor Relations Review* 35: 354–67.

Bird, Graham. 1996. Borrowing from the IMF: The Policy Implications of Recent Empirical Research. *World Development* 24: 1753–60.

Bird, Graham. 2001. The Political Economy of the IMF: A Check List of the Issues. Prepared for delivery at a workshop on The Political Economy of the IMF held at the Fletcher School, Tufts University, April 13.

Bird, G. and D. Rowlands. 2000. IMF Lending: How is it Affected by Economic, Political and Institutional Factors? Mimeo.

Braumoeller, Bear F. 2003. Causal Complexity and the Study of Politics. *Political Analysis* 11: 209–233.

Brune, Nancy, Geoffrey Garrett, and Bruce Kogut. 2004. The International Monetary Fund and the Global Spread of Privatization. *IMF Staff Papers* 51: 309–26.

Bueno de Mesquita, Bruce and Hilton L. Root (eds). 2000. *Governing for Prosperity.* New Haven: Yale University Press.

Bueno de Mesquita, Bruce, Alastair Smith, Randolph Siverson, and James D. Morrow (BdM2S2). 2003. *The Logic of Political Survival.* Cambridge: MIT Press.

Bueno de Mesquita, Bruce, James D. Morrow, Randolph Siverson, and Alastair Smith (BdM2S2). 1999. An Institutional Explanation of the Democratic Peace. *American Political Science Review* 93: 791–807.

Bueno de Mesquita, Bruce, James D. Morrow, Randolph Siverson, and Alastair Smith (BdM2S2). 2002. Political Institutions, Policy Choice and the Survival of Leaders. *British Journal of Political Science* 32 (4) (October): 559–90.

Callaghy, Thomas. 1997. Globalization and Marginalization: Debt and the International Underclass. In a special issue on The Global Economy. *Current History* 96/613: 392–6.

Callaghy, Thomas. 2002. Networks and Governance in Africa: Innovation in the Debt Regime. In *Intervention and Transnationalism in Africa: Global–Local Networks of Power*, edited by Thomas M. Callaghy, Ronald Kassimir, and Robert Latham, pp. 115–48. New York: Cambridge University Press.

Connors, Thomas A. 1979. The Apparent Effects of Recent IMF Stabilization Programs. International Finance Discussion Papers 135. Board of Governors of the Federal Reserve System.

Conway, Patrick. 1994. IMF Lending Programs: Participation and Impact. *Journal of Development Economics* 45: 365–91.

Dixit, Avinash K. 1996. *The Making of Economic Policy: A Transaction–Cost Politics Perspective.* Cambridge: MIT Press.

Drazen, Allan. 2005. Conditionality and Ownership in IMF Lending: A Political Economy Approach. This volume.

Dreher, Axel. 2002. Die Kreditvergabe von IWF und Weltbank: Ursachen und Wirkungen aus politisch-ökonomischer Sicht. PhD dissertation, Mannheim University.

Dreher, Axel. 2003a. The Influence of Elections on IMF Program Interruptions. *The Journal of Development Studies*, forthcoming, August.

Dreher, Axel. 2003b. The Influence of IMF Programs on the Re-election of Debtor Governments. Mimeo.

Edwards, Martin S. 2000. Reevaluating the "Catalytic" Effect of IMF Programs. Prepared for delivery at the 2000 Annual Meeting of the American Political Science Association, Marriott Wardman Park, Washington, DC, August 31–September 3, 2000. Copyright by the American Political Science Association.

Edwards, Sebastian and Julio A. Santaella. 1993. Devaluation Controversies in the Developing Countries: Lessons from the Bretton Woods Era. In *A Retrospective on the Bretton Woods System*, edited by Michael D. Bordo and Barry Eichengreen, pp. 405–55. Chicago: University of Chicago Press.

Goldstein, Morris and Peter J. Montiel. 1986. Evaluating Fund Stabilization Programs with Multicountry Data: Some Methodological Pitfalls. *IMF Staff Papers* 33: 304–44.

Gordon, Sanford and Alastair Smith. 2004. Quantitative Leverage Through Qualitative Knowledge: Augmenting the Statistical Analysis of Complex Causes. Forthcoming Political Analysis.

Gylfason, Thorvaldur. 1987. *Credit Policy and Economic Activity in Developing Countries with IMF Stabilization Programs.* Princeton: Studies in International Finance 60.

International Monetary Fund. 2003. International Financial Statistics CD-ROM. Washington, DC.

Knight, Malcolm and Julio A. Santaella. 1997. Economic Determinants of Fund Financial Arrangements. *Journal of Development Economics* 54: 405–36.

Nelson, Joan M. 1992. Poverty, Equity, and the Politics of Adjustment. In *The Politics of Economic Adjustment: International Constraints, Distributive Conflicts, and the State*, edited by S. Haggard and R.R. Kaufman, pp. 221–69. Princeton: Princeton University Press.

Poirier, Dale J. 1980. Partial Observability in Bivariate Probit Models. *Journal of Econometrics* 12: 209–17.

Przeworski, Adam and James Raymond Vreeland. 2000. The Effect of IMF Programs on Economic Growth. *The Journal of Development Economics* 62: 385–421.

Przeworski, Adam and James Raymond Vreeland. 2002. A Statistical Model of Bilateral Cooperation. *Political Analysis* 10 (2): 101–12.

Putnam, Robert D. 1988. Diplomacy and Domestic Politics: the Logic of Two-Level Games. *International Organization* 42: 427–60.

Ramcharan, Rodney. 2003. Reputation, Debt and Policy Conditionality. Research Department, International Monetary Fund.

Reichmann, Thomas M. and Richard T. Stillson. 1978. Experience with Programs of Balance of Payments Adjustment: Stand-by Arrangements in the Highest Tranches, 1963–72. *IMF Staff Papers* 25: 292–310.

Remmer, Karen L. 1986. The Politics of Economic Stabilization, IMF Standby Programs in Latin America, 1954–1984. *Comparative Politics* 19: 1–24.

Santaella, Julio A. 1996. Stylized Facts Before IMF-Supported Adjustment. *IMF Staff Papers* 43: 502–44.

Spaventa, Luigi. 1983. Two Letters of Intent: External Crises and Stabilization Policy, Italy, 1973–77. In *IMF Conditionality*, edited by John Williamson, pp. 441–73. Washington, DC: Institute for International Economics.

Tsebelis, George. 1995. Decision Making in Political Systems. *British Journal of Political Science* 25: 289–326.

Tsebelis, George. 2002. Veto Players: An Introduction to Institutional Analysis. Unpublished manuscript, UCLA.

Vaubel, Roland. 1986. A Public Choice Approach to International Organization. *Public Choice* 51: 39–57.

Vreeland, James Raymond. 2000. The Institutional Determinants of IMF Programs. Prepared for delivery at the Leitner Work-In-Progress Seminar, Yale University. December 4, 2000.

Vreeland, James Raymond. 2002. The Effect of the IMF Programs on Labor. *World Development* 30: 121–39.

Vreeland, James Raymond. 2003. *The IMF and Economic Development.* New York: Cambridge University Press.

World Bank. 2002. *World Development Indicators on CD-ROM.* Washington, DC: The World Bank.

11 Do PRSPs empower poor countries and disempower the World Bank, or is it the other way round?*

Frances Stewart and Michael Wang

1 Introduction

Policy reforms imposed on developing countries through conditionality have greatly weakened the autonomy of recipient countries. The vast majority of poor countries in Africa, and many in Latin America and Asia, have been subject to a series of IMF and World Bank adjustment packages, especially over the last 20 years. These reforms cover all the major economic decisions – budgets, tax and expenditure policies, exchange rates, trade and tariff policies, price policies, privatization, credit policies – such that countries subject to them have very little control over their economic policies. Moreover, sectoral adjustment policies additionally expand the scope of conditionalities – including education and health policies for example. The Comprehensive Development Framework of the World Bank further extends the realm of potential conditionality into the law and matters of governance. Conditionality thus has been a major source of disempowerment whether or not the policy reforms are in the recipient countries' longer-term interests.

A lack of local enthusiasm for what appeared to be agency-imposed programmes was widely believed to be due to limited country 'ownership' of the programmes, leading to delays or failures in implementation. Consequently, the agencies began to argue the case for greater ownership. The Poverty Reduction Strategy Papers (PRSPs) are the most concrete and widespread manifestation of IMF/WB efforts to increase country ownership. The question we aim to address in this chapter is whether and to what extent PRSPs have effectively empowered poor countries, or whether, as some have suggested[1] they are 'window dressing' which in reality empower neither poor countries nor poor people, but rather enforce the power of the international agencies by giving the appearance of ownership without the reality.

PRSPs explicitly incorporate participation into the IMF/WB lending framework for poor countries. They follow a long history of concern with participation in the development community, spanning nearly four decades. Starting with a series of high-level declarations of support for 'popular participation' by international development organizations in the 1970s, to the re-orientation of bilateral aid projects towards 'customer focus' and 'stakeholder participation' in the 1990s, the concept of participation has increasingly been mainstreamed in donor-developing country policy dialogue.[2]

The International Financial Institutions (IFIs) claim that PRSPs are country driven and nationally owned:

> Country ownership is the guiding principle ... the process and content [of PRSPs] must be designed nationally to suit local circumstances and capacities, and should be useful to the country, *not only* external donors.
>
> (Klugman 2003, our italics)

Moreover, 'participation' of civil society is regarded as essential to achieving the principle of national ownership:

> Poverty Reduction Strategies should be country-driven, promoting national ownership of strategies *by involving broad-based participation by civil society.*
>
> (IMF 2002b, our italics)

PRSPs were first introduced in 1999, and 30 had been produced at the time of writing. Therefore we now have some evidence to permit us to make a preliminary assessment of them, although because of their short history it is only possible to analyse the process and content of the PRSPs, not their impact when implemented. Our concern here is the extent to which they have increased national ownership of programmes, and thereby have empowered the countries. This is a difficult question to answer not least because 'national ownership' is not an unproblematic concept, nor is 'empowerment'.

The term 'ownership' is borrowed from the realm of private property over goods or land, where it generally has a well-defined legal meaning, but also involves a psychological aspect, a perception of possession. When transferred to policy programmes, the legal aspect, which underpins the concept in its normal use, disappears, and we are left with the psychological aspect. This psychological aspect could be just a matter of perceptions, without any change in underlying realities – i.e. that governments/local people are induced to believe they have ownership of what is essentially unchanged reality, by reformed processes, such as the PRSP might bring about. But a genuine change in the underlying reality is likely to be needed to bring about a lasting change in perceptions. This would require that the national contribution to the design of policy programmes substantially increases, even if it does not become exclusive.

There is also a question of what *national* ownership implies: is it a matter of governments' increased contributions to policy design and consequently changed perceptions, or that of civil society, or some combination? From the point of view of the democratic legitimacy of the process, any democratically elected government must be involved; in such cases, the role of civil society is more questionable – it certainly has an important role in helping form and check government policy, but it does not necessarily have an independent right to determine policy;[3] where democracy is limited, or non-existent, however, there is a special need to involve civil society to ensure popular participation in the process. In general, in both democracies and non-democracies, including civil society, the process is likely to help to increase perceptions of national ownership, and improve implementation, since this, of course, involves both government and civil society.

While national ownership can be increased just by changing perceptions, national empowerment cannot. National empowerment means that national actors (government and civil society) have a greater say in the design of policies. Hence we are concerned in this chapter with whether PRSPs bring about a genuine and substantial change towards greater national contribution to the design of policy programmes. We are not so much concerned here with whether PRSPs particularly empower the poor, which is also one of their objectives – not because this is unimportant, but because it is not necessarily relevant to the general issue of national empowerment.

While the PRSP process assumes that participation will increase national ownership, how far it does so must depend on who participates, whether participation actually affects the design of the programmes, or merely provides endorsement to externally designed programmes, as well as the scope and coverage of the PRSP process. It would be possible to have genuine and effective participation (i.e. participation which changes the nature of the programmes), yet to achieve little national empowerment because the arena over which the PRSP rules represents only a small part of the decision making affected by outside agencies.

Specifically, to shed light on these issues we aim to explore:

- who is involved in the PRSP process;
- how far programmes change as a result; and
- what proportion of IFI-affected decision making is covered by the PRSPs.

The remainder of the chapter investigates these questions adopting two perspectives – first, examining the *process* through which countries have developed PRSPs; and second, examining the policies contained in the documents, aiming to assess whether the process has brought about a change in the content of policies and the coverage of the programmes.

The sources consulted consist of countries' completed PRSP documents, as well as some primary and secondary contributions.

The next section first provides a brief overview of PRSPs. Sections 3 and 4 present a general discussion of the meaning of participation and examine the available experience with drafting PRSPs, looking at who has been consulted and in what manner. Section 5 then asks whether or not participation appears to have had an impact on the policy content of PRSP documents. Section 6 examines the importance of PRSPs in the wider realm of IFI decision making, while Section 7 concludes.

2 Overview of PRSPs

PRSPs now form the basis for all multilateral lending to the poorest developing countries. They are policy documents produced by borrower countries outlining the economic, social and structural programmes to reduce poverty, to be implemented over a three-year period. They were developed as the main vehicle to implement the Comprehensive Development Framework (CDF) – the World Bank's new long-term, holistic approach to lending practices which claims to place poverty reduction at the fore and to allow recipient countries to own and direct their development agendas.

Since 1999 recipients of debt relief under the enhanced 'Heavily indebted poor countries' (HIPC) initiative, as well as of concessional IDA lending and the IMF's Poverty Reduction and Growth Facility (PRGF), have been required to produce a PRSP. Finished documents must receive endorsement from the Boards of both the Bank and Fund, part of which, in principle, is based upon an acceptable participatory process.[4] Following one year's implementation, countries which qualify for HIPC relief receive the full cancellation of their agreed-upon debt, the so-called 'completion point'. Countries can access temporary ('decision point') debt relief before completing a full PRSP by producing an interim document (I-PRSP) outlining strategies to be employed in the final document.

Nearly all low-income and highly indebted countries have produced, or are in the process of producing, a PRSP. As of January 2003, the number totalled 77, roughly a third of which (30) have submitted a full PRSP, with the remainder an I-PRSP (22), or in process of producing an I-PRSP (25) (Table 11.1). Of the 30 countries that have submitted a final PRSP, 23 have received approval from the Boards of the Bank and Fund, and eight have been implementing programmes for more than a year (Albania, Bolivia, Burkina Faso, Honduras, Mauritania, Mozambique, Nicaragua, Tanzania, Uganda). In terms of geographic distribution, the majority of countries involved are in Sub-Saharan Africa (SSA) (39), with the remaining distributed fairly evenly across East Asia and the Pacific (11), Europe and Central Asia (11), Latin America and the Caribbean (9) and South Asia (7). The PRSP process is furthest underway in SSA and Europe and Central Asian regions, with most countries possessing either a completed

Table 11.1 Countries in the PRSP process (early 2003)

Full	Interim	Forthcoming
Albania	Armenia	Afghanistan
Azerbaijan	Bosnia and Herzegovina	Angola
Benin	Cape Verde	Bangladesh
Bolivia	The Central African Republic	Bhutan
Burkina Faso	Chad	Burundi
Cambodia	Côte d'Ivoire	Comoros
Cameroon	D.R. Congo	Congo
Ethiopia	Djibouti	Dominica
Gambia	Georgia	East Timor
Ghana	Guinea Bissau	Eritrea
Guinea	Kenya	Grenada
Guyana	Lao	Indonesia
Honduras	Lesotho	Kiribati
Kyrgzstan	Macedonia	Maldives
Malawi	Madagascar	Nepal
Mali	Moldova	Nigeria
Mauritania	Pakistan	Samoa
Mongolia	Sao Tome and Principe	The Solomon Islands
Mozambique	Sierra Leone	St Lucia
Nicaragua	Togo	St Vincent
Niger	Yugoslavia	Sudan
Rwanda		Tonga
Senegal		Uzbekistan
Sri Lanka		Vanuatu
Tajikstan		Zimbabwe
Tanzania		
Uganda		
Vietnam		
Yemen		
Zambia		

Source: World Bank website.

PRSP or I-PRSP (with SSA leading the way in implementation of programmes), and have made least progress in the East Asian and South Asian regions, with the majority of countries still in the process of producing an I-PRSP.

3 The meaning of participation

Participation has been used to mean different things in different contexts. One important distinction is whether it is interpreted to involve 'empowerment', implying significant control over decision making, or whether it simply means rudimentary levels of consultation, where little delegation of decision-making powers occurs (Nelson and Wright 1995). Another distinction is between whether it is viewed as a means or an end (Goulet

1989). An instrumental approach views participation as a means to improving implementation, efficiency and equity, while an empowerment approach values the process of increasing participation as an important end in itself.

At a minimum, participation clearly requires that individuals and groups are in some way involved in the decision-making process. This engagement can assume any of a number of points along a spectrum, which has been defined as ranging from (1) information sharing, (2) consultation, (3) joint decision making, to (4) initiation and control by stakeholders (World Bank 1996; McGee 2000; Narayan *et al.* 2000). At one end 'information sharing' involves very limited decision-making powers but potentially important knowledge transfer. At the other lies 'initiation and control', which implies a high degree of citizen control over decision making. In between, 'consultation' exists when participants are able to express opinions but their perspectives are not necessarily incorporated into the final product; 'joint decision making', on the other hand, gives participants the shared right to negotiate the content of strategy. The boundaries of this classification are of course not clear-cut, and the type of participation involved varies with different stages of the policy-making process (e.g. early stages might involve more information sharing, while later stages more consultation and joint decision making). From the perspective of national empowerment, participation needs to be at the initiation and control end of the spectrum.

There is also the question of who is empowered by the new process, which depends on who is consulted. Early exercises in participation were mainly concerned with development projects, and in this context participation was intended to cover those affected by the projects. Subsequently, Participatory Poverty Assessments (PPAs) were introduced, intended to ascertain what the poor themselves believe about their condition,[5] in which case, it is poor people who should participate. But the PRSPs differ from both these approaches, being centrally concerned with policy. The selection of groups, how representatives are chosen and how capable they are, constitute important factors influencing the legitimacy as well as the effectiveness of the process. The extent of national ownership and empowerment is greatly affected by such considerations. While groups affected by the policies form one important constituency, a democratically elected government, in principle, is the legitimate representative of the people, more so than many Civil Society Organizations (CSOs), such as NGOs, which vary in how representative they are. If national empowerment is to be achieved through PRSPs the government must be the most important participant, with local CSOs a useful adjunct, where they genuinely represent local groups, especially the poor.

Finally, an important consideration relevant to ownership and empowerment lies in the manner in which participants are involved. Issues here are (1) whether the mechanisms for participation (e.g. conferences and voting procedures) are conducive to generating broad-based participation – for example, the timing and location of events can significantly impact the character of participants; (2) whether information is widely available; and (3) the policy areas and stages of the decision-making process in which participation occurs. Equally important is the level at which participation takes place, whether it is confined to the national stage or involves regional and local levels as well.

These considerations suggest that participatory processes can be judged on both the intensity of participants' engagement (e.g. information sharing, consultation or joint decision making) and the degree of inclusion or exclusion of various groups. From the perspective of identifying whether PRSPs are genuinely nationally empowering, the participatory process must

- be towards the initiation and control end of the spectrum;
- be an objective, not merely instrumental;
- give democratically elected governments[6] a central role;
- incorporate a wide range of non-governmental stakeholders, each with capable and representative participation;
- give a much reduced role to *external* actors, official and NGO.

3.1 The World Bank's definition of participation

In its *Source Book for Poverty Reduction Strategies*, the World Bank (2002) defines participation as:

> the process by which stakeholders influence and share control over priority setting, policymaking, resource allocations, and/or program implementation.
>
> (237)

The source book expects the following groups to participate (250, Box 7.6):

1   The general public, particularly the poor and vulnerable groups;
2   The government, including parliament, local government, line and central ministries;
3   Civil Society Organizations such as NGOs, community-based organizations, trade unions and guilds, academic institutions;
4   Private sector actors such as professional associations; and,
5   Donors, both bilateral and multilateral.

From these statements, it would appear that the World Bank envisages participation in PRSPs to be towards the initiation and control end of the spectrum – participants should be able to 'influence' and 'control' policy making and agenda setting, as well as budgeting and implementation. The

World Bank's vision of the participation also suggests an inclusive process, encompassing extremely broad sectors of domestic society and international stakeholders, not only marginalized individuals, but also relevant representative institutions and umbrella groups. However, we should note that the involvement of donors (bilateral and multilateral) in the participatory process weakens the national ownership/empowerment consequences. In order for this involvement not to negate any national empowerment effects, it is important that they do not dominate the process, by setting the agenda, by their articulateness in discussions, and by their implicit financial clout.

In the next two sections we will examine whether the reality of the PRSP participatory process has lived up to the claims of generating national ownership. In assessing participation in PRSPs, we limit ourselves to examining participation only in the policy-making process, not in either budgeting or implementation. We will assess participation along two lines: first in terms of the 'process' of policy formation, assessing the degree of inclusion, asking *who* has participated, in *what manner* they have participated and the *issues* in which they have participated; and second in terms of the *content* of PRSPs, asking whether the PRSP process has affected the policy content of the final documents.

4 The process of formulating PRSPs

4.1 Who participates?

It is difficult to generalize about the range of actors consulted in PRSPs given the diversity of country experiences. In some cases, there has been broad involvement across all the categories outlined in the World Bank's source book. Uganda, Rwanda and Vietnam have been acknowledged both by civil society and donors alike as having fostered such comprehensive participation.[7] In Uganda, broad-based participation was achieved first through Participatory Poverty Assessments (PPAs), which paved the way for constructive consultations between Government and civil society for the PRSP. Participation in the final document was widespread with the Government ensuring heavy public and NGO input through a large scale and high profile media campaign and regional consultation workshops that made concerted efforts to include stakeholders beyond the capital (McGee 2002: 70). The creation of an umbrella organization to channel civil society efforts ensured wide civil society participation in the debate over the final document.

In Rwanda, broad participation was achieved by incorporating existing indigenous participatory practices known as *Ubedehe* into the PRSP process. This involved a bottom-up approach to participatory design, the government targeting 9000 *cellules* to produce public action priority rankings and community development plans, as well as a PPA and Policy

Relevance Test to collect poor people's opinions on the relevance of sectoral policies (Bugingo 2002). Participation appears to have been largely home-grown as a result, with broad consensus that there was grassroots participation at most stages which has helped in the post-conflict reconciliation and peace-building process.

Vietnam is another case of extensive participation. Both donors and civil society observers agree that Vietnam's participatory process involved a broad range of actors, largely the result of good pre-existing relations between government structures and Vietnamese NGOs, particularly at the local level (SGTS *et al.* 2000: 23). The government has involved local NGOs directly in its formal discussions with international donors. In other cases, local NGOs were able to express their perspectives in national policy dialogues through partnerships with international NGOs and donors.

In other countries, some categories of participants were more engaged than others, while some were left out. For example, the private sector was particularly active in Mozambique (McGee and Taimo 2001), while it was notably absent in Rwanda (Mutebi *et al.* 2003: 260). Religious organizations were quite important in Bolivia and Nicaragua but were missing in other countries.

There has been substantial government involvement in almost all countries, with high-level political authority guiding and managing the process of participation, though the breadth of involvement has been variable, with some (e.g. Kenya) exhibiting participation across different levels of government as well as different ministries, while in others the process was led principally by the finance or planning ministry and concentrated at the national level (e.g. Mali and Malawi).[8]

Donors, including IFI representatives, have also displayed differing levels of engagement. In terms of designing the participatory process, it is reported that most have taken a relatively 'hands-off' approach, allowing national government greater room than before in conducting national and regional consultations (e.g. Booth 2001: 27). Donor involvement has ranged from assuming an observer's role to organizing and financing consultations directly. However, when it comes to more substantive issues surrounding policy design, the record is less clear as to whether significant changes have occurred. In some countries such as Ghana, Killick and Abugre (2001) report that IFI representatives specifically avoided excessive involvement in drafting the PRSP (13). But there are reports of heavy IFI involvement in the drafting of Tanzania's I-PRSP (Evans 2003), and little improvement in the transparency of negotiations with IFI officials in Malawi's PRSP (Jenkins and Tsoka 2003). The role of external actors appears even less changed with regard to lending facilities outside the PRSP process, as we will discuss further. These issues have critical bearing for national ownership and empowerment and will be discussed further in Sections 5 and 6.

Despite the variety of experiences several key categories of participants have been excluded from the participatory process consistently across a number of countries. We summarize them briefly:

Groups missing from consultations

- *Parliamentarians:* In a number of countries, the role of national Parliaments in formulating PRSPs has been minimal, particularly in Africa (Booth 2001), although this has also been a problem in Latin America (see Trócaire 2002). In some cases this has resulted from a lack of capacity to become actively involved, in others, because they have been left out of the process. In Malawi, for example, 'only 5 MPS were involved in the process' (cited in Eurodad 2001: 9). In Kenya, less than 10 per cent of MPs attended consultations (Panos Institute 2002: 25). In Senegal and Mali parliamentarians were only officially included in the final ratification of the PRSP (Phillips 2002; Dante *et al.* 2003). Only six of the 83 MPs in Benin participated in meetings (Biershenk *et al.* 2003). In general, it appears that in most African countries there is a tendency for PRSPs to be seen as 'technical planning processes that are properly the affair of the government, and not a subject for party-political debate' (Booth 2001: 41).[9]
- *Trade unions:* The International Conference of Free Trade Unions (ICFTU) reports that trade unions were not systematically consulted in many early PRSP processes. Although in some cases trade unions represent narrow sectional interests, from a participatory perspective their exclusion in many countries is problematic since they generally represent an important group. In Tanzania and Uganda national trade unions were told they could participate in the PRSP process only after the PRSP had already been completed and endorsed by the IFIs (ICFTU 2002). In Mali, neither trade unions nor the important Cotton Producers' Association participated at all (Dante *et al.* 2003). There has been some evidence however of trade unions enjoying substantive participation in transition countries where as a result of the Soviet legacy there have been traditionally close relations between governments and trade unions (ODI 2003b).
- *Women:* In a number of countries, participation of women's groups appear to be weak (World Bank 2001). In Senegal, the United Nations Development Fund for Women (UNIFEM) (2001) found 'Civil Society organizations were ignored, especially women'. Zuckerman (2001) reports that in both Tanzania and Bolivia, consultations with women's groups were very limited (10). McGee (2002) reports that very few women's groups were made aware of consultations in Malawi. But there are reports that some countries made special efforts to include women. In Kenya, the Centre for Gender and Development was instrumental in lobbying for a gender-aware process (ODI 2002: 4), while in Lesotho, a survey found that a majority of communities felt that efforts had been made in the PRSP process to encourage women's participation (Panos Institute 2002: 43).

- *Marginalized groups:* Many CSOs have been critical of national processes for leaving out the poor in consultations. Action Aid (2002) reports that at least five of its country programmes have complained that there has been little direct involvement of associations of the poor in PRSP deliberations. Critics of the process in Bolivia also report that organizations representing certain groups – such as homesteaders, peasants and indigenous peoples – did not themselves attend and were represented by local authorities who were only weakly connected to the poor, particularly indigenous groups (Uriona *et al.* 2002).

In many cases, participation has been excessively selective. Groups out of favour with the government have often not been invited. In Ghana, for example, trade union members reported that 'the Government preferred to consult with more sympathetic institutions, like the Civil Servants Union (which was not a member of the Trades Union Congress), than with bodies which carry real weight within civil society' (quoted in SGTS *et al.* 2000: 19). Christian Aid (2001) reports that in Bolivia, civil society participants felt that the government's selection of participants for the 'National Dialogue' was not impartial or representative of society (14). In Cameroon, the Catholic Relief Services (2001) reports that the government hand-picked participants in civil society consultations, by-passing important civil society institutions such as the Catholic Church which were key campaigners for debt relief (10). In Tanzania, the process for selecting civil society representatives was never made public or transparent (McGee 2002: 66).

In other cases, NGO participation was limited to international NGOs, or NGOs in the capital area. In some cases, smaller and rural NGOs, generally those with the most contact with the poor, were excluded from the process. In Bolivia, for example, only one NGO outside La Paz was invited to initial consultations, while one of the most prominent local NGOs in La Paz was not invited (World Development Movement 2001). In Senegal, smaller CSOs expressed the view that the PRSP process seemed more geared towards large NGOs (Phillips 2002: 56).

Even where a broad range of NGOs have participated, it is not always clear they were necessarily representative of broader societal concerns, while foreign NGOs frequently played an important role. This is particularly a concern in fractionalized communities, where local élite interests may dominate (Hoddinott 2002). Even in fairly homogeneous and united communities, the ability of Civil Society Organizations (CSOs) to be fully representative of the constituencies they claim to represent is often limited by constraints on their outreach capacity; or because they are dominated by urban professionals with little 'natural' constituency among poor communities; or by interest groups more interested in pressing their own case. For example, Killick and Abugre report that the non-state actors involved in drafting Ghana's PRSP were donor-driven and not representative of pro-poor constituencies.[10]

4.2 In what manner?

Countries have employed a variety of strategies for consultation and information dissemination, both formal and informal. These have included national and regional conferences to discuss PRSP drafts and proposals, where representative groups from civil society, sometimes identified by the government or CSOs at the government's behest, were invited to contribute inputs for the analysis of poverty and prioritizing public actions. In some cases national consultations have been general in scope, and in others organized along thematic or sectoral lines. In several countries (e.g. Nicaragua and Bolivia) they built upon participatory mechanisms that had already been enshrined in national legislation (ODI 2003a). Other methods have included local surveys asking villagers for inputs into prioritizing public action and resource allocation, as well as media campaigns ranging from TV, radio and newspaper announcements (e.g. Malawi, Tanzania, Rwanda and Kenya). PPAs have taken place in some countries (e.g. Uganda, Vietnam and Rwanda) to inform the poverty analysis that underpins the PRSP, and have included problem or solution ranking designed to inform policy prioritization and budget allocations. However, there have been problems with the design and implementation of participatory processes, including the timeframe, information sharing and level of consultations.

4.2.1 Time frame

Because debt relief is conditional on producing PRSPs, there is a strong incentive for HIPC-eligible countries (accounting for more than half the countries producing PRSPs) to complete them as soon as possible in order to lock-in debt relief (Adam and Bevan 2001). Considerable evidence suggests this link has compromised the quality of participation. The Mozambique Debt Group (2001) reports that 'the consultation process was driven inordinately by a deadline for the completion of the PRSP, which even with good faith on the part of the government, provided inadequate time to carry out a comprehensive consultation process' (quoted in Christian Aid 2001: 33). In Ethiopia, the government attempted consultations in over 100 districts in just three days (Muwonge *et al.* 2002). In many cases, CSOs were not given sufficient time to prepare for consultation. From a review of its country programmes in six countries in Africa and Latin America, Action Aid (2002) reports that there was

> a lack of adequate prior notice regarding meetings and consultations. Many were informed only 2 or 3 days in advance, and in the case of Nepal, 24-hour prior notice was given on one occasion ... nearly all country programs felt such last minute notification prevented them from preparing adequately for PRS consultations; lengthy reports and

documents could not be commented upon and the views of community partners could not be sought.

(7)

In Bolivia, Honduras and Cameroon, Catholic Relief Services also complained of being given only a day's notice before consultations, with insufficient preparatory information or material.[11] The frequency of participation also appears to have been negatively affected by the PRSP's time frame. In many cases, there have been reports of local consultation workshops taking place only once over the course of a day without any further possibilities for participation at the local level (e.g. Honduras and Cameroon) (Save the Children 2001). This was particularly the case in Tanzania, which had one of the most compressed PRSP timeframes (six months from initiation to cabinet approval) and where the only local consultations took place over the course of a single day (Evans 2003).

4.2.2 Information availability

In general, the consensus has been that access to drafts and final versions of PRSPs and I-PRSPs has been relatively good in most countries. However, there have been a number of cases where the availability of information has been hampered by:

- *Access:* Many CSOs have complained about a lack of access to core World Bank and IMF documents. In Nicaragua, the draft interim PRSP was available in English in Washington before it was available in Managua (ODI 2003a). In a survey of eight PRSP countries McGee (2002) found that the

> sharing of information with CSOs who take an active part in PRSP processes has been patchy. Governments have often appeared reluctant to share early drafts of PRSPs or budgetary information, which would be pertinent in consultative prioritization exercises ... In general, information seems not to have reached rural populations in time to encourage broad and well-informed participation in consultations; civil society has sometimes taken over the task of information dissemination when they consider governments' efforts or plans inadequate (Mozambique).

(9)

It has been reported that in Haiti, civil society groups have had trouble in obtaining even basic information such as, which government ministry is leading the process and the timeline for its formulation (Christian Aid 2001: 14). In Senegal, civil society groups were expected to comment on initial drafts without having received them beforehand, although this appears to have been rectified at later stages of the process (Phillips 2002: 56). In Bolivia, although civil society participants had been promised the opportunity to view and approve the final PRSP at the end of the 'National Dialogue', this opportunity never materialized (Christian Aid 2001: 33). Zambian NGOs also expressed concern that they did not receive all key documents and information necessary for effective participation in PRSP formulation, even basic information such as the amount of interim debt reduction (CRS 2001: 21).

More generally, although many have heard about them, knowledge of exactly what PRSPs involve appears to have been scarce among the populace in many of the first PRSP countries. In a survey of Africa's experience with developing PRSPs, Booth (2001) finds:

> there is a tendency for the facts of the PRSP initiative to be fully grasped only by a small core of government personnel who have been directly responsible for carrying it forward. In some cases, a similar level of understanding is shared by a small number of academics or civil-society representatives ... the availability of even quite elementary information on the subject declines quite steeply as one moves away from these central points.
>
> (20)

- *Language:* The choice of language in several cases has limited civil society participation. For example, Cambodia's PRSP was only made available in Khmer in the final version and not in earlier drafts (NGO Forum on Cambodia 2001). In Bolivia some PRSP documents were initially only produced in English (Christian Aid 2001: 13). A Spanish version followed but documents were never translated into local languages such as Aymara, Quechwa or Guarani (Ibid.).

4.2.3 *Level of consultations*

In some countries, consultations were held mainly in urban areas which limited the participation of rural actors. The ICFTU (2001) reports that consultation has been particularly deficient in rural areas in Africa, despite poverty being most acute there. In Mozambique rural communities and northern districts were far less involved in the consultation process than Maputo-based organizations (Christian Aid 2001: 33). The limited scope of consultations manifested itself in low awareness of the PRSP among civil society outside Maputo (Falck *et al.* 2003). In other countries, consultations were limited to the national level, with few attempts to involve participants at the local level. Tanzanian officials and the PRSP itself state that the poor at the village level were not adequately consulted at the formulation station (McGee 2002: 6). It is precisely the lack of local level consultation that has prompted a number of CSOs to undertake their own grassroots consultations through parallel, civil-society-run PRSP processes (e.g. in Mozambique, Nicaragua, Bolivia, Honduras, Zambia and Malawi).

4.3 About what?

4.3.1 Exclusion from the PRSP drafting process

A recurrent complaint in almost all countries has been that governments have come to discussions with pre-prepared draft frameworks for PRSPs; CSOs have rarely been able to engage in the design of frameworks. CRS (2001) claims this has been the case in Zambia, Honduras and Bolivia:

> In Bolivia, citizen participation in the PRSP drafting process was severely limited. Instead, a small circle of government economists undertook drafting to the PRSP plan for more than four months without including or even informing civil society organizations that had participated in the National Dialogue. Bolivian organizations tried repeatedly to pressure the government to be more inclusive, even appealing to international donors and the World Bank and IMF, but to no avail.
>
> (10)

That the PRSP in Bolivia was drafted in a non-transparent manner is indicated by the fact that the final PRSP was received by CSOs through the German Ministry of International Development (IBIS 2001: 124). In Senegal, a main concern of civil society groups has been that when the PRSP process was launched in June 2001, the government appeared with its analysis already prepared (Phillips 2002: 56). In Zambia, CSOs have been denied representation on the Technical Committee for drafting the PRSP, despite a large and active coalition of groups organized to co-ordinate input into the PRSP (CRS 2001: 11). A UNDP assessment of Lesotho's PRSP found that the procedures were designed to conduct the participatory process *after* the PRSP draft was already prepared instead of before (cited in McGee 2002: 66).

4.4 Summary

Countries implementing PRSPs start from very different positions and, to some extent, processes should be judged relative to starting conditions. National or civil society ownership is unlikely to be as high in countries with unstable or factionalized polities as it would be in more stable and unified societies. Yet, even taking different country conditions into consideration, the fact remains that in many countries key elements of participation have been seriously flawed. Key sections of civil society (e.g. women, religious organizations, workers' movements and rural groups) and government (e.g. line ministries and parliament) have been missing from the process or insufficiently represented. In some cases, this has been because the design of participation has specifically excluded or neglected particular groups. In other cases, participation has been narrowed by rushed timeframes, a lack of information, poor dissemination in appropriate languages and consultation processes which failed to reach local and rural communities. In almost no cases did civil society participate in drafting the framework for initial PRSPs. Most were presented with drafts formulated by small teams of external consultants or central ministry staff. From the perspective of ownership, these limitations to the participatory process have constrained the perception that programmes were popularly owned.

We should note that in all these cases, the complaint is that civil society was not fully involved in the process, which was initiated by governments. However, from our perspective a strong involvement of governments could lead to national empowerment, even if not the empowerment of civil society or the poor. A fundamental issue then is how far the national governments were independent of the IFIs and able to part from the IFI script. This is difficult to ascertain from a process perspective without detailed anthropological enquiry, but we can come to tentative conclusions on the basis of the contents of the programmes – which we turn to next.

5 The content of PRSPs

This section examines whether countries appear to be empowered from the perspective of policy making. Earlier adjustment programmes were criticized for their 'one-size-fits-all' approach to policy design, and the resulting uniformity of reform packages across different countries. If PRSPs are genuinely country-owned we would expect to see considerable variation across country programmes reflecting different national priorities and inputs from participation, and for policies to diverge from standard orthodox packages.

5.1 Has participation by civil society affected the design of programmes?

Participation has had its greatest impact in improving the quality and broadening the scope of poverty diagnostics. In many countries, the official definition of poverty has become much more multi-dimensional in character in the PPA work around the PRSP.[12] ActionAid Vietnam reports that 'PPAs and other consultative exercises ... have created a lot of opportunities for government participants to learn more about the causes of poverty. This has led to national plans becoming more "people-centred and pro-poor"' (quoted in Zaman 2002: 7). The majority of countries have also broadened their definition and analysis of poverty to include such dimensions as security, vulnerability and powerlessness. However, we should note that a move towards a multidimensional approach to poverty has formed an important element in the recent international poverty agenda – for example in the World Bank's *World Development Report* on Poverty (WDR 2000/1) and in the Bank-initiated *Voices of the Poor*. On the World Bank webpage the introduction to poverty states:

> What is poverty?
> Poverty is hunger. Poverty is lack of shelter. Poverty is being sick and not being able to see a doctor. Poverty is not being able to go to school and not knowing how to read. Poverty is not having a job, is fear for the future, living one day at a time. Poverty is losing a child to illness brought about by unclean water. Poverty is powerlessness, lack of representation and freedom.

The three major elements of poverty identified in the WDR 2000/1 – opportunity, empowerment, security – are similar to those emerging from PRSPs – so the broader identification of poverty in the PRSPs can be interpreted as part of a process of advancing the international poverty agenda, rather than as a sign of national ownership of the PRSPs.

Better poverty diagnostics, in turn, has led to a stronger focus on sectoral policies in most countries. All PRSPs emphasize the importance of increasing spending on basic services for the poor. All strategies aim to increase the access of the poor to education, health and clean water, in terms of both coverage and quality. Vietnam's PRSP, for example, commits itself to ensuring the 20/20 initiative is implemented – 20 percent of aid and 20 percent of government expenditure is to be spent on basic social services (Government of Vietnam 2002). Similarly, Nicaragua's PRSP aims to make additional investment in water and sanitation (Government of Nicaragua 2001), while Bolivia's PRSP has allocated social spending according to positive discrimination criteria for the first time, favouring the poorest municipalities (Government of Bolivia 2001). Moreover, PRSPs have emphasized the importance of agricultural sector policies, such as developing food security policies, environmental protection, and increasing agricultural productivity, as well as promoting gender equality and protection of ethnic minorities and the vulnerable (children and the disabled). All these changes, however, are very much in line with the international poverty agenda.

A more significant indication of some genuine contribution made by PRSPs is evidence that specific elements of civil society have been effective in lobbying national government to incorporate affirmative action policies. In Kenya, ODI (2002) reports that pastoralist groups successfully lobbied to have their concerns over access to productive assets, natural resources management and extension services for livestock to be included in the final PRSP document. They also managed to secure higher-than-average funding for education bursaries in pastoralist areas (McGee 2002: 42). Women's groups have also been successful in bringing gender concerns into Kenya's final PRSP and influencing budget allocations (McGee 2002: 43). Action Aid country offices similarly report that HIV/AIDS groups in Malawi and rural peasant producers in Rwanda and Vietnam have been influential in shaping sectoral polices (Zaman 2002). There have also been cases in several countries where CSOs have successfully lobbied to have user fees abolished (Klugman, personal communication).

By and large, however, it appears that participation has had limited impact on the wider content of PSRPs. The perception among many civil society participants and third party observers has been that the recommendations made during consultations have largely not been incorporated in final documents.[13] In Bolivia, civil society participants felt the initial draft bore little relation to the recommendations resulting from the 'National Dialogue' (Christian Aid 2002). Only after mass demonstrations did the policy content shift, but still remained largely void of civil society recommendations for a wider approach to addressing poverty beyond social expenditure, such as land reform and political issues (Bendana 2001). Leading NGO groups were so frustrated with the lack of impact that they lobbied Washington for Bolivia's final document not to be approved (ODI 2003a). The recommendations from parallel PRSP processes initiated and conducted by civil society in Honduras and Nicaragua were also effectively ignored in the final PRSP (IBIS 2001). With respect to Ghana, Killick and Abugre (2001) report that 'it appears that the results of the community consultations did not feed into the analyses and recommendations of the Teams [i.e. core teams for drafting PRSP chapters]' (31). In a survey of civil society recommendations in seven countries, Zaman (2002) found that, while in some countries the adoption of inputs appeared to be good (Rwanda, Vietnam), in the majority, civil society proposals were mostly not incorporated, particularly in areas of tax reform, budget making, and civil service reforms (8). The general lack of tangible impact on policies would appear to corroborate the complaint from many civil society participants that their involvement was limited to information-dissemination and consultation exercises at initial stages of policy design, and that they were excluded from decision making at the latter stages. Indeed very few countries had any civil society representation on teams preparing the drafts following consultations, an exception being Malawi where strong civil society complaint led to their inclusion.

The inability of civil society participation to affect policy is even more evident when it comes to structural reform issues (also see the next section). Most CSOs report that they were barred from participating in macro-economic and structural policy discussions.[14] In a survey of eight countries, McGee (2002) reports that

> There is broad consensus among our civil society sources in Ghana, Malawi, Mozambique, Tanzania, Zambia and Bolivia that NGOs and their coalitions have been totally unable to influence macro-economic policy or even engage governments in dialogue about it.
>
> (13)

In Bolivia, the umbrella NGO organization, CEDLA, complained that the economic model was 'a given' and they were only permitted to tinker around the edges (Christian Aid 2001: 11). Honduran NGOs also complained of being excluded from workshops on the macro-economic chapter of the PRSP, which was included in the final document without ever having been circulated to CSOs or parliamentarians for discussion and input (ODI 2003a: 12). Robb and Scott (2001) report that in six African PRSPs and I-PRSPs policy discussions and workshops rarely discussed sequencing or alternative policies and trade-offs, and in only one (Uganda) was there discussion on the impact of structural adjustment (30).

While national governments have been the agents of this exclusion, it appears they were also constrained in influencing the macro-economic framework. The Honduran NGO network, *Interforos*, was told by government officials that 'the Fund's position with regard to macro-economic policies were not negotiable' (Knoke and Morazan 2002: 16, fn. 2). In Kenya, the Finance Minister was reportedly sacked after a series of public statements that alleged the IMF and the World Bank were forcing the government to undertake unwanted changes in its PRSP (Zaman 2002: 12). In some countries, there has been the perception among government officials that altering the macro-economic framework would prevent endorsement from the Boards of the IFIs, leading to 'self-censorship'. A Finance Minister in a country developing a PRSP is quoted as saying: 'We do not want to second guess the Fund. We prefer to pre-empt them by giving them what they want before they start lecturing us about this and that. By doing so, we send a clear message that we know what we are doing – i.e. we believe in structural adjustment' (quoted in Cheru 2001). In their study of Ghana's PRSP process, Killick and Abugre (2001) similarly describe

> a strong reported tendency towards self-censorship on the part of the Ghanaian authorities, writing into the GPRS drafts wording designed to meet the anticipated demands of the IFIs ... such second-guessing ... does qualify the claim of Ghanaian ownership, which implies the GoG [Government of Ghana] was free to write what it wanted.
>
> (14)

5.2 How far have programmes changed?

Probably, the most effective way to assess whether the PRSPs have empowered countries in decisions about policy making is to explore how far they have altered the basic thrust of reform programmes.

If programmes were truly nationally controlled, we would expect at least some PRSPs to exhibit strategies that differ from the standard policy prescriptions in the past. However, a striking feature of nearly all PRSPs is the consistency among them of their approaches to poverty reduction. All country programmes are based on the premise that private-sector-led growth is the most effective way to reduce poverty. Although this growth is described variously as 'pro-poor' (e.g. Cambodia), 'equity-based' (Burkina Faso) or 'broad-based' (Nicaragua), a general feature of all programmes is that they do not consider alternative approaches to poverty reduction, particularly those with an element of resource redistribution or that are rights-based. Indeed, there is a general disregard for distributional issues; projections of the beneficial impact of growth in country papers tend to assume a scenario where growth is accompanied by neutral distribution (e.g. see Tanzania's PRSP). Even in PRSPs that more explicitly recognize the necessity for redistribution to ensure the poor benefit from growth, policies are either vague about how this should be done in practice (e.g. Azerbaijan, Ethiopia and Sri Lanka) or take redistribution simply to mean increasing the share of social spending devoted to the poor (e.g. Albania, Kyrgyzstan, Malawi and Tajikstan). Where land reforms are mentioned, they usually refer to consolidating property rights and establishing legal titles for the development of property markets rather than re-allocating resources to the landless (e.g. Albania, Benin, Bolivia, Cameroon, Niger, Rwanda, Tajikstan and Tanzania). In only a few countries, e.g. Mozambique and Uganda, are land reforms specifically targeted at improving the access of marginalized groups.

5.3 Familiar reforms

A closer examination of the macro-economic and structural reform policy contents of the 30 completed PRSPs (see Table 11.2) reveals that there is no fundamental departure from the kind of policy advice provided under earlier structural adjustment programmes. Current policies contain all the elements of the first generation of policy reforms designed to promote the role of the market and 'get the prices right', and share a similar format and content involving all of the following: reforms; financial and trade liberalization; privatization; public sector reform; sectoral policies (e.g. infrastructure, energy and manufacturing); and social sector reform.

With regards to fiscal and monetary matters, the emphasis is still on maintaining 'current-account and fiscal balances consistent with low and declining debt levels; inflation in the low single digits; and rising per

Table 11.2 Checklist of reforms contained in PRSPs

Reforms	Albania	Azerbaijan	Benin	Bolivia	Burkina Faso	Cambodia	Cameroon	Chad	Ethiopia	Ghana	Guyana	Honduras	Kyrgyzstan	Malawi	Mali	Mauritania	Mozambique	Nicaragua	Niger	Rwanda	Senegal	Sri Lanka	Tajikistan	Tanzania	Uganda	Yemen	Zambia
Economic management																											
Reliance on macro-economic stability for poverty reduction	x	x	x	x	x	x	x	x	x	x	x	x	x	x	x	x	x	x	x	x	x	x	x	x	x	x	x
Trade policy (tariff reduction/export promotion)	x	x	x	x	x	x	x	x	x	x	x	x	x	x	x	x	x	x	x	x	x	x	x	x	x	x	x
Monetary restraint	x	x	x	x	x	x	x	x	x	x	x	x	x	x	x	x	x	x	x	x	x	x	x	x	x	x	x
Exchange rate policy	x	x	x	x	x	x	x	x	x	x	x	x	x	x	x	x	x	x	x	x	x	x	x	x	x	x	x
Fiscal restraint	x	x	x	x	x	x	x	x	x	x	x	x	x	x	x	x	x	x	x	x	x	x	x	x	x	x	x
Tax and customs reforms	x	x	x	x	x	x	x	x	x	x	x	x	x	x	x	x		x	x	x	x	x	x	x	x	x	x
Price control/wage policies	x	x					x	x				x	x				x	x								x	
User fees	x			x		x						x	x		x	x			x	x		x	x			x	
Sectoral policies	x	x	x	x	x	x	x	x	x	x		x	x	x	x	x		x	x	x	x	x		x	x	x	x
Public sector governance and management																											
Budget management	x	x	x	x	x	x	x	x	x	x	x	x	x	x	x	x	x	x	x	x	x	x	x	x	x	x	x
MTEF	x	x	x	x	x	x	x	x	x	x		x	x	x	x	x		x	x	x	x	x	x	x	x	x	x
Decentralization	x		x	x	x		x	x	x	x	x	x	x	x	x	x	x	x	x	x		x	x	x	x	x	x
Public administration reform	x		x	x	x	x	x	x	x	x	x	x	x	x	x	x	x	x	x	x	x	x	x	x	x	x	x
Anti-corruption	x		x	x	x	x	x	x	x	x	x	x	x	x	x	x	x	x	x	x	x	x	x	x	x	x	x
Financial sector reform																											
Financial institutions	x	x	x				x	x	x	x		x	x	x	x	x		x	x	x	x	x	x	x	x	x	
Financial intermediation policies	x	x	x					x	x	x		x	x	x	x	x	x	x	x	x	x	x	x	x	x	x	
Private sector development																											
Privatization	x	x		x	x		x	x	x	x		x	x		x			x	x	x	x	x		x	x	x	x
Price liberalization	x	x		x	x	x		x	x	x		x	x	x								x	x				x
Legal and judicial reform	x		x	x	x		x	x	x	x	x	x	x	x	x	x	x	x	x	x	x	x	x	x	x	x	x
Land tenure laws	x		x	x	x	x	x	x	x	x	x	x	x	x	x	x		x	x	x	x	x	x	x	x	x	x

Social sector reforms

	1	2	3	4	5	6	7	8	9	10	11	12	13	14	15	16	17	18	19	20	21	22	23	24	25	26	27	28	29	30
Education		x	x	x			x	x	x	x		x	x	x	x		x	x	x	x	x	x	x	x	x	x	x	x	x	x
Health		x	x	x		x	x	x	x	x		x	x	x	x		x	x	x	x	x	x	x	x	x	x	x	x	x	x
Social protection/employment promotion	x	x	x	x	x	x	x	x			x	x	x	x	x	x	x	x	x	x	x	x	x	x	x	x	x	x	x	x
Rural livelihoods	x													x				x	x	x						x			x	
Food security			x	x	x	x		x	x			x	x	x	x	x	x	x	x	x	x	x			x	x				x
Environmental protection	x		x	x		x	x	x			x	x	x	x	x	x	x	x	x	x	x	x	x	x	x	x	x	x	x	x
Ethnic minority protection			x		x					x	x					x				x			x							
Gender equity		x	x	x	x	x	x		x	x		x	x	x	x		x	x	x	x	x	x	x			x	x	x		
Children/disabled		x	x	x			x			x		x	x	x	x	x	x	x		x	x	x	x	x						
Vulnerable groups										x		x	x	x	x	x	x	x	x	x	x	x	x	x	x					
Macro and poverty sections separate?	Y	Y	Y	Y	Y	Y	Y	Y	Y	Y	Y	Y	Y	Y	Y	Y	Y	Y	Y	Y	Y	Y	Y	Y	Y	Y	Y	Y	Y	Y
Ex ante assessment of impact?	N	N	N	N	N	N	N	N	N	N	N	N	N	N	N	N	N	N	N	N	N	N	N	N	N	N	N	N	N	N

Source: Own analysis.

capita GDP' (Ames *et al.* 2001: Box 2). Tight monetary and fiscal policies to control inflation and budget deficits are proposed, along with tax and custom reforms to increase revenues, and a flexible exchange rate or movement towards one (unless part of a monetary union).

The consistency with which countries have espoused policies of monetary and fiscal restraint, including in countries where hyper-inflation is not prevalent, weakens the claim of country ownership. For example, among the 28 countries in SSA with PRSPs or I-PRSPs, only four (Ghana, Malawi, Mozambique and Zambia) had a two-digit level of inflation in 2000, averaging slightly above 20 percent per annum (UNCTAD 2002). The average for the other countries was around 3.5 per cent, and the price level actually fell in five (Burkina Faso, Cape Verde, Côte d'Ivoire, Mali and Sierra Leone) (UNCTAD 2002). Moreover, based on the Participatory Poverty Assessments conducted in many countries (e.g. Ethiopia and Nigeria), the rural poor stress that contractionary macro-economic policies resulting in lower employment and declining wage bills in the public sector are more of a concern than inflation (Narayan *et al.* 2000: 21, 150). Nor does it appear that HIPC Ministers themselves endorse the stance taken with respect to inflation and growth. At the declaration of the 6th HIPC Ministerial Meeting, they urged the IFIs to:

> think more closely about ways to increase growth and employment rather than further reducing inflation, about the supply-side (as well as demand-side) causes of inflation and about defining sustainability of the budget deficit as including grants and debt relief.
>
> (quoted in UNCTAD 2002: 25)

Nevertheless, disinflation continues to be emphasized in PRSPs, partly because it is claimed that inflation generates regressive changes in income distribution.

Other familiar first-generation reforms which re-appear in all PRSPs include measures to de-regulate the financial sector: movement towards market-based interest rates, liberalizing the domestic banking sector and the elimination of exchange controls and opening up of the capital account (see Table 11.2). Yet the connection between these policies and poverty reduction is remote, particularly in the context of poor countries with thin capital markets. Nevertheless, poverty reduction strategies in all Africa PRSPs continue to adhere to these principles.

Trade policy advice in poverty reduction strategy programmes conforms to the view that maintaining rapid integration into the world economy is the best way to combat poverty. In every country, there is commitment to maintaining open and liberal trading regimes. Some countries' strategies emphasize export promotion and diversification, although there is little indication of how this is to be achieved (e.g. Tanzania). A very few cases diverge somewhat from the conventional wisdom.

Mozambique's PRSP, for example, advocates the use of 'case-by-case, selective intervention, limited in time' for manufactured goods (76).

There is also universal emphasis on the continued privatization of state-owned enterprises, reliance on private agents in the provision of public goods, the liberalization of prices for most utilities and key markets; cost-recovery in curative healthcare and secondary/tertiary education; and a general reduction of state involvement in the economy (see Table 11.2). The PRSPs also endorse the second generation reforms, including institutional reform, such as anti-corruption measures; more participatory and accountable public administration with attendant reforms in the civil service; transparency in the preparation and monitoring of budgetary expenditures; and legal reforms aiming at securing property rights and strengthening institutions that affect private sector activity, as well as improving the rule of law.

The purpose here is not to discuss whether the structural strategies pursued in PRSPs are always the most appropriate for combating poverty, but, rather, to highlight the similarity of the policy package contained in PRSPs across countries, and to earlier structural adjustment programmes. Although the emphasis on various reforms differs in different country contexts – for example, transition countries (e.g. Azerbaijan, Albania and Tajikstan) tend to emphasize privatization reforms more than others – the fact remains all countries' documents pursue the same core set of structural reforms. These trends suggest low national control over final documents.

The lack of explicit linkages between macro-economic policies and poverty reduction goals also suggests that these reforms have not been substantially affected by the PRSP process. In every country document, poverty analysis and the macro-economic strategies are presented as two independent sections of the PRSP, with the macro sections largely void of any ex-ante assessments of the impact of structural reforms on poverty apart from considerations of how various growth scenarios will impact poverty levels in the future (see Table 11.3). Only Cambodia's PRSP, and to a lesser extent that of Rwanda, recognize the potential negative impact of various reforms on poverty and the need to conduct qualitative assessments of their possible effects.[15] Nor is there any substantive discussion of the possible trade-offs involved with various policies. Moreover, several country papers (e.g. Albania, Nicaragua and Senegal) exhibit internal inconsistencies, mentioning the failure of adjustment programmes in the past, but going on to advocate the very same policies in the macro section. This together with the separation of the two parts of the documents and the lack of ex ante assessments of poverty consequences of macro-measures, lends support to the view that on the macro side, PRSPs basically endorse the conventional IFI-designed programmes.

Table 11.3 Poverty and macro-reform linkages

	Albania	Azerbaijan	Benin	Bolivia	Burkina Faso	Cambodia	Cameroon	Chad	Ethiopia	Ghana	Guyana	Honduras	Kyrgyzstan	Malawi	Mali	Mauritania	Mozambique	Nicaragua	Niger	Rwanda	Senegal	Sri Lanka	Tajikistan	Tanzania	Uganda	Yemen	Zambia
Links between growth and poverty reduction	x	x	x	x	x			x	x		x	x	x				x	x	x	x	x	x	x	x	x	x	x
Links between poverty and trade policy						x																					x
Links between poverty and monetary policy																				x							
Links between poverty and tax policies/fiscal reform		x																									
Links between poverty and privatization													x							x							x
Links between poverty and legal/judicial reforms						x																					
Links between poverty and civil service reforms						x																					
Links between poverty and financial sector reforms						x																					
Assessment of past policies	x										x	x		x				x			x					x	
Discussion of policy trade-offs					x																						
Poverty impact evaluation																			x	x							

Source: Own analysis.

5.4 Summary

Of course, the issue of who determines policy design is difficult to assess definitively, especially without detailed anthropological work, and the possibility exists that some governments have chosen policies that conform to earlier packages because they genuinely believe them to be the most effective in reducing poverty. Hence it is difficult to be certain that the counterfactual would prevail – i.e. if governments genuinely gained greater control their policies would have looked different. But the fact that so little variation in macro policies exists across an extremely broad range of countries, and that country programmes are conditional on IFI endorsement before qualifying for new lending, strongly suggests that governments were not empowered to any great degree in policy making. The lack of a coherent structure relating macro-policies to poverty reduction goals, and the minimal impact of participation on policies further support the view that governments' independence was greatly constrained.

6 Ownership in the wider context of IFI decision making

PRSPs constitute only one of the programmes through which IFIs disburse funds. At this time it does not seem that the other lending instruments offer anything significant in the way of empowering national decision making.

The Poverty Reduction and Growth Facility (PRGF) continues to play an important role in overall lending to countries. Administered solely by the IMF, they are credits to support monetary policy and fiscal reform. Although they are supposed to be based on the PRSP and to integrate poverty reduction with macro-economic policies, and the IMF states PRGFs should be 'open for public discussion' (IMF 2002a), they do not stipulate either participation or ownership as part of their requirements. In practice, it appears that little has changed in the style of negotiations – non-transparent and confined to a small number of policy actors – or in substance, with a close resemblance to ESAFs (see Adam and Bevan 2001; Killick 2002).

While in theory PRGFs are meant to be based upon PRSPs, it appears in many cases the reverse is true (which may help to explain the lack of coherence between macro-policies and poverty goals). The majority of countries have negotiated PRGFs before formulating a PRSP, and in a number of cases, PRSP endorsement has been postponed as a result of countries missing targets under PRGF agreements. In Kenya, the government negotiated a PRGF with some of the most restrictive sets of conditionalities in its lending history just before finalizing its PRSP (Hanmer *et al.* 2003: 184). In others (e.g. Bolivia, Ghana and Nicaragua) the targets set out in the PRGFs have gone on to form the bases for macro-economic benchmarks and performance targets (ICFTU 2002; Trócaire 2002). Thus, rather than supporting the PRSP, the PRGF appears to be taking the more dominant role in many cases, with macro-economic targets influencing poverty requirements rather than vice versa.[16]

The number of structural conditions in PRGFs has, however, been reduced (so far by about a quarter) in a streamlining exercise, although this has been very variable, with large reductions in some programmes and no change in others (Adam and Bevan 2001). But while detailed structural conditionality appears to be diminishing, there has simultaneously been more emphasis given to governance and public expenditure management (e.g. in Kenya, Killick 2002). Whether or not conditionalities outside the 'core areas' are being reduced in PRGFs is ambiguous. For example, Killick reports they have actually gone up in Zambia,[17] and similarly, a November 2001 stand-by agreement with Romania still included conditions on domestic energy prices, privatization and restructuring of state-owned enterprises (Randel and German 2002). One concern is whether the conditionality being relinquished by the Fund through its streamlining exercise will be taken up by the Bank and bilateral donors. There seems to be no official counterpart effort by the Bank to narrow the scope of its conditionality, leading to the possibility, already backed up by some evidence, that those conditionalities dropped by the Fund will resurface in World Bank credits, resulting in little net reduction. According to a Fund staff report on initial experiences with streamlining (quoted in Killick 2002: 19), the Bank is 'strengthening' its conditionality in areas such as privatization, health system reform and public sector reform, from which the Fund is scaling back.

Poverty Reduction Strategy Credits (PRSCs) are another lending instrument through which IFI conditionality may be imposed. Designed to provide budget support for countries to implement their PRSPs, the PRSC allows the Bank to attach extra conditions to countries' poverty reduction strategies through the Letter of Development Policy (LoDP) that accompanies it. The LoDP is not a public document, and as such extra policy details are not ordinarily available for public discussion. The few PRSCs that have been disbursed so far (e.g. Burkina Faso, Vietnam and Uganda) have allowed the World Bank to modify components of countries' PRSPs, making them differ little from conventional structural adjustment programmes (Eurodad 2001; Killick 2002). Paradoxically, this 'back-door' policy specification undermines the principle of ownership PRSCs are meant to help operationalize.

Thus, although the Bank and Fund have adopted ownership as one of the pillars of the CDF, much of the lending outside PRSPs allows the IFIs to exert considerable policy conditionality.

7 Conclusions

The limited experience with PRSPs so far would suggest that PRSPs have achieved little in the way of increasing national ownership/empowerment over programme design by national governments or civil society, though the process is still at an early stage.

This is not to say, however, that the PRSP exercise has had no impact on the balance of power among stakeholders. In some very limited respects, civil society participants have been empowered compared to their earlier position by being formally included in the policy-making process. But while this inclusion has been quite 'wide' in some instances, involving broad sections of civil society, it has not made much difference, as participation in most countries has been 'shallow', limited to consultation rather than joint decision making. Consequently, PRSPs have done little to empower civil society; and the evidence above suggests that where civil society has been empowered, it is often an assortment of NGOs (including foreign ones), not necessarily representative of society as a whole, or of the poor in particular.

National governments appear to be playing a more prominent role in policy formation, by formally taking charge of the policy-making agenda. However, how far this has been empowering is doubtful. The similarity of the programmes to those that form part of the normal international agenda suggests this is more window dressing than empowerment even with respect to the sectoral or micro agenda, except in a few, usually marginal, instances. When it comes to macro-policies, it appears that there is no national empowerment through the PRSP process, beyond the (usually limited) national contribution to the formulation of macro-programmes that already exists. Moreover, government capacity, which generally was already weak, has been stretched even further with the need to undertake formal consultations and to develop lengthy policy papers.

Governments have also been constrained to involve more stakeholders in the policy process. Indeed, a cynical reading would see the exercise as weakening the legitimacy of national governments by engaging with groups other than governments in designing policy (e.g. Summers 2001). This criticism is particularly telling in the case of democratically elected governments. The insistence on civil society participation by the IFIs bypasses existing institutions and can potentially weaken elected governments. In non-democratic regimes, however, the situation is different and broadening participation may be particularly beneficial, contributing to the democratization of decision making. Of course, most political systems in very poor countries are in the process of democratization – and a widening of consultation and strengthening of civil society may contribute to this process.

Donors' power, in contrast, while seemingly weakened by the relinquishment of policy design to national authorities and civil society participants, may not have actually declined at all significantly. The ultimate endorsement of PRSPs still lies with the Boards of the two institutions, which conditions the dynamics of the process from the start. IFIs exert a considerable indirect influence, as we have discussed in incidences of self-censorship in government design of policies. Moreover, the continued existence of many multilateral programmes outside the PRSP process and unaffected by it, still leaves the IFIs considerable control. Thus, the relative position of donors has not changed much through the PRSP process, and may even have been strengthened to a degree by the veneer of legitimacy and perceptions of ownership that participation lends to the multilateral lending programmes.

On balance, then, it would appear that civil society has been marginally strengthened by PRSPs, the position of national governments may have been somewhat weakened through this, while the position of donors is broadly unchanged. This conclusion is context dependent. Relatively strong governments may be able to use the process to their advantage. But nowhere has the PRSP produced a major change in the balance of power.

To sum up, the PRSP process to date has not empowered developing countries and disempowered the World Bank. It may have changed perceptions and consequently national ownership from this perspective. If so it would appear to have actually helped empower the World Bank, by increasing the effectiveness of programmes through raising national enthusiasm for them and increasing the perception they are home-grown strategies. But this effect is likely to be short-lived unless control over programmes genuinely changes, because eventually perceptions tend to reflect reality.

The evidence assessed thus far is based on only a few years' experience. The PRSP process is still evolving and following reviews of countries' PRSP experiences by the Bank and Fund in January 2002, both institutions have recognized many of the problems highlighted above regarding process and content. The process may be modified as a result.

Notes

* We are grateful for very helpful comments from Jeni Klugman, and to those of the participants at the April conference.
1 For example, 39 organizations and regional networks in 15 African countries agreed at a meeting in Kampala, May 2001, that PRSPs 'were simply window dressing'. See Bretton Woods Project (2001).
2 Cornwall (2000) provides a useful survey of the participatory trends in development policy since the 1970s.
3 See Whitehead (2002) for a subtle overview of the ways the complex relationships between 'democracy' and 'civil society' have been viewed.
4 The Bank has not specified what constitutes an acceptable participatory process, arguing that the great diversity of country contexts and capacities prevents the application of any one standard.
5 See Narayan *et al.* (2000).
6 This is an easy condition to state, but 'democracy' is not at all straightforward to define (see Whitehead 2002), and, almost however defined, in relatively newly established 'democracies' full democratization is unlikely. This itself is a reason to give a large role to civil society.
7 For Uganda see Gariyo (2001); Robb and Scott (2001); and Wordofa (2002).

For Vietnam see SGTS *et al.* (2000). For Rwanda, see references in McGee (2002); Bugingo (2002); Mutebi *et al.* (2003).

8 For Kenya see Hanmer *et al.* (2003); Mali see Dante *et al.* (2003); Malawi see Jenkins and Tsoka (2003).

9 It must be acknowledged, however, that effectiveness of parliamentarians in articulating local priorities depends on the quality and general importance of parliamentary institutions in countries. In some, they do not exist (e.g. Rwanda and Uganda), while in others they are subordinate to the executive or to existing patronage systems (e.g. Ghana and Kenya). As such the lack of parliamentary involvement in some countries may not have made much difference.

10 Killick and Abugre 2001: 32. Nonetheless, there are examples of attempts to ensure that the CSOs are representative. In Uganda, for example, the composition of the task force charged with representing CSOs was determined through an election involving 45 NGOs (Gariyo 2001).

11 Catholic Relief Service 2001: 22.

12 There have been, however, critiques of the poverty analysis in PRSPs, notably regarding the lack of clarity concerning the characteristics of poverty and its causes, as well as a lack of disaggregation of categories of the poor and failure to include those vulnerable to poverty. See Thin *et al.* (2001) and Marcus and Wilkinson (2002).

13 It must be acknowledged, though, that in some cases this resulted because the recommendations from civil society were vague and unimplementable.

14 We should note that this does not apply to the private sector which appears to have influenced macro-economic and investment policy in some cases where NGOs have been unable. See McGee and Taimo (2001).

15 The PRSP source book states that poverty social assessment should be taken for major reforms, but as of yet very few have been undertaken.

16 Indeed, in connection with a recent review of PRGF experiences, the Fund itself admitted a tendency in this direction, from PRGF to PRSP (see IMF review in IMF 2002c).

17 Killick 2002: 5.

References

Action Aid. 2002. *Inclusive Circles Lost in Exclusive Cycles.* Available from http://www.imf.org/external/np/prspgen/review/2002/comm/v2.pdf.

Adam, C.S. and D. Bevan. 2001. *PRGF Stocktaking Exercise on behalf of DFID.* Available from http://www.econ.ox.ac.uk/Members/david.bevan/Reports/PRGFStocktake02.pdf.

Ames, B., W. Brown, S. Devarajan and A. Izquierdo. 2001. Macroeconomic Policy and Poverty Reduction. In *PRSP Handbook.* Washington, DC: IMF.

Bendana, A. 2001. *Poverty Reduction Policy Politics in Bolivia.* Available from aidc.org.za/sapsn/kampala/alejandro_2.htm.

Biershenk, T., E. Thioleren and N. Bako-Arifari. 2003. Benin. *Development Policy Review* 2: 161–78.

Bolivia, Government of. 2001. *Poverty Reduction Strategy Paper.* Available from http://poverty.worldbank.org/files/bolivaprsp.pdf.

Booth, D. 2001. *Overview of PRSP Processes and Monitoring.* Report submitted to the Strategic Partnership with Africa. Available from www.odi.org.uk.

Bretton Woods Project. 2001. PRSPs are Just PR say Civil Society Groups. Available from http://www.BrettonWoodsproject.org/topic/adjustment/a23prspsstats.html.

Bugingo, E. 2002. *Missing the Mark? Participation in the PRSP Process in Rwanda.* Christian Aid Research Report. Available from http://www.christian-aid.org.uk/indepth/0212rwanda/rwanda.pdf.

Catholic Relief Services (CRS). 2001. *Review of the Poverty Reduction Strategy Paper Initiative.* Available from http://www.imf.org/external/np/prspgen/review/2002/comm/v2.pdf.

Cheru, F. 2001. *Economic, Social and Cultural Rights – The Highly Indebted Poor Countries (HIPC) Initiative: A Human Rights Assessment of the Poverty Reduction Strategy Papers (PRSPs).* Report submitted to the 57th Session of the Economic and Social Council of the United Nations, Commission on Human Rights, agenda item 10E/CN.4/2001/56. Available from www.unhchr.ch.

Christian Aid. 2001. *Ignoring the Experts: Poor People's Exclusion from Poverty Reduction Strategies.* Available from http://www.imf.org/external/np/prspgen/review/2002/comm/v2.pdf.

Christian Aid. 2002. *Participation in Dialogue? The Estrategia Boliviana de Reduccion de la Pobreza.* Available from http://www.christian-aid.org.uk/indepth/0204part/particip.htm.

Cornwall, A. 2000. *Beneficiary, Consumer, Citizen: Perspectives on Participation for Poverty Reduction.* Sida Studies no. 2. Stockholm, Swedish International Development Cooperation Agency.

Dante, I., J.-F. Gauteir, M. Marouani and M. Raffinot. 2003. Mali. *Development Policy Review* 2: 217–34.

Eurodad. 2001. *Many Dollars, Any Change?.* Available from www.eruodad.org.

Evans, A. 2003. Tanzania. *Development Policy Review* 2: 271–87.

Falck, H. and K. Landfald. 2003. Mozambique. *Development Policy Review* 2: 235–52.

Gariyo, Z. 2001. *The PRSP Process in Uganda.* Processed. Available from www.eurodad.org.

Goulet, D. 1989. Participation in Development: New Avenues. *World Development* 17 (2): 165–78.

Hanmer, L., G. Ikiara, W. Eberlei and C. Abong. 2003. Kenya. *Development Policy Review* 2: 179–96.

Hoddinott, J. 2002. Participation and Poverty Reduction: An Analytical Framework and Overview of the Issues. *Journal of African Economies* 11 (1): 146–68.

IBIS. 2001. *Input for the PRSP Review. Poverty Reduction and Participation.* Available from http://www.imf.org/external/np/prspgen/review/2002/comm/v2.pdf.

IMF. 2002a. *The IMF's Poverty Reduction and Growth Facility (PRGF): A Factsheet.* Available from http://www.imf.org/external/np/exr/facts/prgf.htm.

IMF. 2002b. *Poverty Reduction Strategy Papers: A Factsheet.* Available from http://www.imf.org/external/np/exr/facts/prsp.htm.

IMF. 2002c. *Review of the Poverty Reduction Growth Facility: Issues and Options.* Available from http://www.imf.org/external/NP/prgf/2002/021402.pdf.

International Conference of Free Trade Unions (ICFTU). 2001. *Submission to IMF/WB Review on PRSP Process,* Brussels: ICFTU.

International Conference of Free Trade Unions (ICFTU). 2002. *Brief to the IMF/World Bank Review on the PRSP Process.* Available from http://www.imf.org/external/np/prspgen/review/2002/comm/v2.pdf.

Jenkins, R. and M. Tsoka. 2003. Malawi. *Development Policy Review* 2: 197–215.

Killick, T. 2002. *The 'Streamlining' of IMF Conditionality: Aspirations, Reality and Repercussions.* Report submitted to DFID. Available from www.eurodad.org.

Killick, T. and C. Abugre. 2001. *Institutionalising the PRSP Approach in Ghana.* Report submitted to the Strategic Partnership with Africa. Available from www.odi.org.uk.

Klugman, J. 2003. *Poverty Reduction Strategy Papers: Objectives, Process and Experience to Date.* Processed. Washington, DC: World Bank.

Klugman, J. Personal communication May 2003.

Knoke, I. and P. Morazan. 2002. *PRSP: Beyond the Theory. Practical Experiences and Positions of Involved Civil Society Organisations.* Available from www. Brot-fuer-die-welt.de.

Marcus, R. and J. Wilkinson. 2002. Whose Poverty Matters? Vulnerability, Social Protection and PRSPs, CHIP Working Paper, 1, London. Available from www.chronicpoverty.org/pdfs/CHIPWorking Paper.pdf.

McGee, R. 2000. *Participation in Poverty Reduction Strategies: A Synthesis of Experience with Participatory Approaches to Policy Design, Implementation and Monitoring.* IDS Working Paper 109. Brighton: IDS.

McGee, R. 2002. *Assessing Participation in Poverty Reduction Strategy Papers: A Desk-Based Synthesis of Experience in Sub-Saharan Africa.* IDS Research Report 52. Brighton: IDS.

McGee, R. and N. Taimo. 2001. *Civil Society in the PRSP Process.* Processed. Report for DFID Mozambique.

Mozambique Debt Group. 2001. Civil Society Participation in the Poverty Reduction Strategy (PRSP), translated. Prepared by Mulhovo, W.A. and S.M. Gomes, unpublished paper, Maputo, Mozambique Debt Group.

Mutebi, F., S. Stone and N. Thin. 2003. Rwanda. *Development Policy Review* 2: 253–70.

Muwonge, J., B. Geleta and S. Heliso. 2002. Working towards an Ethiopian PRSP. In *Masters of Their Own Development?*, edited by A. Whaites, pp. 73–87. Monrovia: World Vision.

Narayan, D., R. Chambers, M. Shah and P. Petesch. 2000. *Voices of the Poor: Can Anyone Hear Us?.* Oxford: Oxford University Press.

Nelson, N. and S. Wright. 1995. Participation and Power. In *Power and Participatory Development*, edited by N. Nelson and S. Wright, pp. 1–18. London: ITDG Publishing.

NGO Forum on Cambodia. 2001. *Results of Initial Discussions among NGOs/CSOs on the National Poverty Reduction Strategy of Cambodia.* Available from www.bigpond.co.kh/users.ngoforum/workshop/att/default.htm.

Nicaragua, Government of. 2001. *A Strengthened Growth and Poverty Reduction Strategy.* Available from http://poverty.worldbank.org/files/Nicaragua_PRSP.pdf.

ODI. 2002. Assessing Participation in PRSPs in Sub-Saharan Africa. *PRSP Synthesis Note 3.* February 2002. Available from www.prspsynthesis.org.

ODI. 2003a. Experience with Poverty Reduction Strategies in Latin America and the Caribbean. *PRSP Synthesis Note 5.* February 2003. Available from www.prspsynthesis.org.

ODI. 2003b. Experience with PRSPs in Transition Countries. *PRSP Synthesis Note 6.* February 2003. Available from www.prspsynthesis.org.

Panos Institute. 2002. *Reducing Poverty. Is the World Bank's Strategy Working?.* Available from www.eurodad.org.

Phillips, W. 2002. All for Naught? An Analysis of Senegal's PRSP Process. In *Masters of their Own Development?*, edited by A. Whaites, pp. 47–71. Monrovia: World Vision.

Randel, J. and T. German. 2002. *Reality of Aid.* London: ActionAid.

Robb, C. and A. Scott. 2001. *Reviewing Some Early Poverty Reduction Strategy Papers in Africa.* IMF policy discussion paper PDP/01/5. Available from www.imf.org.

Save the Children. 2001. *Save the Children UK Submission to the IMF/WB Review of PRSPs.* Available from http://www.imf.org/external/np/prspgen/review/2002/comm/v2.pdf.

SGTS and Associates. 2000. *Civil Society Participation in Poverty Reduction Strategy Papers. Report to the Department for International Development.* Available from www.dfid.gov.uk.

Summers, L. 2001. *Remarks at the World Bank's 2001 Country Director's Retreat.* Available from http://www.jubilee2000uk.org/opinion/Larry_summers120601.htm.

Thin, N., M. Underwood and J. Gilling. 2001. *Sub-Saharan Africa's Poverty Reduction Strategy Papers From Social Policy and Sustainable Livelihoods Perspectives.* Report for DFID. Available from www.eurodad.org.

Trócaire. 2002. *PRSPs – Policy and Practice in Honduras and Nicaragua.* Available from www.eurodad.org.

UNCTAD. 2002. *From Adjustment to Poverty Reduction: What is New?* UNCTAD/GDS/Africa/2. Geneva: UNCTAD.

UNIFEM. 2001. *Contribution to the World Bank and IMF PRSP Review.* Available from http://www.imf.org/external/np/prspgen/review/2002/comm/v1.pdf.

Uriona, R., J. Requena, J. Nunez, R. Eyben and W. Lewis. 2002. Crafting Bolivia's PRSP: 5 Points of View. *Finance and Development* 39 (2): 13–16.

Vietnam, Government of. 2002. *The Comprehensive Poverty Reduction and Growth Strategy.* Available from http://poverty.worldbank.org/files/Vietnam_PRSP.pdf.

Whitehead, L. 2002. *Democratization: Theory and Experience.* Oxford: Oxford University Press.

Wordofa, D. 2002. *The Role of Civil Society Organisations in Formulation of Poverty Reduction Strategies in Uganda.* Processed. Oxford: Oxfam GB.

World Bank. 1996. *The World Bank Participation Sourcebook.* Washington, DC: World Bank.

World Bank. 2000/01. *World Development Report 2000/2001,* Washington, DC: World Bank.

World Bank. 2001. *Gender in the PRSPs: A Stocktaking.* Available from http://www.gtz.de/forum_armut/download/bibliothek/GenderPRSP.pdf.

World Bank. 2002. *Source Book for Poverty Reduction Strategies.* Washington, DC: World Bank.

World Development Movement. 2001. *Policies to Roll-Back the State and Privatise? Poverty Reduction Strategy Papers Investigated.* Available from www.eurodad.org.

Zaman, M. 2002. *Are We Getting Lost in Exclusive Anti-Poor, Adjustment Lending Policy Cycles?.* Action Aid Policy Brief. Available from http://www.esrftz.org/ppa/documents/aa_1.pdf.

Zuckerman, E. 2001. *Engendering Poverty Reduction Strategy Papers, Why it Reduces Poverty and the Rwanda Case.* Available from http://www.wider.unu.edu/conference/conference-2001-2/conference2001-2.htm.

Part III

Possible reforms of the IFIs

12 Macroeconomic adjustment in IMF-supported programs

Projections and reality[*]

Rouben Atoian, Patrick Conway, Marcelo Selowsky, and Tsidi Tsikata

In this chapter, we examine the accuracy of IMF projections associated with 175 IMF-supported programs approved in the period 1993–2001. For each program, the IMF staff prepares a projection of the country's future performance. This projection is based upon the country's initial situation and upon the predicted impact of reforms agreed upon in the context of the IMF program.[1] We focus upon the projections of macroeconomic aggregates – specifically, on the ratios of fiscal surplus to GDP and of current-account surplus to GDP – during the years immediately following the approval of the IMF program. We will compare these projections to the actual data for the same years.

Our comparison is statistical. We begin with descriptive statistics for the two macroeconomic aggregates, and demonstrate that the projection deviates substantially from the observed. We then use a simple vector autoregressive model of the determination of these two aggregates to decompose the deviation into components. We find that the "model" revealed by IMF staff's projections differs significantly from the model evident in historical data. We also find, however, that a substantial amount of the deviation in projections from historical data is due to the incomplete information on which the IMF staff base their projections. We provide summary indicators of our results in this chapter; for more detailed discussion, and for an analysis of the importance of staff revisions of projections, see Atoian *et al.* (2004).

The data we analyze come from two distinct sources. The projections (also called "envisaged" outcomes) are drawn from the Monitoring of Arrangements (MONA) database maintained by the IMF.[2] The data on historical outcomes are drawn from the "World Economic Outlook" (WEO) database of the IMF as reported in June 2002. Given the difference in sources, some data manipulation is necessary to ensure comparability.[3] The data are redefined in each case to be relative to the initial program year: it is denoted "Year T" of the program.[4]

We will examine four projection "horizons" in this study. For each projection horizon, we will compare the IMF staff projection with the historical outcome. The year prior to "Year T" is denoted T − 1. The horizon-T data will be projections of macroeconomic outcomes in period T based upon information available in $T-1$: in other words, a one-year-ahead projection. The horizon-$T+1$ data are projections of macroeconomic outcomes in period $T+1$ based upon information available in $T-1$, and are as such two-year-ahead projections. The horizon-$T+2$ and horizon-$T+3$ projections are defined analogously. The number of observations available differs for each projection horizon due to (a) missing projection data or (b) projection horizons that extend beyond the end of the available historical data. The number of observations available for comparisons for horizons T through $T+3$ is 175, 147, 115, and 79.

We will focus upon two macroeconomic aggregates. The historical fiscal surplus as a share of GDP for country j in year t will be denoted y_{jt}. The historical current-account surplus as a share of GDP will be denoted c_{jt}. The projections of these two variables will be denoted $\hat{y}_{jt}$ and $\hat{c}_{jt}$, respectively. Other variables will be introduced as necessary and defined at that time. It will be useful for exposition to describe projections of these ratios as the change observed in the ratio between period $T-1$ (just before the program began) and the end of the time horizon. We use the notation $\Delta\hat{y}_{jk}$ and $\Delta\hat{c}_{jk}$ to represent the change in the projection ratio between period $T-1$ and the end of horizon k: for example, $\Delta\hat{c}_{jT} = \hat{c}_{jT} - \hat{c}_{jT-1}$. Historical data from WEO are differenced analogously.

Each program is treated as an independent observation in what follows. However, it is important to note that the database includes numerous programs for many participating countries. These programs may overlap for a given country, in the sense that the initial year (Year T) for one program may coincide with a projection year (e.g., Year $T+2$) for a second program in that country.

1 What does the record show?

For an initial pass, we compare the historical outcomes for the countries participating in IMF-supported programs with the outcomes projected by IMF staff when the programs were originally approved.[5] When we compare the mean of $\Delta\hat{y}_{jk}$ and $\Delta\hat{c}_{jk}$ for various projection horizons k with the mean of the actual Δy_{jk} and Δc_{jk}, we find that projections differ substantially from those actually observed. Figure 12.1 illustrates the pattern of mean changes in projected and historical fiscal ratios.[6] The two mean changes are nearly coincident for horizon T, while for longer horizons the historical and envisaged changes diverge sharply. The mean projected change in the fiscal ratio rises with the length of the horizon; at horizon $T+3$, the projected change in the fiscal ratio is 3.5 percentage points. The change actually observed over those time horizons was quite different; 0.68 percentage points for horizon $T+1$ and up to 1.12 percentage points for horizon $T+3$.

Figure 12.2 illustrates the pattern for changes in projected and actual

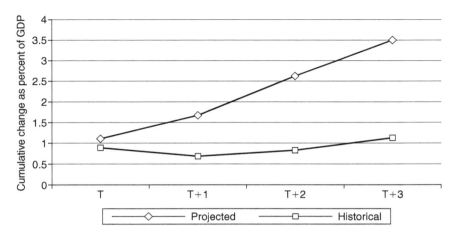

Figure 12.1 Mean historical and projected changes in fiscal ratios.

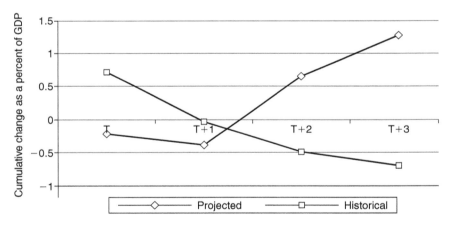

Figure 12.2 Mean historical and projected changes in current-account ratio.

current-account ratios. The mean projected change in the current-account ratio is negative for horizon T and horizon T + 1. The change becomes positive and growing for longer projection horizons. The historical change in current-account ratio for participating countries followed a different dynamic: improvement for horizon T, followed by deterioration in longer horizons. Negative changes in mean current-account ratio continued three and four years after adoption of the IMF program.

While these mean differences are suggestive, they cover up the great variability in projections and realizations for both ratios. As Table 12.1

Table 12.1 Projecting the change in macroeconomic aggregates

Horizon T

Simple statistics

Variable	N	Mean	Standard deviation	Sum	Minimum	Maximum
$\Delta \hat{y}_{jT}$	175	1.08651	2.88011	190.14000	−7.60000	12.50000
Δy_{jT}	175	0.87778	3.25935	153.61161	−11.33896	12.72751
$\Delta \hat{c}_{jT}$	175	−0.22187	3.47920	−38.82699	−13.89236	11.66200
Δc_{jT}	175	0.72340	4.77454	126.59449	−17.68986	14.49604

Correlations

	$\Delta \hat{y}_{jT}$	Δy_{jT}	$\Delta \hat{c}_{jT}$	Δc_{jT}
$\Delta \hat{y}_{jT}$	1.00000			
Δy_{jT}	**0.60489**	1.00000		
$\Delta \hat{c}_{jT}$	0.24256	0.12334	1.00000	
Δc_{jT}	0.19968	0.30303	**0.53486**	1.00000

Horizon T + 1

Simple statistics

Variable	N	Mean	Standard deviation	Sum	Minimum	Maximum
$\Delta \hat{y}_{jT+1}$	147	1.62408	3.22486	238.74000	−5.60000	12.90000
Δy_{jT+1}	147	0.67722	3.93298	99.55073	−19.49935	13.69233
$\Delta \hat{c}_{jT+1}$	147	−0.37867	4.98040	−55.66390	−22.23187	12.01531
Δc_{jT+1}	147	−0.03233	7.07135	−4.75294	−35.61176	25.90529

Correlations

	$\Delta \hat{y}_{jT+1}$	Δy_{jT+1}	$\Delta \hat{c}_{jT+1}$	Δc_{jT+1}
$\Delta \hat{y}_{jT+1}$	1.00000			
Δy_{jT+1}	**0.56182**	1.00000		
$\Delta \hat{c}_{jT+1}$	0.13572	−0.02165	1.00000	
Δc_{jT+1}	0.12453	0.04358	**0.38254**	1.00000

Horizon T + 2

Simple statistics

Variable	N	Mean	Standard deviation	Sum	Minimum	Maximum
$\Delta\hat{y}_{JT+2}$	115	2.59478	3.67922	298.40000	-3.30000	15.60000
Δy_{JT+2}	115	0.81807	4.85553	94.07814	-16.72117	11.88877
$\Delta\hat{c}_{JT+2}$	115	0.64742	4.64897	74.45280	-22.04280	11.68855
Δc_{JT+2}	115	-0.49056	7.32857	-56.41476	-38.14743	21.78397

Correlations

	$\Delta\hat{y}_{JT+2}$	Δy_{JT+2}	$\Delta\hat{c}_{JT+2}$	Δc_{JT+2}
$\Delta\hat{y}_{JT+2}$	1.00000			
Δy_{JT+2}	**0.31046**	1.00000		
$\Delta\hat{c}_{JT+2}$	0.11603	-0.21840	1.00000	
Δc_{JT+2}	-0.03683	-0.11606	**0.32365**	1.00000

Horizon T + 3

Simple statistics

Variable	N	Mean	Standard deviation	Sum	Minimum	Maximum
$\Delta\hat{y}_{JT+3}$	79	3.51000	4.27596	277.29000	-2.70000	19.50000
Δy_{JT+3}	79	1.11918	4.85320	88.41557	-17.48994	13.35470
$\Delta\hat{c}_{JT+3}$	79	1.28198	4.91608	101.27681	-19.89594	14.73079
Δc_{JT+3}	79	-1.37587	12.09842	-108.69398	-81.569321	21.75981

Correlations

	$\Delta\hat{y}_{JT+3}$	Δy_{JT+3}	$\Delta\hat{c}_{JT+3}$	Δc_{JT+3}
$\Delta\hat{y}_{JT+3}$	1.00000			
Δy_{JT+3}	**0.55890**	1.00000		
$\Delta\hat{c}_{JT+3}$	0.14194	-0.12499	1.00000	
Δc_{JT+3}	-0.02829	0.01113	**0.38530**	1.00000

reports, for both historical and envisaged observations the standard error is at least as large as the mean effect. In the correlations between projected and historical changes of the two ratios over the various time horizons,

Horizons	T	T + 1	T + 2	T + 3
Fiscal ratio (Δy_{jk}, $\Delta \hat{y}_{jk}$)	0.61	0.56	0.31	0.56
Current-account ratio (Δc_{jk}, $\Delta \hat{c}_{jk}$)	0.54	0.38	0.32	0.38

There is a good, though not perfect, correlation between projected and historical changes for horizon T. For longer projection horizons the correlation is lower. The horizon $T + 2$ correlations exhibit the lowest values, with horizon $T + 3$ correlations rising again to equal those of $T + 1$.

It is not surprising that the projections are inexact at any projection horizon. Nor is it surprising that the shortest horizon exhibits the closest fit to the actual, since longer-horizon projections require predictions on intermediate-year outcomes that almost surely will be inexact. It will be useful, however, to decompose the projection error into parts – can we learn from the record to identify the source of the projected imprecision?

2 Decomposing projection error

Begin with g_T, a macroeconomic variable observed at time T. Define s_T as the vector of policy-forcing variables observed at time T. Denote the projection of Δg_T to be

$$\Delta \hat{g}_T = f(X_{T-1,}\, \Delta \hat{s}_T) \tag{12.1}$$

with X_{T-1} as a matrix representing the information available to the forecaster at time $T - 1$ and $\hat{s}_T$ as the matrix of projected policy outcomes consistent with the government's Letter of Intent.[7] The actual evolution of the variable g_T can be represented by the expression

$$\Delta g_T = \phi(\zeta_{T-1},\, \Delta s_T) \tag{12.2}$$

with ζ_{T-1} the matrix of forcing variables at time $T - 1$ (including a random error in time T), s_T the matrix of observed policy outcomes and ϕ the true reduced-form model. Projection error can then be represented by the difference $(\Delta \hat{g}_T - \Delta g_T)$.[8]

$$(\Delta \hat{g}_T - \Delta g_T) = \phi(\zeta_{T-1},\, \Delta s_T) - f(X_{T-1},\, \Delta \hat{s}_T) \tag{12.3}$$

There are four potential sources for this projection error. First, the projection model $f(.)$ may not be identical with the true model $\phi(.)$. Second, the historical policy adjustment (Δs_T) may differ from the projected policy adjustment ($\Delta\hat{s}_T$). Third, the information set X_{T-1} available for the projections may not include the same information as the forcing vector ζ_{T-1} for the true process. Finally, there is random error in realizations of the macroeconomic variable.

Consider a simple example. There is a single projection of change in a variable g_T. The forcing matrix is simply the lagged variables g_{T-1} and g_{T-2}.[9] The policy matrix is represented by the single instrument s_T. Equations (12.1) and (12.2) can then be rewritten in the following form:

$$\Delta\hat{g}_T = a_1\Delta\hat{g}_{T-1} + a_2(g_{T-1} + \eta_{T-1}) + b_1\Delta\hat{s}_T \tag{12.1e}$$

$$\Delta g_T = \alpha_1\Delta g_{T-1} + \alpha_2 g_{T-1} + \beta_1\Delta s_T + \epsilon_T \tag{12.2e}$$

The coefficients (α_1, α_2, β_1) represent the true model while (a_1, a_2, b_1) are coefficients from the model used for projections. In the projection rule, the forecaster perceives $\hat{g}_{T-1} = (g_{T-1} + \eta_{T-1})$ with η_{T-1} being a random error. This imprecision may occur because the information set available to the forecaster is less precise than the information set available after later revisions. The variable ϵ_T represents the stochastic nature of realizations of the actual variable.

$$(\Delta\hat{g}_T - \Delta g_T) = [(a_1 - \alpha_1)\Delta g_{T-1} + (a_2 - \alpha_2)g_{T-1} + (b_1 - \beta_1)\Delta s_T] + b_1$$
$$(\Delta\hat{s}_T - \Delta s_T) + [a_2\eta_{T-1} + a_1(\Delta\hat{g}_{T-1} - \Delta g_{T-1})] + \epsilon_T \tag{12.3e}$$

The projection error thus illustrates the four components mentioned above. First, there is the possibility that the forecaster's model differs from that evident in the historical data; this will lead to the errors summarized in the first square bracket. Second, there could be a divergence between the projected policy adjustment and the actual policy adjustment. Third, there is the potential that projection error is due to mismeasurement of initial conditions, or in past forecasts of variable growth. Fourth, the error may simply be due to the stochastic nature of the variable being projected.

In the sections that follow we decompose the projection error into these four parts for the fiscal balance/GDP ratio and the current-account balance/GDP ratio in countries with IMF-supported programs. First, we create a reduced-form model that represents well the evolution of the actual data. We estimate the model implicit in the projected data, and compare the coefficients from this projection model to those from the actual data. Second, we examine the envisaged and historical data for evidence that revisions in the data led to the discrepancies. Third, we perform a decomposition exercise to determine the percentages of deviations of projection from historical that can be attributed to differences in models, differences in initial conditions, differences in policy response, or simply random variation in the historical data.

2.1 *Fiscal and current accounts*

Begin with the macro identity:

$$y_{jt} \equiv c_{jt} - p_{jt} \tag{12.4}$$

holding for all countries j and time periods t. y_{jt} is the fiscal surplus as a share of GDP, c_{jt} is the current-account surplus as a share of GDP, and p_{jt} is private saving as a share of GDP.

Posit as well that there is a "normal"level of private saving specific to each country and to each time period. This normal level p^n_{jt} can be represented by a country-specific component, a component that is common to all countries for a given time period, and a positive relationship between foreign saving opportunities and private saving.

$$p^n_{jt} = \alpha_j + \beta_t + \delta c_{jt} \tag{12.5}$$

Combining Equations (12.4) and (12.5), and defining $e_{jt} = (p_{jt} - p^n_{jt})$ as the excess private saving in any period, yields

$$y_{jt} = -\alpha_j - \beta_t + (1 - \delta)c_{jt} - e_{jt} \tag{12.6}$$

The variables y_{jt} and c_{jt} can be represented by a vector autoregression. With appropriate substitution, this vector autoregression can be rewritten in error-correction form.[10]

$$\Delta y_{jt} = a_o - a_{12}\Delta y_{jt-1} - b_{12}\Delta c_{jt-1} + (a_{11} + a_{12} - 1)y_{jt-1} + (b_{11} + b_{12})c_{jt-1} + \epsilon_{yjt} \tag{12.8a}$$

$$\Delta c_{jt} = b_o - a_{22}\Delta y_{jt-1} - b_{22}\Delta c_{jt-1} + (a_{21} + a_{22})y_{jt-1} + (b_{12} + b_{22} - 1)c_{jt-1} + \epsilon_{zjt} \tag{12.8b}$$

There is in general no way to assign contemporaneous causality in Equations (12.7) and (12.8). If it were possible to assert that the current-account ratio is exogenously determined, for example, then the contemporaneous change Δc_{jt} could be a separate regressor in the Δy_{jt} equation to account for that contemporaneous correlation.

The econometric effects modeled here can be divided into three groups. The first group, represented by the terms in Δc_{jt-1} and Δy_{jt-1}, captures the autoregressive structure of the system. The second group, represented by the terms in y_{jt-1} and c_{jt-1}, captures the adjustment of these variables in response to deviations from the "normal" relationship described in Equation (12.6). The third group represents random errors. Although the direction of contemporaneous causality cannot be verified, there is a version of dynamic causality that can be checked. The coefficients of y_{jt-1} and c_{jt-1} represent the degree to which the current-account and fiscal ratios respond to deviations from the norm.

The system of equations in (12.8) will hold for all t, and thus should be in evidence at time T when the IMF-supported program is introduced. The system has excluded policy interventions from the derivation for simplicity, but it is straightforward, though messy, to introduce them. One way to do so is through definition of a policy response function, by which Δs_{jT} is itself a function of c_{jT-1} and y_{jT-1}. The second is to incorporate the policy variables as exogenous forcing variables. The approach we use will incorporate parts of each.

2.2 Estimation using historical data

The results of Table 12.2a summarize the coefficient estimates from Equations (12.7) and (12.8) for all programs in the sample at horizon T using historical data. Specification testing revealed that lagged first-difference terms with lag length greater than two did not contribute significantly to the regression.[11] The contemporaneous causality imposed upon the model is that changes in the fiscal account are caused by changes in the current account, and not vice versa.[12] The error-correction term (e_{jT-1}) was derived from the regression in levels (i.e., not first-differenced) reported in section A of the Appendix.

For the ratio of fiscal balance to GDP, the estimation results suggest the following insights in the first two columns of Table 12.2a:

Table 12.2a Regression results, historical current, and fiscal account ratios, horizon T

	Δy_{jT}		Δc_{jT}		Δy_{jT}		Δc_{jT}	
	coefficient	S.E.	coefficient	S.E.	coefficient	S.E.	coefficient	S.E.
Δc_{jT}	0.28**	(0.06)			0.25**	(0.05)		
Δy_{jT-1}	0.25**	(0.10)	−0.08	(0.19)	0.23**	(0.10)	−0.04	(0.20)
Δc_{jT-1}	−0.05	(0.05)	−0.04	(0.10)	−0.02	(0.05)	−0.23**	(0.09)
Δy_{jT-2}	0.16**	(0.08)	−0.01	(0.16)	0.14*	(0.08)	0.13	(0.16)
Δc_{jT-2}	−0.07*	(0.04)	−0.02	(0.08)	−0.05	(0.04)	−0.17**	(0.07)
y_{jT-1}	−0.82**	(0.11)	−0.09	(0.21)				
c_{jT-1}	0.16**	(0.07)	−0.40**	(0.12)				
e_{jT-1}					−0.81**	(0.11)	−0.17	(0.22)
N	176		176		176		176	
R^2	0.78		0.56		0.78		0.50	

Notes
Full sample, horizon T. Standard errors (S.E.) in parentheses.
** indicates significance at the 95 percent confidence level, and * indicates significance at the 90 percent confidence level.
A complete set of time and country dummies were included in the regressions, but their coefficients are suppressed for brevity.

- There is significant positive contemporaneous correlation between the two variables, and the normalization chosen here assigns causation to Δc_{jT}. For a 1 percent increase in the current-account ratio, there is a 0.28 percent increase in the fiscal ratio.
- The current first-difference responds positively and significantly to shocks in their own ratio in previous periods. For a unit shock to Δy_{jT-1}, there are other things equal to a 0.25 increase in Δy_{jT}. For a unit shock to Δy_{jT-2}, the transmitted shock is positive and significant at 0.16. Past positive current-account shocks have small negative effects on Δy_{jT} with the two-period lagged effect significant at the 90 percent confidence level.
- The coefficient on y_{jT-1} is significantly different from zero, but not from negative one. It implies that for an average country, a deviation from its "normal" fiscal account ratio will lead to an adjustment in the next period that erases 82 percent of that deviation.

For the ratio of current account to GDP, the estimation explains a lower percentage of the variation (as indicated by the R^2 statistic of 0.56). The second set of columns reports coefficients and standard errors for that specification, and indicates:

- the lagged first-difference terms have no significant effect on the current first-difference;
- the coefficient on c_{jT-1} of -0.40 is significantly different from both zero and negative one. It indicates that 40 percent of any deviations of the current-account ratio from its normal value are made up in the following period.

The last four columns of Table 12.2a report the results of error-correction regressions in which the y_{jT-1} and c_{jT-1} are replaced by e_{jT-1} from Equation (12.6), as implied by a cointegrating relationship between the two variables. As is evident in comparing the first set and third set of results, the cointegrating relationship captures nearly all the explanatory power in the Δy_{jT} regression. The cointegrating relationship is less effective in the Δc_{jT} equation, however, as indicated by the R^2 statistic.[13]

These results are specific to the data for horizon T. When horizon T + 1 is considered, we obtain the results in Table 12.2b. The construction of these data differs somewhat, in that the endogenous variable is a two-period forecast; we chose to use two-period lags on the right-hand side of the equation for comparability. For horizon T + 1, the contemporaneous effect of the current-account ratio on the fiscal ratio is halved – this is perhaps due to the doubling of the length of the time horizon. The autoregressive structure of the fiscal ratio, significant in horizon T, is no longer significant for horizon T + 1. By contrast, the lagged "level" effects have larger coefficients. This effect in the current-account ratio equation

Table 12.2b Regression results, historical current, and fiscal account ratios, horizon T + 1

	Δy_{jT+1}		Δc_{jT+1}		Δy_{jT+1}		Δc_{jT+1}	
	coefficient	*S.E.*	*coefficient*	*S.E.*	*coefficient*	*S.E.*	*coefficient*	*S.E.*
Δc_{jT+1}	0.142**	(0.06)			0.124**	(0.05)		
Δy_{jT-1}	0.093	(0.11)	−0.145	(0.24)	0.079	(0.10)	0.012	(0.26)
Δc_{jT-1}	−0.036	(0.07)	−0.115	(0.16)	−0.006	(0.06)	−0.547***	(0.12)
y_{jT-1}	−1.125***	(0.17)	0.474	(0.37)				
c_{jT-1}	0.230**	(0.10)	−0.833***	(0.21)				
e_{jT-1}					−1.102***	(0.16)	0.273	(0.41)
N	147		147		147		147	
R^2	0.83		0.72		0.83		0.65	

Notes
Variable definition (this table only):
$\Delta g_{jT+1} = g_{jT+1} - g_{jT-1}$
$\Delta g_{jT-1} = g_{jT-1} - g_{jT-3}$
Full sample, horizon T + 1. Standard errors (S.E.) in parentheses.
*** indicates significance at the 99 percent confidence level, ** indicates significance at the 95 percent confidence level, and * indicates significance at the 90 percent confidence level.
A complete set of time and country dummies were included in the regressions, but their coefficients are suppressed for brevity.

is significantly larger, as well, with the coefficient (−0.833) more than double the comparable term for horizon T (−0.40).

2.3 Estimation using the projected data

If we interpret the estimated model of the preceding section to be the true"model (Equation (12.2)), we posit that the model used in forming projections for IMF programs should have a similar form. We can use similar econometric techniques to those of the previous section to derive the economic model implied by the projections. We report the results of this estimation exercise in Table 12.3a for projection horizon T.

The results from estimating the projection model for the fiscal ratio are reported in the first set of columns in Table 12.3a.

• There is significant contemporaneous correlation between the projected fiscal and current-account ratios. For a 1 percentage-point increase to the current-account ratio, there is evidence of a 0.15 percentage-point increase in the fiscal ratio. This is roughly half of the response found in the actual data. By implication, the IMF staff model will project a 0.85 percentage-point increase in the ratio of private net saving to GDP in response to such a current-account shock, while the historical data indicate a 0.72 percentage-point increase in the private saving ratio in response to such a shock.

- A 1 percentage-point increase in last period's fiscal ratio will trigger a 0.15 percentage-point decrease in this period's ratio. This suggests the projection is relying on fiscal policy correction to overcome any inertia in fiscal stance over time and to offset past excesses with current austerity.[14] Also, this response is less than was observed in the historical data.
- There is evidence of an error-correction effect in the data. The coefficients on the lagged ratios have the correct signs, and that associated with $\hat{y}_{jT-1}$ is significantly different from zero. The coefficient -0.44 indicates that the projection is designed to make up 44 percent of any deviation of fiscal ratio from the country's "normal" ratio within a single year. This adjustment is also roughly half of the adjustment observed in the historical data.

The results from estimating the projection model for the current-account ratio are reported in the second set of columns in Table 12.3a.

- There is no significant evidence of an autoregressive structure in Δc_{jt}, just as was true in the historical analysis.
- Past shocks to the fiscal ratio have a significant lagged effect on the current-account ratio, a feature unobserved in the actual data.

Table 12.3a Regression results, envisaged current, and fiscal account ratios, horizon T

	$\Delta\hat{y}_{jT}$		$\Delta\hat{c}_{jT}$		$\Delta\hat{y}_{jT}$		$\Delta\hat{c}_{jT}$	
	coefficient	S.E.	coefficient	S.E.	coefficient	S.E.	coefficient	S.E.
$\Delta\hat{c}_{jT}$	0.15*	(0.09)			0.20**	(0.08)		
$\Delta\hat{y}_{jT-1}$	−0.15	(0.09)	−0.15	(0.12)	−0.14	(0.09)	−0.15	(0.13)
$\Delta\hat{c}_{jT-1}$	−0.09	(0.06)	−0.0004	(0.08)	−0.09	(0.06)	−0.06	(0.09)
$\Delta\hat{y}_{jT-2}$	−0.03	(0.08)	0.16*	(0.10)	−0.05	(0.08)	0.11	(0.11)
$\Delta\hat{c}_{jT-2}$	−0.06	(0.04)	0.04	(0.06)	−0.08*	(0.04)	−0.04	(0.06)
$\hat{y}_{jT-1}$	−0.44**	(0.09)	−0.02	(0.11)				
$\hat{c}_{jT-1}$	0.08	(0.07)	−0.33**	(0.08)				
em_{jT-1}					−0.44**	(0.09)	−0.04	(0.12)
N	165		165		165		165	
R^2	0.85		0.76		0.85		0.69	

Notes
Full sample, horizon T. Standard errors (S.E.) in parentheses.
** indicates significance at the 95 percent confidence level, and * indicates significance at the 90 percent confidence level.
A complete set of time and country dummies were included in the regressions, but their coefficients are suppressed for brevity.

- There is a significant error-correction effect as evidenced by the coefficient on $\hat{c}_{jT-1}$. The coefficient -0.33 indicates that the projection is constructed to make up about a third of any deviation of the current-account ratio from its normal value within a single year. The coefficient on $\hat{y}_{jT-1}$ is insignificantly different from zero. These features are quite similar to those observed in the historical data.

When the envisaged data are examined with cointegrating relationship imposed, the evidence is once again stronger for the fiscal ratio. In that regression, reported in the third set of columns, the cointegrating variable (em_{jT-1}) has explanatory power nearly equal to the lagged $\hat{c}_{jT-1}$ and $\hat{y}_{jT-1}$ reported in the first set of columns. In the equation for the current-account ratio, the results are much weaker.

For time horizon $T + 1$, we observe the outcomes of Table 12.3b. For these envisaged changes, the projection model"for horizon $T + 1$ is quite similar to that of horizon T. The contemporaneous and lagged level"effects are almost identical for the fiscal ratio, as is the lagged level"effect for the current-account ratio. The autoregressive terms differ somewhat, but the differences are not statistically significant. The similarity of error-correction effects is quite striking, as it suggests that the projected adjustment from imbalance occurs totally in horizon T – there is no further adjustment in horizon $T + 1$. This is quite different from the historical record, where adjustment continues in fairly equal increments from horizon T to horizon $T + 1$.

Table 12.3b Regression results, envisaged current, and fiscal account ratios, horizon $T + 1$

	$\Delta\hat{y}_{jT+1}$		$\Delta\hat{c}_{jT+1}$		$\Delta\hat{y}_{jT+1}$		$\Delta\hat{c}_{jT+1}$	
	coefficient	*S.E.*	*coefficient*	*S.E.*	*coefficient*	*S.E.*	*coefficient*	*S.E.*
$\Delta\hat{c}_{jT+1}$	0.158*	(0.08)			0.179**	(0.08)		
$\Delta\hat{y}_{jT-1}$	−0.175*	(0.10)	0.020	(0.16)	−0.165*	(0.09)	0.104	(0.16)
$\Delta\hat{c}_{jT-1}$	0.049	(0.08)	−0.208*	(0.12)	0.034	(0.07)	−0.364***	(0.12)
$\hat{y}_{jT-1}$	−0.462***	(0.11)	−0.029	(0.18)				
$\hat{c}_{jT-1}$	0.048	(0.09)	−0.370***	(0.14)				
em_{jT-1}					−0.474***	(0.11)	−0.128	(0.19)
N	129		129		129		129	
R²	0.86		0.72		0.86		0.68	

Notes
Variable definitions (this table only):
$\Delta\hat{g}_{jT+1} = \hat{g}_{jT+1} - \hat{g}_{jT-1}$
$\Delta\hat{g}_{jT-1} = \hat{g}_{jT-1} - \hat{g}_{jT-3}$
Full sample, horizon T. Standard errors (S.E.) in parentheses.
*** indicates significance at the 99 percent confidence level, ** indicates significance at the 95 percent confidence level, and * indicates significance at the 90 percent confidence level.
A complete set of time and country dummies were included in the regressions, but their coefficients are suppressed for brevity.

2.4 Divergence between projected and actual policy

We note from the preceding discussion that there is substantial evidence of difference between the coefficients in Tables 12.2a and 12.3a, and between Tables 12.2b and 12.3b. We interpret these differences as evidence that the "model" used in IMF projections and the "model" generating the historical data are significantly different. However, as the earlier discussion demonstrated, model differences are only one source of projection errors. In this section, we use the framework of Equation (12.3e) to decompose the observed projection error for horizon T into components.

As the earlier discussion indicated, the projection error can conceptually be decomposed into four parts: differences in models, differences in policy response, mismeasurement of initial conditions at time of projection, and random errors. Projection error is measured directly as the projection of the variable for horizon T minus the realization of the variable. Errors in initial conditions are measured as the difference between projected and historical observations of the level of the variable in period $T - 1$. Two policy variables are considered as indicators of the importance of policy-reform conditions in the error: the difference between projected and historical depreciation of the real exchange rate ($\Delta \hat{e}_{jT} - \Delta e_{jT}$) and the difference between projected and historical change in government consumption expenditures as a share of GDP ($\Delta \hat{w}_{jT} - \Delta w_{jT}$).[15] We hypothesize that the former should have a significant effect on the current account, while the latter should be a significant component of the fiscal surplus.

Estimation of Equation (12.3e) using the error-correction framework presented in Equations (12.7) and (12.8) is complicated by the simultaneity of the macroeconomic balances and the policy variables over which conditions are defined. As Equation (12.3e) indicates, ($\Delta \hat{e}_{jT} - \Delta e_{jT}$), ($\Delta \hat{w}_{jT} - \Delta w_{jT}$), Δe_{jT}, and Δw_{jT} will all be included as regressors in the estimation framework, but all of these are potentially simultaneously determined with the macro balances. We address this by estimating the equations with both OLS and 2SLS, with the 2SLS results presumed to be free of simultaneity bias.[16] For each equation, as implied by Equation (12.6), year-specific dummy variables are included to control for year-to-year differences in capital availability on world markets; we also include significant country-specific dummy variables to control for abnormally large cross-country differences in macro balances. Those results are reported in Table 12.4. The top panel reports the results of regressions in the current-account ratio and the fiscal ratio. There are two columns: the first with OLS estimates, on a slightly larger sample, and the second the 2SLS estimates on a consistent-size sample of 162 observations across all variables. The bottom panel reports the regressions that served as the first stage" of the 2SLS. The first column reports OLS over the largest sample for which data were available for that regression, while the second column reports OLS results over the consistent 2SLS sample of 162 observations.

Table 12.4 Estimation of the projection error equations

$\Delta \hat{c}_{jT} - \Delta c_{jT}$			$\Delta \hat{y}_{jT} - \Delta y_T$		
	OLS	2SLS		OLS	2SLS
c_{jT-1}	0.01	0.04	c_{jT-1}	−0.11**	−0.10**
$\hat{c}_{jT-1} - c_{jT-1}$	−0.41**	−0.31**	$\hat{c}_{jT-1} - c_{jT-1}$	−0.06	−0.07
y_{jT-1}	−0.10	−0.02	y_{jT-1}	0.01	0.04
$\hat{y}_{jT-1} - y_{jT-1}$	−0.19	−0.25*	$\hat{y}_{jT-1} - y_{jT-1}$	−0.34**	−0.30**
Δe_{jT}	−0.0003	−0.002	Δe_{jT}	0.01**	0.01
$\Delta \hat{e}_{jT} - \Delta e_{jT}$	−0.005	−0.001	$\Delta \hat{e}_{jT} - \Delta e_{jT}$	0.007	0.009
			Δw_{jT}	0.10**	0.02
			$\Delta \hat{w}_{jT} - \Delta w_{jT}$	−0.47**	−0.47**
			Δc_{jT-1}	0.03	0.03
			Δy_{jT-1}	−0.08*	−0.08
N	172	162		167	162
R²	0.59	0.59		0.74	0.71

The 2SLS procedure used the estimating equations below for Δe_T, $\Delta \hat{e}_T - \Delta e_T$, Δw_T, and $\Delta \hat{w}_T - \Delta w_T$, and estimated those equations simultaneously with the two reported above. The equations in the following table are all OLS, since they did not include endogenous regressors. The coefficients differ because of the number of observations included: those with 165 were estimated in the simultaneous equation system, while those with other numbers of observations were estimated as single equations.

$\Delta \hat{e}_{jT} - \Delta e_{jT}$			$\Delta \hat{w}_{jT} - \Delta w_{jT}$		
	OLS	OLS		OLS	OLS
$\Delta \hat{e}_{jT-1} - \Delta e_{jT-1}$	0.14**	−0.03	$\hat{w}_{jT-1} - w_{jT-1}$	−0.02	−0.03
Δe_{jT-1}	−0.03**	−0.05**	w_{jT-1}	0.15**	0.14**
			Δw_{jT-1}	−0.06	−0.06
			$\Delta \hat{w}_{jT-1} - \Delta w_{jT-1}$	−0.28**	−0.23**
N	166	162		166	162
R²	0.68	0.68		0.52	0.53

Δe_{jT}			Δw_{jT}		
	OLS	OLS		OLS	OLS
Δe_{jT-1}	0.01**	0.03**	w_{jT-1}	−0.39**	−0.38**
c_{jT-1}	−0.10	0.04	Δw_{jT-1}	−0.13**	−0.16**
y_{jT-1}	0.37	0.28	y_{jT-1}	0.27**	0.29**
N	174	162		173	162
R²	0.65	0.74		0.61	0.60

Notes
** indicates significance at the 95 percent level of confidence, while * indicates significance at the 90 percent confidence level. Standard errors and other regression statistics are available from the authors on demand.

We interpret the results as follows. Take as an example the coefficient on c_{jT-1} in the two regressions. Given our derivation in Equation (12.3e), this coefficient should represent the difference between the projection coefficient and the actual coefficient. When we compare the results of Tables 12.2 and 12.3, we find this to be the case. Consider the 2SLS results. In the fiscal ratio regression of Table 12.4, the coefficient of -0.11 is quite similar to the difference (0.08–0.16) of the coefficients reported in Tables 12.2 and 12.3. For the current-account ratio, the coefficient of 0.04 is also very similar to the difference $(-0.33-(-0.40))$ of the coefficients reported in Tables 12.2a and 12.3a. A positive coefficient in this regression indicates that the projection incorporated a more positive response to that variable than was found in the actual data.

We separate the discussion into the various types of errors.

Differences in modeling. If the projections used a different model from that evident in the actual data, we expect to find significant coefficients on the variables c_{jT-1}, y_{jT-1}, Δc_{jT-1}, Δy_{jT-1}, Δe_{jT}, and Δw_{jT} in the top panel. Our discussion of Tables 12.2a and 12.3a indicated that we anticipated greater evidence of differing models in the fiscal projections than in the current-account projections. This point is partially supported by results reported in Table 12.4. Consider the OLS results. In the fiscal ratio estimation, there are significant coefficients on c_{jT-1} (-0.11), Δe_{jT-1} (0.01), Δy_{jT-1} (-0.08), and Δw_{jT} (0.10). If we consider the last case for illustration: a positive Δw_{jT} should reduce the fiscal balance. The coefficient (0.10) indicates that the IMF projections incorporated less passthrough of increased government expenditures into reduced fiscal ratio than was actually observed, leaving a positive projection error. However, the 2SLS results suggest that differences in modeling are less apparent than is suggested by the OLS estimates, since only the coefficient on c_{jT-1} (-0.10) is significantly different from zero.

For the current-account ratio, there is no significant evidence of differences in modeling. All coefficients on these variables are both small and insignificantly different from zero.

Mismeasurement of initial conditions. Another possible source of projection error is the difference between the initial conditions known to IMF forecasters and the actual initial conditions available in historical data. For these differences to be a significant source of projection error, the coefficients on the variables $(\hat{c}_{jT-1} - c_{jT-1})$ and $(\hat{y}_{jT-1} - y_{jT-1})$ must be significantly different from zero.

In the fiscal ratio regression, the difference in initial fiscal ratios $(\hat{y}_{jT-1} - y_{jT-1})$ is a significant contributor to projection error. The coefficient (-0.30) indicates that when the IMF forecaster had access to artificially high estimates of the previous-period fiscal ratio, she adjusted downward the projected policy adjustment necessary. This forecast response was a rational one, given the error-correction nature of the fiscal ratio, but was based upon an incorrect starting point.

In the current-account ratio regression, the differences in initial conditions are the only significant determinants of projection error. With coefficients (-0.31) for $(\hat{c}_{jT-1} - c_{jT-1})$ and (-0.25) of $(\hat{y}_{jT-1} - y_{jT-1})$, the regressions suggest that the projections were in error largely because of incomplete information about the true value of the current-account ratio in the preceding period.

Differences in policy response. If the projections included a policy response at variance with that actually observed, then the coefficients on $(\Delta\hat{w}_{jT} - \Delta w_{jT})$ and $(\Delta\hat{e}_{jT} - \Delta e_{jT})$ will be significant in the two regressions. In both the 2SLS and the OLS results there is little evidence of this. In the fiscal regression, there is a significant coefficient (-0.47) on $(\Delta\hat{w}_{jT} - \Delta w_{jT})$. This indicates that when the IMF projected smaller expenditure increases than actually occurred, the projection error on the fiscal ratio was on average positive – as expected.

The regressions in the bottom panel hold some clues as to why the projections differed from historical. As is evident in the $(\Delta\hat{w}_{jT} - \Delta w_{jT})$ regression, previous forecast errors were significant determinants of this policy projection error, as was a bias toward more positive projections as the previous-period fiscal ratio rose. The policy projection errors in the real exchange rate depreciation $(\Delta\hat{e}_{jT} - \Delta e_{jT})$ had no significant contribution to either regression in either specification.

Random errors. As the R^2 statistics indicate for the two regressions, the preceding three sources of projection error explain only 59 percent (for the current-account ratio) and 71 percent (for the fiscal ratio) of total projection error. The remainder should be considered random shocks.

3 Accuracy of estimates

Musso and Phillips (2002) suggest evaluating projection accuracy by comparing projected values with a random-walk benchmark projection. Applying their approach to our exercise, we investigate whether the IMF projections of the Year-T and Year-T + 1 values of the variables outperform "random walk"projections – i.e., projected value set equal to the T − 1 value. We draw our conclusions from Theil's U statistic and report results in Table 12.5.[17] Larger values of the U statistic indicate a poorer projection performance.

For the fiscal balance, IMF projections perform significantly better than the random walk for both considered projection horizons. While relative gain in projection performance of MONA projections vis-à-vis the random-walk benchmark decreases from approximately 18 percent for Year-T level to 15 percent for Year-T + 1, the difference still remains quite substantial.

For the current account, only the Year-T projection outperforms the random-walk benchmark. For the T + 1 horizon, IMF projection performance for this variable is about 3 percent worse than that of the random-walk benchmark.

Table 12.5 Test of accuracy (in levels)

Projection model	Number of observations	Fiscal balance ratios	Current account ratios
		Theil's U statistic	
Original program	121	0.695	0.696
Benchmark for OP (random walk)	121	0.788	0.639
First review	120	0.571	0.568
Benchmark for FR (random walk)	120	0.760	0.635

As one would expect, the overall projection performance decreases as the length of projection horizon increases, which is reflected in larger values of U statistic for the Year-T + 1 projections. This observation is valid for both variables and for both types of projections.

4 Conclusions and extensions

Envisaged and historical observations on the fiscal and current-account ratios in countries participating in 175 IMF programs between 1993 and 2001 deviated strongly from one another. Our statistical analysis suggests that the causes can be separated into four components.

First, the IMF staff was apparently working with quite different information about the initial conditions of the program countries than is currently accepted as historical. This difference leads to substantial divergence even if the IMF staff used the model revealed by the historical data. This result is consistent with the conclusions of Orphanides (2001) and Callan *et al.* (2002) on the making of US monetary policy.

Second, the IMF staff did appear to have a different model in mind when making its forecasts. Its model was characterized by gradual fiscal-account adjustment, both in response to contemporaneous current-account shocks and to long-term imbalances, while the model revealed by historical data was characterized by more rapid adjustment to both types of imbalances. Further, its envisaged response was concentrated in horizon T, while the historical response to shocks was roughly equally pro-portioned across horizons T and T + 1.

Third, there is a difference between projected and historical implementation of policy adjustment. Given the level of aggregation of the policy variables investigated (total government consumption expenditures, real exchange rate depreciation) we cannot conclude that the difference is due to a failure to meet the conditions of the program; the differences could also be due to shocks that worsened performance of these aggre-gates even when conditions were fulfilled. This conclusion is contingent upon our choice of policy variable."Here, we use government consump-tion expenditures and real exchange rate depreciation. If we had chosen the fiscal surplus as a þolicy variable"rather than outcome, the results of this chapter suggest that our conclusions would be reversed. This is a question that can, and should, be investigated further.

Fourth, there is ample evidence that IMF projections, as with other macroeconomic projections, are quite inaccurate. The evidence on åccuracy"reported here is instructive – while the projections outperform a random walk most of the time, they are not much better. The Meese and Rogoff (1983) results remind us of the difficulty in projecting exchange rates in time series. The project described here indicates the inaccuracy of simple models in a panel (i.e., time series and cross-section of countries) format.

In a related paper (Atoian *et al.* 2004) we have reported our analyses of IMF staff revisions to its projections, using the methodology of Musso and Phillips (2002). These results indicate that the IMF staff learns from past projection errors and from new information. However, even that learning leaves large gaps to fill. The largest margin for improvement may well be in Just-in-time"data collection, so that the errors due to incomplete information, especially from initial conditions, can be eliminated.

Appendix

A Creating the error-correction residuals

In the following, we use the WEO data set covering those programs with time horizon T. There are 175 observations in general, although somewhat more when considered in levels.

Table 12.A1 Dependent variable: y_{jt} (WEO). Creating the error-correction residual e_{jt}

Analysis of variance					
Source	*DF*	*Sum of squares*	*Mean square*	*F value*	*Pr > F*
Model	86	5518.14566	64.16448	6.58	<0.0001
Error	96	935.61705	9.74601		
Uncorrected total	182	6453.76271			

Root MSE		3.12186	R^2	0.8550
Dependent mean		−4.33059	Adj R^2	0.7252
Coefficient variable		−72.08859		

Parameter estimates					
Variable	*DF*	*Parameter estimate*	*Standard error*	*t value*	*Pr > |t|*
C_{jt}	1	0.09996	0.06203	1.61	0.1103
t93	1	−7.41751	1.72365	−4.30	<0.0001
t94	1	−4.83851	1.91288	−2.53	0.0131
t95	1	−6.31586	1.84898	−3.42	0.0009
t96	1	−5.37486	1.92894	−2.79	0.0064
t97	1	−3.98082	1.88383	−2.11	0.0372
t98	1	−3.63622	1.95216	−1.86	0.0656
t99	1	−4.64533	1.95383	−2.38	0.0194
t00	1	−5.26644	1.97374	−2.67	0.0090
t01	1	−5.92937	1.83106	−3.24	0.0017

This is the formulation used to create the error-correction variable $(e_T - _1 = y_t -$ predicted value) for WEO data. A complete set of country dummies was used as well, but is suppressed here.

The following regression results report the coefficients used in creating the error-correction variable for envisaged data.

Table 12.A2 Dependent variable: y_{jt} (envisaged)

Analysis of variance

Source	DF	Sum of squares	Mean square	F value	Pr > F
Model	95	6449.94187	67.89412	5.29	<0.0001
Error	97	1244.26623	12.82749		
Uncorrected total	192	7694.20810			

Root MSE	3.58155	R^2	0.8383	
Dependent mean	−4.47401	Adj R^2	0.6799	
Coefficient variable	−80.05230			

Parameter estimates

Variable	DF	Parameter estimate	Standard error	t value	Pr > |t|
C_{jt}	1	0.31664	0.07861	4.03	0.0001
t93	1	−6.84332	1.81926	−3.76	0.0003
t94	1	−4.68806	1.95701	−2.40	0.0185
t95	1	−5.69861	1.90593	−2.99	0.0035
t96	1	−3.85602	1.93132	−2.00	0.0487
t97	1	−3.34252	1.93759	−1.73	0.0877
t98	1	−2.74118	1.85499	−1.48	0.1427
t99	1	−4.38718	2.07410	−2.12	0.0370
t00	1	−3.95966	2.08914	−1.90	0.0610
t01	1	−5.05367	2.00406	−2.52	0.0133

A complete set of country dummies was used as well, but is suppressed here.

B Does the timing of approval of IMF-supported programs matter to these results?

One possible explanation for the projection errors analyzed in the text is the uneven timing of approvals of IMF-supported programs. In the text we treat each program as having been approved at the beginning of Year T," so that the projected effects of the program on macroeconomic adjustment have a full year to take hold. In fact, programs are approved at different times within Year T.

Projection errors may reasonably be hypothesized to follow on from earlier approval in Year T. We investigated this hypothesis in two ways. First, we calculated Pearson correlations of the approval month with the size of the projection error for horizons T and T + 1. Second, we regressed the projection error on dummy variables indicating the quarter of Year T in which approval occurred.

The Pearson correlations provide no evidence of a significant approval-time effect in either variable. For the fiscal ratio, there is no evidence of a significant approval-time effect for either Original Program (OP) or First Review (FR) projection errors. For the current-account ratio, a number of coefficients are positive and significant. However, they do not grow uniformly over the sample; the largest deviations from the mean occur for programs approved in the second and third quarters of Year T."

We did the same exercise for the deviation in initial conditions; in that case, the hypothesis is that programs approved later in Year T will have more accurate information on the initial conditions, so that deviations will be lessened. There is no evidence of a significant effect in the Pearson correlations. There is some evidence of this in the regression results, however. For both OP and FR versions of the fiscal ratio and the OP version of the current-account ratio, the deviation in initial conditions is significantly smaller on average for programs approved in the first quarter of Year T than for those approved later in Year T. There is thus a downward bias in the fiscal ratios used as initial conditions in projections created in the first quarter of Year T relative to the historical data, most likely because the IMF staff did not have access to the later revisions when creating its projections.

If there is a value to this information, it should also be evident in the initial conditions as reported in FR relative to OP for each program. In Table 12.B5 we compare the initial conditions, with deviations measured as FR values minus OP values. A similar regression on approval-times within Year T yields little evidence of a systematic bias, with only the current-account ratio showing any deviation of significance. The estimated coefficients are suggestive, though, rising from negative values for quarter 1 approval to ever-increasing values for subsequent quarters.

Table 12.B1 Pearson correlations for projection errors

	Fiscal balance: original program (approval month in T)	Fiscal balance: first review (approval month in T)	Current account: original program (approval month in T)	Current account: first review (approval month in T)
Horizon T	0.01905	−0.02677	0.00687	0.06711
	0.8364	0.7716	0.9406	0.4665
	120	120	120	120
Horizon T + 1	−0.05439	−0.15750	0.14289	0.14916
	0.5853	0.1234	0.1499	0.1406
	103	97	103	99

Table 12.B2 Regressions on quarterly dummies (horizon T) for projection errors

	Fiscal balance (OP)	*Fiscal balance (FR)*	*Current account (OP)*	*Current account (FR)*
Quarter 1	0.06 (0.46)	−0.11 (0.40)	0.44 (0.69)	−0.15 (0.57)
Quarter 2	−0.27 (0.39)	−0.47 (0.34)	1.08* (0.60)	0.94* (0.49)
Quarter 3	0.26 (0.51)	−0.16 (0.44)	1.76** (0.77)	0.26 (0.63)
Quarter 4	0.44 (0.59)	−0.04 (0.51)	0.13 (0.90)	0.63 (0.74)
R^2	0.01	0.02	0.07	0.04
N	120	120	120	120

Notes
** indicates significance at the 95 percent confidence level, and * indicates significance at the 90 percent confidence level.

Table 12.B3 Pearson correlations for discrepancies in initial conditions (actual − projection)

	Fiscal balance: original program (approval month in T)	*Fiscal balance: first review (approval month in T)*	*Current account: original program (approval month in T)*	*Current account: first review (approval month in T)*
All horizons	0.13744	0.10628	0.09385	−0.11611
	0.1328	0.2440	0.3076	0.2028
	121	122	120	122

Table 12.B4 Regressions on quarterly dummies for discrepancies in initial conditions (FR − OP)

	Fiscal balance (OP)	*Fiscal balance (FR)*	*Current account (OP)*	*Current account (FR)*
Quarter 1	−0.80** (0.39)	−0.73** (0.35)	−1.75** (0.73)	1.56 (1.11)
Quarter 2	−0.37 (0.34)	−0.40 (0.31)	−0.95 (0.63)	−0.82 (0.96)
Quarter 3	0.27 (0.44)	0.05 (0.39)	−0.75 (0.82)	0.62 (1.23)
Quarter 4	−0.18 (0.51)	−0.21 (0.46)	−0.34 (0.95)	−2.17 (1.44)
R^2	0.05	0.05	0.07	0.04
N	120	120	120	120

Notes
** indicates significance at the 95 percent confidence level, and * indicates significance at the 90 percent confidence level.

Table 12.B5 Regressions on quarterly dummies (horizon T) for discrepancies in initial conditions (FR − OP)

	Fiscal balance (FR − OP)	Current account (FR − OP)
Quarter 1	−0.072 (0.171)	−0.176 (0.367)
Quarter 2	0.023 (0.148)	0.074 (0.317)
Quarter 3	0.215 (0.190)	0.323 (0.408)
Quarter 4	0.032 (0.222)	0.904* (0.477)
R^2	0.013	0.039
N	120	120

Notes
* indicates significance at the 90 percent confidence level.

Notes

* Thanks to Timothy Lane, T.N. Srinivasan and participants at the Yale University Conference for their comments and critiques.
1 We will hold to a specific definition of þrojections"in this chapter. We do not consider projections to be identical to forecasts."We define a forecast to be the best prediction possible of what is to occur at a given time in the future. A projection in this context is a prediction based upon the participating country undertaking and completing all structural and policy reforms agreed to in the Letter of Intent approved between the participating government and the IMF. The two could diverge if the best prediction includes only partial implementation of policy and structural reform.
2 When an IMF program is approved, the IMF staff uses the best statistics available at that time for current and past macroeconomic data to create projections for the evolution of those variables over the following years. These projections represent the öriginal program" projections for that IMF program. Program performance is reviewed periodically over time, and at each review the IMF staff creates a new set of projections for the macroeconomic data reflecting the best available information of that time. We will use the first review"projections for each program in a later section.
3 For example, the projections are reported on an annual basis but the year is not invariably a calendar year. For some programs, the fiscal year was used as the basis of data collection and forecasting. In those instances, the historical data are converted into fiscal-year equivalents through weighted-average conversion of the calendar-year data.
4 The Year T"of each program is defined by IMF staff to be that fiscal year (as defined by the country) in which the program is approved. Programs are typically not approved at the beginning of Year T, but rather at some point within the year.
5 In this section, we use the projections from the öriginal program."
6 The data on which Figures 12.1 and 12.2 are based are reported in Table 12.1.
7 By contrast, we consider the forecast of Δg_T to be defined $\Delta g^e_T = f(X_{T-1}; s^e_T)$, with s^e_T representing the forecaster's best prediction as of period $T-1$ of the policy vector to be observed in period T.
8 Hendry (1997) provides an excellent summary of the possible sources of projection (in his case forecasting) error when the projection model is potentially different from the actual model. This example can be thought of as a special case of his formulation.

9 g_{T-2} enters the expression through the term Δg_{T-1}.
10 We will refer to the "error-correction form"as one that includes both lagged differences and lagged levels of the two variables as explanatory variables for the current differenced variables. This can be derived from a general AR specification of the two variables; the AR(2) specification is used here for ease of illustration. The form presented in the text can be derived from the following AR(2) set of equations.

$$y_{jt} = a_0 + a_{11}y_{jt-1} + a_{12}y_{jt-2} + b_{11}c_{jt-1} + b_{12}\, c_{jt-2} + \epsilon_{yjt}$$
$$c_{jt} = b_0 + a_{21}y_{jt-1} + a_{22}y_{jt-2} + b_{21}c_{jt-1} + b_{22}\, c_{jt-2} + \epsilon_{cjt}$$

Specification tests are used to choose the lag length appropriate to the empirical work. In a world in which y_{jt} and c_{jt} are non-stationary but are cointegrated on a country-by-country basis, further simplification is possible. If y_{jt} and c_{jt} are non-stationary in the current dataset, then Equation (12.6) represents a cointegrating relationship. The "error correction"variable e $_{jt}$ can then be inserted in the Equations (12.7) and (12.8) in place of the terms in y_{jt-1} and c_{jt-1} and will have the coefficient associated with y_{jt-1} in Equation (12.7). It is impossible to verify a non-stationary relationship in this dataset, given that we have only scattered observations from each country's time series. We do investigate that possibility in the second and fourth columns of Tables 12.2 and 12.3, with support for that interpretation of the error-correction term in the Δy_{jt} equation. Hamilton (1994: chapter 19) provides a clear derivation of this error-correction form from the underlying autoregression.
11 Statistical confidence in this chapter will be measured at the 90 percent, 95 percent, and 99 percent levels. In the text, statistical significance will indicate a degree of confidence greater than 95 percent unless otherwise indicated.
12 This assumption will be justified, for example, if the participating country is constrained in its international borrowing, so that the ratio of current-account surplus to GDP is set by foreign lenders.
13 While imposition of the cointegration condition through the error-correction variable is effective for the fiscal ratio, our comparison of projections with historical data will be based upon the system without this condition imposed. As Clements and Hendry (1995) demonstrate, the imposition of the cointegration condition in estimation when cointegration exists improves forecast accuracy most notably for small (i.e., $N = 50$) samples. For larger samples, the improvements in forecast accuracy are small.
14 We would observe this negative coefficient, for example, if we had a model that required the government to balance its budget over each two-year period. There could be excess spending in odd years, but it would be offset by spending cuts in even years.
15 The variable for government consumption expenditures is available in consistent format in both historical and envisaged data. The variable on real depreciation is constructed in both cases as nominal depreciation minus CPI inflation for the horizon in question. These variables are explicit in the historical data. In the envisaged data, the nominal exchange rate is derived as the ratio between GDP in home currency and GDP in US dollars.
16 Both sets of results are reported because the systems approach to estimation reduces the number of observations usable in estimation. The OLS results thus provide a more comprehensive analysis, although potentially tainted by simultaneity bias.
17 The Theil's U Statistic is: $U = \sqrt{\dfrac{1/N\sum_{jt}(g_{jt} - \hat{g}_{jt})^2}{1/N\sum_{jt}g_{jt}^2}}$

Bibliography

Atoian, R., P. Conway, M. Selowsky, and T. Tsikata. 2004. Macroeconomic Adjustment to IMF-supported Programs: Projections and Reality. Independent Evaluation Office Background Paper 04/2.

Callan, M., E. Ghysels, and N. Swanson. 2002. Monetary Policy Rules with Model and Data Uncertainty. *Southern Economic Journal* 69: 239–65.

Clements, M. and D. Hendry. 1995. Forecasting in Cointegrated Systems. *Journal of Applied Econometrics* 10: 127–46.

Hamilton, J. 1994. *Time Series Analysis.* Princeton: Princeton University Press.

Hendry, D. 1997. The Econometrics of Macroeconomic Forecasting. *The Economic Journal* 107: 1330–57.

Howrey, E.P. 1984. Data Revision, Reconstruction and Prediction: An Application to Inventory Investment. *Review of Economics and Statistics* 66 (3): 386–93.

Meese, R. and K. Rogoff. 1983. Empirical Exchange Rate Models of the Seventies: Do They Fit Out of Sample?. *Journal of International Economics* 14: 3–24.

Musso, A. and S. Phillips. 2002. Comparing Projections and Outcomes of IMF-supported Programs. *IMF Staff Papers* 49 (1): 22–48.

Orphanides, A. 2001. Monetary Policy Rules, Macroeconomic Stability and Inflation: A View from the Trenches. Working Paper, Federal Reserve Board of Governors.

13 The IMF and capital account crises

The case for separate lender of last resort and conditionality functions*

Thomas D. Willett

1 Introduction

What has happened to the push for reform of the international financial architecture that had such momentum during the rash of international financial crises in the 1990s?[1] While not the stuff of dramatic news headlines, a great deal of progress has been made, especially in the areas of increased transparency at the IMF and the growing acknowledgment of the danger of trying to run a stickily pegged exchange rate regime in a world of substantial international capital mobility. Less progress has been made, however, in dealing with another implication of high capital mobility – the need for the IMF (or some other international agent) to have more effective capability to act as a quasi international lender of last resort (ILOLR).[2]

As Barry Eichengreen (2002a) has put it, "On prevention, a number of useful steps have been taken. In terms of how to manage and resolve crisis, in contrast, disappointingly little has been achieved ... disagreement and confusion continue to reign"(52).

In a similar vein, Park and Wang (2002) argue that the G-7 and international financial institutions appear to have lost the zeal to garner the support they need for reform. The ongoing debate on the future direction of international financial reform suggests that most of the problems are likely to remain unchanged. This pessimistic outlook arouses a deep concern in developing countries"(124–5). They go on to argue that much of the interest in regional monetary institutions in Asia has come from frustration at the limited scope of the reforms at the global level.

To be sure, the international community through the IMF has not been idle. Two new financing mechanisms have been created within the IMF for crisis prevention and management. In the judgment of many experts, however, these reforms are far from sufficient. One, the Supplemental Reserve Facility (SRF), has been quite useful but does not go far enough in the view of those who think we need a functional ILOLR. The more radical Contingent Credit Line (CCL) has serious design problems and as yet has not been used.[3]

While debate continues among researchers, public attention largely moved on to the proposal by Anne Krueger, Deputy Managing Director of the IMF, to create some type of debt restructuring facility. The Krueger proposal addressed an important issue but has met with strong political opposition. While current official interest in both ILOLR and debt restructuring mechanisms seems highly muted at the present time, we should not infer from this that our current institutional framework for dealing with international monetary and financial issues is in satisfactory shape.

There have been sharp disagreements in the recent discussions of these issues and this has undoubtedly contributed to the lack of progress. Some of the reasons for disagreement can be clarified by emphasizing the differences in political assumptions made by the disputants. As the reader will see, I share the view of those who argue that there are times where imperfectly functioning markets do present a case for ILOLR-type lending by the IMF (or some other international organization). Furthermore, the growth of international capital mobility and the limited catalytic role played by recent IMF programs in bolstering confidence imply that very large programs will sometimes be called for. Thus there is a strong case for a well-functioning ILOLR-type facility at the IMF.

To the contrary, however, many economists have called for smaller IMF programs. The reason is that in practice, actual IMF programs have often been far from first-best. Some economists and politicians, mostly on the right, have even argued that past IMF programs have worked so badly that it would be best to shut down the institution altogether.

Most middle of the road experts argue that this is too extreme a response, but recognize that the poor-track-record IMF programs present a serious problem. The recent discussion by Barry Eichengreen (2002) is typical of such views. He notes that because there are strong political pressures on the IMF to lend the IMF rarely if ever says no the first time; it says no only after being pushed into a corner by the failure of a long series of loans ... where the short-run prospects of the country are so clearly hopeless that it would be absurd for the IMF to continue lending"(55) The problem is not just that politicians or IMF management like to lend; it is that they fear the uncertain consequences of doing otherwise"(7).

Waste of IMF reserves is not the only consequence of excessive lending. These programs have permitted governments to cling longer ... to unsustainable policies, allowing economic and financial vulnerabilities to build up and creating the potential for very severe political and social dislocations when support is ultimately withdrawn"(7).

Furthermore, such lax lending policies have substantially undermined the value of the IMF's seal of approval, thus requiring large loans to calm current crises. A vicious circle is at work.

In recent years the IMF has shown greater recognition of this problem – and there have been efforts to be tougher under the new management team of Horst Kohler and Anne Krueger. It is still too soon to tell, however, how major a change in IMF policy is at hand, and the guesses of independent experts vary widely. Thus we see that the sources of dispute about a new ILOLR-type facility for the IMF rest as much on judgments about the extent of bureaucratic and political failure as on the extent of market failure.

This suggests that instead of just imposing conditionality on others, it may be necessary for others to impose conditionality on the IMF. Only if the IMF and its political stakeholders demonstrate sufficient reforms in their lending practices is the international community likely to provide the IMF with the increase in resources necessary to operate an effective ILOLR-type facility.

We may interpret in this light the proposals of the majority report of the recent US Congressional Commission (commonly called the Meltzer Report). This report called for abolishing all traditional IMF programs and replacing them with a new ILOLR-type facility that could make large loans, but only for short-time periods and under strict conditions. Many experts and officials dismissed this proposal as being too extreme. From the standpoint of political acceptance this is certainly true. This chapter will argue, however, that while it is unsatisfactory as a comprehensive blueprint, the Meltzer Report and the debate it has stimulated makes an important contribution.

Ironically, while one of the major criticisms of the IMF has been its excessive leniency in lending, another has been the excessive breadth and stringency of the conditions that it imposes. Of course some of the seemingly contradictory nature of these criticisms is that some come from the right and some from the left, but another important cause is the Fund's spotty record of enforcement. The Meltzer Majority Report recommended abandoning ex post policy conditionality altogether and placing exclusive emphasis on meeting preconditions, i.e., ex ante conditionality. While there have been a number of criticisms of the specific preconditions recommended by the Meltzer Report, it has helped spark a valuable debate about ex ante versus ex post conditionality.

This chapter argues that there is a useful role for some of the types of traditional IMF conditionality programs rejected by the Meltzer Report and that we should not yet give up entirely on the ability of the IMF and its political stakeholders to do a better job of running such policies. It has been increasingly widely recognized, however, that the conditions under which such programs can be effective are limited. In particular, considerable national ownership of programs is required.

The development of such ownership generally takes considerable time, however, but in the midst of currency crises rapid action is needed. This chapter proposes that this inherent conflict can be reduced by separating

IMF programs into two major categories. An ILOLR-type facility would provide short-term financing to countries facing liquidity crises who meet a set of preconditions or ex ante conditionality. In a pure liquidity crisis this is all that will be needed, as the Meltzer Report assumed. Frequently, however, crises are a combination of liquidity crisis and genuine problems that are not hopeless, but require reforms over several years. The latter is where traditional IMF conditionality programs can be useful if they are based on sufficient ownership. By providing a separate facility for dealing with the short-term aspects of crises, the ILOLR-type facility would allow more time to negotiate conditionality programs that had a greater chance of success. If it has become politically taboo to talk of lender-of-last-resort-type facilities, we could instead label this a facility for bridge loans while traditional export conditionality programs are being negotiated.

At present these two different types of functions are conflated in IMF facilities – with the partial exception of the Contingent Credit Line. The result is to the detriment of both functions. Such a technical improvement in the division of labor of Fund activities will achieve its potential only in connection with major changes in how the Fund does business. With such a change in attitudes and incentive structures at the Fund and in the willingness of its major shareholders to allow it to operate with less politically motivated interference, however, the separation of LOLR and traditional conditionality programs holds some prospect for helping the Fund operate in a more prudent and effective manner. Thus while Calomiris and the Meltzer Commission majority would "replace ex post negotiations over conditions for IMF lending with ex ante standards for access to IMF lines of credit"(Calomiris 2003: 260), I argue that there is a strong case for seeing these two approaches as complements rather than substitutes.

We begin with a review of a number of important areas of consensus that have developed about reforms of the international financial systems. It is argued that these developments are a necessary precondition for serious consideration of expanding the IMF's capacity to operate as an ILOLR. We then turn to the Meltzer Commission's report and the controversies it has generated. This is followed by more in-depth discussion of several key issues involved in the ILOLR debate: ex ante versus ex post conditionality moral hazard issues, the role of standstills and private sector involvement (PSI), and catalytic effects and the size of Fund programs. We then turn to the case for creating a separate ILOLR function at the IMF, but as a complement to rather than a substitute for, IMF conditionality programs.

2 Areas of consensus about international financial reform

Despite the high degree of controversy about reform of the international financial architecture, a good deal more consensus has developed than would meet the eye of the casual observer. This is especially true with respect to policies of crisis prevention. This is crucial because without this development the case for expanding the IMF's capacity for crisis lending would be much weaker.

One of the most important causes of the IMF's tendency toward excessive leniency in its lending policies, was the pressure to help countries defend regimes of pegged exchange rates. We can imagine circumstances in which such defenses are desirable but they are a small subset of the actual defenses that have occurred over the last several decades. IMF's track record in aiding such defenses has been abysmal. Just think of the recent cases in Argentina, Russia, and Turkey.[4]

Today, the political pressures on the IMF to help countries defend pegged regimes have fallen sharply. For one thing, there are now many fewer pegged regimes.

Second, there is now considerable agreement that pegged exchange rates have been a major (albeit not the only) cause of international currency crisis and that the IMF should not provide financing to countries that follow domestic policies inconsistent with their exchange rate regimes. This view is reflected in both the Meltzer Report and Council on Foreign Relation Report, and statements of the US Treasury and the IMF. There is some evidence of a move back toward heavier exchange rate management by some countries, and some old-fashioned pegs remain in countries such as China and Malaysia. Thus it would be an overstatement to argue that this source of pressure for ill-advised IMF lending has been totally eliminated, but it has surely been sharply reduced.

There is also widespread agreement that the IMF's policy of conditionality must be substantially revamped. The basic idea of conditionality is a good one. IMF lending with no strings attached could help countries postpone necessary but painful adjustments. By making funding contingent on good domestic policies, IMF programs provide both a carrot and a stick to help ease the costs of adjustment for recipient countries while increasing the incentives for them to undertake such policies. A few scholars have criticized the basic theory underlying conditionality,[5] but most criticisms concern its application.

The IMF has done both too much and too little. Over the past decade it greatly expanded the range of its policy conditionality. While often put to good causes, policy conditions became far too intrusive and payed insufficient attention to the appropriate balance between international influence and national responsibility. At the same time, however, the IMF's track record for effectively enforcing its policy conditions was in many cases quite poor.[6]

Political and bureaucratic incentives made it difficult for the IMF to enforce sufficient implementation. The Fund has frequently pulled programs for non-compliance but then started them up again soon after with little or no penalty for previous behavior. A strong consensus has emerged that the IMF should refocus on its core competencies of macro, financial, and exchange-rate economics. Under the new Managing Director, Horst Kohler, the Fund at last began to pay attention to these criticisms, and streamlining conditionality and developing national ownership of programs are now the watchwords.[7] It is too soon to tell just how effective this shift will be, but it is certainly moving in the right direction.

Another area of consensus among most outside experts is that the major powers should stop using the IMF as a backdoor way of funding countries for geopolitical purposes such as the ill-fated Russian loan in the late 1990s. The attractions of using the IMF as a political slush fund by national leaders with short-time horizons are quite understandable; but if continued, such manipulation will undercut the IMF's ability to carry out its prime mandate of promoting international financial stability with long-term costs to all. The combination of the problems just noted has seriously eroded the credibility of IMF programs and reduced the effectiveness of its seal of approval as a signal to private financial markets.[8] More than its billions of cash, its credibility is the Fund's most valuable asset, and this has been dangerously eroded.

Despite the frequent charges that the IMF is an unresponsive and unaccountable international bureaucracy, many of the problems that experts have identified with the operation of the IMF have been due primarily not to the staff of the Fund, but to its management of the Fund and its shareholders (the governments of the member countries) who elect the management.[9] There is, of course, some bureaucratic slippage, but it is much less than in most international organizations. Particular groups of countries may feel that they have little to say on Fund policies, but there is not much the Fund does against the wishes of the major industrial countries.

It is not clear, however, whether the major powers have accepted the argument that continued use of the IMF for political purposes is substantially undercutting its effectiveness. The Bush Administration was sharply critical of excessive IMF lending but then became the leading advocate for big IMF loans to Turkey and Argentina. Geopolitical considerations may be the biggest obstacle faced by advocates of IMF reform. Another important area of consensus is that IMF procedures developed to deal with the early post-war period of low capital mobility need substantial revision in a world of high capital mobility.

The IMF was established in an era where capital controls were widespread and balance of payments difficulties tended to emerge fairly slowly over time and were typically of relatively small size. Indeed, IMF financing was initially intended only to cover current account deficits. The key tasks for IMF programs were to see that countries were initiating appropriate adjustment policies and providing interim financing as these policies began to turn around the balance of payments. IMF funds were paid out in installments. This process helped keep IMF leverage over national policies after a program was agreed. If a country deviated too much on its policy promises, then disbursements could be held up or terminated.

While in practice it has proven difficult for the IMF to manage this process with sufficient toughness, the basic strategy of installment payments linked to policy conditionality was well conceived.

The situation changes drastically, however, in a world of high capital mobility. Payments positions can turn from surplus to deficit quite quickly and the magnitude of the swings can be enormous. This was illustrated in both the Mexican crises in 1994–95 and the Asian crisis in 1997–98. Furthermore, with high capital mobility, crises can spread much more easily from one country to another. In my judgment there were no entirely innocent victims in the wake of the financial contagion stimulated by the recent currency crises – i.e., no countries with strong fundamentals in all dimensions were hit by large, unjustified speculative attacks – but modern international monetary theory stresses that fundamentals do not come in just two flavors – strong and weak.[10] There can be a sizable gray area inbetween and it is countries in this intermediate zone of vulnerability who are the ‟victims"of contagion from international currency crisis today.

Traditional Fund programs were ill-suited to deal with such situations. The international financial community recognized this and has responded with innovations in Fund programs such as the SRF that allow larger financial packages with greater front loading of funding and higher interest charges. These changes have been in the right direction, but they have not gone far enough. The recent CCL facility was a hastily designed political response to the recent currency crises and many international monetary experts believe that it was sufficiently flawed and that it would be better to scrap it and start over again, rather than to continue to tinker with it as the official community has done so far. The IMF understands that the substantial increase in international capital flows generally challenges old ways of doing business and indeed has recently published a study on ‟IMF-Supported Programs in Capital Account Crises"(Ghosh *et al.* 2002). This study is full of cogent analysis and clearly recognizes that the prospect of financial capital running for the exit plays havoc with the traditional IMF policy of doling out money for its programs in tranches over several years. Thus the Fund has moved toward front-loading its loans.

While the IMF study discusses the large overshooting of exchange rates that followed the outbreak of the Asian crisis, it gives little attention to the possibility that greater exchange market intervention financed by the IMF could have substantially reduced this overshooting and hence moderated the effects of the crisis. Because of the large unhedged foreign borrowings by firms in the crisis countries the economy-wide effects of these large depreciations were quite substantial.

The IMF study is not used as a platform to support a request for additional resources to deal with such situations. Rather it emphasizes (quite appropriately) the risk that ‟the financing gap itself becomes endogenous, with greater outflows of private capital enabled by more official money"

(20). This has indeed been a major problem in cases such as Russia where the IMF lent to help a country try to maintain a misaligned pegged rate. Such loans helped capital to rush to the exits at still favorable exchange rates. Thus it is heartening to see this danger emphasized. But once a country has gone to a more flexible exchange rate, as was the case with all of the Fund's programs during the Asian crisis, this consideration would seem less relevant.

Efforts at blame deflection may help explain the IMF study's conclusion that above all, this discussion suggests that there are rather narrow limits to what the available financing tools can do to address an ongoing crisis"(21). This statement, however, begs the question of whether large financing would have been a good idea or whether it just wasn't feasible given the Fund's policies and the size of its resources. For forward-looking policy analysis we need to separate the question of whether the Fund should be faulted for not having done more in the Asian crisis given the constraints it faced from whether these constraints should be changed for the future. The Fund study indicates It is difficult to contemplate official financing packages several times the size of recent ones"(61), but from the standpoint of good future oriented policy analysis that is exactly what we should do. The answer could well be that it's a bad idea, but that's what we need to analyze.

In a similar vein, an influential report from the Council on Foreign Relations (1999a) argues that private capital flows . . . are now just too big to expect Fund-led rescue packages to cover fully all financing gaps faced by emerging economies"(67). In the full report (1999b) the task force argues that We are not persuaded that smaller rescue packages would necessarily make it more difficult to regain the 'confidence' of investors, as experience suggests that this owes more to the speed and determination with which underlying economic problems are addressed"(12).

Both statements are phrased in highly self-serving ways. Arguing that private capital flows are just too big"seems to put an end to the issue. While this statement is certainly true given the current level of Fund resources, this limit is a political not a technical one. Likewise, it is certainly true that pouring more money at the wrong countries would do little to help, but experience suggests that it usually takes time to restore market confidence even when countries are adopting appropriate policies. In such cases it seems unlikely that the quantity of funding available would have no effect. The key may be to get the IMF to be tougher in deciding to fund programs, rather than starving it of cash in general. Indeed, the Institute of International Finance has estimated that in the Asian and Russian crises, international investors lost over $300 billion (Council on Foreign Relations 1999b).

3 The controversy over the Meltzer Commission Report

As we have noted, part of the hesitancy for greatly expanding the IMF's capacity to act as a short-term emerging lender reflects growing recognition that the traditional IMF programs of conditional lending have had a less than stellar track record and that this is endangering the credibility of the IMF's seal of approval. There are also widespread concerns that IMF lending has generated moral hazard problems, and some even argue that the IMF has contributed more to the generation than the amelioration of crises.

Such concerns led to the majority of the recent commission established by the US Congress to study the international financial institutions to make the radical recommendations that all current IMF lending programs be terminated and a new LOLR be created in their place.[11] Ex post conditionality would be entirely eliminated and replaced with ex ante criteria for gaining access to ILOLR lending. While the conditions of access to IMF lending would be much tougher under the Meltzer Majority proposal, and the cost of borrowing higher, the size of permissible Fund loans would be much larger. This is in line with the classic rule for an LOLR proposed by Walter Bagehot: lend freely but at a high rate and only to those with good collateral.[12] In the Meltzer Majority proposal the ex ante conditions play the role for countries that Bagehot's good collateral played for lending to the private sector.

This recommendation drew strong dissents from a minority of the commission members. Such dissent stood in stark contrast to the unanimity on most of the recommendations concerning the IMF. The Meltzer Majority was strongly criticized by the Clinton Administration's Treasury and many international monetary experts for the stringency of its ex ante conditions, for abolishing ex post conditionality, and for requiring very rapid repayment. Some have also criticized it for increasing the potential size of IMF programs rather than reducing them as proposed by the Report of the Task Force for the Council of Foreign Relations (1999a, 1999b).

Kumar *et al.* (2000) emphasize that countries that do not prequalify for the CCL or ILOLR are likely to face a shorter maturity structure of their debt. As a number of recent papers stress (see also, Jeanne (2000b); Fratianni and Pattison (2001)), shorter-term debt provides more discipline but also increases the risk of currency runs. What is unclear is whether the creation of prequalification conditions met by some countries would as a consequence further shorten the debt maturity of the non qualifiers. If so, this might be considered a negative externality. If this increased penalty for poor policies induced substantial increases in good policy effort by the non qualifiers this 'tax" could have net positive effects. Unfortunately there is little evidence to date to give us reason to hope that this type of discipline effect will be large (see Willett (2000b)).

As we will discuss below, some of the specific criticisms of the Meltzer

Commission Majority have considerable merit, but surely the report is right, that with the growth in international financial integration the IMF needs to develop a better capacity to operate as a quasi ILOLR.[13] The question is how can this best be done? This is not to say that for most currency crises ILOLR-type lending would be desirable. As Eichengreen (2002a) points out "most observers are of the view that the majority of crises reflect problems with fundamentals, not investor panic"(xv). Even without panic, however, risk averse behavior can generate sudden reversals in capital flows. While seldom unjustified, such behavior can take on a self-fulfilling character and make the punishment much worse than the crime.

Where the IMF is convinced that the market is overreacting, there is a case for ILOLR-type lending. But in a world of substantial capital mobility, the size of the loan may have to be quite substantial in order to calm markets. This is especially true since the credibility of IMF programs has been called into question. Politically it is easiest for the Fund to make limited loans to many countries. But we have massive evidence that this strategy has serious flaws. The Fund lends to many countries when it should not, but sometimes does not lend enough in the cases where it should lend. The huge magnitude of over-shooting of exchange rates during the Asian crisis is one of the best examples. As capital mobility grows, this problem is heightened.

This is where the Meltzer Commission Report comes in. If we pay attention to the logic, rather than the details of the Commission Majority's recommendations, we can see a strong case for creating a new IMF facility that plays a quasi lender of last function in an effective manner.

4 The Meltzer ex ante conditions

The Meltzer Commission Majority argues that access to the facility should be made conditional on ex ante rather than ex post conditions. While there is much to be said for this approach, the specific recommendations of the Meltzer Commission Majority for preconditions were both too narrow (focusing primarily on financial considerations) and too stringent to enjoy widespread support. Even if one agreed that they were optimal on technical grounds, there is no way that the Fund could credibly commit to lending only under such circumstances. And what is badly needed is to increase IMF credibility, not to saddle it with rules that its major shareholders would never let it enforce.

The Meltzer Commission Majority recommended that to be eligible to borrow from the IMF "a member should meet minimum prudential standards"(IFIAC 2000: 44). This principle is relatively uncontroversial, as are some of the specific recommendations for requirements such as that commercial banks be adequately capitalized, that the maturity structure of outstanding sovereign and guaranteed debt and off-balance-sheet liabilities be published in a timely manner, and that the IMF establish a fiscal requirement to assure that Fund resources are not used to finance irresponsible budget policies."More controversial was the proposed requirement that countries must allow freedom of entry and operation for foreign financial institutions. Many who would agree with this as good policy advice would also question whether it is so essential that such an invasion of traditional national sovereignty is justified.[14]

The dissenting statement by C. Fred Bergsten and others argued that in addition to being unduly stringent in some areas the prequalification criteria are insufficient because they ignore the macroeconomic stance of a country. To this I would add the now widely recommended requirement that loans be prohibited to countries with substantially overvalued pegged exchange rates. A majority of the Commission was critical of pegged rates and recommended that "countries should choose firmly-fixed rates or fluctuating rates"(IFIAC 2000: 49) but these are not included as a precondition for IMF lending.[15] I would argue, however, that it should be one of the most important preconditions.

Conceptually, there is a case for lending to a pegged rate country that is subject to a pure liquidity crisis.[16] There is a substantial moral hazard problem, however, that national officials will argue that outflows due to more fundamental causes are instead due to unjustified speculation or liquidity fears. The track record of IMF lending to countries to help save their pegs is not good at all. Such programs often merely temporarily extend the life of the peg. Argentina, Brazil, Russia, and Turkey are all recent examples.

Ideally the Fund would develop a set of preconditions that would be clearly understood by all. It would be highly preferable to have good rules rather than discretion to determine access to Fund lending, as this would create a less uncertain environment and help protect the IMF from political pressures. However, it is likely to prove difficult in practice to develop a good enough set of objective rules. While the attempt to do this should receive priority attention from the official community and academic researchers it will likely prove impossible to avoid some degree of discretion. The same is likely true for the development of guidelines for private sector involvement in the burden-sharing associated with financial crisis. In both cases, however, the objective should be to make whatever ambiguities remain constructive rather than destructive.

Note that what is called for is to create stable expectations about access that would allow countries to have a pretty good idea of whether they would be judged eligible or not. This would avoid a serious problem involved with the CCL's formal prequalification. The problem is how to deal with a prequalified country that backslides. With clear ex ante conditions the country would just fall out of eligibility. With prequalification, however, the country would have to be decertified of formal prequalification contained in the provisions for the as yet unused CCL. In a purely technocratic public interest world this would not be a major problem, but in the real world of bureaucratic incentives and political pressures, decertification of a country that had slipped backwards in its policies would be extremely difficult.[17] At a time when its credibility has come into question, this is not a burden that should be placed on the IMF.

4.1 Moral hazard issues

Jeanne (2000b) nicely puts one of the key dilemmas of the IMF, "The lender of last resort solves the coordination failure that makes debt runs possible because it is a large lender. Precisely because it is a large lender, however, the Fund[18] is also unable to discipline the government to implement the reform" (20). Of course moving from Jeanne's model to a broader (albeit less rigorous) view of the world, the IMF's size does not make it impossible for it to discipline borrowers, only difficult. This difficulty will almost certainly be greater, the more important is the country in question (for economic or political reasons) and the more likely is a crisis in that country to spread to others.

In part for the latter reason, the IMF is likely to have less effective leverage over the enforcement of policy conditionality in the middle of a crisis than during its aftermath. While a crisis situation increases the costs to both the government and the IMF of failing to reach an agreement on a lending program, it is harder for the IMF to say no to a country that promises policies that the IMF thinks are unlikely to be implemented, than it is for the country to make such promises. This suggests that it would be desirable for the IMF to partially tie its hands during crises by relying primarily on ex ante conditions for making crisis loans. In designing such conditions, however, attention needs to be given not just to what conditions are ideal on economic efficiency grounds under the assumption that the IMF was an optimal welfare manager completely insulated from political pressures, but also on what conditions the IMF might credibly be expected to be able to implement.[19]

This is a type of question on which it is hard to provide solid evidence, and hence the scope to base one's positive analysis on one's normative beliefs is enormous. Thus, it is quite understandable that economists do not like to pose the question in this way. However, ignoring such political economy realities does not make them go away. Nor is just telling the IMF that it should not give into political pressures a viable option. Rather a multi-pronged approach is required. Internal reforms hold at least some scope for reducing the bureaucratic incentives to be too soft. More difficult to implement will be measures to give the Fund greater insulation from short-term political pressures. We can safely conclude that while such efforts are important, they are unlikely to be completely successful. Thus, such issues need to be taken into account in the design of IMF programs.

We can improve the IMF's credibility by minimizing the extent to which it must make pressure-prone decisions such as decertifying a wayward country under the CCL. Separating Fund programs into short-term crisis and medium-term-conditionality types should allow the IMF to be much tougher in the enforcement of its traditional conditionality programs.

It is becoming more widely recognized that national government policies are the primary sources of investor and borrower moral hazards and that IMF programs contribute to moral hazard for the private sector only indirectly through increasing the ability of national governments to make good on their explicit and implicit guarantees.

A second type of moral hazard can operate directly on government policies themselves. Seldom, if ever, would a government have incentives to directly generate a crisis in order to get cheap loans. Even with sizable bailouts, the economic and political costs of crisis are generally just too great. As Meltzer (1998) points out, however, the availability of international loans that reduce the costs of crisis could well induce governments to pursue policies that ran greater risks (albeit not a certainty) of crisis.

What makes this especially likely to be a problem are the time inconsistency problems associated with many types of economic policies combined with short-time horizons of policy makers. Given certain political costs now of adopting crisis reducing policies versus the possibility of increased costs later, governments frequently decide to run the risks, especially if an election is approaching. As Kumar *et al.* (2000) point out, 'in the case of sovereigns who borrow, the moral hazard lies not so much in the incentive to gamble per se as in the failure to put in the necessary 'adjustment effort' after debt has been contracted" (5). Such time inconsistencies provide one of the major rationales for IMF conditionality programs as a source of external discipline. However, where the enforcement of conditionality is weak then it is possible for the moral hazard aspects of Fund programs to dominate their discipline effects.

Kumar *et al.* (2000) suggest that the ILOLR use conditionality as a substitute for the monitoring embodied in the short-term debt extended to the 'non-prequalified' economy" and argue that the authorities can check moral hazard with measures to elicit effort ... if the monitoring of countries via programs allows for conditioning directly on effort" (13). This helps us see the dilemma quite nicely. Ideal conditionality is clearly superior to actual market discipline. On the other hand, ideal market discipline would be superior to IMF conditionality as it has worked in practice. With both imperfect markets and an imperfect IMF, the best course of action is much more difficult to determine and must rest explicitly on political economy as well as technical economic considerations. No wonder there is such a wide range of disagreement about policy. We cannot hope that such differences in view will quickly be resolved, but we can at least begin to make progress by stressing the need for commentators to make clear their political economy as well as their economic assumptions.

In the model developed by Jeanne and Zettlemeyer (2001) "whether international bailouts create excessive moral hazard, and which policy measures best deal with this problem crucially depends on the international allocation of their final costs"(10). They present striking evidence that the fiscal costs of past crises have fallen almost entirely on domestic taxpayers, not on the international taxpayers who finance the IMF. Since the default rate on IMF loans has been low, they argue that there has been little subsidy element in IMF loans and hence little generation of moral hazard at the expense of the global taxpayer.

This conclusion is an important corrective to some of the exaggerated views that have been presented on the moral hazard costs of the IMF – for example the argument that the Mexican bailout was the primary cause of the Asian crisis.[20] However, it has the possibility to mislead. While the concept of international subsidy they advance is certainly a valid one, it is not the only possible concept. Such a "non-subsidized"interest rate could still be well below market rates that rise to temporarily high levels during a crisis. Even with a substantial penalty tax included, IMF lending rates would still be well below market rates in the middle of a banking or currency run. Such LOLR lending would thus still have a type of subsidy element even if the premium was sufficient to remove any expected costs to international taxpayers. This in itself is not bad. It is indeed implied by the efficiency enhancing potential of an LOLR. The fact remains that by lowering the costs of crisis, it can make them more likely.[21] Bagehot sensibly would have us deal with these problems in a domestic context by allowing access only to solvent entities who offer good collateral. As a number of writers have recently emphasized, the international equivalent of the solvency of sovereign countries is much more complicated.[22] It is in part to deal with the international analog of this problem that preconditions and/or ex post conditionality are called for.[23] But in this context ex post conditionality should not also be necessary to ensure repayment. The ex ante conditions for ILOLR-type lending should be set and implemented with sufficient strictness to keep this from being a problem.

Jeanne and Wyplosz (2001) make the important point that with foreign currency denominated debt a country or firm that is insolvent at one exchange rate may be solvent at another. Thus with a large depreciation that is widely believed to have overshot long-term equilibrium, one could have many "temporary"insolvencies. Jeanne and Wyplosz argue, quite convincingly I believe, that evaluations of solvency should be made at normal rather than crisis prices.[24] Implementing this approach could have problems, however. There could be considerable uncertainty about what normal prices should be. Thus, authorities could have considerable discretion. As a consequence they might be subject to strong political pressures to make overly optimistic estimates.

Note that there may be a case for ILOLR lending even to governments that are insolvent. Even where debt restructuring which amounts to partial defaults is required, illiquidity can still magnify the short-term costs of a crisis and these costs might be reduced through temporary loans. Such ILOLR lending would need to have seniority and have a high probability of repayment. It is not always understood that if seniority can be offered, then even an insolvent firm may have good collateral to offer. It is unclear whether solvency in some sense should be included as a precondition for access to an IMF ILOLR facility. This issue requires careful attention, as does the general degree of stringency of preconditions. The Meltzer Majority proposal makes them extremely stringent. The IMF's CCL facility, while not as tight, is clearly aimed at A-list countries. The problem is that most of the countries that have been hit by speculative attacks in recent groups have been at best B-list countries, i.e., ones who are in the intermediate or vulnerable zone. A contagion facility designed only to help completely innocent victims of major speculative attacks could well have no eligible customers.

Jeanne and Zettlemeyer (2001) note where the fiscal cost of the bailout is borne entirely by domestic taxpayer international bailouts could still generate excessive moral hazard but this requires a departure from the benevolent social planner paradigm"(9). Most of those who worry about moral hazard would answer precisely."It is the perceived existence of time inconsistency problems and other sources of political pressures to adopt suboptimal economic policies that provides the classic rationale for the IMF's role as a source of external discipline through its programs of policy conditionality. That the Fund has proven to be much less effective in this role than we might hope is no indication that such political biases do not exist. This suggests that we need to look well beyond concerns with repayment in assessing the design of IMF programs.

Despite their conclusion that there has been little, if any, subsidy element in IMF crises lending, Jeanne and Zettlemeyer do recognize the case for making future IMF loans contingent on the quality of domestic policies – with respect to moral hazard in the financial sector as well as for macroeconomic and exchange rate policies. They provide further support for the growing view that more emphasis needs to be put on ex ante conditionality and suggest that the amount of funds available as well as their interest cost be made contingent on a set of ex ante conditions.[25]

4.2 Standstills and private sector involvement

Of course the provision of an ILOLR is not the only way to deal with a liquidity crisis. Payments standstill and other forms of private sector involvement (PSI) are also possible.[26] Indeed many international monetary experts believe that such measures are likely to be a part of any efficient reform of the international financial architecture. Besides requiring less money for credible IMF programs, PSI would reduce investor moral hazard and to many would seem more equitable since careless or optimistic investment would not be fully bailed out.

Developments on PSI should clearly influence the size of loans from an LOLR. This is presumably a major part of the rationale for the call by the Council on Foreign Relations Task Force that IMF programs should be smaller. Progress on PSI has not been great, however.

This should not be surprising since the collective action problems involved are substantial and so is the political clout of many financial institutions that would just as soon not be involved. The recent IMF study on capital account crisis concludes ëxtensive work on private sector involvement suggests that, short of draconian measures that could jeopardize a country's market access for years to come, there is no simple way to stop the exit of capital once a crisis breaks"(Ghosh   *et al.* 2002: 61–2). Likely the most promising approach is the idea of temporary standstills. This is an element of the Sovereign Debt Restructuring Mechanism (SDRM) proposed by Anne Krueger. It is not clear, however, how broad a coverage is envisioned. If it were limited to sovereign debt alone, its usefulness for dealing with liquidity crises would be quite limited.

While not yet attracting major attention for the official community, many independent experts have expressed support for the possibility of IMF-sanctioned national standstills or for provisions for activating mandatory rollovers for short-time periods at penalty rates such as have been proposed by Buiter and Siebert (1999).[27]

A tradeoff between reducing the costs of a current crisis and increasing the probability of future crises is inevitable, but we can search for better rather than worse tradeoffs.[28] In general it will not be optimal to place weight entirely on minimizing either current costs or the chance of future crisis. Having some degree of PSI in the sense of having major financial actors bear at least some costs from crises is an essential part of finding the efficiency frontier for this trade off. Limits on the extent to which national governments promise to bailout major financial actors should thus be one of the criteria on which eligibility to borrow from the IMF is based. This should be feasible. Obtaining support for broad standstill measures will not be easy, however. In the near term we cannot expect standstills to provide an adequate substitute for an ILOLR-type facility.

4.3 Catalytic effects and the size of loans

Recognition that at present the catalytic effect of Fund programs on private sector capital flows is rather limited also has important implications for the size of IMF lending. The Fund is beginning to recognize that the conventional wisdom about the powerful catalytic effect of IMF programs needs revision, at least temporarily. This indirect route for bailing in"the private sector has not worked well during recent crises. This is documented in the Fund's study of recent capital account crisis. In most of these programs Fund staff projected a positive catalytic effect but in a majority of cases reviewed net capital outflows were recorded and in some cases the differences between projections and outcomes were enormous.[29] This was especially true of the Asian crisis where the forecast errors for Indonesia and Korea were greater than 9 percent of GDP and for Thailand exceeded 17 percent of GDP. (It is a credit to the new transparency at the IMF that these figures have been made public.) For Brazil in 1999, net capital flows remained positive and the forecast error fell to 3.5 percent of GDP.

The IMF's tough bargaining with Argentina since its crisis is consistent with the view that the top officials at the IMF and industrial country finance ministries have finally recognized the importance of worrying about the credibility of IMF programs, but full credibility cannot be earned back overnight.

The IMF requires deep pocket backing to be an effective ILOLR. There is a dilemma here. There is considerable evidence that international financial markets do not always behave with perfect efficiency and that within zones of vulnerability there is scope for self-fulfilling bank or currency runs that present a case for an ILOLR.[30] On the other hand, the IMF's track record on enforcing conditionality leaves a great deal to be desired. Thus it is quite understandable that its shareholders are likely to limit the amount of resources that they are willing to provide to the IMF. In a second best world, institutional failure limits the optimal level of resources that should be provided to the IMF to offset market failures.

There is a danger in making loans too small, however. Jeanne and Wyplosz (2001) show that in the case of twin crises problems (i.e., both banking and currency crises) with high international capital mobility international lending to finance-sterilized intervention in the foreign exchange market will be ineffective and huge amounts of lending could be required of the ILOLR. On the other hand, to the extent that the problem is disorderly markets due to temporarily high risk aversion such as is analyzed in Willett (2000b), sterilized intervention can be effective and much less funding would be needed.

While small compared with the huge funding requirements in a Jeanne–Wyplosz world, the required funding in the Willett scenario in the absence of strong catalytic effects on private capital flows, could still be quite large compared with traditional IMF programs, much less with the recommendations of Goldstein (2001) and the Council on Foreign Relations Task Force (1999a, 1999b) that the size of Fund programs be reduced.

There are definite dangers to making the size of lending too small as well as of making it too large. One can construct models in which a partial bailout is even worse than no bailout at all (see, for example, Zettelmeyer (1999)). It is certainly true that if a loan is too small to stem a crisis of confidence, then all it will do is help some agents get their money out at favorable rates. While this could be an important objective for a government presiding over a regime of crony capitalism, this would hardly be one for the IMF. Still one should not understate the potential helpfulness of limited loans if they are accompanied by stabilizing domestic policy actions. As Roubini (2000) concludes, 'while middle solutions ... may not work in theory they do appear to work in practice as recent episodes (Mexico, Korea, Brazil) seem to suggest"(16).

5 Separating the LOLR and conditionality functions

Serious consideration should be given to separating IMF funding into two components – one to deal with the short-term liquidity crisis and the other to deal with medium-term policy reforms and adjustment. It is widely agreed that Fund programs are much more effective where there is considerable national ownership of its programs.[31] One of the biggest difficulties with developing such ownership is that it takes time to consult broadly, and this is not available in the midst of a crisis.

By creating an explicit ILOLR-type facility in the IMF with only ex ante conditionality, i.e., preconditions, national governments, and the Fund would be given more time to both design and develop political support for a medium-term financing and adjustment package. This is likely to be especially important for issues of financial sector reform where concentrated interests make the political economy of reform even more difficult than in the macroeconomics and exchange rate areas. It seems likely that the existence of a short-term facility without ex post conditionality would thus increase the effectiveness of IMF conditionality for its other programs by reducing the need to reach agreement before sufficient domestic support is obtained.

Of course, it can be argued that by providing immediate short-term financing the IMF will reduce its leverage over future national policy reforms. This concern can easily be overstated, however. The ILOLR funding should carry a substantial penalty rate and, more importantly, should be of short duration. This should keep plenty of pressure on national governments to reach agreement on a medium-term program. The Meltzer Majority's emphasis on making the ILOLR funding short term is well taken.[32]

Of course, if the duration were made too short and rollovers were not allowed then the ability of the loan to calm the market could be compromised. There is a basic tradeoff. The shorter the duration and the greater the difficulty of a rollover, the greater is the pressure on the government to agree to a conditionality program but the greater also is the danger of not quelling the immediate liquidity crisis. Clearly this tradeoff needs to be given careful analysis. Charles Goodhart has suggested that this tradeoff can be improved by imposing a schedule of sharply increasing interest rates as the time before repayment lengthens.[33] The SRF in fact embodies this principle, but in a relatively mild form with the interest surcharge increasing only annually and being capped at 350 basis points.

We have observed in recent crises in emerging market countries a tendency for financial markets to take some time to return to their normal functioning. As a consequence there was a tendency for currency depreciation to frequently initially overshoot.[34] The provision of temporary financing to reduce such overshooting provides another rationale for IMF programs. It is less clear, however, whether financing for this type of problem should be done through an ex ante or an ex post conditionality facility. Here again a policy of time escalating interest rates for the ex ante facility could be helpful, with the rising interest costs giving governments an incentive to negotiate an ex post conditionality program that would carry a lower interest cost. The continuation of this market conditions period of six months or more as occurred during the Asian and Russian crises suggests a case for giving the ex ante facility a maturity longer than would be needed to deal only with outright speculative attacks.

6 Concluding remarks

Because of the combination of the growth of international financial integration and the poor track record of the IMF in enforcing its policy conditionality, the Meltzer Commission Majority were right that the traditional structure of IMF funding programs needs substantial reform. The analysis of potential reforms must go beyond technical economic issues to take into account political economy considerations as well. The latter help explain why past IMF lending policies have been much too lenient and threaten to undermine its credibility.

A substantial reorientation of the behavior of the IMF and its principal shareholders is essential for the IMF to achieve its potential. This will require both changes in attitudes and in institutional mechanisms to better align incentive structures with efficiency considerations.[35]

It is important to recognize, however, that efforts to adopt too stringent a limitation on access to IMF funds will lack credibility and hence defeat their purpose. Much of the current debate about ex ante versus ex post conditionality has been drawn too sharply, with those on each side often implicitly assuming that one type will be effective and the other will not. Basic principles of political economy suggest that neither type is likely to be fully effective and that at least to some degree the two approaches should be viewed as complements rather than substitutes.

A strong tilt toward greater emphasis on preconditions and the removal of ex post conditionality for short-term crisis lending combined with a general increase in toughness would be desirable. By giving more time to develop conditionality programs, such short-term ILOLR-type lending could help facilitate the development of greater national ownership of

IMF policy conditionality programs and give the IMF more cover to say no when insufficient domestic support for programs is forthcoming. This in turn should help the IMF to begin to regain much needed credibility for its programs and restore the traditional catalytic role of the IMF seal of approval.

It is understandable that it is hard for the IMF to say no and then be held responsible for subsequent crises. It may prove impossible for the IMF's incentive structures to be reformed sufficiently for it to perform adequately in this area, but there's a chance, and the IMF should be given the opportunity to make a try. Its recent toughness with Argentina is a hopeful sign, as is the recent emphasis on transparency and the creation of the Fund's new independent evaluation office. So is the Fund's current effort to streamline conditionality. In effect the Fund has itself become the subject of policy conditionality from its shareholders. Notice has clearly been served that if the IMF does not start to be more effective in its policy conditionality, support for increased funding over time will likely decline sharply.

Notes

* This chapter has benefited greatly from comments by, and discussions with, George Anayiotos, Andrew Berg, Graham Bird, Richard Burdekin, Peter Clark, Susan Collins, Arthur Denzau, Michele Fratianni, Charles Goodhart, Olivier Jeanne, Joseph Joyce, Ken Kletzer, Paul Masson, Allan Meltzer, and Jeromin Zettlemeyer, the students in my seminar on international money and finance and discussion at presentations at the annual meetings of the Western Economic Association, the London School of Economics Conference on Euroization, and at the Yale University Conference on the International Monetary Fund and the World Bank. An earlier version was titled Restructuring IMF Facilities to Separate Lender of Last Resort and Conditionality Programs: The Meltzer Commission Recommendations as Complements Rather than Substitutes."

1 For an excellent review of reform discussions, see Kenen (2001).

2 The issues surrounding whether the IMF can be a true ILOLR will be discussed below.

3 The SRF provides larger loans at higher interest rates and has become the facility of choice in recent crises. The CCL was developed in response to fears of contagion and was designed to protect countries with top quality policies from unjustified contagion. In effect it was a preapproved credit line but with the preapproval not absolute. This and fears that an application would be viewed by the market as a signal of looming problems have helped contribute to the failure of any countries to formally apply. For more on the current IMF facilities see Bird (forthcoming) and Kenen (2001, 2002).

4 There is some disagreement about the case of Brazil. While the defense ultimately failed, some argue that the delay generated substantially reduced contagion.

5 See for example, Killick (1996).

6 Summarizing the literature on the effectiveness of Fund conditionality Goldstein (2000) concludes "existing studies suggest that obtaining compliance with Fund conditionality has been a serious problem" and that "The com-

pliance problem has been getting more serious over time"(47). Based on the research to date, Bird (2002) suggests the evidence of the effectiveness of IMF conditionality is neither as low as the Meltzer Commission suggests nor as positive as the IMF implies. He points out that there is a basis for the IMF's rosy glasses if one looks only at effects on the balance of payments, but that the evidence suggests little, if any, systematic effect on other major variables. Such evidence absolves the IMF of the claims from the left that its programs typically harm those they are supposed to be helping; but this should be of only minor consolation. For additional reviews of the effects of IMF programs see Bird (1996, 2002), Killick *et al.* (1998), and ul Haque and Khan (2000).

Note that the full evaluation of effectiveness includes consideration not only of the extent of compliance, but also how much policies changed from what they would otherwise have been as well as what the effects of the policies were. This is in turn a function both of the degree of implementation and of the appropriateness of the policy actions agreed to in the IMF programs. Thus it is not surprising that there is a good deal of controversy about such evaluations.

7 The need for developing strong ownership, i.e., host government commitment to programs, has been stressed in recent IMF documents (see IMF 2001a, 2001b; Khan and Sharma 2001; see also Bird 1998; Bird and Willett forthcoming; Drazen 2002). The concept of ownership is of course full of ambiguities since countries are not unitary actors. Frequently IMF programs are used by some domestic actors to try to gain more political leverage over other domestic actors. How broadly ownership needs to be spread for effective implementation is a crucial question which pure economists have little competency to address. Thus there is a tremendous need for the IMF to develop more capacity for political economy analysis (see Willett (2000c; Bird and Willett forthcoming). More systematic knowledge by IMF staff of the countries in question is another important aspect.

8 See Willett (2000a). Recent work by Bird and Rowlands (2001) fails to find evidence of the commonly assumed catalytic effect of IMF programs on private capital flows but Bussière and Mulder (1999) find that during the crisis of the second half of the 1990s countries with IMF programs were much less vulnerable to contagion, suggesting a positive credibility effect from Fund programs. Mody (2003) also finds evidence of positive catalytic effects under certain circumstances. These results are consistent with the view that the IMF needs to become more selective with its proposals on IMF conditionality as a screening device (see Marchese and Thomas 1999).

9 See Willett (2002a).

10 Often after the initiation of a crisis the financial markets become somewhat indiscriminately conservative for a short period of time resulting in upward pressures on interest rates and downward pressures on stock prices. Major speculative attacks have tended to be much more focused, however. A number of economists have suggested that the speculative attack on Indonesia in the wake of the Thai crisis was not justified by the fundamentals. This is definitely true with respect to traditional economic fundamentals. It becomes much less clear that the speculative outflows are unjustified when financial and political considerations are included in the fundamentals. See Willett (2002b).

11 This report is widely known as the Meltzer Commission Report, after its Chairman, the distinguished economist Allan Meltzer. Its official name is the International Financial Institution Advisory Commission (2000). For reviews of this and other recent reports on international monetary reform see Bird (2000), Kenen (2001, 2002), Willett (2001b), and Williamson (2000a).

12 For a review of what Bagehot (1873) actually said and the earlier analysis by Thornton see Goodhart (1999).

13 There has been a great deal of recent literature on whether the IMF should and whether realistically it could play the role of an international lender of last resort. As Jeanne and Wyplosz (2001) emphasize, there is still considerable ambiguity associated with the notion of international LOLR. Some have argued that since it cannot create its own currency, the IMF cannot be a true LOLR. This ignores, however, the possibility of the IMF being given the authority to issue new Special Drawing Rights. And even without this the IMF could be made a lender of large, albeit not unlimited funds. Thus the Meltzer Commission refers to the role of a quasi LOLR. As is emphasized by Fischer (1999), the crisis manager role of an LOLR is also of considerable importance. For examples of the recent literature on these issues, see Calomiris (1998), Capie (1998), Capie and Wood (1999), Eichengreen (1999, 2002b), Fischer (1999), Giannini (1999), Goldstein (2001), Goodhart (1999, 2000), Goodhart and Huang (2000), Jeanne and Wyplosz (2001), Kenen (2001), Rogoff (1999), Sachs (1999), Srinivasan (1998, 2002), and the papers in Goodhart and Illing (2002).

14 For example, it is not at all clear that such a requirement would meet Feldstein's (1998) suggested criteria for appropriate IMF conditionality that includes that the conditions should be essential for the restoration of access to international financial markets. This recommendation is particularly interesting in light of the Commission's criticism of the infringements of national sovereignty implied by the broadening of IMF policy conditionality.

15 This may have been due to hasty drafting under intense time pressure for completion of the report. Allan Meltzer has indicated that he does support the inclusion of such a requirement. While it is widely agreed that with substantial capital mobility a narrow band adjustable peg is a recipe for currency crisis, it is a more open question whether systems of limited flexibility such as crawling bands are still viable. They have worked well in some cases and not in others. On these issues see Leblang and Willett (2003) and Williamson (2000b).

16 There is, of course, some question whether we ever have pure liquidity crises. Tirole (2002) argues that There is never liquidity without at least some suspicion regarding insolvency"(111).

17 In part to cope with this problem the CCL does not formally provide automatic access to pre-qualified countries. They still require approval of the Executive Board to draw funds. This was probably one of the reasons why no country has asked to be prequalified. In recent revisions to the CCL, the Fund has attempted to make this last stage less of a potential hurdle.

18 The reference here is to any ILOLR, not necessarily the IMF.

19 This point is emphasized in Eichengreen (2000).

20 For recent analysis of the extent of IMF-induced moral hazard see Dell'Ariccia *et al.* (2000) and Lane and Phillips (1999).

21 This does not necessarily connote an inefficiency. Some degree of tradeoff in this area is inevitable. In this context inefficiency from refers to from the choice of policies that fail to give the most efficient tradeoffs.

22 For example, Goldstein (2000) argues that The distinction between illiquidity and insolvency is not regarded as particularly helpful in most crisis situations since the dividing line between the two often rests on the quality of crisis management"(9).

23 For contrasting views on whether the ILOLR should follow Bagehot and lend only on good collateral see Feldstein (1998), Goldstein (2000), and Meltzer (1999).

24 This was also Bagehot's position implicitly.

25 A key issue (which lies beyond the scope of this chapter) is whether access to an ILOLR facility should be all or nothing as recommended in the Meltzer

Commission Report and adopted in the CCL or graduated as favored by the Council in Foreign Relations Task Force, which recommends three categories. Again in assessing this issue it will be important to pay attention to political economy considerations, not just technical economic analysis.

26 For recent discussions and references to other literature on private sector involvement and the restructuring of sovereign debt see Cooper (2002), Eichengreen (1999, 2000), Goldstein (2001), Kumar *et al.* (2000), Rogoff (1999), Roubini (2000), and Williamson (2000a).

  An alternative approach to the ILOLR function has been suggested by Lerrick and Meltzer (2001). They propose, consistent with the spirit of Bagehot, that the IMF and other official lenders stand ready to buy distressed debt to the private sector 'àt a cash price well below its expected restructured value."Such a 'constructive default framework"they argue would fight panic by capping the size of expected losses while avoiding problems of moral hazard. Whether there is in fact a floor price that would meet both objectives is an important question for study.

27 See, for example, Williamson (2000a).

28 Jeanne (2000a) shows that the comparative welfare effects of crisis management policies such as the use of an ILOLR, coordinating creditors, and taxation of short-term capital flows are all highly dependent on the causes of short-term foreign currency debt and the nature of shocks.

29 See Lane *et al.* (1999) and Ghosh *et al.* (2002).

30 See the analysis and references in Willett (2000b).

31 See, for example, Drazen (2002), Khan and Sharma (2001) and the references cited there.

32 I would, however, recommend allowing more rollovers than they propose.

33 In private correspondence to the author.

34 See Willett (2000b).

35 For discussion of bureaucratic and other biases that may affect IMF lending see the analysis and references in Willett (2001a, 2002a).

References

Bagehot, Walter. 1873. *Lombard Street: A Description of the Money Market.* London: The Paternoster Library.

Bird, Graham. 1996. The International Monetary Fund and Developing Countries: A Review of the Evidence and Policy Options. *International Organization* (Summer): 477–511.

Bird, Graham. 1998. The Effectiveness of Conditionality and the Political Economy of Policy Reform. *Policy Reform* 1: 89–113.

Bird, Graham. 2000. Sins of the Commission: the Meltzer Report on International Financial Institutions. *World Economies* (July–September): 17–29.

Bird, Graham. 2002. IMF Programs: Do They Work? Can They Be Made to Work Better?. *World Development* 29 (11) (November): 1849–65.

Bird, Graham. Forthcoming. Restructuring the IMF's Lending Facilities. *The World Economy.*

Bird, Graham and Dane Rowlands. 2001. Catalysts or Direct Borrowing: The Role of the IMF in Mobilizing Private Capital. *The World Economy* 24 (1): 81–98.

Bird, Graham and Thomas Willett. Forthcoming. IMF Conditionality, Implementation and the New Political Economy of Ownership. Prepared for *Comparative Economic Studies*, special issue on the IMF.

Buiter, Willem and A. Siebert. 1999. UNDROP or You Drop: A Small Contribution to the New International Financial Architecture. *International Finance* 2 (2): 227–47.

Bussiėe, Matthieu and Christian Mulder. 1999. External Vulnerability in Emerging Market Economies: How High Liquidity Can Offset Weak Fundamentals and the Effects of Contagion. IMF Working Paper WP/99/88, July.

Calomiris, Charles W. 1998. The IMF's Imprudent Role as Lender of Last Resort. *Cato Journal* 17: 275–95.

Calomiris, Charles W. 2003. Blueprints for a New Global Financial Architecture. In *International Financial Markets*, edited by Leonardo Auernheimer, pp. 259–87. Chicago: University of Chicago Press.

Capie, Forrest M. 1998. Can There Be an International Lender-of-Last-Resort?. *International Finance* 1 (2): 311–25.

Capie, Forrest M. and Geoffrey E. Wood. 1999. The IMF as an International Lender of Last Resort. *The Journal of International Banking Regulation* 1 (3) (September): 208–17.

Cooper, Richard N. 2002. Chapter 11 for Countries?. *Foreign Affairs* 81 (4) (July/August): 90–103.

Council on Foreign Relations. 1999a. The Future of the International Financial Architecture: A Council of Foreign Relations Task Force. *Foreign Affairs* 78 (6) (November/December): 169–84.

Council on Foreign Relations. 1999b. Task Force Report on *Safeguarding Prosperity in a Global Financial System: The Future International Financial Architecture*. Carla Hills and Peter Peterson, co-chairs; Morris Goldstein, Project Director. Washington, DC: Institute for International Economics.

Dell'Ariccia, Giovanni, Isabel Gǟde, and Jeromin Zettelmeyer. 2000. Moral Hazard and International Crisis Lending: A Test. Draft, International Monetary Fund, November.

Drazen, Allan. 2002. Conditionality and Ownership in IMF Lending: A Political Economy Approach. *IMF Staff Papers* 49 (Special Issue): 36–67.

Eichengreen, Barry. 1999. *Toward a New International Financial Architecture*. Washington, DC: Institute for International Economics.

Eichengreen, Barry. 2000. *Can the Moral Hazard Caused by IMF Bailouts be Reduced?* Geneva Reports on the World Economy, Special Report 1, Centre for Economic Policy Research, September.

Eichengreen, Barry. 2002a. *Financial Crises and What to Do About Them*. Oxford and New York: Oxford University Press.

Eichengreen, Barry. 2002b. What Kind of International Financial Architecture for an Integrated World Economy?: Comment. *Asian Economic Papers* 1 (1): 129–45.

Feldstein, Martin. 1998. Refocusing the IMF. *Foreign Affairs* (March/April): 20–33.

Fischer, Stanley. 1999. On the Need for an International Lender of Last Resort. *Journal of Economic Perspectives* 13: 85–104.

Fratianni, Michele and John Patterson. 2000. An Assessment of the Bank for International Settlements. International Financial Institution Advisory Commission (Meltzer Commission). Washington, DC.

Fratianni, Michele and John Patterson. 2001. International Lender of Last Resort: A Concept in Search of a Meaning. Mimeo.

Ghosh, Atish, Timothy Lane, Marianne Schulze-Ghattas, Aleš Bulí ̧ Javier Hamann, and Alex Mourmouras. 2002. *IMF-Supported Programs in Capital Account Crises*. Occasional Paper 210. Washington: International Monetary Fund.

Giannini, Curzio. 1999. Enemy of None but a Common Friend of All?. An International Perspective on the Lender-of-Last-Resort Function. Princeton Essays in International Finance, No. 214, June.

Goldstein, Morris. 2000. Strengthening the International Financial Architecture: Where Do We Stand?. Institute for International Economics Working Paper 00-8, October.

Goldstein, Morris. 2001. An Evaluation of Proposals to Reform the International Financial Architecture. Paper presented at NBER Conference on Management of Currency Crisis, March.

Goodhart, Charles A.E. 1999. Myths about the Lender of Last Resort. *International Finance* (November): 339–60.

Goodhart, Charles A.E. (ed.). 2000. *Which Lender of Last Resort for Europe.* London: Central Banking Publications Limited.

Goodhart, Charles and Haizhou Huang. 2000. A Simple Model of an International Lender of Last Resort. Working Paper 00/75, International Monetary Fund, Washington, DC.

Goodhart, Charles and Gerhard Illing (eds). 2002. *Financial Crises, Contagion, and the Lender of Last Resort.* Oxford: Oxford University Press.

International Financial Institution Advisory Commission (IFIAC). 2000. *Report of the International Financial Institution Advisory Commission.* Washington: no publisher specified; referred to as 'The Meltzer Report."

International Monetary Fund (IMF). 1999. External Evaluation of IMF Surveillance: Report of a Group of Independent Experts (John Crow, Ricardo Arriazu, and Niels Thygesen). Washington, DC: International Monetary Fund, September.

International Monetary Fund (IMF). 2001a. Conditionality in Fund-Supported Programs – Overview. Washington, DC: International Monetary Fund.

International Monetary Fund (IMF). 2001b. Conditionality in Fund-Supported Programs – Policy Issues. Washington, DC: International Monetary Fund.

Jeanne, Olivier. 2000a. Foreign Currency Debt and the Global Financial Architecture. *European Economic Review* 44: 719–27.

Jeanne, Olivier. 2000b. Foreign Currency Debt Maturing and Signaling. Mimeo, IMF.

Jeanne, Olivier and Charles Wyplosz. 2001. The International Lender of Last Resort: How Large is Large Enough?. National Bureau of Economic Research Working Paper No. 8381, July.

Jeanne, Olivier and Jeromin Zettelmeyer. 2001. International Bail-Outs, Moral Hazard, and Conditionality. *Economic Policy* 3: 409–32.

Kenen, Peter B. 2001. *The International Financial Architecture: What's New: What's Missing?.* Washington, DC: Institute for International Economics.

Kenen, Peter B. 2002. The International Financial Architecture: Old Issues and New Initiatives. *International Finance* 5 (1): 23–45.

Khan, Mohsin S. and Sunil Sharma. 2001. IMF Conditionality and Country Ownership of Programs. IMF Working Paper 01/142, International Monetary Fund, Washington, DC.

Killick, Tony. 1996. Principals, Agents, and the Limitation of BWI Conditionality. *World Economy* 19 (2): 211–29.

Killick, Tony, with Ramani Gunatilaka and Ana Marr. 1998. *Aid and the Political Economy of Policy Change.* New York: Routledge.

Kumar, Manmohan S., Paul R. Masson, and Marcus Miller. 2000. Global Financial Crisis – Institutions and Incentives. Working Paper 00/105, International Monetary Fund, Washington, DC.

Lane, Timothy and Steven Phillips. 1999. Moral Hazard in IMF Financing. IMF Working Paper WP/00/168, October.

Lane, Timothy, Marianne Schulze-Ghattas, Steven Phillips, Atish Ghosh, Javier Hamann, and Tsidi Tsikata. 1999. *IMF-Supported Programs in Indonesia, Korea, and Thailand: A Preliminary Assessment.* Occasional Paper 178. International Monetary Fund, Washington, DC.

Leblang, David and Thomas Willett. 2003. Managing the Middle in an Era of Global Capital. Presented at the 2003 Annual Meetings of the International Studies Association, Portland, Oregon.

Lerrick, Adam and Allan Meltzer. 2001. Default without disruption. *Financial Times* May 10: 17.

Marchese, Silvia and Jonathan P. Thomas. 1999. IMF Conditionality as a Screening Device. *The Economic Journal* 109: 111–25.

Meltzer, Allan H. 1998. Asian Problems and the IMF. *The Cato Journal* 17 (3): 267–74.

Meltzer, Allan H. 1999. What's Wrong with the IMF? What Would Be Better?. *Independent Review* 4 (Fall): 201–15.

Mody, A. and D. Saravia. 2003. Catalyzing Capital Flows: Do IMF-supported Programs Work as Commitment Devices? IMF Working Paper WP/03/100.

Park, Yung Chul and Yunjong Wang. 2002. What Kind of International Financial Architecture for an Integrated World Economy?. *Asian Economic Papers* 1 (1): 91–128.

Rogoff, Ken. 1999. International Institutions for Reducing Global Financial Instability. *Journal of Economic Perspectives* 13: 21–42.

Roubini, Nouriel. 2000. Bail-In, Burden-Sharing, Private Sector Involvement (PSI) in Crisis Resolution and Constructive Engagement of the Private Sector. A Primer: Evolving Definitions, Doctrine, Practice and Case Law. Mimeo, NYU.

Sachs, Jeffrey. 1999. International Lender of Last Resort. In *Rethinking the International Monetary System,* edited by Jane Little and Giovanni Oliver. Boston: Federal Reserve Bank.

Srinivasan, T.N. 1998. Strengthening the International Financial Architecture. *Asian Development Review* 16 (2): 1–17.

Srinivasan, T.N. 2002. What Kind of International Financial Architecture for an Integrated World Economy?: Comment. *Asian Economic Papers* 1 (1): 129–45.

Tirole, Jean. 2002. *Financial Crisis, Liquidity, and the International Monetary System.* Princeton: Princeton University Press.

Ul Haque, N. and M.S. Khan. 2000. Do IMF Supported Programs Work?. Presented at the Claremont-Georgetown Workshops on Improving the Credibility of IMF Programs, January. Available from the workshop website at http://spe.cgu.edu/institutes/conference/mainindex.html.

Willett, Thomas D. 2000a. Saving the IMF's Seal of Approval. In *Lessons From Recent Global Financial Crises,* edited by Joseph R. Bisignano, William C. Hunter, and George C. Kaufman, pp. 421–9. Boston: Kluwer.

Willett, Thomas D. 2000b. International Financial Markets as Sources of Crisis or Discipline: The Too Much, Too Late Hypothesis. *Princeton Essays in International Finance.* Princeton: Princeton University, International Finance Section, May.

Willett, Thomas D. 2000c. The Need for a Political Economy Capability at the IMF. Working Paper. Claremont Graduate University.

Willett, Thomas D. 2001a. Upping the Ante for Political Economy Analysis of the International Financial Institutions. *The World Economy* 24 (3) (March): 317–32.

Willett, Thomas D. 2001b. Understanding the IMF Debate. *The Independent Review* (Spring).

Willett, Thomas D. 2002a. Towards a Broader Public Choice Analysis of the International Monetary Fund. In *Organizing the World's Money*, edited by David Andrews, Randall Henning, and Louis Pauly. Ithaca: Cornell University Press.

Willett, Thomas D. 2002b. Why Is There So Much Disagreement About the IMF and Reform of the International Financial Architecture?. Prepared for the IMF Seminar on Current Developments in Monetary and Financial Law, May.

Williamson, John. 2000a. The Role of the IMF: A Guide to the Reports. Institute for International Economics Policy Brief. *Institute for International Economics* 00-5, May.

Williamson, John. 2000b. *Exchange Rate Regimes for Emerging Markets: Reviving the Intermediate Option*. Washington, DC: Institute for International Economics.

Zettelmeyer, Jeronim. 1999. On the Short-Run Effectiveness of Official Crisis Lending. Unpublished Manuscript, International Monetary Fund, December.

14 Should the IMF discontinue its long-term lending role in developing countries?

Graham Bird and Paul Mosley

1 Introduction

The IMF was set up to fulfil three roles: an adjustment role, a short-term financing role and a systemic role. With the collapse of the Bretton Woods system in the early 1970s, it largely lost its traditional systemic role of managing a pegged exchange rate international financial system. However, at the same time, it became more heavily involved in lending to developing countries and eventually to countries in transition (CIT).

From the 1970s, up until the early 1980s, the Fund's involvement was essentially with low income countries. Middle income developing countries had access to private capital and borrowed from private international banks in preference to the IMF. However, after the Third World/Latin American debt crisis arose in 1982, these better-off developing countries turned to the IMF for financial assistance. The Fund's involvement with them has continued as they periodically encounter economic and financial crises. The pattern for them has often been of relatively infrequent but relatively large loans. For poorer countries, the pattern has been rather different. For them, the Fund's involvement has often been fairly prolonged, but the size of the associated lending has represented a relatively small proportion of the Fund's overall lending capacity. Thus, towards the end of the 1990s, the Fund was lending to countries as rich as Korea and as poor as Rwanda. However, the majority of its programmes were with low income countries via its concessionary lending window – the Enhanced Structural Adjustment Facility (which was renamed the Poverty Reduction and Growth Facility in 1999) – while the majority of its lending in quantitative terms was often to the better-off developing countries. A few large loans to relatively large and better-off developing countries or emerging economies frequently dominated the Fund's portfolio of loans.

Against this background, a fairly broad consensus emerged at the end of the 1990s and the beginning of the 2000s that the Fund should withdraw from long-term lending to the poorer developing countries, should abandon the PRGF or relocate it in the World Bank, and should concentrate instead on providing short-term emergency finance to countries in temporary crisis.[1] This re-orientation, it was claimed, would recreate the role for which the Fund was originally intended and would reverse the 'mission-creep' which had seen it evolve into a quasi long-term development agency.

The essence of the argument was that IMF programmes in low income countries had been ineffective and that the World Bank or aid donors had a comparative advantage in dealing with developmental issues. As things turned out, reform moved in a rather different direction. In addition to changing its name, the PRGF incorporated some operational changes as compared with its predecessor, the ESAF. With respect to conditionality in general, the IMF embarked on a strategy of 'streamlining' which was designed, in part, to increase the degree of 'ownership' that countries felt in relation to the programmes they negotiated with the Fund.

The purpose of this chapter is to assess the alternative strategies. Would it be better for the Fund to discontinue its long-term lending role in developing countries? Has conditionality in low income countries been effective or ineffective? If ineffective, is it likely to remain so or will the reforms being pursued improve effectiveness? Would the performance of the PRGF improve if it was relocated to the World Bank? Should financial assistance to low income countries come from aid donors rather than the IMF? Have reforms to the PRGF moved in an appropriate direction and have they gone far enough?

The lay-out of the chapter is as follows. Section 2 briefly examines an analytical framework within which IMF lending to low income countries may be considered; an attempt is made here to identify, in broad terms, the factors that will influence the effectiveness of IMF-supported programmes in poor countries. Section 3 examines the empirical evidence relating to the effectiveness of IMF conditionality in general and its effectiveness in poor countries in particular, under the auspices of the ESAF and the PRGF. Section 4 evaluates the appropriate institutional location for a facility such as the PRGF and examines whether bilateral foreign aid would be superior to financial assistance via the IMF. Section 5 makes some observations about on-going institutional reform and the extent to which it may be expected to strengthen the Fund's record in poor countries. Section 6 offers a brief summary and a few concluding thoughts about the evolving global financial structure and the IMF's future role in developing countries.

2 A simple analytical framework

Countries turn to the IMF when they are in macroeconomic disequilibrium with aggregate demand exceeding aggregate supply. The manifestation of disequilibrium is usually a current account balance of payments deficit; although not all countries experiencing current account deficits will borrow from the IMF since they may have access to, and prefer to use, private loans that do not carry the cost of conditionality. From among developing countries, it will tend to be the poorer ones, which are viewed as uncreditworthy by private international capital markets, that make more frequent use of IMF resources.

Adjustment policy under the auspices of the IMF will be aimed at eliminating macroeconomic disequilibrium to an extent that means that the related current account deficit becomes sustainable. This may be shown within the context of a simple and conventional open economy macroeconomic framework in which

$$X - M = Y - (C + I + G)$$

where X is exports, M is imports, C is consumption, I is investment and G is government expenditure. Balance of payments adjustment will require raising aggregate domestic supply (Y) or reducing aggregate domestic demand $(C + I + G)$. Alternatively, it could involve changing the composition of domestic output so that a higher proportion is exported. However, except in circumstances where there is substantial excess domestic supply capacity, raising aggregate supply or changing the composition of output will tend to be a long-term process. Without adequate capital inflows, policy in the short-to-medium term is likely to have to focus on compressing some component of domestic consumption, private sector investment and government expenditure. Policies traditionally supported by the IMF have not surprisingly therefore incorporated both an expenditure-switching component, in the form of exchange rate devaluation, and an expenditure-reducing component, in the form of contractionary monetary and fiscal policy. The emphasis has been placed on managing aggregate demand.

There are problems in following this policy course of action. While reducing investment and the capital component of government expenditure may generate relatively little short-term domestic political resistance, according to most models it will have an adverse effect on economic growth. This will mean that future period domestic output will be lower than it might otherwise have been, with the implication that the future period current account balance of payments may exhibit a larger deficit. Against this, measures aimed at cutting consumption or the current component of government expenditure are likely to be politically unpopular. They may lead to greater income inequality, as welfare programmes are curtailed and subsidies removed, and therefore to social conflict. This will then create a social and political environment in which it is difficult to maintain the programme of policy reform. Moreover, the effectiveness of devaluation in strengthening the current account of the balance of payments depends on the values of key foreign trade price elasticities. These may be relatively low in poor countries, where some imports are vital to the process of development and exports are primary products which have a low short-term supply elasticity.

Given this analysis, what, in principle, would we expect to be the record of IMF programmes in developing countries? We would expect them to be negatively associated with investment and economic growth. We would also expect them to be poorly implemented because of the social and political problems they encounter. And, furthermore, we would expect them to be relatively unsuccessful in terms of creating balance of payments sustainability, with the result that poor countries would become prolonged users of IMF resources. As will be seen in the next section, this is pretty much the empirical pattern that we observe. If low income countries often encounter structural balance of payments problems, and the Fund attempts to remedy them by advocating policies that focus on depressing aggregate demand, then it follows that the programmes are unlikely to be successful according to a number of criteria.

The IMF's move into structural adjustment lending through the Structural Adjustment Facility, the Enhanced Structural Adjustment Facility and the Poverty Reduction and Growth Facility has been an attempt to eliminate this mismatch between the causes of current account deficits and the policies designed to correct them. The idea behind structural adjustment lending was to provide external financial support over a longer period of time and thereby allow adjustment to be spread out in such a way that it could accommodate supply side measures and overcome political resistance. The intention was to permit adjustment to occur without there being an adverse effect on economic growth. Has this initiative succeeded or failed?

3 The effects of IMF conditionality in developing countries

There are now a large number of empirical studies that set out to examine the effects of IMF programmes.[2] They employ different methodologies and generate somewhat different results. A fundamental problem that they all encounter is the counterfactual; it is impossible to know for sure what would have happened in the absence of an IMF programme. There will always therefore be uncertainties surrounding the extent to which what actually happened may be attributed to IMF conditionality. In a review of the cross-sectional evidence, ul Haque and Khan (1998) claim that 'on balance' IMF conditionality works. However, this judgement relies quite heavily on the apparent impact of IMF programmes on the current account of the balance of payments or the basic balance. From one point of view it would be disconcerting if IMF programmes that focus on improving competitiveness via exchange rate devaluation and depressing aggregate demand did not show a return in terms of the balance of payments.

As ul Haque and Khan acknowledge, the Fund's record in terms of other macroeconomic variables is less strong and may be adverse. Fund-backed programmes appear to have little significant effect on inflation and may have a negative effect, at least in the short term, on the rate of economic growth. Since ul Haque and Khan compiled their survey, other studies using a range of methodologies have tended to confirm the negative growth effects of IMF conditionality (Przeworski and Vreeland 2000; Hutchison 2001; Vreeland 2003), although there is an on-going and unresolved debate about the extent to which poor growth performance in the aftermath of IMF programmes can legitimately be attributed to the IMF. Barro and Lee (2001) claim that, with the appropriate use of instrumental variables to allow for the endogeneity of IMF involvement, the empirical evidence suggests that IMF conditionality has no significant impact on economic growth, whereas without their use, IMF programmes do indeed appear to be associated with a contemporary reduction in the rate of economic growth. But again, there can be legitimate debate about whether Barro and Lee have used appropriate IVs (Bird and Rowlands 2001a).

In a more recent on-going study, Baqir *et al.* (2003) assess the effects of IMF programmes relative to the targets that were established at their outset. They confirm that programmes seem to surpass expectations relating to the balance of payments and reserves but are generally disappointing in failing to achieve output and growth targets. Since many studies also find that IMF conditionality seems to be associated with a fall in the investment rate, which in turn might reasonably be seen as having adverse consequences for economic growth, it would appear that the balance of the evidence suggests that IMF conditionality will be associated with negative growth effects. Unless the expansionary impact of devaluation is fairly powerful, this empirical finding is largely consistent with the theoretical priorities outlined in the previous section.

But there is another empirical question which is of more interest to us. The studies referred to above tend to aggregate all IMF programmes together. However, structural adjustment within the context of SAFs, ESAFs and PRGFs was supposed to be different. Here, a stronger emphasis was placed on enhancing economic growth. Indeed, the very name of the PRGF emphasises its growth orientation. At the same time, much of the criticism that has been levelled at IMF conditionality by the reports of the Meltzer Commission and the Task Force of the Overseas Development Council has concentrated not on conditionality in general but rather conditionality in the context of structural adjustment lending. So what does the evidence on the effectiveness of the ESAF/PRGF tell us?

Here again there is considerable disagreement. Early internal reviews of the ESAF were generally positive (Schadler *et al.* 1993). However, outsiders criticised the methodologies used and the conclusions drawn (Killick 1995). An external review commissioned by the Fund was also critical of the design of the ESAF (Botchwey *et al.* 1998) with members of the review team going on to offer further critical assessment (Collier and Gunning 1999), arguing that the ESAF had little impact on poverty reduction and had tended to result in a tapering out of foreign aid.[3] The difficulties in assessing the track record of ESAF are nicely captured by a recent investigation that shows that, while using a modified control group to model the counterfactual, results are generated that suggest statistically significant beneficial effects of ESAF programmes on output growth and the debt/service ratio over the period 1986–91, diagnostic tests cast doubt on the reliability of the estimates (Dicks-Mireaux *et al.* 2000). Early internal reviews of the PRGF claim that it has had positive growth effects and has helped to redirect government expenditure in ways that contribute to reducing poverty (IMF 2002).

Further evidence on the effectiveness of ESAF/PRGF conditionality based on control group comparisons is presented in Tables 14.1 through 14.3. The results reported here compare the performance of a sample of countries that received ESAF/PRGF credits from the Fund in the period since the mid 1990s with a control group selected to be similar apart from their lack of Fund involvement.[4] Economic growth is found to be higher in the ESAF/PRGF group, with the difference in the sample means being significant at the 1 percent level. This confirms one of the findings in the study by Dicks-Mireaux *et al.* for the earlier period reported above. Leading on from the discussion in section 2 the Table then seeks to understand the association between ESAFs/PRGFs, inequality and political tension. It appears that countries with ESAF (PRGF) programmes have a more 'pro-poor' mix of stabilisation and expenditure policies and a significantly higher level of political stability. However, it is important to understand the causal mechanism by which these results come about, and also to learn lessons from the outliers.

A typical IMF programme involves cuts in public expenditure; historically the IMF has been concerned with the macroeconomic magnitude and impact of these cuts, and not with their composition. Their composition, however, certainly determines the incidence on different segments of the population, and thus the distribution of income; which in turn influences the level of investment and growth (Alesina and Rodrik 1994; Alesina and Perotti 1996). The longer time period for adjustment allowed by the ESAF/PRGF provides an opportunity for a government, conscious of these influences, to plan public expenditure programmes, and cuts in them, in a manner that minimises the growth costs of adjustment, and the negative impact on poor people. It also provides an opportunity and time for the communication of this logic, and for participation in public expenditure decision making at local level, in a manner, which helps build social capital and minimises the risk of political tension.

A good illustration of these opportunities being seized is Uganda, the recipient of four ESAFs between 1990 and 1999, which during a period of retrenchment and dialogue with the IMF in 1994 determined to exempt the sectors of primary health and education, agricultural research and extension, and rural roads and water from expenditure cuts because of its belief that expenditure on these sectors was likely to be especially

Table 14.1 Purchases and loans from the IMF, financial year ended 30 April 2002 (in millions of SDRs)

Member	Reserve tranche	Stand-by/credit tranche	Extended fund facility	SRF	Total purchases	PRGF loans	Total purchases and loans
Albania	–	–	–	–	–	–	5
Antigua and Barbuda							
Argentina	–	1529	–	4393	5922	–	5922
Armenia		–	–	–	–	10	10
Azerbaijan						16	16
Belarus						–	
Bolivia						19	19
Bosnia and Herzegovina		14				–	14
Brazil		1960	–	3317	5277	–	5277
Bulgaria		32	52		84	–	84
Burkina Faso						17	17
Burundi	6				6	–	6
Cambodia						17	17
Cameroon						32	32
Cape Verde						1	1
Chad						21	21
Côte d'Ivoire						59	59
Djibouti	–					4	4
Ecuador		113			113	–	
Egypt	120				120	–	120
Ethiopia						41	41
Gambia, The						7	7
Georgia						9	9
Ghana	–				–	105	105
Guinea						13	13
Honduras	–				–	16	16
Indonesia	–		585		585	–	585

Jordan	–	–	30	–	30	–	30
Kyrgyz Republic	–	–	–	–		12	12
Lao PDR	–	–	–	–		5	5
Lesotho	–	–	–	–		7	7
Madagascar	–	–	–	–		11	11
Mali	–	–	–	–		18	18
Mauritania	–	–	–	–		12	12
Mongolia	–	–	–	–		4	4
Mozambique	–	–	–	–		8	8
Niger	–	–	–	–		17	17
Pakistan	–	210	–	–	210	172	382
Papua New Guinea	–	19	–	–	19	–	19
Romania	–	52	–	–	52	–	52
Rwanda	–	–	–	–		10	10
Senegal	–	–	–	–		18	18
Sierra Leone	–	–	–	–		56	56
Tajikistan	–	–	–	–		6	6
Tanzania	–	–	–	–		40	40
Turkey	–	12819	–	3181	16000	–	16000
Ukraine, The	–	–	291	–	291	–	291
Uruguay	–	273	–	–	273	–	273
Vietnam	–	–	–	–		41	41
Yemen	–	–	–	–		69	69
Yugoslavia	–	150	–	–	150	–	150
Zambia	–	–	–	–		50	50
Total	126	17219	958	10891	29194	952	30146

Source: IMF, Annual Report 2002: table 14.11.7.

Table 14.2 Outstanding IMF credit by facility and policy, financial years ended 30 April 1992–99 (in millions of SDRs and percent)

	1993	1994	1995	1996	1997	1998	1999	2000	2001	2002
Stand-by arrangements[a]	1971	1381	13055	9645	3183	27336	14325	15706	13093	39438
Extended arrangements	1242	779	2335	8381	1193	3078	14090	6582	–9	0
ESAF (after 1999, **PRGF**) arrangements[b]	527	1170	1197	1476	911	1738	998	641	1249	1781
Total	3789	3357	16587	19684	5287	32152	29413	22929	14333	41219

Notes
a Includes outstanding credit tranche and emergency purchases.
b Includes outstanding associated loans from the Saudi Fund for Development.
c Less than $\frac{1}{2}$ of 1 per cent of total.

	1992	1993	1994	1995	1996	1997	1998	1999
	Percent of total							
Stand-by arrangements[a]	35	37	32	41	49	45	46	38
Extended arrangements	32	34	32	28	24	28	22	25
Supplemental reserve facility	–	–	–	–	–	–	13	19
Compensatory and contingency financing facility	20	15	12	8	4	3	1	4
Systemic transformation facility	–	–	9	10	9	10	7	5
Subtotal (GRA)	87	86	85	87	86	85	89	90
SAF arrangements	6	5	5	3	3	2	1	1
ESAF arrangements[b]	6	8	9	9	11	12	10	9
Trust Fund	1	1	–c	–c	–c	–c	–c	–c
Total	100	100	100	100	100	100	100	100

Source: IMF, Annual Report 2002: table 14.21.

Notes
The control group is selected to have similar income and other initial conditions to the ESAF group, except for the fact of not receiving ESAF support. For this purpose, the countries of the control sample are selected pairwise in relation to countries within the treatment sample (e.g. Ethiopia is matched with Eritrea, Uzbekistan is matched with Albania, etc.)
a This is defined as ratio of real devaluation to increase of indirect tax rates, 1994–99.
b AM = Adelman-Morris index of social capacity; Obs = Observer Human Rights Index.
c Start date of the 5 year period is 1995 or year after inception date of ESAF (if different) (a) donates data for 1995–98 only.

Table 14.3 ESAF countries and control group: fund agreements, economic performance and indicators of 'social capacity', 1995–2001

Country	Date of most recent Fund agreement and type of agreement	Mix of stabilisation instruments[a]	Social capability indicators[b] AM	Social capability indicators[b] Obs	Growth 1995–99[c]	PPE index[d] (change 1994–98)	Political stability indicator[e] Level 2000/01	Political stability indicator[e] change (1997–2001)
PRGF countries (average per capita GDP = $426)								
Uganda		6.4	-1.22	20.0	6.3	0.0022	-1.31	NA
Malawi		3.7	-1.57	13.7	6.0 (a)		0.03	-0.01
Tanzania		5.1	-1.22	22.4	1.7(a)	-0.113	-0.34	0.91
Mozambique		7.1	–	-16.2	6.1(a)		0.20	NA
Nicaragua		6.5	0.88	27.7	2.5(a)		0.31	0.65
Bolivia		4.7	-0.35	21.2	2.4(a)	0.5295	-0.61	-0.47
Albania	ESAF 11 (1995)	1.8	–	-38.6	5.5(a)		-0.6	0.4
Vietnam	ESAF 11 (1994)	7.2	-0.49	29.7	5.7		0.44	-0.21
Sri Lanka	ESAF 111 (1995)	1.4	0.35		3.6		-1.63	0
Pakistan	ESAF 1 (1994)	1.3		56.5	2.2(a)		-0.39	0.26

Table 14.3 continued

Country	Date of most recent Fund agreement and type of agreement	Mix of stabilisation instruments[a]	Social capability indicators[b]		Growth 1995–99[c]	PPE index[d] (change 1994–98)	Political stability indicator[e] Level 2000/01 change (1997–2001)
			AM	Obs			
Zimbabwe		1.8	0.14	18.9	0.9	0.4787	−1.25 −0.14
Ethiopia		3.2	−0.99	12.2	3.0		−0.55 −0.69
Bangladesh		2.7		30.5			−0.57 −0.17
PRGF countries average		3.8		24.7	3.1	0.34	Change 1997–2001: −0.21
Non-PRGF countries (average per capita GDP = $497)						−0.16	Change 1997–2001: 0.11
Nepal		3.1		27.4		0.4377	
Sierra Leone		1.9		14.4			
Eritrea		0.6		26.3	2.1		
Rwanda		2.3	−0.64		–	−0.26	
Sudan		0.8		46.2	2.5		
Haiti		1.4		25.3			

Vanuatu	1.1				0.5
Tonga	0.9				−2.5(a)
Congo (Dem. Rep.)	0.4	9.1			−4.5
Congo (Rep.)	0.2	42.5			
		41.1			
Lesotho				−0.06	−0.4
Non-ESAF average	1.3	31.7			
t-stat[f]	4.23**	1.29	4.13**	2.71**	1.15

Notes and sources:

** The control group is selected to have similar income and other initial conditions to the ESAF group, except for the fact of not receiving ESAF support. For this purpose, the countries of the control sample are selected pairwise in relation to countries within the treatment sample (e.g. Ethiopia is matched with Eritrea, Moldova is matched with Albania, etc.).

a This is defined as ratio of real devaluation to increase of indirect tax rates, 1994–99; data from IMF *Government Expenditure Statistics Yearbook*.

b AM + Adelman-Morris index of social capacity (as given in Temple and Johnson (1996); Obs = Observer Human Rights Index.

c Start date of the 5-year period is 1995 or year after inception date of ESAF (if different) (a) denotes data for 1995–98 only.

d The PPE (pro-poor expenditure) index' is calculated as $((E + A + S - M)$/public expenditure), where E = primary educational expenditure, A = agricultural development expenditure (research and extension), S = other social expenditures' (housing and rural infrastructure) and M = military expenditure. This is conceived as an index of those most likely to achieve poverty impact. For further details of the construction of the index see annex 1 of Mosley *et al.* (2003). All data from IMF *Government Expenditure Statistics Yearbook*.

e Political stability indicator from World Bank Governance Indicators: http://info.worldbank.org/governance/kkz/sc_chart.asp.

f T-statistic is defined for difference between sample means and is calculated

$$\frac{X_1 - X_2}{\sqrt{\dfrac{S_1^2 + S_2^2}{(n_1 \quad n_2)}}}$$

poverty-reducing. This approach has been broadened into a national poverty strategy which has been widely acknowledged to be successful; poverty fell from 50 percent to 32 percent between 1992 and 2000, and universal primary education was achieved in 2002. In a less spectacular way Ghana, Mozambique, Tanzania and Ethiopia have been associated with a similar process in which the extended time period of ESAF/PRGF (and associated aid) resources has been consciously used to achieve a pattern of public expenditure which is more resilient to the need for occasional stabilisation. Through what we have called elsewhere the new political economy of adjustment' (Mosley 2003) the same approach of using the pattern of public expenditure to build up social capacity could be extended to other countries. As shown by the data in Table 14.1 this has been an encouragingly frequent pattern in the context of ESAF/PRGF.

However, there are also plenty of outliers which failed to grasp the opportunities offered by longer-term adjustment under the auspices of ESAF/PRGF; for example, Eritrea, Sierra Leone, Zambia and Zimbabwe. The tragedy, particularly in Zimbabwe, is that during the 1980s, the government tried to carry through a pro-poor, small-scale agriculture-first public expenditure strategy very similar to the one that has delivered some success in Uganda and Ethiopia; but it failed to preempt resentments based both on tribal and on vertical inequalities. The expenditure instrument which had failed to deliver consensus was then switched into costly military adventures, with agricultural yields as a consequence falling (Addison and Laakso 2003). This experience provides a warning that extended adjustment facilities are not remotely a sufficient condition for effective adjustment. On the other hand, there is now enough evidence to make a case that the ESAF/PRGF has been relatively effective in facilitating economic growth and in helping to build social capacity. It is through economic growth that developing countries will eventually become less reliant on the Fund (Bird 1996a), and it is by building social capacity that the scope for effective economic management may be raised on a sustainable basis. Long-term lending by the IMF may therefore be helping to create the conditions in which traditional stabilisation measures may be made more effective.

A broader political economy assessment of the ESAF/PRGF which goes beyond the conventional criteria for evaluating success, and examines the social and political environment in which economic adjustment is to be pursued, suggests that the facility has made a positive contribution. Abandoning it, and focusing on conventional short-term programmes based on managing aggregate demand could, in isolation, lead to a loss of effectiveness, not only because the economic conditions would be less conducive to its success but also because the political/social capacity to sustain the related policies would be in place to a lesser extent and could indeed be damaged by too abrupt a process of stabilisation. The argument is not that macroeconomic stability is unnecessary: clearly it is. But in many developing countries macroeconomic stabilisation may be most sustainably achieved in the kind of economic and social environment which long-term lending by the IMF may be helping to create.

But what about relocating this long-term lending function into the World Bank as the ODC Task Force and others suggest? Where there is a justification for structural adjustment, should it be the World Bank rather than the IMF that is institutionally responsible for encouraging it? Or should it be left to domestic governments supported by foreign aid donors?

4 Institutional comparative advantage: the IMF, the World Bank and aid donors

Through its involvement in structural adjustment lending in the context of the ESAF and PRGF, has the IMF encroached too much into the territory of the World Bank and aid donors? Whatever its record, would it be preferable for the Fund to withdraw in favour of the Bank and aid donors? Certainly the overlap between the IMF and the World Bank has become much greater than was envisaged when the institutions were originally established.[5] At that time, the IMF was seen as a balance of payments agency with a short-term and demand side focus. It was a monetary institution and its assistance was based on programmes. The Bank was a development agency with a long-term and supply side focus. It was a development institution and its assistance was based on projects. During the 1980s both institutions embarked on policy-based structural adjustment lending with the result that the demarcation between them became opaque. Would the World Bank perform the structural adjustment-lending role in poor countries better if the Fund withdrew from this role? The argument for such change is based on a view of institutional comparative advantage; the Bank has the expertise in the microeconomics of economic development and is stronger on the supply side.

There are a number of counter-arguments. First, the World Bank's track record on structural adjustment has been criticised in many ways, ranging from design, to implementation and effectiveness (Mosley *et al.* 1995). Even where countries are seen as pursuing appropriate policies, researchers have found this to be generally unconnected with World Bank lending (Burnside and Dollar 2000; Dollar and Svensson 1998; Collier and Dollar 1998), alleging in some cases that the effectiveness of conditionality is zero.[6] Although this judgement may be excessive, there is reason to believe that the Fund's leverage may well exceed that of the Bank's in specific areas; notably in the development of tax capacity. Dependence on aid flows blunts the incentive to build up a tax base (Moore 1998); what fragile regime, faced with the choice between financing through a tax increase or financing through reversion to a loyal aid donor, will see it as politic to choose the former? As Table 14.4 shows, PRGF countries have

Table 14.4 ESAF borrower countries and control group: IMF agreements, aid, taxation, and private investment

Country	Most recent IMF agreement: date and type	Aid flow/GNP Ratio 1997	Aid flow/GNP Change since 1990	Tax revenue/GDP Ratio	Tax revenue/GDP Change since latest IMF agreement	Private foreign Ratio	Private foreign Change since 1990
ESAF countries							
Uganda		12.8	−3.4	11.2	+4.0	2.7	+2.4
Malawi		13.7	−15.1			0.1	
Tanzania		13.9	−16.4	11.1	+0.6	2.1	+2.0
Bangladesh		2.3	−4.6			0.2	+0.1
Mozambique		29.6	−16.0			1.0	+0.5
Nicaragua		22.7	−18.3	23.9	+3.8		
Bolivia		9.2	−3	15.0	+3.2	10.2	+14.4
Albania		6.7	+6.1	16.6		1.7	+0.6
Vietnam		4.2	+0.1			7.7	+7.7
Sri Lanka		2.3	−7.0	18.5	0.0	3.7	+3.4
Pakistan		1.5	−0.5	12.9	−1.8	3.3	+3.0
Ethiopia		15.8	+4.7	11.9	+8.5	0.1	+0.4
ESAF countries average		11.2	−5.8	15.1	+2.6	3.0	+3.4
Non-ESAF countries							
Sierra Leone		16.0	+7.9			0.2	−4.5
Eritrea			+14.8			0	0
Rwanda		11.6	+18.2			0.05	
Sudan				6.7	−0.8		
Congo (Dem. Rep.)				4.9	−0.3		
Burkina Faso		12.3	+3.3			0	
Congo (Rep.)		9.9	+4.8			0	
Uzbekistan		0.5	+.02			0.05	
Vanuatu						1.4	+1.8

Western Samoa						
Haiti	11.8	+6.0	8.1	+2.4	0.1	−0.6
Nepal	8.3	−3.5			0.6	+0.4
Average, non-ESAF countries	10.0	+6.4	6.5	+0.6	0.3	−0.6
t-statistic for difference between sample means	0.34	3.75**	3.58	1.98*	2.87	4.25**

Source: IMF, *World Economic Outlook* and (for tax data) *Government Finance Statistics Yearbook*; data on timing of IMF agreements are also from IMF *Annual Report*; private investment data from World Bank, *World Development Report 1999/2000*, tables 1 and 2.1.

Notes

i Note on PPE and its significance.

ii This is not a role which the Fund has learnt with ease, and indeed in 1996 it took sustained pressure from the Bank to force the Fund to allow Mozambique to avoid cutting social expenditures. For the details of this episode, see Mosley (2001: xx).

had significantly (at the 5 percent level) greater success in building up their tax bases than a control group of non-PRGF countries. The first reason therefore for preferring the Fund to have a role in the poorest countries is that the Fund has shown more awareness of the need for long-term measures to build the tax capacity of weak states.

Second, of the two institutions, it is the Fund that is responsible for designing the macroeconomic framework within which a poverty reduction strategy will be placed. It will be within this framework that the pattern of expenditure will be determined. Since the sectoral allocation of budgets will be set at the same time as the overall budget is discussed, the question of a pro-poor expenditure pattern needs to be considered at this stage. By the time the World Bank becomes more heavily involved, expenditure patterns may already have been determined.

Third and finally, an important question when discussing the effects of involvement by the IMF and World Bank in developing countries is their effect on other capital flows. Is World Bank involvement likely to be more effective than IMF involvement in encouraging private capital markets and aid donors to lend? The available empirical evidence suggests not. There is no evidence to support the idea of a significant World Bank catalytic effect (Bird and Rowlands 2001b). Although the econometric evidence suggests that the IMF's impact is weak, managers of mutual funds and pension funds certainly report that they pay more attention and attach greater weight to IMF programmes than to those of the World Bank (Bird and Rowlands 2000). Moreover, to the extent that it exists, the catalytic effect of IMF lending seems to be strongest in terms of official flows. Indeed it has been in the context of ESAF that this form of catalysis has been most significant (Bird and Rowlands 2002a); a finding that is inconsistent with the idea that the IMF drives aid out at precisely the time that it is needed. The data in Table 14.4 also suggest that through the ESAF/PRGF the IMF has exhibited some success in attracting private foreign investment.

This assessment overall would lead us to conclude that the current policy of seeking closer co-ordination and co-operation between the IMF and the World Bank in the context of the PRGF and related Poverty Reduction Strategy Papers is better than a World Bank take-over of the PRGF.

But what about relying more heavily on aid donors and less on the IMF to assist poor countries? A problem here is that aid may be used by recipients to finance fiscal deficits. There is a moral hazard issue. Recent evidence suggests that aid is effective when combined with a good policy environment (including avoiding large fiscal deficits) as well as with strong social capacity to accommodate economic reform.[7] Aid without the IMF may be less potent in improving economic performance. In any case, given evidence of a positive correlation between IMF lending and aid, there is reason to believe that without the IMF aid flows would decline further.

So where does this leave us? The stark reality is that there is no sharp dividing line between development and the balance of payments and therefore no equivalently clear delineation between the World Bank and the IMF. Developing countries often have long-term balance of payments problems and the IMF is a balance of payments institution. Overlap cannot be avoided. The above evidence gives no compelling reason to believe that phasing out the role of the IMF in long-term lending to developing countries and building up the role in the World Bank will necessarily have beneficial consequences. Relying more heavily on aid donors to provide long-term finance could be unwise given the track record of aid, especially in terms of long-term objectives such as the building up of tax capacity and could simply be unrealistic given the political economy of aid flows. Moreover, it is rather inconsistent for the Meltzer Commission to recommend a greater reliance on bi-lateral aid because of increasing political influences over IMF lending. While this could make the politics involved in international lending more overt it would almost certainly increase the degree to which financial assistance depends on politics.[8]

5 Moving forwards rather than backwards

Section 3 of this chapter claimed that there is some evidence that the PRGF has had positive effects on economic growth and has contributed to creating the social capacity necessary for economic reform. Section 4 argued that the performance of the PRGF would not be improved by relocating it to the World Bank. However, this is not to argue that there is no scope for beneficial reform in terms of the IMF's role in poor countries. We have already noted that there are cases where the PRGF has not had the degree of success that it has had elsewhere; its performance has been patchy. In addition to this, there is aggregate evidence that structural adjustment, in general, has been unsuccessful in delivering economic growth (Easterly 2003). Furthermore, concentrating on a sample of Countries in Transition and users of the ESAF/PRGF, Baqir *et al.* (2003) claim that actual growth has fallen significantly short of the target set in IMF programmes. Mussa and Savastano (1999) show that SAF/ESAF programmes exhibited a low rate of implementation as measured by the proportion of credits disbursed and a rather poorer record than stand-bys in terms of full disbursement. Finally, the Fund's Independent Evaluation Office (2002) shows that the growth in the prolonged use of IMF resources is largely associated with lending under the ESAF and PRGF. While, in one sense, prolonged use may simply reflect the fundamental and long-term nature of the problems that poor countries confront, it also reveals that ESAF and PRGF programmes have not allowed them to graduate away from the IMF. This evidence suggests that there is certainly room for improvement; indeed it is easy to see why some have concluded – erroneously in our view – that it may be sensible for the Fund to terminate its long-term lending to developing countries.

Our response is that the evidence helps to identify ways in which the

Fund's involvement in poor countries may be strengthened. Reform should move in this direction. The Fund's own internal reviews report ambivalent findings concerning the record of the PRGF and recommend ways in which it should be reformed. The overall conclusion reached is that there is scope for a more systematic application of best practices'. Gupta *et al.* (2002) summarise the recommendations as follows:

- More systematic discussion and analysis of macroeconomic frameworks and policies.
- Continued improvements in differentiating between the roles of the IMF and the World Bank.
- Further efforts on public expenditure issues.
- A clearer setting out of the PRGF's role in a country's overall poverty reduction strategy.
- Increased focus on the sources of growth.
- More extensive and effective communication.
- A routine description of related poverty and social impact analyses (PSIAs).
- Further capacity building.
- A greater recognition of the diverse circumstances of low income countries.

While it is difficult to disagree with such general statements, the problem is in making them operational. Outside critics have tended to reach rather harsher conclusions, suggesting that the reforms embedded in the PRGF have been more cosmetic than real. They claim that macroeconomics still dominates, that at heart PRGF programmes are little different from conventional IMF programmes, that wider consultation is strictly constrained and that ultimate decisions remain squarely with the IMF and, to a lesser degree, the World Bank.

Rather than becoming embroiled in all these issues we instead opt to make a limited number of observations about reforming the PRGF as the Fund's chosen modality for assisting poor countries. First, there is a wide scientific consensus surrounding macroeconomic stabilisation. Excessive fiscal deficits and monetary expansion lead to economic and often ultimately political and social problems. Rapid inflation is no friend of the poor and currency overvaluation brings with it more costs than benefits. PRGF programmes therefore need to retain a mandatory macroeconomic framework. Second, there is no equivalent consensus surrounding the causes of economic growth or the causes of poverty. While it is sensible to have a policy blueprint for dealing with these issues, maximum discretion for designing it should therefore be left in the hands of governments. This emphasis may be expected to encourage ownership and the fuller implementation of reform. However, governments need to be held to account for the implementation of reforms. Third, there is likely to be a short-term trade-off between macroeconomic stabilisation and economic growth as well, perhaps, as poverty reduction. This needs to be addressed by additional short-term external financing. Without it, adjustment may be starved of the necessary financial support and prove unsuccessful. Extra external finance will allow countries to stay within a given macroeconomic framework without having to make the economic sacrifices that would otherwise be involved and that might be unsustainable politically. Additional external finance is most unlikely to come from private capital markets and therefore needs to be supplied either by the IMF or by bilateral aid donors. The amounts of finance involved would be small relative to the overall lending capacity of the Fund and could be achieved either by expanding the existing financial arrangements underpinning the PRGF or by making additional allocations of SDRs to countries that agree to implement PRGF programmes.[9] It is important that the Fund pays as much attention to generating adequate capital inflows as it does to designing programmes of economic reform. Indeed the two will tend to stand or fall together.[10]

6 Concluding remarks

In reforming the global financial architecture an important issue is to examine the roles of the principal international financial institutions. A consensus seemed to emerge at the end of the twentieth century that the IMF had become too heavily involved in long-term tending to developing countries and that it was ill-equipped to undertake this role.[11] While the Fund was seeking to make its concessionary long-term lending facility – the Poverty Reduction and Growth Facility – more effective, critics argued that the PRGF should be abandoned altogether or be relocated within the World Bank.

In this chapter we reach a different conclusion. The heavy involvement of the IMF in poor countries reflects the fact that they need assistance from the Fund. Moreover, we present evidence to suggest that the PRGF and its predecessor, the Enhanced Structural Adjustment Facility, has already delivered some success in important areas, promoting pro-poor government expenditure, expanding taxable capacity and helping to create an economic and political environment in which conventional stabilisation measures stand a better chance of working.

This is not to argue that reform is unnecessary. Success is far from universal and there is also evidence that shows the weaknesses of the Fund's involvement in poor countries. However, rather than discontinuing the Fund's lending role, we suggest ways in which the PRGF could be made more effective. At the same time, it is important not to expect too much. Poor countries wrestle with a complex range of economic, social and political problems and to expect the IMF to rapidly overcome all of them is to have unrealistic expectations. The more reasonable test is to see whether the Fund is making a positive contribution. While it has certainly not perfected its role in poor countries, there are enough positive signs to suggest that the Fund's current attempts to strengthen its contribution to economic development should be supported rather than abandoned. These attempts do not require the Fund to step outside its traditional areas of competence in terms of the design of conditionality; it is appropriate that countries should be encouraged to play the principal role in designing their own strategies for encouraging economic growth and poverty reduction. In this context, the Fund's role should be in helping to finance economic reform and in providing incentives for governments to implement the programmes that they have played a pivotal role in designing. An implication is that the Fund may need to expand rather than contract its long-term lending to poor countries.

In terms of the institutional division of labour, we argue that there is little reason to believe that the World Bank or aid donors would be more effective in poor countries without the involvement of the Fund. Indeed, more strongly than this, the positive contribution that the Fund makes would be lost. The less clear demarcation between the Fund and the Bank in poor countries that now exists reflects the nature of the problems that are encountered. This implies that mutual involvement and closer co-ordination is what is required. Under the Poverty Reduction Strategy Papers initiative this is what is being sought. While the jury may still be out in terms of whether appropriate co-ordination between the institutions will actually be achieved, it would seem premature to conclude that it will not be and that the World Bank and aid donors should take over all responsibility for long-term lending to poor countries.

Notes

1 This view found expression in a report by the International Financial Institution Advisory Commission (the Meltzer Commission) established by the US Congress (United States 2000), but it was also advocated by task forces' sponsored by the Council on Foreign Relations (CFR 1999) and the Overseas Development Council (2000). Similar views have been expressed by influential economists such as Laurence Summers (1999) and Joseph Stiglitz (2003).
2 Some of the most cited ones include Conway (1994) and Killick (1995). ul Haque and Khan (1998) provide a reasonably comprehensive survey of the empirical studies available at the time, although their judgement on whether Fund-supported programmes work can be questioned (Bird 2001).
3 Collier and Gunning (1999) criticise the ESAF because of what they see as its flawed design'. They claim that ESAF programmes have sometimes had adverse consequences for the poor either directly through reducing incomes or indirectly through reductions in social provision'. However, their principal criticism relates to the sequencing of reform rather than the content. Too much early attention has been paid to financial liberalisation so they claim. They also argue that ESAF conditionality has transferred sovereignty away from governments in a dysfunctional' way and that inadvertently ESAF programmes have resulted in a misallocation of aid. ESAF support, so they claim,

has tended to go to countries with poor policies where it is unlikely to reduce poverty. Countries complying with ESAF conditionality will tend to find aid tapering out.

4 Details relating to the control group are available from the authors. Again it may be worth emphasising that control group comparisons are only one, albeit imperfect, way of constructing a counter factual. Clearly it is impossible to select countries that are identical in all respects other than the involvement of the IMF. Thus it remains scientifically unsound to claim that differences in performance can be unambiguously attributed to IMF involvement. However, the difficulty is that there is no way of perfectly capturing the counterfactual; other methodologies encounter their own problems. By exercising care in choosing the control group and by interpreting the results as merely indicative rather than definitive, our intention is to provide at least some empirical evidence pertaining to the track record of the ESAF.

5 For a discussion of the increasing overlap and a consideration of possible organisational structures see Bird (1994).

6 Perhaps for this reason while the IMF retains confidence in conditionality as a modus operandi, the World Bank, in contrast, no longer does. Having depended on conditionality throughout the 1980s and most of the 1990s as its main instrument for increasing the effectiveness of policy in developing countries, by its 2000 *World Development Report* it was writing:

> studies in the 1990s showed little systematic relationship between conditionality and policy changes, though case studies do find positive effects under some conditions, especially where conditionality supports the hand of reforming groups. The dynamics between aid donors and recipients explain *why conditionality fails* (our emphasis). Recipients do not see the conditions as binding, and most donors are reluctant to stop giving aid when conditions are not met. As a result, compliance with conditions tends to be low, while the release rate of loan tranches tends to be high. Thus aid has often continued to flow despite the continuation of bad policies.
>
> (World Bank 2000: 193)

7 The literature on aid effectiveness is very large. Burnside and Dollar (1997) provide evidence to suggest that aid when combined with a good policy environment is effective, although additional research suggests that this environment does not depend on World Bank structural adjustment. More recently Tarp and Hansen (1999, 2002) have cast doubt on the view that aid only works where policies are 'good'. Their key result establishes a link between aid effectiveness and not the conventional index of good policy, but rather the Adelman-Morris index of social capacity. This provides further empirical support for the argument that the building up of social capacity, which may be assisted by the ESAF and PRGF, according to the results reported in the text, is important for the long-term economic success of developing countries. Foreign aid alone, however, clearly does not guarantee it. Aid flows are generally inversely correlated with tax effort. Poor countries can become trapped in a vicious circle in which aid dependence is both the consequence and the continuing cause of an inability to build up a democratic, accountable political system (Moore 1998).

8 For a fuller discussion of the extent to which IMF lending is influenced by political and institutional variables as well as economic ones see Bird and Rowlands (2001b, 2002b).

9 Bird (2003) provides a more detailed discussion of these reform proposals. See also Mosley *et al.* (2003).

10 In this chapter we have avoided a detailed discussion of IMF conditionality, the theory behind it and the ways in which it might usefully be reformed. Bird (1996b) provides an overview of issues surrounding conditionality in the context of developing countries and discusses some proposals for reform. Mosley (1987) provides an early analysis of conditionality in the context of a bargaining model and goes on to develop a simple theoretical framework within which the theory underlying conditionality may be conceptualised (Mosley 1992). Analyses of the effectiveness of conditionality which emphasise the degree of commitment to policy reform and the idea of ôwnership' include Bird (1998) and Killick (1997). In similar vein Collier *et al.* (1997) offer a wide-ranging critique of conditionality. It should be underlined that to argue that the IMF should continue to play a role in developing countries is not to endorse the status quo but rather to argue that more may be achieved by evolutionary reform along the lines that have been seen over recent years than by radical change.

11 As noted in the introduction, richer developing countries place time variant claims on the IMF's resources as their creditworthiness with private capital markets comes and goes. When it ǵoes' the IMF becomes involved in emergency lending in the context of currency crises. Given the Asian crisis in 1997/98, it is unsurprising that this aspect of IMF activity received most attention and is certainly the focus of the Meltzer Commission. It is in the context of these crises that much has been made of the moral hazard associated with IMF lending which is not an issue for poor countries that do not in general have access to private capital markets. Although in quantitative terms programmes with emerging economies dominate Fund lending they represent only a very small proportion of its activity in terms of the number of programmes. A case may be made that lending to these richer countries has been excessive and loans could be better provided by other agencies (Bird and Rajan 2002) and that the Fund should concentrate on encouraging private capital markets to lend to these countries, bailing in rather than bailing out private lenders. (For a discussion of these issues see, for example, Eichengreen 1999; Bird 1999.) For the poorest countries of the world the IMF needs to substitute for private capital and it is to these countries that the analysis in this chapter relates.

References

Addison, Tony and Lisa Laakso. 2003. The Political Economy of Zimbabwe's Descent into Conflict. *Journal of International Development* 15 (4): 457–71.

Alesina, Alberto and Dani Rodrik. 1994. Distributive Politics and Economic Growth. *Quarterly Journal of Economics* (May): 465–90.

Alesina, Alberto and Roberto Perotti. 1996. Income Distribution, Political Instability, and Investment. *European Economic Review* 40: 1203–28.

Baqir, Reza, Rodney Ramcharan and Ratna Sahay. 2003. IMF Program Design and Growth: What is the Link?. Mimeo.

Barro, Robert J. and Jong-Wha Lee. 2001. IMF Programs: Who is Chosen and What Are the Effects?. Paper presented to 2nd IMF Research Conference.

Bird, Graham. 1994. Changing Partners: Perspectives and Policies of the Bretton Woods Institutions. *Third World Quarterly* 15 (3): 483–503.

Bird, Graham. 1996a. Borrowing from the IMF: The Policy Implications of Recent Empirical Research. *World Development* 24 (11): 1753–60.

Bird, Graham. 1996b. The IMF and Developing Countries: A Review of the Evidence and Policy Options. *International Organisation* 50 (3): 477–512.

Bird, Graham. 1998. The Effectiveness of Conditionality and the Political Economy of Policy Reform: Is It Simply a Matter of Political Will?. *Journal of Policy Reform* 1: 89–113.

Bird, Graham. 1999. Crisis Averter, Crisis Lender, Crisis Manager: The IMF in Search of a Systemic Role. *The World Economy* 22 (7): 955–75.

Bird, Graham. 2001. IMF Programmes: Do They Work, Can They Be Made to Work Better. *World Development* 29 (11): 1849–66.

Bird, Graham. 2003. Growth, Poverty and the IMF. Mimeo, Surrey Centre for International Economic Studies.

Bird, Graham and Dane Rowlands. 2000. The Catalyzing Role of Policy-based Lending by the IMF and the World Bank: Fact or Fiction?. *Journal of International Development* 12: 951–73.

Bird, Graham and Dane Rowlands. 2001a. World Bank Lending and Other Financial Flows: Is There a Connection?. *Journal of Development Studies* 37 (5): 83–103.

Bird, Graham and Dane Rowlands. 2001b. IMF Lending: How is it Affected by Economic, Political and Institutional Factors?. *Journal of Policy Reform* 4 (3): 243–70.

Bird, Graham and Dane Rowlands. 2002a. The Pattern of IMF Lending: An Analysis of Prediction Failures. *Journal of Policy Reform* 5 (3): 173–86.

Bird, Graham and Dane Rowlands. 2002b. Do IMF Programmes Have a Catalytic Effect on other International Capital Flows?. *Oxford Development Studies* 33 (3): 229–49.

Bird, Graham and Ramkishen Rajan. 2002. The Evolving Asian Financial Architecture. *Essays in International Economics*. No. 226. Princeton University.

Botchwey, Kwesi, Paul Collier, Jan Willem Gunning and Koichi Hamada. 1998. *External Evaluation of the Enhanced Structural Adjustment Facility*. Washington, DC: IMF.

Burnside, Craig and David Dollar. 1997. Aid Policies and Growth. World Bank Policy Research Working Paper No. 1777. Washington, DC: World Bank, subsequently published in *American Economic Review* 90 (4): 847–68.

Burnside, C. and D. Dollar. 2000. Aid Policies and Growth. *American Economic Review* 90: 847–68.

Collier, Paul and David Dollar. 1998. Aid Allocation and Poverty Reduction. Mimeo, World Bank.

Collier, Paul, Patrick Guillamont, Sylviane Guillamont and Jan W. Gunning. 1997. Redesigning Conditionality. *World Development* 25 (9): 1399–407.

Collier, Paul and Jan Willem Gunning. 1999. The IMF's Role in Structural Adjustment. *Economic Journal* 109 (November): F634–52.

Conway, Patrick. 1994. IMF Programmes: Participation and Impact. *Journal of Development Economics* 45: 365–91.

Council on Foreign Relations (CFR). 1999. *Safeguarding Prosperity in a Global Financial System: The Future International Financial Architecture*. Report of Independent Task Force. Washington, DC: Institute for International Economics.

Dicks-Mireaux, Louis, Mauro Mecagni and Susan Schadler. 2000. Evaluating the Effect of IMF Lending to Low-income Countries. *Journal of Development Economics* 61: 495–526.

Dollar, David and Jakob Svensson. 1998. What Explains the Success or Failure of Structural Adjustment Programmes?. World Bank Policy Research Working Paper, No. 1998. Washington, DC: World Bank.

Easterly, William. 2003. Can Foreign Aid Buy Growth?. *Journal of Economic Perspectives* 17: 23–48.

Eichengreen, Barry. 1999. *Towards a New International Financial Architecture.* Washington, DC: Institute for International Economics.

Gupta, Sanjeev, Mark Plant, Thomas Dorsey and Benedict Clements. 2002. Is the PRGF Living up to Expectations?. *Finance and Development* 39 (2): 17–20.

Hutchison, Michael M. 2001. A Cure Worse than the Disease: Currency Crises and the Output Costs of IMF Supported Stabilization Programs. Forthcoming in *Managing Currency Crises in Emerging Markets*, edited by H. Dooley and J.A. Frankel. Chicago: University of Chicago.

IMF. 2000. *Evaluation of the Poverty Reduction and Growth Facility.* Washington, DC: IMF.

Independent Evaluation Office. 2002. *Evaluation of the Prolonged Use of IMF Resources*, Vol I, Main Report and Vol II, Report of the Case Studies. Washington, DC: IMF.

Killick, Tony. 1995. Can the IMF Help Low Income Countries? Experiences with Its Structural Adjustment Facilities. *The World Economy* 18 (4) July: 603–16.

Killick, Tony. 1997. *Aid and the Political Economy of Policy Change*. London: Routledge.

Moore, Mick. 1998. Death Without Taxes: Democracy, State Capacity and Aid Dependence in the Fourth World. In *The Democratic Developmental State: Politics and Institutional Design*, edited by Mark Robinson and Gordon White. Oxford: Oxford University Press.

Mosley, Paul. 1987. Conditionality as Bargaining Process: Structural Adjustment Lending, 1980–86. *Essays in International Finance*, No. 168, Princeton University.

Mosley, Paul. 1992. A Theory of Conditionality. In *Development Finance and Policy Reform*, edited by P. Mosley. London: St Martins Press.

Mosley, Paul. 2003. Pro-poor Politics and the Modern Political Economy of Stabilisation. Unpublished conference paper, forthcoming: *Development and Change*.

Mosley, Paul, Jane Harrigan and John Toye. 1995. *Aid and Power: The World Bank and Policy-based Lending*, 2nd edition. New York and London: Routledge.

Mosley, Paul, John Hudson and Arjan Verschoor. 2003. Aid, Poverty Reduction and the New Conditionality. Mimeo.

Mussa, Michael and Miguel Savastano. 1999. The IMF Approach to Economic Stabilization. IMF Working Paper, WP/99/104. Washington, DC: IMF.

Overseas Development Council. 2000. *Task Force Report: The Future Role of the IMF in Development.* Washington, DC: ODC.

Przeworski, Adam and James R. Vreeland. 2000. The Effect of IMF Programs on Economic Growth. *Journal of Development Economics* 62 (2): 385–421.

Schadler, S., F. Rozwadowski, S. Tiwari and D.O. Robinson. 1993. Economic Adjustment in Low Income Countries: Experience under the Enhanced Structural Adjustment Facility. Occasional Paper No. 106. Washington, DC: IMF.

Stiglitz, Joseph. 2003. *Globalisation and Its Discontents.* New York: Norton.

Summers, Laurence. 1999. Speech at London Business School. Available at www.lbs.ac.uk.news-events . . . scripts.summers.

Tarp, F. and H. Hansen. 1999. Aid Effectiveness Disputed. In *Foreign Aid and Development*, edited by F. Tarp, chapter 4. London: Routledge.

Tarp, F. and H. Hansen. 2002. Aid and Growth Regressions. *Journal of Development Economics* 64: 547–70.

ul Haque, Nadeem and Mohsin Khan. 1998. Do IMF-Supported Programmes Work? A Survey of the Cross Country Empirical Evidence. *IMF Working Paper WP/98/169*, December.

US Department of the Treasury. 2000. *Report of the International Financial Institution Advisory Commission* (Meltzer Report'). Washington, DC: US Department of the Treasury.

Vreeland, James R. 2003. *The IMF and Economic Development*. Cambridge: Cambridge University Press.

15 IFIs and IPGs

Operational implications for the World Bank[*]

Ravi Kanbur

1 Introduction

When people talk of the International Financial Institutions (IFIs), they mean the two Bretton Woods institutions, the International Monetary Fund and the World Bank. Of course, strictly speaking, any multilateral organization with financial operations is an IFI – for example, the regional multilateral banks, regional monetary authorities, some agencies of the UN that disburse funding, etc. However, in practice, by IFIs is meant the two global IFIs – the Fund and the Bank. In recent years there has been growing discussion of the role of these institutions in the provision of International Public Goods (IPGs). An aid-fatigued public in the rich North, beset by its own internal budgetary problems (for example, the looming social security crisis of an aging population) and convinced by tales of waste and corruption in aid flows, has grown weary and wary of conventional country-specific development assistance. In contrast, the notion of IPGs seems attractive to Northern publics – at least their representatives have adopted the IPG refrain in international fora.[1]

But what exactly is an IPG? Given the "aura" that the term seems to have developed, there is clearly an incentive to justify any activity by any agency as an IPG, and aid agencies have not been shy in doing this. At its most general level, development in poor countries is being argued to be an IPG, and hence an argument for continuing conventional aid – disenchantment with which turned the Northern public to IPGs in the first place. On the other hand, highly specific activities like research into vaccines for tropical diseases are also being labeled as the provision of an international public good. If we are not careful, everything will be labeled an IPG, and the concept will lose not only its analytical cutting power, but also its capacity to mobilize Northern resources.

This chapter begins by carefully defining IPGs and characterizing their key dimensions (section 2). It argues that the concept is subtle and multifaceted, and that in practice there are many different types of IPGs. The mechanisms for provision of these IPGs need to be equally subtle and multifaceted. The IFIs have not been slow off the mark in claiming the mantle of "IPG providers," but the theory of IPGs provides a framework in which to evaluate the claims of the IFIs for resources in the name of IPGs. The chapter then discusses World Bank practice for specific IPGs (section 3), and considers reforms to better articulate the comparative advantage of the Bank with the requirements of IPG provision (section 4). The chapter concludes (section 5) with an outline of areas for further research and analysis.

2 IPG theory

As noted above, there is an understandable tendency to fit almost any IFI activity under the IPG umbrella – for example, financial support for vaccine research, in-house economic research on development, capacity-building for research in developing countries, collation and dissemination of research, convening international summits on global pollution, developing international trading mechanisms for national pollution permits, multicountry environmental and water preservation projects, raising money from financial markets at lower cost, disseminating and evaluating information on economic and financial conditions in individual countries, developing and monitoring of banking standards, coordinating aid flows from disparate donors, etc.

It is important at the outset to clarify terms and set up a clear framework for identifying IPGs and their key characteristics.[2] The technical definition of a pure public good is a commodity or activity whose benefits are non-rival and non-excludable. "Non-rival" means that one entity benefiting from it does not diminish the benefit to another entity. By non-excludable is meant that no entity can in fact be denied the benefit. An international public good is one where the entities in question are conceptualized as nations rather than individuals. There are two important points to be made with regard to these two criteria. First, although they help sharpen conceptualization, in most practical cases they will only be met partially. Second, while rivalry can be characterized as a property given by technology, excludability is man made.

IPGs relate very closely to spillover effects or externalities between countries, and it is worth clarifying the concept of such international externalities. Consider a collection of nation states that have jurisdictional authority and control over different policy instruments within their own boundaries. However, there are spillover effects of events and policies in one country on other countries, near and far. Civil war in one country sends refugees into nearby neighbors. Carbon dioxide emissions from one country affect all countries through their impact on global climate. Water use in one country lowers the available water supply for others who share the same water table. Infectious diseases incubated in one place spread to another. Financial contagion, as the name suggests, spreads from country to country; lack of confidence in one country's financial future may unfairly taint other countries in a peer group. Activities that mitigate negative externalities and promote positive ones then satisfy the criteria defining IPGs.

All of the above are examples of cross-border externalities, spillovers that are not mediated by competitive markets. Certain key features of these spillovers will be relevant for our discussion of IPGs and IFIs. The first feature to highlight is the spread of the spillover – what sorts of countries are involved at the two ends of the spillover? It is useful to distinguish between (i) spillovers across developing countries only and (ii) spillovers that include both developing and developed countries. The next feature to consider is the direction of the spillover – is it unidirectional or does the spillover go both ways? Characterization of this is a subtle and intricate matter, and is not independent of the particular circumstances of time and place. The standard example of a multidirectional spillover currently is air pollution, where developed and developing countries are inflicting spillovers on each other. Farm protection policies in North America and the EU, which create a surplus and depress world prices, are a unidirectional spillover from developed to developing countries. Infectious diseases are in principle multidirectional but in the specific conditions of today the issue is framed as unidirectional – poor infectious-disease control in developing countries spreading (through travel) to developed countries.

Perhaps the most famous example of a unidirectional spillover, at least as it is portrayed in much of the current discussion, is development itself. This argument is being used with increasing force by donor agencies in general, and the IFIs in particular, to justify maintenance and increase of official development assistance. But there are at least two caveats. The first is a certain unease with the "there's something in it for us" line of argument bolstering the case for development assistance to an aid-fatigued public. While recognizing that this seems to be working at the moment, at least if statements of politicians are anything to go by, it can be argued that this undermines the more solid moral basis for assistance based on a common humanity and alleviation of suffering.

The second caveat is perhaps more pertinent for the discussion in this chapter, and is in any case relevant to the critique noted above. This is that the whole argument rests on the assumption that the transfer in question actually makes the recipient better off. The theoretical literature in international economics is replete with analyses showing immiserizing transfers can paradoxically occur. Indeed, one can theoretically get a situation in which the transfer makes the donor better off and the recipient worse off – and many NGOs have argued that this is what the aid system, both bilateral and multilateral, actually does. The evidence on the efficacy of aid in promoting development is decidedly mixed and, before the IFIs and other agencies are allowed to use the "development is good for developed countries too" argument, those arguments should be scrutinized to find whether aid is actually good for development.[3]

This chapter will not elaborate further on the argument that the development and poverty reduction in poor countries is an IPG. That is, it will not deal any further with the generalized unidirectional externality that flows from lack of development in poor countries to added well-being of rich countries (and other poor countries). Rather, it will focus on more specific activities that (i) although they take place primarily in developed countries, imply a unidirectional positive externality to several developing countries simultaneously, (ii) coordinate multidirectional externalities among groups of developing countries, and (iii) benefit developed and developing countries simultaneously, the benefits in all cases being non-rival and non-excludable.

A leading example of the first type of public good is basic research – such things as tropical agriculture, or medicine, or even, some would argue, on the development process itself. Examples of the second category of public goods are regional or sub-regional level agreements on transport or water. Finally, global mechanisms to control carbon dioxide emissions, or financial contagion, are examples of the third type of public good.

In the case of multidirectional spillovers, whether between developing countries or between developed and developing countries, the central issue is coordination failure: each country ignores the negative consequences of its actions on others. All countries could be better off if they took this into account and coordinated their actions. In this case it is the coordination *mechanism* that is the IPG. Once coordination is in place, countries as a whole benefit, and it is not easy to exclude any one country from this pool of benefit (or the coordination wouldn't work in the first place). However, very many different types of coordination are possible, which determine not only the total gains but also the division of these gains. There is thus a range of possible IPGs, each with different consequences for different countries.

This last point leads to a very important consideration. Coordination mechanisms may satisfy the technical definition of an International Public Good, but it is important to analyze the distribution of benefits from the coordination – in particular, how are they divided between developing and developed countries? To the extent that the benefits are very unevenly divided against developing countries, the mechanism might not be so much an IPG as a cartel of developed countries pursuing their own interests. This distinction between an IPG and an international cartel is well worth bearing in mind when we move to a discussion of IFI practice.

The final theoretical consideration[4] follows from the principle of subsidiarity. This says that all other things being equal, the coordination mechanism must be as close as possible to the jurisdictions being coordinated. Under this rubric, there is a priori no strong argument for a *global* institution to coordinate the water rights problems of just three countries in Africa – rather, what is needed is an institution as close to the three countries as possible. Economies of scale may suggest a regional-level institution to deal with coordination issues between countries in that region – but it is unlikely that they will suggest a global-level institution, capable of tackling coordination problems across any group of countries anywhere in the world. Going against this argument is one on economies of scope: that IPG issues in a particular sector (for example, health) could best be combined under a single institution (like the WHO). In practice we may end up with a combination of regional and technical institutions to handle coordination problems within developing countries.[5] But arguments that a global institution should handle everything should be treated skeptically.

3 World Bank practice

How does the actual practice of the IFIs compare to the theory of IPGs? How much of what IFIs do can reasonably be characterized as provision of IPGs? The Bank and the Fund are of course complex entities with multifaceted operations in scores of countries and many sectors. They are also controlled primarily by the developed countries, especially by the G7. It is important to bear this political fact in mind, and also to be clear which parts of their operations are being discussed (e.g., financial versus research, country specific versus multicountry, etc.) and the criteria for evaluation. The bulk of the operations of the two institutions are country specific in nature and this is unlikely to change in the future.

In the rest of this chapter we focus on the World Bank. Of its administrative budget of around $1.4 billion in FY01, about half went directly to support country operations ("Regions").[6] If we take away the "overhead" expenditure of administration, corporate management, etc., the share of country operations is even higher. This therefore raises two questions. First, to what extent can the Bank's country specific operations take on the mantle of international public goods? Second, is there a case for a shift to more multicountry operations, and what would this entail? Under multicountry activities, research and dissemination of research (the budget headings of Development Economics and World Bank Institute) account for around $100 million of the total administrative budget. The Development Grant Facility, from which a range of global activities is funded in the form of grants, was around $150 million in FY01. "Networks" account for almost $120 million: it is not clear how much of this allocation is for multicountry activities and how much for supporting country operations, but if we allocate 1 in 8 (roughly, the ratio of research and dissemination to research, dissemination and country operations) of this to multicountry activities, we get $265 million ($100m + $150m + $15m) as the allocation of the administrative budget to this category, compared to $805 million ($700m + $105m) to country specific activities.[7]

It is important to realize that any evaluation of the Bank will stand and fall, for many years to come, on the efficacy of its country specific operations. Let us focus, however, on the non-country specific operations. We start with IPGs for small groups of developing countries and work our way up to global IPGs. What is striking is that multicountry operations across small groups of developing countries facing cross-border externalities are few and far between. To the extent that they exist, they are generally outside the normal realm of Bank instruments, relying on grants from the Bank's net income, rather than loans from IBRD or IDA. The hugely successful River Blindness project is often put forward as an example in which the Bank supplied an IPG with (in concert with other donors) a multicountry project to counter a vector-borne disease – a classic negative externality across geographically adjacent countries. The project benefited these countries in a manner that was at least partly non-rival and non-excludable.[8]

But there are at least two questions that arise, in light of the theoretical discussion in the previous section. First, does the Bank necessarily have to be involved in such IPGs? The principle of subsidiarity suggests that it should be regional institutions that should have the responsibility for these activities. Even if it can be argued that at the time of the project regional institutions in Africa were not strong enough to take over this task, and even if they are not strong enough now, should we not be aiming for a time when they will be capable of supplying such localized IPGs? Second, how, if at all, can the Bank's standard loan instruments be used in the supply of such public goods? To the extent that they cannot, this surely implies a move in the direction of more grant financing from the Bank as a whole. These questions will be taken up in the next section.

Staying with multicountry coordination, let us move to the case where the coordination required is across developing and developed countries – in other words, a truly global coordination mechanism, the supply of which would undoubtedly count as the supply of an IPG. The Bank is involved in a number of these types of exercises. The global coordination, jointly with the IMF, of debt relief for the poorest countries (the HIPC initiative) is a leading example. It is clear that even for a single debtor country with many creditors there is a major coordination problem in debt relief, since it is in the interest of every creditor to be repaid at the expense of the other creditors. Such coordination mechanisms exist for commercial debt (London club) and official bilateral debt (Paris club), but there needs to be a mechanism for coordination across these, as well as of course for multilateral debt itself. Some of the debt issues are quite intricate – for example, the Soviet era debt owed to Russia by African countries, while Russia is itself a debtor to Western nations. The case for coordination is strong, but not without questions. Should the Bank be involved at all or should this be left to the IMF? How can either the Bank (or the IMF) be a legitimate coordinator between creditors and debtors when its own debt is at stake?

A second leading example of coordination across developing and developed countries would be the Bank's work in the environment, especially air pollution. Global coordination problems on the use of the seas, on fishing disputes, etc. are dealt with by specialized agencies of the UN and various trade organizations, and the Bank does not have a major role. However, for the case of carbon dioxide emissions or ozone depletion the Bank has taken a lead role in conjunction with UN agencies such as UNDP and UNEP. The Global Environmental Facility, for example, was incubated in the Bank but it is now a separate entity, with the Bank listed as an implementing agency, through its regular country operations in countries that participate in GEF projects. This shows another aspect of practice that is of interest. Global coordination will often require country specific projects. To the extent that the Bank's country programs purposively finance such projects (for example, the Aquatic Biodiversity Conservation project in Bangladesh as a part of the overall objective of global biodiversity conservation) they are part of the supply of IPGs. But this raises yet more questions. What is the trade off between resources for such projects and resources for national development pure and simple? And is it better to use loan or grant instruments for such projects?

Consider now a non-rival, non-excludable and unidirectional positive externality from activities primarily in the developed countries, or in the IFIs, to developing countries as a whole. One example would be generalized lifting of trade barriers, or immigration restrictions against developing countries by developed ones. But the more commonly discussed examples are basic research – for example, into tropical agriculture, tropical diseases, or into the development process itself.

Rather like the River Blindness project, the work of the CGIAR (Consultative Group on International Agricultural Research) is often used by the Bank as an example of an IPG that it is instrumental in helping to supply. Despite the usual problems of an aging institution, most evaluations of CGIAR generally applaud its achievements in helping to increase agricultural yields in developing countries as a whole. Indeed they call on it to do more, in light of the slow down in yield growth that has been experienced in the last fifteen years. There is a strong argument for increased financial support of the CGIAR, subject to the usual caveats of institutional reform. By extension, there is strong argument for the Bank to increase its support, which is in the form of grants from its net income. But notice an interesting point. Whatever the Bank's initial role in getting CGIAR off the ground (it can be argued that Foundations such as Rockefeller played an even more crucial incubating role), its current contribution is essentially as a financier (through its Development Grant Facility) rather than provider of substantive input (for example, based on its country operations). This raises again a question on the link between the Bank's role as an IPG provider and its bread and butter country-specific operations.

Similar to the Bank's contribution to the CGIAR, its contribution to various proposed funds for research into diseases prevalent in developing countries satisfies the criteria for helping the supply of an IPG. Basic research that leads to an anti-malaria vaccine, for example, could benefit poor countries enormously. While this benefit will of course depend on the specifics of how the vaccine is disseminated, the output of the research itself is non-rival, and furthermore non-excludable provided the right institutional framework is in place that does not create private property rights in its findings. As is well known, the development community faces a difficult trade off between using the private sector's efficiency in pursuing research goals, and giving private property rights on the outcomes as an incentive, since the benefits would not then be non-excludable. There is the added issue that vaccines or treatments for the diseases of poor people may not be profitable enough. One way to square these various circles is the well-discussed device of the Vaccine Purchase Fund, which would act as an incentive to the private sector to do basic research on poor country diseases and then, effectively, make the findings available (at a price). From the point of view of developing countries, the Vaccine Purchase Fund is indeed an IPG, a positive unidirectional externality from the Fund to the countries as a whole.

But once again the question arises, is there anything other than the Bank's financing in the final product of the IPG? In the case of the Vaccine Purchase Fund (rather like in the case of the HIPC fund), it is clear that the Bank's "convening role" has been important, that (along with a small number of individuals and foundations) it was able to nurture the basic idea and then expand it to other partners to the point where it could become operational. This convening and incubating role will be discussed again in the next section.

As a final example of World Bank practice in the supply of IPGs, let us consider its role in producing research on the development process itself. The World Bank, in particular, projects itself as the "Knowledge Bank," and sees its role as a synthesizer of country-specific development experience for the benefit of all countries – an IPG. While the Fund does not project itself quite so aggressively in this mode, it offers the general experience of its staff in a range of countries to policy makers from specific countries, and it also has a large research department. Taking the World Bank specifically, there are two major issues of interest. First is the actual mechanism through which the vast amount of information generated by its operations is synthesized – much is made of the role of new information technology in this process. But second, there is the issue of how and in what framework the synthesis takes place.

Leaving to one side complex technical and institutional issues of managing knowledge flow, the central issue is that frameworks for understanding and interpreting information and knowledge in the development process are contested. In this context, the Bank can take an open stance of allowing a range of issues to be debated and discussed, with dissenting voices invited and given their proper place, or it can present a particular synthesis and stand behind it to the exclusion of other perspectives. In practice the outcome is somewhere in the middle, with a definite stance on some policy issues (for example capital account liberalization till a few years ago, and trade liberalization now), which reflect and are reflected in country-specific operations, but a more open stance on others (for example, on reducing gender discrimination).

Is Bank (and Fund) research an IPG? It is clearly non-rival, in the sense that once the output of the Bank's research goes on to its comprehensive website, access by one person anywhere in the world does not diminish access for another. And the Bank does a very good job at wide dissemination of its findings. It is also non-excludable in the sense that anyone who wishes to have access to the Bank's research can in principle do so. But this is a case where satisfying these technical criteria is not enough – we have to look deeper into the consequences of making this research available widely. The consequences depend upon whether the research is believed, and by whom. To the extent that there is a perception, and perception is what matters, that the research is blinkered and dedicated to showing particular results, it will not have general impact. In this context, effective mechanisms of collecting, organizing, and disseminating information through electronic means can only deepen suspicion. The recent discussion of civil society's deep reservations on the Development Gateway is a case in point.[9]

The central question is whether research in institutions like the Bank, who have to take stances and views on policy in their operations, can ever command wide enough trust to be an IPG. This in no way impugns the motives of the many fine individuals who do research in these institutions. But they do face constraints, and this is entirely to be expected in an operational organization. The point is not whether there should or should not be a research organization in an operational institution – any such institution will need a group dedicated to specific analysis and to interacting with outside analysis. The point rather is whether IFI research can claim the mantle of an IPG, and thence the aura and the resources that flow from it in the current climate favoring IPGs. My conclusion on this is a skeptical one, at least when there is a widespread perception that the research is in the service of a particular line or policy stance to the exclusion of others. This is perhaps more likely in social science research where, unlike research in the natural sciences, much of the terrain is contested and there is no uniform, unifying framework in which research and its findings can be assessed.

4 Reform to promote IPGs

Almost by definition, IPGs will tend to be undersupplied in the world. And this undersupply will often adversely affect developing countries. The World Bank is engaged in a wide variety of activities whose direct (and sometimes indirect) objective is to supply various types of IPGs. Indeed, it (and other international agencies) are using this fact to argue for continued support in a climate where conventional development assistance is out of favor. Before this argument is accepted, it is worth asking whether there are reforms that could make the Bank better at supplying IPGs. The theory of IPGs in section 2, and the review of some examples of World Bank practice in section 3, suggest some useful directions.

Let us start with the (reasonable) assumption that over the next ten to fifteen years the World Bank will essentially remain an organization the bulk of whose operations are country-specific projects and programs. As noted earlier, we do not consider here the argument, increasingly stridently made, that since development itself is an IPG, the Bank's (and other agencies') country programs should be supported as IPGs. Suffice it to say that the argument hinges on the efficacy of these country programs in promoting development, and the debate on that will continue. What is important for us here, however, is that the culture of the institution, and the bulk of its detailed knowledge and experience, is and will continue to come from its country operations. Reform of the Bank to promote the supply of IPGs will have to take this basic fact on board, and weave a pragmatic path between current reality and the ideal suggested by the theory of IPGs.

Recalling the discussion of spillovers between adjacent developing countries in section 2, a coordination mechanism requires simultaneous actions by a number of countries, and financing the cost of these actions, as well as the cost of the coordination mechanism itself, is an IPG. The fundamental disconnect between the requirements of the theory and Bank practice is that the Bank (IBRD or IDA) enters into loan agreements with *individual* countries, while what is clearly needed, if the loan route is to be pursued, are creative mechanisms whereby a number of countries can jointly be given a loan. This expansion of the scope of Bank lending is the first implication of the reasoning developed in this chapter.

To the extent that multicountry loans are difficult to develop and roll out because of structural impediments in a sovereign debt framework, this argues strongly for the development of grant instruments *as a normal part of the Bank's country operations*. There is of course a big debate about whether *all* of the Bank's operations, certainly in the poorest countries, should be on a grant basis. The practicality of financing coordination mechanisms between adjacent developing countries adds its weight to the side of the debate arguing for conversion to grant instruments. Thus greater use of grants is the second set of operational implications of an IPG focused look at the World Bank's operations.

The theoretical principle of subsidiarity states that it should ideally be regional level institutions, not a global institution like the World Bank that should be addressing cross-border spillovers between small numbers of adjacent countries. In the short term there is often a strong argument for continued or even strengthened World Bank involvement in these local level IPGs. But over the long term there should be a strengthening of regional institutions to deal with these issues, through transfer of knowledge and skills. To the extent that the World Bank's financial resources are used for this, they will be helping to supply IPGs indirectly. A similar argument can be made for strengthening sectoral organizations that are currently relatively weak but are needed on IPG issues – health and WHO is an obvious example. Thus a systematic program of strengthening of regional and specific sectoral organizations is thus the third operational implication of our reasoning.

On basic research into tropical agriculture and tropical diseases, World Bank practice and IPG theory are quite closely aligned; there are spectacular successes in the past and promising avenues being pursued currently. An expansion of financial resources into these operations is strongly suggested. However, there is scope for reform of World Bank practice from a closer examination of theory and practice. First, given that for the foreseeable future the bulk of the Bank's operations will be country specific, there should be a systematic attempt to feed the lessons of country practice into these global initiatives – this would give a substantive strategic role to the Bank over and above its financial role. The details of this need to be worked out, of course, but the key is the word "systematic" – the use of new technology to collect and collate information through to global initiatives is something at which the Bank should excel.

But the experience of the various successful global initiatives highlights a second issue. In a number of cases the Bank played a central role as a catalyst, using its convening power, and then took a less central role in discussions while perhaps maintaining its financial role intact. This "entrepreneurial role" of the Bank has been useful in the past and should be maintained and strengthened. This requires a certain amount of "blue sky thinking" to identify problems and potential solutions, and to start down the road of global consensus building on the issue. An expanded fund for pursuing such innovative ideas on IPGs, perhaps through an expanded Development Grant Facility, is thus the fourth operational implication of the arguments in this chapter.

As noted in the previous section, the Bank spends significant resources on general social science research into the development process itself, and to dissemination of the findings of this research. The Bank as a whole no doubt has a huge base of experience to report on from its country operations. A systematic and independent collation of this information would be an IPG. Reform suggests itself first of all in developing mechanisms that will enable raw information to be accessed the world over. New technology holds out some hope in this regard, and the Bank is already moving in this direction. But there is the fundamental problem referred to in the previous two sections. Social science is not like natural science. It is contested terrain to a much greater extent. Moreover, the Bank as a whole cannot possibly be viewed as an independent arbiter of social science research. It is owned by the rich countries, and it has operational policies that need to be defended. These features mean that social science research done by the Bank itself cannot fully lay claim to the mantle of an IPG. The issue is sharply seen in much of the "cross-country regression analysis" that is done at the Bank. Whatever one's views on the quality of this research, there is weak comparative advantage justification for this type of research to be done at the Bank – it does not rely on information peculiarly available to the Bank because of its country operations, nor on methods and techniques that are peculiar to the Bank. The fifth and final implication of the reasoning in this chapter is that more of the research at the Bank should be farmed out to universities and transparently independent institutions, where at least perceived independence will enhance its value as an IPG.

5 Conclusion

To summarize, the arguments in this chapter have (at least) five implications for the operations of the World Bank. First, the development of multicountry loan instruments. Second, a stronger move in the direction of grant instruments, which will mean an increased charge on net income. Third, use of grants to support build-up of key regional and sectoral organizations. Fourth, increased use of grants to support basic research initiatives, and innovative development of new IPGs, through an expansion of the Development Grant Facility. Fifth, a greater farming out of social science research to independent institutions.

This chapter has only begun the systematic and detailed investigation of international aid agencies as suppliers of IPGs. It has focused on the World Bank, but many other agencies – the IMF and various UN specialized agencies, in particular – can and should be subjected to the same scrutiny. The details of the practice will differ in each case, of course, as will the application of the theory of IPGs in each case. Such analysis will contribute to an overall sense of what resource reallocation is needed in international agencies to address undersupply of IPGs. At the same time, it will highlight overlaps and duplications in the supply of IPGs – all international agencies are claming their activities are essential as providers of IPGs, and they cannot all be right.

But the case of the World Bank itself, as the biggest aid agency of all, needs more detailed analysis than has been possible here. We have used broad budget headings to characterize country-specific operations and different types of multicountry operations that could be interpreted, or have been claimed by the Bank to be, IPGs. With the availability of more detailed budgets (more detailed than those available publicly in the Annual Reports), a more careful accounting would be possible to sort out items under country operations that should be reclassified to country-specific operations and vice versa. While this may not lead to a big change in the overall proportions, it is an exercise worth doing. A concomitant of this exercise, however, would be a much more detailed set of operational and resource reallocation implications than the general ones developed here. For example, the overall set of activities currently lumped under Networks, Development Economics, and World Bank Institute need to be examined against the criteria of IPGs. A more fine-grained conclusion on the research budget could then be reached.

There is, finally, a "big" question that we have left untouched. This is the issue of the World Bank (or the IMF) as an IPG per se. The IDA part of the Bank, for example, coordinates and acts as the channel for aid flows whose origins are not the Bank's own borrowing or its net income, but are from donor countries who have chosen to send them through this mechanism rather than through direct bilateral arrangements. It is argued that in this sense IDA provides the IPG and, it is argued by some, because of this mechanism aid flows are greater than they otherwise would be, and hence developing countries benefit as well. This is a different argument from multicountry activities that IDA funds could support, or the positive externality that country-specific use of IDA funds generates as the country in question develops and grows. Rather, it is that this mechanism for country-specific programs is better than others, better specifically than the alternative of all bilateral flows, and in providing this very mechanism the Bank provides an IPG. In the end, this may turn out to be the strongest IPG argument in favor of the World Bank.

Acknowledgment

This chapter was originally published as: Ravi Kanbur, "IFIs and IPGs: Operational Implications for the World Bank," in Ariel Buira (editor), *Challenges to the World Bank and IMF: Developing Country Perspectives*, Anthem Press, 2003. Reprinted with permission of the Anthem Press.

Notes

* This chapter was prepared as a paper for the G24 Technical Group meeting, March 1–2, 2002. The paper was also presented at the 5th Annual Conference of the Centre for the Study of Globalisation and Regionalisation, University of Warwick, March 15–17, 2002. I am grateful to participants at these meetings for their helpful comments.
1 The rising interest in the policy arena has led to an explosion of analytical work at the intersection of IPGs and development assistance: see, for example, Jayaraman and Kanbur (1999), Kanbur *et al.* (1999), Kaul *et al.* (1999), Sagasti and Bezanson (2001), Gerrard *et al.* (2001), Arce and Sandler (2002), and Ferroni and Mody (2002).
2 There are a number of studies that set out the basic theory of public goods. See for example Cornes and Sandler (1996), Sandler (1998), Kanbur *et al.* (1999).

3 There is of course a huge literature on aid effectiveness. Some recent examples include: Burnside and Dollar (2000), Tarp (2000), and Kanbur (2000).

4 There are a number of other theoretical considerations that will not be considered further in this chapter. One example is how exactly actions in different countries contribute to the public good. These issues of the technology of public good provision are dealt with, for example, in Jayaraman and Kanbur (1999), Kanbur *et al.* (1999), and Arce and Sandler (2002).

5 This is further discussed in Kanbur (2001).

6 The figures that follow are from the annual report of the World Bank (2001), Appendix 1, "World Bank Expenditures by Program Fiscal 1997–2001." The table can be downloaded from http://www.worldbank.org./annualreport/2001/pdf/appendix.pdf.

7 Of course, this is a very rough and ready order of magnitude calculation. Sometimes Development Economics and the World Bank Institute will support country operations, just as sometimes Regions will support multicountry activities. A more sophisticated analysis can be conducted with more detailed budgetary data.

8 Other initiatives like the regional Water Initiative for the Middle East and North Africa, http://lnweb18.worldbank.org/mna/mena.nsf/Sectors/MNSRE/AA7510D24BEE223C85256B58005A5026?OpenDocument, are at the stage of seminars and meetings, with "normal" project activity projected some time into the future.

9 See Wilks (2001) on the Gateway. For a discussion of the pressures on the World Bank from its major shareholder see Wade (2002).

References

Arce, M., Daniel, G. and Todd Sandler. 2002. *Regional Public Goods: Typologies, Provision, Financing and Development Assistance.* Stockholm: Almkvist and Wiksell International.

Burnside, Craig and David Dollar. 2000. "Aid, Policies and Growth. *American Economic Review.* (September): 847–68.

Cornes, Richard and Todd Sandler. 1996. *The Theory of Externalities, Public Goods and Club Goods,* 2nd Edition. Cambridge: Cambridge University Press.

Gerrard, Christopher D., Marco Ferroni and Ashoka Mody (eds). 2001. *Global Public Policies and Programs: Implications for Financing and Evaluation.* Washington, DC: The World Bank.

Jayaraman, Rajshri and Ravi Kanbur. 1999. International Public Goods and the Case for Foreign Aid. In *Global Public Goods: International Cooperation in the 21st Century,* edited by I. Kaul, I. Grunberg, and M.A. Stern, pp. 418–35. New York: Oxford University Press.

Kanbur, Ravi and Todd Sandler, with Kevin Morrison. 1999. *The Future of Development Assistance: Common Pools and International Public Goods.* Washington, DC: Johns Hopkins Press for the Overseas Development Council.

Kanbur, Ravi. 2000. Aid, Conditionality and Debt in Africa. In *Foreign Aid and Development: Lessons Learnt and Directions for the Future,* edited by Finn Tarp, pp. 409–22. London: Routledge.

Kanbur, Ravi. 2001. Cross Border Externalities, International Public Goods and Their Implications for Aid Agencies. Cornell working paper. http://aem.cornell.edu//research/researchpdf/wp0103.pdf.

Kaul, I., I. Grunberg and M.A. Stern (eds). 1999. *Global Public Goods: International Cooperation in the 21st Century.* New York: Oxford University Press.

Sagasti, Francisco and Keith Bezanson. 2001. *Financing and Providing Global Public Goods: Expectations and Prospects.* Stockholm: Fritzes Kundservice.

Sandler, Todd. 1998. Global and Regional Public Goods: A Prognosis for Collective Action. *Fiscal Studies* 19 (3): 221–47.

Tarp, Finn (ed.). 2000. *Foreign Aid and Development: Lessons Learnt and Directions for the Future.* London: Routledge.

Wade, Robert. 2002. US Hegemony and the World Bank: the Flight Over People and Ideas, *Review of International Political Economy* 9(2): 215–43.

Wilks, Alex. 2001. Development Through the Looking Glass: The World Bank in Cyberspace. Paper prepared for the 6th Oxford Conference on Education and Development, Knowledge Values and Policy, September 2001. http://www.brettonwoodsproject.org/.

World Bank. 2001. *Annual Report 2001.* http://www.worldbank.org/annualreport/2001/wbar2001.htm.

16 Ownership, Dutch Disease and the World Bank

Gustav Ranis

In this chapter I intend to briefly assess the changing role of the World Bank as a purveyor of capital, a generator of ideas, and an instrument for changing policy in aid recipient countries. While the Bank has shown a good deal of flexibility in recent years in addressing some of the issues cited below, in my view the picture presented here is still more or less accurate, even though, for effect, it may be slightly exaggerated at times. I will then proceed to recommend changes and departures from the present situation which may enhance the impact of the World Bank's actions on its proclaimed objectives in the Third World.

1 Evolving behavior of the Bank

I think there can be little doubt, even among its most severe critics, that the Bank has made a major contribution as a global storage facility of knowledge and as a reference point both with respect to data, research findings, and at least the Bank's interpretation of the developing-country experience. While the Bank can be faulted for disproportionately taking in its own intellectual linen and being guilty of a relative neglect of outside academic contributions, even its critics widely use its formidable storehouse of data, research, and policy papers accumulated over the years. While its role as a "knowledge bank," if biased in favor of an only slowly changing orthodoxy, has become more pronounced, the Bank has clearly become less important as a purveyor of capital. Private capital has increasingly dwarfed its own contributions to total flows, for example, since 1990, the World Bank's share has declined from 50 percent of the total to 5 percent today, but it should also be remembered that those private capital flows go mainly to 13 of the middle-income developing countries, even while the poorest countries, especially IDA recipients, still desperately need public capital. Partly as a consequence of becoming a relatively minor player in terms of total flows, the Bank has thus over time neither fulfilled its initially perceived critical role as a substitute for private capital (i.e., acting counter-cyclically) when private flows fail, nor acted as a catalyst in leveraging private flows by way of providing confidence or a

"Good Housekeeping Seal of Approval." Indeed, given the current reality of overall reverse net flows in many country cases, Michael Clemmons[1] finds that the World Bank may well be discouraging subsequent private flows, either due to information failure or because it has not affected the productivity of private capital in a positive direction.

But all of this very much relates to how well or poorly the Bank has functioned in terms of affecting the quality of performance in the Third World as a consequence of its provision of dollars and advice, coupled with conditionality. The Bank's catalytic effect, for better or worse, must really be located in terms of the policies it preaches, the extent to which this affects behavior in the recipient countries, and not principally in terms of the dollars provided, which can be seen mainly as a lubricant. In other words, such dollars can, of course, be helpful in easing adjustment pains, buying off vested interests, alleviating inflationary pressures, etc., but it is the conditionality accompanying such capital flows which is critical, has been most controversial, and will be the main focus of my attention here.

There seems to be general agreement, even within the Bank, that traditional conditionality, given the experience with the structural adjustment lending that has taken place over past decades, has not been very successful. The Bank's own major evaluation report in 1998 admitted to "a long legacy of failed adjustment lending where there was no domestic constituency for reform." While William Easterly[2] points out that the probability of receiving an additional structural adjustment loan did not decrease with the number of loans already received – some countries received between 20 and 30 – a number of researchers have also found no difference in performance between structural adjustment loan countries and non-structural adjustment loan countries, although there are admittedly research findings still to be found on both sides of the issue.

A number of reasons have been put forward to account for the lack of relative success of conditionality in the past. To my mind, the most important reason remains the Bank's persistent "disbursement dilemma" which, in spite of all efforts to the contrary, continues to focus attention on the *quantity* of the lending today rather than the *quality* of the results down the road. Ever since the days of McNamara when annual global and country lending targets were established at the Bank, such quantitative targets have continued to overcome all else as indicators of success. There has, of course, been an evolution of what is meant by quality, given the changing set of topics warranting priority attention at the Bank, as well as in the general development community; indeed there is hardly a new idea, from basic needs to human development to institutional reform which is not appropriated sooner or later by the Bank. But the question is how much of this evolving search for *the* key lever or levers for successful development really affects lending decisions.

In order to further clarify this point, one has to acknowledge the continued existence of two circulatory systems in operation within the Bank: one encompasses the President's office, the Bank's research departments, and sometimes even the chief economist in some of the regions, and is concerned with the realm of ideas and focuses on the ever-changing subjects for emphasis, whether generated within the Bank or appropriated from outside the Bank. This system enhances the quality of policy papers, of country analyses, and of the annual World Development Reports. The other system resides in the realm of the operating departments, where the continuous flow of project and program lending commitments is what matters and where it is generally recognized that the longer-term chances for promotion and recognition are still largely tied to lending volume. Of course, lip service is paid to the intellectual flavor of the year and additional relevant indices need to be produced, but, very much in the tradition of ex post cost/benefit analysis, this is not what determines lending decisions. Instead, given these two circulatory systems, with relatively little capillary action between them, the Bank continues to suffer from a case of schizophrenia, this in spite of admittedly valiant efforts by the Wolfensohn administration to alleviate the problem.

Thus, while there is no explicit adherence to country lending levels, in spite of all protestations to the contrary, resource commitments continue to take precedence over a concern with the quality enhancement of loan or grant instruments, the accompanying conditionality, and the overall impact of the total package on borrower performance. What the Wappenhans Report found in terms of the priority of project approval over project supervision and implementation also holds for structural adjustment and program support of various types, which has become the dominant feature of World Bank lending. It is very hard to keep the juices from flowing in the direction of making loans and "getting on with it" since it is very difficult to change the culture within the Bank. It is no mean task to be able to reward loan officers for the success down the road of country programs rather than getting commitments out the door today. At a luncheon discussion last year with Mr. Wolfensohn on the issue of the Bank's internal incentive system, his response was that he recognized the problem and was appointing a committee to look into it.

As a consequence, even as the Bank is complaining about its lack of capital and as its relative importance in this dimension has shrunk considerably, dollars continue to chase programs and projects. Fast-disbursing sector and program loans continue to be most attractive to recipients; yet we observe the Bank continuing to feel the need to take the initiative and construct resource-*cum*-conditionality packages for the recipients to "ask for." Of course, at the formal level all lending has always been request-based, as recipient "ownership" is appealed to loudly and clearly in all corners. But, in fact, the Bank, directly or indirectly, usually takes the initiative, convinces the borrowing country of what it should ask for, of what it must do in the way of policy change, and what terms of conditionality it should accept. The need to lend continues to be overwhelmingly strong, a fact not lost on recipients. In fact it is no exaggeration to say that both the Bank and the recipients, having gone through this particular procedure many times in the past, already recognize full well that, while loans may be linked to conditionality, ultimately that need to lend is likely to overcome the need to ensure that the conditions have really been fully internalized. What results, at the risk of some exaggeration, is a rather time-consuming and expensive repeated ritual dance. Few tranche releases get cancelled, even if at times they may be delayed. Few countries, certainly not politically important ones, have ever had prolonged breakdowns in their lending relations with the Bank. Most importantly, conditions which have never really become part of the body politic are set aside or partially met. It is no surprise, therefore, that the lending process has become subject to mounting cynicism and fatigue, and has become increasingly unproductive in terms of delivering on its usually well-articulated development objectives.

The use of the World Bank and/or the IMF as convenient lightning rods to blame for unpopular policies, as well as to permit the reform wing of a government to convince its more recalcitrant ministers, all of which represent hoary arguments in support of the present system, has also definitely begun to wear thin. For one, the argument does not have a long half-life in a necessarily repeated game context; moreover, it is always easy and convenient for the borrower to blame the lender both for his excessive intervention in domestic affairs and subsequently for the failure of the program. Taking a more passive posture on the part of the Bank would force recipient governments to get their house as much in order as possible at the outset, including deciding on what few things the executive branch is capable of delivering and whether or not the legislative branch, if it has a voice, as well as other stakeholders, are likely to accept their responsibilities, politically as well as technically.

Another dimension of the decreased credibility in program lending associated with conditionality is that donor motives have become more suspect over time, including the exercise of political pressures, given the impact of past loans or asset negotiations, private donor country investor pressure, etc., leading to the differential treatment of recipients. Indeed, political pressure by donors through the multilateral agencies has undoubtedly increased as bilateral aid has declined and as the needed quick responses to balance of payments crises and other rescue operations have multiplied in recent years. Indeed it is sometimes argued, in terms of the principal-agency framework, that it is not the Bank as the principal and the recipient country as the agent, but private sector interests within the G7, acting as the principal, with the Bank as the agent, given the official assignment to help eliminate poverty through growth and the unofficial assignment to safeguard "under the carpet" G7 interests. The fact that some World Bank profits have gone to MIGA capital increases instead of IDA should raise eyebrows in that connection.

Also contributing to the lack of credibility of the process has been the addition of ever larger numbers of conditions, sometimes as the result of cross-conditionality with the IMF and bilateral donors, which makes it politically easy to determine that enough conditions have reasonably been complied with to continue the disbursement of tranches, as well as sufficiently frustrating to recipients, given the implied intrusiveness and lack of realism of a substantial number of requirements. Indeed, while the average number of conditions has been reduced from 60 in the 1980s to 30 in 2000, this is still a very large set in terms of countries' implementation capability. As a consequence, both parties go through the motions, but they are time-consuming and irritating motions, causing cynicism and fatigue.

It is sometimes claimed that foreign capital, like an abundance of natural resources, can have a negative influence on developing country performance via the so-called "Dutch Disease" which, in its narrow definition, focuses on the exchange rate, rendering it unduly strong and thus discouraging possible labor-intensive exports. Given the diminishing role of World Bank lending in most countries, this relatively narrow interpretation of the Dutch Disease probably does not carry a lot of weight. But there is also an extension of the Dutch Disease into decision making which, in fact, may be a critical component of the present landscape, in my view. This extended version of the Disease depends on the ritual nature of the annual donor–recipient dance previously described, in the sense that since both parties know that the funds will ultimately flow, World Bank lending may, in fact, have the effect of taking the pressure off and permitting countries to remain with present policies instead of being a catalyst for change.

All of this is, of course, hard to demonstrate conclusively. With development clearly a multi-cook endeavor, it is virtually impossible to pinpoint how to attribute credit or blame for success or failure in the process; in spite of substantial efforts made by the Bank, which should be acknowledged, ex post evaluation remains a very imperfect science because it is hard to assess the counter-factual, for instance, how the recipient would have fared in the absence of the package. Undoubtedly, lots of learning has been going on and the reputation and the influence of failures of the past have not been lost on recipients. We do know that the structural adjustment lending evaluations have concluded that implementation changes on average take at least twice as long as anticipated, and that results have consistently been overstated as countries continue to receive one adjustment loan after another. Whether this relative failure is due to the misplaced nature of the principal–agency framework previously mentioned or to the effects of the extended Dutch Disease phenomenon is difficult to assess since we cannot be sure, as is often claimed, that these countries would have done better in the absence of the conditionality and accompanying aid packages. What we can be sure of is that the present system is limping badly, has lost credibility, and, in spite of current efforts to repair it, remains in need of fundamental reform.

2 Suggestions for reform

First of all, it should be agreed that non-project or program lending, accompanied by policy-based agreements, should be retained as an important and flexible instrument for World Bank lending in order to facilitate required reforms clearly needed in many poor countries. Such policy-based non-project lending, in spite of its unsatisfactory perform-ance in the past, remains a potentially excellent instrument to help devel-oping-country borrowers achieve graduation into "sustained growth with improved equity and poverty alleviation." Second, there needs to be a real-ization that, without joint conceptualization and genuine ownership, no amount of conditionality can be expected to work. Achieving such genuine ownership will clearly not be an easy task, but it requires, in my view, the Bank acting much more like a bank and assuming a much more passive stance, while leaving it to recipient countries to propose reform programs to which the Bank would, as part of the international donor community, respond and, of course, negotiate about. In terms of the prin-cipal–agency framework, it should probably be virtually reversed, for instance, with the developing country as the principal and the lenders as a second agent, although negotiations would, of course, be in order.

Realistically speaking, it is probably politically impossible to get away completely from some form of routine annual country lending levels. But in order to achieve major results in terms of country-focused, policy-based lending, it will be important for the Bank to be in a position to sit back and encourage would-be borrowers to approach with fully-owned plans: fully-owned politically as well as technically. Such a new approach for transacting World Bank business would entail a number of other changes in the culture of the Bank:

1   Conditionality cannot be and should not be avoided, but it would have to take a different form, that of "self-conditionality," highly dif-ferentiated by country and put together by the recipient in the first instance, even though negotiations with donors can, of course, always be expected to take place. Such "self-conditionality" would be part of the package proposed by the recipient and presented to the Bank and the international community. It would be reasonably restrictive in the number of conditions contained and would put the developing country itself on notice that, in order to ensure the continued flow of resources, tranche releases, etc., in the case of non-compliance, the rules, presumably more credible and home-grown, would have to be adhered to. If you rely only on the external carrot or stick, once they are removed, behavior has been seen to revert.

2   I am in full agreement with the emerging consensus that any checklist of conditions should be substantially shortened; especially when one realizes that most countries can only accomplish, at a maximum, three or four reform items over any planning period. There is an adverse relationship between the number of conditions and their credibility. It is also necessary to count on a longer time horizon since institutional and political realities must be taken into account. This clearly requires a more fundamental, longer-term assessment and proposal to the international community, with financial resources clearly required not only to buy off vested interest groups and ease the pain of adjustment but also to provide the required reassurance to all present stakeholders. Self-conditionality should, moreover, preferably focus on policy change rather than on the level of policy currently in vogue. This would avoid one current problem, for instance, that as countries do better and better in terms of some definition of "good behavior" there has been a tendency for conditions to become tougher and tougher. If both parties agree on what is the right policy framework, using a gap reduction approach between the present and the ideal would seem to make more sense.

3   This process probably means – in addition to "business as usual" on a country project basis – opening a separate window, permitting the ballooning of World Bank and other donor assistance when and if such packages are presented to the Bank and the rest of the donor community. This so-called "New Window" would give the Bank an opportunity to initiate a somewhat fresh approach to its lending programs. It would assume substantial country selectivity, but also that the anticipated success of the approach would itself lead to increased resources and a greater willingness of Part I countries to support the Bank's role over time. This new kind of selectivity would not be a reward for good past performance as proposed by President Bush at Monterrey, but selectivity based on self-conditionality-*cum*-aid packages, which includes both the political as well as the technical elements of ownership by all the relevant parties. The Millennium Challenge Account unveiled at Monterrey unfortunately still proposes 16 criteria for purposes of assessment and is heavily biased toward a handful of already good performers. If properly adjusted, it could become the model for the "New Window" suggested here.

4   Where the local capability to fashion such genuinely owned packages is deficient – and this may be the case in some of the least developed countries – an effort needs to be mounted to supplement it by international action, possibly by helping build capacity through third-party- and/or World Bank-provided financial support. It is important, however, to have the intellectual inputs offered by independent third parties rather than World Bank personnel, for example, by independent university teams, think tanks, networks, etc., in order to ensure

both continuity and the building up of domestic reputation and trust as extremely important for the longer term. Such a procedure would recognize both the increased professional competence of Less Developed Country personnel as of a given point in time as well as the need for their competence to be enhanced over time when necessary.

5   Everything clearly depends on the reality of the genuine ownership of the program posited here and on who exercises the initiative. Reversing the principal–agency framework reduces the extended Dutch Disease problem and comes much closer to what was envisioned in the post-World War II Marshall Plan context, with the added possibility of regional peer reviews of country self-conditionality accompanied by donor resource flows.

The type of selectivity proposed here is perhaps the best way to protect developing countries' sovereignty while also ensuring that IFI dollars are appropriately used. It clearly requires the willingness of the World Bank to sometimes lend less, at least for a time, and to cut off loans when necessary, thus holding off political demands from G7 countries. Neither current ritual dance procedures nor the proposed selectivity via front-loading for conditions already met comes close to curing the present malaise. As a relatively minor actor in the financial resource dimension, the Bank would be well advised to respond to country proposals with heavy reliance on its own analytic abilities and its willingness, when necessary, to finance the enhancement of recipient capabilities. By protecting the sovereignty of Third World nation states in this fashion, the Bank can expect to regain its own impact and relevance.

Notes

1 In "World Bank Capital Neither Complements Nor Substitutes for Private Capital," Center for Global Development, Working Paper No. 20, December, 2002.
2 "What Did Structural Adjustment Adjust?," Center for Global Development, Working Paper No. 11, October, 2002.

Part IV

Reflections on the international infrastructure

17 Why it matters who runs the IMF and the World Bank[1]

Nancy Birdsall

1 Introduction

The debate about globalization is fundamentally a debate about who's running the global economy, and in whose interests. It is about politics and power as much as about the technical questions of currency regimes, prudential standards and the financial underpinning of global economic stability. Most economists, finance officials and central bankers agree that the benefits of global, market-based integration can more than offset the costs for the poorest countries and the poor within countries. Most social activists, in contrast, emphasize that so far potential has not been realized. The more pragmatic among them advocate moving well beyond the current reform agenda for the international financial architecture to broader and deeper reform of the system of global economic governance. Those activists see the Financial Stability Forum, the Bank for International Settlements, the International Monetary Fund, and the World Trade Organization as undemocratic. They see the overall system as controlled by corporate and financial insiders, not by the world's median income voter; by the United States Treasury and Wall Street not middle-income consumers; by Ministers of Finance and Governors of Central Banks not Ministers of Health, Labor, nor Social Affairs.[2] They are suspicious of the Bretton Woods institutions, where country votes reflect economic power, compared to the more democratic United Nations, where in the General Assembly at least, every country has a single vote.[3]

Independent of the merits or demerits of these various views, they all contain a core truth, namely that the global economic and financial system overall is not particularly representative of the poor of the world. As a result, even sensible enlightened policies – for example to liberalize further international trade rules and increase market access for the poorest countries – lack legitimacy and fail to command the energies and commitment of activists around the world.

Were the system of global economic governance more representative of the interests of the poorest countries and of the poor within countries, it might be not only more legitimate but also more effective, and thus more conducive to rapid reductions in global poverty and faster convergence of the income of the poorest countries toward that of the richest. Of course the mechanisms by which better representation would make the system more effective and bring faster poverty reduction are neither obvious nor straightforward. Below I discuss some possible links between poor representation and lower effectiveness for the cases of the IMF and the World Bank.

For those two institutions there has been increasing discussion in the last decade of the poor representation, in terms of voting power, of their borrowing member countries compared to the non-borrowing industrialized countries.[4] Given their mission of reducing global poverty, it does seem that a first step toward better representation of the interests of the global poor in the global economic system would be to increase the influence and representation of the developing countries, where the world's poor are concentrated, in those two institutions. This would not and should not imply a shift to the UN system of one-country, one-vote; in the financial institutions, the greater power of the advanced economies is key to their continued financial commitments. Moreover, even among the developing countries as a group, one-country, one-vote would make little sense given that China and Indonesia have populations and economies thousands of times greater than Sao Tome or Mongolia. It should imply adjustments, however, that better reflect the real changes in the relative weight of the developing countries in the global economy, and the potential to increase the institutions' legitimacy and effectiveness by giving countries most affected by their activities greater power in setting their agendas and policies.[5]

This is no longer the pipe dream it seemed to be a decade or so ago. Public criticism of the peculiar way in which the most recent appointment of the current Managing Director of the IMF occurred is one example; there is now increasing concern in the international community about the potential costs to the global financial system of what is a highly political and thus unpredictable (in terms of the qualifications and experience of the appointee) appointment process, at the World Bank as well as the IMF.[6] The fact that 24 African nations are represented by only two Board members in the IMF and the World Bank is now often remarked upon.[7] That matters because governance in these two institutions is not only a function of votes but of the technical and administrative capacity to use "voice" in the Board to affect decisions. At the same time, though actual decisions, particularly on lending, are almost always made by consensus in the Boards, the nature of the apparent consensus on many issues is naturally shaped by voting power, even when that power is not explicitly invoked. The G-24 (the club of finance officials of the developing countries) has openly argued for a change in the quota system and thus the representation of developing countries in the IMF. A coalition of non-governmental organizations has been formed to support reform of the governance of the institutions, and some member governments have begun actively discussing the options.[8] Finally, and tellingly, the issue of developing country representation was on the agenda of the 2003 spring meetings of those Bretton Woods institutions.

It must be said that increasing representation of developing countries in the global financial institutions, as difficult as it may be to achieve politically, would still be only a modest step toward making those institutions more representative. Even a system that was more "democratic" in representing all countries at the international level would not necessarily be "democratic" in representing well the poor within countries, particularly in the case of the many developing countries that are not themselves mature democracies.[9] However, it would be a start in the right direction, and is surely necessary if not sufficient.

I proceed with a brief discussion of why good global economic governance matters for reducing global inequality and poverty while sustaining politically a global, market-based economic system (section 2). I then set out the arguments for why better representation of developing countries would make the institutions more effective (section 3). I use the example of the Inter-American Development Bank to bring out some differences in its decisions and in some cases in its institutional effectiveness compared to the World Bank (section 4). I conclude with some comments on the dilemma of reconciling the financial power and resulting accountability of the rich countries in the international financial institutions, with the need for voice and ownership by the poorer countries, if the system of global economic governance is to be effective as well as legitimate.

2 Why good global economic governance matters

One of the great challenges of the twenty-first century is surely to eliminate worldwide poverty. Indeed, in the year 2000, the nations of the world all signed on to the Millennium Development Goals, which include the reduction by half of income poverty by the year 2015. Why does good global economic governance (including improving the international financial architecture), matter for reducing global poverty? Let me suggest two reasons: that the market fails (or as it is more generally put in the textbooks, there are missing markets and market failures); and, ironically, that the market, for the most part, works.[10]

First, markets fail in many domains. The market will never reflect the full social costs of a particular firm's pollution. In the absence of taxes or penalties, local polluters will pollute too much from a social point of view, since they need not internalize the costs to their communities of the pollution they generate. Similarly at the global level, any one country will not necessarily internalize the costs to the global community of its greenhouse gas emissions in the absence of collectively agreed taxes or penalties. In the absence of a market, the rich countries that have historically emitted the highest per capita greenhouse gas emissions can and have imposed costs – of future prevention or of mitigation – on not only their own children and grandchildren but on future generations in the poorer countries. The costs in prevention or mitigation are likely to be relatively greater, as a proportion of total income, in poorer countries. In that sense, the effect of this global public "bad" is asymmetric.

Financial contagion across countries, affecting even those emerging market economies with relatively sound domestic policies, is another example of how market failures can have asymmetric effects. Emerging market economies are less able to manage the same global financial shock as the richer countries. They are less able to borrow domestically, because their own financial markets are relatively shallow. They are more reliant on debt issued in other currencies than their own, creating market doubts about their ability to sustain debt. As a result, they are often forced to resort to tight fiscal and monetary policy to reestablish market confidence, just when in the face of recession they would ideally implement macroeconomic measures to stimulate their economies. Such pro-cyclicality, with its costs in terms of interest rates, unemployment, and reduced spending on social programs, is the opposite of what the industrial economies implement during recessions. In that sense at least, the global market failure creates an asymmetry of greater costs to poorer countries, and to the poor within those countries. We know that the effects of unemployment and bankruptcy can be permanent for the poor; in Mexico, increases in child labor that reduced school enrollment during the 1995 crisis were not reversed, implying some children did not return to school when growth resumed.[11]

The risks of global warming and the problems of global financial contagion are only two examples of market failures that entail asymmetric costs and risks for poor countries and poor people. The same can be said of contagious disease that crosses borders, of transnational crime, and of potentially beneficial but risky new technologies such as genetically modified foods. Similarly, poor countries that protect global resources such as tropical forests and biological diversity are paying the full costs but are unable to capture the full benefits of these global goods. Within countries, governments temper market failures through regulations, taxes and subsidies, and fines; and they share the benefits of such public goods as public security, military defense, management of natural disasters and public health through their tax and expenditure decisions. Ideally the latter are made in a democratic system with fair and legitimate representation of all people, independent of their wealth. In nations, such political systems seldom work perfectly (as the proponents of campaign finance reform in the US would argue). In the global community, a comparable political system just barely exists.

Ironically, it is also the case that because markets work reasonably well, the poor and weak can be left behind. Markets that are bigger and deeper reward more efficiently those who already have productive assets: financial assets, land, physical assets, and perhaps most crucial in the technologically driven global economy, human capital. For that reason, markets alone do not necessarily generate equal opportunity. This is true not just across people but across countries too. Countries that are already ahead – with stable political systems, secure property rights, adequate banking supervision, reasonable public services, and so on – are better able to exploit new opportunities generated by the global market. Countries without these institutional assets can be caught in an "institutional poverty trap." One symptom of such traps is the reality that global capital goes where it is already most abundant rather than most scarce, because it is in the former not the latter that its return is highest. That turns out to be settings where governance is reasonably good and other institutional assets are adequate to ensure a reasonable return to capital. Indeed, in a global financial system, even local financial capital will go abroad if expected returns are too low at home. Thus most foreign direct investment goes to developed countries, and little if any to sub-Saharan Africa (Lucas 1990).

At the individual level, the best example of how healthy markets can generate unequal opportunities is the rising returns throughout the world to higher education. The effect of having a university education compared to secondary education or less has been increasing for almost two decades everywhere. This is true despite the fact that more and more people are going to university. In the global economy, with the information and communications revolution, the supply of university-educated people has apparently not been keeping up with ever-increasing demand. In the United States the highly educated have enjoyed healthy earnings gains for three decades, while those with high school education or less have suffered absolute wage losses. In Latin America, between 1991 and 1995, the period of intense liberalization, the wage gap between the skilled and unskilled increased for six of seven countries for which reliable wage data are available. In Eastern Europe, with the fall of Communism, the wage difference between those with and without post-secondary education has widened considerably.[12] In most settings, education has been reinforcing initial advantages instead of compensating for initial handicaps.

The global market for skilled and talented people is another example of how markets can hurt the already weak. In today's global economy the highly skilled are highly mobile. Indian engineers can quadruple their earnings by moving from Kerala to Silicon Valley, and Indian PhD biochemists from Delhi to Atlanta or Cambridge. For the individuals concerned, this is a good thing, and eventually this brain drain can generate offsetting remittances and return investments if the institutional and policy setting in India and other poor countries improves.[13] In the short term, however, it makes the task of poorer countries, trying to build those institutions and improve those policies, tougher. The annual loss to India of its brain drain to the US is estimated at $2 billion, about equal to all the foreign aid it receives.[14] The farmers and workers whose taxes finance education in poor countries are subsidizing the citizens of the rich countries – whose tax revenues are boosted by the immigrants' contributions (and whose cultures by the way are also greatly enriched).

In modern market economies, national governments provide for the regulatory, taxing and subsidy arrangements for mitigating market failures. These are not always perfect – indeed there is always the question about whether some intervention is better than none – but the governance structure exists should the commonwealth decide to use interventions to minimize the problems market failures entail. In varying degrees, modern market economies also have social and other policies explicitly designed to temper the excess inequalities of income and opportunity that efficient markets easily generate. The resulting social contract may not be perfect, but it exists at the national level. Progressive tax systems provide for some redistribution, with the state financing at least minimal educational opportunities for all and some social and old-age insurance.

There is never likely to be an exact analogue of the domestic government with its regulatory and taxing authorities at the global level. But global asymmetries underline the need for a system of global economic governance which would minimize the costs and risks of global market failures and through transfers would help ensure something much closer to equal opportunity for the world's poor than we currently have.

The World Bank and the IMF are among the global economic institutions that represent a start in that direction.[15] I turn now to a discussion of whether and how better representation of the poor within them (through better representation of developing countries) might increase their effectiveness in these tasks.

3 Linking representation and effectiveness

How might better representation of developing countries in the World Bank and the IMF make those institutions more effective? There is no simple way to address such a question, since there is little agreement on the definition of the institutions' effectiveness in the first place.[16] However, imagine a simple definition of effectiveness as maximizing global poverty reduction by raising and efficiently allocating as much of members' political and financial resources as can be used at positive rates of return (in reducing poverty). With that in mind, I suggest four possible arguments linking increased developing country representation to increased institutional effectiveness.

The first has to do with the ability of an institution to acquire additional resources in the face of real additional needs. In the case of the IMF, Buira (2002) notes that limited representation of developing countries has contributed to a stalemate among shareholders regarding any increase in its resources. That has made the Fund less able to play its stabilizing role; its resources have declined from 58 percent of world trade to less than 6 percent today (and a smaller proportion still of capital flows). Many of the larger emerging market economies, such as Brazil and Korea, have lower quotas and fewer votes than Belgium and Denmark, though the former two countries now have a greater potential impact on the global financial stability that the IMF is charged to protect. But the industrial countries have resisted any increase in the capital (or quotas), in part because negotiating the allocation of such an increase would open the Pandora's box of restructuring possibilities, at possible cost to their own influence and power. With any increase there would be pressure to restructure the quota system so as to better align economic size and voting power, allowing Korea, Brazil, and South Africa for example, to increase their quotas and thus their contributions to the Fund's resources.[17]

This argument applies less well to the World Bank (and the other multilaterals) where there is less immediate concern on the part of the borrowers that they could effectively use more capital for their traditional loan operations. However, any recurrence of the pressures for financial support that the financial crises of the late 1990s created, when the World Bank (as well as the Asian Development Bank and the Inter-American Development Bank) were called upon to commit loans to Korea and later Brazil and Argentina, to supplement the IMF commitments, might add to the view that the banks, because they are short of sufficient capital, are ineffective in providing the kind of countercyclical support that emerging market economies with fragile financial systems need in an increasingly volatile global system.[18]

A second argument is implicit in the view of those who believe the institutions are unduly powerful and "intrusive," especially in the poorest countries most dependent on them, and end up pushing for reforms that are not politically sustainable and are thus ineffective.[19] This view is most often associated with critics of so-called Washington Consensus (or "neoliberal") policies, who argue that the IMF and the World Bank have actually done borrowers harm by using loan conditions to pressure them into capital market liberalization before their financial sectors were resilient enough, or into privatization programs that ended up enriching corrupt insiders.[20] In this view, implicitly if not explicitly, better representation of developing countries on the boards of the institutions would give the borrowing countries more influence in resisting pressure for constant liberalization of their markets, and might create pressure to hire more professional staff with broader backgrounds, including more non-economists and more economists trained in other than the mainstream Anglo-Saxon neoclassical tradition.

A related argument, widely held even by many who endorse the general direction of the institutions' policy advice, is that the imbalance of power makes them prone to prolonged reliance on universal (and in some cases, possibly wrong-headed) "recipes" for economic reform, and less open than they otherwise would be to home-grown approaches taking into account local institutional and political constraints.[21]

(Of course, the merit of these related points linking poor representation of developing countries to their ineffectiveness rests, in fact, on highly contentious positions about what policies and strategies are in fact most conducive to growth and development strategies, which clearly cannot be resolved here.)

Oddly enough, a third argument is based on the evidence that as intrusive as these institutions may seem to be in recipient countries' policies and programs, in fact in the end they are not powerful at all but weak and ineffective. The evidence of weakness and thus ineffectiveness comes from the long record in many borrowing countries of repeated failures to implement agreed programs, compounded by the institutions' providing repeated waivers of pre-agreed loan conditions and continuing to disburse loans (Willett 2003). This may be because the borrowers are gaming the system (what Willett calls "strategic reneging"), i.e., signing up knowing conditionality will not be enforced; or because they fail to anticipate the difficulties of undertaking agreed programs when circumstances change (what might be called willfully myopic behavior); or because there are different actors in the recipient government, and "reformers" who hoped to use the leverage of external conditionality to implement changes, subsequently fail. In any event, the fact is that in the poorest countries of Africa, where the record of program implementation is weakest, the institutions have often seemed powerless, politically or bureaucratically or both, to cut off lending,[22] and that has raised questions about their overall effectiveness, given that their lending is not associated with implementation of the programs they are trying to support.

The response of the institutions to the accumulating evidence that borrowing countries were not implementing programs successfully has been to emphasize the need for borrowing countries to demonstrate "ownership" of their reform programs, in the hope that they will make the governments' decisions more likely to be sustained politically. That creates the new need for staff assessment of whether a government is likely to fulfill its promises (independent of whether it is willing to sign on to such promises, given the past record of repeated failures of programs followed by renegotiations).[23] The only sense in which this new requirement has been specified has to do with the idea of "participation" of citizens through civil society groups in discussion of the proposed programs. Staff in the World Bank are required to confirm to the Board that there has been such participation when bringing a country's "Poverty Reduction Strategy Paper" (PRSP) and debt relief programs to the Board for approval.

In fact, ownership on the part of the citizenry, even if adequately reflected in "participation," is only one dimension of the issue. In most settings the political sustainability of an agreed program will be related to the relative power and influence of the executive and the legislature, the positions of any relevant political parties, the interplay of various interest group pressures, and the likelihood that beneficiaries of a policy change (such as future exporters benefiting from a more open trade regime) will themselves have political influence. As a result, the new standard actually requires much more than an assessment of the role of civil society groups in discussing a program; it requires acknowledging more explicitly that borrowing governments are making political as well as technical decisions, and increasing the staff time and resources needed to do the necessary political impact analysis.

A subtext of this argument that local politics matters arises from its relevance for the ability of the institutions to be effective in their primary objective, i.e., reducing poverty by ensuring that the programs they support ultimately benefit the poor. Most programs supported by the IMF and the World Bank implicitly assume a common interest of the lender and the country policy makers; on the other hand the use of conditionality makes no sense if there is not some conflict of interest (Drazen 2005). Coate and Morris (2005) note that conditionality may simply induce a government to shift the way it allocates its resources, in order to comply with an agreed loan condition, but in the direction of a less efficient (and presumably even less transparent) transfer mechanism.

Coate and Morris emphasize the overall reduction in efficiency. But it is easy to imagine that the new "transfer mechanism" would protect (in many cases continue to protect) powerful entrenched interests, not the poor. Vreeland's (2003) analysis suggests that such "misfires" on the part of the IMF or World Bank in terms of conditionality have ended up hurting the poor. In the same spirit, Birdsall and James (1993) apply the theory of public choice to social spending in developing countries. They observe that prior to any particular allocation of resources there is a political equilibrium; if the advice or resources (or conditions) of the World Bank or any other external force leads to pressure to increase public spending on the education sector so as to put more poor children into school and make the distribution of public expenditures more progressive, there is likely to be a countervailing reaction to return to the initial equilibrium – for example via reductions in the overall tax burden on the wealthy, or an increase in spending within education on universities that meet the needs of better-off households.

Classic examples of such misfiring are when a government agrees to a program of fiscal reform, which then ends up leading to expenditure cuts that harm the poor while insulating the rich (made famous in the 1987 UNICEF-sponsored study *Adjustment with a Human Face*) and when a government undertakes a trade opening which leads to the collapse of local production on which the poor and unskilled relied for jobs and income. Whether particular examples are true or not (or in the short term but not the long term), the implication is that effectiveness requires explicit understanding of the political economy of borrowing country governments, and what might be called "political impact analysis" of the efficiency and the equity implications of agreed policy and program changes. Since agreed reforms can be manipulated by entrenched interests, such analysis seems absolutely key to the institutions' effectiveness in reducing global poverty.

My final argument takes as given the institutions' partial loss of legitimacy in the last decade or two, and links loss of legitimacy to reduced effectiveness. The perception that the institutions have been not only ineffective in helping the poor, but worse actually harmful, has contributed to the questioning of their legitimacy on the part of many groups who are committed to global social justice. A similar process occurred earlier, especially for the World Bank, on environmental issues. If the IMF and the World Bank become the scapegoat for failure, that in turn risks a further loss of effectiveness. A worrying example is the attack on the institutions on the part of the indigenous peoples' movement in Latin America, who see Washington, America, the IMF and so on as illegitimate in their apparent defense of international financial and corporate interests. To the extent that IMF and World Bank programs become a political liability for local leaders, and are associated with political uncertainty and the risk of political instability, they will discourage rather than encourage local and foreign creditor and investor confidence.[24] This is a particular problem for the IMF, whose effectiveness is closely linked to its ability to trigger confidence in an economy by agreeing to its economic program, particularly when the programs it endorses in fact rely on the private confidence they are meant to trigger.

The institutions have and are responding to these incursions on their legitimacy. The question is whether such incremental responses as the emphasis on "participation" and the increased rhetoric about poverty reduction (such as the IMF's renaming of its Enhanced Structural Adjustment Facility as the Poverty Reduction and Growth Facility) will make a difference in themselves, as long as the prevailing doubts about legitimacy extend to the imbalance in their governance itself.

On the one hand, it is not obvious that better representation of borrowing member countries in the governance of the institutions would translate directly into more "ownership" of institutional programs by borrowing member governments, or into greater savvy about the political economy situation of borrowers as it bears on ability and willingness to carry out reform and investment programs. Nor is it clear, as noted above, that greater representation of developing countries through their political leadership would translate into better effective representation of the needs of their own poor. On the other hand, it would be wrong to write off the possibility just because it is not easy to demonstrate, or to adhere to the status quo because the right move away from the status quo is politically difficult to imagine. I turn now to a discussion of the Inter-American

Development Bank as an example of the possible effects of better representation of borrowers on institutional effectiveness, and how it might operate.

4 Representation and decisions at the Inter-American Development Bank

The Inter-American Development Bank (IDB) has a number of characteristics that make it one of the five major multilateral banks – World Bank, African Development Bank, Asian Development Bank, European Bank for Reconstruction and Development, and IDB – and the IMF, the institution in which the developing countries and the poor within developing countries are probably best represented. These include the following:

- 50 percent of the voting shares are controlled by the borrowing members.
- The President is effectively elected by the borrowers. [25]
- Of the 14 chairs of the Board of Executive Directors, nine are held by the borrowers.
- All country members of the IDB are democracies.

A comment on the last point is needed. Activists are concerned, often with good reason, that even when poor countries have adequate representation in international institutions, the poor within those countries may not be represented well. Obviously those who represent their countries in official fora are among the best educated and trained a country has. The question is whether their views reflect narrow interests or the interests of their countries as a whole. To the extent that all members of the IDB are democracies, of course at varying stages of maturity, there is a somewhat better case that their representatives speak for a larger majority of their countries' populations.

Table 17.1 provides summary indicators of the governance structures of the six international financial institutions. The other institution with a governance structure similar to that of the IDB is the African Development Bank. However, most lending commitments of the latter bank (more than 40 percent) are made from the highly concessional ("soft") window which is financed by the non-borrowing OECD members. Thus AfDB lending is highly dependent on the continued support of those countries. The non-borrowers have in effect a short leash over the shareholders as a group. In contrast, only about 5 percent of annual lending commitments are made from the IDB soft window. The bulk of IDB lending is financed not by contributions but by the bank's borrowing in the global capital market. This borrowing is backed primarily by the paid-in capital and guarantees of non-borrowers, which constitute a more permanent and largely irreversible commitment of the non-borrowers (Table 17.2). It is best thought of as a much longer and looser leash.

Table 17.1 International financial institutions (IFIs): governance structure

IFI	Voting share (%)				Directors					President
	US	Other G-7	Other non-borrowers	Developing country borrowers	US	Other G-7	Other non-borrowers	Developing country borrowers	Total	
IMF	17.1	28.2	16.7	38.0	1	6	6	11	24	Non-borrower
WB	16.4	26.6	18.2	38.8	1	6	7	10	24	Non-borrower
IDB	30.0	15.7	4.3	50.0	1	4	0	9	14	Borrower
ADB	13.0	27.4	14.6	45.0	1	4	1	6	12	Non-borrower
EBRD	10.1	46.5	30.2	13.2	1	6	12	4	23	Non-borrower
AfDB	6.6	21.0	12.4	60.0	1	4	1	12	18	Borrower

Sources: ADB, AfDB, and IDB Annual Reports 2001, WB, EBRD, and IMF Annual Reports 2002. Website data on shares, AfDB, IDB, IMF, and WB.

Notes

IFI = International financial institution; IMF = International Monetary Fund; WB = World Bank; IDB = Inter-American Development Bank; ADB = Asian Development Bank; EBRD = European Bank for Reconstruction and Development; AfDB = African Development Bank.

Table 17.2 International financial institutions (IFIs): selected indicators (2001)

	Total authorized capital (US$ billions)	Non-borrowers' capital (US$ billions)	Non-concessional lending commitments (% total[a])
IMF[b]	289	176.3	86.7
WB	189.5	98.5	73.3
IDB	100.9	49.1	94.4
ADB	48.4	32.3	74.5
EBRD	20.2	2.6	99.1
AfDB	22.3	8.9	58.4

Sources: IDB 2001; WB 2002; IMF 2002; ADB 2001; AfDB 2001; Gwin 2002.

Notes
IFI = international financial institution; IMF = International Monetary Fund; WB = World Bank; IDB = Inter-American Development Bank; ADB = Asian Development Bank; EBRD = European Bank for Reconstruction and Development; AfDB = African Development Bank.
a Percentage of non-concessional annual lending commitments during 2000–02 (concessional lending figures obtained from: International Development Agency at the World Bank – IDA; Heavily Indebted Poor Countries Initiative – HIPC at the IMF; Fund for Special Operations at the IDB; African Development Fund at the AfDB; Asian Development Fund at the ADB; Special Funds at the EBRD).
b IMF's financial resources (closest equivalent to capital).

In addition, at the time of the seventh capital replenishment of the IDB, in 1989, the shareholders agreed that a defined group of the smallest countries in the region (many but not all of which are among the poorest countries as well) should have a quota of a minimum of 35 percent of all lending from the Bank. No doubt this decision was pressed upon all the shareholders by a coalition of the non-borrowers and the small countries; presumably the non-borrowers wanted to prevent the larger borrowers (Mexico, Brazil, Argentina, Venezuela) from crowding out access of the smaller countries. Its result in terms of governance is that it is the weak equivalent of secured minority rights, and in that sense ensures somewhat greater access and voice for the small and usually relatively poorer countries in the institution.

Table 17.1 indicates that the United States is by far the largest single shareholder in the IDB. The US has substantial power by reason of its voting share and the financial commitment that it represents (though by no means an outright veto on lending from the hard window). That power, however, is primarily negative. The US can easily prevent lending and policy changes it opposes, but except in the context of negotiating new capital infusions, it is constrained to comment and suggest as opposed to making demands. It was at the time of the third capital replenishment that the US secured the IDB's collaboration in helping to finance the adjustment programs in Latin America under the Brady Plan, with the kind of conditionality that the World Bank began imposing in the late

1980s.[26] It was at the time of the fourth capital replenishment, in 1994, that the US introduced and pushed through such changes as the introduction of greater disclosure and the implementation of the independent inspection procedure, both of which had been introduced at the World Bank through the normal Board decision-making process. But except for the leverage it had in the context of contributing to the capital of the Bank, the US can only prevent damage at the IDB, not promote new initiatives or policies.

Perhaps the best evidence for the difficulty the non-borrowers including the US have in pushing their own agendas at the IDB is that the big borrowers (Mexico, Brazil, and others) have successfully resisted the transfer of net income from ordinary capital lending (the hard window) to the IDB's soft window, which is similar to the IDA window of the World Bank and lends on highly concessional terms to five of the region's poorest and most indebted borrowers. Such transfers are made regularly in the World Bank. The large borrowers object to such transfers since they raise their costs of borrowing (essentially by reducing the potential for increasing reserves); in their view such transfers amount to them bearing a burden of foreign aid that the rich countries ought to be bearing completely. Similarly, the big borrowers in the IDB have resisted use of net income to finance the IDB's obligations for debt relief and reduction under the HIPC (heavily indebted poor country) initiative.[27] The HIPC obligations have been covered only after extensive and contentious negotiations among IDB shareholders, finally with the big borrowers securing other benefits in return for their willingness to "give up" some of the control they had earlier negotiated over use of IDB resources held in their countries in the local currency of their countries.

A second manifestation of borrower power in the IDB has been the borrowers' interest in restraining growth of the IDB's administrative budget. The reason is the same; an increase in the administrative budget for a given amount of outstanding loan assets, implies a higher cost that must be borne by the borrowers to sustain the same level of reserves, provisions, and so on. Budget restraint on the part of the borrowers explains the much lower spending in the IDB compared to the World Bank on research and on economic and sectoral studies that are not clearly tied to loans. In the mid-1990s such budget restraint meant that in real terms the IDB administrative budget was declining slightly, while in the World Bank, the shareholders through the Board agreed to management's proposal for a "Strategic Compact" which involved a substantial increase in the real administrative budget (admittedly designed in principle to be one-time).

These points are evidence not of greater effectiveness but of the fact that voting power and other formal arrangements of governance matter to institutional decisions, even in institutions where the critical decisions regarding programs and lending all seem to result from "consensus." (Indeed some would argue that the IDB would be *more* effective if its large borrowers had agreed to transfer some profits to its concessional window, or if more of its administrative budget had been spent on research over the years.)

Is there evidence that the IDB has been more effective than it might have been as a result of its relatively greater borrower representation compared say to the World Bank? Without a counterfactual, it is not possible to answer systematically. However here are several points that at the least suggest the question is not unreasonable.

First, the ownership issue. The IDB is widely seen as closer to its borrowers. The regional borrowers for all practical purposes set the agenda in the IDB; it was their influence that led to a heavy emphasis from the IDB's founding on support for regional integration and for lending for social programs. (The IDB began immediately lending for water and sanitation in 1961, and for many years heavily supported higher education when the World Bank did not.) The Presidents of the IDB can and have used the institution as a platform for shaping new priorities at the regional level; early in the 1990s President Iglesias brought together leaders of the judicial sector and defined with them a set of priorities for judicial reform and anti-corruption programs – before these issues now discussed under the rubric of "governance" became prominent on the international development agenda. The IDB also does seem to secure, and its loans seem to reflect, substantial "ownership" by its borrowers of the programs for which they are borrowing. Conditionality in IDB loans in the 1990s did suffer (as at the World Bank and IMF) from overkill. But the general impression is that borrowers had more control over the details of conditions in the IDB setting, and often saw conditionality as useful in signaling to private creditors their commitment to the reforms supported by IDB loans. Much of the time it was probably the staff more than the Board that was demanding in terms of conditionality and agreement to waivers of conditionality for release of tranches.

The fact of greater borrower ownership is, perhaps ironically, most evident in the periodic concern of World Bank staff that the IDB is "too close" to the borrowers and thus all too willing to lend, independent of the merits of the program being financed. In the 1980s the IDB made a series of "program loans" to support public spending of countries struggling to reduce fiscal deficits and increase trade surpluses as they adjusted following the debt crisis early in the decade, at a time when the World Bank was agreeing to such budget support only in the context of highly conditional structural adjustment loans. Similarly the IDB supported more willingly spending on university programs in Latin America, at a time when the World Bank was pushing for relatively greater spending on primary and secondary education, and for imposition of tuition fees at the university level. These differences in policy on the part of the two banks almost certainly reflected the differences in governance.[28]

Second, because the IDB is seen as more closely reflecting the needs of its borrowers, it does not seem to have suffered the same loss of legitimacy as have the IMF and the World Bank. That it is smaller and less visible has almost certainly helped; still the fact is that it is much less associated with, for example, the "Washington Consensus" among the critics of the neoliberal interpretation of that consensus. That may have helped preserve its ability to remain effective in encouraging certain difficult and unpopular reforms – though there is no obvious way to demonstrate this.

Third, the IDB is seen as politically savvy, at least relative to the World Bank. Its longstanding support for university education, for example, could be interpreted as implicit recognition that it was better to reinforce a program that had domestic political salience, even if second best, than to push for changes that would create a more costly backlash, or the kinds of countervailing pressures mentioned above, for example a decline in taxpayer support for public spending on basic education. More important is the likelihood that IDB staff and the Board, because they are more familiar with the local political economy in more countries, will better anticipate the risk that conditionality will misfire to the detriment of the poor, as described above. Unfortunately it is impossible to distinguish between the effects of truly better political understanding, and the greater likelihood of less "tough" conditionality in general.

One reason for at least the potential for more savvy political understanding is that in the IDB the borrowers are better represented at the senior staff level. There are many staff at the senior level in the World Bank from borrowing member countries. But in contrast to the IDB they are not likely to be working in their own regions of origin, and much less likely to speak the language of the borrowing country governments with which they are negotiating. Indeed Latin American countries are said to have resented the dominance of World Bank staff from Asia in work on their countries during the late 1980s and much of the 1990s, though not objecting to the particular persons, all of whom were seen as smart and committed. (In the last few years, under James Wolfensohn, the World Bank does seem to have made efforts to have more staff from Latin America working in the region, and similarly to have made senior appointments in Africa of staff from that region.)

In part the difference between the two banks is the simple fact that staff in the IDB working on Latin America have not and will not ever work on Africa or Asia. However, there is more to it. World Bank staffing and promotions are highly meritocratic and largely apolitical. Staff are thus relatively isolated from their own countries; indeed success, including promotions in the World Bank, requires that staff spend a considerable amount of time interacting with each other. In the case of the IDB, many more senior staff from borrowing countries are appointed from outside the bureaucracy itself. Their appointments are more likely to reflect political pressures from their own countries, who have relatively more political sway in the IDB because of their greater representation on the Board.

Ironically, as a result those senior staff are more alert to their own countries' interests and policies and politics, and less concerned with proving their merits inside the IDB bureaucracy. Their careers are after all likely to be determined elsewhere. The IDB is thus more "politicized" than the World Bank, but that has its benefits; it is also more porous and its staff are more client-oriented – and possibly more effective.

Fourth, the IDB is highly supportive of what might be called regional public goods. As in the World Bank, there is no good instrument for supplying global or regional public goods. The "loan" is the IDB's most important product, and cannot easily be made to finance a public good with benefits to many countries because of the problem of allocating costs across the various countries. However, much more than the World Bank, the IDB has found ways to support regional trade agreements, including for the past nine years substantial technical work on the Free Trade Agreement of the Americas; cross-border infrastructure projects (including the electricity grid in Central America); and the strengthening of sub-regional banks including the Andean Development Bank[29] (the CAF – Corporacion Andina de Fomento) and the Central American Development Bank (CABEI – the BCIE Banco Centroamericano de Integracion Economica).[30] Much of this support has come from the very scarce concessional funds available (but not from net income as noted above). The weight of regional programs is not simply the result of the IDB being itself a regional rather than a global institution. The Asian Development Bank (where the Presidency is controlled by the Japanese) and the African Development Bank (where the borrowers are more dependent on the non-borrowers to finance their relatively large concessional lending program) came relatively later to regional programs and have not committed as much on regional programs as a portion of total commitments (though regional programs in all the banks are small).

5 Concluding note: a dilemma

Increasing global integration has made the challenge of reducing global poverty and inequality and advancing human development more achievable than ever, and more dependent than ever on the legitimacy and effectiveness of the two global institutions with the particular responsibility for those tasks – the World Bank and the IMF. Yet their legitimacy and effectiveness are being increasingly questioned – in part because developing countries, whose governments and peoples are the main objects and the beneficiaries of this task, are poorly represented in their governance structures.

Governance of the two institutions reflects the historically greater financial capacity of today's richer countries, and their governance has had the advantage of securing the continuing financial and political support of the rich countries. But times have changed. The developing countries have become a bigger factor in the global economy (as the financial crises of the late 1990s suggested all to well); they affect and are affected by the stability and prosperity of the global system much more than they were five decades ago. In addition, the demands of the global economy have gradually increased the role of the IMF and the World Bank in advising and influencing domestic economic policy in the borrowing countries. As a result, the people of those countries, including the poor, are increasingly affected by decisions made at the international level. Finally, there has been increased attention from an increasingly global civil society movement to the two institutions, with greater scrutiny of their roles and increased questioning of their legitimacy.

The dilemma at the global level is reconciling the continuing need for financial support of the rich countries with the ability of the institutions to remain legitimate and effective in a changing world. There is at least some evidence that their effectiveness is reduced directly by lack of developing country influence, and indirectly because that dearth of influence reduces their legitimacy. The evidence, based loosely on the effects of greater influence of borrowers in the Inter-American Development Bank, is not only that the developing countries need the multilateral institutions, but that institutions can benefit from their greater influence.

In short, it is possible that in the long term, the institutions' legitimacy and effectiveness in their vital task of addressing the challenge of reducing global poverty will be increasingly at risk, in the absence of some change in their governance structures. The issue thus should no longer be whether any change at all is warranted, but exactly what that change should be and how to overcome the political gridlock that is preventing it.

Notes

1 This chapter is based on remarks originally presented at the Commonwealth Secretariat Conference in London on July 3, 2002, and revised for the Yale conference. An earlier version was titled "Global Economic Governance and Representation of Developing Countries: The IDB Example" (available at www.cgdev.org). I am grateful to Euric Bobb for his help in clarifying issues regarding the Inter-American Development Bank, and to James Adams, Ariel Buira, William Cline, Kemal Dervis, T.N. Srinivasan, Sandip Sukhtankar, Ngaire Woods, and John Williamson for their comments on earlier versions.
2 Joseph Stiglitz makes this point (2002).
3 The view of the UN as more democratic (and more friendly to developing countries) is surprising given that its most fundamental decisions are controlled in the Security Council, where six countries have a veto. On security issues, the traditional cleavage has been between east and west, however, not between the "north," i.e., the industrialized countries, and the "south," i.e., the developing countries, and as a result on some issues, some countries of the north have often been unable to push through decisions they favored.
4 On the IMF, see Buira (2002). Woods (2000) and Kapur (2002) discuss additional mechanisms besides voting for improving representation of developing countries, including staffing, location of the institutions, use of outside experts, etc.

5 The European Union (EU) system of representation provides one model for representing countries which differ in population and economic size, while protecting the rights of smaller countries. See Woods (2000) for the relevance of the EU model, including the EU system of double qualified majorities (number of countries, and proportion of EU population).

6 Kahler (2001).

7 See for example, the minutes of recent seminars organized by Ngaire Woods and funded by the Government of Canada (Woods 2002; Buira 2002).

8 The coalition is called New Rules for Global Finance. See Caliari and Schroeder (2003). The Executive Director for Germany at the World Bank has made proposals for change (Deutscher 2003).

9 I discuss this point at greater length in Birdsall (2001).

10 This portion is based heavily on Birdsall (2002).

11 Székely 1998.

12 For more on the United States see Levy (1998) and Cline (1997); on Latin America see Duryea and Székely (1998) and Behrman *et al.* (2001); on Eastern Europe see Terrell (2000) and Terrell and Garner (2001). Of course it is also true that the emigration of unskilled workers from poor to rich countries constitutes a windfall for the latter, since they arrive at an age when they can contribute to the economy.

13 Kapur and McHale forthcoming.

14 UNDP 2001, 1998.

15 Others include the World Trade Organization and the various UN agencies that finance technical assistance and other transfer programs in developing countries.

16 One oft-used measure is the proportion of lending operations that are reported to be "satisfactory" during implementation and in project completion reports, as in the Wapenhans 1992 report of the World Bank. But this project-level assessment is itself a narrow measure of overall effectiveness, since the domestic policy environment appears to be a critical factor affecting project success. Thus comparisons over time between these internal measures of projects would almost certainly show little difference between the World Bank in Latin America and the Inter-American Development Bank, as long as country allocations over time were similar.

17 Recognition of the increasing stake of the emerging market economies in the global economy, and their potential to affect its growth and stability, has led to efforts to include them in discussions of the international financial architecture, through creation of the "G-20" (G-7 plus Argentina, Australia, Brazil, China, India, Indonesia, Mexico, Russia, Saudi Arabia, South Africa, South Korea, and Turkey).

18 Fernandez-Arias and Hausmann (2000) and Griffith-Jones and Ocampo (2001) argue that the lack of sufficient transfer of capital from the rich to the poor world is a fundamental problem. The Meltzer Commission (2000) took the opposite view.

19 Woods and Narlikar (2001) describe the "new intrusiveness" of these organizations in the context of growing concern about the merits of their advice. The tendency to insist on universal recipes is one way to interpret Stiglitz's (2002) critique of the IMF's emphasis on fiscal austerity in East Asia during the financial crisis of 1997–98, and its emphasis (along with the US Treasury and the World Bank) on rapid privatization in Russia in the early 1990s. The evidence that opening the capital account prematurely can exacerbate the vulnerability of emerging market economies to financial crises is another example.

20 Stiglitz (2002) describes the IMF as both intrusive and wrong.

21 Rodrik (2001) is particularly critical of the imposition of universal approaches

implied in WTO-agreed disciplines. See also Rodrik (2003). For an eloquent argument for greater reliance on home-grown institutions, see Hausmann and Rodrik (2002).

22 Birdsall *et al.* (2004) show this is a particular problem in the case of low-income countries with high accumulated debt to the multilaterals; those countries have been able to borrow independent of the quality of their own policies.

23 Willett (2003) notes that the IMF Managing Director has the duty of certifying that he believes that not only is the policy to be supported good, but that the prospects for its implementation are good.

24 In Ecuador recently, as reported by Reuters from Quito and described in the daily summary of news issued by the IMF, "President Lucio Gutierrez pleaded with Congress to . . . keep the IMF loan deal on track. I want to ask lawmakers to reflect. This is not a bill imposed by the IMF . . . This is a necessity for Ecuador.'" In Bolivia, the leaders of the indigenous group movement that succeeded in forcing President Sanchez de Lozada of Bolivia to resign in October 2003, were in part objecting to his record of reform supported by the US and the Bretton Woods institutions, and associated with encouraging foreign investment and engagement.

25 The election of the President requires a majority of the regional member countries. The US and Canada are regional members, but of course the effective majority is with borrowers.

26 During much of the 1980s, the IDB had continued lending, but generally with fewer demands on governments for fiscal and other reforms.

27 The big borrowers might well agree to higher costs of borrowing if they had more control over the subsequent use of the incremental net income higher charges would generate – for example for increased financing of regional public goods. See Carnegie Endowment 2001, for discussion of this issue.

28 It is in fact much less clear today than was understood within the institutions at the time that domestic policy including emphasis on import substitution industrialization were for all purposes the only underlying cause of the debt build-up and subsequent lost decade in Latin America; today somewhat more emphasis would be put on the effects of external shocks interacting with domestic policy shortcomings. Similarly in the case of education, it is much less obvious today that there are not unmeasured positive externalities or spillovers associated with university education, and that, though reform of university financing is critical, political realism dictates broad-based reform of the kind initiated now in Brazil, not only or primarily an immediate imposition of higher tuition.

29 The Andean Development Bank no longer relies on borrowing from official sources to finance its lending operations. It now borrows on the private capital market. It is a notable example of a multilateral that has captured the benefits of a cooperative, since it now has a higher credit rating than any single one of its members, all of whom are borrowers.

30 The IDB is able to make loans without the recipient government or governments guaranteeing repayment; this has made it easier for it to provide loans to the subregional development banks. On the other hand, it is likely that the heavy presence of borrowers on the Board of the IDB has made it easier to secure approval of these loans.

References

African Development Bank (AfDB). 2001. *Annual Report.* Abidjan, Ivory Coast. Available at: www.afdb.org.

Asian Development Bank (ADB). 2001. *Annual Report.* Singapore. Available at: www.adb.org.

Behrman, Jere, Nancy Birdsall, and Miguel Székely. 2001. Economic Policy and Wage Differentials in Latin America. PIER Working Paper 01-048. Philadelphia: Penn Institute for Economic Research.

Birdsall, Nancy. 2001. Global Finance: Representation Failure and the Role of Civil Society. *Economic Reform Project Discussion Paper.* No. 2. Washington, DC. Carnegie Endowment for International Peace. Available at: http://www.ceip. org/files/publications/gf.asp.

Birdsall, Nancy. 2002. Asymmetric Globalization: Global Markets Require Good Global Politics. Working Paper No. 12. Washington, DC. Center for Global Development. Available at: www.cgdev.org.

Birdsall, Nancy and Estelle James. 1993. Efficiency and Equity in Social Spending: How and Why Governments Misbehave. In *Including the Poor,* edited by Michael Lipton and Jacques van der Gaag. New York: Oxford University Press.

Birdsall, Nancy, Stijn Claessens, and Ishac Diwan. 2004. Policy Selectivity Foregone: Debt and Donor Behavior in Africa. *World Bank Economic Review.* Also at www.cgdev.org.

Boughton, James and Alexandros Mourmouras. 2002. Is Policy Ownership an Operational Concept?. International Monetary Fund Working Paper No. 02/72.

Buira, Ariel. 2002. An Analysis of IMF Conditionality. G-24 Working Paper. Available at: www.cid.harvard.edu.

Caliari, Aldo and Frank Schroeder. 2003. Reform Proposals for the Governance Structures of the International Financial Institutions. Available at: www.new-rules.org.

Carnegie Endowment for International Peace. 2001. *The Role of the Multilateral Development Banks in Emerging Market Economies.* Findings of the Commission on the Role of the MDBs in Emerging Markets. Washington, DC: Carnegie Endowment for International Peace. Available at: www.ceip.org/econ.

Cline, William. 1997. *Trade and Income Distribution.* Washington, DC: Institute for International Economics.

Coate, Stephen and Stephen Morris. 2005. Policy Conditionality. This volume.

Cornia, Giovanni Andrea, Richard Jolly, and Frances Stewart. 1987. *Adjustment with a Human Face: Protecting the Vulnerable and Promoting Growth.* Oxford: Oxford University Press and UNICEF.

Corporacion Andina de Fomento. 2002. *Annual Report.* Available at: www.caf.com.

Deutscher, Eckhard. 2003. The World Bank Calls for Reform: On the Inefficiency of the Multilateral Development Structures. *Development and Change,* 2003.

Drazen, Allan. 2005. Conditionality and Ownership in IMF Lending: A Political Economy Approach. This volume.

Duryea, Suzanne and Miguel Székely. 1998. Labor Markets in Latin America: A Supply Side Story. Working Paper Research Department. No. 374. Washington, DC: Inter-American Development Bank.

Emerging Markets Eminent Persons Group (EMEPG). 2001. Rebuilding the International Financial Architecture. *EMEPG Seoul Report.* Seoul.

European Bank for Reconstruction and Development. 2002. *Annual Report.* Available at: www.ebrd.org.

Fernandez-Arias, Eduardo and Ricardo Hausmann. 2000. The Redesign of the International Financial Architecture: Who Pays the Bills?. Working Paper No. 440. Washington, DC: Inter-American Development Bank Research Department.

Griffith-Jones, Stephany and Jose Antonio Ocampo. 2001. Facing the Volatility and Concentration of Capital Flows. In *Reforming the International Financial System: Crisis Prevention and Response,* edited by Jan Joost Teunissen, pp. 31–63. The Hague: FONDAD.

Gwin, Catherine. 2002. *IDA's Partnership for Poverty Reduction: An Independent Evaluation of Fiscal Years 1994–2000.* Washington, DC: World Bank Operations Evaluation Department, World Bank.

Hausmann, Ricardo and Dani Rodrik. 2002. Economic Development as Self-Discovery. NBER Working Paper No. W8952. May.

Inter-American Development Bank. 2001. *Annual Report.* Washington, DC. Available at: www.iadb.org.

International Monetary Fund. 2002. *Annual Report.* Washington, DC. Available at: www.imf.org.

Kahler, Michael. 2001. *Leadership Selection in the Major Multilaterals.* Washington, DC: Institute for International Economics.

Kapur, Devesh. 2001. Reforming the International Financial System: Key Issues. *Global Financial Reform: How? Why? When?.* Ottawa: North-South Institute.

Kapur, Devesh. 2002. Do as I Say Not as I Do: A Critique of G-7 Proposals on Reforming the MDBs. Working Paper No. 16. Washington, DC: Center for Global Development. Available at: www.cgdev.org.

Kapur, Devesh. Forthcoming. International Human Capital Flows: The Case of India. Center for International Development. Harvard University.

Kapur, Devesh and John McHale. Forthcoming. *The War for Global Talent: Implications for Developing Countries.* Washington, DC: Center for Global Development.

Levy, Frank. 1998. *The New Dollars and Dreams: The Changing American Income Distribution.* New York: The Russell Sage Foundation.

Lucas, Robert. 1990. Why Doesn't Capital Flow from Rich to Poor Countries?. *American Economic Review* 80 (2): 92–6.

Meltzer Commission. 2000. Report of the International Financial Institution Advisory Commission. Available at: http://www.house.gov/jec/imf/meltzer.pdf.

Ocampo, Jose Antonio. 2002. Recasting the Internacional Financial Agenda. *External Liberalization, Economic Performance, and Social Policy.* New York: Oxford University Press.

Rodrik, Dani. 2001. Trading Illusions. *Foreign Policy.* March–April.

Rodrik, Dani. 2003. Growth Strategies. NBER Working Paper W10050. Cambridge, MA: National Bureau of Economic Research.

Sewell, John, Nancy Birdsall, and Kevin Morrison. 2000. The Right Role for the IMF in Development. ODC Policy Brief (May). Washington, DC: Overseas Development Council.

Stiglitz, Joseph. 2002. *Globalization and its Discontents.* New York: Norton.

Székely, Miguel. 1998. *The Economics of Poverty, Inequality and Wealth Accumulation in Mexico.* London: Macmillan.

Terrell, Katherine. 2000. Worker Mobility and Transition to a Market Economy: Winners and Losers. In *New Markets, New Opportunities? Economic and Social Mobil-*

ity in a Changing World, edited by Nancy Birdsall and Carol Graham. Washington, DC: Brookings Institution Press.

Terrell, Katherine and Thesia I. Garner. 2001. Some Explanations for Changes in the Distribution of Household Income in Slovakia: 1988 and 1996. University of Michigan Working Paper.

United Nations Development Programme (UNDP). 2001. Making New Technologies Work for Human Development. *Human Development Report. Report 2001*. New York: Oxford University Press.

United Nations Development Programme (UNDP). 1998. *Indian Human Development Report*. Bangalore, India: India Country Office.

Vreeland, James Raymond. 2003. *The IMF and Economic Development*. New York: Cambridge University Press.

Wapenhans, Will. 1992. Effective Implementation: Key to Development Impact. *Report of the World Bank's Portfolio Management Task Force*. Washington, DC: World Bank.

Willett, Thomas D. 2003. IMF Conditionality and the New Political Economy of Ownership. Mimeo.

Woods, Ngaire. 2000. The Challenge of Good Governance for the IMF and the World Bank Themselves. *World Development* 28 (5): 823–41.

Woods, Ngaire. 2002. Report of the Working Group on Institutional Reform, chaired by Ngaire Woods, sponsored by the International Development Research Council. Reports and proceedings available at: http://users.ox.ac.uk/~ntwoods/wg3.htm.

Woods, Ngaire and Amrita Narlikar. 2001. Governance and the Limits of Accountability: the WTO, the IMF, and the World Bank. *International Social Science Journal* 53 (170): 569–83.

World Bank. 2002. *Annual Report*. Washington, DC: World Bank. Available at: www.worldbank.org.

18 Do as I say not as I do

A critique of G-7 proposals on "reforming" the MDBs[1]

Devesh Kapur

1 Introduction

In recent years, reforming the Multilateral Development Banks (MDBs) has engaged the attention of a variety of blue ribboned commissions and groups. The most recent of these proposals was made by the G-7 at its summit in 2001. Considering the source, they are also the most noteworthy. While most of these reports and recommendations have focused on the key MDB – the World Bank – others have focused on the MDB system and, more broadly and ambitiously, the workings of the International Financial Institutions (IFIs). The principal recommendations of these different reports (including the G-7's recommendations) are summarized in an Appendix.[2] This chapter focuses on the World Bank and, where necessary, on other MDBs and the IMF.

The chapter addresses three key issues raised by the G-7:

1   The restructuring of the International Development Association (IDA) with a part of its lending in the form of grants rather than loans.
2   Harmonization of procedures, policies and overlapping mandates among MDBs.
3   The volume of support by MDBs for Global Public Goods (GPGs) and the rankings and priorities among these.

But like the dog that did not bark, the G-7 proposals are just as interesting for the issues they are silent on, as for the issues they choose to emphasize. This chapter highlights three omissions: the Bank's research and its contribution to GPGs; the high transaction and opportunity costs of World Bank lending and their implications for harmonization of the MDBs' procedures and policies; and issues of governance and accountability that fundamentally affect the "what" and "how" these institutions go about their business. Finally, the chapter examines the structural realities of the LDCs, and questions two strongly held beliefs about the MDBs that are virtually deemed axiomatic. One, whether the MDBs' goal of poverty alleviation is best achieved by their lending in social sectors; and second, whether in their quest for a larger IDA, LDCs might be sacrificing their larger interests in the global system.

Renewed attention to the MDBs is occurring in a geopolitical and economic context that presents LDCs, especially the poorest ones, with limited and bleak options. The end of the Cold War removed much of the rationale for foreign aid and recent studies questioning its efficacy have further vitiated the atmosphere for foreign aid. The steady decline of bilateral foreign aid has correspondingly increased financial pressures on no new multilateral institutions. As a result, multilateral institutions with greater financial autonomy, in particular, those less dependent on direct appropriations of public funds, have become relatively more important. Since a swift response to crisis requires rapid access to additional financial resources, the increased financial stringency coupled with an increase in disasters and crises, both natural and man-made, has enhanced the "liquidity premium" of multilateral institutions. Consequently, multilateral institutions that can commit new resources rapidly without having to seek recourse to budgetary appropriations from member governments – essentially the IFIs – are becoming more important, and consequently more prone to political pressure from major shareholders. As a result the MDBs' status as *multilateral* institutions is facing greater stress than ever before.

The LDCs themselves are more divided than ever before. The compact between the larger and stronger LDCs and their weaker counterparts has weakened considerably. Weaker LDCs, faced with fewer options, are more susceptible to political pressure and more amenable to being bought out. Stronger LDCs are less willing to spend their political capital on behalf of the weaker countries, further reducing the latter's bargaining power. The result has been a downward spiral of the capacity for collective action by LDCs. The larger LDCs have implicitly taken the foreign policy advice the late Deng Xiaoping gave his compatriots as he launched China on its growth path more than two decades ago: "keep a cool head, maintain a low profile, and never take the lead." Just as China, shedding Maoist exhortations of pursuing a "revolutionary foreign policy" aligned itself with the United States at the turn of the 1980s in pursuit of hard-nosed national interest, the larger LDCs (Brazil, China, India, Mexico, Pakistan to name a few) are less willing to expend their political capital championing "Third World" causes.

The structural reality of growing heterogeneity in preferences and severe collective action problems among LDCs must be kept in mind in examining the G-7 proposals. Any alternatives to the G-7 proposals must be seen to be in the interest of borrowers from both the hard and the soft windows of the MDBs, or else the recurring reality of fragmented LDC interests will result in the G-7 proposals once again carrying the day.

2 IDA and the "aidization" of the Bank

With regard to IDA, the G-7 called for an increased use of grants within IDA-13 and a review of lending terms for the blend countries, such that the terms for blend countries would be hardened while those for the IDA-only borrowers further softened. At first glance this proposition seems obviously worthy of strong support. However, a strategic review of what IDA has done to the Bank, and by implication the LDCs, might give pause.

IDA's accession to the Bank transformed both the scale and content of the institution's operations. On the one hand it helped finance repayments to the IBRD while also mitigating pressures on the IBRD to make loans to countries with low creditworthiness. On the other, it made the Bank less risk averse and more willing to experiment, especially in sectors that were more poor-oriented. At the same time, IDA expanded the institution's administrative budget, further softening what was already not a very hard budget constraint. The institution now had administrative resources to undertake a plethora of studies, analysis, reflections, conferences – all of which leveraged it head and shoulders above any alternative by the mid-1970s.

But what IDA gave to the Bank in the short term, it took away in the long term. In particular, IDA reduced institutional autonomy and fundamentally subverted the institution's governance. The market-based autonomy that the IBRD had gained for itself began to be eroded slowly, but surely, by the public monies that were the mainstay of IDA. The seeds were contained in the replenishment procedures of IDA – its periodicity and burden-sharing procedures – which rendered it extremely susceptible to the goodwill of major shareholders. In any burden-sharing scheme, the most powerful member sets the tone. From the late 1960s onwards, as the US began a long process of reducing its financial share, other donors began to link their contributions to that of the US – which paradoxically increased the bargaining power of the US even as its contributions declined. The periodicity meant that every three (sometimes four) years, new demands could be made of the institution. The peculiarities of the US budgetary process, wherein annual Congressional authorizations were an additional choke-point, not only ensured that the exercise became perennial but further enhanced US influence. Slowly but surely IDA became the tail that wagged the Bank dog with increasing vigor.

Through the 1960s and (especially) 1970s, the Bank managed to secure increases in IDA while maintaining a considerable degree of operational autonomy. This state of affairs began to change from the early 1980s onwards when the US began to exercise its muscle in a much more unilateral and preemptory manner. Any occasion when the Bank group asked its shareholders for additional funds was now seized by its non-borrowing shareholders as an opportunity to exercise leverage. Since capital increases for the IBRD, IFC, and MIGA were increasingly rare (just twice each in the last two decades), IDA replenishments became the principal mechanism for exercising leverage. The Bank both oversold the benefits of IDA and complied with each additional demand. The many small and poor LDCs, desperate to obtain any money, signed on to conditionalities without much intention (and even less capacity) to see them through. Other governments soon began to imitate the US, and donor interference in Bank decision making increased in the 1980s. IDA-9 was particularly significant coming as it did at the end of the Cold War. IDA deputies explicitly linked IDA replenishments to changes in the World Bank group's policies. As a result the locus of major policy decisions de facto shifted from the IBRD's Executive Board – the body charged by its Articles to make policy decisions – to the IDA deputies, and by extension to the richer countries. It is also one reason why donor countries have refused to lengthen the replenishment cycle of IDA (from three to five years as called for in the initial guidelines), since that allows the Bank to be kept on a shorter leash.[3]

Financial autonomy is the key to bureaucratic autonomy and can also be the crucial instrument to leverage change. Indeed, the IFIs' relative financial autonomy from their member governments annual (or biannual) budgetary vicissitudes has been central in giving them greater salience relative to the UN family. Pressed to give LDCs greater financial resources, IDA's – and hence the Bank group's – reliance on governmental monies increased. This not only amplified the power of major shareholders but also resulted in a shift in power (most acutely in the US) from the executive branch to the legislative branch and non-government actors. Given the reality that "the dynamics of the transnational advocacy process itself campaigns to focus on *available* pressure points – for example, in the case of US environmental NGOs lobbying the US Congress to pressure the Bank,"[4] this "availability," whether of the US Congress or another northern legislature, does not necessarily enhance the welfare of poor countries. To begin with, indirect channels of US influence are unsurpassed relative to any other shareholder: the much higher percentage of Bank staff educated in the US than in its early years; and the shaping of key Bank policies by a wide array of US non-governmental actors – academia, think-tanks, NGOs, and the like – a natural corollary both of the institution's geographical location but also the intellectual strength of US institutions.

Many of the latter factors had been true throughout the Bank's history. But with the end of the Cold War and the withering of US bilateral aid programs (as well as the Bank's own perceived vulnerabilities), they exercised substantially greater influence in the 1990s. The US has good reason to promote "participation" of NGOs, particularly in policy formulation. Participatory institutions can often yield highly inequitable outcomes as a result of the inequality of the participation process in already unequal settings, resulting from unequal consciousness of needs and the unequal ability to articulate demands or transform these demands into decisions. While the growth of NGOs is, on balance, a welcome trend, with thousands of NGOs globally to choose from, it should come as no surprise that, with a few notable exceptions, the agenda of the most vocal and media- and politically-savvy matters.

This strategic review of IDA holds several lessons for evaluating the G-7 proposals. At one level, the belief that a switch to grants will necessarily improve developmental prospects has weak analytical and empirical foundations. The debt problems of the HIPC countries occurred for a variety of causes ranging from the Cold War to egregious domestic leadership to exogenous shocks to poorly designed and executed foreign aid policies, not because IDA was not an outright grant. Perhaps the strongest argument for grants is that projects and programs run by non-state actors can be supported, which is important in "failed states" or states where the government is clearly not interested in the welfare of its citizens. However, IDA's articles permit lending without government guarantees, and although the institution has seldom exercised this option, it could move further in this direction.

As a series of IDA briefing notes (prepared for IDA-13) made clear, the principal implications of grants is that the long-term financial future of IDA is much bleaker, especially after a decade. This stems from the fact that just over half of IDA's resources are from fresh donor contributions.[5] The rest are from reflows and transfers from IBRD's net income. Given the reality of development over the past four decades, it stretches credulity to believe that the need for IDA (or some equivalent) would severely drop after a decade. One would be equally delusional to believe that the additional funds to supplement the loss of reflows to IDA would be easily forthcoming. In all probability the pressure on loan charges to IBRD borrowers would sharply increase to make for increased net income and thereby transfers to IDA. Indeed the IDA-13 agreement makes it clear that the IDA deputies "placed great importance on continued and substantial transfers to IDA and the HIPC program out of available IBRD net income during IDA 13."[6]

The final agreement on IDA-13 settled on grants being between 18–21 percent of the total replenishment resources. The grant proposal also deepened an emerging rift between IBRD and IDA-only borrowers, with the latter naturally inclined to support the G-7 proposals. As I will discuss later, IBRD borrowers are increasingly paying a high price – in the form of higher financial costs and much higher transaction and opportunity costs – for the institution's IDA fix. The root of the problem is that policy decisions relating not just to IDA, but to the institution as a whole, are increasingly being made by the IDA deputies (the representatives of the donor countries). Even as donors insist on the importance of participation and ownership, they routinely insist on IDA priorities that differ from those of borrowers. The latter for instance attach low priority to areas such as strengthening civic participation or promoting equitable treatment of women – both high in the priorities of donors (and IDA).[7] The result has been a creeping constitutional coup that has fundamentally subverted the role of the Executive Board in the World Bank's governance. Although for the first time the meetings of the Deputies of IDA-13 were opened to a modest extent to representatives of borrowing countries, in effect a parallel government has been created. It must be emphasized that there is a strong case to use a part of the IBRD's net income for global public goods – but these should be such as to benefit *poor people* more generally (as distinct from poor countries). These funds could also underwrite the Bank's role as a venture capitalist to support social entrepreneurship which benefit poor people in both IBRD and IDA countries. A good example of the latter is the innovative Development Marketplace program launched by the Bank a few years ago.[8] It is an open question that if the Bank were to ratchet up funding for the program (say by 20 percent a year for the next five years), the welfare implications for the world's poor would not be better than the status quo distribution of soft funds.

3 Governance and accountability

Debates on governance and accountability of the IFIs have largely been two-dimensional, focusing on governance and accountability issues in borrowing countries and the IFIs themselves. The third dimension – that of the major shareholders and "donors" – has been largely glossed over.

The design of Bretton Woods had built-in accountability of major shareholders by imposing a larger financial burden on them through larger cash outlays and contingent liabilities. Over its history, as the MDBs' financial strength grew and took firmer root, the cost of "ownership" fell: easier access to capital markets and comfortable equity reduced the need for additional paid-in capital, and higher reserves and the track record on defaults diminished the risks to the callable part of subscribed capital. As a result, the influence that came with ownership has become less expensive – indeed almost cost-free – and therefore more attractive. If capital increases in the MDBs are really that much of a burden (relative to the benefits of influence), then the major shareholders should only have been too happy to agree to a reduction in their shareholding. The fierce intensity of disputes centered on even slight changes in capital share, underscores the reality that the cost of influence is practically zero.

The growing disjuncture between influence and accountability of major shareholders and donors has become the *bête noire* of the World Bank in particular. Thus, transfers from IBRD net income to IDA allow major shareholders to retain the power of their voting shares over IDA while limiting their financial outlays. The Bank transferred $150 million from its net income to partially pay for the capital increase of the Multilateral

Investment Guarantee Agency (MIGA, an affiliate organization) in 1998. This transfer, which took place even as the Bank's management lamented the trends in net income, meant that, in effect, IBRD borrowers paid for the Bank's non-borrowers to retain their voting power in MIGA!

The G-7 proposals understandably made no mention of the governance of the MDBs and their own accountability for how they govern and pressure the MDBs. The rhetoric on the importance of governance and accountability of the MDBs and LDCs is in stark contrast to their determination that they may not be subjected to these same standards. This chapter has argued that IDA has increasingly served both to subvert the governance of the World Bank as well as the donors' accountability since it allows them to distance themselves from any developmental failures. These are inevitably attributed to the Bank and/or the borrowers but never the result of donor fads and political pressure. The Bank is hardly an innocent ingénue, but it has also become a convenient scapegoat.

The burden of leadership seldom meets universal acclaim, and the owners of multilateral institutions are particularly adept at shifting blame to multilateral institutions when the terrain gets rough, as the UN learnt in Somalia, Bosnia, and Iraq, and the IFIs have learnt in Africa, Bosnia, Gaza, and Russia. It must be emphasized that the IFIs' policy prescriptions and operational stances are all approved – more or less unanimously – by their owners, exercising their prerogatives through their executive directors. Even more, as has been the case with the instructions of the IDA deputies in the context of IDA replenishments (and quota increases in the case of the IMF), many policies have been imposed on the institution by some of its major shareholders for a variety of domestic reasons. The record on this is unambiguous. Consequently, to whatever extent the IFIs have "failed," their dominant shareholders bear the brunt of the responsibility.

The governance structures of the Bretton Woods institutions had tried to balance power, represented by larger shareholdings, with accountability, in the form of larger financial contributions to the IBRD's capital. Over time, financial trends in the IBRD led to a weakening of this link to the extent that today, the marginal cost of influence is virtually negligible. It is this de-linking of power from accountability that has created a form of moral hazard, that has emerged as the critical governance issue in all IFIs.[9]

Thus even as donors insist on "increasing selectivity" and urge the Bank to be more flexible and not be weighed down by bureaucratization, each IDA replenishment comes up with additional issues. These are then applied to the institution as a whole, including the IBRD, even as the donors sing hosannas on the importance of borrowing country "ownership." Observers of government bureaucracies have long recognized that multiplicity of missions impairs bureaucratic incentives and erodes institutional autonomy.[10] Insisting on high standards on multiple issues is at best pointless and in all likelihood inimical in countries with the most limited institutional resources. In retrospect this was the case with the WTO agreements which were an "inappropriate diagnosis and an inappropriate remedy, one incompatible with the resources they [developing countries] have at their disposal" (Finger and Schuler 1999).

This has become the case with IDA as well. On the one hand donors insist that stakeholders be involved in Bank projects. However, when it comes to Bank policies, especially lending priorities, they are much more reticent. A survey of preferences of opinion leaders from IDA borrowing countries found that the "Northern" agenda is near the bottom of the list (IDA 2001b: tables 3 and 4).

The donors would like IDA to put greater stress on post-conflict countries, an eminently sensible idea. But to ensure that the funds will be spent wisely, there are all sorts of progress indicators – no less than 29. IDA-13's objectives total 23 and its recommendations/actions total no less than 62 (one of which is "increasing selectivity"!).[11] To the many well-meaning goals has been added the laudable objective of "anti-money laundering" with the deputies stressing that IDA "should help borrower countries improve the regulatory and supervisory systems for the financial sector, strengthen the legal framework for combating money laundering and similar crimes, and promote transparency and good governance principles (para. 57)." One might have thought that given the existence of other institutions with greater expertise and work in the financial sector (the IMF and the Financial Sector Task Force (FATF)), an institution whose core function is poverty reduction would be a tad more focused. Many of the same donors that insist on "curbing non-productive including [excessive] military expenditure reviews" are also the ones that line up on arms sales.

A reading of the IDA-13 document makes clear that the need to feel good and be *seen* to do good has vastly outstripped any sense of realism. This can only happen in a context where accountability is severely asymmetrical; while donors cannot be held accountable in any substantively meaningful sense, recipients have to live up to multiple objectives over the next three years. An additional problem arises from the fact that unless targets match underlying objectives precisely, they tend to create perverse incentives. They divert innovation from productive enterprises to the pursuit of targets. When the measure becomes a target, it ceases to be a good measure. The solution is not to produce yet more prescriptive rules, but unfortunately that is precisely what has happened.

That matters have come to this pass reflects, at least in part, the failures of the institution's management and Board. The Executive Board, long deprived of real power both by management and by their countries, has done little to improve governance, handicapped by the fact that few members appear to rise above the parochial interests of their constituencies to dwell on long-term institutional interests. Its caliber is often indifferent, with appointments from LDCs often reflecting complex political compromises both within countries as well as among constituencies. Nominally, the Bank's principals – its Executive Board – act on behalf of the members to exercise oversight. But built-in structural features of the Board – ranging from the frequency of rotation for Executive Directors to widely varying agendas – make its task of oversight difficult.[12]

While asymmetric information between principals and agents can strengthen the agent's hand, the problem is particularly acute in the case of the Bank, where differing interests among principals and the inherent ambiguities in ascribing specific outcomes on the ground to specific institutional actions further strengthen the agents' hands. In any case, borrowing country members of the Board are both principals and agents, which leads them to oppose, or at best reluctantly support, tight budgets.

The roots of this attitude lie in a collective action problem. Borrowing countries are individually unwilling to publicly cross swords with management on the budget, fearing that their programs will be singled out to bear the burden of cuts.[13] They are also wary of subjecting loans to critical analysis fearing that "what goes around comes around."[14] Consider for instance the recent (in January 2002) announcement by President Wolfensohn at the Afghanistan reconstruction donors' conference in Tokyo, that the Bank would commit itself to $500 million for the reconstruction of that country. That decision was announced without the approval of the Executive Board, even though a sum of that magnitude is bound to have repercussions for other IDA countries. Despite strong private reservations, publicly the Executive Board simply rubber stamped the decision, given the political sensitivity of the issue. On Iraq, even as the US was pressing the World Bank to get involved in reconstruction, once again it was one of the few donors that had not provided the necessary commitment authority when the IDA-13 replenishment came into effect in April 2003.

A different tack in shaping institutional priorities has been the use of "trust funds," by some donors. By supplementing the institution's budgetary resources, countries have sought to influence institutional priorities and governance by bypassing the Bank's budgetary process.[15] To the extent that budgets reflect the priorities of an institution, the growing share of off-budgetary funds in financing administrative expenses changes micro-incentives within organizations. It provides a mechanism for change from below, even when change from above is stymied by the lack of change in formal institutional governance structures. But Trust Funds are fundamentally a form of off-balance sheet financing. And as Enron has proven, while off-balance sheet transactions offer considerable flexibility and foster entrepreneurship, their very seductiveness can carry large risks. And in this case, the risk is the governance of the Bank itself.

4 Harmonization and cost of lending

The G-7 proposals also called for greater MDB coordination and harmonization in policies and procedures. It is indeed surprising that in a variety of operational areas ranging from procurement to financial and audit procedures, even today the MDBs do not have common procedures. In this specific regard the G-7 proposals can only be welcomed and it is a measure of the collective action abilities of LDCs, that even on an issue of such obvious importance to them, they have been unable until now to press the MDBs to do more in this direction.

However, it is clear that the G-7 call for harmonization goes well beyond *procedures* to encompass *policies* as well. In particular, the G-7 is pressing for reducing the operational overlap among the MDBs as well as imposing common and higher standards in MDB policies, with the World Bank serving as the yardstick. For a variety of reasons, the G-7 has been unable to get the Regional Development Banks to adopt as stringent safeguards as the World Bank was forced to adopt due to the pressures brought by the environmental NGOs and the US Congress, using IDA as leverage (Table 18.1). The MDB with the fewest safeguard policies in place, the EBRD, is also the one where LDCs are least involved.

At one level, pressure from the G-7 for the MDBs to identify their comparative advantages and provide justification for any overlapping seems an obvious way to cut flab from the MDB system. It could also be in concordance with the global movement recognizing the benefits inherent in decentralization, with the MDB system reconfiguring by promoting the

Table 18.1 Safeguard area policies in MDBs, 2001

Safeguard area	AfDB	AsDB	EBRD	IDB	IBRD/IDA
Environmental assessment	Guideline	Policy	Policy	Guideline	Policy
Forestry	Policy	Policy	NR	Policy	Policy
Involuntary resettlement	NR	Policy	NR	Policy	Policy
Indigenous peoples	Policy	Policy	NR	Guideline	Policy
International waterways	NR	NR	NR	NR	Policy
Dam safety	Guideline	Guideline	NR	NR	Policy
Natural habitats	NR	Guideline	NR	NR	Policy
Pest management	Guideline	NR	NR	NR	Policy
Cultural resources	Guideline	Guideline	NR	NR	OPN
Projects in disputed areas	NR	NR	NR	NR	Policy

Source: IBRD 2001a: table 3.

Notes
NR: No Requirement; OPN: Operational Policy Note (being converted into a policy).

principle of subsidiarity with greater resources and responsibilities devolving to regional (and sub-regional) organizations. And more coordination is usually better, especially in countries with limited coordinating capabilities.

But at the same time it is curious why, if competition is deemed so virtuous in economic and political markets, cartel-like arrangements and not competition is the preferred solution to restructuring the MDB system. The argument that competition (or institutional overlap) is undesirable in the case of public institutions has weak analytical basis. Consider for instance theories of "polycentricity" (Ostrom *et al.* 1961; Ostrom 1999) where a political system has multiple coexisting centers of decision making that are formally independent of one another. In practice, however, they may function independently or form interdependent links, and they may support or thwart each other.

However, the interdependence follows some set of general norms and can thus be somewhat predicted. In such systems, this ordered set of relationships underlies and reinforces the fragmentation of central authority and overlapping of jurisdiction that would otherwise be deemed chaotic. The fragmentation of authority inherent in such a system is often seen to be inefficient (most notably in the case of metropolitan polities in the US where the theory was first applied) with the presence of various governmental bodies at different levels and overlapping jurisdiction leading to the phenomenon of too many governments but too little government. In practice, however, it has been demonstrated that polycentrism can be as, if not more, efficient than monocentric political systems, especially in the provision of public goods.

Another desirable feature of overlapping mandates is that given the limited "voice" option available to poor countries in the IFIs, exit is the only weapon of the weak. Even then for a majority of poor countries exit is not a viable option – leaving them with Hobson's choice, an enforced loyalty. The "market" for international organizations is for the most part not contestable except in the few areas where both regional and global institutions exist. "Forum shopping" allows borrowers to have at least a modicum of choice between a regional development bank and the World Bank and harmonization can be the slippery slope to cartelization.[16] For LDCs, overlapping (especially vertical) jurisdictions are preferable to non-competing cartel-like clauses.

That the MDB system is a high-cost system is not in doubt. But the costs are not because of institutional overlap. Rather, they are due to overregulation of the MDBs, and are manifest in higher budgetary expenditures, higher borrowing rates, higher overall borrowing costs, and high opportunity costs of sectors and programs where lending has dwindled because of substantially greater transactional costs and risks.

The regulatory burden is most onerous at the World Bank. There is no disputing the reality that many Bank projects have had problems and in some case have created serious problems, both ecological and human. But there is another reality, wherein the Bank is a small actor whose efforts for the most part have been dwarfed by much more powerful forces – whether the sheer scale of demographic pressures, the rising material aspirations of billions of people, the informatics revolution, external shocks both political and economic, technological scale and its own smallness (other than in the small poor countries). The physical and human costs of poor policies, poor investments, and poor national leadership and the meddlings of the super powers have vastly exceeded the worst efforts of the World Bank. In contrast, the benefits of the efforts of MDBs in persuading borrowers, donors, and the private sector to eschew white elephant projects are seldom visible.

Beset by external pressures, the Bank has created innumerable safeguards to ring-fence itself from risk. The additional administrative costs of these new safeguard/fiduciary policies were estimated to be about $81 million in FY01. Borrower costs in meeting these requirements were estimated to be $118–215 million (IBRD 2001: table 18.1.2). But a different cost might be the most expensive for LDCs in terms of its development impact – the changing composition of lending. In the last five years, Bank lending for infrastructure has declined sharply – for electric power and energy from $2 billion to $0.75 billion; for transportation by 28 percent over the same period; and for water and sanitation by 25 percent. It is noteworthy that the decline began when the Inspection Panel was formed. Is there a connection?

In all international organizations, the principals (national governments) delegate a task to an agent (the Bank) but with imperfect information about how the agent is going about it. While shareholders need to monitor the Bank to ensure that it is going about it in the way they want, the institution has better information than anyone else on how good a job it is doing. Since the mid-1980s, a variety of well-publicized Bank project disasters led to mounting skepticism about the ability and willingness of the Bank to monitor itself and eventually resulted in the creation of an independent Inspection Panel despite the presence of two internal monitoring mechanisms (Internal Audit and the Ombudsman) and one quasi-independent one (OED, the Operations Evaluation Department). The common assumption was that increased public scrutiny would keep the institution honest and save the world's poor from the depredations of the institution.

However, as Prendergast (2001) has argued, external monitoring may be no better because outside monitors (independent overseer departments, the press and so on) rely on complaints to initiate investigations. This means that the activities of the Inspection Panel will be skewed toward cases where complaints are filed. This will invariably be in cases where the project was poorly conceived and/or executed (and even there they may not all be justified), *not the cases where good projects were incorrectly not pursued.*

In the absence of full information available to the external overseers, Bank staff now face what appears to be a perverse choice: aggressively pushing loans at the risk of individually bearing the costs of complaints brought by outsiders, or letting things slide in the knowledge that the costs of loans forgone will be borne by the country, and any resulting criticism (e.g., stagnant lending) will be borne by the institution collectively, and not them individually. This does not mean that institutions such as the Inspection Panel were necessarily a retrograde step, but rather that monitoring agents in the public sector, where outputs are often by their nature unclear and diffuse, are more complex than it may appear. Moreover, since the mandate of the Bank's Inspection Panel explicitly rules out investigating inappropriate major shareholder pressure on Bank management and staff, its policing role is inherently limited.

The concern with quality is obviously quite valid. But there are trade-offs and while the changing pattern of Bank lending may satisfy major shareholders and their civil society, all of them enjoy the privileges of the infrastructural services that the Bank is now wary of lending to LDCs. The Bank's involvement in infrastructure projects, more often than not, reduces both the scope of corruption and inappropriate policies, which can impose substantial costs on a country. It is a measure of the power of donor country interest groups that in contrast to environmental costs these opportunity costs are seldom highlighted, even though their impact on the poor could well dwarf environmental costs.[17] Moreover, the multiple safeguards have turned the Bank to a high cost operation whose administrative costs have little to do with lending, and a lot to do with the bells and whistles that keep many other constituencies satisfied. Of the $1.2 billion administrative budget in 2001, *just $94 million – less than 8 percent –* was for lending (i.e., preparation of projects). "Client services" were $564 million, less than half of the total budget. And expenditure on the corporate secretariat (mainly the Executive Board) itself was $67 million, more than two-thirds that on lending! The rest reflects major shareholder driven mandates (whether directly or through their "stakeholders") and presidential proclivities which are not challenged by IBRD borrowers.

The individual interests of all concerned parties have meant that opposition to such a high cost operation has been muted. IBRD borrowers have worried about private costs, management and staff about their livelihood, and major shareholders and western NGOs about the loss of a useful mechanism for putting pressure on borrowing governments. Major shareholders in particular have used their control rights to secure their particularistic objectives. By caving into such pressures, the Bank has raised its transactions costs and undermined an important comparative advantage built over the years as one of the finest global financial intermediaries. Additionally, the undue optimism with regards to the volumes and virtues of private capital flows, has meant that this comparative advantage of the Bank has been underutilized in the interests of LDCs.

5 Global public goods

The Bank is involved in 70 global programs the majority of which are less than five years old.[18] Thirty of these programs are managed partially in the Bank and the rest outside. In 2001 it spent $30 million of its administrative budget, $120 million from the Development Grant Facility (financed by transfers from net income) and another $500 million from Bank administered trust funds for global programs. Of the 70 global programs, 13 provide global public goods, 30 national public goods with potential transnational spillovers, 20 national public goods without spillovers and 7 merit goods.[19]

The IDA Deputies and the G-7 have pressed the Bank to focus on GPGs, and have asked that "fighting infectious diseases, promoting environmental improvement, facilitating trade and promoting financial stability" be the "MDBs' main priorities in the field of GPGs." There is little evidence on why this list, and not some other, might be the institution's priorities. Despite much ado about GPGs, there is little substantive analysis that would help IO members to rank global public goods in order of their relative contribution to global welfare. This analytical hiatus gives both principals (the Bank's major shareholders) and agents (the Bank's management and staff) greater discretion. It allows them to press for private interests in the guise of GPGs. With foreign aid budgets declining and the remaining budgets further constrained by bilateral objectives, the resources of the World Bank – whether its administrative budget or its net income – have been viewed as a cash-cow by interest groups wishing to finance both genuine GPGs as well as narrower private goods.

Just 20 of the Bank's global programs provide investments. Knowledge creation and global consensus on best practice are viewed by Bank staff and managers as potentially the most useful contribution of these programs to global public goods. However, "most have not built the capacity of developing countries to access new knowledge and achieve empowerment."[20] For the most part these programs do not focus on global public policy formulation nor do they try to enhance the quality and effectiveness of developing countries' participation in international negotiations. Developing countries are involved in implementation but have little voice in "design, governance, and management of most global programs."[21]

In seeking to reinvent the Bank's public image, its management and staff have tended to label all kinds of activities or "networks" as GPGs, meriting involvement on the basis of the moral claims that public goods invoke, and their ready slogan-appeal for Northern taxpayers. While many initiatives certainly do meet the criteria of public goods, the management also includes what one might call "Potemkin GPGs." A good example was the Bank's initiative related to the World Faiths Development Dialogue. The burden of financing GPGs in the case of the World Bank has fallen increasingly on IBRD borrowers. It is indeed true that IBRD loans have a subsidy element in that they are cheaper than market alternatives, but is balanced by much lower default rates on IBRD loans and substantially higher transaction costs faced by borrowers.

In recent years international financial institutions have witnessed a perceptible shift in burden sharing, with borrowers now picking up a greater part of the burden; the World Bank provides an excellent case in point. Over the past half century, the IBRD has witnessed a steady downward trend in the share of usable capital in total usable equity – more than two-thirds of its usable equity now comes from retained earnings and less than a third from usable capital. However, control rights have essentially remained unchanged in these institutions. Consequently, the priorities implicit in the selective support of Global Public Goods reflect historical control rights in the IFIs, not the changing patterns of burden sharing in the past three decades.

6 Is research a global public good?[22]

A critical feature of the IMF and World Bank that distinguishes them from other international organizations is an extensive (and expensive) commitment to research. Developing countries for the most part have not critically examined the IFIs' research activities, be it the quantum of resources devoted to research, the distribution of those resources among different research activities or the optimal institutional mechanisms to generate the research. Consider for instance the following hypothetical questions:

1   If the Bank's and Fund's budgets were cut by half and the resulting savings were put into research in those diseases, agriculture, and energy technologies that are *sui generis* to poor countries, would the global welfare of the poor improve or decline?
2   If the Bank were to double its funding for research in the health sciences and halve the expenditures in the social sciences, would the global welfare of the poor increase or decline?
3   If the Bank's research activities were more akin to a National Science Foundation (NSF) type funding activity rather than in-house research, would LDCs gain or lose?

A large array of studies has demonstrated the high rates of return in publicly funded research (Salter and Martin 2001). The knowledge that investments in R&D have high rates of social return do not, however, provide any guidance either on which areas to finance investment in nor the precise mechanism to undertake this task. Although most research shows high rates of return to public research, average values are of little use when deciding whether to increase (or decrease) funding for public research or what mechanism would yield the best results (resource allocation decisions require some sense of marginal rather than average rates of return). Moreover, there is no analytical framework that would help answer if IFIs should themselves conduct research, outsource it (by funding universities or research centers), promote research joint ventures, promote exchange of personnel, or build research networks.

The dilemmas are compounded by the reality that research capabilities are located in the North while many of the issue areas with the highest rates of social return to public investments in research are in resource-poor countries. Furthermore, even if the World Bank were to out-source its research and fund more research, what mechanisms should it follow? In areas where research is undersupplied because of severe market failures (such as tropical diseases, where pharmaceutical firms do not invest fearing that were they to actually develop a product, they would face severe public pressure to sell the product at a price that would not justify the initial investment), a novel mechanism is for public agencies to guarantee buying vaccines meeting predetermined specifications for a certain price (Kremer 2000).

But while a "tournament" approach has much to speak for it, it does little to build developing countries' own capabilities. While this is not important in those areas where delay has high human costs, the issue is quite different in policy research. Consider for instance the participation of researchers at the flagship Annual World Bank Conference on Development Economics. As Table 18.2 indicates, researchers based in LDCs are barely 4 percent of the authors.

The figures for the Annual IMF conference are scarcely better (Table 18.3). One example is the IMF's conference (in November 1999) on "Second Generation Reforms" seeking to understand "why stabilization and structural adjustment programs of the past, while successful in jump-starting economies, have not been able to ensure the quality and sustainability of renewed growth."[23] None of the twenty authors and discussants were based in an LDC, the ostensible object of the reforms over the past two decades. This is despite the reality that development economics is for the most part a peripheral field in mainstream economics.[24] The mainline prestigious journals, usually give articles with micro-data painstakingly collected in an LDC short shrift (Bardhan 2003). These journals act as

Table 18.2 Annual World Bank conferences on development economics, 1995–2000

	Location of affiliation			Total
	US	Non-US North	LDCs	
Papers				57
Authors	58	15	3	76
Discussants	53	12	16	83

Table 18.3 Annual IMF research conferences, 2000–01

	Location of affiliation			Total
	US	Non-US North	LDCs	
Papers				24
Authors	46	7	4	57
Discussants	22	2	2	26

gatekeepers of knowledge as well as reputation, important for the who, how, and what that dominates the IFIs' research agenda. For the most part this service is positive, given the concentration of talent in these institutions. But the fact is that unless a researcher is part of this circuit, she is marginalized.

The meager representation of LDC-based researchers in these conferences is a sad testimony to the structures of knowledge production. And if knowledge is power, it underlies the powerlessness of LDCs. It is true that the IFIs organize conferences on issues in which there are many more participants from the countries who are the nominal beneficiaries of these exercises. However, on subjects that have *systemic* (as opposed to country-specific) implications, the contributors are invariably from a narrow base.

There are several good reasons why concerns on this score may not be warranted. For one, there are typically participants from developing countries in these conferences. It just so happens that their institutional base is in the US. Second, the idea that one's analytical position is an isomorphic reflection of one's nationality and/or geographical base is rather specious. Third, one could argue that the IFIs should only be drawing on the best talent to understand difficult issues, and if it so happens that the talent is North American based, so be it. Fourth, the fears of lack of diversity are misplaced given the vigorous debates and differences that are integral to the academic and intellectual culture in the US. And finally, the skewed participation may simply reflect the realities of the global production of knowledge, in which LDCs themselves have played a not insignificant role by running their own universities and knowledge production systems to the ground.

However, there are grounds for unease as well. For long, an important ingredient of East Asian success was the "embeddedness" of the state manifest in "thick" networks of business–government relations. Following the crisis, the other side of these networks became apparent in what was termed as "crony capitalism." Intellectual networks are similarly double-edged. They reduce selection costs and can serve as reputational mechanisms but can also be prone to a form of "crony intellectualism." There is an inherent tendency to inbreeding which has negative consequences for biological species or for intellectual advancement. Researchers, like other societal groups, also have interests. From research funding to access to data and visibility – research involvement with the IFIs has substantial payoffs. It also skews the priorities of research staff in these institutions – the cognitive payoffs of delivering a paper on Africa are substantially greater in Cambridge, Massachusetts than in Côte d'Ivoire. In turn that means that the questions and methodologies will, at least at the margin, be such as to ensure that it will be received well in the former, even though the latter audience might have a different set of priorities as to research questions and have more at stake.

An important strategic benefit – and potentially critical for developing countries – of publicly funded research is the creation of capabilities, in particular the vital linkage between research and the supply of skilled graduates. To put it differently, the process of research creates capabilities that allows for better consumption or use of knowledge. Additionally, public funding of research in different environments plays an important role in the creation of diverse options. The importance of diversity is particularly important in the context of an uncertain future (Stirling 1998). Moreover, diversity may matter in and of itself on the grounds that there should be at least a minimum degree of participation by those likely to be affected by the consequences of the actions resulting from ideas emanating from these institutions. Diversity may also be important for its instrumentality – it diversifies risk, a not unimportant criterion given limited knowledge and the consequences of misplaced advice.

The virtual absence of researchers based in developing countries in the more prestigious development conferences cannot be attributed simply to exclusionary networks. Given the outpouring of reports on key global debates involving the IFIs, networks and reputation are critical screening mechanisms. On both counts, a base in a developing country virtually ensures extinction. The developing countries – especially the larger ones – have much to answer for themselves, having failed to develop and maintain reputational institutions in the social sciences.[25] The poor quality of developing country academic institutions in the social sciences leads the IFIs to not only draw their research staff from US universities (which then creates research networks between these staff and faculty in those universities), but when these institutions want to train and support developing country students or send their own staff for training it is invariably again at US universities.[26] Given the outstanding quality of the latter, the short-term compulsions of the Bretton Woods institutions are quite understandable, but their long-term consequences are inimical. These practices have strengthened already strong research institutions in the US while further weakening developing country institutions – creating conditions for perpetuating the practice. The process has generated a vicious circle with results that are in line with models of statistical discrimination. The more the World Bank and the IMF in effect discriminate against researchers from LDCs, the more the incentive of these researchers to migrate out of the countries either to these institutions themselves or to developed countries where their credibility is enhanced by their association with a developed country institution, furthering the decline of LDC research institutions.

Indeed, in some issue areas, the quest for supplying public goods at the global level may be amplifying the deficit at the national level. Agricultural research is a case in point. According to one estimate, while nearly a third of the hundreds of agricultural researchers who routinely attend the CGIAR's annual "Centers' Week" meetings at the World Bank were originally from LDCs, only one in twenty were still actually affiliated with LDC national research institutes or universities.[27] With donors viewing the building of research capacity in LDCs as "elitist," research as a public good is seen to be better supplied at the global rather than the national level. However, it may well be the case that in areas ranging from agricultural to economical research, LDC researchers faced with rewards that are much greater in international rather than national research organizations, gravitate toward the former. As a result, while the supply of global public goods (in the form of research in agriculture and economics) is reasonably adequate, public goods deficits at the national level, involving the production of country specific knowledge, may be increasing.

As a result, a half century into "development," developing countries still seem incapable of thinking for themselves on issues (to put it crudely) critical to their own welfare, at least as measured by the lack of meaningful contributions that would find a place at the high seats of social science research. What have the Bretton Woods institutions done in the last half-century to build institutions in developing countries that could help them think for themselves?

For the most part the answer is "not much." Research is centralized in both institutions – and to the extent that ideas shape agendas, centralized control of research is an excellent unobtrusive approach to set the agenda. Large salary differentials offered by these institutions and developing country research institutions (with the exception of some Latin American countries) means that they often draw out limited talent in developing countries. Moreover, for nearly two decades the IFIs have been chary of supporting institutions of higher learning, directing resources to primary and secondary education and justifying this shift both on equity and efficiency grounds. Foundations have also joined the bandwagon against supporting research institutions in developing countries on the grounds that they were elitist and that instead, "grass-roots" institutions needed more support. In both cases there was more than ample justification for the shift – but in the process both the IFIs and the foundations have thrown the baby out with the bathwater. It has meant that developing country researchers are by and large restricted to data collection and country specific applied work, incapable of contributing anything meaningful to "big ideas" on debates ranging from global financial architecture to second generation reforms.

The IFIs have never seriously attempted to subject their substantial research expenditures to rigorous rate-of-return calculations. Admittedly the task would be analytically difficult, but there are few incentives within the institutions to do so. Arguably, if even a third of this expenditure was instead redirected at creating endowments for regional research centers in developing countries, it is at least an open question if the welfare of those societies may not be better. It may help LDCs to think for themselves – and take responsibility for the actions resulting from their ideas – rather than be the perennial objects of received wisdom.

The rhetoric of the World Bank and IMF on institutions notwithstanding, they have been tepid in supporting initiatives to develop research capacity in LDCs, although over the last decade the World Bank has made some efforts to support regional research centers.[28] Kanbur (2001) has argued that the World Bank's research as a global public good is undermined by its lack of independence, real or perceived, and without this independence, the Bank's research will always be found wanting as a global public good. The IDB has been more creative in this regard. It has been coordinating the Latin American Research Network, created in 1991, and funds leading research centers in the region to conduct research on economic and social issues in Latin America and the Caribbean.[29]

The World Bank-supported Global Development Network (GDN, which has now been spun off as an independent entity) is an interesting innovation aimed at linking researchers and policy institutes involved in the field of development. The network also aims at skill and reputation building. This is a commendable effort, although it is too early to gauge its impact. However, even the GDN is unlikely to address the problem of how developing country researchers can overcome the high reputational barriers that exist on research and policies related to systemic issues. That requires a receptivity and openness in the IFIs themselves which is structurally difficult. Virtually all the links in the research web sites of the IFIs are to researchers in developed countries, a reflection of the quality of research from LDCs but also an indication of the personal networks of research staff in these institutions. A potentially bigger weakness of the GDN is that to the extent its links are more with LDC think-tanks and research centers that are not university-based, it could perversely undermine university research (and long-term training) even further, as researchers flee to the more flexible, connected and better paying think-tanks if LDCs do not act to reform their corroding public university systems.

It should be emphasized that in-house research at the Bank is expensive, even when compared to US universities, let alone LDCs. Consequently, it would appear that all factors, from operating costs to opportunity costs (using the resources to build capabilities in LDCs), would seem to support a serious reconsideration of the allocation of research resources by the World Bank. The only reason why this may not be advantageous is if there are operational externalities for the World Bank in that the possibility of being able to undertake research at the Bank, attracts higher quality personnel (especially economists) who then contribute positively to the operations side of the Bank.[30]

Research and international discourse on the international financial system have been dominated by the Bretton Woods institutions and US academia. This domination reflecting in part the outstanding quality of the latter, has several undesirable consequences. It skews the questions, methodologies, and other priorities of research. As a result, those directly affected by the policies of the IFIs are underrepresented in setting the research and policy agenda. Furthermore, it narrows the diversity of views, which, given limited knowledge and the possibility of wrong advice, could amplify risk in the international system.

7 Prospects for the future and what can be done

The bargaining hand of LDCs in international fora has weakened considerably in recent years. On the one hand they face an adverse political and economic environment. On the other, LDCs increasingly have diverse political and economic interests which have reduced their capacity for collective action, be it international trade negotiations, concessional financing, or IFI reform. Selectively targeting benefits to specific LDCs has ensured that money buys silence. The high discount rates of LDC governments has led them to bargain away their interests in issues that affect their long-term future – barriers to their exports; intellectual property rights; environmental and labor standards – for very modest amounts of additional financial resources. An important lesson of IDA is that LDCs should be more wary of donors bearing gifts.

This chapter has attempted to critically analyze the G-7's MDB reform proposals. It has argued that reconstituting IDA in the form of grants will have significant financial repercussions for IDA in the medium term. Consequently, it would be best if only a modest fraction of IDA was in the form of grants, and the final IDA-13 agreement appears to veer in this direction. However, it has to be stated that it is the donors' prerogative to decide how much of their contributions should be used in the form of grants. LDCs should, however, hold the line on the transfer of IBRD net income to IDA. Since the policy and strategic decisions with regard to IDA are being made de facto outside the policy making body of the World Bank (the Executive Board), transfers from IBRD's net income should be placed in a separate pool whose principal objective would be to fund projects that maximize the welfare of *poor people* rather than *poor countries* and the allocation decisions should rest solely with the Executive Board.

The LDCs should also insist that the role of IDA deputies should be sharply curtailed, if not scrapped altogether. Additionally, the replenishment period of IDA should be increased to five years coinciding (roughly) with the contractual term of the appointment of the World Bank's president. The short duration of the IDA replenishment process imposes high transaction costs on all parties. Senior managers and staff as well as officials from donor countries spend inordinate amounts of time on raising resources with no downtime between successive replenishments. The short cycle has also led the MDBs to be locked into short time-horizons that respond to the impatient demands of donors, changing academic fashions, and internal bureaucratic imperatives. The process has amplified donor country interest group pressures, thereby undermining the governance of the World Bank.

The G-7 has proposed that the Bank group focus on four global public goods: infectious diseases, environment, trade and financial stability. While there is strong consensus on the first, the others are more problematic. It is unclear what precisely constitutes the "environment" and why the last two rank so high in priority relative to alternatives is a mystery. It is strange that there is no mention of support for the one GPG that the Bank can rightly be proud of, namely agriculture innovation through support for the CGIAR system. Support for research on tropical and dry land agriculture, non-conventional energy and cheap water purification technologies are likely to affect the well-being of the poor in more fundamental ways than trade. In any case, LDCs should first insist on better analytical and empirical evidence before prioritizing GPGs. With regard to the harmonization of procedures and policies among the MDBs, it is strongly in the interest of the LDCs that procedures, especially those related to procurement and financial reporting, be common to all MDBs. However, it is equally in their interest that harmonization of policies and overlapping of jurisdictions *not* be formalized. While informal co-ordination is welcome, each MDB should decide its own priorities rather than having them imposed from above.

Finally, this chapter has argued that increasingly stringent compliance standards of the World Bank in particular are imposing high financial and opportunity costs on the Bank's borrowers. It is trivially easy for the major shareholders to insist on standards whose costs they do not bear. The most inimical aspect of this pressure is that it has forced the Bank to shift lending toward sectors where it has little comparative advantage (and indeed where it cannot have comparative advantage) and away from the very sectors where it does have comparative advantage.

In recent years it has become a matter of dogma that the MDBs' principal goal of poverty alleviation is best achieved through broadly defined "social development" projects. LDCs should have serious misgivings about the *instruments* to exercise the 29 universally accepted goals. International organizations with *universal* membership will invariably impose *universal* standards and norms. And more than ever before, the universal standards that come attached to external resources, bring with them their own priorities, consultants, values, and technologies. It is one thing to deploy these resources for physical infrastructure, for knowledge production especially in areas that affect the well-being of the poor in the low income countries (such as research on tropical diseases, tropical agriculture, non-conventional energy resources), but it is quite another for the resources to be focused almost exclusively on social development, which is much more context specific, being deeply rooted in a society's culture, norms, and values.

The importance of social development and the need to give it greater priority cannot be overemphasized. But that priority should fundamentally be met by LDCs themselves. The case for *external* resources for social development is much weaker and involves substantial risks for LDCs because it will inevitably come with conditionalities that will have a particular bias. In recent years there is one truism of development – more money inevitably means more conditionality, implicit or explicit. The best that LDCs can hope for is that the budgetary envelope of foreign aid does not continue the decline apparent in recent years. If LDCs press for increased external financing for social development, there will be a large opportunity cost ranging from the crowding out of lending for other sectors to conditionalities on areas that societies regard as their core norms and values. And there is no evidence that this will be better for the well-being of their citizens.

The interest of LDCs would be much better served if they prepared a strategic compact whereby they themselves would undertake to provide their citizens with key elements of social development – basic education and basic health, legal frameworks that do not discriminate against sections of their citizenry – and in return donors would fund the complementary inputs for development (the sorts of areas mentioned earlier). Virtually all aspects of social development (example basic education and basic health) are neither capital nor foreign exchange intensive. Regrettably we have conflated what is good for development with what the MDBs should do without much regard to the very issue that LDCs have been forced to confront: comparative advantage and the fungibility of public expenditures.

If a country is *unwilling* to act sufficiently vigorously on its own in the matter of primary education and health, that country is clearly uninterested in development and deserves little support from the international community. And if a country is *unable* to even undertake these basic tasks, then the problem is a much deeper one: is that country a viable state to begin with? And if not, is the Bank (and the IFIs in general) the appropriate institutional mechanism to deal with this issue or should the task be entrusted to the UN family and NGOs? By incessantly confusing what is good for development with what the Bank should be engaged in, borrower countries have been saddled with poverty projects with multiple criteria and implementation standards whose overall economywide effects are often questionable. The result: projects reflecting donor preferences, foreign exchange debt in sectors where it is quite unnecessary, and an undermining of efforts at self-reliance in areas that are the most basic responsibilities of a government. It is a lesson LDCs may well ponder as they reflect on their response to the G-7.

For a long time, obtaining greater concessional resources has been the highest priority of LDCs. This chapter has argued that the LDCs have been paying increasingly higher non-pecuniary costs which have offset any gains in additional "concessional" resources. Consequently, it is time LDCs reevaluated their priorities, and ponder whether their cause would be better served by asking rich countries not for more "positive freedoms" (through say additional financial resources) but fewer "negative freedoms" allowed them in the international system, e.g., lower barriers to their exports; lower greenhouse gas emissions; weaker insistence that LDCs conform to imposed artificial high standards be it those on intellectual property rights or MDB lending; a strong international regime controlling exports of small arms that wreak havoc in the civil wars afflicting many developing countries, etc. . . . The relative benefits of these measures for LDCs are likely to far exceed those from any politically feasible increase in concessional flows.

Acknowledgment

An earlier version of this chapter was published as: Devesh Kapur (2003), "Do as I say not as I do: A Critique of G-7 Proposals on Reforming' the World Bank," G-24 Discussion Paper No. 20. Reprinted with permission.

Appendix

International Financial Institution Advisory Commission (Meltzer Commission)

Issue	*Reform recommendations*
IDA	• Grants should replace loans for the provision of physical infrastructure and social services, and should increase when used productively.
	• Grants should be paid directly to legitimate and verify service providers to eliminate opportunities for government corruption.
	• Institutional Reform Loans should be offered at subsidized interest rates (10–90 percent) to support reform strategies developed by borrowing governments and approved by the MDBs.
	• MDBs and creditor nations should write off all claims against the HIPC, conditional on effective economic strategies.
IBRD	• Phase out lending to countries with capital market access (investment grade international bond rating), or with per capita incomes over $4000, over five years.

	• Limit official assistance to countries with a per capita income over $2500.
Global public goods	• Shift World Bank focus to provision of global public goods, including treatment of tropical diseases and AIDS, environmental management, and inter-country infrastructure.
	• World Bank should be technical assistance center to RDBs.
	• MDB services should be awarded as accounts on a competitive basis to private and public sector agencies (including NGOs). Cost of service provision should be shared between the donor agency and recipient government, with the amount of subsidy varying between 10–90 percent (depending on levels of development).
	• MDBs should not engage in financial crisis lending.
Governance/ representation	• None applicable.
Financial windows	• MIGA should be eliminated.
Relations with regional MDBs (RDBs)	• All country and regional programs should become the responsibility of the corresponding development bank.
	• World Bank should maintain care of African states and the poor countries of Europe and the Middle East until appropriate regional MDBs are ready to assume responsibility.
	• Excess callable capital should be reallocated to RDBs and should be reduced in line with declining World Bank loan portfolios.
Other	• The World Bank should change its name to the "World Development Agency" to reflect these reforms.

Source: www.econ.lsa.umich.edu/~alandear/topics/meltzer.html.

G-7 proposals on MDB reform activities

Issue	Reform recommendations
IDA	• Analyze financial and practical implementation issues related to the increased use of grants within IDA-13, and review terms for blend countries.
IBRD	• Review lending instruments and pricing, including an assessment of rationalizing and streamlining existing intra- and inter-MDB instruments.
Global public goods	• MDBs' main priorities in this field should be to fight infectious diseases, promote environmental improvement, facilitate trade, and support financial stability.
	• World Bank's and RDBs' roles in this area should be defined clearly on the basis of comparative advantage.
Governance/ representation	• Establish and/or strengthen compliance and inspection mechanisms and enhance evaluation.
	• Institute reforms to promote wide consultation, coordination, and debate. Include an annual review of information disclosure policies to improve transparency.

	• Establish a more transparent budget process by better linking institutional priorities to resource allocations.
	• MDBs should institute periodic consultations between Executive Directors and senior management to better monitor organizational structure.
Financial windows	• All Country Assistance Strategies should eventually incorporate financial sector issues.
	• MDBs should assist borrowers in developing the capacity and strategies to meet international codes and standards, including FATF anti-money laundering standards.
Relations with regional MDBs (RDBs)	• MDBs should identify their comparative advantages and justify any overlap. Work Plans should be developed in accordance with this comparative advantage.
Other	• Country Strategies should include a review of countries' governance, focusing on public sector management, accountability, and anti-corruption measures.

The Commonwealth Secretariat on IMF/World Bank issues

Issue	*Reform recommendations*
IDA	• The criteria as set out by IDA-12 are sufficient.
	• Distribute IDA aid so as to reward good performance and penalize poor performance.
	• Carefully consider applying "normal" performance to states emerging from conflict. Appropriate criteria should emphasize reconciliation processes, reconstruction attempts, and market promotion/liberalization projects.
	• On partially replacing IDA lending with grants, especially for AIDS programs and post-conflict states, the Secretariat recognizes concerns associated with the long-term viability of IDA, dependency on grants, and moral hazard.
IBRD	• Recent declines in IBRD and IDA lending or net transfers (to $-\$6.2$ billion in 2001) are inappropriate. This decline should raise questions about the impact on IBRD's net income and its procedures and loan charges.
	• Resolve any lack of clarity on the level of conditionality to be attached to Bank loans.
Global public goods	• None applicable.
Governance/representation	• None applicable.
Financial windows	• None applicable.
Relations with regional MDBs (RDBs)	• No specific recommendations.
Other	• None applicable.

Source: www.thecommonwealth.org/papers/_alandear/topics/meltzer.html.

Bretton Woods Committee Symposium: reassessing MDBs' role in emerging markets

Issue	Reform recommendations
IDA	• Oppose the disbursement of grants, which would lead to major reductions in, and the eventual elimination of, Bank aid.
IBRD	• Phase out lending for projects that are privately financeable.
	• Increase interest rates as countries achieve graduation criteria. Perhaps implement price differentiation and create an internal credit rating system to graduate borrowers.
Global public goods	• Focus on sectors such as education and health that are crucial for development and that are neglected by the private sector. Such lending has been important for institution-building, infrastructure and policy development.
	• MDBs should continue as flexible tools in the resolution of economic crises. Such lending is an effective instrument in targeting expenditure, developing and maintaining monitoring systems and strengthening the private sector.
Governance/representation	• None applicable.
Financial windows	• None applicable.
Relations with regional MDBs	• Oppose a strict delineation of duties among MDBs – the competition created by the overlapping of duties is advantageous to both the borrowing countries and the private market.
Other	• None applicable.

Source: www.brettonwoods.org/july13_2000symposium_report.htm.

Commission on the Role of the MDBs in Emerging Markets: Carnegie Endowment for International Peace

Issue	Reform recommendations
IDA	• None applicable.
IBRD	• Continue lending to emerging market economies, as access to private capital remains risky, expensive, and unreliable.
	• As countries get richer, make declining dependence on MDB loans voluntary. This process should be joined by incentives that allow MDBs flexibility in addressing individual countries' needs.
	• Simplify conditionality and focus it on equity and growth issues. Conditions should be determined via transparent public debate that engages civil society.
Global public goods	• MDBs should lend in times of market and

	economic crises, but maintain their long-term development goals.
Governance/representation	• None applicable.
Financial windows	• None applicable.
Relations with regional MDBs (RDBs)	• None applicable.
Other	• Emerging Market Economies should establish a borrower's club (on the model provided by the Andean Development and Nordic Investment Banks) to complement MDBs and enable members to "own" policies and set their own development mandate.

Task force on Multilateral Development Banks

Issue	*Reform recommendations*
IDA	• None applicable.
IBRD	• To strengthen "ownership," borrowers should take the lead in project and sector work, especially when this involves major policy reforms.
Global public goods	• None applicable.
Governance/representation	• Make information on MDB activities more readily available, in part to better justify MDBs' actions.
	• Open up and formalize new channels of dialogue to take account of advice and opinions from borrowing countries and international specialists.
	• Executive Boards should define the scope of the MDB activities, and demand a system that sets clear objectives at all policy levels. Establish clear and public benchmarks against which institutions' progress can be measured.
	• Boards should discuss and agree on country assistance strategies, to which management should adhere. Measure results by generally accepted and comparable objective criteria.
	• Boards should ensure that MDBs' administrative resources are appropriate and used efficiently, and that budgetary practices allow for flexibility and greater responsiveness.
Financial windows	• None applicable.
Relations with regional MDBs (RDBs)	• Make objective evaluative criteria to improve MDB accountability common to the five MDBs. Meetings between the MDBs' evaluation units should develop shared evaluation standards and performance indicators.
Other	• None applicable.

Source: Development Committee, Washington, DC, 1996.

Notes

1 This chapter was originally prepared for the G-24. It draws on earlier work, Devesh Kapur 2002a, 2002b, 2001, 2000 and Devesh Kapur *et al.* 1997. I'd like to thank Nancy Birdsall, John Briscoe, Gerry Helleiner, Michael Kremer, Urjit Patel, Dani Rodrik, Richard Webb, and Ngaire Woods for helpful comments.

2 While this list is by no means exhaustive it gives a flavor of the more influential reports on this contentious issue. Other contributions include Birdsall and Deese (2001) and Jong Il-You (2000).

3 See footnote 19, in Kapur *et al.* 1997: 1129.

4 Jonathan Fox and L. David Brown. 1998. Introduction. In *The Struggle for Accountability: The World Bank, NGOs and Grassroots Movements*, edited by Jonathan Fox and David Brown, p. 15, emphasis added. Cambridge: MIT Press 1998.

5 Of the IDA-13 replenishment amount of SDR 18 billion, SDR 10 billion, or 55 percent is from new donor contributions. The rest is from reflows (SDR 7.3 billion) and transfers from IBRD's net income.

6 IDA. 2002. Additions to IDA Resources: Thirteenth Replenishment: para. 5.

7 IDA. 2002. Sounding out borrowers about IDA's Policy Framework: Report on a Survey. May, Table 4.

8 Through this program which annually provides between $3–4 million, the Bank has awarded more than $12 million in start-up funding for social entrepreneurs with previously no access to Bank funds. As of early 2002 more than 3800 projects had been submitted to this program from more than 1000 groups in 100 countries.

9 See Woods (2001) for a more thorough analysis of the links between global governance and accountability.

10 James Q. Wilson. 1989. *Bureaucracy: What Government Agencies Do and Why They Do It.* New York: Basic Books. For a more formal analysis of these results see Dewatripont *et al.* 1999.

11 IDA. 2002. Annex 3.

12 See Naim 1996.

13 Another alleged reason is the fear of developing countries that budget cuts would adversely affect the nationals employed in the Bank.

14 Whether moving from open to secret voting rules in the Board would result in shareholders' votes being more closely aligned to their "true" preferences, is an open question.

15 By the end of fiscal year 2001, the World Bank was administering 2024 trust fund accounts whose fiduciary assets totaled $2.7 billion, of which the Bank group itself provided $0.42 billion. Disbursements totaled $1.85 billion of which nearly $1 billion was accounted by just three programs – Heavily Indebted Poor Countries (HIPC), the Global Environmental Facility (GEF), and the Poverty and Human Resources Development Fund (PHRD). See note H, in Appendix in 2001 World Bank *Annual Report.*

16 For instance, following the onset of the Asian crisis, the idea of an Asian Monetary Authority was shot down by the major powers and the Asian Development Bank was severely criticized when it attempted to adopt a position different from the prescriptions of the IMF. The monopoly power of the IMF was reaffirmed, and the possibility of exit denied.

17 On the power and influence of environmental lobbies on the World Bank see Wade 2001.

18 Operational Evaluation Unit. 2002. The World Bank's Approach to Global Programs: An Independent Evaluation. Phase I Report. August.

19 Ibid.

20 Ibid: p. x.
21 Ibid: p. xi.
22 This section draws on Kapur (2000).
23 http://www.imf.org/external/pubs/ft/seminar/1999/reforms/index.htm.
24 According to Ellison (2000: table 18.19, Appendix B) the fraction of develop-
    ment related papers in the most prestigious journals has declined from 3.8
    percent in the 1970s to 1.6 percent in the 1990s.
25 The case of India is illustrative. In the 1990s of the 2312 articles in the top five
    journals in economics (*AER, EJ, JPE, QJE*, and *Rev of Economic Studies*), 138 were
    by Indians outside India and just 7 were from Indians in India – a factor of 20!
26 At the beginning of the 1990s, 80 percent of the research staff at the World
    Bank had graduate degrees from US and UK institutions (nearly two-thirds
    from the US). While similar data from the IMF is unavailable, it is unlikely to
    be less. Since then, widening quality differences between US and developing
    country academic institutions are likely to have increased the skewness.
    Nicholas Stern. 1997. "The World Bank as Intellectual Actor." In *The World
    Bank: Its First Half Century*, edited by Devesh Kapur *et al.*, Table 18.12.6. Wash-
    ington, DC: The Brookings Institution.
27 Robert Paarlberg, personal communication, April 24, 2002.
28 These include the Africa Economic Research Consortium (AERC) and the
    Joint Vienna Institute (cosponsored with the BIS, the EBRD, the IMF, and the
    OECD). But the output of these institutions is not geared to addressing sys-
    temic issues – as attested by the fact that it is rarely cited by the sponsoring
    institutions themselves on debates related to those issues.
29 The research topics are determined through consultation with IDB and exter-
    nal professionals. The network annually sends requests for project proposals to
    all of its 240 members on a number of specific topics. Project funding runs
    around $35 000–$50 000 on average with a few projects receiving up to $70 000.
30 I am grateful to Michael Kremer for pointing this out.

References

Bardhan, Pranab. 2003. Journal Publication in Economics: A View from the
    Periphery. *The Economic Journal* 113 (488) (June): F332–7.
Birdsall, Nancy and Brian Deese. 2001. Multilateral Development Banks in a
    Changing World Economy. Carnegie Endowment for International Peace.
Dewatripont, M., I. Jewitt, and J. Tirole. 1999. The Economics of Career Concerns.
    Part II. Application to Missions and Accountability of Government Agencies. *The
    Review of Economic Studies* 66 (1) (January): 199–217.
Ellison, Glenn. 2000. The Slowdown of the Economics Publishing Process. June.
    Available at: http://econ-www.mit.edu/faculty/gellison/papers.htm.
Finger, J. Michael and Philip Schuler. 1999. Implementation of Uruguay Round
    Commitments: The Development Challenge. Policy Research Working Paper
    No. 2215, World Bank, October.
IBRD. 2001. Cost of Doing Business: Fiduciary and Safeguard Policies and Com-
    pliance. SecM2001-0469, July 17.
IDA. 2001a. Sounding Out Borrowers about IDA's Policy Framework. May.
IDA. 2001b. Additions to IDA Resources: Thirteenth Replenishment. November
    20.
IDA. 2002. Additions to IDA Resources: Thirteenth Replenishment. IDA/SecM
    2002-0488, September 17.

Jong Il-You. 2002. The Bretton Woods Institutions: Evolution, Reform and Change. In *Governing Globalization: Issues and Institutions*, edited by Deepak Nayyar, pp. 209–37. Oxford: Oxford University Press.

Kanbur, Ravi. 2001. Cross-Border Externalities, International Public Goods and Their Implications for Aid Agencies. Available at: http://www.people.cornell.edu/pages/sk145/papers/IPGWB.pdf.

Kapur, Devesh. 2000. Reforming the International Financial System: Key Issues. In *Global Financial Reform: How? Why? When?* Ottawa: North-South Institute.

Kapur, Devesh. 2001. Expansive Agendas and Weak Instruments: Governance Related Conditionalities of International Financial Institutions. *Policy Reform 4* (3): 207–41.

Kapur, Devesh. 2002a. The Common Pool Dilemma of Global Public Goods: Lessons from the World Bank's Net Income and Reserves. *World Development* 30 (3) (March): 337–54.

Kapur, Devesh. 2002b. Anatomy of Governance in the World Bank. In *Re-inventing the World Bank*, edited by Jonathan R. Pincus and Jeffrey A. Winters. Ithaca: Cornell University Press.

Kapur, Devesh, John Lewis, and Richard Webb. 1997. *The World Bank: Its First Half Century. Volume 1: History*. Washington, DC: The Brookings Institution.

Kremer, Michael. 2000. Creating Markets for New Vaccines – Part I: Rationale, Part II: Design Issues. *Innovation Policy and the Economy* 1: 35–118.

Naim, Moises. 1996. From Supplicants to Shareholders: Developing Countries and the World Bank. In *The International Monetary and Financial System*, edited by G.K. Helleiner, pp. 293–323. London: Macmillan Press Ltd.

Ostrom, Vincent. 1999. Polycentricity (Part 1). In *Polycentricity and Local Public Economies: Readings from the Workshop in Political Theory and Policy Analysis*, edited by Michael D. McGinnis, pp. 52–74. Ann Arbor: University of Michigan Press.

Ostrom, Vincent, Charles M. Tiebout, and Robert Warren. 1961. The Organization of Government in Metropolitan Areas: A Theoretical Inquiry. *American Political Science Review* 55 (December): 831–42.

Prendergast, Candice. 2001. Selection and Oversight in the Public Sector. NBER Working Paper No. 8664, December.

Salter, A.J. and B.R. Martin. 2001. The Economic Benefits of Publicly Funded Research: A Critical Review. *Research Policy* 30: 509–32.

Stirling, A. 1998. On the Economics and Analysis of Diversity. SPRU Working Papers. Brighton: University of Sussex.

Wade, Robert. 2001. The U.S. Role in the Malaise at the World Bank: Get up Gulliver. Discussion paper prepared under the research program of the Intergovernmental Group of Twenty-Four on International Monetary Affairs (G-24). Available at: http://ksghome.harvard.edu/~drodrik/WadeG24.pdf.

Woods, Ngaire. 2001. Accountability in Global Governance. Background Paper for HDR 2002, draft, October.

World Bank. 2001. Annual Report. Washington, DC.

Author index

Subject index